The
Black-White
Test Score
Gap

The Black-White Test Score Gap

Christopher Jencks
and
Meredith Phillips
Editors

BROOKINGS INSTITUTION PRESS
Washington, D.C.

Copyright © 1998 by
THE BROOKINGS INSTITUTION
1775 Massachusetts Avenue, N.W., Washington, D.C. 20036

Library of Congress Cataloging-in-Publication data
The black-white test score gap / Christopher Jencks and Meredith Phillips, editors.
    p. cm.
Includes bibliographical references and index.

ISBN 0-8157-4610-5 (cloth : acid-free paper)
ISBN 0-8157-4609-1 (pbk. : acid-free paper)
1. Discrimination in education—United States. 2. Educational tests and measurements—United States. 3. Test bias—United States.
I. Jencks, Christopher. II. Phillips, Meredith.
    LC212.2 .B53   1998
    371.26'01'3--ddc21

                                                              98-25316
                                                                   CIP

9 8 7 6 5 4 3

The paper used in this publication meets the minimum requirements of the American National Standard for Information Sciences—Permanence of Paper for Printed Library Materials, ANSI Z39.48-1984.

Typeset in Adobe Garamond

Composition by Cynthia Stock
Silver Spring, Maryland

Printed by
R. R. Donnelly & Sons
Harrisonburg, Virginia

Acknowledgments

T HE PUBLICATION of *The Bell Curve* by Richard Herrnstein and Charles Murray in 1994 generated a surge of interest in the idea that cognitive skills have become the most important determinant of personal success in modern societies. This idea was not new, of course. Bill Clinton had said much the same thing many times during his first run for the presidency in 1992. Clinton's close friend Robert Reich, who served as secretary of labor from 1993 to 1996, had been making the same argument for years. Indeed, Michael Young had laid out many of Herrnstein and Murray's arguments in his brilliant fictional dystopia, *The Rise of the Meritocracy*, published in 1958. But unlike Young, Herrnstein and Murray saw no alternative to the meritocracy they thought America was becoming. And unlike Clinton or Reich, they thought cognitive inequality was largely explained by genetic inequality. Indeed, they even thought the test score gap between blacks and whites was partly innate. These claims aroused far more controversy than anything Young, Reich, or Clinton had said about the subject.

Capitalizing on popular interest in these issues, Susan Mayer and Christopher Jencks organized a year-long faculty workshop on "meritocracy" at the University of Chicago in 1995. This seminar was sponsored by Chicago's Irving B. Harris Graduate School of Public Policy Studies and funded by the Russell Sage Foundation. It brought together scholars from many disciplines and universities, all of whom shared an interest in the changing role of cognitive skills and schooling in American society. Its goal was to familiarize participants with the current state of knowledge about these issues, not to assess *The Bell Curve*. As part of this effort, Mayer and Jencks organized a day-long workshop in May 1995 for scholars who were studying the causes of the black-white test score gap. (Mayer and Paul Peterson also organized a conference on schooling and meritocracy in September 1996 supported by the Russell Sage Foundation. The papers presented at that conference will be published in a separate volume.)

The papers presented at both the workshop and other meetings of the faculty seminar pointed to two broad conclusions about the black-white test score gap that surprised many participants. First, the test score gap between blacks and whites turned out to play a much larger role in explaining racial disparities in educational attainment and income than many had realized. Second, many common explanations for the test score gap, including racial disparities in family income, school resources, and innate ability, did not seem to be as important as their proponents claimed. But like everything involving race in America, these conclusions were controversial, even among experts. It therefore seemed important to assemble the supporting evidence in one place. In the summer of 1995 Jencks and Meredith Phillips decided to edit a book on the black-white test score gap. They also decided that such a book should discuss a wide range of possible explanations for the gap and should discuss theories about why the gap has narrowed as well as theories about its causes. The Andrew W. Mellon Foundation agreed to underwrite this effort.

Although the Mellon Foundation provided primary support for our work, others contributed as well. Jencks worked on the book at Northwestern University's Center for Urban Affairs and Policy Research (now the Institute for Policy Research) and completed work on it while he was a fellow at the Center for Advanced Study in the Behavioral Sciences, supported by the National Science Foundation Grant SBR-9602236. Phillips worked on the book while she was supported by the Taubman Center for State and Local Government at Harvard University's John F. Kennedy School of Government and completed her work on it while she held a Spencer Foundation fellowship. The Malcolm Wiener Center for Social Policy at Harvard's John F. Kennedy School of Government also provided office space and logistical support.

A number of individuals also helped make the book possible. Sara Miller Acosta organized the 1995 workshop at the University of Chicago so skillfully that it seemed effortless. Laurie Pielak at Northwestern University's Institute for Policy Research managed the Mellon Foundation grant with her usual patience and competence. William Bowen and Harriet Zuckerman of the Mellon Foundation were unfailingly helpful and understanding. William Dickens and James Flynn provided extraordinarily detailed critiques of every chapter. Nancy Davidson and Robert Faherty at Brookings were enthusiastic about the project, put up with our tardiness, and were helpful at every stage of the production process. Tanjam Jacobson and Jim Schneider edited the manuscript, Carlotta Ribar proofread the pages, and Robert Elwood compiled the index. All the contributors responded to endless requests for revisions with unfailing good humor.

Social scientists have been trying to understand the black-white test score gap since World War I, when test scores collected from the U.S. Army's wartime recruits first demonstrated its existence. But empirical research on the subject has proceeded in fits and starts. By now this cycle has become predictable. First someone claims that the black-white gap is largely innate. Then skeptics challenge this claim. The debate starts off largely unencumbered by evidence, but it eventually precipitates a number of useful empirical studies. The issue is not fully resolved, but the number of plausible explanations is smaller at the end of the debate than at the beginning. This happened in the 1920s. It happened again in the 1970s, after Arthur Jensen published "How Much Can We Boost IQ and Scholastic Achievement?" in the *Harvard Education Review* in 1969. It seems to be happening again now, at least partly as a result of *The Bell Curve*. This book tries to help the reader understand where the debate has come from and where it is likely to go next.

CHRISTOPHER JENCKS
MEREDITH PHILLIPS

Contents

The
Black-White
Test Score
Gap

CHRISTOPHER JENCKS
MEREDITH PHILLIPS

1 | The Black-White Test Score Gap: An Introduction

A FRICAN AMERICANS currently score lower than European Americans on vocabulary, reading, and mathematics tests, as well as on tests that claim to measure scholastic aptitude and intelligence.[1] This gap appears before children enter kindergarten (figure 1-1), and it persists into adulthood. It has narrowed since 1970, but the typical American black still scores below 75 percent of American whites on most standardized tests.[2] On some tests the typical American black scores below more than 85 percent of whites.[3]

---

1. We are indebted to Karl Alexander, William Dickens, Ronald Ferguson, James Flynn, Frank Furstenberg, Arthur Goldberger, Tom Kane, David Levine, Jens Ludwig, Richard Nisbett, Jane Mansbridge, Susan Mayer, Claude Steele, and Karolyn Tyson for helpful criticisms of earlier drafts. But we did not make all the changes they suggested, and they are in no way responsible for our conclusions.

2. These statistics also imply, of course, that a lot of blacks score above a lot of whites. If the black and white distributions are normal and have the same standard deviation, and if the black-white gap is one (black or white) standard deviation, then when we compare a randomly selected black to a randomly selected white, the black will score higher than the white about 24 percent of the time. If the black-white gap is 0.75 rather than 1.00 standard deviations, a randomly selected black will score higher than a randomly selected white about 30 percent of the time.

3. Although this book concentrates on the black-white gap, similar issues arise when we compare either Hispanics or Native Americans to whites or Asians. We have concentrated on the black-white gap because far more is known about test performance among blacks and whites than among other groups. This reflects the fact that white American scholars have traditionally been more concerned

1

Figure 1-1. *Vocabulary Scores for Black and White Three- and Four-Year-Olds, 1986–94*

Percent of population

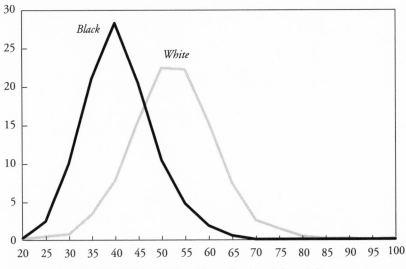

PPVT-R score (black median = 40; white median = 52)

Source: National Longitudinal Survey of Youth Child Data, 1986–94. Black N = 1,134; white N = 2,071. Figure is based on black and white three- and four-year-olds in the Children of the National Longitudinal Survey of Youth (CNLSY) data set who took the Peabody Picture Vocabulary Test-Revised (PPVT-R). The test is the standardized residual, coded to a mean of 50 and a standard deviation of 10, from a weighted regression of children's raw scores on their age in months, age in months squared, and year-of-testing dummies. See chapter 4 for details on the CNLSY and the PPVT-R.

The black-white test score gap does not appear to be an inevitable fact of nature. It is true that the gap shrinks only a little when black and white children attend the same schools. It is also true that the gap shrinks only a little when black and white families have the same amount of schooling, the same income, and the same wealth. But despite endless speculation, no one has found genetic evidence indicating that blacks have less innate intellectual ability than whites. Thus while it is clear that eliminating the test score gap would require enormous effort by both blacks and whites and would probably take more than one generation, we believe it can be done.

about the plight of blacks than about the plight of other minorities, as well as the fact that blacks were (until recently) far more numerous than Native Americans, Asians, or even Hispanics.

This conviction rests mainly on three facts:

—*When black or mixed-race children are raised in white rather than black homes, their preadolescent test scores rise dramatically.* Black adoptees' scores seem to fall in adolescence, but this is what we would expect if, as seems likely, their social and cultural environment comes to resemble that of other black adolescents and becomes less like that of the average white adolescent.[4]

—*Even nonverbal IQ scores are sensitive to environmental change.* Scores on nonverbal IQ tests have risen dramatically throughout the world since the 1930s.[5] The average white scored higher on the Stanford-Binet in 1978 than 82 percent of whites who took the test in 1932.[6] Such findings reinforce the implications of adoption studies: large environmental changes can have a large impact on test performance.

—*Black-white differences in academic achievement have also narrowed throughout the twentieth century.* The best trend data come from the National Assessment of Educational Progress (NAEP), which has been testing seventeen-year-olds since 1971 and has repeated many of the same items year after year. Figure 1-2 shows that the black-white reading gap narrowed from 1.25 standard deviations in 1971 to 0.69 standard deviations in 1996. The math gap fell from 1.33 to 0.89 standard deviations.[7] When Min-Hsiung Huang and Robert Hauser analyzed vocabulary scores for adults born between 1909 and 1969, the black-white gap also narrowed by half.

In a country as racially polarized as the United States, no single change taken in isolation could possibly eliminate the entire legacy of slavery and Jim Crow or usher in an era of full racial equality. But if racial equality is America's goal, reducing the black-white test score gap would probably do

4. See chapter 3.

5. Flynn (1987); Neisser (1998).

6. The 1932–78 comparison for whites is derived from Flynn (1984), who shows that IQ scores rose by roughly 13.8 points between 1931–33 and 1976–80. Tuddenham (1948) reported an equally dramatic improvement in the test performance of American soldiers between World War I and World War II. Since the trend found by Flynn appears to have been roughly linear, the net increase between 1917 and 1978 was probably close to 18 points (1.2 standard deviations). Flynn (personal communication) reports that restandardization of the Wechsler intelligence tests shows a further increase in mean IQ since 1978.

7. The standardized black-white gap always looks larger in NAEP than in other surveys, because NAEP reports standard deviations that have been corrected for measurement error. In addition, the standard deviation of seventeen-year-olds' reading and math scores has fallen over time, making the pre-1996 gaps look larger than they would if they were expressed in contemporary standard deviations. Five other major national surveys of high school seniors conducted since 1965 also show black-white convergence (see chapter 5), as do surveys of younger children (see chapter 6 and chapter 7).

Figure 1-2. *NAEP Reading and Mathematics Scores for Black and White Seventeen-Year-Olds, 1971–96*

Standardized score using 1996 mean and SD

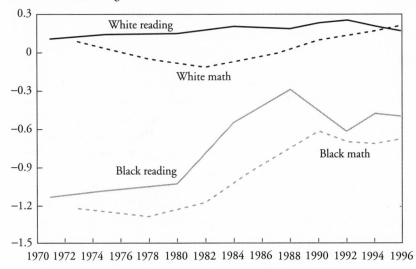

Source: National Assessment of Educational Progress. Tests in all years are in a common metric and have been rescaled so that the 1996 population mean is zero and the 1996 standard deviation is 1.00.

more to promote this goal than any other strategy that commands broad political support. Reducing the test score gap is probably both necessary and sufficient for substantially reducing racial inequality in educational attainment and earnings. Changes in education and earnings would in turn help reduce racial differences in crime, health, and family structure, although we do not know how large these effects would be.

This judgment contradicts Christopher Jencks and his colleagues' 1972 conclusion in *Inequality* that reducing cognitive inequality would not do much to reduce economic inequality. The reason is simple: the world has changed. In 1972 the best evidence about what happened to black workers with high test scores came from a study by Phillips Cutright, who had analyzed the 1964 earnings of men in their thirties who had taken the Armed Forces Qualification Test (AFQT) between 1949 and 1953.[8] Over-

8. Cutright (1972, 1974). Cutright's sample, which was 30 to 37 years old in 1964, included both veterans and nonveterans. His checks suggested that it was quite representative of men in this age

Figure 1-3. *Black Annual Earnings as a Percentage of White Earnings among Employed Men Aged 30 to 37 in 1964 or 31 to 36 in 1993, by Percentile Rank on a Military Test Taken When the Men Were Aged 18 to 23*

Percent

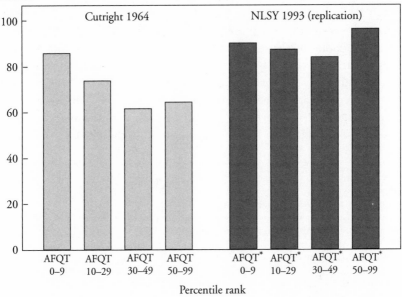

Percentile rank

Sources: Cutright (1972) and authors' tabulations from the NLSY. Cutright's version of the AFQT included tests for vocabulary, arithmetic, and spatial relations. Our NLSY approximation of his AFQT included tests for word knowledge, numerical operations, and mechanical reasoning (AFQT*). See the notes in the text for details on the samples and standard errors.

all, employed black men earned 57.5 percent of what whites earned. Among men with AFQT scores above the national average, black men earned 64.5 percent of what whites earned (figure 1-3).[9] In such a world, eliminating racial differences in test performance did not seem likely to reduce the earnings gap very much.

---

group. His earnings data came from the Social Security Administration and were therefore limited to those in covered employment. Social security withholding covered only the first $4,800 of earnings in 1964, so Cutright estimated the total 1964 earnings of those who reached the $4,800 ceiling by assuming that they continued to earn the amount they received in the quarter before they reached the ceiling.

9. Using five AFQT intervals, Cutright (1972) reported mean annual earnings for black and white men who worked. We collapsed the top two intervals, because Cutright's sample of 4,051 employed blacks included only 53 men in his top AFQT interval (80th to 99th percentile), and because our

Today's world is different. The best recent data on test scores and earnings come from the National Longitudinal Survey of Youth (NLSY), which gave the Armed Services Vocational Aptitude Battery to a national sample of young people in 1980.[10] Among employed men who were 31 to 36 years old in 1993, blacks earned 67.5 percent of what whites earned, a modest but significant improvement over the situation in 1964.[11] The big change occurred among blacks with test scores near or above the white average. Among men who scored between the 30th and 49th percentiles nationally, black earnings rose from 62 to 84 percent of the white average. Among men who scored above the 50th percentile, black earnings rose from 65 to 96 percent of the white average.[12] In this new world, raising black workers' test scores looks far more important than it did in the 1960s.[13]

---

comparison sample of 736 black men from the National Longitudinal Survey of Youth includes only 21 men in this interval.

10. Almost all members of Cutright's sample took a version of the AFQT that included equal numbers of questions on vocabulary, arithmetic, and spatial relations. The Armed Services Vocational Aptitude Battery (ASVAB) did not include a spatial relations test, so we could not exactly reproduce the 1950–53 AFQT. To approximate the 1950–53 test we summed men's scores on the ASVAB tests of word knowledge, numerical operations, and mechanical reasoning. Our results did not change appreciably when we used other ASVAB tests instead.

11. To match Cutright's sample, we selected men who took the ASVAB between the ages of 18 and 23. Cutright had no data on whether respondents were Hispanic. We treated Hispanics as white, but our results hardly changed when we dropped Hispanics. Cutright's data were limited to men who worked in jobs covered by social security in 1964, whereas our NLSY sample covered all men of the relevant age.

12. Cutright (1972) reported the mean earnings of black and white men with AFQT scores in each interval. He also reported the linear regression of men's unlogged earnings on their AFQT percentile score (coded 0 to 99). We estimated a similar regression. To express coefficients in a common metric, we divided each coefficient by the mean earnings of the relevant group in the relevant year. The regression coefficients (B), standard errors (SE), and unweighted sample sizes (N) were as follows:

	Blacks 1964	Blacks 1993	Whites 1964	Whites 1993
B	.52	1.33	.69	.82
(SE)	(.11)	(.11)	(.03)	(.05)
N	4,051	7,362	5,022	1,842

13. ASVAB scores explain more of the racial gap in annual earnings in figure 1-3 than in chapter 14 by William Johnson and Derek Neal. This discrepancy has at least six sources, most of which derive from our effort to maintain comparability with Cutright. First, unlike Johnson and Neal we include respondents with military earnings. Second, whereas Johnson and Neal include anyone with positive earnings between 1990 and 1992, we include only individuals with positive earnings in 1993, which excludes more black men with weak labor force attachment. Third, unlike Johnson and Neal, we top-coded earnings (at 3.16 times the white mean, as in Cutright), raising the black-white earnings ratio by about 0.03. Fourth, we used different ASVAB tests from Johnson and Neal, although this makes very little difference. Fifth, we included men from all the NLSY sampling strata and used sample weights, whereas Johnson and Neal excluded the poor white oversample and the military sample and

Some skeptics have argued that scores on tests of this kind are really just proxies for family background. As we shall see, family background does affect test performance. But even when biological siblings are raised in the same family, their test scores hardly ever correlate more than 0.5. Among children who have been adopted, the correlation falls to around half that level.[14] The claim that test scores are only a proxy for family background is therefore false. Furthermore, test score differences between siblings raised in the same family have sizable effects on their educational attainment and earnings.[15] Thus while it is true that eliminating the black-white test score gap would not reduce the black-white earnings gap quite as much as figure 1-3 implies, the effect would surely be substantial.

Reducing the black-white test score gap would reduce racial disparities in educational attainment as well as in earnings. The nationwide High School and Beyond survey tested twelfth-graders in 1982 and followed them up in 1992, when they were in their late twenties. At the time of the followup only 13.3 percent of the blacks had earned a B.A., compared with 30 percent of the non-Hispanic whites. Many observers blame this disparity on black parents' inability to pay college bills, black students' lack of motivation, or the hostility that black students encounter on predominantly white college campuses. All these factors probably play some role. Nonetheless, figure 1-4 shows that when we compare blacks and whites with the same twelfth grade test scores, blacks are *more* likely than whites to complete college. Once we equalize test scores, High School and Beyond blacks' 16.7 point disadvantage in college graduation rates turns into a 5.9 point advantage.[16]

Eliminating racial differences in test performance would also allow colleges, professional schools, and employers to phase out the racial preferences that have caused so much political trouble over the past generation. If selective colleges based their admission decisions solely on applicants' predicted college grades, their undergraduate enrollment would currently

---

did not weight their data. Sixth, we included men who took the ASVAB between the ages of 18 and 23, whereas Johnson and Neal included men who took it between the ages of 15 and 18, so our ASVAB scores are more likely than theirs to have been affected by the length of time men spent in school.

14. See Jencks and others (1972, appendix A); Loehlin (1980); and Cherny and Cardon (1994).

15. Korenman and Winship (forthcoming).

16. The results shown in figure 1-4 do not change if we use years of schooling rather than college graduation as the dependent variable. Similar results can be found in samples dating back to the early 1960s, so they are not attributable to affirmative action. Affirmative action mainly affects *where* blacks go to college, not *whether* they go.

Figure 1-4. *Gap in Eventual College Graduation Rates among Blacks and Whites Who Were in Twelfth Grade in 1982, Controlling Socioeconomic Status and Test Scores, 1992*
Black-white gap in percent with a B.A.

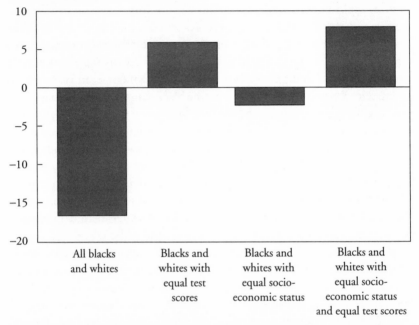

Source: Authors' tabulations from High School and Beyond 1992 followup. Test score is the sum of vocabulary, reading, and math scores. Socioeconomic status includes parents' income, occupation, schooling, possessions in the home, marital status, number of siblings, urbanism, and region. The standard error for black-white gap is about 2.5 percentage points.

be 96 or 97 percent white and Asian. To avoid this, almost all selective colleges and professional schools admit African Americans and Hispanics whom they would not admit if they were white. Racial preferences of this kind are politically unpopular.[17] If selective colleges could achieve racial diversity without making race an explicit factor in their admission decisions, blacks would do better in college and whites would nurse fewer political grudges.

17. Proposition 209 banned racial preferences in California's public institutions but did not cover private institutions. The Fifth Circuit's *Hopwood* v. *State of Texas* decision banned such preferences in both public and private institutions throughout Texas, Louisiana, and Mississippi. The U.S. Supreme Court refused to review *Hopwood*, so it does not apply elsewhere in the United States. Should the Supreme Court endorse the *Hopwood* principle in the future, it would cover both public and private institutions throughout the nation.

Advocates of racial equality might be more willing to accept our argument that narrowing the test score gap is crucial to achieving their goals if they believed that narrowing the gap was really feasible. But pessimism about this has become almost universal. In the 1960s, racial egalitarians routinely blamed the test score gap on the combined effects of black poverty, racial segregation, and inadequate funding for black schools. That analysis implied obvious solutions: raise black children's family income, desegregate their schools, and equalize spending on schools that remain racially segregated. All these steps still look useful, but none has made as much difference as optimists expected in the early 1960s.

—The number of affluent black parents has grown substantially since the 1960s, but their children's test scores still lag far behind those of white children from equally affluent families. Income inequality between blacks and whites appears to play some role in the test score gap, but it is quite small.[18]

—Most southern schools desegregated in the early 1970s, and southern black nine-year-olds' reading scores seem to have risen as a result.[19] Even today, black third-graders in predominantly white schools read better than initially similar blacks who have attended predominantly black schools. But large racial differences in reading skills persist even in desegregated schools, and a school's racial mix does not seem to have much effect on changes in reading scores after sixth grade or on math scores at any age.[20]

—Despite glaring economic inequalities between a few rich suburbs and nearby central cities, the average black child and the average white child now live in school districts that spend almost exactly the same amount per pupil.[21] Black and white schools also have the same average number of

18. See chapter 4.

19. See chapter 6.

20. Phillips (1997) found that a 10 point increase in the percentage of white students was associated with a .027 standard deviation increment in third-grade reading scores, holding "true" first-grade scores constant. Attending a 90 percent white school rather than an all-black school could therefore raise third-grade reading scores by .243 standard deviations. The estimated effect was smaller in later elementary grades and often changed signs. For math the effects were smaller than for reading and changed sign in high school.

21. Tabulations by William Evans show that the average black student lived in a district that spent $5,387 in 1992, while the average white student lived in a district that spent $5,397. In 1972 the figures (in 1992 dollars) were $3,261 for blacks and $3,397 for whites. These estimates come from a file that matches expenditure data collected by the Census of Governments in 1972, 1982, and 1992 with demographic data on Census tracts in 1970, 1980, and 1990. A few districts cannot be matched. For details on the samples see Evans, Murray, and Schwab (1997).

teachers per pupil, the same pay scales, and teachers with almost the same amount of formal education and teaching experience.[22] The most important resource difference between black and white schools seems to be that teachers in black schools have lower test scores than teachers in white schools. This is partly because black schools have more black teachers and partly because white teachers in black schools have unusually low scores.[23]

For all these reasons, the number of people who think they know how to eliminate racial differences in test performance has shrunk steadily since the mid-1960s. While many people still think the traditional liberal remedies would help, few now believe they would suffice.

Demoralization among liberals has given new legitimacy to conservative explanations for the test score gap. From an empirical viewpoint, however, the traditional conservative explanations are no more appealing than their liberal counterparts. These explanations fall into three overlapping categories: the culture of poverty, the scarcity of two-parent black families, and genes.

—In the 1960s and 1970s, many conservatives blamed blacks' problems on a culture of poverty that rejected school achievement, the work ethic, and the two-parent family in favor of instant gratification and episodic violence. In the 1980s, conservatives (as well as some liberals) characterized the "black underclass" in similar terms. But this description only fits a tiny fraction of the black population. It certainly cannot explain why children from affluent black families have much lower test scores than their white counterparts.

—Conservatives invoke the decline of the family to explain social problems almost as frequently as liberals invoke poverty. But once we control a mother's family background, test scores, and years of schooling, whether she is married has even less effect on her children's test scores than whether she is poor.[24]

22. On teacher-pupil ratios see chapter 9. On salaries, teacher training, and teacher experience, see Boozer, Krueger, and Wolkon (1992, p. 299). Boozer, Krueger, and Wolkon's data cover secondary schools. Because most teachers prefer high-scoring students, and experienced teachers get preference in assignments, we would expect blacks to get less experienced teachers than whites in the same high school. We have not seen comparable recent data on elementary schools. For earlier data see Coleman and others (1966) and Mosteller and Moynihan (1972).

23. See chapter 9 by Ronald Ferguson. Ferguson's data come from Alabama and Texas, but the same pattern almost certainly recurs in other states.

24. See chapter 4.

—Scientists have not yet identified most of the genes that affect test performance, so we have no direct genetic evidence regarding innate cognitive differences between blacks and whites. But we have accumulated a fair amount of indirect evidence since 1970. Most of it suggests that whether children live in a "black" or "white" environment has far more impact on their test performance than the number of Africans or Europeans in their family tree.[25]

Taken as a whole, then, what we have characterized as the "traditional" explanations for the black-white test score gap do not take us very far. This has led some people to dismiss the gap as unimportant, arguing that the tests are culturally biased and do not measure skills that matter in the real world. Few scholars who spend time looking at quantitative data accept either of these arguments, so they have had to look for new explanations of the gap. These new explanations can mostly be grouped under two overlapping headings: culture and schooling.

In the late 1960s and early 1970s, many blacks and some whites dismissed cultural explanations of the test score gap as an effort to put down blacks for not thinking and acting like upper-middle-class whites. Since then, cultural explanations have enjoyed a slow but steady revival. In 1978 the Nigerian anthropologist John Ogbu suggested that caste-like minorities throughout the world tended to do poorly in school, even when they were visually indistinguishable from the majority.[26] Later, Ogbu argued that because blacks had such limited opportunities in America, they developed an "oppositional" culture that equated academic success with "acting white."[27] By linking black culture directly to oppression, Ogbu made it much easier for liberals to talk about cultural differences. Jeff Howard and Ray Hammond added another important strand to this argument when they suggested that academic competence developed partly through competition, and that "rumors of inferiority" made blacks reluctant to compete academically.[28] More recently, Claude Steele has argued that people of all races avoid situations in which they expect others to have negative stereotypes about them, even when they know that the stereotype does not apply. According to Steele, many black students "disidentify" with school because

---

25. See chapter 3.
26. Ogbu (1978).
27. Ogbu (1986); Fordham and Ogbu (1986). Philip Cook and Jens Ludwig discuss the empirical evidence for the "acting white" theory in chapter 10.
28. Howard and Hammond (1985).

constructing a personal identity based on academic competence entails a commitment to dealing with such stereotypes on a daily basis.[29]

Social scientists' thinking about "school effects" has also changed since the late 1960s. The 1966 Coleman Report and subsequent "production function" studies convinced most economists and quantitative sociologists that school resources had little impact on achievement.[30] Since 1990, however, new statistical methods, new data, and a handful of genuine experiments have suggested that additional resources may in fact have sizable effects on student achievement. The idea that resources matter cannot in itself explain the black-white achievement gap, because most school resources are now fairly equally distributed between blacks and whites. But certain crucial resources, such as teachers with high test scores, are still unequally distributed. And other resources, such as small classes and teachers with high expectations, may help blacks more than whites.[31] The idea that resources matter also suggests that "compensatory" spending on black schools could be valuable, at least if the money were used to cut class size and implement policies that have been shown to help.

This book tries to bring together recent evidence on some of the most controversial and puzzling aspects of the test score debate.[32] Section I examines the role of test bias, heredity, and family background in the black-white gap. Section II looks at how and why the gap has changed over the past generation. Section III examines educational, psychological, and cultural explanations for the gap. Section IV analyzes some of the educational and economic consequences of the gap. The book concludes with a commentary by William Julius Wilson. The rest of the introduction summarizes the book's main findings and then discusses some of their implications.

Test Bias

Many blacks and some whites believe that all cognitive tests are racially biased. In chapter 2 Christopher Jencks discusses five possible varieties of racial bias in testing. He concludes that two of the five constitute serious problems and that three are probably of minor importance.

---

29. Steele (1992, 1997).
30. Coleman and others (1966); Mosteller and Moynihan (1972); Jencks and others (1972); and Hanushek (1989).
31. See chapters 8 and 9.
32. The reader who wants a more complete survey should look at Miller (1995); Brody (1992, chap. 10); Snyderman and Rothman (1990); Vernon (1979); and Loehlin, Lindzey, and Spuhler (1975).

Labeling Bias

What Jencks calls "labeling bias" arises when a test claims to measure one thing but really measures something else. This is a major problem when tests claim to measure either intelligence or aptitude, because these terms are widely used to describe innate "potential" as well as developed abilities. The notion that intelligence and aptitude are innate seems to be especially salient in discussions of racial differences. Thus, the statement that "blacks are less intelligent than whites" is widely understood as a statement about innate differences. Yet almost all psychologists now agree that intelligence tests measure developed rather than innate abilities, and that people's developed abilities depend on their environment as well as their genes. Even psychologists who believe that racial differences in test performance are to some extent innate agree that intelligence tests overstate the difference one would observe if blacks and whites grew up in identical environments. Intelligence tests therefore constitute a racially biased estimate of innate ability, which is what nonpsychologists often mean by the word "intelligence." Test designers cannot eliminate this bias by changing the content of intelligence tests. The only way to eliminate it is to change the tests' labels so as to emphasize the fact that they measure developed rather than innate skills and abilities.

Content Bias

"Content bias" arises when a test contains questions that favor one group over another. Suppose, for example, that black and white children spoke mutually unintelligible versions of English. A test given in white English would then underestimate black children's skills and vice versa. This kind of content bias does not appear to be a significant problem for the tests discussed in this book. If one takes a standard vocabulary test and winnows out words with unusually large black-white differences, for example, the black-white gap does not shrink much. Likewise, if one compares black children to slightly younger white children, blacks and whites find the same words easy and difficult. Nor is the black-white gap on tests that measure familiarity with the content of American culture consistently larger than the gap on nonverbal tests that do not measure familiarity with any particular culture. Because the racial gap in children's test performance is not confined to items that measure exposure to white language, culture, or behavior but is dramatically reduced when black children are raised in white homes, Jencks suggests that it may reflect differences in the way blacks and whites are taught to deal with what they do not know and in the emphasis they put on learning new cognitive skills.

Methodological Bias

Methodological bias arises when we assess mastery of some skill or body of information in a way that underestimates the competence of one group relative to another. Methodological bias would be important if, say, having black rather than white testers changed the relative standing of black and white test takers. That does not appear to be the case. There is some evidence that describing a test in different ways can affect different groups' relative performance, but we do not yet know how general this is.[33]

Prediction Bias

A generation ago many egalitarians argued that using the SAT to screen applicants for selective colleges was unfair to blacks because tests of this kind underestimated black applicants' academic potential. For most colleges, academic potential means undergraduate grades. Almost all colleges have found that when they compare black and white undergraduates who enter with the same SAT scores, blacks earn *lower* grades than whites, not just in their first year but throughout their college careers.[34] Likewise, when firms compare black and white workers with the same test scores, blacks usually get slightly lower ratings from their supervisors and also do a little worse on more objective measures of job performance.[35] In psychological parlance, this means that tests like the SAT do not suffer from "prediction bias."

Selection System Bias

The test score gap between black and white job applicants has traditionally averaged about one standard deviation. When employers do not screen workers, the performance gap is likely to be much smaller—typi-

---

33. See chapter 11.
34. See chapters 12 and 13.
35. Hartigan and Wigdor (1989); and Wigdor and Green (1991).

cally more like two-fifths of a standard deviation.[36] The reason for this discrepancy is not that blacks perform better than whites with the same test scores. The reason is that test scores explain only 10 to 20 percent of the variation in job performance, and blacks are far less disadvantaged on the noncognitive determinants of job performance than on the cognitive ones.

Because blacks perform no better on the job than whites with similar scores, many people assume that using tests to select workers is racially fair. But if racial fairness means that blacks and whites who could do a job equally well must have an equal chance of getting the job, a selection system that emphasizes test scores is almost always unfair to most blacks (and to everyone else with low test scores). Imagine a company that has 600 applicants for 100 openings. Half the applicants are black and half are white. If the firm hires all applicants as temporary workers and retains those who perform best on the job, and if the performance gap between blacks and whites averages 0.4 standard deviations, about 36 blacks will get permanent jobs. If the firm selects the 100 applicants with the highest scores, about 13 blacks will get permanent jobs.[37] Jencks argues that the first outcome should be our yardstick for defining racial fairness. Using this yardstick, the second system is clearly biased against blacks. In effect, Jencks says, the second system forces blacks to pay for the fact that social scientists have unusually good measures of a trait on which blacks are unusually disadvantaged.

The Heredity-Environment Controversy

When the U.S. Army launched the world's first large-scale mental testing program in 1917, it found that whites scored substantially higher than

---

36. A test score gap of 1 SD implies a job performance gap of 0.4 SDs if the correlation between test scores and performance is 0.4 or—more realistically—if the correlation between test scores and performance is 0.25 and the gap between blacks and whites with the same test score averages 0.15 SDs (Hartigan and Wigdor, 1989).

37. In the test score case the black mean is –0.5 SDs and the white mean is +0.5 SDs. If the within-race SDs are equal, they are both $(1 - 0.5^2)^{0.5} = 0.866$. If the cutpoint is set at +1 SD, blacks must be $1.5/0.866 = 1.73$ SDs above the black mean, whereas whites must be only $0.5/0.866 = 0.577$ SDs above the white mean. The selection rates are then 4.2 percent for blacks and 28.3 percent for whites. Blacks will therefore get $4.2/(28.3 + 4.2) = 13$ percent of the jobs. In the case of temporary workers the black mean is –0.2 SDs, the white mean is +0.2 SDs, and the within-race SDs are 0.98, so blacks must be $1.2/.98 = 1.22$ SDs above the black mean and whites must be $0.8/.98 = 0.816$ SDs above the white mean. The selection rates are then 11.1 percent for blacks and 20.8 percent for whites, so blacks get $11.1/(11.1 + 20.8) = 36$ percent of jobs.

blacks. Biological determinists immediately cited these findings as evidence that whites had more innate ability than blacks, but cultural determinists quickly challenged this interpretation. By the late 1930s most social scientists seem to have been convinced that either genetic or cultural factors could explain the gap. Neither side had a convincing way of separating the effects of heredity from the effects of culture, so the debate was an empirical standoff.

After 1945 the horrors of the Holocaust made all genetic explanations of human differences politically suspect. Once the U.S. Supreme Court declared de jure racial segregation unconstitutional in 1954, genetic explanations of racial differences became doubly suspect because they were identified with southern resistance to desegregation. As a result, environmentalism remained hegemonic throughout the 1960s. Then in 1969 Arthur Jensen published an article in the *Harvard Educational Review* arguing that educational programs for disadvantaged children initiated as part of the War on Poverty had failed, and that the black-white test score gap probably had a substantial genetic component.[38] Jensen's argument went roughly as follows:

—Most of the variation in white IQ scores is genetic.[39]

—No one has advanced a plausible environmental explanation for the black-white gap.

—Therefore it is more reasonable to assume that part of the black-white gap is genetic than to assume it is entirely environmental.

Jensen's article created such a furor that psychologists once again began looking for evidence that bore directly on the question of whether racial differences in test performance were partly innate. Richard Nisbett reviews their findings in chapter 3.

Two small studies have tried to compare genetically similar children raised in black and white families. Elsie Moore found that black children adopted by white parents had IQ scores 13.5 points higher than black

---

38. Jensen (1969).

39. Based on his estimates of the correlations between twins reared together and apart, adopted siblings, and other kinds of relatives, Jensen suggested that 80 percent of the variance in white children's test scores was traceable to genetic differences. More recent estimates usually put the percentage between 30 and 70 percent (Jencks and others, 1972, appendix A; Plomin and DeFries, 1980; Rao and others, 1982; and Chipuer, Rovine, and Plomin, 1990). We regard 50 percent as a reasonable middle-of-the-road estimate for white children. Recent work (summarized in Plomin and Petrill, 1997) suggests that genes explain more of the variance in adults' scores than in children's scores, perhaps because adults are in a better position to choose environments compatible with their genetic propensities.

children adopted by black parents.[40] Lee Willerman and his colleagues compared children with a black mother and a white father to children with a white mother and a black father. The cleanest comparison is for mixed-race children who lived only with their mother. Mixed-race children who lived with a white mother scored 11 points higher than mixed-race children who lived with a black mother.[41] Since the black-white IQ gap averaged about 15 points at the time these two studies were done, they imply that about four-fifths of that gap was traceable to family-related factors (including schools and neighborhoods).[42]

A better-known study dealt with black and mixed-race children adopted by white parents in Minnesota. The mixed-race children were adopted earlier in life and had higher IQ scores than the children with two black parents. When the 29 black children were first tested, they scored at least ten points higher than the norm for black children, presumably because they had more favorable home environments than most black children.[43] When these children were retested in their late teens or twenties, their IQ scores had dropped and were no longer very different from those of Northern

40. Moore (1986) studied 23 white and 23 black families. The sample included 20 biracial children and 26 all-black children. In black families the 6 biracial children scored 2.8 points higher than the 17 all-black children. In white families the 14 biracial children scored 1.5 points lower than the 9 all-black children.

41. Willerman, Naylor, and Myrianthopoulos (1974) studied 129 four-year-olds, 101 of whom were raised by a white mother and 28 of whom were raised by a black mother. Among the married mothers the 50 children raised by a white mother and a black father had mean IQs of 104.7, while the 17 children raised by a black mother and a white father had mean IQs of 96.4. Among single mothers, who provide a cleaner comparison of the effects of growing up in a "white" rather than a "black" environment, the 51 children raised by a white mother had mean IQs of 99, while the 11 children raised by a black mother had mean IQs of 88. The mixed-race children raised by black and white mothers presumably had about the same mixture of "African" and "European" genes, but the parents may have been subject to different forms of genetic selection relative to others in their racial group.

42. Children raised by, say, black and white single mothers usually grow up in different neighborhoods and attend different schools. Nonetheless, black children raised by white parents are unlikely to have exactly the same overall environment as white children raised by the same parents. We do not know how white parents treat their black and white children, but there could be important differences favoring either group. We do know that teachers often treat black and white children somewhat differently (see chapter 8), and strangers are even more likely to do so. In addition, black and white children see themselves somewhat differently and may choose different environments as a result.

43. Most adoptees were first tested between the ages of four and sixteen. Weinberg, Scarr, and Waldman (1992, table 2) report data indicating that at the time of initial testing IQ scores averaged 97 for adoptees known to have had two black parents (N = 29), 109 for adoptees known to have had one black and one white parent (N = 68), and 109 for adoptees with a black mother and a father of unknown race (N = 33). The IQ gap between all-black and mixed-race children was much larger in the Minnesota study than in other studies (Moore, 1986; see also Flynn, 1980, on Eyferth).

blacks raised in black families.[44] The most obvious explanation for this drop is that the adoptees had moved out of their white adoptive parents' homes into less favorable environments.[45] But because the study did not cover black or mixed-race children adopted by black parents, it does not seem to us to provide strong evidence on either side of the heredity-environment debate.

Racially Mixed Children

Race is not a well-defined biological category. It is a social category, whose biological correlates vary geographically and historically. America has traditionally classified people as black using the "one drop" rule, under which anyone with known black ancestors is black. As a result, people are often treated as black even though they have a lot of European ancestors. If blacks with a lot of European ancestors had the same test scores as those with no European ancestors, we could safely conclude that the black-white test score gap was a by-product of social classification rather than heredity. But when we find that light-skinned blacks score higher than dark-skinned blacks, we cannot rule out the possibility that this difference is environmental. Light skin has traditionally been a social asset for black Americans, and the correlation between light skin and test performance could reflect this fact. To get around this problem, we need less visible genetic markers. Two studies have used blood markers to estimate the percentage of Europeans in a black child's family tree. Neither study found a correlation between the number of "European" blood markers and IQ.[46]

44. Weinberg, Scarr, and Waldman (1992) report data suggesting that when the Minnesota adoptees were retested, the IQ means were 89 for black adoptees (N = 21), 99 for mixed-race adoptees (N = 55), and 99 for those whose father's race was unknown (N = 25). Adjusting for changes in test norms makes the decline about 2 points larger (Waldman, personal communication, August 6, 1997).

45. It is also conceivable that genetic differences between blacks and whites become more important in adolescence. McCartney and others' (1992) meta-analysis of twin studies suggests that the relative importance of home environment falls in adolescence and that the relative importance of genes increases. Thus if black adoptees had average test scores prior to adolescence because the negative effects of their genes were offset by the positive effects of their adoptive homes, and if their home environment exerted less influence after they reached adolescence, their test scores might fall.

46. Loehlin, Vandenberg, and Osborne (1973) and Scarr and others (1977). These studies would be more convincing if blood group classification were more reliable. With today's technology it should be possible to classify children more accurately along the European-versus-African ancestry continuum, but conducting such a study would be politically difficult.

Although racially mixed children are culturally black in America, and are almost always raised by black parents in black communities, this is not true everywhere. Klaus Eyferth studied the illegitimate children of black and white soldiers stationed in Germany as part of the army of occupation after World War II. All these children were raised by their German mothers.[47] There was considerable prejudice against blacks in Germany at the time, and any child of a German mother who looked black was also presumed to be illegitimate, which carried additional stigma. But mixed-race German children did not attend predominantly black schools, live in black neighborhoods, or (presumably) have predominantly black (or mixed-race) friends. When Eyferth gave these children a German version of the Wechsler IQ test, children with black fathers and white fathers had almost identical scores.[48]

Taken in isolation, none of these studies would carry much weight. The samples are small, and the comparisons could be distorted by unmeasured genetic or environmental influences. But Nisbett argues that their consistency gives them far more weight that they would have if taken one by one.[49] We agree. We read these studies as supporting three tentative conclusions:

—When "black" genes are not visible to the naked eye and are not associated with membership in a black community, they do not have much effect on young children's test scores.

—Growing up in an African-American rather than a European-American family substantially reduces a young child's test performance.

—When black Americans raised in white families reach adolescence, their test scores fall.

47. The most detailed summary of this study in English is found in Flynn (1980). Eyferth sampled roughly 5 percent (N = 181) of the children known to have been fathered by black French and American soldiers between 1945 and 1953. He then constructed a matched sample of 83 children fathered by white soldiers. The two samples were matched only on characteristics of the mother and location, not characteristics of the father, which were largely unknown. Eighty percent of the black fathers were American and 20 percent were French Africans. Flynn reports that in the U.S. army of occupation the black-white gap on the Army General Classification Test (a predecessor of the AFQT) was about four-fifths that in the general population.

48. The means were 96.5 for mixed-race children and 97.2 for all-white children. The sampling error of this difference is about 4 points.

49. Although the published results are quite consistent, there is some risk that unpublished studies might show a different pattern, especially if liberal authors engage in self-censorship or liberal reviewers have higher scientific standards for papers that they see as dangerous. But while political correctness could have posed an important obstacle to publication in sociology and education journals, a number of psychology journals regularly publish papers suggesting that the black-white gap is partly innate.

These studies do not prove that blacks and whites would have exactly the same test scores if they were raised in the same environment and treated the same way. But we find it hard to see how anyone reading these studies with an open mind could conclude that innate ability played a *large* role in the black-white gap.[50]

Effects of Family Background

Chapter 4, by Meredith Phillips, Jeanne Brooks-Gunn, Greg Duncan, Pamela Klebanov, and Jonathan Crane tries to estimate the effect of specific family characteristics on young children's test scores. This is not easy. Hundreds of different family characteristics correlate with children's test performance. Disentangling their effects is a statistical nightmare. Almost any family characteristic can also serve as a proxy for a child's genes. We know, for example, that a mother's genes affect her test scores and that her test scores affect her educational attainment. Thus when we compare children whose mothers finished college to children whose mothers only finished high school, the two groups' vocabulary scores can differ for genetic as well as environmental reasons. Even when a child is adopted, moreover, the way the adoptive parents treat the child may depend on the child's genes. Parents read more to children who seem to enjoy it, for example, and whether children enjoy being read to may well depend partly on their genes.[51]

The best solution to such problems is to conduct experiments. In the 1970s, for example, the federal government conducted a series of "negative income tax" experiments that increased the cash income of randomly se-

---

50. Skeptics may wonder whether other experts read this literature the way we do. That question is not easy to answer. Snyderman and Rothman (1987) asked a sample of over 1,000 psychologists, sociologists, and educational researchers, "Which of the following best characterizes your opinion of the heritability of the black-white differences in IQ?" Of the 661 "experts" who returned a questionnaire, 14 percent declined to answer this particular question, 24 percent said the data were insufficient to support a reasonable opinion, 1 percent thought the gap was "due entirely to genetic variation," 15 percent thought it was "due entirely to environmental variation," and 45 percent thought it was "a product of both genetic and environmental variation." It is not clear how many of those who gave the "both" response would accept our conclusion that genes do not play a *large* role in the black-white gap. Nor is it clear how many of Snyderman and Rothman's respondents had read the research that Nisbett reviews.

51. For a general review see Plomin and Bergeman (1991). For data on parental treatment of adopted children and twins see Braungart, Fulker, and Plomin (1992).

lected low-income families. These experiments did not last very long, the samples getting any given "treatment" were small, and the results were poorly reported, so it is hard to know exactly what happened. Short-term income increases did not have statistically reliable effects on low-income children's test scores, but that does not mean their true effect was zero.[52] As far as we know, these are the only randomized experiments that have altered families' socioeconomic characteristics and then measured the effect on children's test scores.

In theory, we can also separate the effects of parents' socioeconomic status from the effects of their genes by studying adopted children. But because adoption agencies try to screen out "unsuitable" parents, the range of environments in adoptive homes is usually restricted. The adoptive samples for which we have data are also small. Thus while parental SES does not predict adopted children's IQ scores as well as it predicts natural children's IQ scores, the data on adopted children are not likely to persuade skeptics.[53]

Anyone who wants to estimate the impact of specific family characteristics on children's test scores must therefore rely heavily on surveys of children raised by their natural parents. The best source of such data is the National Longitudinal Survey of Youth (CNLSY) that Phillips and her colleagues use in chapter 4. Black five- and six-year-olds in their sample scored about 16 points (one standard deviation) below whites on the Peabody Picture Vocabulary Test (PPVT). Traditional measures of educational and economic inequality do not explain much of this gap. Measures of a mother's socioeconomic position when she was growing up and measures of her current parenting practices explain considerably more.

---

52. See the summary in Mayer (1997).

53. The only convincing way to deal with unmeasured restrictions in the range of adoptive children's home environments is to compare the regression of IQ on parental SES for adopted and natural children in the same families. Scarr and Weinberg (1978) report much larger correlations for natural than adopted children in a postadolescent sample. Comparisons involving younger samples are ambiguous. The IQ-SES correlations for adopted children in Scarr and Weinberg (1976) do not differ in any consistent way from the correlations for natural children in (more or less) the same families (Scarr and Weinberg, 1978). The IQ-SES correlations for natural and adopted children in Loehlin, Horn, and Willerman (1989) also seem inconclusive. For early studies without a comparison group of natural children raised in the same family see Jencks and others (1972, p. 80). For a small recent study of separated identical twins with an unusually large variance for parental education see Bouchard and others (1990).

Parental Schooling

Early in the twentieth century white parents typically completed two or three more years of school than blacks.[54] By 1991 the gap between black and white mothers with children in first grade had fallen to 0.8 years.[55] Many observers have suggested that this change played a significant role in reducing the black-white gap in children's test scores.[56] But if parental schooling correlates with children's test scores mainly because it is a proxy for parental genes, changing the distribution of schooling will not affect the distribution of test scores, either for individuals or for groups.

When Phillips and her colleagues control a mother's family background, the estimated effect of an extra year of school on her child's PPVT score falls from 1.73 to 1.15 points.[57] When they also control the mother's AFQT score (their proxy for her cognitive genotype), the effect falls to somewhere between 0.5 and 0.6 points.[58] This suggests that a two-year reduction in the black-white education gap among mothers would cut the PPVT gap by about a point. Of course, if the schooling gap narrowed because black and white parents had grown up in more similar homes or had more similar test scores, the predicted reduction in the PPVT gap between black and white children would be larger.[59] The CNLSY suggests that cutting the

54. Hauser and Featherman (1976) show, for example, that the fathers of black men born between 1907 and 1916 had 2.6 years less schooling than the fathers of white men born in these years. We could not find comparable data on mothers.

55. This estimate comes from the Prospects sample that Phillips, Crouse, and Ralph describe in chapter 7. The racial disparity in mother's education is smaller in CNLSY than in Prospects (0.2 versus 0.8 years), at least partly because the CNLSY data that Phillips and her colleagues analyzed underrepresent older mothers, who are disproportionately white and highly educated.

56. See chapters 5 and 6, as well as Armor (1992).

57. See Chapter 4, table 4-3.

58. Phillips and her colleagues include some mothers whose test scores were measured after they had had different amounts of schooling. For these mothers, differences in schooling contribute to differences in AFQT scores as well as the other way round. Winship and Korenman (1997) estimate that an extra year of schooling raises test scores by an average of 0.18 SDs. Phillips and her colleagues estimate that with maternal education controlled a 1 SD increase in a mother's AFQT score raises her child's test score by 0.23 SDs. Since the coefficient of mother's schooling with AFQT controlled is 0.52, the sum of the direct and indirect effects of an extra year of maternal schooling on a child's PPVT score is $0.52 + (0.18)(0.23) = 0.56$ points. This estimate assumes that a mother's IQ genotype has no partial correlation with her educational attainment once we control her AFQT score.

59. Black and white CNLSY parents also attended schools of differing quality. The CNLSY shows that the percentage of whites in a mother's high school had a significant positive effect on her children's PPVT score, independent of her own race, years of schooling, and AFQT score. Teacher turnover also had a significant negative effect.

schooling gap between black and white fathers would have a smaller effect than cutting the gap between black and white mothers. But this may not be true for older children, for whom the effects of mother's and father's education are roughly equal.[60]

Income Effects

White CNLSY parents reported 73 percent more income than their black counterparts. When Phillips and her colleagues compared black and white children whose families had had the same average annual income since the child was born, the PPVT gap narrowed by 2.4 points. But once again it does not follow that raising all black families' incomes by 73 percent would raise their children's PPVT scores by 2.4 points. To estimate the effect of increasing black parents' incomes without changing the traits that cause the current income gap, we need to know how much parental income affects children's test scores when we compare parents with the same family background, test scores, and schooling. These controls cut the estimated effect of parental income on PPVT scores by about three-fifths. Even this estimate is probably on the high side, because it does not control either the father's test scores or his family background. Thus, the CNLSY suggests that eliminating black-white income differences would cut the PPVT gap by less than 1 point.[61] Eliminating the causes of the black-white income gap might, of course, have a much larger effect. Racial disparities in parental wealth have almost no effect on children's test scores once Phillips and her colleagues control income, schooling, and the mother's test scores.

Single-Parent Families

Once Phillips and her colleagues hold constant the mother's family background, educational attainment, and test scores, children who have grown up in an intact family score no higher on the PPVT than children

---

60. See table 5B-3 of chapter 5.

61. This estimate is based on the fact that (a) equation 4 in table 4-3 of chapter 4 shows that controlling the natural log of mean family income since birth reduces the test score gap from 16.27 to 13.89 points, and (b) equations 5 and 7 in the same table show that controlling parental schooling, mother's AFQT, maternal grandparents' SES, and a set of location variables lowers the coefficients of the parental income dummies by an average of 60 percent. The estimated reduction in the black-white PPVT gap due to income per se is thus about $(16.27 - 13.89)(0.40) = 0.95$ points, or 6 percent of the initial gap.

from single-parent families. Other studies find slightly larger effects, but the effects are never large enough to be of any substantive importance.[62]

Parenting Strategies

Knowing parents' education and income tells us something about how they raise their children, but not much. The CNLSY tried to measure parenting practices directly, both by asking parents what they did and by asking interviewers how mothers treated their children during the interview. Parenting practices appear to have a sizable impact on children's test scores. Even with parental education, family income, and the mother's AFQT scores controlled, racial differences in parenting practices account for between a fifth and a quarter of the racial gap on the PPVT. This suggests that changes in parenting practices might do more to reduce the black-white test score gap than changes in parents' educational attainment or income. We cannot be sure how large these effects would be, however, because the way parents treat their children is a proxy for all kinds of unmeasured parental characteristics, as well as for the child's own genes.[63]

Grandparents

Upwardly mobile parents often raise their children the way they themselves were raised. Phillips and her colleagues find that racial differences in parenting practices are partly traceable to the fact that even when black and white parents have the same test scores, educational attainment, income, wealth, and number of children, black parents are likely to have grown up in less advantaged households. Phillips and her colleagues also find that

62. Using the 1980 High School and Beyond data, Mulkey, Crain, and Harrington (1992) found that even without controlling parental test scores, controls for parental schooling and race reduced the estimated effect of living with a single mother on tenth-grade vocabulary scores to 0.06 standard deviations. McLanahan and Sandefur (1994, p. 44) report that living with a single mother reduced quartile rank (coded 1-4) by 0.11 points, which is equivalent to a reduction of (0.11)(25) = 3 percentile points. This is consistent with Mulkey, Crain, and Harrington's findings.

63. On genetic determinants of parenting practices see Plomin, DeFries, and Fulker (1988); Braungart, Fulker, and Plomin (1992); and Plomin (1994). Although these data suggest that children's genes have some effect on parenting practices, the effects appear to be small and the standard errors of the estimates are large.

this can lower black children's test scores. In other words, it can take more than one generation for successful families to adopt the "middle-class" parenting practices that seem most likely to increase children's cognitive skills.

Changes in the Black-White Gap

Chapter 5, by Larry Hedges and Amy Nowell, analyzes changes since 1965 in the black-white test score gap at the end of high school. As figure 1-2 showed, this gap has narrowed substantially. Nonetheless, racial disparities are still very large, especially near the top of the distribution. In both 1982 and 1992 white high school seniors were about ten times more likely than black seniors to score in the top 5 percent of the national distribution on a composite measure of academic skills. These test score disparities near the top of the distribution put blacks at a severe disadvantage in competition for places at selective colleges and professional schools. They are also likely to have a major impact on the racial composition of the nation's professional and managerial elite.

David Grissmer, Ann Flanagan, and Stephanie Williamson also examine changes in the black-white gap in chapter 6. Unlike Hedges and Nowell, they analyze trends in black and white achievement separately, asking what could have caused the changes they document for each group. This approach focuses attention on a puzzle that neither they nor anyone else has been able to resolve fully. It is easy to identify changes in both families and schools that might account for the improvement in black achievement. Increased parental education, smaller families, smaller classes, and rising enrollment in academically demanding courses are all plausible candidates. But these changes have all affected whites as well as blacks. The changes were smaller for whites than for blacks, but they were still substantial. If changes of this kind raised black scores, they should also have raised white scores. Yet as figure 1-2 indicates, white seventeen-year-olds' reading and math scores rose by only 0.1 standard deviations between the early 1970s and 1996.

One way to solve this puzzle is to assume that improvements in schooling were more valuable to blacks than to whites. But while there is some evidence that blacks benefit more than whites from small classes and highly educated mothers, such advantages always confer some benefit on whites as well. Grissmer and his colleagues therefore looked for changes that might plausibly be expected to raise blacks' scores without affecting whites' scores. School desegregation in the South is one example. Desegregation seems to have pushed up southern blacks' scores a little without affecting whites either way. Grissmer and his colleagues also speculate that the civil rights movement, the War on Poverty, and affirmative action may have changed black parents' and students' attitude toward school achievement without affecting whites, but this hypothesis is hard to test in a rigorous way.

The authors also suggest that the decline in black teenagers' reading scores after 1988 could be related to the surge in violence among black teenagers that began in the late 1980s. All else equal, the surge in violence should also have depressed black adolescents' math scores.[64] But the negative effect of violence on math scores may have been offset by the fact that more black adolescents were studying geometry and second-year algebra. Among non-Hispanic whites, who were also taking more demanding math courses and were not murdering one another at a higher rate, math scores have risen steadily since 1982, while reading scores have remained flat.

Does the Gap Widen with Age?

Discussions of how schooling affects the black-white achievement gap have long been bedeviled by disagreement about how the gap should be measured. Those who think the gap widens with age almost always describe achievement in terms of grade levels or years. When a first-grader scores at the 16th percentile of the first-grade distribution, for example, she has a vocabulary roughly comparable to the average kindergartner. One way to describe this situation is to say that she is "one year below grade level." When a seventh-grader scores at the 16th percentile of the seventh-grade distribution, she has a vocabulary roughly comparable to that of the average fifth-grader, so we can say she is now "two years below grade level." But it is not clear that a child who consistently scores at the 16th percentile is really farther behind at age twelve than at age six. That makes us reluctant to discuss the black-white gap in these terms, and none of the contributors to this volume does so.

---

64. Precise comparisons between trends in reading and math achievement are impossible before 1990 because NAEP did not give its reading and math tests in the same years. We have no data on math achievement in 1988, when black reading achievement peaked. Thus, we do not know whether black seventeen-year-olds' math achievement deteriorated as much as their reading achievement between 1988 and 1990. There was no clear trend in either reading or math achievement among black seventeen-year-olds from 1990 to 1996.

Instead, they focus on where blacks fall in the national distribution at a given age. They usually describe their findings in terms of "standard deviations." If the average black scores at the 16th percentile, the average white scores at the 50th percentile, and the distribution is normal, the black-white gap is one standard deviation. Sometimes contributors simply report the average black child's percentile rank in the overall distribution of scores. If every black child falls at the same percentile of the overall distribution at age eighteen as at age six, what psychometricians call "age standardized" measures will show no change in the gap. Chapter 7, by Meredith Phillips, James Crouse, and John Ralph, shows that the age-standardized black-white gap hardly changes for reading between first and twelfth grades. The math gap increases a little. The vocabulary gap appears to increase more, but the vocabulary data are not as good as the reading or math data, so it is hard to be sure.[65]

Such findings have persuaded some social scientists that schools do not contribute much to the black-white gap. This conclusion strikes us as premature. If stability were the natural order of things and did not need to be explained, the fact that blacks typically score at about the same percentile in first and twelfth grades would be evidence that schools did not contribute to the gap. In human development, however, change is at least as common as stability. That means we have to explain stability as well as change.

Consider a simple example. Suppose we give children a vocabulary test at the end of kindergarten. Twelve years later we retest both blacks and whites who scored at the 16th percentile of the white distribution in kindergarten. Since we have selected white children with unusually low first-grade scores, most are likely to have come from homes that were considerably worse than the average white child's home. But home environments change in unpredictable ways between first and twelfth grades. Mothers who are constantly irritated by small children sometimes do much better with older children. Fathers who drink too much sometimes go on the wagon. Unstable jobs and living arrangements sometimes stabilize. Children's envi-

---

65. Both Entwisle, Alexander, and Olson's (1997) Baltimore data and the CNLSY show that the standardized black-white gap on reading and math tests is quite small for five- and six-year-olds. In the case of the CNLSY, this may be because the reading and math tests for five- and six-year-olds have poor psychometric properties. The PPVT-R, which is less sensitive to formal instruction, shows less increase in the standardized black-white gap with age. Even tests that are sensitive to formal instruction, like math tests, do not show much increase in the standardized black-white gap after the first few years of school.

ronments also expand as they get older. Some children of neglectful parents encounter dedicated teachers. Some children from semiliterate homes make friends with children who read a lot, while others discover libraries. Because these changes have a large random element, children whose homes were unusually bad during their first five years of life tend to have somewhat better environments later in life.[66] This process is often called "regression to the mean," but that is only a label, not an explanation. Readers may find the reasons for regression to the mean easier to understand if they focus on the child whose home ranked at the very bottom at the end of kindergarten. Twelve years later, this child's home is still likely to be relatively bad, but it is unlikely to be the very worst.

Because every child's environment changes, white children who started school at the 16th percentile seldom score at exactly the 16th percentile in twelfth grade. Nor do their scores spread out in a completely random way. Some score below the 16th percentile in twelfth grade, but most score above it. This happens because the luck of repeated environmental draws moves most children with low initial scores closer to the average.[67] A reasonable guess is that the average white child who starts school scoring at the 16th percentile will finish school scoring at about the 27th percentile.[68]

Now consider the black children who started school scoring at the 16th percentile of the white distribution. If the black-white gap does not change with age and is always one standard deviation, blacks who score at the 16th percentile in first grade will still score at the 16th percentile in twelfth grade. Black and white children who start out at the 16th percentile will therefore end up with quite different scores in twelfth grade, with the average white at the 27th percentile and the average black at the

66. The genes that affect test performance may also have different effects at different ages, which would produce the same regression effects.

67. Readers should also bear in mind that 16 percent of children always score below the 16th percentile, regardless of the children's age. The fact that children who start near the bottom tend to move up therefore has to be offset by the fact that other children who started with higher scores move down to fill the bottom rungs of the ladder. Since 84 percent of all children start out above the 16th percentile, only a small minority of this large group needs to slip below the 16th percentile to replace those who move up.

68. This estimate assumes that the observed correlation between first- and twelfth-grade verbal scores is 0.52. The estimate comes from a sample of 753 children in Boulder, Colorado, who took the California Test of Mental Maturity in first or second grade and took the Lorge-Thorndike intelligence test in eleventh grade (Hopkins and Bracht, 1975). Assuming an average test-retest reliability of 0.85 for verbal IQ at these ages, the true correlation is 0.52/0.85 = 0.61. The estimate is meant to be heuristic, not exact.

16th percentile. Something must cause this difference. That "something" could involve genes, home environments, school environments, or other factors.[69]

Phillips and her colleagues' best guess is that if we followed representative samples of black and white children from first to twelfth grade we would find that about half the black-white gap in twelfth-grade reading and math scores was explained (in a statistical sense) by differences in their first-grade scores. The other half would then be attributable to things that happened between the ages of six and eighteen. But this estimate need not mean that schools cause half the difference between black and white twelfth-grade scores. A number of studies show, for example, that the test score gap between economically advantaged and disadvantaged children widens more over the summer, when children are not in school, than it does during the winter.[70] This suggests that racial differences in how much children learn between the ages of six and eighteen depend partly on what happens outside the schools. Nonetheless, schools are society's main instrument for altering the distribution of cognitive skills. Their role in widening or narrowing the black-white gap therefore requires strict scrutiny.

What Can Schools Do?

Instead of asking whether schools cause the black-white test score gap, Ronald Ferguson asks what they can do to reduce it. In chapter 8 he deals with the vexed question of teacher expectations. His survey of the evidence leads him to five conclusions.

—Teachers have lower expectations for blacks than for whites.

—Teachers' expectations have more impact on black students' performance than on white students' performance.

—Teachers expect less of blacks than of whites because black students' past performance and behavior have been worse. Ferguson finds no evi-

---

69. Some readers may think it is obvious that whites should regress to the white mean and that blacks should regress to the black mean. These readers should reframe the puzzle in terms of a simple regression model. Let T denote a test score, let the subscripts 1 and 2 denote time, let W be a dichotomous variable with a value of 1 for whites and 0 for nonwhites, and let e be an error term. Then $T_2 = B_0 + B_1 T_1 + B_w W + e$. The question is why B_w should be positive even after correcting T_1 for measurement error.

70. On summer versus winter learning, see Heyns (1978, 1987) and Entwisle and Alexander (1992) and the sources they cite.

dence that teachers' expectations differ by race when they are asked to assess children who have performed equally well and behaved equally well in the past.

—By basing their expectations on children's past performance and behavior, teachers perpetuate racial disparities in achievement.

—Exhorting teachers to have more faith in black children's potential is unlikely to change their expectations. But professional development programs in which teachers actually see disadvantaged black children performing at a high level can make a difference.

In chapter 9 Ferguson reviews school policies that might help reduce the black-white test score gap. A substantial number of randomized experiments suggest that smaller classes raise test scores.[71] The largest of these studies is the Tennessee class-size experiment, which covered 6,572 children in 76 schools. It found that cutting class size by a third between kindergarten and third grade (from about 23 to about 15) raised both reading and math scores by about a third of a standard deviation for blacks and by a sixth of a standard deviation for whites. After children moved to larger classes in fourth grade, the benefits associated with having been in smaller classes began to diminish, especially for blacks. But the benefits were still sizable at the end of the seventh grade, which is the last year for which we currently have data.[72]

History is never as tidy as a randomized experiment, but the historical record seems consistent with the hypothesis that reducing class size raises reading scores. Averaged across all grade levels, the pupil-teacher ratio fell from 26:1 in the early 1960s to 17:1 in the early 1990s. About half the extra teachers were used to cut the number of students in regular classrooms. The size of the average class therefore fell from 29 in 1961 to 24 in 1991.[73] Ferguson finds that changes in the pupil-teacher ratio predict changes in the black-white reading gap among NAEP nine-year-olds quite well.[74] The pupil-teacher ratio fell substantially in the 1970s. Both black and white nine-year-olds' reading scores rose during this period, but blacks' scores rose more, which is what the Tennessee results would predict. Unfortunately, nine-year-olds' math scores did not rise in tandem with their reading scores. Black nine-year-olds' math scores rose only a little during

71. Glass and others (1982).
72. Mosteller (1995). For a far more skeptical view see Hanushek (1998).
73. Lewitt and Baker (1997).
74. See also chapter 6.

the 1970s, and white nine-year-olds' math scores hardly changed at all.[75] Perhaps the impact of smaller classes on math scores was offset by other countervailing influences, such as a less demanding curriculum.

Counting the number of teachers in a school is easier than measuring their competence. Ferguson argues that a teacher's test score is the best readily available indicator of the teacher's ability to raise children's test scores. No one has done randomized experiments to see whether hiring teachers with higher test scores improves student achievement, but a large body of non-experimental research by Ferguson and others suggests that high-scoring teachers are more effective. Ferguson therefore concludes that using competency exams to screen out low-scoring teachers will help children in the long run. Screening out teachers with low scores should benefit blacks even more than whites, because black children are now considerably more likely than whites to have teachers with low scores. But competency exams will not do much to raise students' test scores unless the passing score is high enough to eliminate a substantial fraction of potential teachers. At present, few states or school districts set the cut point on competency tests very high.

Unfortunately, raising the passing score on teacher competency exams will also reduce the percentage of blacks who qualify for teaching jobs. This is a major political problem. It may also be a pedagogic problem, since Ferguson finds some evidence that black children learn more from black teachers. But this evidence is far weaker and less consistent than the evidence that teachers with high test scores will raise black children's scores.

School desegregation can also raise black children's achievement under some circumstances. The findings of David Grissmer and his colleagues strongly suggest that desegregation raised southern black nine-year-olds' test scores in the 1970s. In a study covering the early 1990s, Meredith Phillips also found that attending a whiter school probably had a positive effect on black students' reading scores in the early grades. But she found less evidence that the racial mix of middle schools and high schools affected reading scores. Nor did a school's racial mix have a consistent influence on black students' math scores.[76] Since racially mixed schools have higher-scoring teachers, and since we often assume that teachers in racially mixed schools have higher expectations for their students, this finding is puzzling.

75. Both black and white nine-year-olds' math scores did rise after 1982, but class size has not changed much since the late 1970s.
76. Phillips (1997).

One common hypothesis about why black children derive such modest benefits from attending what seem to be better schools is that racially mixed schools track black students into classrooms where their classmates are mostly black and their teachers expect very little. Ability grouping is obviously a contentious issue even in racially homogeneous schools. Students in low-ability classes usually cover less material than those in mixed-ability classes, but covering less material does not necessarily mean that students learn less. Ability grouping is supposed to increase the odds that slower learners get instruction appropriate to their skills. If that happened, slow learners could be better off.

Public debates about ability grouping seldom pay much attention to empirical evidence about its impact, perhaps because the evidence does not fit either side's preconceptions. Ferguson's review suggests that assigning children to separate classrooms on the basis of their presumed ability has no significant effect, positive or negative, on the test scores of children in the middle or bottom third of the distribution. This kind of grouping may help high-scoring students a little, but if so the effect is very small.[77] Assigning students to heterogeneous classrooms and then grouping them by ability *within* a heterogeneous classroom appears to increase math achievement for all children, but there have been only a handful of randomized experiments with this kind of grouping, so it is hard to be sure.[78] The impact of ability grouping on reading skills is apparently unknown. Research on this subject is now mostly qualitative. Only one experimental study of ability grouping and test performance has been conducted since 1974.

At the high school level, black and white students are almost equally likely to say they are in the college preparatory program, but white students are substantially more likely to take academically demanding classes, such as second-year algebra, geometry, or Advanced Placement courses of various kinds. Ferguson finds that class assignments depend on students' pre-

---

77. In a review limited to randomized experiments, Mosteller, Light, and Sachs (1996) found ten studies covering 2,641 students that compared heterogeneous classrooms to classrooms tracked on the basis of estimated ability or past achievement ("XYZ grouping"). Averaged across all students, the mean difference in achievement between the two methods was exactly zero. There was some evidence that the least skilled students learned less and that the most skilled students learned more under XYZ grouping, but this difference was not statistically significant.

78. Mosteller, Light, and Sachs (1996) found only three experimental studies that compared the effect of ability grouping within heterogeneous classrooms with the effect of ungrouped heterogeneous classrooms.

vious grades, test scores, and socioeconomic background, but not on their race per se. We do not know *how* socioeconomic background affects course assignments. High-SES parents may encourage their children to take more demanding courses even when their children's test scores or grades are marginal. High-SES parents may also pressure schools to let their children take such courses. It would be a mistake to fault schools for letting high-SES students take demanding courses, however. Instead, we should probably fault schools for not pushing more low-SES students into such courses.

Fear of "Acting White"

An influential 1986 article by Signithia Fordham and John Ogbu drew attention to the fact that academically successful black adolescents often said their classmates disparaged them for "acting white." Some black students also reported that they had stopped working hard in order to avoid such taunts. Since 1986 many successful black adults have also reported such experiences. So have other ethnographers. Indeed, this explanation for blacks' academic problems has become part of American folklore and is often repeated in the mass media. Philip Cook and Jens Ludwig were apparently the first scholars to test such claims quantitatively with national data.[79] Chapter 10 describes their findings.

If black students were less committed to academic success than white students, we would expect blacks to do less homework and skip school more often. Cook and Ludwig find that few students, black or white, do much homework. The median black, like the median white, spends between two and four hours a week doing homework outside school. The hardest-working whites do more homework than the hardest-working blacks, but even for these students the difference is not huge: 14 percent of white tenth-graders report spending more than ten hours a week on homework, compared with 10 percent of blacks. When it comes to skipping school, racial differences are negligible.

Cook and Ludwig also investigate the social costs of academic success for blacks and whites. They do not challenge Fordham and Ogbu's claim that working hard or getting good grades can lead to charges of racial disloyalty. But white students who work hard are also taunted as "nerds" and

---

79. For a more recent analysis along the same lines see Ainsworth-Darnell and Downey (forthcoming)

"geeks." Black students' fear of "acting white" can only exacerbate the black-white test score gap if academic success has higher social costs for blacks than for whites, or if blacks are more responsive than whites to such social costs. Since Fordham and Ogbu studied an all-black high school, they could not investigate these issues.

In 1990 the National Education Longitudinal Survey (NELS) asked tenth-graders whether they had been physically threatened at school, whether they often felt put down by other students in their classes, whether other students thought of them as popular, whether other students thought of them as part of the "leading crowd," and whether they were popular with the opposite sex. Cook and Ludwig use these measures to assess the social consequences of getting A's in math and of being a member of the student honor society. Their analysis yields two findings.

—Getting A's in math is almost unrelated to being threatened, feeling put down by other students, and feeling unpopular. Honor society members appear to feel *less* threatened and *more* popular than other students.

—The social costs and benefits of academic success are about the same for blacks and whites. Where racial differences do arise, blacks usually benefit slightly more than whites from academic success.

Cook and Ludwig's findings suggest that while academic success can have social costs, it also has benefits. If schools can reduce the costs or increase the benefits, student achievement is likely to improve. Judging by Cook and Ludwig's findings, however, the improvement would be as large for whites as for blacks. If that were the case, the racial disparity in academic achievement would not change much.

Ferguson challenges these conclusions in his comment on Cook and Ludwig's chapter. His most important criticism is that they are asking the wrong question. He agrees that fear of acting white probably plays a minor role in *creating* the black-white test score gap that we observe in American high schools, but it may nonetheless be an important obstacle to *reducing* the gap. Ferguson compares American high schools to a mile-long race in which two competitors are nearing the end of the course. They are separated by forty yards. Both are jogging. Neither is out of breath. Observing this scene, we could ask why the black runner was behind. But we could also ask why the black runner was not trying to catch up. The "acting white" hypothesis does not seem to explain why black high school students are behind their white classmates. But it may well explain why they are not making more effort to catch up.

"Stereotype Threat"

Claude Steele and Joshua Aronson argue in chapter 11 that academically successful blacks worry about the possibility that getting a low score on a test will confirm the stereotype that blacks are not academically talented. This kind of anxiety, they argue, can actually impair successful blacks' performance. They ran a series of ingenious experiments in which a white experimenter gave Stanford undergraduates a test composed of difficult verbal questions from the Graduate Record Exam. Black students made substantially more mistakes when they were asked to record their race before taking the test. Blacks also made more mistakes when they were told that the test measured "verbal reasoning ability" than when they were told that the study focused on "psychological factors involved in solving verbal problems." White students' performance did not depend on the way the experimenter described the test or on whether they recorded their race.

Steele and Aronson's findings strongly suggest that anxiety about racial stereotypes and intellectual competence can sometimes depress able black students' test performance. But their findings do not tell us how general this phenomenon is. Steele believes that what he calls "stereotype threat" is mainly a problem for blacks who have an emotional investment in seeing themselves as good students.[80] He also believes that it helps explain why so many black students "disidentify" with school.[81] We do not yet know whether stereotype threat affects the amount of time black students spend studying or how much they learn when they study. But we do have some indirect evidence.

Steele believes that "remedial" programs for black undergraduates can exacerbate stereotype threat and depress blacks' academic performance. Working with colleagues at the University of Michigan, he initiated an alternative program for a random sample of all students entering in the early 1990s. This program described itself as *more* demanding than the normal first-year curriculum. It seems to have boosted black students' undergraduate grades not just while they were in the program but afterwards.[82]

80. Frederick Vars and William Bowen's finding in chapter 13 that grade disparities between black and white undergraduates increase as their SAT scores increase is consistent with the hypothesis that stereotype threat is more of a problem among high-achieving blacks.
81. Osborne (forthcoming) presents evidence that the correlation between high school grades and self-esteem falls during the high school years for blacks but not whites.
82. Steele and others (1997).

This outcome suggests that the best way to improve black undergraduates' performance may be to treat them like everyone else and expect more than we do now. This may also be the best way to counter the perception that blacks are less intelligent than whites—a perception that has faded over the past twenty years but is still widespread.[83] Ferguson's review of research on teachers' expectations suggests that this logic also applies to younger black students.

Test Scores and College Admissions

A number of American colleges limit admission to students who, by one standard or another, seem to be in the top 5 percent of their cohort. If these colleges based their admissions decisions entirely on test performance and only accepted students who scored above the 95th percentile, less than 2 percent of their students would be black.[84] In practice, most colleges use a combination of test scores and high school grades to predict applicants' college grades. This increases blacks' chances of qualifying for a selective college on the basis of academic merit alone, but if predicted college grades were the sole criterion for choosing among applicants, blacks would remain badly underrepresented in selective colleges.

83. The 1990 General Social Survey (GSS) asked respondents to rate various groups on a scale that ran from 1 ("unintelligent") to 7 ("intelligent"). Among white respondents, 31 percent gave blacks a score of 3 or less, 16 percent gave southern whites a score of 3 or less, and 6 percent gave all whites a score of 3 or less. We do not know how these ratings have changed over time, but we do have trend data on a related question. Since 1977 the GSS has repeatedly asked respondents why blacks have worse jobs, income, and housing than whites. One possible answer is that "most blacks have less inborn ability to learn." In 1977, 26 percent of whites agreed that this was one possible explanation for black poverty. By 1994, just before the publication of The Bell Curve, only 14 percent agreed. In 1996, only 10 percent agreed. This question almost certainly understates the percentage of whites who entertain doubts about blacks' intellectual ability. To begin with, Americans are far more likely to blame poverty on laziness than stupidity, and the GSS shows that this pattern holds for black poverty as well. This means that even whites who doubt blacks' intellectual ability may not think this is an important factor in explaining black poverty. In addition, some whites probably think blacks are unintelligent for environmental reasons, and others are probably reluctant to report politically incorrect views. Nonetheless, we believe the downward trend is real. We are indebted to Joseph Swingle for analyzing the GSS for us.

84. Roughly 15 percent of school-age children are black. Hedges and Nowell show that whites were ten times more likely than blacks to score in the top 5 percent of the national test score distribution. The estimate in the text assumes that the ratio would still be at least eight to one if we compared all nonblacks to blacks.

Fortunately, selective private colleges have never based their admissions decisions solely on predicted grades. They also favor applicants who are good at football, who edited their high school newspaper, who play the trombone, or who have extremely rich fathers. When selective colleges began trying to increase their black enrollment in the late 1960s, they simply added race to the list of attributes that could push an otherwise marginal applicant above the threshold for admission. This policy was always controversial, but it survived more or less unchanged until the mid-1990s. In 1995 the University of California's Board of Regents voted to ban racial preferences in admissions. In 1996 the Fifth Circuit Court of Appeals banned racial preferences throughout Texas, Louisiana, and Mississippi.[85] Such bans may well spread in the years ahead.

Thomas Kane analyzes the extent of racial preferences in chapter 12, using data from the 1980s. Most American colleges admit most of their applicants. These colleges do not need racial preferences to maintain a racially diverse student body. Kane finds that such preferences are important only at the most selective fifth of four-year colleges. An applicant's race makes a big difference at these institutions. In 1982 selective colleges were as likely to admit a black student with total SAT scores of 1100 and a B+ average as they were to admit a white student with total SAT scores of 1300 and an A- average.[86] Kane does not present comparable data for the 1990s, but we doubt that the extent of racial preferences changed much between 1982 and 1995. The situation has certainly changed since 1995 in California, Texas, Louisiana, and Mississippi. It may also have changed elsewhere.

Advocates of color-blind admissions usually argue that racial preferences are unfair to whites and Asians. To support this argument, they often point out that blacks who attend selective colleges earn lower undergraduate grades and are less likely to graduate than their white and Asian classmates. In some cases, advocates of color-blind admissions go further and argue that racial preferences are actually a disservice to their nominal beneficiaries, who would be better off at less demanding institutions. If this were true, racial preferences would certainly be hard to defend. But it seems to be false.

85. *Hopwood* v. *State of Texas*, 95 F 3d 53; U.S. App. Lexis 22891.
86. Estimated from table 12-2 of chapter 12 by Thomas Kane. The effect of race on an applicant's chance of admission obviously varies from one selective institution to the next, but Kane does not try to estimate the extent of this variation.

When Kane tracks high school students matched on SAT scores, high school grades, and family background, those who attend more selective colleges have about the same undergraduate grades as those who attend less selective colleges. If a B at Stanford or Northwestern represents a higher level of accomplishment than a B at San Jose State or Northern Illinois, Kane's findings imply that marginal students are learning more at selective colleges.

Attending a more selective college does not reduce a student's chance of graduating, either. Holding applicants' academic qualifications constant, Kane finds that those who attend more selective colleges are actually *more* likely to graduate. Perhaps students at selective colleges are more highly motivated to begin with. Perhaps they stick around because life at a selective college is more interesting or because a degree from Stanford or Northwestern is worth more than a degree from San Jose State or Northern Illinois. (Among students who looked similar at the end of high school, those who attended a more selective college earned a little more when they were in their late twenties, but this could be because they were more ambitious to begin with.)

Selective colleges often justify their exclusiveness on the grounds that unusually talented students need an unusually demanding curriculum, which would merely frustrate less talented students. This argument may well be correct, but it has never been tested empirically, because the United States has never collected data on how much students learn in different colleges. At the elementary school level, where we do have data, putting high- and low-ability children in separate classes does not seem to have much impact on how much they learn. But twenty-year-olds probably learn more from their classmates than ten-year-olds do, and studies of elementary school ability grouping measure mastery of very simple skills. Kane finds that the *economic* value of attending a selective college is actually higher for students with low SAT scores than for students with high SAT scores. This could be because selective colleges only take low-scoring applicants who have other virtues, but we doubt it.

Kane's findings suggest to us that when all else is equal students usually benefit from attending the most selective college that will admit them. Selective colleges cannot, by definition, admit everyone who would benefit from attending. If they did, they would no longer be selective, and the value of attending them would fall. At present, selective colleges allocate scarce places by trying to balance two ill-defined ideals: merit and diversity. Those who oppose racial preferences want selective colleges to allocate places on merit alone. For some, this means relying entirely on predicted college grades. For others, it leaves room for football players, trombone players, and student newspaper editors.

The claim that selective colleges should only consider "merit" could mean that colleges should only consider an applicant's past accomplishments, treating admission as a prize that goes to the most deserving. Most college admissions offices view merit somewhat differently. They think their task is to predict applicants' future accomplishments. These two versions of "merit" have very different implications. A young man from a wealthy family is likely to exert a lot of influence on the world, even if his SAT scores are not especially impressive. He may also give the college a lot of money. Few selective colleges think they should ignore either of these facts. A college that sees itself as training America's future leaders also knows that excluding applicants with SAT scores below 1300 will exclude almost all the nation's future black leaders. Selective colleges are also reluctant to ignore this risk, since they do not want to position themselves as "white" (or even "white and Asian") institutions in an increasingly multiracial society. Faced with a difficult problem that has no perfect solution, one might expect a society committed to laissez-faire to let every college pursue its own conception of virtue mixed with self-interest. But when racial preferences are the issue, Americans often lose their enthusiasm for laissez-faire.

Frederick Vars and William Bowen also explore the consequences of racial preferences in chapter 13, using data on all the students who entered eleven highly selective colleges and universities in 1989. Like Kane, they find that blacks earn lower college grades than whites with the same SAT scores, although the magnitude of the discrepancy varies from campus to campus. Black students' low grades are not attributable to the fact that they come from families with less money or less schooling than the average white. Among applicants with the same SAT scores and high school grades, the measures of family background that college admissions offices collect do not predict college grades.[87]

Vars and Bowen's most disturbing finding is that the black-white disparity in college grades is widest among students with high SAT scores. Elite colleges apparently have particular difficulty engaging their most promising black students.[88] This could be because black students tend to social-

---

87. Kane controls a more extensive list of SES measures in his analysis of the High School and Beyond data. He too finds that SES has a negligible effect on college grades once SAT scores and high school grades are controlled, although he does not display the coefficients in chapter 12.

88. Steele and others' (1997) intervention program at the University of Michigan yielded its largest benefits for high-scoring black students.

ize with one another. A well-prepared black student may therefore have worse-prepared friends and study partners than an equally well-prepared white student. If racially delimited friendship patterns depress promising black students' grades, the problem might diminish if selective colleges set a higher threshold for admitting black applicants. But color-blind admissions could also have the perverse effect of forcing selective colleges to admit only those minority students whom they currently have the greatest difficulty motivating.

Faced with such uncertainty, we need more information. Over the past generation, some colleges have kept the black-white test score gap quite small while others have allowed it to grow very large. According to *The Bell Curve* the SAT gap at selective colleges in 1990–92 ranged from a high of 288 points at Berkeley to a low of 95 points at Harvard.[89] If large racial preferences have any effect on black students, positive or negative, we should have been able to measure this effect by comparing places like Berkeley to places like Harvard. Because colleges do not normally report the extent to which they favor black applicants, we have no studies of this kind.[90]

Test Scores and Wages

Many American whites believe that large employers favor blacks over whites when making hiring and promotion decisions because such employers want to "make their numbers look good." Many American blacks, in contrast, assume that they have to be more qualified than any white applicant to get a job or promotion. Both groups are presumably right some of the time. Some employers clearly favor black applicants for some jobs. Others clearly favor whites for some jobs. Such evidence as we have suggests, however, that whites are favored considerably more often than blacks.[91] The obvious question is why.

William Johnson and Derek Neal investigate test scores' contribution to racial differences in wages and employment in chapter 14. Their findings vary dramatically by gender. When they compare all black and white women in their late twenties, black women work about as many hours a

89. Herrnstein and Murray (1994). Kane reproduces the relevant table in chapter 12.

90. The report from which Herrnstein and Murray (1994) took most of their estimates of the black-white SAT gap is only available to participating institutions' admissions offices, not to social scientists.

91. Turner, Fix, and Struyk (1991) show that when matched black and white "testers" apply for jobs listed in the "Help Wanted" section of the newspaper, whites are favored more often than blacks.

year as white women but earn about 17 percent less per hour.[92] When Johnson and Neal compare women who had similar AFQT scores in adolescence, this picture changes dramatically. Black women work 15 percent more hours and earn 5 percent more per hour than white women with the same scores.[93] These findings could conceivably mean that employers prefer black women to equally skilled white women, but few employers say that is the case.[94] A more plausible explanation is that black women's small apparent wage advantage is a product of either sampling error or racial differences in geographic location, and that black women work more hours than equally skilled white women because black men work less, earn lower wages, and are less likely to live with their children.[95]

Among men, the picture is quite different. Black men in their late twenties work 30 percent fewer hours than whites and earn 24 percent less per hour. As a result, black men earn about half as much per year as white men.[96] When Johnson and Neal compare men with the same adolescent AFQT scores, black men still work 20 percent fewer hours than whites and earn 9 percent less per hour.[97] This means that the skills measured by the AFQT explain only half the racial disparity in men's annual earnings. We do not know why black men work less than white men with comparable cognitive skills, but the fact that this pattern does not hold among women rules out many possible explanations. One plausible hypothesis is that employers have more negative stereotypes of black men than of black women. An-

92. The coefficients of race in equations predicting the log of mean hourly wages and mean annual earnings for 1990–92 are –0.277 and –0.272, so the implied coefficient of race in an equation predicting these individuals' hours is .005. This estimate omits women who did not work at any time during 1990, 1991, or 1992, who constituted 20 percent of the total sample.

93. The apparent effect of test scores could reflect the fact that family background influences both test scores and wages, but this bias is quite small (Korenman and Winship, forthcoming).

94. Kirschenman and Neckerman (1991).

95. Johnson and Neal do not analyze racial differences in hours worked by married women, but we would expect to find that black wives worked more than white wives with equally well paid husbands. Black wives' marriages are even less stable than white wives' marriages, so black wives have even more reason than white wives to keep working so that they will be able to support themselves and their children in the event of a divorce.

96. Johnson and Neal's estimate covers men who had earnings in any of three years (1990, 1991, or 1992). Most other racial comparisons are limited to men with positive earnings in a single year. Focusing on a single year excludes more men with weak labor force attachment and raises the black-white earnings ratio.

97. Table 14-1 of chapter 14 shows that controlling test scores reduces the logged black-white hourly wage gap among men from 0.277 to 0.098. Table 14-5 shows that the coefficient for annual earnings drops from .640 to .329. Subtraction yields the implied coefficients for the natural log of annual hours, which are .363 without test scores controlled and .231 with test scores controlled.

other possibility is that black men are less willing than black women to take the low-wage jobs that America now offers unskilled workers of both sexes.

Can We Explain More of the Gap?

The evidence summarized in the first eleven chapters of this book shows that traditional explanations for the black-white test score gap do not work very well. If genes play any role, it is probably quite small. Poverty probably plays some role, but it too is modest. School desegregation probably reduced the black-white gap in the South during the 1970s, and desegregating northern elementary schools might raise blacks' reading scores today, but the gain would be modest. Reducing class size in the early grades would probably raise scores more for blacks than whites, and reducing class size in later grades might help preserve these black gains, although this latter conclusion is based on conjecture rather than firm evidence. Screening teachers for verbal and mathematical competence is also likely to raise black children's scores.

The United States ought to be conducting large-scale experiments aimed at reducing uncertainty about the effects of schools' racial mix, class size, teacher selection systems, ability grouping, and many other policies. We do such experiments to determine the effects of different medical treatments, different job training programs, and many other social interventions. But the U.S. Department of Education, which should in principle be funding experiments from which every state and school district would benefit, has shown almost no interest in this approach to advancing knowledge about education. The most important piece of educational research in the past generation, the Tennessee class-size experiment, was funded by the Tennessee legislature, not the U.S. Department of Education. Experimental assessments of other educational policies that have a major impact on school spending—salary levels, teacher selection systems, education for the physically and mentally disabled, and bilingual education, for example—have been almost nonexistent.

If we did more experiments, we might eventually develop better theories. At present, theorizing about the causes of the black-white gap is largely a waste of time, because there is no way to resolve theoretical disagreements without data that all sides accept as valid. Most theories about human behavior start out as hunches, anecdotes, or ideological predispositions. Such theories improve only when they have to confront evidence that the theorist cannot control. In education, that seldom happens.

Our best guess is that successful new theories about the causes of the black-white gap will differ from traditional theories in at least three ways:

—Instead of looking at families' economic and educational resources, successful theories will probably pay more attention to the way family members and friends interact with one another and with the outside world. A good explanation of why white four-year-olds have bigger vocabularies than black four-year-olds is likely to focus on how much parents talk to their children, how they deal with their children's questions, and how they react when their children either learn or fail to learn something, not on how much money the parents have in the bank.[98]

—Instead of looking mainly for resource differences between predominantly black and predominantly white schools, successful theories will probably pay more attention to the way black and white children respond to the same classroom experiences, such as having a teacher of a different race or having a teacher with low expectations for students who read below grade level.

—Instead of trying to trace the black-white test score gap to economic or demographic influences, successful theories will probably have to pay more attention to psychological and cultural differences that are harder to describe accurately and therefore easy to exaggerate. Collecting accurate data on such differences would require a massive investment of effort, perhaps comparable to what psychologists invested in developing cognitive tests during the first half of the twentieth century. It would also require far closer cooperation between psychologists, ethnographers, and survey researchers than one ordinarily sees in academic life.

Can We Narrow the Gap?

We have argued that reducing the black-white test score gap would do more to move America toward racial equality than any politically plausible alternative. This argument rests on two problematic premises: first, that we know how to reduce the gap, and second that the policies required to reduce the gap could command broad political support.

When readers try to assess what experts know, they should start by drawing a sharp distinction between policies that are expensive but easy to implement and policies that are cheap but hard to implement. (Most policies that are cheap, easy to implement, and clearly effective—like teaching

---

98. See, for example, Hart and Risley (1992).

children the alphabet or the multiplication tables—are already universal.) The two policies that seem to us most likely to combine effectiveness with ease of implementation are cutting class size and screening out teachers with weak academic skills. Cutting class size is clearly expensive, although we might be able to make some progress by moving existing teachers back into regular classes.[99] Selecting teachers with higher test scores would not be expensive in districts that now have more applicants than openings, but it would require higher salaries in many big cities.[100]

When educators look for less expensive ways of improving black children's achievement, they usually find themselves considering proposals that are quite difficult to implement. Raising teachers' expectations is not inherently expensive, for example, but how does a school administrator do it? Big-city school districts are besieged by advocates of curricular innovation who claim their programs will raise black children's test scores. These programs usually require complex and relatively subtle changes in classroom practice. School boards and administrators cannot impose such changes by decree, the way they can reduce class size or require new teachers to pass an exam. Nor can teachers make such changes by a single act of will, the way they might adopt a new textbook. As a result, schools seldom implement these programs in exactly the way their designers expected or intended. A program may work well initially, when it is closely supervised by a dedicated innovator, but may have no detectable effect when the innovator tries to bottle it and sell it off the shelf.[101]

Proposals for reducing the black-white test score gap also arouse passionate white resistance if they seem likely to lower white children's achievement. Both school desegregation and the elimination of academically

99. Taken at face value, Lewitt and Baker's (1997) data imply that during the hours when students were in class in 1991 about 17/24 = 70 percent of teachers were in class. In 1961 the figure was 26/29 = 90 percent. Part of this apparent reduction in teachers' classroom time may be spurious, however. Schools now have more specialized teachers for disabled children, bilingual instruction, and slow readers. These teachers' classes tend to be smaller than regular classes and may not be included in the estimates of average class size.

100. If wages did not rise in central cities, emphasizing teachers' test scores might actually widen the achievement gap between minority students in the central city and predominantly white students in the surrounding suburbs, since it might improve the quality of instruction more in districts that now have a surplus of applicants for every opening.

101. The program with the best-documented success record seems to be Robert Slavin's Success for All. Ferguson discusses this program in more detail in chapter 9. Success for All is more expensive than many of its competitors. For an excellent account of an apparently successful intervention that cost considerably less see Farkas (1996).

selective classes often arouse such fears. School desegregation probably raises black elementary school students' reading scores. Whether it lowers white scores is unclear. But once black enrollment in a neighborhood school expands past something like 20 percent, most white parents become reluctant to move into the neighborhood. If black enrollment remains low enough to keep whites comfortable, many blacks feel uncomfortable. There is no simple way out of this dilemma. It takes years of patient work to create stable, racially mixed schools with high black enrollments, and such schools remain unusual.

Ferguson's review suggests that the struggle over ability grouping at the elementary level is largely symbolic. Eliminating such classes would not do black children much good, and it would probably not do whites much harm either. At the secondary level, eliminating demanding courses seems ridiculous. We should be trying to get more black students to take such classes, not trying to eliminate them as an option for whites, who will respond by sending their children elsewhere. Any politically workable educational strategy for reducing the black-white test score gap has to promise some benefits for whites as well as blacks. Reducing class size, requiring greater academic competence among teachers, and raising teachers' expectations for students who have trouble with schoolwork all meet this test.

Although we believe that improving the nation's schools could reduce the black-white test score gap, we do not believe that schools alone can eliminate it. To begin with, competition for educational resources is fierce. The typical American voter might accept a system of educational finance that gave schools with unusually disadvantaged students 10 or 20 percent more money per pupil than the average school. But few Americans would accept a system that gave disadvantaged schools 50 or 100 percent more money than the average school. If smaller classes in disadvantaged schools improve children's reading skills, for example, more affluent parents will want smaller classes too. In a system of school finance that relies heavily on local funding, affluent parents who want smaller classes will usually be able to get them. Even ensuring equal funding for black and white schools is a constant struggle. Creating a system in which black schools get far more money than white schools is politically inconceivable.

Even if resources were not a constraint, the cognitive disparities between black and white preschool children are currently so large that it is hard to imagine how schools alone could eliminate them. Figure 1-1 showed that among three- and four-year-olds the typical black child's vocabulary score falls below the 20th percentile of the national distribution. Relying entirely on educational reform to move such a child up to the 50th percentile does not strike us as realistic. If we want equal outcomes among twelfth-graders, we will also have to narrow the skill gap between black and white children before they enter school.

Broadly speaking, there are two ways of improving three- and four-year-olds' cognitive skills: we can change their preschool experiences and we can change their home experiences. Changing preschools is less important but easier than changing homes. Black preschoolers are concentrated in Head Start. At present, the program does not concentrate on teaching cognitive skills. Few Head Start teachers are trained to do this, and some oppose the idea on principle. Steven Barnett's review of research on preschool effects strongly suggests that cognitively oriented preschool programs can improve black children's achievement scores, even though the benefits fade somewhat as children age.[102] Getting Head Start to emphasize cognitive development should therefore be a higher priority than merely expanding its enrollment.

Parenting practices almost certainly have more impact on children's cognitive development than preschool practices. Indeed, changing the way parents deal with their children may be the single most important thing we can do to improve children's cognitive skills. But getting parents to change their habits is even harder than getting teachers to change. Like teachers, parents are usually suspicious of unsolicited suggestions. This is doubly true when the suggestions require fundamental changes in a parent's behavior. But once parents become convinced that changing their behavior will really help their children, many try to change, even when this is quite difficult. As a practical matter, whites cannot tell black parents to change their practices without provoking charges of ethnocentrism, racism, and much else. But black parents are not the only ones who need help. We should be promoting better parenting practices for *all* parents, using every tool at our disposal, from Head Start outreach programs and home visits by nurses to television sitcoms or anything else that might affect parents' behavior.[103]

A successful strategy for raising black children's test scores must also try to convince both blacks and whites that the gap is not genetic in origin.

102. Barnett (1995). Currie and Thomas (1995) find that Head Start's effect on children's test scores fades after a few years among blacks but not among whites. Currie and Thomas (1998) argue that this is because white children go on to better schools.

103. See Olds and others (1998) on the uneven cognitive effects of home visits by nurses.

This is not a simple task. Genetic variation does explain a substantial fraction of the variation in cognitive skills among people of the same race. But so does environmental variation. Once hereditarianism percolates into popular culture, it can easily become an excuse for treating academic failure as an inescapable fact of nature. Teaching children skills that do not seem to "come naturally" is hard work. If our culture allows us to avoid such work by saying that a child simply lacks the required aptitude to master the skill, both teachers and parents will sometimes jump at this as an excuse for not trying. This often makes everyone's life pleasanter in the short run, but in the long run it is a formula for failure. Emphasizing heredity is likely to have especially negative consequences for African Americans, who start out behind whites and therefore need to work even harder than whites if they are to catch up.

The agenda we have sketched would not be easy to implement. We are not optimistic about expanding federal support for efforts of this kind. Popular distrust of federal education programs is now quite pervasive and shows no sign of receding. We are more optimistic about state and local efforts to narrow the black-white test score gap. Everyone recognizes that racial conflict is one of the nation's most pressing and persistent problems. Other strategies for dealing with this problem, which emphasize the use of racial preferences to overcome the adverse effects of discrimination, the test score gap, or both, are clearly in political trouble. Public support for efforts to narrow the test score gap, while tempered by suspicion that "nothing works," still seems fairly widespread. One reason is that the beneficiaries appear so deserving. Hardly anyone blames black first-graders' limited vocabulary on defects of character or lack of ambition. First-graders of every race seem eager to please. That was why Lyndon Johnson placed so much emphasis on helping children in his original War on Poverty.

We recognize that few readers will find our sketchy agenda for reducing the black-white test score gap entirely persuasive. Such skepticism is completely reasonable. While we are convinced that reducing the gap is both necessary and possible, we do not have a detailed blueprint for achieving this goal and neither does anyone else. This book tries to update the reader's knowledge about many aspects of the problem, but almost every chapter raises as many questions as it answers. This is partly because psychologists, sociologists, and educational researchers have devoted far less attention to the test score gap over the past quarter century than its political and social consequences warranted. Most social scientists have chosen safer topics and hoped the problem would go away. It didn't. We can do better.

References

Ainsworth-Darnell, James, and Douglas Downey. Forthcoming. "Assessing the Oppositional Explanation for Racial/Ethnic Differences in School Performance." *American Sociological Review.*

Armor, David. 1992. "Why Is Black Educational Achievement Rising?" *Public Interest,* no.
108 (Summer): 65–80.

Barnett, Steven. 1995. "Long-Term Effects of Early Childhood Programs on Cognitive and
School Outcomes." *Future of Children* 5 (3): 25–50.

Boozer, Michael, Alan Krueger, and Shari Wolkon. 1992. "Race and School Quality since
Brown v. *Board of Education.*" *Brookings Papers on Economic Activity (Microeconomics)*:
269–326.

Bouchard, Thomas, and others. 1990. "Sources of Human Psychological Differences: The
Minnesota Study of Twins Reared Apart." *Science,* 250 (October 12): 223–28.

Braungart, Julia, David Fulker, and Robert Plomin. 1992. "Genetic Mediation of the Home
Environment during Infancy: A Sibling Adoption Study of the Home." *Developmental
Psychology,* 28: 1048–55.

Brody, Nathan. 1992. *Intelligence.* San Diego: Academic Press.

Cherny, Stacey, and Lon Cardon. 1994. "General Cognitive Ability," in John DeFries, Robert Plomin, and David Fulker, eds., *Nature and Nurture in Middle Childhood.* Oxford:
Blackwell.

Chipuer, Heather, Michael Rovine, and Robert Plomin. 1990. "LISREL Modeling: Genetic and Environmental Influences on IQ Revisited." *Intelligence* 14 (1): 11–29.

Coleman, James, and others. 1966. *Equality of Educational Opportunity.* Department of
Health, Education, and Welfare.

Currie, Janet, and Duncan Thomas. 1995. "Does Headstart Make a Difference?" *American
Economic Review,* 85 (3): 341–64.

———. 1998. "School Quality and the Longer-Term Effects of Headstart," Working Paper
6362. Cambridge, Mass.: National Bureau of Economic Research.

Cutright, Phillips. 1972. "Achievement, Mobility, and the Draft: Their Impact on the Earnings of Men," DHEW (SSA) 73-11854. Department of Health, Education, and Welfare.

———. 1974. "Academic Achievement, Schooling, and the Earnings of White and Black
Men." *Journal of Social and Behavioral Sciences,* 20 (3): 1–18.

Entwisle, Doris, and Karl Alexander. 1994. "Winter Setback: The Racial Composition of
Schools and Learning to Read." *American Sociological Review,* 59 (June): 446–60.

Entwisle, Doris, Karl Alexander, and Linda Steffel Olson. 1997. *Children, Schools, and
Inequality.* Boulder: Westview Press.

Evans, William N., Sheila Murray, and Robert Schwab. 1997. "School Houses, Court
Houses, and State Houses after Serrano." *Journal of Policy Analysis and Management,* 16
(January): 10–31.

Farkas, George. 1996. *Human Capital or Cultural Capital? Ethnicity and Poverty Groups in
an Urban School District.* Aldine de Gruyter.

Flynn, James. 1980. *Race, IQ, and Jensen.* London: Routledge and Kegan Paul.

———. 1984. "The Mean IQ of Americans: Massive Gains 1932 to 1978." *Psychological
Bulletin,* 95 (1): 29–51.

————. 1987. "Massive IQ Gains in 14 Nations: What IQ Tests Really Measure." *Psychological Bulletin*, 101 (2): 171–91.

Fordham, Signithia, and John Ogbu. 1986. "Black Students' School Success: Coping with the 'Burden of Acting White.'" *Urban Review*, 18(3): 176–206.

Glass, Gene, and others. 1982. *School Class Size*. Beverly Hills: Sage Publications.

Hanushek, Eric. 1989. "The Impact of Differential Expenditures on School Performance." *Educational Researcher*, 18 (4): 45–51.

————. 1998. "The Evidence on Class Size," occasional paper 98-1. University of Rochester, W. Allen Wallis Institute of Political Economy.

Hartigan, John, and Alexandra Wigdor, eds. 1989. *Fairness in Employment Testing: Validity Generalization, Minority Issues, and the General Aptitude Test Battery*. Washington: National Academy Press.

Hauser, Robert, and David Featherman. 1976. "Equality of Schooling: Trends and Prospects." *Sociology of Education*, 49: 99–120.

Herrnstein, Richard, and Charles Murray. 1994. *The Bell Curve: Intelligence and Class Structure in American Life*. Free Press.

Heyns, Barbara. 1978. *Summer Learning and the Effects of Schooling*. Academic Press.

————. 1987. "Schooling and Cognitive Development: Is There a Season for Learning?" *Child Development*, 58: 1151–60.

Hopkins, Kenneth, and Glenn Bracht. 1975. "Ten-Year Stability of Verbal and Nonverbal IQ Scores." *Educational Research Journal*, 12: 469–77.

Howard, Jeff, and Ray Hammond. 1985. "Rumors of Inferiority." *New Republic*, September 9: 18–23.

Jencks, Christopher, and others. 1972. *Inequality: A Reassessment of the Effect of Family and Schooling in America*. Basic Books.

Jensen, Arthur. 1969. "How Much Can We Boost IQ and Scholastic Achievement?" *Harvard Educational Review*, 39: 1–123.

Kirschenman, Joleen, and Kahryn Neckerman. 1991. "We'd Love to Hire Them But . . .: The Meaning of Race for Employers." In Christopher Jencks and Paul Peterson, eds. *The Urban Underclass*, pp. 203–32. Brookings.

Korenman, Sanders, and Christopher Winship. Forthcoming. "A Reanalysis of *The Bell Curve*: Intelligence, Family Background, and Schooling," In Steven Durlauf and Samuel Bowles, eds., *Meritocracy and Society*. Princeton University Press.

Lewitt, Eugene, and Linda Schumann Baker. 1997. "Class Size." *Future of Children*, 7 (3): 112–21.

Loehlin, John. 1980. "Recent Adoption Studies of IQ." *Human Genetics*, 55: 297–302.

Loehlin, John, Steven Vandenberg, and R. T. Osborne. 1973. "Blood Group Genes and Negro-White Ability Differences." *Behavior Genetics*, 3: 263–70.

Loehlin, John, Gardner Lindzey, and J. N. Spuhler. 1975. *Race Differences in Intelligence*. San Francisco: W. H. Freeman.

Loehlin, John, Joseph Horn, and Lee Willlerman. 1989. "Modeling IQ Changes: Evidence from the Texas Adoption Project." *Child Development*, 60: 993–1004.

Mayer, Susan. 1997. *What Money Can't Buy: Family Income and Children's Life Chances*. Harvard University Press.

McCartney, Kathleen, Monica Harris, and Frank Bernieri. 1990. "Growing Up and Growing Apart: A Developmental Meta-Analysis of Twin Studies." *Psychological Bulletin*, 107 (2): 226–37.

McLanahan, Sara, and Gary Sandefur. 1994. *Growing Up with a Single Parent.* Harvard University Press.

Miller, L. Scott. 1995. *An American Imperative: Accelerating Minority Educational Advancement.* Yale University Press.

Moore, Elsie. 1986. "Family Socialization and IQ Test Performance of Traditionally and Transracially Adopted Black Children." *Developmental Psychology,* 22 (3): 317–26.

Mosteller, Frederick. 1995. "The Tennessee Study of Class Size in the Early Grades." *Future of Children,* 5 (2): 113–27.

Mosteller, Frederick, and Daniel P. Moynihan, eds. 1972. *On Equality of Educational Opportunity.* Random House.

Mosteller, Frederick, Richard Light, and Jason Sacks. 1996. "Sustained Inquiry in Education: Lessons from Skill Grouping and Class Size." *Harvard Educational Review,* 66 (4): 797–842.

Mulkey, Lynn, Robert Crain, and Alexander Harrington. 1992. "One Parent Households and Achievement: Economic and Behavioral Explanations of a Small Effect." *Sociology of Education,* 65 (January): 48–65.

Neisser, Ulrich, ed. 1998. *The Rising Curve: Long-Term Gains in IQ and Related Measures.* Washington: American Psychological Association.

Ogbu, John. 1978. *Minority Education and Caste: The American System in Cross-Cultural Perspective.* Academic Press.

———. 1986. "The Consequences of the American Caste System." In Ulrich Neisser, ed., *The School Achievement of Minority Children: New Perspectives,* pp. 19–56. Hillsdale, N.J.: Erlbaum.

Olds, David L., and others. 1998. "Prenatal and Infancy Home Visitation by Nurses: A Program of Research." Washington: American Enterprise Institute.

Osborne, Jason. Forthcoming. "Race and Academic Disidentification." *Journal of Educational Psychology.*

Phillips, Meredith. 1997. "Does School Segregation Explain Why African Americans and Latinos Score Lower than Whites on Academic Achievement Tests?" Paper prepared for the annual meeting of the American Sociological Association.

Plomin, Robert. 1994. *Genetics and Experience: The Interplay between Nature and Nurture.* Newbury Park, Calif.: Sage.

——— and John DeFries. 1980. "Genetics and Intelligence: Recent Data." *Intelligence* 4: 15-24.

Plomin, Robert, and C. S. Bergeman. 1991. "The Nature of Nurture: Genetic Influence on 'Environmental' Measures." *Behavioral and Brain Sciences,* 14 (3): 373–427.

Plomin, Robert, and Stephen Petrill. 1997. "Genetics and Intelligence: What's New?" *Intelligence,* 24 (1): 53–77.

Plomin, Robert, John DeFries, and David Fulker. 1988. *Nature and Nurture in Infancy and Early Childhood.* Cambridge University Press.

Rao, D. C., and others. 1982. "Path Analysis under Generalized Assortative Mating." *Genetical Research,* 39: 187–98.

Scarr, Sandra, and Richard Weinberg. 1976. "IQ Test Performance of Black Children Adopted by White Families." *American Psychologist,* 31: 726–39.

———. 1978. "The Influence of 'Family Background' on Intellectual Attainment." *American Sociological Review,* 43 (October): 674–92.

Scarr, Sandra, and others. 1977. "Absence of a Relationship between Degree of White Ancestry and Intellectual Skills within a Black Population." *Human Genetics*, 39: 69–86.

Snyderman, Mark, and Stanley Rothman. 1987. "Survey of Expert Opinion on Intelligence and Aptitude Testing." *American Psychologist*, 42 (2): 137–44.

———. 1990. *The IQ Controversy, the Media, and Public Policy.* New Brunswick, N.J.: Transaction Books.

Steele, Claude. 1992. "Race and the Schooling of Black Americans." *Atlantic Monthly*, April: 68–78.

———. 1997. "A Threat in the Air: How Stereotypes Shape Intellectual Identity and Performance." *American Psychologist*, 52 (6): 613–29.

Steele, Claude, and others. 1997. "African American College Achievement: A 'Wise' Intervention." Stanford University Department of Psychology.

Tuddenham, Reed. 1948. "Soldier Intelligence in World Wars I and II." *American Psychologist*, 3:54–56.

Turner, Margery, Michael Fix, and Raymond Struyk. 1991. *Opportunities Denied, Opportunities Diminished.* Washington: Urban Institute.

Vernon, Philip. 1979. *Intelligence: Heredity and Environment.* San Francisco: W. H. Freeman.

Weinberg, Richard, Sandra Scarr, and Irwin Waldman. 1992. "The Minnesota Transracial Adoption Study: A Follow-Up of IQ Performance at Adolescence." *Intelligence*, 16: 117–35.

Wigdor, Alexandra, and Bert Green, eds. 1991. *Performance Assessment in the Workplace*, vol. 1. Washington: National Academy Press.

Willerman, Lee, Alfred Naylor, and Ntinos Myrianthopoulos. 1974. "Intellectual Development of Children from Interracial Matings: Performance in Infancy and at 4 Years." *Behavior Genetics*, 4 (1): 83–90.

Winship, Christopher, and Sanders Korenman. 1997. "Does Staying in School Make You Smarter? The Effect of Education on IQ in *The Bell Curve*." In Bernie Devlin and others, eds., *Intelligence, Genes, and Success*, pp. 215–34. Copernicus.

PART I

Test Bias, Heredity, and Home Environment

CHRISTOPHER JENCKS

2 | *Racial Bias in Testing*

M ANY AMERICANS discount racial differences in test performance on the grounds that all cognitive tests are either racially or culturally biased. This chapter provides a lay reader's guide to the bias debate. I discuss three kinds of bias—which I call labeling bias, content bias, and methodological bias—that can arise when psychometricians create a test. In addition, I discuss two kinds of bias that can arise when a test is used to predict performance. I call these prediction bias and selection system bias. Readers should be warned that most of these names do not match conventional psychometric usage. They do, however, have the advantage of indicating the causes of each problem and how it might be remedied.

Labeling bias arises when tests claim to measure one thing but actually measure something else.[1] This kind of bias is a major problem in tests that

I am indebted to James Crouse, William Dickens, James Flynn, Jane Mansbridge, and Meredith Phillips for helpful comments on drafts of this chapter.

1. When a test does not measure what it claims to measure, psychologists usually say that it lacks construct validity. But psychologists normally limit discussions of construct validity to whether a test measures what its designers intended to measure. They seldom deal with discrepancies between the labels that psychologists give their tests and the ways in which nonpsychologists interpret these labels, which is my concern here.

55

claim to measure either "intelligence" or "aptitude." Many people—including federal judges—think that both intelligence and aptitude are innate traits. Many of these people also assume that when tests claim to measure intelligence or aptitude, they are claiming to measure something innate. Yet almost all psychologists now agree that while an individual's score on an intelligence or aptitude test depends partly on his or her genetic makeup, it also reflects a multitude of environmental influences. All but a handful of psychologists also agree that these environmental influences play some role in the black-white test score gap.[2] Intelligence and aptitude tests are therefore racially biased estimates of the innate traits that many nonpsychologists think such tests are claiming to measure. Psychologists cannot eliminate this bias by changing the content of such tests. The only way to eliminate this kind of bias is to change the names of the tests, so that they no longer connote anything innate.

Content bias is closely related to labeling bias. It arises when a test claims to measure something that could in principle be measured in an unbiased way, but fails to do so because it contains questions that favor one group over another. Suppose, for example, that French- and English-speaking Canadians take a "vocabulary" test. If the test is in English, it will underestimate the vocabulary of French-speaking children. The tester can cure this problem either by relabeling the test as a measure of English vocabulary or by including equal numbers of French and English words. Whether the test's critics describe it as suffering from labeling bias or content bias should therefore depend on which cure they prefer.[3]

Setting aside tests that claim to measure intelligence and aptitude, this kind of content bias does not appear to be a significant problem for the tests discussed in this book. Unlike French- and English-speaking Canadians, for example, black and white Americans with equally large vocabularies know pretty much the same words. Conventional vocabulary tests therefore yield a relatively accurate estimate of each group's total vocabulary.

Methodological bias arises when a test assesses mastery of some skill or body of information using a technique or method that underestimates the competence of one group relative to another. Claude Steele and Joshua Aronson show in chapter 11 in this book, for example, that able black

---

2. Snyderman and Rothman (1987) surveyed 1,020 social scientists with some expertise on testing. Of the 661 who responded, only 8 said they believed that the black-white test score gap was entirely genetic in origin.

3. What I here call content bias, psychologists would call a group difference in construct validity.

students get lower scores on a difficult test if they are told that it measures "verbal reasoning ability" than if no reference is made to "ability." Others have argued (with far less supporting evidence) that blacks do worse when the tester is white. Using multiple choice questions rather than essays, or tests where students are under severe time pressure, could in theory pose similar problems. (Content bias can also be seen as a special form of methodological bias.) It is not clear how much these kinds of methodological biases distort black-white comparisons, but no one has produced a testing methodology that sharply reduces the black-white gap.

Prediction bias can arise whenever a test is used to predict an individual's future performance. Colleges, for example, often use the Scholastic Assessment Test (SAT) to predict applicants' college grades, and the military uses the Armed Forces Qualification Test (AFQT) to predict new recruits' job performance. If black undergraduates typically earned higher grades than whites with the same SAT scores, most people would probably conclude that the SAT was biased against blacks. Likewise, if black recruits performed better in most military jobs than whites with similar AFQT scores, most people would say that the AFQT was biased against blacks. But that is not what we find. White undergraduates usually earn higher grades than blacks with the same SAT scores, and white recruits perform slightly better in most jobs than blacks with the same AFQT scores.[4] This does not mean that either the SAT or AFQT is biased against whites. It merely means that whites who compete with blacks tend to have other advantages besides higher test scores. Unless blacks and whites are equally advantaged on the unmeasured determinants of performance, we will *always* find prediction bias in one direction or the other.

Selection system bias sounds like prediction bias but is fundamentally different. It can easily arise when prediction bias is not a problem. It can also be absent when prediction bias is a serious problem. Selection system bias arises when three conditions are met: (1) performance depends partly on cognitive skills and partly on other traits; (2) it is easy to measure cognitive skills but hard to measure the other traits that determine performance; and (3) the racial disparity in cognitive skills is larger than the racial disparity in the other, unmeasured traits that influence performance. When these

---

4. For data on college grades, see chapters 12 and 13. For a review of evidence on racial differences in military performance, with AFQT scores controlled, see Wigdor and Green (1991, pp. 173–81). Data are available on both "objective" and "subjective" assessments of military performance. For data on possible racial bias in these performance assessments, see Oppler and others (1992).

three conditions hold, both educational institutions and employers have strong incentives to adopt a selection system that emphasizes test scores. Such a selection system is "unfair" to anyone whose competitive rank on the cognitive test is lower than their rank on the other unmeasured determinants of performance. As a result, it puts blacks (and Hispanics) at a greater disadvantage than a selection system based on actual performance. In effect, blacks and Hispanics have to pay for the fact that social science is better at measuring the skills they lack than the skills they have.

This chapter assesses the importance of these five forms of bias for tests that purport to measure intelligence or aptitude, tests that measure vocabulary, and tests used to predict college grades and job performance.

Labeling Bias in Intelligence and Aptitude Tests

Suppose that I give a representative sample of American tenth-graders a dozen quadratic equations to solve. I will almost surely find that European Americans score higher than African Americans. Now consider two scenarios. In the first, I conclude that the white tenth-graders are better at solving quadratic equations than the black tenth-graders. If that is all I say, hardly anyone will challenge my conclusion or raise questions about cultural bias. In the second scenario I argue that solving quadratic equations depends partly on native intelligence and that my test is therefore a proxy for native intelligence. I conclude that blacks score below whites because blacks have less innate mathematical ability than do whites. In this case, many people will rightly denounce my test as racially or culturally biased.

What has changed between scenario one and scenario two? Not the test—only what I say about it. Any test that yields an unbiased estimate of two groups' current ability to solve quadratic equations is likely to yield a biased estimate of their native intelligence. That is because no two groups have exactly the same incentives and opportunities to learn algebra. Even if two groups differ in their innate mathematical ability, a test of their mathematical competence in tenth grade will almost surely either overstate or understate the innate difference between them.

Most tests provide a relatively unbiased estimate of something that is hard to label and biased estimates of many other things that we care more about. In principle, therefore, testers should be able to rebut most charges of cultural bias by labeling their products more accurately. In practice, those who design, market, and analyze tests are often reluctant to relabel their products. Test distributors usually want to claim that their products measure quite broad traits, like "intelligence," "aptitude," or "reading comprehension." Cautious scholars often prefer narrower labels, like "vocabulary," "digit span," or "analogies." But most widely used tests combine items covering many domains and measure more than one psychological trait. Debates about labeling bias are therefore likely to remain a permanent feature of the testing business.

Intelligence Tests

In colloquial usage, intelligence almost always includes the capacity to learn new facts, understand complicated ideas, apply familiar facts and ideas to unfamiliar problems, foresee unintended consequences, and so on. "And so on" is important. Everyday usage does not set any clear limits on what counts as intelligent behavior.[5] If mental skills were unrelated to one another, uncertainty about which skills counted as intelligence would make the term almost useless. But mental skills are related. Children who learn algebra easily also tend to have large vocabularies and be good at visual puzzles. Most people use the word "intelligence" to describe whatever it is that explains these positive correlations, and most psychologists have adopted this usage.

Today, most psychologists equate intelligence with the "general factor" (known as g) that emerges from analyzing the correlations among a wide range of tests.[6] Sometimes psychologists estimate g from correlations among

5. Both Lewis Terman, who developed the first American IQ test (the Stanford-Binet) and David Wechsler, who developed and gave his name to the Stanford-Binet's principal competitor, believed that intelligence tests ought to measure not only people's capacity for relatively abstract reasoning but also their ability to cope with the practical problems of everyday life. In describing why teachers gave poor estimates of children's IQ scores, for example, Terman (1916, p. 29) noted that only a small minority of teachers paid attention to "resourcefulness in play, capacity to adjust to practical situations, or any other out-of-school criteria." David Wechsler wrote in 1975, "What we measure with tests is not what tests measure—not information, not spatial perception, not reasoning ability. . . . What intelligence tests measure, what we hope they measure, is something much more important: the capacity of an individual to understand the world about him and his resourcefulness to cope with its challenges" (quoted in Elliott, 1987, p. 73). This sounds more like what many critics of intelligence testing say the concept *ought* to encompass than what its defenders usually say it measures. Compare, for example, the discussion in Cleary and others (1975).

6. Thurstone (1938) preferred four factors to one. Cattell (1971) and his followers prefer two: "fluid" and "crystallized" intelligence. The Educational Testing Service reports separate verbal and mathematical test scores for college applicants; it reports three separate scores for students applying to

the subtests of a single intelligence test, such as the Stanford-Binet or the Wechsler. Sometimes they estimate g from a collection of other tests. Fortunately, these diverse estimates of g are very highly correlated with each other. Whether g corresponds to an underlying biological phenomenon or is merely a statistical construct remains controversial.

Innate versus Developed Intelligence

Ordinary people often use the terms "intelligence" and "innate intelligence" almost interchangeably. But they also use the word intelligence to describe an individual's *current* capacity for intelligent behavior. For these two usages to be consistent, our genes would have to completely determine our capacity for intelligent behavior throughout life. This is not the case. Most efforts to synthesize the available evidence suggest that genes can explain between one-third and two-thirds of the variation in measured IQ among children.[7] Genes may explain more of the variance in IQ among adults than among children, but that is not yet certain.[8] In any event, all psychologists agree that people's developed capacity for intelligent behavior often differs in predictable ways from their innate potential.

Ph.D. programs. In principle, there can be as many scores (or factors) as test items. The number of summary statistics psychologists choose to report depends partly on what they want to predict and partly on whether they want to maximize R^2 or the number of people who remember and use their results.

7. For reviews of data on the heritability of intelligence, see, for example, Plomin and DeFries (1980) and Chipuer, Rovine, and Plomin (1990). Readers should be warned that when psychologists say that genes explain a certain proportion of the variance in IQ scores, this sets no upper bound on the explanatory power of environmental factors. Genetic differences can explain phenotypic variation by affecting people's environment. The genes that affect skin color, for example, affect the ways in which people are treated and the environments they choose for themselves. Standard estimates of the heritability of intelligence do not distinguish between genetic effects that work through the external environment and genetic effects that work through purely physiological mechanisms.

8. Many genes exert more influence as people get older. A Y chromosome, for example, exerts more influence in adolescence than in childhood. Studies of twins suggest that the correlation between genotype and measured IQ is somewhat higher among adolescents than among younger children, but the evidence is not conclusive; see McCartney, Harris, and Bernieri (1990). The correlation between genotype and IQ may continue to rise in adulthood (Plomin and others, 1994; McClearn and others, 1997), but there are not enough data on twins between the ages of eighteen and sixty-five to justify strong conclusions on this issue. High heritabilities among those over the age of sixty-five probably tell one more about the importance of genes for aging than about their importance for cognitive growth earlier in life.

Psychologists can only measure people's developed capacity for intelligent behavior, not their innate potential. As often happens in the social sciences, psychologists tend to assume that what they can measure defines the word they use to describe it. This convention works well enough when psychologists talk to one another, but it creates endless misunderstandings when they try to communicate with the rest of the world, where intelligence can still mean either innate or developed intelligence. Such misunderstandings are especially common (and dangerous) when they involve racial comparisons. The following logic summarizes the way many nonpsychologists think about race and intelligence:

—if intelligence means innate ability to learn,

—and if blacks and whites have the same innate ability to learn,

—and if blacks score below whites on tests that claim to measure intelligence,

—then intelligence tests must be biased against blacks.

This logic makes clear not only why blacks think that intelligence tests are culturally biased, but also why they object to endless repetition of the fact that they score below whites on such tests.

The case of *Larry P.* v. *Riles* provides a dramatic illustration of the problems that can arise when psychologists who equate intelligence with developed ability confront nonpsychologists who equate intelligence with innate ability. In 1971 a group of black plaintiffs sued the San Francisco Unified School District in a federal court, arguing that IQ scores should not be used as a criterion for assigning black students to special classes for the "educably mentally retarded" (EMR). Judge Robert Peckham issued a preliminary injunction barring the use of IQ tests for this purpose in 1972, and he extended it to cover all California schools in 1974. Five years later, after a lengthy trial, he made the injunction permanent.[9] Peckham's injunction was based on his finding that intelligence tests are culturally biased against blacks. He seems to have concluded that if a test both claimed to measure intelligence and was used to label children as retarded, it ought to measure innate rather than developed ability. He also believed that blacks and whites had the same innate ability. He therefore inferred that intelligence tests must be biased against blacks. The state's argument that intelli-

9. In Illinois, another federal district judge upheld the Chicago Board of Education's right to use intelligence tests when assigning slow learners to special classes. Elliott (1987) describes both cases in detail.

gence tests measure developed competence, not innate ability, left him unmoved.[10]

Many psychologists view Peckham's decision as an example of "shooting the messenger." As they see it, Peckham was blaming psychological tests for a much deeper social problem, namely, black students' difficulties both in school and in other areas of life that require abstract reasoning of various kinds. This reaction seems to me to miss the point of the case. *Larry P.* was not a challenge to testing in general. It was a challenge to intelligence testing. The plaintiffs did not ask the court to bar the use of achievement tests that measured children's reading comprehension or their ability to solve arithmetic problems, even though such tests often show racial disparities as large as those on the Stanford-Binet or the Wechsler. The plaintiffs asked Peckham to bar the use of tests that claimed to measure intelligence, and that is what he did.[11]

Both the plaintiffs and Judge Peckham focused on intelligence tests because they felt that these tests stigmatized blacks in ways that other tests did not. This judgment was surely correct. The statement that blacks cannot read as well as whites makes many blacks uncomfortable, but it is widely accepted as correct and seldom denounced as racist. The statement that blacks are less intelligent than whites is very different. It implies that black-white differences in skills such as reading and mathematics are, or at least may well be, innate and irremediable. The fact that professional psychologists no longer think intelligence tests measure innate ability does not change how most people interpret such a statement, because professional psychologists have neither the legal authority nor the political power to redefine the words they appropriate from everyday language.

---

10. My conclusions about what Judge Peckham believed are based on Elliott's (1987) lengthy excerpts from Peckham's opinion and his courtroom discussions with counsel for the plaintiffs and for the defendants.

11. The plaintiffs would probably not have brought the *Larry P.* case if California had used reading and mathematics tests rather than intelligence tests to select students for EMR classes, but it is not obvious that using different tests would have altered the legal situation. Any test would have produced EMR classes that were disproportionately black. This would not have posed a legal problem if students with low scores had benefited from EMR classes, which were about half the size of normal classes and had specially trained teachers. But the state introduced no evidence that EMR classes improved children's cognitive skills, and the plaintiffs assumed that the social cost of being labeled a "retard" outweighed any cognitive gains associated with the program. Once a judge concluded that the program was harmful, *no* rationale for assigning more blacks than whites to it would have had much chance of surviving strict scrutiny. Of course, if the EMR program harmed those it was meant to help, it was also a huge waste of money, and litigating the question of who should be forced to enroll in it was absurd.

Lloyd Humphreys provided a dramatic illustration of this problem when he testified as an expert witness for the state of California in the *Larry P.* case. Humphreys had spent a lifetime studying cognitive tests. He had argued for years that intelligence should be defined as a set of developed rather than innate abilities, and that the developed abilities that define intelligence were those that intelligence tests measured.[12] He was also critical of psychologists who saw black-white differences on such tests as evidence of innate racial differences.[13] At the *Larry P.* trial, the following interchange took place between the plaintiffs' attorney and Humphreys:

"Doctor, it is your view, is it not, that black people have less intelligence than white people?"

"By my definition at the current point in history, the answer is yes."

"And you will agree with me that your definition is going against 2,000 years of tradition?"

"Yes."[14]

Humphreys clearly feared that his response to the first question would be construed as a statement that blacks were innately less intelligent than whites. He tried to forestall this inference by prefacing his response with the qualifiers "by my definition" and "at the current point in history," but these qualifiers were insufficient to offset the impact of his final yes. The lead lawyer for the plaintiffs thought that Humphreys' response to this question played a critical role in convincing Judge Peckham that the tests were biased.[15] The oddest part of the interchange is Humphreys's acknowledgment that his definition of intelligence was at odds with tradition. Despite this, he still preferred the risk of being seen as a racist—and losing the case—to changing the word he used to describe what the Stanford-Binet or the Wechsler measured.

Not all psychologists share Humphreys's commitment to the claim that IQ tests measure intelligence. Robert Thorndike, for example, renamed

12. See Humphreys (1971). Humphreys did not explicitly equate intelligence with what intelligence tests measured, but he argued that there was "consensus among psychologists as to the kinds of behavior that are labeled intellectual," and that "the Stanford-Binet and the Wechsler tests both exemplify and define the consensus" (p. 19).

13. See Cleary and others (1975), a report to the American Psychological Association of which Humphreys appears to have been the lead author. This report does not rule out the possibility of genetic differences. It merely says that the evidence is insufficient to justify any conclusion.

14. Quoted in Elliott (1987, p. 77).

15. Elliott (1988, p. 335). Elliott argues, to the contrary, that Judge Peckham had already made up his mind when he issued a preliminary restraining order in 1972, long before Humphreys testified.

the Lorge-Thorndike Intelligence Test, calling it the Cognitive Abilities Test. But most psychologists who study cognitive skills see no reason for such a change. As they see it, the discrepancy between what intelligence tests measure and what nonpsychologists mean by the word is evidence of lay ignorance, not evidence that the tests are mislabeled.

This stance is partly a matter of disciplinary pride. Psychologists have been trying to measure intelligence since the late nineteenth century. The tests they have used for this purpose have not changed much since World War I and have hardly changed at all since World War II. But while the tests have not changed much, psychologists' understanding of what the tests measure has changed substantially. Instead of thinking that intelligence tests measure biological potential, psychologists now think of them as measuring developed abilities. But psychologists never signaled this change in their thinking by renaming the tests. Instead, they redefined intelligence to fit their new view of what they were measuring. In effect, they assumed that their discipline owned the word *intelligence* and could use it in any way that members of the discipline found acceptable. Renaming intelligence tests would be a public acknowledgment that the discipline does not, in fact, own this particular term and cannot control its use.

Renaming the tests would be particularly galling to psychologists who believe that the public seriously underestimates both the heritability of IQ and its stability over time. Such psychologists think their job is to change the way the public thinks about intelligence, not capitulate to ignorance. But changing everyday usage is like trying to force-feed a fish. Experts can introduce new terms into everyday language ("IQ," for example). Experts can also introduce new meanings for old terms. But experts cannot suppress traditional uses of familiar terms. Thus if the public uses the word intelligence in many different ways today, the situation is unlikely to improve any time soon. The worse the confusion, the stronger the case for relabeling IQ tests.

Aptitude Tests: The Case of the SAT

Tests that claim to measure academic aptitude raise the same issues as tests that claim to measure intelligence. The best known test of this kind is the Scholastic Aptitude Test. The SAT was developed in the 1930s to help selective colleges identify "diamonds in the rough"—talented students from mediocre high schools who performed poorly on traditional achievement tests because they had not studied the relevant subject matter. At the time, many testers still believed they could measure innate ability. They also thought that a measure of innate ability would predict college success better than traditional achievement tests did. The SAT's designers therefore tried to create a test that was relatively insensitive to whether a student had attended a strong or weak secondary school. The SAT was supposed to measure how much college applicants had learned from experiences that they had all shared (or could have shared if they had been sufficiently motivated). The mathematics test required no formal training beyond first-year algebra, which almost all college applicants had studied. The verbal test required skills that voracious readers could acquire at home, even if their school never asked them to read anything more complex than *Dick and Jane* primers.

Claiming that the SAT measured aptitude was a good way of selling it to college admissions officers, but it also had important costs. One risk was that successful high school students who scored poorly on the test might conclude that they were incapable of doing intellectually demanding academic work. The College Entrance Examination Board initially hoped to avoid this problem by not telling students their scores, but it abandoned this strategy in the early 1950s. It is hard to know how students with good high school grades and low SAT scores really interpret their scores, but many students with relatively low scores certainly do competent work at academically demanding colleges. At the selective colleges that Fredrick Vars and William Bowen discuss in chapter 13, for example, the average student had a combined SAT score of 1,289 and earned college grades averaging roughly B+. These schools did not admit many students with SAT scores as low as 1,000, but those whom they did admit earned grades averaging roughly B.[16] The difference between an average SAT score and an unacceptable SAT score therefore implied a decline of only a third of a letter grade in academic performance.[17] Anyone who has graded undergraduates knows that this is not a large difference. Indeed, it is the smallest difference that most college grading systems bother to record.

16. See chapter 13, tables 13-1 and 13A-1. The predicted grade point average of students with SAT scores of 1,000 is 2.93. The mean for all students is 3.25. The difference is thus 0.32 points.

17. The low-scoring students admitted to these colleges undoubtedly had other strengths. My point is only that low SAT scores taken in isolation should not convince an otherwise competent student that he or she cannot do good work. Crouse and Trusheim (1988, 1991) analyze the predictive power of the SAT in more detail.

A second drawback of claiming that the SAT measured aptitude became obvious in the 1960s, when the dearth of black students in selective colleges became a political issue. Black college applicants scored below whites on all sorts of tests. But whereas low scores on conventional achievement tests merely suggested that black students were poorly prepared for college, low scores on something called an "aptitude" test suggested that blacks might suffer from some kind of innate disability. The Educational Testing Service (ETS), which administers the SAT, disavowed this interpretation but was reluctant to change the name of its most successful product. ETS tried to deal with the problem by saying that the SAT measured abilities developed over many years, but this strategy worked no better than psychologists' attempt to redefine intelligence as developed rather than innate ability. Experts got the message, but the public often did not.

The Educational Testing Service finally threw in the towel in 1995 and renamed the SAT—sort of. It chose a name, the Scholastic Assessment Test, that allowed it to retain the test's original acronym, which had become part of everyday language. "SAT" still appears on every document describing the test; "Scholastic Assessment Test" is much harder to find. Few students who take the SAT seem to know that its name has changed. If, as Claude Steele and Joshua Aronson suggest in chapter 11, able black students underperform on tests that claim to measure intellectual ability, they may have as much trouble with the new SAT as with the old one.

Content Bias

Relabeling aptitude and intelligence tests can reduce concerns about racial bias, but it cannot settle the issue entirely. If blacks score far below whites on a test with real-world consequences, people will want to know who selected the questions and why they chose those questions instead of others. If the test measures things that are taught in school, that is usually a sufficient rationale for its content. But tests like the Stanford-Binet and the SAT also try to test skills that schools do not teach in any direct way. Deciding which skills to include therefore involves somewhat arbitrary judgments. (Were that not the case, all intelligence tests would have the same subtests.) If tests like the Stanford-Binet and the SAT emphasized domains in which blacks were unusually disadvantaged, one would have reason to think these tests were biased against blacks, no matter what their creators or distributors called them.

Every test includes some items that appear to favor one cultural group over another. But intuitive judgments about cultural bias do not seem to predict the racial gap on a given item. In 1951, for example, a doctoral student named Frank McGurk selected 226 items from group intelligence tests and asked a panel of seventy-eight judges to rate them for cultural bias. The judges showed some consensus on 184 items. McGurk then constructed a 74-item test for high school students, composed of 37 culturally loaded items and 37 items that were less culturally loaded but of equal difficulty. He gave this test to black and white seniors at fourteen New Jersey and Pennsylvania high schools and analyzed the results for a subsample of 213 blacks and 213 whites of comparable socioeconomic status. The black-white gap was twice as large for the items that the judges had rated "least cultural" as for those they rated "most cultural."[18]

Another way to assess content bias is to abandon a priori judgments and simply ask how much the black-white gap varies from one question to the next. The Peabody Picture Vocabulary Test (PPVT), for example, tries to measure the size of an individual's English vocabulary. The tester reads a word aloud in standard English and asks the test taker which of four pictures best approximates the word's meaning. If black and white children spoke relatively distinct languages, as some experts on black English claim, one might expect black and white children with vocabularies of equal size to know somewhat different words. In that case, the PPVT should show much larger black-white gaps for some words than for others. But that is not what psychologists have found. The percentage of white children who know a PPVT word correlates 0.98 with the percentage of slightly older black children who know the same word.[19] Black children, in other words, learn pretty much the same words as white children. The black children just tend to learn these words somewhat later.[20] Black children never catch up, however, so black adults know fewer words than white adults. These

18. Summarized in Jensen (1980, pp. 524–27). By matching the test takers on socioeconomic status and school experience, McGurk minimized both the size of the black-white gap and the likely influence of cultural bias. But matching did not eliminate the gap entirely, and the fact that it was smaller for the more culture-bound items is still striking.

19. Jensen (1980, p. 571). Some experts believe that black and white English have become more distinct over the past generation. If so, the correlation between black and white pass rates on PPVT items may have fallen over time. Because the search for biased items has generally yielded negative results, research on the issue has become relatively rare.

20. In times past, the likelihood that test takers would know a word seems to have depended mainly on the frequency with which it appeared in American newspapers, magazines, and books (Jensen, 1974, p. 193). In the 1990s, television may play a larger role.

findings suggest that black and white English differ more in their pronunciation and syntax than in their vocabulary. (I return to pronunciation differences below.)

A few words are unique to black English. In the early 1970s Robert Williams developed the Black Intelligence Test of Racial Homogeneity (BITCH), which measured knowledge of black street language. As one would expect, black high school students scored higher than whites on this test. But blacks' scores on the BITCH were negatively correlated with their scores on other tests.[21] Since the number of words unique to black street language is very small relative to the total number of English words, this negative correlation implies that blacks who did well on the BITCH had smaller total vocabularies than blacks who did poorly on the BITCH. Thus when the goal is to measure the total size of an individual's English vocabulary, tests designed by and for whites are probably not very biased against blacks. The main reason why blacks score lower than whites on these tests is probably that black children have fewer opportunities and incentives to expand their vocabulary, not that conventional tests significantly underestimate the number of words that black children know.

A third approach to assessing content bias in intelligence and aptitude tests is to ask whether the black-white gap is larger on tests that measure familiarity with the content of American culture than on "nonverbal" tests that do not measure familiarity with a particular culture. Larry Hedges and Amy Nowell have reviewed all the national surveys that have tested high school seniors (see chapter 5). These surveys no longer include nonverbal tests, but in 1965 and 1972 the black-white gap was marginally larger on tests of "nonverbal reasoning" than on tests dealing with vocabulary, reading, and mathematics.[22]

The large difference between blacks and whites on many different tests and items suggests that race must play a much broader and deeper role in depressing black scores than many critics assume. There is nothing distinctively white or middle class about the content of the Block Design test, in which a tester asks a child to reproduce two-dimensional red and white designs using a set of colored blocks. Race must affect performance on this

---

21. Brody (1992, p. 292).

22. In the 1965 Equality of Educational Opportunity Survey, the gap on vocabulary, reading, and mathematics tests averaged 1.04 standard deviations, compared to 1.09 standard deviations on the nonverbal reasoning test. In the National Longitudinal Survey of the high school class of 1972, the gap averaged 0.97 standard deviations for vocabulary, reading, and math, compared to 0.99 standard deviations for nonverbal reasoning.

test by affecting black and white children's approach to learning, solving problems, and taking tests, not by affecting their familiarity with the content of the test.

These findings underscore a fact that is easily forgotten. Culture is not merely a body of knowledge and skills. It is also a set of strategies for dealing with the unknown and with tasks that seem difficult.[23] Culture can affect people's willingness to think about unfamiliar questions, their strategies for seeking answers that are not obvious, their motivation to persist in the face of frustration, their confidence that such persistence will be rewarded, and their interest in figuring out what the tester thinks is the right answer. No one knows how large a role cultural differences of this kind play in the black-white test score gap.[24] But we do know that the size of the gap does not depend in any simple, predictable way on the nominal content of the test.

Methodological Bias

Standardized tests assess people's skills and knowledge using methods that some test takers find puzzling, frustrating, anxiety-provoking, or silly. The person giving the test is usually a stranger and more often white than black. The content of some subtests is completely unfamiliar, which may unsettle some people more than others. The instructions for administering the tests are quite rigid, so some people give the wrong answer because they do not understand the question. These and other features of standardized tests have led critics to suspect that blacks might do poorly for reasons that have more to do with the method of assessment than with racial differences in actual skills.

Succcess on the PPVT, for example, depends on knowing what a word means, recognizing the word when it is pronounced in standard English, and recognizing the picture that matches the word. If black preschoolers only recognize a word when it is pronounced with a black accent, the PPVT will understimate their vocabulary. Even preschool children spend a lot of time watching television, so they have almost all had considerable exposure to standard English, but some black preschoolers may still find standard English pronunciation hard to understand. Among three- and four-year-

23. Swidler (1986).
24. But see the classic study by Hess and Shipman (1964) and the observations of Moore (1986).

olds tested in 1986–88 as part of the Children of the National Longitudinal Survey of Youth (CNLSY) survey, for example, the black-white gap averaged 1.01 standard deviations. When these children were retested in 1992, the black-white gap had fallen to 0.90 standard deviations.[25] The gap could have fallen because black children had learned more new words than white children. But the gap could also have fallen because attending school made black children more familiar with standard English pronunciation. A series of studies by Lorene Quay in the early 1970s found no evidence that black children did better when they took a version of the Stanford-Binet that had been translated into black English, but pronunciation plays a smaller role in the Binet than in the PPVT.[26]

Many people also assume that blacks do better when the tester is black. The evidence on this issue is inconsistent, but if the tester's race matters at all, the effect is clearly small.[27] But the way a test is presented can have quite large effects, at least for some students. As mentioned earlier, Steele and Aronson show that black Stanford undergraduates make substantially more mistakes on a difficult verbal test when they are told that the test measures intellectual ability. They also do worse when they are asked to record their race before taking the test. These contextual factors do not affect the performance of white students. Steele and Aronson argue that able black students do worse when they fear that poor performance might confirm the stereotype that blacks are not as intelligent as whites. Steele reports similar findings for able women taking difficult mathematics tests.[28]

Such findings raise the question of what we mean by test bias. When I first read Steele and Aronson's work, I assumed that the "true" black-white gap was the gap observed when students were neither asked to record their race nor told that the test measured intellectual ability. It seemed to me that results obtained under more threatening conditions were more biased. But when blacks and whites attend college together, everyone knows everyone else's race, and students constantly make judgments about one another's

---

25. Among the 195 blacks and 236 whites tested at the age of three or four in 1986 and retested at the age of nine or ten in 1992, the PPVT gap shrank from 1.05 to 0.88 standard deviations. Among the 224 blacks and 371 whites tested at the age of three or four in 1988 and retested at the age of seven or eight in 1992, the gap shrank from 0.97 to 0.92 standard deviations. These estimates all use the CNLSY standard deviations, not the published PPVT norms. Meredith Phillips did the tabulations.

26. See Quay (1974) and the earlier studies cited there. See also Jensen (1980, pp. 603–04).

27. See the review by Jensen (1980) and the sources cited there.

28. See chapter 11 below; Steele (1997).

intellectual ability. Thus if a college wants to predict the classroom performance of black and white applicants, a test administered under "threatening" conditions may yield better predictions than one administered under more neutral conditions. On reflection, I think that the goal of calculating a single "true" black-white gap is a chimera. The true gap, like the measured gap, depends to some extent on the context.

Prediction Bias

Prediction bias can arise whenever a school uses a test to predict students' academic performance or an employer uses a test to predict job performance. Psychologists say that a test suffers from prediction bias when blacks and whites with the same score on the test—the SAT, for example—perform differently on the outcome that they are trying to predict—college grades, for example. Many psychologists also assume that if these predictions are racially unbiased, the system in which they are embedded is "fair." As I show below, this definition of fairness is quite problematic. In this section, I discuss only the extent and possible causes of prediction bias.[29]

College Grades

In the late 1960s, when selective colleges began trying to explain why their black enrollments were so low, they often blamed a shortage of black applicants with SAT scores comparable to those of their top white applicants. Skeptics responded by arguing that the SAT underestimated the academic potential of black applicants. Their reasoning usually went roughly as follows.

—Other things being equal, innate ability probably has some effect on both SAT scores and college grades.

—Blacks have the same innate ability as whites.

—But blacks score lower on the SAT than whites.

—Therefore, the average black with a total SAT score of 1,000 must have started life with more innate ability than the average white with the same score.

---

29. In standard psychometric parlance, these issues are known as threats to predictive validity.

—So, blacks should earn higher college grades than whites with the same SAT scores (because blacks have greater innate ability than whites with the same score).

—Furthermore, if colleges were to treat black applicants with an average SAT score of 1,000 like white applicants with a higher score, the lower-scoring blacks would start college at a disadvantage because of poor preparation but would eventually catch up, because they would have the same innate ability.

This line of reasoning turned out to be wrong. In practice, black undergraduates earn lower grades than whites with the same SAT scores. This is true not only for freshman grades, but for cumulative grades over all four years of college. At selective colleges, moreover, the racial disparity in grades is wider among students with the highest SAT scores.[30]

The fact that blacks earn lower college grades than whites with the same scores does not mean that the SAT is really biased against whites. Individuals with the same SAT scores usually differ in many other ways, such as how much they know about academic subjects when they enter college, how hard they work while at college, and how efficiently they organize their studying.[31] If blacks are disadvantaged on these unmeasured traits, one would expect them to earn lower grades than whites with the same SAT scores.[32]

Prediction Bias and Cultural Bias

The SAT does not measure students' mastery of the subjects they study in secondary school. If blacks attend worse high schools than whites, as most people assume, they presumably know less about history, literature, science, and calculus than whites with the same SAT scores. In that case, one should not be surprised to find that blacks earn lower college grades

---

30. On overprediction of grades among black undergraduates, see chapters 12 and 13. On the widening of the racial gap in grades as SAT scores rise, see both chapter 13 and Crouse and Trusheim (1988).

31. On study habits, see Treisman (1985, 1992).

32. Because critics often claim that the SAT is not a valid predictor of college performance for blacks, research has tended to focus on whether the black and white regression slopes differ, not on whether the intercepts differ. This emphasis probably misconstrues the critics' real concern, which is that such tests underestimate the average performance of black students, not that they fail to distinguish blacks who will earn high grades from those who will earn lower grades.

than whites with the same SAT scores. If the SAT did measure how much students had learned in high school, it might predict college grades more accurately. But it might also show an even larger black-white gap than the SAT.

I emphasize the possibility that making the SAT less "fair" to students from weak high schools could improve its predictive power for college grades because critics of the test often assume the opposite. Like the psychologists who originally developed the SAT, its modern critics often assume that an "aptitude" test would predict college grades more accurately if it were less contaminated by social and cultural influences. This is possible, but hardly self-evident. Consider an extreme case. Suppose that a blood test could identify all the genes that influence cognitive skills, and that colleges could use this information to predict the performance of each applicant if—and this is a crucial if—the applicant had been raised in an average American home and had attended average schools. I doubt that selective colleges would find this information as useful as the SAT. Colleges do not admit students at the moment of conception; they admit applicants whose minds have been developing in different ways for seventeen or eighteen years. What matters to them is not the genes with which applicants were born, but what applicants are likely to do *after* having grown up in a specific environment.

No one knows exactly how genes shape mental development. But genes do not appear to be like oil, which can sit in the ground unused for centuries without losing its value as an energy source. By the time students are old enough to apply to college, their minds have developed in particular ways: some neural paths have grown strong and others have atrophied. The mental differences among seventeen-year-olds do not completely determine their future, but neither are they easy to change. Those who have not yet heard any English can still learn to speak the language, but they will almost always speak with an accent, and some will never become fully fluent. Those who have heard no language of any kind may never speak at all. People who think that a measure of innate ability would predict college grades better than the SAT tacitly assume that genetic advantages are worth more in the long run than environmental advantages. That may be true, but it is not obvious.

Why Use the SAT?

No other country uses a test like the SAT to screen university applicants. Other countries use tests that cover (and largely determine) what prospective applicants have studied in secondary school. These tests resemble university examinations more closely than the SAT does, and they predict university grades more accurately.[33] By relying on achievement tests to choose among applicants, universities abroad also reap other benefits. First, weak secondary schools know what their best students must learn in order to get into a good college. This probably improves the courses offered by weak schools. Second, because admission is contingent on how much applicants have learned, ambitious teenagers have more incentive to study hard. America's selective colleges do give an applicant's high school grades substantial weight when making admissions decisions. But American students know that their SAT scores will count nearly as much as their grades, so their incentive to work hard is lower than it would be in Europe or Japan.[34] As a result, even ambitious American high school students seem to begin their higher education knowing less than their counterparts in other countries.

The fact that American colleges care as much about SAT scores as high school grades not only gives teenagers less incentive to study hard, but encourages them to value what the English aristocracy used to call effortless superiority. In such a student culture, the best kind of A is the kind one gets without studying. The A one has to earn by hard work may be worth considerably less than the B+ one gets without working. This kind of student culture can have a particularly negative effect on blacks, who know that their chances of doing well on aptitude tests like the SAT are low. Without an ethos that supports hard work, their chances of success fall even further. But while there is a strong pedagogic case for replacing the SAT with achievement tests, no one should assume that this would improve the competitive position of blacks in the short run.

33. In Great Britain, Choppin and colleagues (1973, 1976) found that an aptitude test modeled on the SAT was a far worse predictor of university grades than the achievement tests traditionally used in Britain. As a supplement to achievement tests, an SAT-like test made a small contribution to the prediction of grades in the social sciences—which are not taught in British secondary schools—but made almost no contribution to the prediction of grades in other subjects.

34. Using high school grades to motivate students has two drawbacks. First, such a system creates an adversary relationship between students and teachers. A system of national exams, in contrast, puts students and teachers on the same side: both are trying to ensure that the student does as well as possible on somebody else's examination. A second drawback is that when high school grades matter, students resent classmates who work hard, because they know that other students' extra effort "raises the curve" and lowers the grades that they themselves can expect to get for any given level of effort (Bishop, 1996). With national exams, this latter problem almost vanishes.

Job Performance

Research on the relationship between test scores and job performance yields conclusions broadly similar to those on test scores and college grades. A decade ago, after an extensive review of roughly 700 studies using the General Aptitude Test Battery (GATB), a panel appointed by the National Academy of Sciences reached the following conclusions about its predictive power:[35]

1. The GATB predicts performance in almost all kinds of jobs, including relatively unskilled jobs.

2. GATB scores do not predict job performance very well. If two workers' GATB scores differ by one standard deviation, their supervisor's rating of their performance will typically differ by a quarter of a standard deviation.

3. For reasons that nobody understands, the GATB's ability to predict job performance has been falling. In the 1950s and 1960s, workers whose GATB scores differed by one standard deviation typically got performance ratings that differed by almost two-fifths of a standard deviation.[36]

4. In the twenty studies that compare blacks and whites on both objective measures of job performance and supervisors' ratings, the racial gap on

35. Hartigan and Wigdor (1989).

36. Ibid., pp. 169–71. Earlier in the 1980s the U.S. Employment Service (USES, 1983), reported much higher predictive validities for the GATB. USES's validity estimates exceed Hartigan and Wigdor's partly because USES relied on studies conducted before 1972, which turned out to have higher validities than studies conducted later. In addition, USES assumed a reliability of 0.80. Finally, USES assumed that restrictions of range on the GATB reduced its standardized coefficient by a fifth, whereas Hartigan and Wigdor assumed the reduction was only a tenth. I have accepted Hartigan and Wigdor's estimates of reliability and restriction of range not because they produce better evidence for their estimates than USES produced but because an NAS panel is under more pressure to reflect the professional consensus. I have no idea whether this consensus is correct.

Hartigan and Wigdor (1989, pp. 166–68) argue against any correction for restriction of range, on the grounds that employers need to know how much using GATB would improve their choices relative to the actual pool of applicants, not relative to choosing randomly from the entire labor force. Although correcting for restriction of range in the applicant pool might mislead employers about how much they could improve the performance of their workers by using GATB, the (standardized) slope coefficient corrected for restriction of range is the best available way of describing the likely benefit of choosing a worker with a score of X over a worker with a score of X'. Assuming that Hartigan and Wigdor's estimates of restriction in range are correct, my best guess is that a difference of one population standard deviation between two workers' GATB scores was associated with an increase of 0.385 standard deviations in their supervisors' mean ratings before 1972, and with an increase of between 0.242 and 0.275 standard deviations after 1972. (This calculation accepts Hartigan and Wigdor's assumption that individual supervisors' ratings have a reliability of 0.80.)

the supervisors' ratings is only 0.06 standard deviations larger than the gap on the objective measures.[37]

5. In the seventy studies that compared blacks and whites with the same GATB scores, white supervisors typically rate whites who score at the mean on the GATB about 0.23 standard deviations higher than blacks who score at the mean.[38] The fact that the racial gap is smaller on objective measures of performance suggests that some of this difference could be due to racial bias among supervisors.

6. The racial disparity in supervisors' ratings is greater among workers with high GATB scores than among those with low scores.[39] Putting this point slightly differently, the GATB is more likely to identify high-performing whites than high-performing blacks.

These results are broadly similar to those for college grades. In both cases, test scores have a moderate correlation with performance. In both cases, whites perform a little better than blacks with the same test scores. In both cases, the gap between blacks and whites grows wider as their test scores rise. And in neither case, as the next section shows, do these facts tell us whether using tests to select students or workers is "fair."

37. Hartigan and Wigdor (1989, p. 187) report a mean black-white performance gap of about 0.2 standard deviations on both objective measures of performance and supervisors' subjective judgments. But Ford, Schechtman, and Kraiger (1986) show that supervisors slightly overestimate the racial gap in actual job performance, while underestimating the (larger) racial gap in job knowledge. This need not mean that the racial gap in supervisors' ratings of job performance is motivated by racial prejudice. Instead, ratings of black workers' job performance may be contaminated by the racial disparity in job knowledge, which is often easier to observe than actual performance. On the other hand, most of the supervisors who rated workers in these studies were white, and Oppler and others (1992) report that both blacks and whites get somewhat higher ratings from supervisors of their own race than from supervisors of a different race.

38. Ibid., table 9-5. This estimate of the racial difference in supervisors' ratings comes from a larger sample of studies than the finding that the racial gap is 0.06 standard deviations greater for supervisors' ratings than for objective ratings. Therefore one cannot use the latter estimate to "correct" the former.

39. Ibid., tables 9-6 to 9-8. Pooling blacks and whites and estimating performance from a single prediction equation overestimates the ratings given to black workers by 0.05 standard deviations for workers with GATB scores one standard deviation below the black mean, 0.13 standard deviations for workers whose scores are at the black mean, and 0.18 standard deviations for workers with scores one standard deviation above the black mean. These estimates, like those in the previous note, come mainly from white supervisors. The gap for workers with scores one standard deviation above the black mean is presumably smaller than the gap in the previous note because the intercept of the estimating equation in these tables is for a pooled sample of blacks and whites, rather than for whites alone.

Selection System Bias

Selection system bias, like prediction bias, arises when a test is used to predict performance. Nonetheless, there is no necessary association between the two types of bias. Consider a firm that uses a battery of cognitive tests to select workers for white collar jobs. For simplicity, assume the firm relies solely on test scores to choose workers. In fact, few firms do this, but the logical structure of the problem usually remains the same when tests are combined with other predictors. Only the magnitude of bias changes. As I indicated in the previous section, prediction bias exists when blacks and whites with the same scores on the test perform differently on the job. Selection system bias, using my definition of it, exists when blacks and whites who would perform equally well if they got a job have different chances of getting it. If a firm relies entirely on test scores to select workers, selection system bias will arise whenever the standardized racial gap in job performance is smaller than the standardized racial gap in test performance. In the absence of prediction bias, this outcome is almost inevitable, because the absence of prediction bias guarantees that the racial disparity in job performance will be smaller than the racial disparity in test performance.[40]

---

40. In formal terms, let P be a standardized performance measure of some kind, let E be a firm's standardized estimate of a worker's performance, and let the subscripts b and w denote the black and white means of P and E. If the selection system is "top-down," always picking the applicants with the highest values on E, selection system bias will exist when $P_w - P_b < E_w - E_b$. This cannot happen if predictions are perfectly accurate ($r_{PE} = 1$). But estimates of P always contain some error (e). Thus, $P_i = r_{PE}E_i + e_i$, where the subscript i denotes the value for the ith individual. For simplicity, assume a selection system based solely on test scores (T). Then let M be a dichotomous variable with a value of 1 for blacks and 0 for everyone else. If the test suffers from prediction bias and we estimate

(1) $P_i = B_1 T_i + B_2 M_i + e_i$,

B_2 will be positive. If $B_2 = 0$, we have no prediction bias and equation 1 reduces to

(2) $P_i = B_1 T_i + e_i$.

Since all variables are standardized, moreover, $B_1 = r_{PT}$. Thus when there is no prediction bias, $P_w - P_b = r_{PT}(T_w - T_b)$. Since $r_{PT} < 1$, the standardized racial gap on the performance measure ($P_w - P_b$) must by definition be smaller than the standardized racial gap on the test $(T_w - T_b)$. Thus, if a selection system is based solely on test performance, if blacks score lower than whites on the test, and the test does not suffer from prediction bias, there will *always* be selection system bias. Indeed, even if there is prediction bias in favor of blacks (B_2 in equation 1 is negative), there will still be selection system bias against blacks unless B_2 is large enough to offset the fact that r_{PT} is less than 1.00. If the black-white test score gap is 1 SD, for example, and if $r_{PT} = 0.30$, B_2 will need to be roughly -0.70 to make $P_w - P_b = E_w - E_b$, eliminating selection system bias.

If there is no prediction bias, there are two ways of eliminating selection system bias. One alternative is to eliminate the error term in equation 2 by adding enough predictors to make $R^2 = 1$. The other alternative, which would only make sense in selection systems that care more about racial equity

Selecting Workers

In the late 1970s, testing enthusiasts began urging the U.S. Employment Service (USES) to use the General Aptitude Test Battery to assess everyone who came in looking for work. If USES gave high-scoring applicants priority in its referrals to employers, they argued, more employers would use the service. This proposal appealed to USES, which had become the employment service of last resort, serving the nation's most marginal workers. But emphasizing the GATB posed an obvious problem: blacks scored roughly one standard deviation below whites, and the Supreme Court's 1971 decision in *Griggs* v. *Duke Power Co.* barred the use of a test that had an adverse impact on the job prospects of blacks unless the test had a demonstrated relationship to job performance.

There was no practical way of proving that the GATB predicted performance in all the diverse jobs to which USES referred applicants. The service therefore decided to renorm the GATB so as to eliminate its adverse impact on blacks. Instead of ranking everyone who took the GATB on a single scale, USES ranked blacks relative to other blacks and whites relative to other whites. This kind of "race norming" ensured that blacks and whites would have the same distribution of percentile scores, no matter how much their raw scores differed.

In 1986 William Bradford Reynolds, Assistant Attorney General for Civil Rights, informed the U.S. Employment Service that his office viewed race norming as illegal. USES responded by asking the National Academy of Sciences (NAS) to determine whether the GATB was a valid predictor of job performance and whether it should be race normed. The NAS review panel concluded that the GATB was a valid predictor of job performance, but that USES should nonetheless rank job applicants relative to others of their race, not relative to a single national standard.[41]

---

than maximizing the performance of workers, would be to augment the predicted values from equation 2 by adding a random error term with the same variance as e_i. But while including the random error term from equation 2 will make $P_w - P_b = E_w - E_b$ and thus make the selection system racially unbiased, this solution will lower the mean performance of those selected. Worse, it will lower mean performance *more* than racial quotas combined with top-down selection within racial groups. No system can maximize the expected performance of those selected while ensuring that equally competent blacks and whites have equal chances of selection, because no system can currently measure most of the traits that differentiate blacks who will perform well on the job from those who will perform badly.

41. Hartigan and Wigdor (1989).

The panel's rationale for this startling recommendation was not that the GATB underestimated the job performance of individual minority workers relative to that of whites with identical scores. That was not the case. Nonetheless, the panel argued that relying primarily or exclusively on unadjusted GATB scores to rank-order job applicants, as USES had been urged to do, would drastically underestimate the percentage of blacks who could perform as well as the whites. The panel's recommendation that race-norming continue did not go down well with the public or with Congress, however, and the Civil Rights Act of 1991 made race norming illegal.

To understand how the NAS panel arrived at what the public regarded as a completely illogical conclusion, one must begin with some facts. First, even after making reasonable corrections for measurement error, the GATB explains less than 15 percent of the variance in supervisors' ratings of workers. Other unmeasured differences between workers, between workplaces, or in the ways that workers and workplaces affect one another must by definition explain the rest.[42] Second, the racial gap on the GATB is much larger than the racial gap on the other, unmeasured (but in the aggregate more important) determinants of job performance.[43] A third fact follows from the first two: the racial disparity in supervisors' ratings is far smaller than the racial disparity in test performance. In the absence of any prescreening, the black-white gap in supervisors' ratings would probably average about 0.4 standard deviations.[44] The racial gap on the GATB is more like 1.0 standard deviation. It follows that if the U.S. Employment

42. The estimates in the text are corrected for measurement error (see note 36) and are, if anything, high for post-1972 data.

43. Once test scores are controlled, the racial gap in performance averages about 0.12 standard deviations. If one assumes that the unmeasured determinants of performance account for all of the variance not accounted for by test scores, they must account for at least 85 percent of the nonerror variance. Thus if one could create a standardized index of all these unmeasured factors, the implied black-white gap would be 0.13 standard deviations ($0.12/0.85^{0.5}$). The racial gap on the GATB, in contrast, is about one standard deviation.

44. The standardized disparity in job performance is (roughly) the sum of the standardized disparity predicted by the racial difference in GATB scores and the standardized effect of race with GATB scores controlled. After correcting for restrictions of range in the GATB, its standardized coefficient in post-1972 samples averages 0.26 standard deviations (see note 36). Assuming racial difference of one standard deviation in GATB scores, the standardized racial difference in supervisors' ratings from this source is therefore 0.26 standard deviations. The standardized racial difference in supervisors' ratings with GATB scores controlled averages 0.13 standard deviations at the black mean. Thus if one ignores the fact that controlling race probably lowers the estimated coefficient of the GATB, the overall racial difference in performance is about 0.39 standard deviations (0.26 + 0.13). William Johnson and Derek Neal's data in chapter 14 also suggest that the standardized wage gap is far smaller than the gap in standardized test scores, and that test scores explain most but not all of the wage gap.

Service were to rank job applicants on the basis of the GATB alone, without race norming, black job seekers' chances of getting to the head of the queue would be far lower than if they were ranked on the basis of their past supervisors' ratings. Likewise, employers who used the GATB to select workers would hire far fewer blacks than employers who hired a lot of temporary workers and retained those who performed best.

The conflict between what I will call test-based and performance-based selection systems would vanish if employers could measure all the traits that influence job performance, and could therefore predict exactly how well each applicant would do. In that case, randomly selected blacks would presumably rank only about 0.4 standard deviations below randomly selected whites on predicted performance. But employers cannot measure in advance most of the traits that affect job performance.[45]

This leaves America in a bind. The predictor that social scientists can measure most accurately—namely, cognitive skills—is the predictor on which blacks are most disadvantaged. If employers (or USES) were to rely largely on test scores to rank applicants, blacks would have to pay for the limitations of social science. If employers (or USES) decide to ignore test scores, society as a whole pays for the limitations of social science.

The problem posed by the GATB is analogous to what would happen if professional basketball teams stopped observing potential recruits on the courts and began screening them on the basis of "objective" criteria. In such a world, coaches might well screen on height. A lot of good basketball players would be excluded, the quality of the game would deteriorate, and shorter players would claim that the system was unfair. Such a system would also reduce the number of black basketball players, because blacks and whites are almost equally likely to be tall, whereas blacks are much more likely than whites to be outstanding basketball players.

Psychologists have worried about these issues since the early 1970s.[46] They have not found any good solutions. As far as I can tell, there are none. When employers cannot or will not observe the actual performance of their workers, fairness and efficiency are bound to conflict.[47] Six conclusions seem warranted.

45. One reason why test scores predict better than measures of character or personality is that high test scores are harder to fake than diligence, congeniality, and other social virtues. Every worker who goes for an interview tries to put his or her best foot forward. Most people who take paper and pencil personality tests try to do the same.

46. Thorndike (1971) seems to be the first statement of the problem.

47. One can think of fairness to low-scoring applicants as requiring that their chances of getting any given job be proportional to their chances of doing well in the job. If 66.7 percent of workers who

—Using tests to select workers will usually exclude more competent blacks than whites.

—Using tests to select workers will usually raise the average level of job performance above what it would be if employers selected workers randomly.

—Hiring more inexperienced applicants than one needs and retaining those who perform best will usually yield a more competent permanent workforce than hiring applicants with high test scores.

—Performance-based selection will also increase the percentage of blacks who make the cut relative to test-based selection.

—The economic benefits of getting the best possible workers will not always exceed the cost of hiring, training, and firing a lot of less capable workers. Airlines, for example, seldom think that trial and error is a good way to select pilots. When the costs of hiring mistakes are high, employers may find that it pays to rely on test scores, even if doing so excludes more competent blacks than competent whites.

—If a firm cannot select workers based on actual (or simulated) performance, the only way to prevent it from using tests to screen workers is to make this illegal. This policy has some economic costs.[48]

College Admissions

Suppose that a selective college wants an admissions policy that makes black applicants' chances of admission proportional to their chances of earning high grades as students. Suppose, in other words, that the college's goal is group fairness. This college faces the same dilemma that the U.S. Employment Service faces when deciding which job seekers should get priority in referrals. Simply admitting the applicants with the highest predicted grades will not achieve the college's goal. This seemingly equitable

---

score above the mean on the GATB do outstanding work, compared with 33.3 percent of low-scoring workers, fairness requires that employers choose two high-scoring workers for every low-scoring worker. But no sane employer would want to do this. Because employers cannot tell in advance which low-scoring workers will do outstanding work, they will choose only high-scoring applicants. Who can blame them?

48. For reasons discussed by Hartigan and Wigdor (1989), the estimated cost of not using tests is far lower than the figures that USES circulated in the 1980s. The cost to society of not using tests to select workers is quite different from the cost to a specific employer. A firm that tests job applicants when its competitors do not may gain a large advantage. If all firms use tests, the overall increase in economic efficiency will be much smaller because the overall supply of good workers will not expand, at least in the short run.

strategy will fail because blacks are more disadvantaged on the measures that predict college grades best (that is, SAT scores and high school grades) than on the other, unmeasured—and apparently unmeasurable—determinants of college grades.

Among members of the high school class of 1982 who attended four-year colleges, about 11 percent earned college grade point averages (GPAs) closer to A than B—that is, above 3.5.[49] Blacks and Hispanics earned GPAs about a third of a letter grade below those of non-Hispanic whites, which implies that roughly 5 percent of blacks and Hispanics had GPAs above 3.5.[50] Now imagine a college whose goal is to admit only the top 11 percent of all applicants to four-year colleges. The grade data suggest that if the college could identify these people, it would admit about 5 percent of all blacks and Hispanics. If the college selected students on the basis of SAT scores alone, it would admit only 2 percent of blacks and Hispanics.[51] If it relied on both SAT scores and high school grades, it would admit more than 2 percent but less than 5 percent of blacks and Hispanics.

Although it is intuitively appealing to admit blacks and Hispanics in proportion to their chances of earning high grades, this goal has two serious drawbacks. First, there is no color-blind mechanism that will achieve this goal. Because blacks rank far below whites on the best currently available predictors of college performance, a college must use some system of racial preferences to offset this disadvantage. That is bound to be controversial, and in some jurisdictions it is now illegal. The second drawback of trying to base admissions policy on the estimated percentages of blacks and whites who "could" earn the highest grades is that there is no good way to identify the students who really *will* earn the highest grades. In practice, therefore, racial quotas will not mean that selective colleges admit black and white students who earn the same grades. Instead, the average black

49. These estimates are based on the sample covered by chapter 12, table 12-5. These students' mean GPA is 2.65, with a standard deviation of 0.68 (Thomas Kane, personal communication). A GPA of 3.5 therefore represents a z score of 1.25. If grades are normally distributed, 11 percent of students score above this level.

50. See chapter 12, table 12-5. I assume that blacks and Hispanics constituted 15 percent of four-year college students, that other nonwhites had the same mean as whites, and that black and Hispanics therefore had a mean GPA of 2.38. Assuming that GPAs are normally distributed and that the standard deviation for blacks and Hispanics is also 0.68, 5 percent of the black and Hispanic distribution would have GPAs above 3.5 ($z > 1.65$).

51. Assuming that blacks and Hispanics score 0.8 standard deviations below the population mean, and that a college sets its SAT cutoff point so that 10 percent of all students qualify ($z = 1.28$), blacks and Hispanics would have needed a z of 2.08, which excludes all but the top 2 percent.

admitted to a college that pursues this policy will get lower grades than the average white. The only way to solve these two problems would be to admit all applicants and then ask those with a grade point average below, say, 3.5 to leave after their first year. Since students are risk-averse, a college that adopted this policy would have great difficulty attracting good students.

Conclusions

Charges that standardized tests are racially biased will not go away. But while some forms of bias are a major problem, others are not.

Labeling bias. When a test claims to measure aptitude or intelligence, the charge that it suffers from labeling bias seems to me reasonable. Millions of Americans think of aptitude and intelligence as innate traits, at least some of the time. This interpretation is especially common when race is involved. People hear statements like "blacks are less intelligent than whites" or "blacks have less academic aptitude than whites" as claims that blacks are innately inferior. Few psychologists believe that racial differences in either IQ scores or SAT scores suffice to prove the existence of racial differences in innate ability. Those psychologists who claim that these tests measure intelligence or aptitude must therefore be either oblivious or indifferent to the way their words are often interpreted.

Content bias. Blacks score lower than whites (and Asians) on a wide range of tests that cover both subjects taught in school and skills that are not taught in school. The gap is no greater on tasks that appear to measure familiarity with the content of "white" or "middle class" culture than on tasks that appear to be more culturally neutral. Furthermore, the gap on IQ tests is similar to that on many tests of academic achievement. This means that black-white differences go far beyond such apparently trivial matters as knowing who wrote *Faust* or what a sonata is.

Methodological bias. I have not seen much evidence that the way psychologists measure cognitive skills has a sizable impact on the black-white gap. The exception is Steele and Aronson's work with Stanford undergraduates, which shows that the psychological context in which a test is given can sometimes make a big difference. How often this happens is still uncertain.

Prediction bias. Cognitive tests seldom underestimate the future performance of black test takers, either at college or on the job. This is because blacks are also somewhat disadvantaged in other ways that cognitive tests do not capture.

Selection system bias. Despite the absence of prediction bias, selection system bias is a major issue. Relying on tests to select either college applicants or job applicants will exclude far more blacks (and Hispanics) than performance-based selection will. In principle, performance-based selection can yield both better workers and a more diverse labor force than test-based selection. But the practical costs of performance-based selection are often substantial.

If these conclusions are correct, it seems fair to say that the invention of standardized tests has harmed blacks as a group, both because of labeling bias and because of selection system bias. This does not mean the tests themselves are flawed. The skill differences that the tests measure are real, and these skills have real consequences both at school and at work. But inability to measure the other predictors of performance, on which blacks seem to be far less disadvantaged, poses a huge social problem.

References

Bishop, John. 1996. "Nerd Harassment, Incentives, School Priorities, and Learning." Cornell University, Consortium for Policy Research in Education.

Brody, Nathan. 1992. *Intelligence.* San Diego, Calif.: Academic Press.

Cattell, Raymond. 1971. *Abilities: Their Structure, Growth, and Action.* Boston: Houghton-Mifflin.

Chipuer, Heather, Michael Rovine, and Robert Plomin. 1990. "LISREL Modeling: Genetic and Environmental Influences on IQ Revisited." *Intelligence* 14 (1):11–29.

Choppin, Bruce, and Lea Orr. 1976. *Aptitude Testing at Eighteen-Plus.* Windsor, England: National Foundation for Educational Research.

Choppin, Bruce, and others. 1973. *The Prediction of Academic Success.* Slough, England: National Foundation for Educational Research.

Cleary, Anne T., and others. 1975. "Educational Uses of Tests with Disadvantaged Students." *American Psychologist* 30:15–41.

Crouse, James, and Dale Trusheim. 1988. *The Case against the SAT.* University of Chicago Press.

———. 1991. "How Colleges Can Correctly Determine Selection Benefits from the SAT." *Harvard Educational Review* 61(2):123–47.

Elliott, Rogers. 1987. *Litigating Intelligence: IQ Tests, Special Education, and Social Science in the Courtroom.* Dover, Mass.: Auburn House.

———. 1988. "Tests, Abilities, Race, and Conflict." *Intelligence* 12:333-50.

Ford, Kevin, Susan Schechtman, and Kurt Kraiger. 1986. "Study of Race Effects in Objective Indices and Subjective Evaluations of Performance: A Meta-Analysis of Performance Criteria." *Psychological Bulletin* 99(3):330-37.

Hartigan, John, and Alexandra Wigdor, eds. 1989. *Fairness in Employment Testing: Validity*

Generalization, Minority Issues, and the General Aptitude Test Battery. Washington: National Academy Press.

Hess, Robert D., and Virginia C. Shipman. 1964. "Early Experience and the Socialization of Cognitive Modes in Children." *Child Development* 36:869–86.

Humphreys, Lloyd. 1971. "Theory of Intelligence." In Robert Cancro, ed., *Intelligence: Genetic and Environmental Influences.* New York: Grune and Stratton.

Jensen, Arthur R. 1974. "How Biased Are Culture-Loaded Tests?" *Genetic Psychology Monographs* 70:185-244.

———. 1980. *Bias in Mental Testing.* Free Press.

McCartney, Kathleen, Monica Harris, and Frank Bernieri. 1990. "Growing Up and Growing Apart: A Developmental Meta-Analysis of Twin Samples." *Psychological Bulletin* 107:226-37.

McClearn, Gerald, and others. 1997. "Substantial Genetic Influence on Cognitive Abilities in Twins 80 or More Years Old." *Science* 276 (June 6):1560–63.

Moore, Elsie. 1986. "Family Socialization and the IQ Test Performance of Traditionally and Transracially Adopted Black Children." *Developmental Psychology* 22(3):317-26.

Oppler, Scott, and others. 1992. "Three Approaches to the Investigation of Subgroup Bias in Performance Measurement: Review, Results, and Conclusions." *Journal of Applied Psychology* 77 (2):201–17.

Plomin, Robert, and John C. DeFries. 1980. "Genetics and Intelligence: Recent Data." *Intelligence* 4:15–24.

Plomin, Robert, and others. 1994. "Variability and Stability in Cognitive Abilities Are Largely Genetic Later in Life." *Behavior Genetics* 24 (3):207–15.

Quay, L. C. 1974. "Language, Dialect, Age, and Intelligence Test Performance in Disadvataged Black Children." *Child Development* 45:463–468.

Schmidt, Frank, and John Hunter. 1981. "Employment Testing: Old Theories and New Research Findings." *American Psychologist* 36:1128–1137

Snyderman, Mark, and Stanley Rothman. 1987. "Survey of Expert Opinion on Intelligence and Aptitude Testing." *American Psychologist* 42 (2):137–44.

Steele, Claude. 1997. "A Threat in the Air: How Stereotypes Shape Intellectual Identity and Performance." *American Psychologist* 52 (6):613-29.

Swidler, Ann. 1986. "Culture in Action: Symbols and Strategies." *American Sociological Review* 51:273–86.

Terman, Lewis. 1916. *The Measurement of Intelligence.* Boston: Houghton-Mifflin.

Thorndike, Robert. 1971. "Concepts of Culture-Fairness." *Journal of Educational Measurement* 8 (2):63–70.

Thurstone, Louis Leon. 1938. *Primary Mental Abilities.* University of Chicago Press.

Treisman, Uri. 1985. "A Study of the Mathematics Performance of Black Students at the University of California, Berkeley." University of California.

———. 1992. "Studying Students Studying Calculus: A Look at the Lives of Minority Mathematics Students in College." *College Mathematics Journal* 23 (November 5):362–72.

Wigdor, Alexandra, and Bert Green, eds. 1991. *Performance Assessment in the Workplace,* vol. 1. Washington: National Academy Press.

RICHARD E. NISBETT

3 | Race, Genetics, and IQ

THE QUESTION OF whether IQ differences between blacks and whites have a genetic basis goes back at least a thousand years. When the Moors invaded Europe, they speculated that Europeans might be congenitally incapable of abstract thought.[1] By the nineteenth century, however, most Europeans probably believed that their intellectual skills were congenitally superior to those of Africans. The IQ test, developed early in the twentieth century, seemed to reinforce this view: for decades, whites scored about 15 points higher than blacks.

If this difference were wholly or substantially genetic in origin, the implications for American society could be dire. It would mean that even if the environmental playing field were leveled, a higher proportion of blacks than whites would have trouble supporting themselves, and a lower proportion of blacks than whites would be professionals and successful execu-

I am indebted to William Dickens, Greg Duncan, Adye Bel Evans, James Jones, Derek Neal, Craig Ramey, Sandra Scarr, Claude Steele, Robert Sternberg, and Edward Zigler for advice and assistance. A version of this chapter appears in *The Bell Curve Wars* (Fraser, 1994).

1. J. B. S. Haldane, cited in Flynn (1980). Swarthy southern Europeans had their doubts about pale northern Europeans for even longer. Cicero warned the Romans not to purchase British slaves because they were so difficult to train (Sowell, 1994, p. 156), although Caesar felt they had a certain value for rough work (Churchill, 1974, p. 2).

tives. A recent example of this claim can be found in the phenomenally successful book *The Bell Curve*, by Richard Herrnstein and Charles Murray.[2]

In this chapter I review the evidence on whether the black-white IQ difference is wholly or substantially due to genetic factors—other than obvious factors like skin color, which affect the way Americans treat each other. Because *The Bell Curve* has played such a central role in recent discussions of this issue, I often focus on its claims. For present purposes, I accept the mainstream view on IQ tests and their correlates, including the following assumptions:

—IQ tests measure something real about intelligence, as defined in the modern West.

—Children's IQ scores predict important life outcomes, such as school success, delinquency and crime, and productive economic behavior. This relationship persists even when one controls for family background and other social correlates of IQ.

—Among whites, variation in IQ is heritable to a substantial extent. That is to say, IQ scores vary independent of environmental conditions. Expert estimates suggest that anywhere between 30 and 80 percent of the variation in IQ scores is determined by genetic factors. The best available studies indicate that heritability is somewhat greater than .70.[3]

—Estimates of heritability *within* a given population need not say anything about the degree to which differences *between* populations are genetically determined. The classic example is an experiment in which a random mix of wheat seeds is grown on two different plots of land. Within either plot, the environment is kept uniform, so the difference in height among the plants is largely or entirely genetically determined. Yet the average difference *between* the two plots is entirely environmental, because the mix of genotypes in each plot is identical.[4]

Despite the fact that the heritability of a characteristic within a population has no necessary relationship to the heritability of differences between populations, many people believe that the large IQ difference between blacks and whites must be partly genetic in origin. They argue that if the heritability of IQ within populations is high (especially if it is as high as 80 percent), and if the IQ difference between blacks and whites is as large as

2. Herrnstein and Murray (1994).

3. See Neisser (1996).

4. For a particularly lucid account of heritability and the genetic contribution to IQ, see Block (1995).

one standard deviation, then one must assume implausibly large environmental differences between blacks and whites to explain the IQ gap in exclusively environmental terms. Meredith Phillips, Jeanne Brooks-Gunn, Greg Duncan, Pamela Klebanov, and Jonathan Crane explore this argument in more detail in chapter 4. For present purposes, it is sufficient to point out, first, that heritability of IQ within populations is considered by most scholars to be lower than 80 percent. Second, the IQ gap is no longer 15 points, but something closer to 10 points.[5] Third, the environmental differences between blacks and whites on variables known to be related to IQ are indeed quite large.[6] And fourth, there may well be environmental differences between blacks and whites of a qualitative nature, having to do with socialization practices, for example, that operate so as to increase the IQ difference between blacks and whites.[7]

Evidence bearing on the heritability of the IQ difference between blacks and whites is of two broad types. The first comprises studies that assess heritability directly, correlating the IQ scores of African Americans with the percentage of their genes that are "European." These are by far the most relevant studies. They are also relatively easy to perform in the United States, where individuals are classified as "black" even when they have a very large percentage of "white" ancestors. As much as 30 percent of the "black" American gene pool consists of "European" genes. The conventional genetic hypothesis is that blacks with more European genes should have higher IQ scores. Nevertheless, such a correlation could also arise for environmental reasons. Blacks with lighter skins and more Caucasian features might have social and economic advantages that would make them more likely to have high IQs. Consequently, if little or no association were found between Caucasian ancestry and IQ within the black population, this would be particularly damaging to the genetic explanation of the black-white IQ gap.

The second type of evidence comes from studies that examine the effects of the family environments in which black children are raised. The strong genetic hypothesis is that rearing blacks in family environments similar to those of whites should result in little or no gain in their IQ scores. Yet even when black children are reared in white homes, they are probably subject to other cultural and social influences that might depress their IQ scores. Consequently, if growing up in a typical white family environment

5. Nisbett (1995); chapters 5 and 6 below.
6. Chapter 4 below; Dickens, Kane, and Schultze (forthcoming).
7. Heath (1983); Moore (1986); Scarr (1981); Young (1970).

were shown to have a large effect on black IQ scores, this would damage the genetic hypothesis.

Despite the assertions of some scholars, including Herrnstein and Murray, a review of the evidence in both areas provides almost no support for genetic explanations of the IQ difference between blacks and whites.

Studies That Directly Assess Heritability

Five types of studies have some bearing on the heritability of the IQ gap between blacks and whites. Three of these estimate how European is the genetic heritage of individual blacks—by assessing skin color and facial features, by examining blood groups, and by simply asking them about their parents and grandparents. The fourth and fifth types study mixed-race children.

SKIN COLOR. Studies relating skin color and IQ are easy to perform and many have been reported over the years. This literature consistently shows that the correlation of IQ with skin color within the black population is quite low. Even Audrey Shuey, one of the most vehement supporters of the view that the IQ difference between blacks and whites is genetic in origin, concludes that IQ is only weakly associated with skin color.[8] Typical correlations with skin color are around 0.15. Correlations between IQ and those facial features rated as "negroid" are even lower. Even if one ignores the advantages that probably accrue to blacks with light skin, a correlation of 0.15 does not suggest that European ancestry strongly influences IQ.

However, many of the studies reviewed by Shuey use small samples and dubious sampling procedures. Besides, skin color is not as straightforward an indicator of degree of European ancestry as it may seem to be. Skin color varies substantially among sub-Saharan African populations. As a result, some Africans have relatively light skin for reasons that have nothing to do with European ancestry. Arthur Jensen and Sandra Scarr disagree about whether one would expect a very high correlation between skin color and IQ, even if there were a strong correlation between IQ and European ancestry.[9] A strong test of the European ancestry hypothesis therefore requires a more reliable indicator than skin color.

8. Shuey (1966).
9. Jensen (1981); Scarr (1981).

BLOOD GROUP INDICATORS. The frequency of different blood groups varies by race. Under the genetic hypothesis, blacks with more European blood types should have more European genes, and hence higher IQs. But Sandra Scarr and her colleagues find the correlation between IQ and European heritage, assessed on the basis of blood groups, to be only 0.05 in a sample of 144 pairs of black adolescent twins.[10] When skin color and socioeconomic status are controlled, the correlation drops to –0.02. It is important to note that they also find the typical correlation of 0.15 between skin color and IQ. This suggests that the comparable correlations between skin color and IQ in other studies are due not to European genes, but to some other factor associated with skin color in the black population.

John Loehlin and colleagues use blood groups as their unit of analysis rather than individuals. They "obtained, for each of 16 blood group genes, two items of information. First, the extent to which it was more common in the white than in the black sample, and second, its association with ability in the black sample" (p. 124). They then examine the correlation between these two measures in two small samples of blacks.[11] In one sample they find a 0.01 correlation between IQ and the extent to which blood group genes are more characteristic of European than African populations. In the other sample they find a nonsignificant –0.38 correlation, with the more African blood groups associated with higher IQ.

A problem common to the studies led by Scarr and Loehlin is that one does not know exactly what correlation to expect under various hypotheses about the degree of heritability of the black-white IQ gap, in part because one does not know the precise validity of the racial diagnoses for the respective blood group tests employed. What is known, however, is that these studies provide no support whatever for a large role of genetics in the IQ difference between blacks and whites.

REPORTED WHITE ANCESTRY. A third approach to estimating the white ancestry of blacks is to ask them about their family histories. Assuming a 15 point IQ difference that is fully genetic in origin, imagine two groups of blacks: one with only African genes and the other with 30 percent European genes. According to the pure genetic model, the first group would be expected to have an IQ that is 4.5 (15 × 0.30) points lower than the second. This mean difference would translate into very great differences at the

---

10. Scarr and others (1977).
11. Loehlin and others (1973).

tails of the IQ distribution. If one singled out everyone with an extremely high IQ—say, 140—one would expect to find several times as many individuals in the group with 30 percent European genes as in the pure African gene group.

A study by Martin Jenkins using a sample of black schoolchildren in Chicago identifies 63 children with IQs of 125 or above and 28 with IQs of 140 or above.[12] On the basis of the children's own reports about their ancestry, the investigators classified them into several categories of Europeanness. Those with IQs of 125 or above, and also those with IQs of 140 or above, have slightly *less* European ancestry than the best estimate for the American black population at the time. This study is not ideal. It would have been better to compare the degree of European ancestry of the black Chicago children with high IQs to that of other black Chicago children, rather than to the entire black population. Moreover, the reliability of the reports of ancestry is unknown and may not be high. But once again, the results are consistent with a model of zero genetic contribution to the IQ difference between blacks and whites—or, perhaps, a slight genetic advantage for Africans.

CHILDREN BORN TO AMERICAN SOLDIERS IN POSTWAR GERMANY. Eyferth examines the IQs of several hundred German children fathered by black American GIs during the occupation of Germany after 1945 and compares them with the IQs of children fathered by white GIs.[13] The children fathered by black GIs were found to have an average IQ of 96.5. Those fathered by white GIs were found to have an average IQ of 97. Inasmuch as the black-white IQ gap in the U.S. military as a whole was close to that in the general population at the time of the occupation, these data imply that the IQ difference between blacks and whites in the U.S. population as a whole is not genetic in origin.[14] Note also that the children of the two groups of GIs had similar IQs even though common sense would suggest that environmental conditions were probably inferior for black children.

MIXED-RACE CHILDREN: WHITE VERSUS BLACK MOTHERS. If the black-white IQ gap is substantially or entirely genetic, children of mixed parentage should have the same average IQ, regardless of which parent is black. By

12. Jenkins (1936).
13. Eyferth (1961).
14. Flynn (1980, pp. 87–88).

contrast, if one assumes that mothers are very important to the intellectual socialization of their children—more important than fathers—and if the socialization practices of whites favor the acquisition of skills that result in high IQ scores, children of white mothers and black fathers should score higher than children of black mothers and white fathers. In fact, a study by Lee Willerman, Alfred Naylor, and Ntinos Myrianthopoulos finds that children of white mothers and black fathers have a 9 point IQ advantage over children with black mothers and white fathers.[15] Taken at face value, this result suggests that most of the IQ difference between blacks and whites is environmental. In fact, since mothers do not represent the sole environmental influence on their children's IQ scores, the 9 point difference might be regarded as a conservative estimate of the environmental contribution.

ALTERNATIVE INTERPRETATIONS. All of the studies described above are subject to alternative interpretations. Most important, whites who mate with blacks may have lower IQs than whites in general, and blacks who mate with whites may have higher IQs than blacks in general. If whites who mate with blacks have particularly low IQs, for example, their European genes would convey relatively little IQ advantage. Yet the degree of self-selection would have to be extreme to produce no difference at all between children of purely African heritage and those of partially European origin. Self-selection for IQ was probably not very great under slavery. It is unlikely, for example, that the white males who mated with black females had lower IQs than other white males. Indeed, if such unions mostly involved male slave owners, and if economic status was positively related to IQ (as it is now), these whites probably had above average IQs. It seems similarly unlikely that the black females in interracial unions would have had IQs much higher than those in the black population as a whole. It stretches credulity to propose that white males sought intelligence rather than attractiveness in the black women with whom they mated. It should also be noted that self-selection would have been on phenotypes (that is, visible properties), not on genotypes. Since genotype differences in such a case would be less than phenotype differences, self-selection would have to have been in excess even of the 15 points required by the pure genetic model.

The self-selection explanations of studies of populations arising from contemporary interracial unions are not very plausible either. For example,

15. Willerman, Naylor, and Myrianthopoulos (1974).

James Flynn shows that self-selection is highly unlikely as an explanation of IQ parity between the children of black and white GIs in Eyferth's study. Moreover, his analysis of the children in the study by Willerman and colleagues suggests that the IQ difference between mixed-race children of black and white mothers cannot be accounted for by any reasonable assumptions about selective mating and parental IQ.[16]

Studies That Examine the Effects of Family Environment

Three adoption studies speak to the question of the heritability of the IQ difference between blacks and whites. An adoption study of truly experimental design, with random assignment, could be highly informative on the question of heredity versus environment. But no such study exists. Those that do exist are flawed by both small samples and possible selection biases.

BLACK VERSUS WHITE ADOPTIVE FAMILIES FOR BLACK CHILDREN. Elsie Moore studied black and mixed-race children raised in black and in white adoptive families.[17] Under the conventional genetic model, it should make relatively little difference whether the children are raised by black or white families, but it should make a substantial difference whether the children are of mixed or "pure" African descent. However, under the assumption that black families are less likely to instill the orientations that lead to high IQ scores, Moore predicts that children raised by white adoptive parents would have higher IQs than those raised by black adoptive parents, even if both set of parents are relatively middle-class. She finds that children raised by blacks have an average IQ of 104. Those raised by whites have an average IQ of 117. Black and biracial children raised by blacks have similar average IQs, as do those raised by whites.

It is possible that some sort of self-selection might account for these results. The only source of self-selection that Moore reports is that black parents expressed a wish for black rather than mixed-race children. Such a bias could have affected the results only if the (genotypically) less intelligent black children were assigned to black families. But adoption agencies ordinarily only have information on the social class and education of the

16. Flynn (1980, pp. 94, 180).
17. Moore (1986).

natural mother, scarcely sufficient indicators to predict the 13 point difference in IQ between children raised in black and in white families.

Another important aspect of this study is that Moore finds some differences between the parenting behavior of whites and blacks that might be related to their children's IQ scores. When helping their children work on a difficult cognitive task, white mothers tended to be more supportive and less critical of a child's mistakes than were black mothers.

BLACK AND WHITE CHILDREN REARED IN THE SAME ENVIRONMENT. Tizard, Cooperman, and Tizard compare black and white orphans raised from infancy in the same highly enriched institutional environment.[18] At age four or five, the white children have IQs of 103, the black children have IQs of 108, and the children of mixed race have IQs of 106. These results are most compatible with the assumption of a slight genetic advantage for blacks. The black children in this experiment were West Indian and the white children were English. While it is possible that the black parents of these children had unusually high IQs, Flynn argues that selective migration of West Indians to Britain could not have raised IQ scores by more than a few points—perhaps enough to eliminate the observed black superiority but not enough to reverse it.[19]

WHITE ADOPTIVE FAMILES FOR BLACK VERSUS WHITE CHILDREN. The well-known Minnesota adoption study by Scarr and Richard Weinberg compares the IQs of adopted children from different racial backgrounds.[20] Some of the adopted children have two white biological parents, some have two black biological parents, and some have one black and one white biological parent. This study is harder to interpret than the two adoption studies discussed above, one of which holds race constant and assigns children to different environments, and the other of which holds the environment constant and assigns children of different races to it. The Scarr and Weinberg study assigns children of different races to different environments. Moreover, the black children in the study were adopted at a substantially later age than the other children, which Scarr and Weinberg note is a factor associated with lower IQ in later life. The black children's natural mothers also had less education than the average for black women in the region.

18. Tizard, Cooperman, and Tizard (1972).
19. Flynn (1980).
20. Scarr and Weinberg (1983).

There is no educational discrepancy for white mothers. In addition, the "quality of placement" in terms of social class and education of the adoptive parents is higher for white children. Thus for reasons having nothing to do with race, the expected IQ of the white adoptees is clearly higher than that for black or interracial adoptees, although the magnitude of their expected advantage is uncertain. Consequently, one does not know what to predict under either the pure genetic model or the environmental model.

At about seven or eight years old, the average IQ of the white children in the study was 112, of the interracial children 109, and of the black children 97. These results are consistent with the conclusion that adoption into middle class families has a strong positive effect on IQ, at least for the white and interracial children. The data are also consistent with the supposition that a substantial portion of the IQ difference between blacks and whites is genetic in origin, since the IQs of the black children are substantially lower than those of the others. (The slight difference between white and interracial children might seem to indicate that there is little genetic contribution to the IQ gap, but the interracial children were adopted even younger than the white children.)

As adolescents, the white children had an average IQ of 106, the mixed race children 99, and the black children 89.[21] The finding that the IQs of the black and mixed-race children dropped somewhat more than those of the white children provides even more support for the hypothesis that the IQ difference between blacks and whites is partly genetic, because the genetic contribution to IQ increases with age. Weinberg, Scarr, and Waldman maintain, however, that because of the vagaries of the study's design and the severe adjustment problems that seemed to plague their black and interracial teenage subjects, no clear interpretation of the differential drop in IQ is possible.

Implications of the Direct Evidence on Heritability

Suppose one simply takes at face value all the available evidence—the many different types of evidence and the dozens of different studies. The Scarr and Weinberg results are consistent with a large genetic contribution to the IQ gap between blacks and whites. But all the other evidence is most consistent with a zero or near-zero genetic contribution: all of the other

21. Weinberg, Scarr, and Waldman (1992).

studies described above suggest genetic equality between the races or very small genetic differences favoring one race or the other.

Advocates of the genetic hypothesis can always invent the equivalent of Ptolemaic "epicycles" to explain these results. But there would have to be a good many such convolutions to make much headway. It would have to be the case that either whites in the past who contributed European genes to the black gene pool of the present had extremely low IQs or blacks who mated with whites in the past had extremely high IQs; *and* that either the black GIs who mated with German women following World War II had extremely high IQs, or the white GIs had extremely low IQs, or both; *and* that in the study of children born to unions of blacks and whites, either the white mothers had much higher IQs than the black mothers or the black fathers had much higher IQs than the white fathers; *and* that in the study of black and mixed-race children reared by black and by white families, black and mixed-race children with low IQ genotypes were much more likely to be placed with black families and those with high IQ genotypes with white families; *and* that in the study of the enriched orphanage environment, the black Caribbean children had unusually high genotypic IQs, or the white English children had unusually low genotypic IQs, or both. And yet Flynn has shown that most of these alternative explanations are implausible taken one at a time.[22]

Trying to weave a coherent theory for the ensemble of alternatives across different circumstances, countries, and historical eras would be a daunting project. That is presumably why Herrnstein and Murray make no serious effort to propound alternative explanations for the studies that fail to support their genetic hypothesis. They mention only a few of the negative studies, typically dismissing them with ad hoc selection explanations. By contrast, they spent a great deal of time discussing the one study that is consistent with a strong genetic interpretation favoring whites: the Scarr and Weinberg study. But they do not mention the fact that this study is subject to the same sorts of selection bias as most of the studies with negative findings. They also ignore the most comprehensive and sophisticated treatment of the genetic hypothesis and its alternatives: that of Flynn.[23] By conventional academic standards, Herrnstein and Murray's review of the evidence on the heritability of the IQ difference between blacks and whites is shockingly incomplete and biased.

22. Flynn (1980).
23. Flynn (1980).

Indirect Arguments for Genetic Determination of the IQ Difference between Blacks and Whites

If this summary of the direct genetic evidence is correct, why pay any attention to the possibility that the black-white IQ gap is genetically determined? There are three main reasons (as Herrnstein and Murray would agree, judging by the amount of space they devote to them). First, at every level of socioeconomic status, blacks have lower IQs than whites. Hence it is difficult to argue that poor socioeconomic conditions alone account for the low scores of blacks.

Second, blacks and whites have different ability profiles.[24] Whites of low socioeconomic status with an overall IQ score of, for example, 105, show the same average ability pattern as whites of high socioeconomic status with an IQ score of 105. But this is not the case for blacks. For example, blacks having an IQ of 105 are likely to be better than either low or high socioeconomic status whites at recalling digit strings, but they tend to be worse at solving mazes.

Third, blacks and whites differ most in performing "*g*-loaded" tasks. *G* is the general intelligence factor that some psychologists believe permeates all abilities. Blacks do as well or better than whites on tasks involving simple memory or reaction time, but are slower than whites on tasks involving complex memory or reaction time. These latter tasks are considered more *g*-loaded, because they predict overall IQ scores better. The same racial difference applies to more obviously cognitive skills, such as form perception (low *g*-loading) and vocabulary (high *g*-loading).

I consider each of these points in turn.

Socioeconomic Status

On its face, it is hard to reconcile the finding that blacks have lower IQs than whites at every socioeconomic level with the notion that it is merely poor opportunity that causes blacks to have lower IQs. It is somewhat misleading, however, to compare the IQs of blacks with those of whites in the higher socioeconomic ranges. Whites in the top socioeconomic quintile (based on income) have more than twice the wealth of blacks in

---

24. Jensen and Reynolds (1982).

the top quintile.[25] More important, statistically equating blacks and whites on measures of environment that include not only traditional indicators of socioeconomic status but also measures of family and quality of neighborhood reduces the black-white IQ gap by at least a third, even after controlling for mother's IQ.[26] These results are most consistent with an interpretation of the IQ difference between blacks and whites as partially environmental and partially genetic.

Nonetheless, like the authors of chapter 4, I am skeptical about regression analyses of this type, because they depend heavily on the reliability and validity of the measures that go into them and on whether all the relevant variables have been measured. In addition, the results presented in chapter 4 suggest that the IQs of black and white children differ for reasons related to child-rearing practices that are somewhat independent of socioeconomic status. Both the study showing that mixed-race children having white mothers have higher IQs than those having black mothers and the study in which white mothers demonstrate more supportive patterns of interaction when their children work on cognitive tasks also suggest this. All ethnic groups try to socialize children for the roles they are expected to play in the world. Socialization patterns, including peer influences, cannot be expected to change completely in a generation in response to change in socioeconomic status.

Ability Profiles

Differences in ability profiles do not provide strong evidence for genetic determination of the overall IQ gap. Systematic differences between the socialization of black and white children begin in the cradle.[27] Shirley Bryce Heath has shown marked differences in the socialization practices of underclass blacks and working class whites that plausibly could result in substantial differences in relative mental skills. For example, underclass black children are not read to, receive almost no training in abstractions such as form and color of objects, and are not taught to "decontextualize" information learned in one domain and apply it in another. On the other hand, they hear many similes and metaphors in everyday life and are often asked

25. Smith (1998).
26. See chapter 4 below.
27. See, for example, Heath (1983).

to tell "what that's like." Not surprisingly, blacks do better on similarities, compared to whites, than on any other IQ subtest, a fact reported by Loehlin, Lindzey, and Spuhler but not commented upon by them.[28]

The General Intelligence Factor

Whether g is a real entity or a statistical artifact is a matter of heated debate that would lead us far afield. But even accepting the view that g is a cognitive reality as opposed to a statistical one, the black-white gap on complex reaction time tasks may well be explained by motivational differences. In informal work conducted many years ago, I found that white college students with high achievement motivation had faster complex reaction times—but not faster simple reaction times—than those with low achievement motivation.

More important, the g-loading argument also obtains for tasks that one thinks of as genuinely intellectual.[29] For skills such as spatial reasoning and form perception, the g-loading is relatively low and the black-white gap is relatively small. For the even more vital and general skills exercised in reading comprehension, mathematics, vocabulary, and information tests, the g-loading is high and the black-white gap is great. According to Jensen, this shows that race differences are greatest for those tasks that tap into general intelligence most strongly. But his argument loses force in view of two critical facts.

First, Flynn observes that IQ gains as great as 15 points have occurred over as short a period as a generation in Western countries in recent decades.[30] This fact in itself gives substantial weight to the possibility that the IQ difference between blacks and whites might be entirely due to environmental factors, since the gene pool of Western countries is not changing at a rate remotely rapid enough to produce a genotypic difference in intelligence of one standard deviation. Moreover, it seems entirely plausible that, with respect to factors relevant to IQ, the environments of blacks today more nearly resemble the environments of whites a generation ago than they do the present environments of whites. Second, and more pointed, the advances in IQ over time are greatest for g-saturated abstract and "cul-

28. Loehlin, Lindzey, and Spuhler (1975).
29. Jensen (1985).
30. Flynn (1984, 1987).

turally neutral" tests.[31] It is particularly implausible that generational differences would be so large for those tests that allegedly tap most directly into true genetic factors.

Just as important, these allegedly highly heritable, heavily *g*-loaded skills are being shown to be highly modifiable by a variety of strategies. Interventions given to black children at any age, from infancy to college, can dramatically alter IQ and achievement differences between blacks and whites. Whether these strategies would narrow the gap if they were also applied to whites has not received much attention. But the little research that exists indicates that they can do so—especially at the college level. Moreover, it has been shown that some interventions at the elementary and middle school levels can raise minority performance well in excess of national norms. And perhaps most telling, the evidence strongly indicates that the IQ gap between blacks and whites has been closing nationally, as would be expected after decades of improved opportunity and economic advance for blacks.[32]

Conclusion

The studies most directly relevant to the question of whether the IQ difference between blacks and whites is genetic in origin show no association between IQ and African, as opposed to European, ancestry. A few older studies of skin color are consistent with European superiority, but most are not. The best modern study shows no relationship between IQ and European ancestry as defined by blood group factors, thus indicating that although there is a weak relationship between skin color and IQ, this has nothing to do with European ancestry. One other modern study of blood types also suggests that there is no genetic difference in IQ between the races, while the other weakly suggests African superiority. Studies of the children of black as against white GI fathers in Germany and of the European heritage of black children in Chicago show no advantage of European over African genes. A study of mixed-race children shows that those with white mothers and black fathers have much higher IQs than those with black mothers and white fathers.

---

31. Dickens, Kane, and Schultze (forthcoming).

32. For reviews of the general potential of interventions, see Bennett (1987); and Selvin (1992). For research on blacks and whites together, see Steele and others (1987); Treisman (1985). On minorities in elementary and middle schools, see Selvin (1992). For the closing of the gap nationally, see chapters 5 and 6 below; Nisbett (1995).

And all of the studies that examine home environment indicate strong environmental effects on the IQ of blacks. One of these is most consistent with no genetic difference between the races, one with moderate African genetic superiority, and one with substantial European genetic superiority.

In sum, the most relevant studies provide no evidence for the genetic superiority of either race, but strong evidence for a substantial environmental contribution to the IQ gap between blacks and whites. Almost equally important, rigorous interventions do affect IQ and cognitive skills at every stage of the life course. Moreover, the IQ difference between blacks and whites in the United States has narrowed in recent decades. The evidence thus indicates that if there are genetically determined IQ differences between the races, they are too small to show up with any regularity in studies covering a wide range of populations and using a wide range of methodologies. This is an extraordinarily important conclusion.

References

Bennett, William J. 1987. *Schools That Work*. U. S. Department of Education.

Block, Ned. 1995. "How Heritability Misleads about Race." *Cognition* 56:99–108.

Churchill, W. 1974. *A History of the English-Speaking Peoples*. Bantam.

Dickens, William, Thomas J. Kane, and Charles Schultze. Forthcoming. *Does the Bell Curve Ring True?* Brookings.

Eyferth, K. 1961. "Leistungen verschiedener Gruppen von Besatzungskindern in Hamburg-Wechsler Intelligenztest für Kinder (HAWIK)." *Archiv für die gesamte Psychologie* 113:222–41.

Flynn, James R. 1980. *Race, IQ and Jensen*. London: Routledge and Kegan-Paul.

———. 1984. "The Mean IQ of Americans: Massive Gains 1932 to 1978." *Psychological Bulletin* 95:29–51.

———. 1987. "Massive IQ Gains in 14 Nations: What IQ Tests Really Measure." *Psychological Bulletin* 101:171–91.

Fraser, Steven, ed. 1994. *The Bell Curve Wars*. Basic Books.

Heath, Shirley Bryce. 1983. *Ways with Words: Language, Life, and Work in Communities and Classrooms*. Cambridge University Press.

Herrnstein, Richard J., and Charles Murray. 1994. *The Bell Curve: Intelligence and Class Structure in American Life*. Free Press.

Jenkins, Martin D. 1936. "A Socio-Psychological Study of Negro Children of Superior Intelligence." *Journal of Negro Education* 5:175–190.

Jensen, Arthur R. 1981. "Obstacles, Problems, and Pitfalls in Differential Psychology." In Sandra Scarr, ed., *Race, Social Class, and Individual Differences in IQ*. Hillsdale, N.J.: Erlbaum.

———. 1985. "The Nature of the Black-White Difference on Various Psychometric Tests: Spearman's Hypothesis." *Behavioral and Brain Sciences* 8:193–258.

Jensen, Arthur R., and C. R. Reynolds. 1982. "Race, Social Class and Ability Patterns on the WISC-R." *Personality and Individual Differences* 3:423–38.

Loehlin, John C., Gardner Lindzey, and J. N. Spuhler. 1975. *Race Differences in Intelligence.* Freeman.

Moore, Elsie G. J. 1986. "Family Socialization and the IQ Test Performance of Traditionally and Transracially Adopted Black Children." *Developmental Psychology* 22:317–26.

Neisser, Ulrich, and others. 1996. "Intelligence: Knowns and Unknowns." *American Psychologist* 51:77–101.

Nisbett, Richard E. 1995. "Race, IQ and Scientism." In *The Bell Curve Wars*, edited by Steven Fraser. New York: Basic Books.

Scarr, Sandra, ed. 1981. *Race, Social Class, and Individual Differences in IQ.* Hillsdale, N.J.: Erlbaum.

Scarr, Sandra, and R. A. Weinberg. 1983. "The Minnesota Adoption Studies: Genetic Differences and Malleability." *Child Development* 54:260–67.

Scarr, Sandra, and others. 1977. "Absence of a Relationship between Degree of White Ancestry and Intellectual Skills within a Black Population." *Human Genetics* 39:69–86.

Selvin, P. 1992. "Math Education: Multiplying the Meager Numbers." *Science* 258:1200–01.

Shuey, Audrey. 1966. *The Testing of Negro Intelligence.* Social Science Press.

Smith, J. P. 1998. "Racial and Ethnic Differences in Wealth Using the HRS." *Journal of Human Resources.*

Sowell, Thomas. 1994. *Race and Culture: A World View.* Basic Books.

Steele, Claude M., and others. 1998. "African American College Achievement: A 'Wise Intervention.'" Stanford University.

Tizard, B., A. Cooperman, and J. Tizard. 1972. "Environmental Effects on Language Development: A Study of Young Children in Long-Stay Residential Nurseries." *Child Development* 43:342–43.

Treisman, Uri. 1985. "A Study of Mathematics Performance of Black Students at the University of California, Berkeley." Unpublished Program Report, Department of Mathematics, University of California.

Weinberg, Richard A., Sandra Scarr, and I. D. Waldman. 1992. "The Minnesota Transracial Adoption Study: A Follow-Up of IQ Test Performance at Adolescence." *Intelligence* 16: 117–35.

Willerman, Lee, Alfred F. Naylor, and Ntinos C. Myrianthopoulos. 1974. "Intellectual Development of Children from Interracial Matings: Performance in Infancy and at 4 Years." *Behavior Genetics* 4:84–88.

Young, V. H. 1970. "Family and Childhood in a Southern Negro Community." *American Anthropologist* 72:269–88.

MEREDITH PHILLIPS
JEANNE BROOKS-GUNN
GREG J. DUNCAN
PAMELA KLEBANOV
JONATHAN CRANE

4

Family Background, Parenting Practices, and the Black-White Test Score Gap

IN 1994 Richard Herrnstein and Charles Murray's *The Bell Curve* reignited debate over the role of genetic and environmental factors in explaining the black-white test score gap. Many Americans suspect that blacks perform poorly on standardized tests because of their social and economic disadvantages. But Herrnstein and Murray argued that contemporary racial differences in socioeconomic status are not large enough to explain the gap. They also argued that social and economic inequalities are weak predictors of children's test scores and that apparent environmental effects may merely be proxies for genetic effects.

In this chapter we use recent survey data from two samples of young children to investigate Herrnstein and Murray's claims about the association between family background and young children's cognitive skills. This is a difficult task because almost every family characteristic we include in our statistical equations may be a proxy for both a child's environment and his or her genes. Many studies of the effects of family background on chil-

We are indebted to William Dickens, James Flynn, Christopher Jencks, and David Rowe for thoughtful comments. We also thank the Mellon Foundation, the Spencer Foundation, and the National Institute for Child Health and Human Development's Research Network on Child and Family Wellbeing for their financial support. They are in no way responsible for our errors or our conclusions.

dren ignore the fact that family members share not only environments but genes. Years ago, Arthur Jensen referred to social scientists' disregard of genetic effects as the "sociological fallacy."[1] We attempt to deal with it here by statistically controlling a mother's test scores, her rank in her high school class, and an interviewer's rating of her understanding of the interview, which we can think of as imperfect proxies for the mother's genetic "potential" and hence for the genes she passes along to her children. Although this approach cannot settle the question of whether family characteristics explain the entire black-white gap in children's test scores, it can give us some sense of which characteristics are likely to be most important.

We begin by examining the contribution of parental education and income to the test score gap among five- and six-year-olds. Although parents' education is fairly strongly related to children's test scores, we find that eliminating the black-white gap in parents' years of schooling would not shrink the gap in children's test scores much because black and white parents now have very similar amounts of schooling. Compared with the education gap, the average black-white income gap is large. But eliminating the income gap might not do much to reduce the test score gap, either, because at least in one of our data sets, family income does not seem to be strongly related to children's test scores.

We then look at a much larger set of family environment indicators, including grandparents' educational attainment, mothers' household size, mothers' high school quality, mothers' perceived self-efficacy, children's birth weight (a proxy for prenatal environment), children's household size, and mothers' parenting practices. Blacks are much more disadvantaged than whites when ranked on this set of measures than when ranked on the measures of socioeconomic status considered by Herrnstein and Murray. We find that racial inequalities on these measures account for more than half the test score gap between black and white five- and six-year-olds. If we add measures of mothers' cognitive skills, we can account for about two-thirds of the gap. To the extent that our family environment measures are really proxies for children's genes, these reductions are too large. But if our statistical models omit other aspects of the environment that affect children's test scores and on which blacks are disadvantaged, and especially if they omit aspects of the environment that vary between but not within races, the environmental differences between blacks and whites may explain the entire test score gap.

---

1. Jensen (1969). See Scarr and Weinberg (1978) for supporting evidence.

The Data

Most of our analyses use data from the Children of the National Longitudinal Survey of Youth (CNLSY).[2] The CNLSY, which began in 1986, covers all children born to the 6,283 women in the National Longitudinal Survey of Youth (NLSY). The NLSY is a longitudinal study of people who were between the ages of fourteen and twenty-two in 1979 when the survey began. The NLSY oversampled low-income and minority youth. We focus on 1,626 African-American and European-American five- and six-year-olds who took the Peabody Picture Vocabulary Test-Revised (denoted hereafter as the PPVT-R).[3] Because we have no PPVT-R scores before 1986 or after 1992, our sample is limited to children born between 1980 and 1987.[4] As a result, it does not include children whose mothers were older than age thirty at the time of the child's birth. Children born to mothers in their late twenties are also underrepresented relative to children of younger mothers.

We use data from the Infant Health and Development Program (IHDP) to supplement our CNLSY analyses.[5] The IHDP is an eight-site randomized clinical trial, designed to test the efficacy of educational and family support services for low-birth-weight, preterm infants during their first three years of life.[6] Infants born at the eight participating hospitals during 1984–85 were eligible if they weighed 2,500 grams or less at birth. Two-thirds

---

2. See Chase-Lansdale and others (1991).

3. See Dunn and Dunn (1981) for details on the PPVT-R. We excluded nineteen children whose normed PPVT-R scores were more than three standard deviations below the mean. When the same child had been tested twice, we retained the earliest test score. The CNLSY also administered Peabody Individual Achievement Tests (PIATs) in mathematics and reading to children who were at least five years old. We used these tests in an earlier version of this chapter but abandoned them because they did not provide a strong test of the hypothesis that family environment can explain the black-white test score gap. The PIAT tests' distributions are non-normal among five-, six-, and seven-year-olds for reading, and among five- and six-year-olds for math. The black-white gaps on these tests are also unusually small. When we ran analyses similar to those reported in this chapter using the math and reading PIATs for eight- and nine-year-olds, controlling a large set of family characteristics like those in column 5 of table 4-5 reduced the math and reading gaps nearly to zero. Crane (1994) found similar results using the PIATs and a CNLSY sample of five- to nine-year-olds assessed in 1988. (The PIAT distributions for eight- and nine-year-olds are reasonable, but the unadjusted black-white gaps are still small.)

4. This chapter was written before the 1994 data became available. Because the CNLSY does not administer the PPVT-R to all children in all years, however, the 1994 data would have contributed only about 265 children to our sample.

5. See Chase-Lansdale and others (1991); and Brooks-Gunn and others (1993, 1994, 1995) for a more complete description of these data sets.

6. Infant Health and Development Program (1990).

of these infants were randomly assigned to a control group that got no treatment (over and above extensive follow-up surveillance).[7] We focus exclusively on the control group.[8] After dropping children whose birth weight was 1,000 grams or less, children with incomplete data, and children who were neither black nor white, our IHDP sample includes 315 children.

Like the CNLSY, the IHDP gave children the PPVT-R. Although the PPVT-R has been called a short-form IQ test, it measures only verbal comprehension and vocabulary. A tester shows a child a card with four pictures and asks the child to point to the picture that best represents the meaning of a particular word. In the first example on the test, the tester shows the child a card with pictures of a fork, a table, a car, and a doll and asks the child to point to the doll.

The IHDP also gave five-year-olds the full Wechsler Preschool and Primary Scale of Intelligence (WPPSI).[9] Both the PPVT-R and WPPSI are age-standardized in "IQ" metric, which yields a national mean of 100 and standard deviation of 15.

Table 4-1 presents descriptive statistics for blacks and whites in both samples. In the larger and more representative CNLSY, the black-white gap on the PPVT-R averages about 17.1 points, which is somewhat larger than the gap one ordinarily finds in representative national samples.[10] A combination of factors seems to explain why the PPVT-R gap in the CNLSY is relatively large. First, the national norms used to standardize the test are probably wrong. If we restandardize the test based on the entire sample of CNLSY five- and six-year-olds, including Latinos, the weighted gap shrinks from 17.1 to 14.7 points. A gap of 14.7 points is closer to gaps in other samples, especially when we take into account the fact that vocabulary gaps tend to be larger than gaps for reading comprehension or mathematics.[11] Second, most estimates of the black-white gap are based on older children. Among children tested twice in the CNLSY, the PPVT-R gap tends to narrow somewhat with age.[12] This could be because the PPVT-R requires

7. Constantine and others (1993); Spiker and others (1991); and Kraemer and Fendt (1990). Of the 1,302 infants who met enrollment criteria, 21 percent were eliminated because consent was refused and another 3 percent were withdrawn before entry into their assigned group.

8. For more on the results of the intervention see Brooks-Gunn and others (1994).

9. Wechsler (1989).

10. See chapter 7.

11. See chapters 5 and 7.

12. Analyses not reported here show that among five- and six-year-olds tested in 1986 or 1988 and retested in 1992, black children gained an average of 4.94 more points (in IQ metric) on the PPVT-R than white children did.

children to recognize spoken words, which presumably puts those who do not speak standard English at some disadvantage. If schooling increases such children's familiarity with standard English, their PPVT-R scores should improve faster than those of most other children.[13]

The black-white PPVT-R gap is much larger (25.6 points) in the IHDP than in the CNLSY. The black-white gaps on the socioeconomic status measures in the IHDP are also much larger than those in the CNLSY. The IHDP apparently includes a disproportionate number of very disadvantaged black mothers. Yet white mothers in the IHDP are somewhat more advantaged than white mothers in the CNLSY, probably because IHDP mothers are much older on average.

The CNLSY mothers also took the Armed Services Vocational Aptitude Battery (ASVAB) when they were 15 to 23 years old. The ASVAB covers both academic and vocational skills. The AFQT, or Armed Forces Qualification Test, combines the ASVAB tests that measure mathematics skills, reading comprehension, and vocabulary. The penultimate row of table 4-1 shows that black mothers in our CNLSY sample scored about 14 points lower than white mothers on the AFQT.

A mother's AFQT score is a product of her environment as well as her genes.[14] In this chapter, however, we treat AFQT scores as an imperfect proxy for the cognitive genes that mothers pass on to their children. Because part of the reason mothers with high AFQT scores have children with high PPVT-R scores is environmental, this approach underestimates

---

13. Our hypothesis that black English may play a role in the larger PPVT-R gaps among younger children conflicts somewhat with Quay's (1974) results, however. He found no interaction between child age and whether an IQ test had been translated into black English. But his sample only included children in the third and sixth grades. The relevant changes may occur very quickly after children start school. It is also possible that an interaction between child's dialect and the dialect of the tester matters more on the PPVT-R than on other tests, since the PPVT-R measures verbal comprehension. If this were the case, this bias would deflate black children's scores, making the black-white PPVT-R gap seem unusually large. We cannot test this hypothesis in the CNLSY because we do not know the ethnicity or race of the tester, let alone his or her dialect. However, most evidence (albeit dated) suggests that the PPVT-R is not affected much by the race of the tester. Of the studies of race-of-tester effects that Jensen (1980) reviewed, five tested children on the PPVT-R. None found a statistically significant difference between the scores of black children tested by white testers and those tested by black testers. One of these studies is especially relevant, since it measured dialect directly. France (1973) tape-recorded four white and four black test administrators giving the PPVT-R to 128 white and 124 black elementary school children. The black children scored equally well with the black and white testers. The white children scored somewhat better with the white testers. See Quay (1971, 1972, 1974) for additional evidence on the effect of black English on black children's IQ scores.

14. See Winship and Korenman (1997) for evidence on how education affects AFQT scores.

Table 4-1. *Means and Standard Deviations of Selected Variables for Children in the CNLSY and IHDP, by Ethnicity*

	CNLSY		IHDP	
Independent variable	Whites	Blacks	Whites	Blacks
PPVT-R	98.92	81.86	97.37	71.77
	(15.21)	(14.59)	(19.70)	(17.81)
WPPSI	. . .	. . .	103.88	84.67
			(17.28)	(14.13)
Gender	0.52	0.50	0.51	0.47
	(0.50)	(0.50)	(0.50)	(0.50)
Average family income	36,717	21,242	38,176	16,859
(dollars)	(21,748)	(15,471)	(18,965)	(12,890)
Household size	4.12	4.59	4.42	5.41
	(0.95)	(1.55)	(1.30)	(1.87)
Mother's education	12.33	12.17	14.01	12.12
	(2.03)	(1.82)	(2.83)	(1.52)
Mother's age at child's birth	23.30	21.93	28.12	23.08
	(3.31)	(3.29)	(5.86)	(5.60)
Single-parent household	0.29	0.75	0.28	0.79
	(0.45)	(0.43)	(0.45)	(0.41)
AFQT (normalized and	99.71	85.66	. . .	. . .
in IQ metric)	(12.37)	(10.81)		
N	985	641	125	190

Sources: See text.

a. See Data Appendix for description of variables. CNLSY data are weighted by the child weights.

the overall impact of a child's home environment. But it does help us begin to purge our other family background measures of their genetic component. Moreover, our treatment of AFQT scores as a proxy for cognitive genes parallels Herrnstein and Murray's use of these scores in *The Bell Curve*.

The Importance of Genotype-Environment Correlation

Test scores run in families for both genetic and environmental reasons. By comparing twins, siblings, and adopted children reared together and apart, behavioral geneticists have concluded that about half of the variance in children's IQ scores can be attributed to genetic differences among individuals. This estimate tends to be somewhat lower (about 40 percent) for young children such as those in our sample, and may be somewhat higher among adults.[15]

Does this mean that black-white differences are genetic as well? Not necessarily. Genes can affect variation within groups without having any effect on variation between groups. Herrnstein and Murray use a version of Richard Lewontin's famous metaphor to communicate this idea to their readers.[16] They dare anyone who doubts Lewontin's argument to "take two handfuls of genetically identical seed corn and plant one handful in Iowa, the other in the Mojave Desert, and let nature (i.e., the environment) take its course. The seeds will grow in Iowa, not in the Mojave, and the result will have nothing to do with genetic differences."[17] But Herrnstein and Murray also challenge readers to name "mysterious environmental differences" between blacks and whites that are as stark as the environmental differences that differentiate Iowa from the Mojave. Our results suggest that it is possible to account for at least two-thirds of the black-white test score gap without having to appeal to environmental mysteries or genetic differences between blacks and whites. But before discussing our results, it may help to spell out the ways in which genetic effects within groups can masquerade as environmental effects and thus bias estimates of how much we could improve children's test scores by changing their environments.

Robert Plomin, J. C. DeFries, and John Loehlin distinguish three ways in which genes may influence the environment.[18]

Passive correlation occurs when parents' genes affect both the environments they provide for their children and their children's genes. Suppose, for example, that parents' genes affect their reading skills and that parents who are better readers read more to their children. Suppose too that how much parents read to their children is related to children's vocabulary scores. If the correlation between reading frequency and vocabulary scores occurred entirely because reading to children raised their vocabulary scores, we would *not* need to worry about the fact that parents with "better genes" read to their children more often. All we would need to worry about is getting parents who find reading difficult to read to their children more. If, however, the correlation between reading frequency and vocabulary scores oc-

15. See Plomin and Petrill (1997) and the sources cited there.
16. Lewontin (1976).
17. Herrnstein and Murray (1994, p. 298).
18. Plomin, DeFries, and Loehlin (1977).

curred partly because parents with "better genes" transmitted those genes to their children, and those genes raised the children's vocabulary scores, we *would* need to worry about controlling for genetic effects. If we did not, encouraging parents to read to their children would not raise the children's vocabulary scores as much as we expected.

Active correlation occurs when children's genes cause them to seek out particular environments. Psychologists generally believe that this mechanism becomes more important with age. Nonetheless, we always need to worry about active correlation when estimating the effect of the environment on children's scores. Suppose, for example, that children's genes affect how much they enjoy being read to, which in turn affects how much parents enjoy reading to the children. If this is the case, any relationship between reading frequency and children's vocabulary might reflect reverse causation—that children who picked up new words easily encouraged their parents to read to them more. If reverse causation explained most of the correlation between reading frequency and vocabulary scores, changing parents' reading practices would have a smaller effect on children's test scores than we would expect if we assumed that a given parent was equally likely to read to all children, regardless of how they responded.

Reactive correlation occurs when the environment reacts differently to individuals with different genes. This type of correlation between genes and the environment is particularly relevant to the question of whether the black-white test score gap is genetic in origin. In the United States, blacks and whites tend to look different from one another, recognize those differences, and respond to them. Ironically, this implies that as long as race remains a socially meaningful concept, the black-white test score gap must, in one sense, be genetic in origin.[19] Hereditarians' "genetic" story is that black skin and facial features are correlated with other genes that affect cognitive skills. Environmentalists' "genetic" story is that black skin and facial features cause social and economic inequalities that affect cognitive skills. Thus, as long as the typical black and white look different from one another and these differences have some social significance, the test score gap may be partially genetic and yet have absolutely nothing to do with black-white differences in innate cognitive ability.

The analyses that follow estimate the within-group effects of family environment on children's test scores, while trying to reduce the genetic contamination of our estimates that occurs because of passive and active genotype-environment correlation. At the end of the chapter, we revisit the

19. Jencks (1980).

issue of reactive correlation and the relative contributions of between-group environmental and genetic factors to the black-white test score gap.

Inequality of Educational Attainment and Schooling

The most easily obtained and widely used measure of a child's socio-economic status is the mother's educational attainment. When we rank black and white children in the CNLSY on this measure, the black and white medians are identical (twelve years). This similarity reflects both racial convergence in educational attainment since 1970 and the fact that our CNLSY sample underrepresents highly educated mothers.

One way to think about the effects of parental education on the black-white PPVT-R gap is to ask how big the gap would be if black and white parents not only attended school for the same length of time but attended the same schools or schools of comparable quality. Column 1 in table 4-2 shows the unweighted black-white vocabulary gap when we control only gender and age. Adding mothers' and fathers' highest grade of school or college completed reduces the gap slightly, from 16.3 to 16.1 points (column 2). This reduction is small because the educational attainment of black and white parents in our sample is so similar.

Even when whites and blacks attend school for the same number of years, however, whites usually attend better schools than blacks. These racial differences in the quality of a mother's schooling may influence her child's PPVT-R scores in two ways. First, they can make each extra year of school more valuable for whites than blacks. In our sample, however, the opposite is the case. An extra year of maternal schooling raises a black child's vocabulary score more than a white child's.[20]

---

20. Mothers' years of schooling has a larger effect on PPVT-R scores among blacks than among whites. This interaction was highly significant in all equations. When we added the interaction to equation 5 in table 4-2, for example, its coefficient was 1.39, with a standard error of .38. The coefficient on the main effect of mothers' education (the effect for whites) was −.25, with a standard error of .29. Because we did not find consistent interactions of race with the other socioeconomic status or cognitive variables, we excluded the race-by-mothers'-education interaction from the models shown in our tables. To check our assumption that the overall model fit equally well for blacks and whites, we regressed students' actual PPVT-R scores on the scores we predicted from the single equation in column 9 of table 4-5, plus an interaction between this predicted score (centered) and race. The coefficient of the race-by-predicted-PPVT-R-score interaction was negative, suggesting that a single equation fits worse for blacks than whites, but this interaction was not statistically significant at the .05 level. Our finding of generally similar coefficients for blacks and whites is consistent with Rowe, Vazsonyi, and Flannery's (1994) argument that the association between family processes and academic achievement does not differ by race.

Table 4-2. *Effects of Parental Education on the Black-White PPVT-R Gap among Five- and Six-Year-Olds in the CNLSY*[a]

Independent variable	(1)	(2)	(3)	(3a)	(4)	(5)
Black	−16.27	−16.07	−12.75	−10.57	−11.51	−9.36
	(0.82)	(0.84)	(0.99)	(1.07)	(1.08)	(1.14)
Mother's education	...	1.73	1.15	0.52	1.06	0.27
		(0.22)	(0.23)	(0.25)	(0.23)	(0.25)
Father's education	...	0.86	0.65	0.69	0.63	0.65
		(0.23)	(0.24)	(0.23)	(0.23)	(0.23)
Percent disadvantaged in mother's high school	...	...	...	...	0.022	0.025
					(0.024)	(0.023)
Percent white students in mother's high school	...	...	...	...	0.038	0.041
					(0.018)	(0.018)
Percent teachers in mother's high school with M.A.s or Ph.D.s	...	...	...	...	−0.023	−0.013
					(0.020)	(0.019)
Student-teacher ratio	...	...	...	...	−0.20	−0.21
					(0.12)	(0.11)
Percent teacher turnover	...	...	...	...	−0.125	−0.144
					(0.057)	(0.058)
Mother reports that high school is somewhat to very unsafe	...	...	...	...	−0.94	−0.46
					(1.18)	(1.14)
Mother reports that teachers know their subjects very well	...	...	...	...	−0.67	−0.43
					(1.15)	(1.12)
Mother's AFQT score	...	...	...	0.23	...	0.18
				(0.04)		(0.04)
Mother's class rank in high school (rank/class size)	...	...	...	...	...	−3.03
						(2.04)
Interviewer's assessment of mother's understanding ("good" is the omitted category)						
Mother had fair understanding of interview	...	...	...	...	...	−3.03
						(0.93)
Mother had poor understanding of interview	...	...	...	...	...	−4.72
						(2.26)
Mother's family background	no	no	yes	yes	yes	yes
Adjusted R^2	0.22	0.29	0.31	0.33	0.32	0.34

Source: See text.

a. Standard errors are in parentheses and are corrected for the nonindependence of siblings. All equations also control child's age in months, child's gender, and dummies for missing data. See Data Appendix for description of the variables. N = 1,626.

A second possibility is that better-quality schooling for mothers could raise their children's vocabulary scores regardless of how much schooling the mothers completed. Fortunately, the NLSY collected some data on mothers' high schools. Before examining the influence of these school characteristics we must first control the available measures of mothers' family background, including parents' educational attainment and occupational status. This reduces the original black-white PPVT-R gap dramatically— from 16.1 to 12.8 points (column 3, table 4-2). When we then control all the characteristics of mothers' high schools, the black-white vocabulary gap shrinks to 11.5 points (column 4). Mothers' perceptions of school safety and teachers' competence do not seem to influence their children's PPVT-R scores.[21] Nor does the percentage of teachers with advanced degrees. However, black-white differences in the percentage of white students in a mother's high school and in the amount of teacher turnover at the school seem to account for some of the PPVT-R gap between these mothers' five- and six-year-old children. The student-teacher ratio at the mother's high school is also a marginally significant predictor of her child's PPVT-R score. These results hold even when we control our measure of the mother's cognitive skills (column 5). Table 4-2 suggests, therefore, that models of children's achievement that only control mothers' years of schooling miss some effects of mothers' school quality.

CNLSY mothers mostly finished high school between 1976 and 1984. Black mothers attended high schools that averaged 41 percent white, while white mothers attended high schools that averaged 86 percent white. All else equal, a 45 point increase in the percentage of whites at the mother's school is associated with a 1.71 point increase in a child's PPVT-R score, a relatively large effect. Even when we control a mother's cognitive skills, as measured by her AFQT score in 1980, her class rank in high school, and the interviewer's rating of her understanding of the interview, the racial mix of her high school affects her child's PPVT-R score (column 5). This suggests that the effect of racial mix operates via a social or cultural channel rather than a cognitive channel.[22]

We do not know the racial composition of mothers' elementary schools, but many of the southern mothers attended elementary school in the late

---

21. A host of additional measures of the climate of the mother's high school also had no influence on her child's PPVT-R score.

22. This is consistent with other literature that finds only small effects of desegregation and racial composition on children's *cognitive* skills; see Cook (1984) and Phillips (1997) for evidence, and Schofield (1995) for a review. It is also consistent with a suggestive literature on the positive relationship between school desegregation and long-term *social* outcomes; see Wells and Crain (1994) for a review.

1960s before most southern schools were desegregated. If school racial mix has more of an effect in the first few years of school, additional controls for the racial mix of mothers' elementary schools might have reduced the black-white vocabulary gap even further.[23]

Higher education is also somewhat segregated by race, partly because a large minority of blacks still choose to attend historically black institutions and partly because blacks who attend historically white institutions are concentrated in the less academically selective institutions (see chapter 12). Traditional socioeconomic status models typically do not control college selectivity. Nor do the models we present in this chapter. This is not a problem if attending a selective college influences children's outcomes only by influencing traditional socioeconomic status measures such as educational attainment and income.[24] But if attending a selective college has other benefits, it could affect a child's PPVT-R score even after controlling the mother's educational attainment and income.

The relationship between teacher turnover and children's vocabulary scores is statistically significant, but the black-white difference in teacher turnover is only about 1 percent. All else equal, a 1 percent reduction in teacher turnover in a mother's high school is associated with about a one-seventh of a point increase in her child's PPVT-R score.

Inequality of Educational Outcomes

A second way to think about how parental education affects the black-white PPVT-R gap is to ask how big the gap would be if black and white parents knew the same amount when they left school. This would be a difficult standard to meet, because eliminating the black-white gap in parents' test scores would require major changes not just in their school experiences but also in their home environments as children. It might also require changes in the larger cultural environment. Nonetheless, if we statistically equate black and white mothers not only on the amount and quality of their schooling but also on their cognitive skills, the black-white gap shrinks by more than 2 points (table 4-2, columns 4 and 5). This is a substantial reduction.

---

23. On the effect of school racial mix see Crain and Mahard (1983) and Phillips (1997).

24. Kane shows in chapter 12 that attending a more selective college increases both a woman's chance of graduating and her future earnings, but the CNLSY captures these benefits by measuring educational attainment and earnings directly.

Unfortunately, this estimated reduction may be either too small or too big. These estimates take no account of the benefits that might flow from equalizing fathers' cognitive skills because the CNLSY did not collect data on children's fathers. If we were to compare black and white children whose mothers *and* fathers were matched on schooling and test performance, the PPVT-R gap would probably narrow more. But as we discussed earlier, when we estimate the effect of any environmental characteristic on children's test scores, we ought to hold children's genetic endowment constant. This is particularly true when we want to estimate the effect of parents' cognitive skills on their children's cognitive skills. Since we cannot measure children's genes directly, table 4-2 does not control their effects. As a result, it overstates the impact of changing parents' test scores. If something like half the correlation between a mother's test scores and her child's test scores is genetic in origin, as most heritability estimates suggest, raising a mother's cognitive skills by improving her schooling is likely to have about half as much an effect as our estimate implies.[25]

Overall, table 4-2 indicates that even when black and white parents have similar schooling and similar cognitive skills, their children still end up with very different vocabulary scores.

Family Income

A second common explanation for the test score gap is that black parents are poorer than white parents. The black-white income gap is much larger than the education gap. Using one year of income data, we find that the typical black child in the CNLSY ranks at the 19th percentile of the white distribution. The income gap in the Current Population Survey (CPS) is very similar.[26] Because the CNLSY is a longitudinal survey, we can average parental income over a child's lifetime (in this case, from birth to age five or six), thus producing a better indicator of a family's economic status. Using average family income, we find that the typical black child in our CNLSY sample is at the 16th percentile of the white income distribution.

Table 4-3 shows the relationship between family income and children's vocabulary scores. A comparison of columns 2 and 3 shows that replacing

25. See Jencks and others (1972).

26. The CPS shows that among children aged four to six in 1995 the household income of the median black child also fell at the 19th percentile of the white income distribution. We thank Gretchen Caspery for these analyses.

Table 4-3. *Effects of Parental Income and Wealth on the Black-White PPVT-R Gap among Five- and Six-Year-Olds in the CNLSY*[a]

Independent variable	(1)	(2)	(3)	(4)	(5)	(6)	(7)	(8)	(9)
Black	-16.27	-14.88	-14.08	-13.89	-13.60	-8.28	-8.25	-13.18	-8.15
	(0.82)	(0.84)	(0.84)	(0.85)	(0.85)	(1.19)	(1.19)	(0.88)	(1.19)
Total family income last year (in $1,000s)	...	0.13	...	...	...	...	...	...	...
		(0.02)							
Average total family income over five or six years (in $1,000s)	...	...	0.17	...	...	...	...	...	...
			(0.02)						
Natural log of average total family income over five or six years	...	...	...	4.86	...	...	...	...	...
				(0.58)					
Average income as dummies ($0 to $12,500 is the omitted category):									
$12,501 to $25,000	...	...	...	...	2.84	...	1.74	2.50	1.77
					(1.05)		(1.06)	(1.08)	(1.08)
$25,001 to $35,000	...	...	...	...	7.16	...	3.56	6.39	3.65
					(1.17)		(1.35)	(1.29)	(1.39)
$35,001 to $50,000	...	...	...	...	8.45	...	2.83	7.32	2.85
					(1.21)		(1.41)	(1.40)	(1.49)
$50,001 or more	...	...	...	...	11.30	...	4.88	9.16	4.59
					(1.45)		(1.78)	(1.80)	(1.93)
Mother's occupational status	...	...	...	...	...	0.005	-0.005	...	-0.003
						(0.034)	(0.035)		(0.035)
Father's occupational status	...	...	...	...	...	0.006	-0.004	...	-0.008
						(0.033)	(0.034)		(0.034)

Single-parent household	...	...	...	...	...	-1.34	-0.67	...	-0.88
						(0.98)	(1.01)		(1.01)
Household size	...	...	...	...	...	-1.40	-1.53	...	-1.52
						(0.28)	(0.29)		(0.29)
Mother worked some during child's first three years of life	...	...	...	...	...	0.39	-0.21	...	-0.30
						(0.88)	(0.89)		(0.89)
Parental wealth as dummies: (less than $0 is the omitted category)									
$0 to $2,184	...	...	...	...	...	...	...	2.13	1.72
								(1.22)	(1.11)
$2,185 to $10,194	...	...	...	...	...	...	...	3.01	1.87
								(1.29)	(1.20)
$10,194 to $34,011	...	...	...	...	...	...	...	1.79	0.27
								(1.39)	(1.31)
$34,012 or more	...	...	...	...	...	...	...	4.60	1.80
								(1.58)	(1.50)
Everything in column 5, table 4-2, including mother's family background	no	no	no	no	no	yes	yes	no	yes
Adjusted R^2	0.22	0.25	0.26	0.26	0.27	0.35	0.35	0.27	0.35

Source: See text.

a. Standard errors are in parentheses and are corrected for the nonindependence of siblings. All equations also control child's age in months, child's gender, and dummies for missing data. See Data Appendix for description of the variables. N = 1,626.

income for one year with income averaged over the child's lifetime reduces the black-white gap by about 0.80 points. If we then allow the effect of income to differ at the top and bottom of the income distribution, either by taking its log (column 4) or by splitting it into categories (column 5), the black-white gap shrinks by up to another half point.[27]

The income effects in column 5 seem to suggest that black-white differences in parental income explain almost 3 points of the PPVT-R gap. But this estimate is too high. When we control other CNLSY variables that affect both parental income and children's PPVT-R scores (grandparents' characteristics, parents' educational attainment, and the mother's AFQT score), the effects of parental income on children's test scores are sharply reduced. The point estimates in column 7 imply that black-white differences in parental income explain about 1 point of the gap.[28] This effect is not trivial but it is small.[29] Even if we assume that sampling error has biased this estimate downward, it is unlikely that parental income explains more than 2 points of the PPVT-R gap, and it could explain as little as 0.2 points. Income effects may be larger for other types of tests for other samples, however.[30]

Family income does not capture all financial differences between black and white parents. White CNLSY parents' median wealth (assets minus debts) is $18,161, compared with only $1,161 for black parents.[31] Despite this large difference, however, parental wealth does not seem to explain much of the black-white score gap among five- and six-year-olds. When we add dummy variables for quintiles of parental wealth to an equation that includes parental income and causally prior variables, the effect of wealth

27. We chose cut points for the dummy variables that maximized the reduction in the black-white gap. The medians for the five categories are $8,896, $18,294, $29,795, $41,251, and $60,035. Although the dummy specification reduces the gap more than the log specification, a log specification fits just as well if not better if we first bottom-code average income to the median of those in the bottom income category and then take the log.

28. Note that we cannot judge the importance of income simply by comparing the black-white gaps in columns 6 and 7 because income mediates some of the effect of the causally prior variables. To estimate the effect of eliminating black-white income differences on the test score gap, we need to multiply each income coefficient by the difference in the proportion of blacks and whites in each category. This yields an estimated effect of 1.05 PPVT-R points.

29. We can reject the hypothesis that all the income coefficients in equation 6 are equal to zero at the .10 level.

30. See Duncan and Brooks-Gunn (1997) and Mayer (1997) for extensive studies of the effects of family income on a variety of child and adolescent outcomes.

31. See Oliver and Shapiro (1995) for more data on black-white wealth differences.

on children's test scores is small and statistically insignificant (column 9).[32] Parental wealth may be more important for older children because savings and inheritances may affect children's chances of living in good school districts, but we do not examine these effects in this chapter.[33]

The CNLSY data suggest that the economic component of socioeconomic status accounts for little of the black-white gap in vocabulary scores once we control causally prior measures. Our confidence in this conclusion is somewhat diminished, however, by IHDP-based evidence, presented later, that suggests a larger effect of income on children's vocabulary scores and on a full-scale IQ test.

Attitudes and Values

A common but controversial explanation for black children's low test scores is that black parents do not have attitudes and values that support children's learning. The NLSY asked parents about their educational expectations, self-efficacy, self-esteem, and whether they would go on welfare if they needed to support their families. It also asked the interviewer to assess the respondent's attitude during the interview. These data were collected before the children in our sample were born. Table 4-4 shows what happens to the black-white gap among five- and six-year-olds when we equate black and white parents on these values and attitudes. With nothing else controlled, black-white differences in mothers' attitudes and values explain less than half a point of the gap in their children's vocabulary scores. After controlling the causally prior variables that affect both mothers' values and their children's scores, the attitudes and values reflected in column 4 explain none of the gap in children's vocabulary scores. Other attitudes and values may explain more, but we are not aware of any empirical evidence to that effect.

---

32. We categorized wealth into dummies based on quintile splits for our sample. This specification fits better than a quadratic specification. Nonetheless, we cannot reject the joint hypothesis that the coefficients of all the wealth dummies are equal to zero ($p = .30$).

33. Housing is worth more when it is located in a school attendance area that feeds into a high-scoring elementary school (Black, 1996), but the difference is small. We do not have data on housing prices and the value added by schools. Nor do we know how much impact parental wealth has on a family's chances of purchasing such a house near a good school once other parental characteristics are controlled.

Table 4-4. *Effects of Mothers' Attitudes and Values on the Black-White PPVT-R Gap among Five- and Six-Year-Olds in the CNLSY*[a]

Independent variable	(1)	(2)	(3)	(4)
Black	−16.27	−15.85	−8.87	−8.95
	(0.82)	(0.82)	(1.06)	(1.11)
Educational expectations (1979)	...	1.01	...	0.08
		(0.20)		(0.21)
If couldn't support family, probably	...	−1.70	...	−0.67
would go on welfare (1979)		(0.84)		(0.77)
What happens to me is my own doing	...	1.10	...	0.91
(1979)		(0.40)		(0.37)
When I make plans, I am almost certain	...	1.13	...	0.75
that I can make them work (1979)		(0.40)		(0.38)
Self-esteem index (1980)	...	0.94	...	0.25
		(0.42)		(0.41)
Interviewer's assessment of mother's attitude toward interview (1979) ("friendly, interested" is the omitted category)				
"Cooperative, not interested"	...	−2.14	...	0.13
		(0.97)		(0.92)
"Impatient, restless" or "hostile"	...	−5.92	...	−3.90
		(2.08)		(1.81)
Everything in column 5, table 4-2, including mother's family background but excluding parents' educational attainment	no	no	yes	yes
Adjusted R^2	0.22	0.28	0.34	0.34

Source: See text.

a. Standard errors are in parentheses and are corrected for the nonindependence of siblings. All equations also control child's age in months, child's gender, and dummies for missing data. See Data Appendix for description of the variables. N = 1,626.

Tables 4-2 through 4-4 indicate that common explanations for the test score gap do not work very well, at least for five- and six-year-olds in the CNLSY.[34] These results support Herrnstein and Murray's contention that socioeconomic factors cannot be much of the explanation for the gap. But

---

34. Another popular explanation for the test score gap is "the decline of the family." We experimented with two measures of family structure. One measured whether the child resided in a single-

the variables in these tables do not come close to capturing children's total environment. Table 4-5 tries to explain the gap as the culmination of a historical process that began generations ago. The results show that more extensive measures of a child's family environment may account for about two-thirds of the gap.

Grandparents

Grandparents can affect their grandchildren in two ways. First, they can pass along their advantages and disadvantages to parents, who then pass them along to the next generation of children. Most quantitative social scientists implicitly assume that this simple sequence captures the full effect of grandparents on grandchildren, and that grandparents have no direct effect on their grandchildren except through the parents.[35] If this model is correct, equalizing black and white parents' education or income in one generation should exert its full effect in the next generation. Analytic models that include only parents' characteristics should then yield an unbiased estimate of the contribution of socioeconomic status to the black-white gap. But if having advantaged grandparents affects children's test scores independently of their parents' educational and economic advantages, reaping the full benefits of educational or economic equality could take several generations, and ignoring grandparents would underestimate the overall contribution of socioeconomic status to the black-white gap.

Table 4-5 first shows the overall impact of maternal grandparents' characteristics on their grandchildren's test scores. Column 1 shows the 16.3 point test score gap we observe among five- and six-year-olds in the CNLSY. Column 2 shows that the gap narrows by about 25 percent when we compare children whose mothers were raised in same region by parents who had the same amount of schooling, the same occupational status, the same

parent home during some or all of his or her life. The other measured whether the child lived with his or her biological father in the year of testing. With no other controls, these variables are both highly statistically significant but reduce the gap by only 1.3 and 1.0 points, respectively. After controlling the mother's family background, high school quality, cognitive skills, and educational attainment, neither of the family structure variables is an even marginally statistically significant predictor of her child's PPVT-R score.

35. Warren and Hauser (1997) present evidence that this model is correct when predicting grandchildren's educational attainment and occupational status in the Wisconsin Longitudinal Study (WLS).

Table 4-5. *Three-Generational Model of the Effects of Family Background on the Black-White PPVT-R Gap among Five- and Six-Year-Olds in the CNLSY*[a]

Independent variables	(1)	(2)	(3)	(4)	(5)	(6)	(7)	(8)	(9)
Black	-16.27	-11.91	-10.88	-9.06	-7.25	-11.41	-11.81	-7.64	-5.64
	(0.82)	(0.93)	(1.06)	(1.21)	(1.19)	(0.87)	(0.87)	(1.21)	(1.22)
Maternal grandparents' educational	...	0.98	0.84	0.72	0.56	...	...	0.61	0.44
attainment		(0.20)	(0.19)	(0.19)	(0.18)			(0.18)	(0.18)
Maternal grandparents' occupational	...	0.08	0.03	0.01	0.02	...	...	0.01	0.02
status		(0.03)	(0.03)	(0.03)	(0.03)			(0.03)	(0.03)
Southern roots	...	-1.61	-1.21	-1.04	-0.68	...	...	-0.69	-0.29
		(0.48)	(0.47)	(0.60)	(0.59)			(0.61)	(0.59)
Mother's number of siblings	...	-0.78	-0.73	-0.53	-0.42	...	...	-0.49	-0.37
		(0.21)	(0.21)	(0.20)	(0.19)			(0.20)	(0.19)
Mother's number of older siblings	...	0.77	0.75	0.64	0.51	...	...	0.62	0.49
		(0.24)	(0.23)	(0.22)	(0.21)			(0.21)	(0.20)
No one in mother's family subscribed to	...	-2.90	-1.94	-1.63	-0.41	...	...	-1.28	-0.06
magazines, newspapers, or had library card		(1.14)	(1.14)	(1.07)	(1.08)			(1.06)	(1.06)
Percent white students in mother's high	...	...	0.049	0.042	0.045	...	...	0.043	0.044
school			(0.019)	(0.018)	(0.018)			(0.018)	(0.017)
Student-teacher ratio	...	...	-0.22	-0.18	-0.17	...	...	-0.20	-0.18
			(0.12)	(0.11)	(0.11)			(0.11)	(0.11)
Percent teacher turnover	...	...	-0.142	-0.096	-0.111	...	...	-0.110	-0.120
			(0.059)	(0.054)	(0.053)			(0.054)	(0.053)
Educational expectations (1979)	...	...	0.49	-0.07	-0.10	...	...	-0.17	-0.23
			(0.20)	(0.22)	(0.22)			(0.22)	(0.21)

What happens to me is my own doing (1979)	0.96 (0.38)	0.72 (0.38)	0.60 (0.37)	...	...	...	0.71 (0.37)	0.59 (0.35)
When I make plans, I am almost certain that I can make them work (1979)	0.92 (0.38)	0.85 (0.38)	0.56 (0.37)	...	...	...	0.75 (0.37)	0.45 (0.36)
Self-esteem index (1980)	0.80 (0.40)	0.25 (0.40)	−0.35 (0.39)	...	...	...	−0.01 (0.40)	−0.64 (0.40)
Interviewer's assessment of mother's attitude toward the interview (1979) ("friendly, interested" is the omitted category)								
"Cooperative, not interested"	−1.02 (0.92)	−0.69 (0.89)	−0.58 (0.87)	...	...	...	0.34 (0.90)	0.36 (0.89)
"Impatient, restless" or "hostile"	−5.91 (1.97)	−4.73 (1.79)	−4.53 (1.77)	...	...	...	−2.92 (1.71)	−2.78 (1.67)
Mother's age at child's birth	...	−0.30 (0.17)	0.05 (0.19)	...	...	...	−0.25 (0.17)	0.13 (0.19)
Child's birthweight in ounces	...	0.05 (0.02)	0.05 (0.02)	...	...	...	0.05 (0.02)	0.05 (0.02)
Child's birth order	...	−2.25 (0.50)	−1.84 (0.48)	...	...	...	−2.36 (0.49)	−1.93 (0.47)
Mother's education	...	0.40 (0.28)	0.23 (0.28)	...	...	...	−0.02 (0.29)	−0.20 (0.29)
Father's education	...	0.35 (.24)	0.24 (.23)	...	...	...	0.41 (.23)	0.29 (.22)
Single-parent household	...	−1.34 (1.02)	−0.82 (1.00)	...	...	...	−1.13 (1.00)	−0.62 (0.98)

Table 4-5 (continued)

Independent variables	(1)	(2)	(3)	(4)	(5)	(6)	(7)	(8)	(9)
Household size	...	...	...	-0.61	-0.35	...	...	-0.63	-0.37
				(0.31)	(0.30)			(0.30)	(0.29)
Average income as dummies ($0 to $12,500 is the omitted category)									
$12,501 to $25,000	...	...	...	1.87	1.82	...	...	1.56	1.44
				(1.06)	(1.03)			(1.07)	(1.03)
$25,001 to $35,000	...	...	...	3.63	2.99	...	...	2.89	2.19
				(1.34)	(1.30)			(1.37)	(1.33)
$35,001 to $50,000	...	...	...	2.56	1.87	...	...	1.68	0.91
				(1.45)	(1.41)			(1.47)	(1.44)
$50,001 or more	...	...	...	4.07	3.46	...	...	3.43	2.70
				(1.89)	(1.83)			(1.90)	(1.85)
Home score—cognitive scale (age 5 or 6)	...	...	...	...	0.10	...	...	...	0.09
					(0.03)				(0.03)
Home score—emotional scale (age 5 or 6)	...	...	...	...	0.08	...	...	...	0.08
					(0.03)				(0.03)
Home score—cognitive scale (age 3 or 4)	...	...	...	...	0.01	...	...	...	0.02
					(0.04)				(0.04)
Home score—emotional scale (age 3 or 4)	...	...	...	...	0.11	...	...	...	0.11
					(0.04)				(0.04)
Number of days per year mother reads to child (every day = 365, age 5 or 6)	...	...	...	...	0.010	...	...	...	0.011
					(0.003)				(0.003)

Number of books child has (10 or more = 15, age 5 or 6)	...	...	...	...	0.28	...	...	...	0.27
					(0.09)				(0.09)
Mother's AFQT score	...	...	...	...	...	0.40	0.30	0.15	0.17
						(0.03)	(0.04)	(0.04)	(0.04)
Mother's class rank in high school (rank/class size)	...	...	...	...	...	...	−2.56	−3.08	−2.29
							(2.08)	(2.06)	(2.02)
Interviewer's assessment of mother's understanding of interview ("good" is the omitted category)									
"Fair" understanding of interview	...	...	...	...	...	...	−4.04	−2.61	−2.39
							(0.96)	(0.95)	(0.95)
"Poor" understanding of interview	...	...	...	...	...	...	−5.63	−4.24	−3.98
							(2.31)	(2.03)	(1.93)
Adjusted R^2	0.22	0.29	0.32	0.36	0.40	0.30	0.31	0.38	0.41

Source: See text.

a. Standard errors are in parentheses and are corrected for the nonindependence of siblings. All equations also control child's age in months, child's gender, and dummies for missing data. See "Data Appendix" for description of the variables. N = 1,626. Equations 2, 3, 4, 5, 8, and 9 also control whether the maternal grandmother worked when daughter was fourteen and whether the mother lived in single-parent family at age fourteen. Equations 3, 4, 5, 8, and 9 also control the percentage of disadvantaged people in the mother's high school, the percentage of teachers in mother's high school with M.A.s or Ph.D.s, whether the mother reported that her high school was somewhat to very unsafe, whether the mother reported that her teachers knew their subjects very well, and whether the mother reported in 1979 that if she could not support her family, she probably would go on welfare. Equations 4, 5, 8, and 9 also control whether the child lived in a rural area for at least one year, whether the child lived in the South for at least one year, whether the child was breast fed, the mother's occupational status (MSEI score) averaged over the child's lifetime, the father's occupational status (MSEI score) averaged over the child's lifetime, whether the mother worked during the child's first three years of life, and parental wealth in categories. Equations 5 and 9 also control whether the mother spanked her child last week, and the mother's report that she would spank or hit her child if her child hit her (age five) or swore or said "I hate you" (age six).

reading materials in their home, and the same number of children. This result implies that the effects of historical inequalities persist for more than one generation, but it does not tell us how this occurs. The estimate is also probably too low, both because the NLSY did not collect very detailed information on maternal grandparents and because it did not collect any information at all on paternal grandparents. But it may also be biased upward because grandparents and grandchildren are genetically related.

Column 3 of table 4-5 suggests that maternal grandparents' educational attainment and how many children they had affect their grandchildren's test scores even after controlling parents' educational attainment, the racial mix of the mother's school, the grandchild's family income and wealth, the mother's cognitive skills, and the mother's perceived self-efficacy. Of course, grandparents' characteristics may only be serving as proxies for other poorly measured or unmeasured parental characteristics. In fact, column 9 suggests that grandparents' characteristics are proxies for mother's parenting practices. Comparing columns 8 and 9, we can see that controlling mothers' parenting practices reduces the coefficients of the grandparent characteristics, especially the coefficient on mothers' access to reading materials when they were children. This suggests that changes in families' class position take more than one generation to alter parenting practices. It could therefore take several generations for educational or economic changes to exert their full effect on the black-white test score gap.

Parenting Practices

Both the CNLSY and the IHDP used the Home Observation for Measurement of the Environment (HOME) scale to measure the quality of children's home environment. The HOME scale is based on interviewer observations and questions that the interviewer asks the mother. It includes measures of learning experiences outside the home (trips to museums, visits to friends, trips to the grocery store), literary experiences within the home (child has more than ten books, mother reads to child, family member reads newspaper, family receives magazine), cognitively stimulating activities within the home (materials that improve learning of skills such as recognition of letters, numbers, colors, shapes, sizes), punishment (whether child was spanked during the home visit; maternal disciplinary style), maternal warmth (mother kissed, caressed, or hugged the child during the visit; mother praised the child's accomplishments during the visit), and the physical environment (whether the home is reasonably clean and uncluttered; whether the child's play environment is safe). The CNLSY used a short form of the HOME scale; the IHDP used the original longer form.[36]

The HOME scale assigns high values to activities and practices that psychologists believe are good for children. Such activities and practices are more common in families with a high socioeconomic status.[37] Readers who think of socioeconomic status as a cultural rather than an economic or social construct may want to treat the HOME scale as "just another measure of it." Readers who think of socioeconomic status as a cultural or economic construct may want to treat the HOME scale as "just another measure of socioeconomic status."

The HOME is an important predictor of children's test performance, even after controlling other measures of children's family environment. In the CNLSY, five- and six-year-olds' vocabulary scores are about 4 points higher when their mothers read to them daily as opposed to not at all. In the IHDP, children score 9 points higher on the PPVT-R and the WPPSI when their families score one standard deviation above the mean on all the HOME measures (table 4-6). These are large effects. Moreover, since the HOME score is an imperfect measure of the home environment to which children are exposed, our results are more likely to be biased downward than upward.[38] For parents who want their children to do well on tests (which means almost all parents), middle-class parenting practices seem to work.

The frequency of middle-class parenting practices also explains part of the relationship between test performance and race. Column 9 of table 4-5 adds various components of the HOME scale to an equation predicting CNLSY children's vocabulary scores. Even after controlling all the parental characteristics in column 8, black-white differences in parenting practices explain an additional 2 points of the black-white gap. Of course, parenting practices also mediate some of the influence of other parental characteristics. Overall, the HOME variables in our CNLSY equations account for

---

36. Bradley and others (1994); Berlin and others (1995).

37. For example, the HOME cognitive scale, measured at age five or six, correlates .29 with mothers' years of schooling. It correlates .34 with family income averaged over the child's lifetime.

38. The CNLSY did not collect extensive observational data on how much the parents talked to their children or how much they disciplined their children physically. Hart and Risley's (1992) results suggest that systematic study of how parents treat their children might account for much of the variation in young children's test scores, although their results do not control genetic influences.

Table 4-6. Effects of Family Background on the Black-White PPVT-R and WPPSI Gaps among Five-Year-Olds in the IHDP[a]

Independent variables	CNLSY PPVT-R		IHDP PPVT-R				WPPSI			
	(1)	(2)	(1)	(2)	(3)	(4)	(1)	(2)	(3)	(4)
Black	-16.27	-14.22	-24.93	-16.11	-14.98	-10.30	-17.76	-9.22	-8.42	-3.89
	(0.82)	(0.88)	(2.49)	(2.55)	(2.70)	(2.73)	(2.07)	(2.06)	(2.17)	(2.13)
Household size (averaged over child's lifetime)	...	-1.74	...	-2.15	-2.15	-1.48	...	-1.39	-1.41	-0.74
		(0.30)		(0.48)	(0.48)	(0.48)		(0.39)	(0.39)	(0.38)
Family income (averaged over child's lifetime)	...	0.11	...	0.24	0.22	0.13	...	0.28	0.26	0.16
		(0.03)		(0.08)	(0.08)	(0.08)		(0.06)	(0.07)	(0.06)
Female-headed household (during some or all of child's life)	...	-0.70	...	-1.64	-1.71	-0.48	...	-1.20	-1.34	0.02
		(0.90)		(2.44)	(2.45)	(2.36)		(1.97)	(1.97)	(1.84)
Mother's educational attainment (in years)	...	1.59	...	1.49	1.44	0.92	...	1.76	1.69	1.14
		(0.23)		(0.55)	(0.55)	(0.54)		(0.44)	(0.44)	(0.42)
Mother's age at child's birth	...	-0.28	...	0.11	0.08	0.06	...	-0.10	-0.14	-0.14
		(0.13)		(0.19)	(0.19)	(0.18)		(0.15)	(0.15)	(0.14)
Fraction of neighbors with income less than $10,000	...	...	...	...	-6.75	0.56	...	...	-0.02	6.11
					(8.48)	(8.30)			(6.82)	(6.48)
Fraction of neighbors with income greater than $30,000	...	...	...	...	3.86	7.80	...	...	10.42	13.07
					(11.42)	(11.01)			(9.19)	(8.59)
Home learning environment (12 months)	...	...	...	...	...	0.21	...	...	...	0.15
						(0.08)				(0.07)
Home learning environment (36 months)	...	...	...	...	...	0.24	...	...	...	0.32
						(0.10)				(0.08)
Home warmth (36 months)	...	...	...	...	...	0.16	...	...	...	0.13
						(0.07)				(0.05)
Adjusted R^2	0.22	0.31	0.33	0.47	0.47	0.52	0.28	0.47	0.47	0.55

Source: See text.

a. Standard errors are in parentheses. IHDP equations control gender, age, and site. IHDP N = 315. CNLSY equations control gender, birthweight, neonatal health, and dummies for missing data. CNLSY N = 1,626.

more than 3.5 points of the gap.

Notably, the "effects" of the HOME variables are hardly reduced once we control our proxies for children's cognitive genes (compare columns 5 and 9). These results imply that most of the relationship between the HOME and children's vocabulary scores is environmental rather than genetic. It is still possible, however, that an active correlation between children's cognitive genes and mothers' parenting practices biases these results. It is also possible that vocabulary scores and parenting practices are correlated because of genes that influence noncognitive traits. Suppose, for example, that genes influence depression and that depressed children tend not to pay much attention to mothers' reading or that mothers read to them less because depressed children give mothers less positive reinforcement. Since we have not controlled any proxies for children's genes for depression, the relationship between reading frequency and vocabulary scores may be spurious or it may reflect reverse causation.[39] In fact, behavioral geneticists have found some evidence that the relationship between the home environment and children's cognitive skills is partially genetic but that it is not mediated by genes for cognitive skills. For example, Julia Braungart, David Fulker, and Robert Plomin found that the correlation between the HOME and infants' cognitive skills was larger in nonadoptive families than in adoptive families.[40] C. S. Bergeman and Plomin report, however, that parental characteristics such as socioeconomic status, IQ, specific cognitive abilities, and major personality dimensions have hardly any effect on the correlation between the HOME and infant cognitive skills.[41] We have seen no evidence on the extent to which genes of any sort mediate the relationship between the HOME and five- and six-year-olds' vocabulary scores.

When we add parenting measures to the IHDP, the unexplained effect of race falls even more than in the CNLSY: from 15 to 10 points for the PPVT-R and from 8 to 4 points for the WPPSI (see table 4-6).[42] This large

39. The problem with the logic of such a story is that it requires that different genes influence cognitive skills at different ages. Otherwise, if a mother passed on the genes for depression to her five- or six-year-old, she also probably felt depressed as a child, and did not pay attention to her mother's reading or was less responsive and thus read to less, which would have also had some effect on her cognitive skills and thus on her measured AFQT, which our models control.

40. Braungart, Fulker, and Plomin (1992).

41. Bergeman and Plomin (1988).

42. These findings leave open the question of why black-white differences in parenting practices persist even after controlling for measured socioenconomic status. The relative importance that mothers place on many child-oriented activities and skills may be related to group identity or membership,

reduction probably occurs because we have fewer controls for other aspects of family environment, no adequate proxies for child's genotype, and more detailed measures of parenting practices.[43]

Table 4-6 also compares results from the IHDP with those from the CNLSY. The IHDP includes an unusually large number of very poor black children, many of whom also have very low PPVT-R scores (see table 4-1). As a result, the black-white gap on the PPVT-R is 8 points larger than in the CNLSY. Partly because black and white children's socioeconomic status and family structure differ more in the IHDP than in the CNLSY, and partly because income has larger effects on children's test performance in the IHDP than in the CNLSY, controlling socioeconomic status and family structure narrows the black-white PPVT-R gap far more in the IHDP than in the CNLSY. With "traditional" socioeconomic status and family structure controls, the PPVT-R gap decreases from 16 to 14 points in the CNLSY and from 25 to 16 points in the IHDP. The gap on the WPPSI falls even more—by 50 percent. Thus the IHDP data suggest that income and other measures of socioeconomic status contribute considerably to between- and within-group differences in test scores, particularly on the full-scale WPPSI IQ test.[44] We suspected that the greater reduction in the WPPSI gap might be attributable to the fact that it measures a number of cognitive skills, whereas the PPVT-R measures only verbal comprehension. However, the reduction in the black-white gap on the verbal subscale of the WPPSI is almost identical to the reduction on the full-scale WPPSI.[45]

Neighborhood Effects?

The importance of neighborhood income for children's cognitive development is still uncertain. However, large racial differences in neighborhood poverty do suggest that traditional measures of socioeconomic status

---

over and above socioeconimic status. See, for example, Goodnow (1985). Others have suggested that some groups of African-American and European-American parents may differ culturally in how they nurture children's cognitive skills. See, for example, Boykin (1986) and Allen and Boykin (1992).

43. The IHDP did administer the PPVT-R to mothers in the sample. But despite extremely large black-white differences on the PPVT-R among mothers in the IHDP, mothers' scores explain none of the large black-white gap in their children's PPVT-R or WPPSI scores.

44. Note, however, that the difference between the income effect on the PPVT-R in the CNLSY and the IHDP is not statistically significant.

45. See Brooks-Gunn, Klebanov, and Duncan (1996).

understate the difference between black and white children's environments. For example, data from the national Panel Study of Income Dynamics (PSID) indicate that about 57 percent of black children born between 1978 and 1980 lived in census tracts where a fifth or more of their neighbors were poor compared with only 7 percent of white children. Even among children whose own family was not poor between 1980 and 1985, nearly half of the black children but only 6 percent of the white children resided in neighborhoods where at least a fifth of their neighbors were poor.[46] The IHDP provides data on the income of other families in the child's census tract. Equation 3 in table 4-6 suggests that having high-income neighbors may be beneficial to a child's test scores, although the coefficients are not statistically significant.[47] Jeanne Brooks-Gunn and colleagues found effects of high-income neighbors on age three Stanford-Binet IQ scores in the IHDP that are statistically significant and twice the size of those reported in table 4-6. The different neighborhood results for three- and five-year-olds may be attributable to the fact that the IHDP neighborhood data were collected at the time of the child's birth. Five-year-olds are more likely than three-year-olds to have moved from their original census tracts. Moreover, the demographic characteristics of the original tracts are more likely to have changed over a five-year interval than over a three-year interval.[48]

Overall Effects of Family Environment

Our results suggest that racial differences in socioeconomic status, broadly conceived, are larger than Herrnstein and Murray imply. They calculate that "the average environment of blacks would have to be at the 6th percentile of the distribution of environments among whites . . . for racial differences to be entirely environmental." According to them, "environ-

---

46. Duncan, Brooks-Gunn, and Klebanov (1994).

47. See Brooks-Gunn, Klebanov, and Duncan (1996). The neighborhood coefficients and standard errors are large because the measures are scaled so that a one-unit change is equivalent to moving from a tract with no low- or high-income neighbors to one with exclusively low- or high-income neighbors. Since a standard deviation change in the IHDP sample is only about 0.16 for both measures, readers should divide the coefficients and standard errors in table 4-6 by 6 to approximate a 1.0 standard deviation change.

48. Brooks-Gunn and others (1993) also found that having high-income neighbors is a significant predictor of dropping out of high school and teenage out-of-wedlock childbearing in the Panel Study of Income Dynamics (PSID), after controlling variables similar to those in column 3 of table 4-6.

mental differences of this magnitude . . . are implausible."[49] When we construct an index of all the measures in column 5 of table 4-5, however, we find that the average black child's "environment" ranks at the 9th percentile of the distribution of environments among whites. When we construct an index that also includes measures of the mother's cognitive skills (all the measures in column 9 of table 4-5), the average black child's "environment" ranks at the 8th percentile of the white distribution. Other social inequalities not included in table 4-5 could easily push the average black child's "environment" a few percentiles lower.

Herrnstein and Murray also argue that measured differences in parents' socioeconomic status account for only a third of the racial gap in children's test scores.[50] Although this is true if we use traditional measures of socioeconomic status, the measures in column 5 of table 4-5 explain more than half of the black-white gap in vocabulary scores among five- and six-year-olds. When combined with measures of the mother's cognitive skills, these variables explain about two-thirds of the gap (see column 9 in table 4-5).[51] The IHDP results suggest that better parenting measures might well explain even more of the gap. The IHDP results also suggest that socioeconomic status, family structure, and parenting practices may explain more of the racial gap for full-scale IQ than for vocabulary scores.[52]

49. Herrnstein and Murray (1994, p. 299). Their calculation is based on the assumption that the typical black ranks at the 16th percentile of the white IQ distribution, and that 60 percent of the variance in test scores in due to genetic effects within groups. They claim that 60 percent is "a middle-ground estimate" of test-score heritabilities. We think 50 percent is closer to the middle ground and that 40 percent may be more descriptive of IQ heritabilities for children as young as those in our sample, but we stick with Herrnstein and Murray's assumption here. See Jensen (1973) for calculations using higher heritabilities.

50. Herrnstein and Murray (1994, p. 286).

51. We reestimated all our CNLSY models after restandardizing the PPVT-R on the entire population of five and six-year-olds in the CNLSY, including Hispanics. Although the coefficients of the family background variables changed depending on whether we used the standardized PPVT or the restandardized PPVT-R as the dependent variable, the percentage of the black-white gap explained by each model was nearly identical across the dependent variables.

52. These results seem to resemble those of Mercer and Brown (1973), who tried to explain the black-white and Latino-white test score gaps among 540 elementary school children in Riverside, California, in the late 1960s. Controlling socioeconomic status, broadly conceived, including residence in an integrated neighborhood, mothers' participation in formal organizations, mothers' self-efficacy, mothers' information about their children's schools, and the children's general anxiety, Mercer and Brown reduced the correlation between race and PPVT-R score by 55 percent and the correlation between race and WPPSI full-scale IQ by 70 percent.

Table 4-7. *Correlations among Family Environment Proxy, Cognitive Genotype Proxy, and Child's PPVT-R Score in the CNLSY*[a]

Variables	(1)	(2)	(3)	(4)
Family environment proxy	1	. . .	. . .	. . .
Cognitive genotype proxy	0.45	1	. . .	. . .
Child's PPVT-R score	0.62	0.46	1	. . .
Race (black = 1)	–0.50	–0.40	–0.47	1

Source: See text.

a. Family environment proxy is a composite of all the variables in column 5 of table 4-5, except race, weighted by their coefficients in column 9 of table 4-5. Cognitive genotype proxy is a composite of all the variables in column 7 of table 4-5, except race, weighted by their coefficients in column 9 of table 4-5. Correlations are unweighted because the regressions in table 4-5 are unweighted.

Herrnstein and Murray are correct, however, to reiterate Arthur Jensen's concern about the sociological fallacy.[53] Some of the measures in our tables are contaminated by genetic effects that operate within groups. To estimate the extent of this contamination, we created two indices: one labeled "family environment proxy," which includes all the CNLSY measures in column 5 of table 4-5, weighted by their coefficients in column 9, and another labeled "cognitive genotype proxy," which includes all the CNLSY measures in column 7 of table 4-5, weighted by their coefficients in column 9. Table 4-7 shows the correlations between these indices and children's PPVT-R scores. The family environment proxy is strongly correlated with the cognitive genotype proxy ($R = .45$) and with the child's PPVT-R score ($R = .62$). When we standardize all three variables and regress children's PPVT-R scores on the two indices plus race, we get

(1)   PPVT-R = –.16*black + .46*family environment proxy + .19*cognitive genotype proxy.

These results indicate that the cognitive genotype proxy reduces the standardized coefficient of our family environment proxy from .62 to .46, which implies that about 26 percent of the apparent effect of family environment in table 4-5 is a genetic effect. This reduction is slightly greater than the 18 percent reduction that Loehlin and his colleagues found when they compared socioeconomic status–IQ correlations between samples of adopted

53. Jensen (1969).

and biological children.[54] And the reduction is identical to the one Sandra Scarr and Richard Weinberg found when they compared correlations between black children's IQ scores and the educational attainment of their biological and adoptive parents.[55]

Unfortunately, equation 1 cannot tell us for sure that raising children's family environments from the 16th to the 50th percentile would really raise their vocabulary scores by almost half a standard deviation. The standardized coefficient on our family environment proxy could easily be too large or too small.

Upward Biases

We have no proxy for the fathers' cognitive genes, because the CNLSY did not collect fathers' test scores. Because children receive half of their genes from each parent, on average, it is very likely that our environmental estimate would be smaller if we had a better proxy for fathers' genetic contribution to their children's cognitive skills. Of course, since mothers' and fathers' test scores tend to be correlated, controlling fathers' scores would also reduce the apparent effect of mothers' scores.

Our estimate of the family environment effect may also be biased upward because our proxies for the cognitive genes that mothers pass on to their children are imperfect.[56] To be certain that we had adequately con-

54. See Loehlin, Horn, and Willerman (1989). Their measure of socioeconomic status included parents' education and father's occupational status.

55. See Scarr and Weinberg (1976). We averaged the correlations for mother's and father's education and then compared the average correlation for adoptive parents (r = .28) with that for natural parents (r = .38). Children in their sample ranged from four years old to more than sixteen, with a mean age of seven.

56. Besides worrying that the AFQT is not a valid measure of children's genes, we might also worry that its unreliability biases its coefficients downward. Using estimates for the reliabilities of its components from Bock and Moore (1986) and correlations among its components for mothers in our sample, we estimate the reliability of the AFQT score at .94. When we reestimated the equations in table 4-5, assuming a reliability for AFQT of .94, this increased the AFQT coefficient in the column 6 equation from .40 to .43, and reduced the remaining black-white gap from −11.41 to −11.01. Correcting mothers' AFQT scores for unreliability also increased the AFQT coefficient in column 9 to .21 and reduced the remaining gap from −5.64 to −5.38. Because Currie and Thomas (1995) reported that the math components of the ASVAB were more weakly associated with children's PPVT-R scores than the verbal components, we also reestimated the equations in table 5 using just the word knowledge and paragraph comprehension components of the ASVAB. Without correcting the tests for measurement error, the coefficient on word knowledge is slightly smaller than that on the AFQT, and the coefficient on paragraph comprehension is considerably smaller. If we correct word knowledge for unreliability and include it in an equation identical to that in column 9, the black-white gap shrinks to

trolled all the effects of children's cognitive genes, we would need to map the genes and then measure their effects. Molecular geneticists have only just begun to locate the genes associated with cognitive skills.[57]

Finally, our environmental estimates may be biased upward because we have not controlled all the genes for noncognitive traits that may affect the acquisition of cognitive skills. Genes for all sorts of traits could conceivably influence how children shape their own cognitive environments. Since we have not captured these genes with our cognitive genotype proxy, we have probably overstated the effect of improving children's family environments.

Downward Biases

The variables we have used as proxies for cognitive genotype also measure children's cognitive environment. To the extent that mothers' cognitive skills create more cognitively stimulating environments for their children, factoring out the effect of mothers' cognitive skills as we did in equation 1 gets rid of some environmental effects. This argument holds regardless of whether mothers' cognitive skills are genetic or environmental in origin.

Table 4-5 also omits many factors that vary among individuals and also affect children's vocabulary scores. These factors range from lead exposure to familiarity with standard English. Unmeasured aspects of children's home environments probably also matter a lot. Recall that the CNLSY HOME measures in our sample were collected during two interviewers' visits separated by two years. More detailed measures of the home environment collected at more frequent intervals and validated across observers might have a much larger effect on children's test scores.[58]

To get some sense of how much our family environment estimate is biased by omitted variables, we can ask how well equation 9 in table 4-5 explains the correlation among siblings' PPVT-R scores. Equation 9 explains 41 percent of the variance in these scores. If siblings had identical

---

−5.19. If we correct paragraph comprehension for unreliability and include it in an equation identical to that in column 9, the gap shrinks to −3.55 points.

57. See Plomin and Petrill (1997) for a discussion of what is currently known about DNA markers for genes associated with cognition.

58. See Hart and Risley (1992) for data on the relationship between children's IQ scores and parenting practices observed at frequent intervals before, during, and after the children learned to talk.

values on all the variables in equation 9, therefore, their PPVT-R scores would have to correlate at least .41. In fact, siblings do not have identical values on all the variables in equation 9, partly because families' circumstances change, partly because parents treat children differently, and partly because equation 9 includes variables such as birth weight that vary independently of family circumstances. For the 266 pairs of siblings in our PPVT-R sample, the values predicted using equation 9 correlate .83. Thus if equation 9 included everything that contributed to resemblance between siblings, their PPVT-R scores would correlate (.83)(.41) = .34. The actual correlation among siblings' PPVT-R scores is .51.

Analyses of resemblance between adopted children almost never find test score correlations as high as .34. This may be partly because the range of environments in adoptive families is very restricted, but no analysis of resemblance between relatives suggests that shared environmental factors explain as much as 34 percent of the variance in children's test performance. This suggests that some of the variables in equation 9 must also serve as proxies for children's genes.

Environmental and Genetic "X Factors"

The coefficient of the black variable in table 4-5 is an estimate of the test score gap that is not explained by variables that affect both black and white children. If we had controlled all the environmental variables that affected both black and white children's scores, any remaining gap would have to be caused by genes that differ by race. But as we emphasized at the outset, such genes need not be directly linked to cognition; they may merely be linked to appearance. As long as blacks and whites look different from one another and those differences have social meaning, there can be environmental factors that are unique to one racial group or the other. These so-called X factors may explain the remaining test score gap we observe in table 4-5.[59] What might these X factors be? Racial prejudice and discrimination are the most likely candidates, but we need data on exactly *how* they affect children's test scores. Claude Steele and Joshua Aronson's stereotype threat is a perfect example of an X factor, but we do not yet know whether it affects young children's test scores.[60] If the effects of environmental X factors are constant across all situations, these effects will be indistinguish-

---

59. Jensen (1973). See also Flynn (1980) for a discussion of possible X factors.
60. See chapter 11 of this volume.

able from genetic X factors, because both will be perfectly correlated with being socially identified as black. If some of these X factors are situation specific, or even manipulable, as stereotype threat appears to be, future research may uncover explanations for the black-white test score gap that take us beyond traditional explanations based on socioeconomic status.

Conclusion

Herrnstein and Murray claim in *The Bell Curve* that socioeconomic status explains about a third of the black-white test score gap. Larry Hedges and Amy Nowell reach the same conclusion in chapter 5 of this volume. Such estimates seem to be roughly correct when we define socioeconomic status in strictly social and economic terms. Parental education affects children's test scores, even after controlling causally prior variables, but the black-white gap in years of schooling now averages less than a year.[61] Judging from table 4-2, eliminating this difference would reduce the PPVT-R gap by only 1 or 2 points. If we take a more expansive view of educational equality, its effects could be larger. The CNLSY hints that when black and white parents have attended the same schools, their children's test scores may be more alike. Also, if we define educational equality as a situation in which black and white parents with the same amount of schooling also have the same skills, the CNLSY suggests that this could reduce the test score gap by 3 or 4 points. Moreover, our results imply that it takes at least two generations for changes in parental socioeconomic status to exert their full effect on parenting practices. Consequently, the long-term effects of educational inequality may be larger than 3 or 4 points.

The CNLSY also suggests that black-white differences in economic well-being have only a modest effect on the black-white test score gap among young children. After controlling other causally prior variables, black-white differences in family income reduce the PPVT-R gap by about 1 point. Adding other measures of parents' economic resources, such as wealth and occupational status, does not improve our prediction of young children's test scores in the CNLSY. The picture is somewhat different in the less representative IHDP data, which show considerably larger income effects on both the PPVT-R and the full-scale WPPSI. At least in the CNLSY, we

---

61. The gap is 0.8 years among the eighth-graders whose parents NELS surveyed in 1988 and 0.8 years among the first-graders whose parents Prospects surveyed in 1992.

find that reducing economic inequality between black and white parents would probably not reduce the black-white gap much.

Some readers may find this conclusion discouraging. But the conclusion that income plays a minor role in the test score gap is only discouraging if you think it would be easier to equalize black and white parents' incomes than to change some of the other factors that contribute to the gap. Recent history does not suggest that equalizing incomes would be at all easy. Despite dramatic changes in the social position of blacks, including improvements in their educational attainment and occupational status, the income gap between black and white parents has remained remarkably stable since the early 1970s. Hedges and Nowell's estimates in chapter 5 suggest, for example, that black parents' incomes were 62 percent of white parents' incomes in 1992, compared with 63 percent in 1972. Thus, if children's test scores are more sensitive to the correlates of parental income than to income per se, that may be good news, not bad news.

Even though traditional measures of socioeconomic status account for no more than a third of the test score gap, our results show that a broader index of family environment may explain up to two-thirds of it. Racial differences in grandparents' educational attainment, mothers' household size, mothers' high school quality, mothers' perceived self-efficacy, children's birth weight, and children's household size all seem to be important factors in the gap among young children. Racial differences in parenting practices also appear to be important.

We also found that many of our measures of family environment are linearly related to the test score gap. This has implications for Sandra Scarr's controversial argument that family environments "in the normal range of experience" have little or no effect on children's development.[62] Our results suggest that environments provided by ordinary families do influence children's cognitive development.

This chapter cannot tell us the true effect of family environment on children's vocabulary scores. Nor can it settle the question of whether the black-white test score gap is entirely or only partially environmental in origin. But it does help identify the family characteristics that matter most for the gap. It also suggests that eliminating environmental differences between black and white families could go a long way toward eliminating the test score gap.

62. Scarr (1992, 1993). See Baumrind (1993) and Jackson (1993) for responses.

Data Appendix

Our CNLSY sample contains the 1,626 black and white children who were five or six years old when they were tested in 1986, 1988, 1990, or 1992. If the same child was tested twice, we retained the earlier test score. We also deleted 19 children who scored over 3 standard deviations below the mean on the PPVT-R. All our regressions are unweighted and include dummies for missing data. Our descriptive statistics are weighted, using the child weight for the year in which the child was tested. The standard errors in our regressions are corrected for the nonindependence of siblings. We describe below how we recoded and combined some of the CNLSY variables for our analyses.

Maternal grandparents' educational attainment. The mean of maternal grandfather's and maternal grandmother's highest grade completed.

Maternal grandparents' occupational status. We first recoded the 1970 census occupational codes for maternal grandmother and maternal grandfather to MSEI scores.[63] We then averaged these MSEI scores.

Southern roots. This variable equals 2 if the child's mother was born in the South, 1 if either the child's maternal grandmother or the child's maternal grandfather was born in the South, and 0 otherwise. We coded the maternal grandparents' state of birth according to the NLSY definition of the South (see attachment 100 in the NLSY Codebook Supplement 1979–1992).

No one in mother's family subscribed to magazines, newspapers, or had a library card. The CNLSY has three dichotomous variables that ask whether anyone in the household when the mother was aged fourteen received magazines, newspapers, or had a library card. Our variable sums these dichotomous variables and then recodes them to equal 1 if no one in the household received magazines, newspapers, or had a library card and 0 otherwise.

Mother lived in a single-parent family at age fourteen. The CNLSY asked the respondent whom she lived with at age fourteen. We coded this variable 1 if the respondent lived with only one adult caregiver, and 0 otherwise.

Student-teacher ratio. The ratio of the school administrator's reports of the total enrollment in the mother's high school to the number of full-time-equivalent teachers in the school.

Teacher turnover. The school administrator's response to a question about what percentage of full-time teachers in the school at the end of the previous year had since left for reasons other than death or retirement.

---

63. See Stevens and Featherman (1981).

Mother reports that high school is somewhat to very unsafe. This variable equals 0 if mother answered "not true at all" to the statement, "I don't feel safe at this school," and 1 otherwise.

Mother reports that teachers know their subjects very well. This variable equals 1 if mother answered "very true" to the statement, "Most of my teachers really know their subjects well," and 0 otherwise.

What happens to me is my own doing. This item comes from Julian Rotter's locus-of-control measure. It is asked in two parts. First, the respondent replies to the statement, "What happens to me is my own doing . . . sometimes I feel that I don't have enough control over the direction my life is taking," by choosing one of two responses, "in control" or "not in control." Then the respondent is asked whether her last statement is "much closer" or "slightly closer" to her opinion. We coded the item into an ordinal scale where "in control and much closer" equals 4, "in control and slightly closer" equals 3, "not in control and slightly closer" equals 2, and "not in control and much closer" equals 4. We then standardized this scale to a mean of zero and standard deviation of 1.

When I make plans, I am almost certain that I can make them work. This item also comes from the Rotter measure. It reads: "When I make plans, I am almost certain that I can make them work . . . it is not always wise to plan too far ahead, because many things turn out to be a matter of good or bad fortune anyhow." We recoded it to an ordinal 4 point scale using the same procedures outlined above. Two other locus-of-control items are available in the NLSY. These two items were not related to children's PPVT-R scores. Nor were these other items correlated highly enough with the two items we describe here to justify combining them all into one index.

Self-esteem index. This is an index of ten Likert-scaled items: "I feel that I'm a person of worth, at least on an equal basis with others. I feel that I have a number of good qualities. All in all, I am inclined to feel that I am a failure. I am able to do things as well as most other people. I feel I do not have much to be proud of. I take a positive attitude toward myself. On the whole, I am satisfied with myself. I wish I could have more respect for myself. I certainly feel useless at times. At times I think I am no good at all." We constructed the index by recoding some of the items so that high values indicated high self-esteem and then taking the mean of all the nonmissing items. We then standardized this variable to a mean of 0 and standard deviation of 1. The index's reliability is .83.

Mother's AFQT score. We converted the 1989 version of the AFQT score from the percentile scale to a standardized normal distribution, with a mean of 0 and standard deviation of 1. We then age-standardized these scores based on the entire weighted NLSY sample of both men and women. We then recoded these scores to an "IQ" metric (a mean of 100 and standard deviation of 15).

Mother's education. Mother's highest grade completed in year of child's testing. If it was missing, we used the value for the previous year.

Father's education. Highest grade completed by mother's spouse or partner in year of child's testing. If it was missing, we used the value for the previous year.

Mother's occupational status. We recoded mothers' census occupational codes to MSEI scores.[64] We then averaged the nonmissing scores over the child's lifetime (five years for the five-year-olds, six years for the six-year-olds).

Father's occupational status. We recoded spouses' census occupational codes to MSEI scores.[65] We then averaged the nonmissing scores over the child's lifetime (five years for the five-year-olds, six years for the six-year-olds).

Single-parent household. This variable equals 1 if a man was not present in the child's household for at least one year of the child's lifetime, 0 otherwise.

Mother worked some during child's first three years of life. This variable equals 1 if the mother worked at least one year during the first three years of the child's life, 0 otherwise.

Average total family income over five or six years. The mean of nonmissing values of total family income in 1992 dollars, averaged over the child's lifetime (five years for the five-year-olds, six years for the six-year-olds). Respondents with an average income of zero dollars were coded as missing.

Natural log of average total family income. Natural log of the child's lifetime average family income, after bottom-coding the average to $2,000.

Parental wealth. The NLSY asked respondents about the value of their assets and debts. We recoded validly skipped asset and debt items to $0 and then computed an asset and debt variable for each year. Wealth equals assets minus debts. We then averaged wealth over as many years of a child's lifetime as were available, excluding data reported in 1989 because reports in that year were not highly correlated with reports in previous or later years. We then split the wealth variable into quintiles.

HOME scores. HOME scores are the standardized scores reported by the CNLSY, transformed to a mean of 100 and standard deviation of 15.

---

64. See Stevens and Featherman (1981).
65. Ibid.

Number of days a year mother reads to child. Mothers were asked how often they read aloud to their children, with possible responses of "never, several times a year, several times a month, about once a week, at least three times a week, and every day." We recoded these responses to estimates of the number of days a year mothers read to their children (0, 3, 36, 52, 156, and 365).

Number of books child has. Mothers were asked how many books the child has, with possible responses of "none, 1 or 2, 3 to 9, and 10 or more." We recoded these responses to 1, 1.5, 6, and 15, respectively.

References

Allen, Brenda A., and A. Wade Boykin. 1992. "African-American Children and the Educational Process: Alleviating Cultural Discontinuity through Prescriptive Pedagogy." *School Psychology Review* 21(4): 586–96.

Baumrind, Diana. 1993. "The Average Expectable Environment Is Not Good Enough: A Response to Scarr." *Child Development* 64(5): 1299–1317.

Bergeman, C. S., and Robert Plomin. 1988. "Parental Mediators of the Genetic Relationship between Home Environment and Infant Mental Development." *British Journal of Developmental Psychology* 6(1):11–19.

Berlin, Lisa J., and others. 1995. "Examining Observational Measures of Emotional Support and Cognitive Stimulation in Black and White Mothers of Preschoolers." *Journal of Family Issues* 16(5): 664–86.

Black, Sandra E. 1996. "Do 'Better' Schools Matter? Parents Think So." Department of Economics, Harvard University.

Bock, R. Darrell, and Elsie E. J. Moore. 1986. *Advantage and Disadvantage: A Profile of American Youth.* Hillsdale, N. J.: L. Erlbaum.

Boykin, A. Wade. 1986. "The Triple Quandary and the Schooling of Afro-American Children." In Ulric Neisser, ed., *The School Achievement of Minority Children*, pp. 57–92. Hillsdale, N. J.: L. Erlbaum.

Bradley, Robert H., and others. 1994. "Early Indications of Resilience and Their Relation to Experiences in the Home Environments of Low Birthweight, Premature Children Living in Poverty." *Child Development* 65(2): 346–60.

Braungart, Julia M., David W. Fulker, and Robert Plomin. 1992. "Genetic Mediation of the Home Environment during Infancy: A Sibling Adoption Study of the HOME." *Developmental Psychology* 28(6): 1048–55.

Brooks-Gunn, Jeanne, Pamela K. Klebanov, and Greg J. Duncan. 1996. "Ethnic Differences in Children's Intelligence Test Scores: Role of Economic Deprivation, Home Environment, and Maternal Characteristics." *Child Development* 67(2): 396–408.

Brooks-Gunn, J., Pamela K. Klebanov, and Fong-Ruey Liaw. 1995. "The Learning, Physical, and Emotional Environment of the Home in the Context of Poverty: The Infant Health and Development Program." *Children and Youth Services Review* 17(1/2): 251–76.

Brooks-Gunn, Jeanne, and others. 1993. "Do Neighborhoods Influence Child and Adolescent Development?" *American Journal of Sociology* 99(2): 353–95.

Brooks-Gunn, Jeanne, and others. 1994. "Early Intervention in Low Birthweight, Premature Infants: Results through Age 5 Years from the Infant Health and Development Program." *Journal of the American Medical Association* 272(16): 1257–62.

Chase-Lansdale, P. Lindsay, and others. 1991. "Children of the NLSY: A Unique Research Opportunity." *Developmental Psychology* 27(6): 918–31.

Constantine, Wendy L., and others. 1993. "Recruitment and Retention in a Clinical Trial for Low Birthweight, Premature Infants." *Journal of Developmental Behavioral Pediatrics* 14(1): 1–7.

Cook, Thomas D. 1984. "What Have Black Children Gained Academically from School Integration?: Examination of the Meta-Analytic Evidence." In Thomas Cook and others, *School Desegregation and Black Achievement*, pp. 6–42. Washington, D.C.: National Institute of Education.

Crain, Robert, and Rita E. Mahard. 1983. "The Effect of Research Methodology on Desegregation-Achievement Studies: A Meta-Analysis." *American Journal of Sociology* 88(5): 839–54.

Crane, Jonathan. 1994. "Race and Children's Cognitive Test Scores: Empirical Evidence that Environment Explains the Entire Gap." University of Illinois at Chicago.

Currie, Janet, and Duncan Thomas. 1995. "Race, Children's Cognitive Achievement, and *The Bell Curve*." University of California, Los Angeles.

Duncan, Greg J., and Jeanne Brooks-Gunn, eds. 1997. *The Consequences of Growing Up Poor*. Russell Sage.

Duncan, Greg J., Jeanne Brooks-Gunn, and Pamela K. Klebanov. 1994. "Economic Deprivation and Early Childhood Development." *Child Development* 65(2): 296–318.

Dunn, Lloyd M., and Leota M. Dunn. 1981. *Peabody Picture Vocabulary Test—Revised*. Circle Pines, Minn.: American Guidance Service.

Flynn, James R. 1980. *Race, IQ, and Jensen*. London: Routledge & Kegan Paul.

France, Kenneth. 1973. "Effects of 'White' and of 'Black' Examiner Voices on IQ Scores for Children." *Developmental Psychology* 8(1): 144.

Goodnow, Jacqueline. 1985. "Change and Variation in Ideas about Childhood and Parenting." In Irving E. Sigel, ed., *Parental Belief Systems: The Psychological Consequences for Children*, pp. 235–70. Hillsdale, N. J.: L. Erlbaum.

Hart, Betty, and Todd R. Risley. 1992. "American Parenting of Language-Learning Children: Persisting Differences in Family-Child Interactions Observed in Natural Home Environments." *Developmental Psychology* 28(6): 1096–1105.

Herrnstein, Richrd J., and Charles Murray. 1994. *The Bell Curve: Intelligence and Class Structure in American Life*. Free Press.

The Infant Health and Development Program Staff. 1990. "Enhancing the Outcomes of Low Birthweight, Premature Infants: A Multisite Randomized Trial." *Journal of the American Medical Association* 263(22): 3035–42.

Jackson, Jacquelyne F. 1993. "Human Behavioral Genetics, Scarr's Theory, and Her Views on Interventions: A Critical Review and Commentary on Their Implications for African-American Children." *Child Development* 64(5): 1318–32.

Jencks, Christopher, and others. 1972. *Inequality: A Reassessment of the Effect of Family and Schooling in America*. Basic Books.

Jencks, Christopher. 1980. "Heredity, Environment, and Public Policy Reconsidered." *American Sociological Review* 45(5): 723–36.

Jensen, Arthur R. 1980. *Bias in Mental Testing*. Free Press.

———. 1973. *Educability and Group Differences*. Harper and Row.

———. 1969. "How Much Can We Boost IQ and Scholastic Achievement?" *Harvard Educational Review* 39(1): 1–123.

Kraemer, Helena C., and Kay H. Fendt. 1990. "Random Assignment in Clinical Trials: Issues in Planning (Infant Health and Development Program)." *Journal of Clinical Epidemiology* 43(11): 1157–67.

Lewontin, Richard C. 1976. "Race and Intelligence." In N. J. Block and Gerald Dworkin, eds., *The IQ Controversy*, pp. 85–90. Pantheon Books.

Loehlin, John C., Joseph M. Horn, and Lee Willerman. 1989. "Modeling IQ Change: Evidence from the Texas Adoption Project." *Child Development* 60(4): 993–1004.

Mayer, Susan E. 1997. *What Money Can't Buy: Family Income and Children's Life Chances*. Harvard University Press.

Mercer, Jane R., and Wayne C. Brown. 1973. "Racial Differences in IQ: Fact or Artifact?" In Carl Senna, ed., *The Fallacy of IQ*, pp. 56–113. Third Press.

Oliver, Melvin T., and Thomas M. Shapiro. 1995. *Black Wealth/White Wealth: A New Perspective on Racial Inequality*. Routledge.

Plomin, Robert, and Stephen A. Petrill. 1997. "Genetics and Intelligence: What's New?" *Intelligence* 24(1): 53–77.

Plomin, Robert, J. C. DeFries, and John C. Loehlin. 1977. "Genotype-Environment Correlation in the Analysis of Human Behavior." *Psychological Bulletin* 84(2): 309–22.

Phillips, Meredith. 1997. "Does School Segregation Explain Why African Americans and Latinos Score Lower than Whites on Academic Achievement Tests?" Paper prepared for the annual meeting of the American Sociological Association.

Quay, Lorene C. 1974. "Language Dialect, Age, and Intelligence-Test Performance in Disadvantaged Black Children." *Child Development* 45(2): 463–68.

———. 1972. "Negro Dialect and Binet Performance in Severely Disadvantaged Black Four-Year-Olds." *Child Development* 43(1): 245–50.

———. 1971. "Language, Dialect, Reinforcement, and the Intelligence Test performance of Negro Children." *Child Development* 42(1): 5–15.

Rowe, David C., Alexander T. Vazsonyi, and Daniel D. Flannery. 1994. "No More Than Skin Deep: Ethnic and Racial Similarity in Developmental Process." *Psychological Review* 101(3): 396–413.

Scarr, Sandra. 1993. "Biological and Cultural Diversity: The Legacy of Darwin for Development." *Child Development* 64(5): 1333–53,

———. 1992. "Developmental Theories for the 1990s: Development and Individual Differences." *Child Development* 63(1): 1–19.

Scarr, Sandra, and Richard A. Weinberg. 1978. "The Influence of 'Family Background' on Intellectual Attainment." *American Sociological Review* 43(5): 674–92.

———. 1976. "IQ Test Performance of Black Children Adopted by White Families." *American Psychologist* 31(10): 726–39.

Schofield, Janet W. 1995. "Review of Research on School Desegregation's Impact on Elementary and Secondary School Students." In James A. Banks and C. A. McGee Banks, eds., *Handbook of Research on Multicultural Education*, pp. 597–616. Macmillan.

Spiker, Donna, and others. 1991. "Design Issues in a Randomized Clinical Trial of a Behavioral Intervention: Insights from the Infant Health and Development Program." *Journal of Developmental Behavioral Pediatrics* 12(6): 386–93.

Stevens, Gillian, and David L. Featherman. 1981. "A Revised Socioeconomic Index of Occupational Status." *Social Science Research* 10: 364–95.

Warren, John Robert, and Robert Hauser. 1997. "Social Stratification across Three Generations: New Evidence from the Wisconsin Longitudinal Study." *American Sociological Review* 62(4): 561–72.

Wechsler, D. 1989. *Wechsler Preschool and Primary Scale of Intelligence.* San Antonio: Psychological Corp.

Wells, Amy Stuart, and Robert L. Crain. 1994. "Perpetuation Theory and the Long-Term Effects of School Desegregation." *Review of Educational Research* 64(4): 531–55.

Winship, Christopher, and Sanders Korenman. 1997. "Does Staying in School Make You Smarter? The Effect of Education on IQ in *The Bell Curve.*" In Bernie Devlin and others, eds., *Intelligence, Genes, and Success,* pp. 215–34. Copernicus.

PART II

How and Why
the Gap Has Changed

LARRY V. HEDGES
AMY NOWELL

5

Black-White Test
Score Convergence
since 1965

U NTIL THE 1960s, studies of black-white differences in test performance relied on samples of convenience rather than widely representative samples, making the study of
trends almost impossible. The 1965 Equality of Educational Opportunity
(EEO:65) survey was the first to both measure the performance of a national sample of students and include a measure of race. Since then, such
surveys have become quite common. This chapter uses all available nationally representative samples to describe changes since 1965 in the average
test performances of black and white seventeen-year-olds and in the relative proportions of blacks and whites with very high and very low scores.

History

Many scholars have reviewed the evidence on black-white differences
in cognitive skills, and they report substantial disparity.[1] Unfortunately,
most of the studies reviewed use convenience samples that cannot be gen-

---

1. See, for example, Woodworth (1916); Garth (1925); Klineberg (1944); Dreger and Miller (1960,
1968); Kennedy, Van de Riet, and White (1963); Shuey (1966); Osborne and McGurk (1982).

eralized to the nation as a whole. Even sophisticated reviewers have not always come to grips with the sample problem. For example, Arthur Jensen, a leading advocate of the measurement of black-white differences in test scores, identifies two studies as providing the best available evidence on the distribution of scores in the black population. One of the two is restricted to schoolchildren in five southeastern states, and the other is based on data from job applicants at firms that use a specific test for screening prospective employees.[2] Neither is representative of the U.S. population.

However, studies that have used nationally representative data to describe black-white test score differences have also found large gaps favoring whites. At the same time, the National Assessment of Educational Progress (NAEP) suggests that the gap has narrowed since the 1970s.[3]

David Grissmer and colleagues have recently tried to assess whether changes in social class and family structure can explain the decline in the black-white test score gap.[4] They use the National Education Longitudinal Study of 1988 (NELS:88) and the National Longitudinal Survey of Youth (NLSY:80) to describe how students' social class (as defined by parents' educational attainment and family income) and family structure (that is, number of siblings, household composition, and mothers' work status) relate to their achievement in eighth grade and between the ages of fifteen and eighteen. They then use historical data from the Current Population Survey (CPS) of the Bureau of Labor Statistics to estimate changes in these measures of social class and family structure among blacks and whites between 1970 and 1988–92. They show that if all else had remained equal, both black and white academic achievement should have risen over the twenty-year period (1971–90) for which the National Assessment of Educational Progress survey had collected data. Comparing actual changes in achievement to those predicted by changes in social class and family structure, Grissmer and colleagues find that the achievement of black students increased substantially more than predicted, whereas the achievement of white students increased less than predicted. They attribute the difference between actual and predicted trends to educational policies that have especially helped blacks.

---

2. See Jensen (1980). The studies are Kennedy, Van de Reit and White (1963) and Wonderlic and Wonderlic (1972), respectively.

3. Examples of nationally representative studies are Coleman and others (1966); Osborne (1982); Bock and Moore (1986); and Herrnstein and Murray (1994). For the NAEP, see Mullis and others (1994).

4. Grissmer and others (1994).

While the analysis of Grissmer and colleagues is useful, it has several limitations. First, they estimate the effects of social class and family structure at only one point in time and then assume that these effects remain constant over the entire twenty-year period. Second, they assume that the effects of family characteristics on achievement are the same in the NLSY:80, the NELS:88, and the NAEP. Third, and more fundamental, they attribute all unexplained changes in the black-white gap to educational policies. If unmeasured changes in family structure, social class, the structure of economic opportunity, or cultural norms have also played a part in narrowing the black-white gap, then the role of educational policy may be overstated.

Data

We analyze data from six large surveys conducted between 1965 and 1992, all of which attempted to test nationally representative samples of high school seniors. The tests used in these surveys are described in appendix A.

The Equality of Educational Opportunity survey collected data on public school students enrolled in grades 1, 3, 6, 9, and 12 in the spring of 1965. We use only the twelfth grade sample: a total of 97,660 seniors completed the 169 minute ability test battery.[5]

The National Longitudinal Study of the High School Class of 1972 (NLS:72) surveyed a national probability sample of seniors at public and private high schools in spring 1972. A total of 16,860 students completed a 69 minute test battery measuring both verbal and nonverbal skills.[6]

High School and Beyond (HSB:80, HSB:82) surveyed tenth and twelfth grade students in public and private high schools in spring 1980, and resurveyed the tenth graders as twelfth graders in 1982. We use test scores from seniors in 1980 and 1982. To maintain comparability with our other samples, we limit the 1982 sample to students still enrolled in school. In the 1980 survey, 25,068 seniors completed a 68 minute test battery very similar to that used in the NLS:72. In the 1982 survey, 23,246 seniors completed a test battery of the same length, but with somewhat different content.

5. Coleman and others (1966).
6. Rock and others (1985).

The National Longitudinal Surveys of Youth of 1980 includes three independent probability samples: a cross-section of noninstitutional civilian youth aged between fourteen and twenty-two on January 1, 1979; a supplemental oversample of civilian Hispanic, black, and poor white youth in the same age range; and a sample of youth aged between seventeen and twenty-one as of January 1, 1979, who had been serving in the military as of September 30, 1978. Over 90 percent of the 11,914 individuals sampled completed Form 8A of the Armed Services Vocational Apptitude Battery (designed to select and sort new recruits into appropriate training programs and jobs) in spring or summer 1980.[7] To maintain comparability with our other samples, we use only the scores of the 1,184 NLSY twelfth graders who completed the test.

The National Education Longitudinal Study of 1988 is a national probability sample of 24,599 students enrolled in eighth grade in 1988. The same students were resurveyed in 1990 and 1992. We analyze data from the 16,114 twelfth graders who completed the 85 minute test battery in the 1992 followup (NELS:92).

The National Assessment of Educational Progress program was established in 1969 to monitor the academic achievement of nine-, thirteen-, and seventeen-year-olds currently enrolled in school. The NAEP periodically tests national probability samples of 70,000 to 100,000 students in reading, mathematics, science, and writing. We analyze statistics computed from the NAEP trend samples, which are asked exactly the same questions under the same procedures year after year.[8] During the 1970s and early 1980s, these trend samples ranged from 31,000 to 8,000 students; however, since the mid-1980s, they have covered only from 5,500 to 3,600 students, so the reported black-white gaps have much larger sampling errors.

Analysis

We estimate the national mean and standard deviation of each test in each survey separately for blacks and whites. The variance ratio is the square of the standard deviation of blacks divided by that of whites. We compute

7. See Bock and Moore (1986).
8. See Mullis and others (1994).

effect sizes (*d*) by subtracting the estimated national mean for whites from that for blacks, and then dividing by the estimated standard deviation for the entire population (including members of other races). A negative *d* implies that blacks score lower than whites, whereas a positive *d* implies that blacks score higher.

We also estimate for each test and survey the number or proportion of blacks and whites who score in the upper 5, 10, 25, and 50 percent and the bottom 5, 10, and 25 percent. We then compare the estimated proportion of blacks in each group to the estimated proportion of whites in each group. Because test scores are discrete, one cannot always make this calculation. For example, if two wrong items correspond to the ninety-sixth percentile and three wrong items correspond to the ninety-third percentile, one cannot say how many blacks or whites score above the ninety-fifth percentile. Such cases are noted in the tables. We combine results from different surveys using standard meta-analytic methods.[9]

The results of our analysis follow.

Group Differences in Central Tendency

Test score data can be summarized by using a composite score. To do so, we add vocabulary, reading, and mathematics test scores. Table 5-1 shows the standardized mean difference (*d*) between blacks and whites on this composite score in the following surveys: Equality of Educational Opportunity, 1965; National Longitudinal Study of the High School Class of 1972; High School and Beyond, 1980 and 1982; National Longitudinal Surveys of Youth, 1980; and National Education Longitudinal Study, 1992. Since the white mean is higher than the black mean, all these effect sizes are negative. They are also all large, ranging from 0.82 to 1.18 standard deviations. With the exception of the NLSY:80, the differences decrease between 1965 and 1992. This decrease averages 0.13 standard deviations per decade, which is statistically significant ($p < 0.05$), but still small relative to the initial difference of 1.18 standard deviations.

---

9. See Hedges (1992). We use fixed effects models to correct differences between surveys whenever our statistical tests indicate that this is necessary. Fixed effects models seem particularly appropriate in this context (unless they are explicitly rejected), since the large sample sizes produce specification tests with considerable power.

Table 5-1. *Black-White Differences in Composite Test Scores*[a]

Study	Effect size[b]	Variance ratio[c]
EEO:65	−1.18	0.93
	(0.020)	(0.029)
NLS:72	−1.12	0.73
	(0.028)	(0.031)
HSB:80	−0.94	0.72
	(0.053)	(0.056)
NLSY:80	−1.15	0.79
	(0.138)	(0.161)
HSB:82	−0.95	0.70
	(0.068)	(0.071)
NELS:92	−0.82	0.84
	(0.107)	(0.131)

Source: Authors' calculations based on data from on-line publicly available data bases.

a. Standard errors are in parentheses.

b. Standardized mean difference (*d*). Since standard errors are multiplied by the study design effect, studies of similar size may have standard errors of different magnitudes.

c. Square of the ratio of the standard deviation for blacks to the standard deviation for whites.

Appendix table 5B-1 shows analogous results for specific tests. The effect sizes for these measures are generally smaller than those for the composites. This is to be expected since the components of the composites are positively correlated. However, there is considerable variation in the racial gap both across tests and over time. The gap in science achievement is about 1.0 standard deviation, for example, compared to approximately 0.64 standard deviations in social science. With the exception of social science achievement and associative memory, these differences are all large.

The racial gap appears to be getting slightly smaller over time for each measure except social science achievement. This narrowing is most evident in comparisons of abilities that have been measured in each survey over the full range of years. The NLSY:80 shows a larger racial gap than one would expect from the other surveys. The decrease per decade is large and statistically significant for reading comprehension ($b = 0.12$, $p < .001$) and approaches significance for mathematics ($b = 0.06$, $p = 0.058$). The gap does not narrow significantly for vocabulary, science, or perceptual speed.

The National Assessment of Educational Progress trend studies, which use exactly the same tests and sampling procedures each time, provide even better evidence about trends over time, but one cannot construct composite scores from these data. Table 5-2 shows NAEP trend data on reading, mathematics, science, and writing achievement for seventeen-year-olds. The racial gaps in reading, mathematics, and science appear to be somewhat larger in the NAEP than in the other surveys. This is because the NAEP standard deviations have been corrected for measurement error, making them smaller. When the standard deviations in the other surveys are similarly corrected for measurement error, the racial gaps are very close to those obtained with the NAEP.[10]

The racial gap narrows for all tests administered as part of NAEP during the 1980s. After 1988 or 1990, it widens again in science and mathematics. Nevertheless, differences in all areas were smaller in 1994 than in 1971. There is a significant decrease per decade in the gaps for both reading ($b = 0.26$, $p < 0.05$) and science ($b = 0.15$, $p < 0.05$). If these rates of change were to persist, the gap in reading would completely disappear in approximately twenty-five years, and that in science in approximately seventy years. Neither the gap in mathematics nor that in writing shows a significant narrowing over the years. In fact, from 1990 the gap in mathematics appears to be increasing, although the trend coefficient computed for 1990, 1992, and 1994 is not significant.

Group Differences in Variance

The variance ratios presented in table 5-1 show that the composite test scores of blacks vary less than those of whites in surveys other than the NAEP. Table 5B-1 indicates that this is also true for most of the specific tests. The major exception is perceptual speed, where blacks have more variable scores than whites. In the NAEP, the variances for blacks are of the same magnitude as those for whites, but this may be an artifact of the derivation of the statistics from this survey.[11] The linear time trend in variance ratios is not statistically significant for any of the outcomes, either in the NAEP or in tests from the other surveys.

---

10. See Hedges (1981).

11. In the conditioning model for imputations in NAEP, so-called plausible values for test scores are obtained by sampling from a posterior distribution. However, the prior distribution used to obtain this posterior (which is conditional on certain student background variables, including race) is constrained to have the same variance for all individuals, which may make the variances of different groups more similar.

Table 5-2. *Black-White Differences among Seventeen-Year-Olds in NAEP Trend Sample Scores, 1971–94*[a]

	Effect size				Variance ratio			
Year	*Reading*	*Mathematics*	*Science*	*Writing*[b]	*Reading*	*Mathematics*	*Science*	*Writing*[b]
1971	-1.15 (0.045)	...	...	...	1.05 (0.020)	...	...	...
1975	-1.19 (0.050)	...	...	...	1.21 (0.035)	...	...	...
1977	...	...	-1.28 (0.038)	...	...	...	1.06 (0.024)	...
1978	...	-1.07 (0.046)	...	...	...	0.97 (0.031)	...	...
1980	-1.19 (0.051)	...	...	...	1.09 (0.035)	...	...	...
1982	...	-0.98 (0.048)	-1.25 (0.046)	...	...	0.92 (0.025)	1.01 (0.034)	...
1984	-0.79 (0.038)	...	...	-0.83 (0.133)	0.94 (0.022)	...	...	1.08 (0.095)

1986	...	-0.93 (0.076)	-1.01 (0.079)	...	...	0.82 (0.046)	0.99 (0.059)	...
1988	-0.55 (0.073)	...	...	-0.75 (0.118)	0.99 (0.042)	...	...	0.98 (0.070)
1990	-0.72 (0.064)	-0.68 (0.096)	-1.04 (0.101)	-0.67 (0.074)	0.98 (0.057)	0.89 (0.057)	1.18 (0.066)	0.95 (0.044)
1992	-0.86 (0.060)	-0.87 (0.079)	-1.07 (0.080)	-0.97 (0.039)	1.12 (0.048)	0.94 (0.047)	0.94 (0.039)	0.95 (0.054)
1994	-0.66 (0.095)	-0.89 (0.072)	-1.08 (0.080)	-0.68 (0.070)	0.98 (0.039)	1.12 (0.050)	0.97 (0.046)	1.01 (0.048)
Trend 1971–94	0.026* (0.009)	0.015 (0.006)	0.015* (0.004)	0.002 (0.023)	-0.005 (0.004)	0.005 (0.007)	-0.003 (0.006)	-0.003 (0.008)

Source: Authors' calculations based on data published in Mullis (1994). Data for 1994 provided by the National Center for Education Statistics. Asterisk denotes statistically significant at or below the 0.05 level.

a. Standard deviations are corrected for measurement error. Standard errors are in parentheses.

b. Trend samples for writing are measured for grade 11 rather than for seventeen-year-olds.

Group Differences in Very High and Very Low Scores

The racial mix of students at the top and bottom of the national distribution of test scores is often even more politically important than differences between the means of the distributions for blacks and for whites. Table 5-3 compares the proportions of the black population and white population that score above and below various cutoff points in the national distributions of all the surveys except the NAEP. A ratio larger than one indicates that blacks are overrepresented. A ratio smaller than one indicates that blacks are underrepresented. Blacks are almost always overrepresented in the bottom tail of the composite test score distribution and underrepresented in the upper tail. Because there is less variance in the black distribution than in the white distribution, black underrepresentation in the upper tail is somewhat more extreme than black overrepresentation in the lower tail. The proportion of blacks who score in the lowest 5 percent of the distribution is four to eight times the proportion of whites who score in that tail, but the proportion of whites who score in the upper 5 percent is ten to twenty times the proportion of blacks.

Table 5-3. *Black-White Proportion Ratios in Composite Test Scores*[a]

Study	Ratio of proportions of blacks to whites						
	Below 5th percentile	Below 10th percentile	Below 25th percentile	Above 50th percentile	Above 75th percentile	Above 90th percentile	Above 95th percentile
EEO:65	14.16	10.20	5.33	0.240	0.120	0.069	0.051
	(2.197)	(0.843)	(0.209)	(0.011)	(0.011)	(0.013)	(0.016)
NLS:72	7.78	6.10	3.54	0.233	0.092	0.066	0.061
	(0.692)	(0.358)	(0.111)	(0.017)	(0.015)	(0.021)	(0.029)
HSB:80	5.87	4.96	3.16	0.314	0.200	0.132	0.120
	(1.014)	(0.572)	(0.196)	(0.035)	(0.041)	(0.054)	(0.073)
NLSY:80	7.07	7.56	3.82	0.236	0.120	0.064	0.050
	(4.243)	(3.238)	(0.823)	(0.070)	(0.071)	(0.081)	(0.099)
HSB:82	6.57	5.58	3.32	0.314	0.177	0.118	0.095
	(1.695)	(0.940)	(0.298)	(0.044)	(0.049)	(0.064)	(0.081)
NELS:92	4.12	3.45	2.63	0.399	0.221	0.154	0.104
	(1.386)	(0.801)	(0.338)	(0.077)	(0.087)	(0.118)	(0.138)

Source: Authors' calculations based on data from sources for table 5-1.

a. Ratio of the proportion of blacks scoring above or below a given percentile to the corresponding proportion of whites. Standard errors are in parentheses. Since standard errors are multiplied by the study design effect, studies of similar size may have standard errors of different magnitudes.

Racial disparities have diminished over time in the lower tail, but not in the upper tail. In the lowest tenth of the distribution, for example, black overrepresentation has decreased significantly over time ($p < 0.01$). In the top tenth of the distribution, however, black underrepresentation has not changed significantly. Appendix table 5B-2 shows that this pattern also holds for specific tests in these surveys. Changes over time in the racial composition of the bottom tenth are statistically significant for reading comprehension ($p < 0.05$), science ($p < 0.01$), and perceptual speed ($p < 0.025$), but not for mathematics. In general, changes over time for the top tenth are not significant.

Why Is There No Change at the Top?

If the shapes of the black and white distributions were the same, and only the means of the two distributions differed, the gap between blacks and whites at, say, the tenth or ninetieth percentile of their respective distributions would be the same as the gap between the means. If the black variance were smaller than the white variance, but the shape of the two distributions were the same in other respects, the differences between corresponding percentiles would increase in the top tail of the distribution and decrease in the bottom tail. The first panel of figure 5-1, using the composite score on the 1992 National Education Longitudinal Study, illustrates what one would expect if the racial gap were 0.82 standard deviations and the black variance were 84 percent of the white variance. The graph shows the predicted size of the black-white gap, measured in population standard deviations, at any given percentile of the two distributions.

The second panel of figure 5-1 shows that the actual black-white gaps are not what would be expected from the simple model used to construct the first panel. Group differences in composite scores are smallest at the bottom of the distribution, largest in the middle, and somewhat smaller near the top. The third, fourth, and fifth panels show that this pattern also holds for reading comprehension, mathematics, and science. However, as the sixth panel shows, the pattern is reversed for perceptual speed, with large differences at the bottom and small differences at the top.[12]

---

12. Throughout these figures, the high degree of nonnormality of scores on the High School and Beyond tests is revealed by their somewhat different patterns; the standardized differences at the fiftieth percentiles (medians) are frequently quite different than the corresponding standardized mean differences.

Figure 5-1. *Standardized Percentile Differences for Various Tests and Samples*

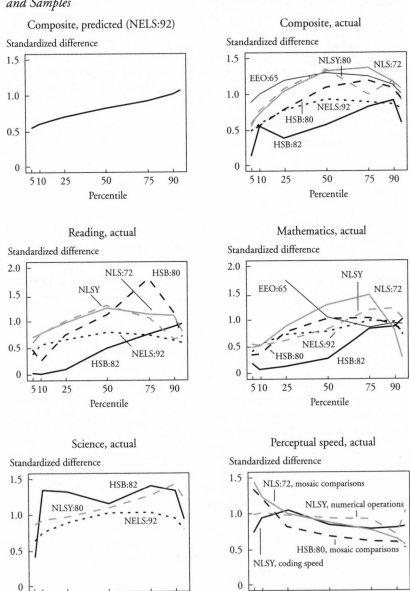

Source: Authors' calculations based on data from sources for table 5-1.

For the NAEP, the best way to investigate changes over time in the shapes of the black and white distributions is to look at changes in the scores of blacks and whites at different points in their respective distributions. The first two panels of figure 5-2 depict the standardized change since 1971 in reading percentiles for whites and blacks, respectively.[13] There was relatively little change at any point on the black distribution between 1971 and 1975. From 1980 to 1988 there was a substantial increase at all points on the black distribution, with much greater change in the lower percentiles. Increases for whites were more modest. The third and fourth panels of figure 5-2 show a similar pattern of increases in mathematics scores for blacks and whites at selected percentiles, and the fifth and sixth panels show increases in science scores. Unfortunately, for mathematics and science the trend data are not available until 1977–78.

The Effects of Social Class on Group Differences

The relationship between test scores and socioeconomic status is one of the most widely replicated findings in the social sciences.[14] All the surveys that we consider try to measure parental socioeconomic status, but they seldom do so in the same way. We use students' reports of their mothers' and fathers' education and their family income as proxies for socioeconomic status because this information is available in the same form in each survey. Table 5-4 shows that controlling these three standard proxies reduces the racial gap on our composite scores by approximately 0.3 standard deviations. The exception is the National Longitudinal Study of the High School Class of 1972, where the composite difference is reduced by 0.46 standard deviations. The coefficients for the social class measures themselves show no substantial trends across years (see appendix table 5B-3). The trend in the racial gap on the composite score is 0.13 standard deviations per decade ($p < 0.05$), and it is virtually the same in the uncontrolled and controlled scores. Likewise, after adjusting for socioeconomic status the trends in reading ($b = 0.11$) and mathematics ($b = 0.08$) gaps remain virtually the same as those in the unadjusted scores, although the trends are not statistically significant once one imposes this control. Therefore our

13. To provide changes over time in comparable units, the differences are divided by the average standard deviation for the appropriate group taken over all years of data presented in the graphs.

14. See, for example, Neff (1938); White (1982).

Figure 5-2. *Standardized Gain since 1971 for NAEP Tests, by Race*

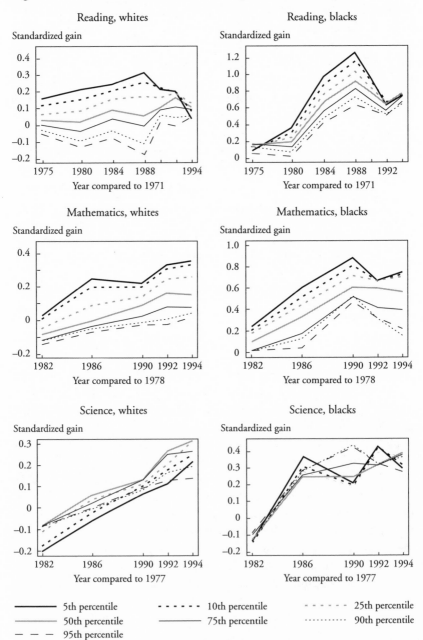

Source: Authors' calculations based on data in Mullis (1994). Data for 1994 provided by the National Center for Education Statistics.

Table 5-4. *Socioeconomic Status and Black-White Differences in Cognitive Test Scores*[a]

Test and study	Unadjusted effect size	Adjusted effect size
Composite		
EEO:65	–1.18	–0.89
	(0.019)	(0.020)
NLS:72	–1.12	–0.66
	(0.032)	(0.030)
HSB:80	–0.94	–0.67
	(0.055)	(0.053)
NLSY:80	–1.15	–0.81
	(0.165)	(0.165)
HSB:82	–0.95	–0.64
	(0.066)	(0.061)
NELS:92	–0.82	–0.65
	(0.095)	(0.090)
Reading		
EEO:65	–1.00	–0.74
	(0.020)	(0.022)
NLS:72	–0.94	–0.54
	(0.032)	(0.031)
HSB:80	–0.81	–0.59
	(0.054)	(0.054)
NLSY:80	–0.96	–0.70
	(0.170)	(0.177)
HSB:82	–0.78	–0.52
	(0.065)	(0.065)
NELS:92	–0.70	–0.53
	(0.096)	(0.093)
Vocabulary		
EEO:65	–1.13	–0.83
	(0.019)	(0.020)
NLS:72	–0.94	–0.55
	(0.032)	(0.032)
HSB:80	–0.83	–0.59
	(0.055)	(0.053)
NLSY:80	–1.14	–0.84
	(0.165)	(0.168)

Table 5-4 *(continued)*

Test and study	Unadjusted effect size	Adjusted effect size
HSB:82	–0.97	–0.66
	(0.064)	(0.060)
Mathematics		
EEO:65	–0.99	–0.79
	(0.020)	(0.022)
NLS:72	–1.02	–0.62
	(0.032)	(0.031)
HSB:80	–0.85	–0.61
	(0.056)	(0.054)
NLSY:80		
Mathematics knowledge	–0.83	–0.48
	(0.172)	(0.170)
Arithmetic reasoning	–1.06	–0.83
	(0.168)	(0.176)
HSB:82	–0.85	–0.57
	(0.067)	(0.063)
NELS:92	–0.82	–0.61
	(0.095)	(0.090)
Perceptual speed		
NLS:72	–0.91	–0.69
	(0.033)	(0.034)
NLSY:80		
Numerical operations	–0.92	–0.70
	(0.171)	(0.182)
Coding speed	–0.79	–0.65
	(0.174)	(0.187)
HSB:80	–0.74	–0.63
	(0.058)	(0.060)
Science		
NLSY:80	–1.03	–0.70
	(0.169)	(0.169)
HSB:82	–1.04	–0.80
	(0.064)	(0.063)
NELS:92	–0.97	–0.79
	(0.094)	(0.091)

Table 5-4 *(continued)*

Test and study	Unadjusted effect size	Adjusted effect size
Associative memory		
NLS:72	–0.67	–0.47
	(0.033)	(0.035)
HSB:80	–0.32	–0.22
	(0.058)	(0.060)
Nonverbal reasoning		
EEO:65	–1.09	–0.82
	(0.020)	(0.021)
NLS:72	–0.99	–0.62
	(0.032)	(0.032)
Vocational information		
NLSY:80		
Auto and shop information	–1.04	–0.91
	(0.168)	(0.181)
Electronics information	–0.99	–0.76
	(0.169)	(0.179)
Mechanical comprehension	–1.04	–0.85
	(0.170)	(0.180)
Spatial ability		
HSB:80	–0.70	–0.60
	(0.058)	(0.059)
Social sciences		
HSB:82	–0.60	–0.40
	(0.068)	(0.068)
NELS:92	–0.67	–0.47
	(0.097)	(0.093)
General information		
EEO:65	–1.14	–0.85
	(0.019)	(0.020)
Writing		
HSB:82	–0.82	–0.61
	(0.066)	(0.064)

Source: Authors' calculations based on data from sources for table 5-1.

a. Socioeconomic status is measured in terms of mother's education, father's education, and family income; except for the EEO:65, where income is proxied by possessions in the home (see discussion in text). Standard errors are in parentheses. Since standard errors are multiplied by the study design effect, studies of similar size may have standard errors of different magnitudes.

analysis, like those of Grissmer and colleagues, suggests that convergence in parental education and income between 1965 and 1994 does not account for the convergence in the test performances of black and white twelfth graders.[15]

We also compute the trend coefficients separately for the periods 1965–72 and 1972–92 in the composite, reading, mathematics, and vocabulary scores. We find that once socioeconomic status is controlled, the black-white gap narrows significantly for the composite (b = 0.33, p < 0.001), reading (b = 0.29, p < 0.001), mathematics (b = 0.24, p < 0.001), and vocabulary (b = 0.40, p < 0.001) from 1965 to 1972. However, in the later period the trends in the gap are small and statistically insignificant for all the tests.

While it is tempting to conclude that the trend changed around 1972, the results of both the Equality of Educational Opportunity survey and the National Longitudinal Study of the High School Class of 1972 are somewhat puzzling. Controlling for socioeconomic status reduces the black-white gap in the NLS:72 more than in any other survey. By contrast, controlling for socioeconomic status in the EEO:65 reduces the black-white gap less than in any other survey. It is possible that the effects of socioeconomic status are underestimated in the EEO:65 because it is the one survey that does not provide a direct measure of family income.[16] If adjusting for socioeconomic status had reduced the gap in the EEO:65 as much as it did in the NLS:72, the trends in the adjusted racial gaps would have been much smaller for the composite and for reading, and essentially zero for mathematics.

Conversely, it is also possible that the adjustment for socioeconomic status in the EEO:65 is appropriate but that the adjustment in the NLS:72 is too large. The only argument we can advance in favor of this hypothesis is the size of the adjustment in the NLS:72. However, there are reasons to believe that such an adjustment should be larger for 1972 (and probably also for 1965) than for later years. School policies and programs dating from this era were designed to promote the achievement of disadvantaged children and thus reduce the effects of socioeconomic status on achieve-

15. See Grissmer and others (1994); also, chapter 6 below.
16. We use a measure of possessions in the home as a proxy for income in the EEO:65 analyses. The NLS:72 includes both family income or possessions in the home, and controlling either reduces the black-white gap by the same amount. Unfortunately, there is no way to be sure that this would have been true of the EEO:65.

ment. Hence adjustments for socioeconomic status should have been smaller in studies conducted after these measures had begun to take effect.

Conclusions and Discussion

Our review includes every major national survey of high school students since 1965 that has tested both blacks and whites. The data provide convincing evidence that racial differences have decreased over time. They also suggest that socioeconomic convergence cannot entirely explain black-white test score convergence. The decreases in both the unadjusted black-white gaps and those adjusted for socioeconomic status follow a similar trajectory, with one exception: the decrease in the adjusted gap was substantially larger over the period 1965–72 than in later years, although this change may be overestimated. Nonetheless, blacks' expectations grew dramatically during this period and it is possible that achievement rose because black students viewed success in school as a possible way to fulfill these increased expectations.

Blacks are hugely underrepresented in the upper tails of the achievement distributions, and this underrepresentation does not seem to be decreasing. If very high scores are needed to excel in a field, or if gatekeepers believe that this is so, the fact that whites are ten to twenty times more likely to have high scores makes it almost impossible for blacks to be well represented in high-ranking positions. This underrepresentation seems to hold for all types of tests: the consequences are not limited to scientific or technical fields.

Although our discussion has emphasized academic tests, the same patterns hold for vocational tests. Military research has found these scales to have substantial predictive validity for many blue-collar occupations. Although these are sometimes described as occupations in which blacks should be better represented, half of all young blacks scored below the twentieth percentile on all three of the 1980 National Longitudinal Surveys of Youth vocational information tests.

These data cannot identify which policies might further reduce group differences in test performance. The finding that parental education and income have played such a role in the past does, however, suggest that further reducing differences in socioeconomic status between blacks and whites might narrow the gap in test performance still more. At the same time, it is important to consider educational policies that would make children's test scores less dependent on their parents' education and income.

Appendix A: Test Content of Surveys Used

This appendix provides information about the content of the tests in the surveys that we analyze.

Equality of Educational Opportunity

Reading Read passages of prose and poetry about a wide variety of topics and answer questions that require interpretation and inference.

Verbal ability Choose synonyms and correct words to complete sentences.

Mathematics Demonstrate understanding of mathematical concepts and ability to compute.

General information Demonstrate knowledge of natural sciences, humanities, social science, and practical arts. Focus is on knowledge obtained out of school.

Nonverbal reasoning Determine which of six figures is different, and generalize relationship between two figures to a different set of figures.

Composite Reading + vocabulary + mathematics.

National Longitudinal Study of the High School Class of 1972

Vocabulary Choose correct synonyms for moderately difficult words.

Reading Read five short passages and answer questions requiring comprehension, analysis, or interpretation.

Mathematics Indicate whether two quantities are equal, one is greater than the other, or their relationship cannot be determined based on the available information. Test does not require specific algebraic, geometric, or trigonometric skills.

Letter groups Use inductive reasoning to identify which of several groups of letters share a common characteristic.

Picture number Study drawings of objects paired with numbers, and then try to recall the number associated with each type of object.

Mosaic Use perceptual skills involving both speed and accuracy to detect small differences between otherwise identical tile-like patterns.

Composite Reading + vocabulary + mathematics.

High School and Beyond, 1980

Tests are similar (92 percent of items identical) to those for the NLS:72, but letter groups is replaced by visualization in three dimensions.

Visualization Indicate what a figure would look like if it were manipulated in three-dimensional space.

Composite Reading + vocabulary + mathematics.

High School and Beyond, 1982

Vocabulary, reading, and mathematics tests are similar but not identical to those for the NLS:72. None of the other tests from the NLS:72 or the HSB:80 batteries are included. Instead, tests on science, writing, and civics are added.

Science Answer questions about general science, biology, chemistry, physics, and scientific method.

Writing Identify errors in capitalization, punctuation, form, and style.

Civics Answer questions about reading graphs, American history and government, and current issues, requiring inferential reasoning.

Composite Reading + vocabulary + mathematics.

National Longitudinal Surveys of Youth

Arithmetic reasoning Choose the correct mathematical operation to solve problems expressed verbally and then perform the operation. The problems involve addition, subtraction, multiplication, and division using whole numbers and fractions.

Mathematics knowledge Answer questions using knowledge of mathematical terms and concepts, as well as algebra skills. This is the most academic of the tests, since success depends heavily on having taken secondary school mathematics courses.

Word knowledge Choose synonyms for words.

Paragraph comprehension Read brief passages and then answer questions about them. Since the readings contain general information that is not especially unusual or difficult, a well-informed person could answer the questions without having read the passages.

General science Demonstrate familiarity with topics from the physical and biological sciences.

Numerical operations Demonstrate speed at adding, subtracting, multiplication, and division. The scale is created so that few students have time to complete all fifty items.

Coding speed Match words with numbers, based on a key at the beginning of each problem. This test emphasizes quickness and accuracy.

Auto and shop information Demonstrate knowledge about the principles of automobile repair and about metal and wood shop procedures and use of tools.

Mechanical comprehension Demonstrate knowledge about mechanical principles, as well as interpreting and visualizing motion in schematic drawings.

Electronics information Demonstrate practical knowledge of electronics.

Composite Paragraph comprehension + word knowledge + mathematics knowledge + arithmetic reasoning.

National Education Longitudinal Study of the Eighth Grade Class of 1988

Reading Read five short passages and answer questions on comprehension and interpretation.

Mathematics Indicate whether two quantities are equal, one is greater than the other, or their relationship cannot be determined based on the available information, and also demonstrate general mathematics knowledge.

Science Answer questions from the physical and biological sciences that assess scientific knowledge and ability for scientific reasoning.

Social studies Answer questions that assess knowledge of U.S. history, civics, and government.

Composite Reading + mathematics.

National Assessment of Educational Progress

Reading Read passages and then answer questions in multiple-choice format and with short constructed responses.

Mathematics Demonstrate knowledge of numbers and operations, measurement, geometry, statistics, data analysis, and algebra and functions.

Science Answer multiple-choice items on life sciences, physical sciences, and earth and space sciences. Test assesses ability to solve problems, design experiments, and interpret data.

Writing Respond to either two twenty-five minute or one fifty minute writing prompt.

Appendix B: Data

Table 5B-1. *Black-White Differences in Specific Abilities*[a]

Test and study	Effect size[b]	Variance ratio[c]
Reading		
EEO:65	−1.00	1.04
	(0.021)	(0.033)
NLS:72	−0.94	0.88
	(0.028)	(0.037)
HSB:80	−0.81	0.80
	(0.052)	(0.061)
NLSY:80	−0.96	1.17
	(0.144)	(0.238)
HSB:82	−0.78	0.71
	(0.068)	(0.070)
NELS:92	−0.70	0.86
	(0.107)	(0.134)
Vocabulary		
EEO:65	−1.13	0.98
	(0.020)	(0.031)
NLS:72	−0.94	0.63
	(0.029)	(0.026)
HSB:80	−0.83	0.81
	(0.052)	(0.031)
NLSY:80	−1.14	1.14
	(0.144)	(0.232)
HSB:82	−0.97	1.07
	(0.066)	(0.107)
Mathematics		
EEO:65	−0.99	1.07
	(0.021)	(0.034)
NLS:72	−1.02	0.76
	(0.029)	(0.032)
HSB:80	−0.85	0.75
	(0.053)	(0.058)
NLSY:80		
Arithmetic reasoning	−1.06	0.45
	(0.132)	(0.091)
Mathematics knowledge	−0.84	0.62
	(0.137)	(0.125)

Table 5B-1 *(continued)*

Test and study	Effect size[b]	Variance ratio[c]
HSB:82	−0.85	0.62
	(0.069)	(0.063)
NELS:92	−0.82	0.80
	(0.107)	(0.125)
Perceptual speed		
NLS:72	−0.91	1.31
	(0.029)	(0.055)
HSB:80	−0.74	1.40
	(0.054)	(0.111)
NLSY:80		
Numerical operations	−0.92	1.32
	(0.148)	(0.269)
Coding speed	−0.79	0.88
	(0.142)	(0.179)
Science		
NLSY:80	−1.03	0.75
	(0.137)	(0.154)
HSB:82	−1.04	0.93
	(0.067)	(0.094)
NELS:92	−0.97	0.82
	(0.106)	(0.128)
Associative memory		
NLS:72	−0.67	0.97
	(0.029)	(0.041)
HSB:80	−0.32	1.26
	(0.054)	(0.096)
Nonverbal reasoning		
EEO:65	−1.09	1.49
	(0.020)	(0.047)
NLS:72	−0.99	1.40
	(0.028)	(0.059)
Vocational information		
NLSY:80		
Auto and shop information	−1.04	0.67
	(0.135)	(0.136)
Mechanical comprehension	−1.04	0.62
	(0.136)	(0.127)
Electronics information	−0.99	0.76
	(0.138)	(0.154)

Table 5B-1 (continued)

Test and study	Effect size[b]	Variance ratio[c]
Spatial ability		
HSB:80	–0.70	0.71
	(0.054)	(0.055)
Social sciences		
HSB:82	–0.60	1.03
	(0.070)	(0.105)
NELS:92	–0.67	0.86
	(0.108)	(0.134)
General information		
EEO:65	–1.14	0.82
	(0.020)	(0.026)
Writing		
HSB:82	–0.82	1.00
	(0.068)	(0.101)

Source: Authors' calculations based on data from sources for table 5-1.

a. Standard errors are in parentheses.

b. Standardized mean difference (*d*). Since standard errors are multiplied by the study design effect, studies of similar size may have standard errors of different magnitudes.

c. Square of the ratio of the standard deviation for blacks to the standard deviation for whites.

Table 5B-2. Black-White Proportion Ratios in Specific Abilities[a]

Test and study			Ratio of proportions of blacks to whites				
	Below 5th percentile	Below 10th percentile	Below 25th percentile	Below 50th percentile	Below 75th percentile	Below 90th percentile	Below 95th percentile
Reading comprehension							
EEO:65	6.05	5.43	3.87	0.320	0.190	0.133[b]	0.102
	(0.702)	(0.369)	(0.139)	(0.012)	(0.014)	(0.018)	(0.026)
NLS:72	4.87	4.00	3.11	3.510	0.162	0.120	0.126
	(0.045)	(0.233)	(0.105)	(0.244)	(0.020)	(0.025)	(0.035)
HSB:80	3.35	3.18	2.77	0.377[b]	0.255	0.123	0.116
	(0.540)	(0.374)	(0.185)	(0.037)	(0.046)	(0.049)	(0.065)
NLSY:80	4.77	4.18	3.06	0.372	0.252	0.151[b]	· · ·
	(2.702)	(1.633)	(0.649)	(0.087)	(0.106)	(0.126)	
HSB:82	3.10[b]	2.91[b]	2.44[b]	0.439[b]	0.272	0.157[b]	0.151[b]
	(0.695)	(0.442)	(0.211)	(0.047)	(0.053)	(0.065)	(0.081)
NELS:92	3.13	2.90	2.18	0.457	0.268	0.211	0.161
	(1.097)	(0.706)	(0.302)	(0.081)	(0.096)	(0.138)	(0.172)
Vocabulary							
EEO:65	16.82	11.00[b]	5.12	0.270	0.150	0.090	0.069
	(2.983)	(0.934)	(0.195)	(0.011)	(0.013)	(0.016)	(0.020)
NLS:72	5.54[b]	4.41	3.11	0.293	0.160	0.092[b]	0.093[b]
	(0.571)	(0.276)	(0.099)	(0.018)	(0.021)	(0.023)	(0.032)
HSB:80	5.20	3.95	2.90	0.384	0.239	0.175	0.141
	(1.013)	(0.405)	(0.181)	(0.036)	(0.043)	(0.058)	(0.078)

NLSY:80	13.43[b] (9.279)	7.39 (3.166)	3.93 (0.851)	0.264 (0.073)	0.231 (0.100)	0.132[b] (0.110)	0.222 (0.214)
HSB:82	6.25 (1.434)	5.61 (0.937)	3.59 (0.322)	0.376 (0.043)	0.238 (0.055)	0.174 (0.073)	0.120 (0.082)
Mathematics							
EEO:65	...	4.64 (0.272)	2.73 (0.067)	0.430 (0.012)	0.110 (0.011)	0.052 (0.012)	0.045 (0.015)
NLS:72	5.93 (0.532)	4.34 (0.245)	3.18 (0.103)	0.282 (0.018)	0.139 (0.019)	0.073[b] (0.024)	...
HSB:80	5.14 (0.914)	3.68 (0.425)	2.70 (0.174)	0.367 (0.037)	0.214 (0.042)	0.145 (0.054)	0.098 (0.065)
NLSY:80							
Arithmetic reasoning	4.47 (2.559)	5.28 (2.167)	3.68 (0.799)	0.196 (0.063)	0.088 (0.061)	0.027 (0.052)	...
Mathematics knowledge	3.00 (1.671)	2.74 (1.012)	2.62 (0.559)	0.367 (0.085)	0.183 (0.089)	0.089 (0.096)	0.064 (0.108)
HSB:82	3.70 (0.912)	3.38 (0.571)	2.66 (0.223)	0.190 (0.050)	0.190 (0.050)	0.120 (0.062)	0.108 (0.080)
NELS:92	4.48 (1.449)	3.79 (0.855)	2.61 (0.333)	0.401 (0.078)	0.249 (0.093)	0.127 (0.108)	0.064 (0.109)
Perceptual speed							
NLS:72	6.86 (0.583)	5.54 (0.311)	3.05 (0.095)	0.355 (0.020)	0.339 (0.030)	0.397 (0.053)	0.374 (0.073)
HSB:80	4.59 (0.765)	4.03 (0.453)	2.58 (0.165)	0.424 (0.041)	0.371 (0.058)	0.479 (0.109)	0.559 (0.170)

Table 5B-2 (continued)

Test and study	Ratio of proportions of blacks to whites						
	Below 5th percentile	Below 10th percentile	Below 25th percentile	Below 50th percentile	Below 75th percentile	Below 90th percentile	Below 95th percentile
NLSY:80							
Numerical operations	6.31	3.95	2.67	0.369	0.313	0.269[b]	...
	(3.552)	(1.476)	(0.556)	(0.083)	(0.117)	(0.150)	
Coding speed	3.36	2.84	2.19	0.447	0.177	0.113	0.135
	(1.809)	(1.048)	(0.046)	(0.092)	(0.084)	(0.103)	(0.158)
Science							
NLSY:80	13.52	8.40	3.44	0.300	0.157	0.076	0.075
	(10.651)	(3.881)	(0.748)	(0.078)	(0.084)	(0.088)	(0.119)
HSB:82	5.57	5.82	3.50	0.309	0.169	0.135	0.094
	(1.401)	(1.010)	(0.296)	(0.041)	(0.046)	(0.067)	(0.078)
NELS:92	4.84	4.22	3.31	0.306	0.168	0.106	0.057
	(1.605)	(0.956)	(0.398)	(0.070)	(0.076)	(0.097)	(0.101)
Associative memory							
NLS:72	3.72	3.18	2.20	0.516	0.368	0.367	0.325[b]
	(0.339)	(0.196)	(0.080)	(0.024)	(0.031)	(0.050)	(0.061)
HSB:80	2.03	1.85	1.52	0.759	0.791[b]	...	...
	(0.382)	(0.241)	(0.119)	(0.048)	(0.074)		
Nonverbal reasoning							
EEO:65	9.46	7.71	4.34	0.300	0.180	0.116	0.084[b]
	(1.307)	(0.543)	(0.156)	(0.012)	(0.013)	(0.016)	(0.021)
NLS:72	5.83	4.24	2.85	0.328	0.205	0.140	...
	(0.518)	(0.248)	(0.094)	(0.020)	(0.023)	(0.030)	

Vocational information

NLSY:80

Auto and shop information	6.16	5.82	3.61	0.219	0.126	0.193	0.052
	(3.605)	(2.371)	(0.776)	(0.066)	(0.074)	(0.150)	(0.106)
Mechanical comprehension	8.28	5.86	3.55	0.245	0.152	0.073	0.074
	(5.348)	(2.335)	(0.737)	(0.071)	(0.082)	(0.087)	(0.122)
Electronics information	5.59	5.29	3.41	0.281	0.192	0.195	0.173
	(3.262)	(2.103)	(0.747)	(0.075)	(0.091)	(0.150)	(0.200)
Spatial ability							
HSB:80	3.10[b]	3.05[b]	2.16	0.462	0.242	0.191[b]	0.157
	(0.436)	(0.419)	(0.149)	(0.041)	(0.051)	(0.072)	(0.093)
Social sciences							
HSB:82	2.39[b]	2.16[b]	2.06	0.585[b]	0.462	0.366[b]	...
	(0.514)	(0.302)	(0.194)	(0.051)	(0.060)	(0.075)	
NELS:92	2.44	2.54	2.30	0.496	0.308	0.178	0.223
	(0.918)	(0.639)	(0.316)	(0.085)	(0.104)	(0.127)	(0.204)
General information							
EEO:65	12.08	9.54	5.54	0.240	0.110	0.062	0.050
	(1.910)	(0.744)	(0.221)	(0.011)	(0.011)	(0.012)	(0.015)
Writing							
HSB:82	2.97	3.20	2.50	0.362	0.230	0.173	0.050
	(0.817)	(0.512)	(0.226)	(0.047)	(0.051)	(0.056)	(0.015)

Source: Authors' calculations based on data from sources for table 5-1.

a. Ratio of the proportion of blacks scoring above or below a given percentile to the corresponding proportion of whites. Standard errors are in parentheses. Since standard errors are multiplied by the study design effect, studies of similar size may have standard errors of different magnitudes.

b. Percentile cannot be well approximated.

Table 5B-3. Regression Coefficients for Socioeconomic Status and Family Characteristics

Test and study	Family income (× 10,000)	Mother's education			Father's education			Mother working	Number of siblings	Race	Family income	Missing variables[a]			
		Less than high school degree	Some college	College degree	Less than high school degree	Some college	College degree					Mother's education	Father's education	Mother working	Number of siblings
Composite															
EEO:65	0.080	-0.144	0.188	0.195	-0.094	0.151	0.247	-0.011	-0.012	-0.482	-0.353	-0.252	-0.186	0.007	-0.107
NLS:72	0.566	-0.177	0.152	0.162	-0.092	0.169	0.331	0.126	-0.003	0.105	-0.155	-0.428	-0.379	-0.320	-0.251
HSB:80	0.112	-0.182	0.137	0.304	-0.108	0.186	0.442	0.072	-0.034	-0.328	-0.183	-0.324	-0.237	-0.194	-0.151
NLSY:80	0.087	-0.181	0.062	0.319	-0.167	-0.017	0.442	-0.003	-0.057	-0.433	-0.083	-0.154	-0.012	0.116	n.a.
HSB:82	0.072	-0.118	0.108	0.255	-0.122	0.173	0.506	0.060	-0.042	n.a.	-0.424	-0.327	-0.187	-0.039	-0.228
NELS:92	0.028	-0.052	0.202	0.313	-0.208	0.134	0.359	0.138	-0.014	-0.689	-0.237	-0.252	-0.065	0.085	-0.278
Reading															
EEO:65	0.081	-0.098	0.174	0.148	-0.084	0.123	0.191	-0.002	-0.008	-0.377	-0.386	-0.268	-0.137	0.023	-0.138
NLS:72	0.378	-0.131	0.154	0.140	-0.091	0.134	0.275	0.098	-0.008	0.074	-0.118	-0.402	-0.330	-0.310	-0.248
HSB:80	0.065	-0.150	0.124	0.239	-0.077	0.172	0.332	0.070	-0.032	-0.379	-0.185	-0.285	-0.229	-0.168	-0.129
NLSY:80	0.072	-0.187	-0.068	0.081	-0.155	0.003	0.369	0.033	-0.056	-0.197	-0.103	0.093	0.010	0.295	n.a.
HSB:82	0.044	-0.086	0.093	0.239	-0.064	0.163	0.418	0.069	-0.035	n.a.	-0.356	-0.300	-0.170	-0.031	-0.223
NELS:92	0.021	-0.018	0.185	0.280	-0.170	0.146	0.305	0.131	-0.014	-0.737	-0.217	-0.271	-0.035	0.071	-0.290
Vocabulary															
EEO:65	0.083	-0.157	0.213	0.214	-0.110	0.164	0.268	-0.012	-0.018	-0.402	-0.309	-0.267	-0.185	0.096	-0.057
NLS:72	0.575	-0.160	0.148	0.184	-0.085	0.168	0.309	0.131	-0.023	0.155	-0.126	-0.318	-0.282	-0.226	-0.215
HSB:80	0.092	-0.162	0.137	0.322	-0.081	0.176	0.397	0.065	-0.044	-0.260	-0.153	-0.301	-0.187	-0.152	-0.111
NLSY:80	0.066	-0.212	0.002	0.244	-0.143	0.122	0.381	0.022	-0.064	-0.561	-0.031	-0.086	0.023	0.139	n.a.
HSB:82	0.065	-0.146	0.090	0.228	-0.115	0.156	0.434	0.066	-0.054	n.a.	-0.355	-0.308	-0.176	-0.054	-0.264

Mathematics															
EEO:65	0.048	-0.128	0.118	0.159	-0.059	0.115	0.199	-0.014	-0.007	-0.489	-0.241	-0.141	-0.172	-0.087	-0.084
NLS:72	0.529	-0.169	0.109	0.119	-0.070	0.146	0.287	0.107	0.012	0.068	-0.152	-0.386	-0.360	-0.289	-0.202
HSB:80	0.123	-0.174	0.107	0.243	-0.116	0.143	0.413	0.053	-0.017	-0.309	-0.157	-0.276	-0.212	-0.193	-0.154
NLSY:80															
Arithmetic reasoning	0.065	-0.985	0.141	0.447	-0.079	-0.090	0.235	-0.050	-0.034	-0.155	-0.036	-0.304	0.005	-0.086	n.a.
Mathematics knowledge	0.097	-0.140	0.125	0.324	-0.203	-0.081	0.549	-0.017	-0.048	-0.599	-0.117	-0.224	-0.075	0.084	n.a.
HSB:82	0.076	-0.100	0.099	0.239	-0.127	0.150	0.480	0.041	-0.030	n.a.	-0.416	-0.281	-0.166	-0.031	-0.162
NELS:92	0.031	-0.079	0.191	0.303	-0.218	0.101	0.365	0.123	-0.011	-0.529	-0.222	-0.195	-0.086	0.071	-0.224
Perceptual speed															
NLS:72	0.354	-0.047	0.063	0.022	-0.061	0.031	0.030	0.039	0.004	-0.042	-0.018	-0.247	-0.233	-0.126	-0.159
HSB:80	0.079	-0.088	0.035	0.027	-0.048	0.054	0.144	0.067	-0.009	-0.513	-0.025	-0.168	-0.048	-0.082	-0.121
NLSY:80															
Coding speed	0.084	-0.106	-0.080	0.004	-0.118	-0.170	0.196	0.121	-0.013	0.106	-0.133	-0.224	0.022	0.122	n.a.
Numerical operations	0.099	-0.020	0.135	-0.002	-0.201	-0.031	0.250	0.062	-0.037	0.033	0.017	-0.253	-0.053	0.064	n.a.
Science															
NLSY:80	0.065	-0.123	0.031	0.278	-0.106	0.022	0.549	0.028	-0.073	-0.513	-0.153	-0.227	-0.038	-0.009	n.a.
HSB:82	0.050	-0.077	0.082	0.188	-0.112	0.119	0.336	0.083	-0.035	n.a.	-0.352	-0.287	-0.193	-0.043	-0.165
NELS:92	0.019	-0.067	0.197	0.255	-0.211	0.099	0.323	0.070	-0.016	-0.698	-0.212	-0.160	-0.135	0.065	-0.195
Associative memory															
NLS:72	0.108	-0.035	0.047	0.002	-0.040	0.084	0.121	0.048	0.013	-0.126	-0.010	-0.221	-0.245	-0.202	-0.159
HSB:80	0.090	-0.061	0.027	0.024	-0.047	0.011	0.052	0.087	-0.004	-0.218	-0.002	-0.155	-0.064	-0.029	-0.099
Nonverbal reasoning															
EEO:65	0.103	-0.117	0.112	0.101	-0.084	0.102	0.138	0.007	-0.001	-0.357	-0.432	-0.199	-0.138	0.009	-0.235
NLS:72	0.354	-0.101	0.115	0.094	-0.088	0.045	0.121	0.064	0.021	-0.002	-0.021	-0.378	-0.398	-0.299	-0.271

(continues)

Table 5B-3 (continued)

Test and study	Family income (× 10,000)	Mother's education			Father's education			Mother working	Number of siblings	Race	Missing variables[a]				
		Less than high school degree	Some college	College degree	Less than high school degree	Some college	College degree				Family income	Mother's education	Father's education	Mother working	Number of siblings
Vocational information NLSY:80															
Electronics information	0.014	-0.097	0.022	0.185	-0.093	-0.100	0.244	-0.057	-0.071	-0.659	-0.083	-0.069	-0.035	-0.155	n.a.
Mechanical comprehension	-0.023	-0.082	0.040	0.371	-0.111	-0.114	0.199	-0.025	-0.046	-0.331	-0.028	-0.189	-0.128	0.116	n.a.
Auto and shop information	-0.011	-0.176	0.032	0.288	-0.044	-0.086	-0.022	-0.071	-0.045	-0.884	-0.019	-0.264	0.061	-0.107	n.a.
Spatial ability HSB:80	0.034	-0.088	0.069	0.151	-0.071	0.133	0.247	0.042	-0.002	-0.182	-0.064	-0.148	-0.113	-0.097	-0.048
Social sciences															
HSB:82	0.035	-0.051	0.089	0.189	-0.080	0.123	0.314	0.041	-0.027	n.a.	-0.365	-0.322	-0.101	-0.114	-0.219
NELS:92	0.024	-0.045	0.140	0.239	-0.223	0.171	0.357	0.125	-0.015	-0.883	-0.226	-0.236	-0.123	0.197	-0.274
General information EEO:65	0.083	-0.151	0.176	0.199	-0.096	0.143	0.211	-0.018	-0.015	-0.783	-0.368	-0.224	-0.184	-0.119	-0.353
Writing HSB:82	0.017	-0.091	0.111	0.160	-0.068	0.116	0.346	0.064	-0.026	n.a.	-0.440	-0.396	-0.104	-0.137	-0.288

Source: Authors' calculations based on data from sources for table 5-1.
a. "Not applicable" (n.a.) indicates no cases missing.

References

Bock, R. Darell, and Elsie Moore. 1986. *Advantage and Disadvantage: A Profile of American Youth.* Hillsdale, N.J.: Erlbaum.

Coleman, James C., and others. 1966. *Equality of Educational Opportunity.* Government Printing Office.

Dreger, Ralph M., and Kent S. Miller. 1960. "Comparative Studies of Negroes and Whites in the United States." *Psychological Bulletin* 57(September):361–402.

———. 1968. "Comparative Psychological Studies of Negroes and Whites in the United States." *Psychological Bulletin* 70(September):1–58.

Garth, Thomas R. 1925. "A Review of Racial Psychology." *Psychological Bulletin* 22(June): 343–64.

Grissmer, David W., and others. 1994. *Student Achievement and the Changing American Family.* Santa Monica, Calif.: Rand Corporation.

Hedges, Larry V. 1981. "Distribution Theory for Glass's Estimator of Effect Size and Related Estimators." *Journal of Educational Statistics* 6(summer):107–28.

Herrnstein, Richard J., and Charles Murray. 1994. *The Bell Curve: Intelligence and Class Structure in American Life.* Free Press.

Jensen, Arthur R. 1980. *Bias in Mental Testing.* Free Press.

Kennedy, Wallace A., Vernon Van de Reit, and James C. White. 1963. "A Normative Sample of Intelligence and Achievement of Negro Elementary School Children in the Southeastern United States." *Monographs of the Society for Research on Child Development* 28(6).

Klineberg, Otto, ed. 1944. *Characteristics of the American Negro.* Harper and Brothers.

Mullis, Ina V., and others. 1994. *NAEP 1992 Trends in Academic Progress.* Government Printing Office.

Neff, W. S. 1938. "Socioeconomic Status and Intelligence." *Psychological Bulletin* 35(December):727–57.

Osborne, R. Travis. 1982. "National Longitudinal Study of the High School Class of 1972: An Analysis of Sub-Population Differences." In R. T. Osborne and F. C. J. McGurk, *eds., The Testing of Negro Intelligence,* vol. 2. Athens, Ga.: Foundation for Human Understanding.

Osborne, R. Travis, and Frank C. J. McGurk, eds. 1982. *The Testing of Negro Intelligence,* vol. 2. Athens, Ga.: Foundation for Human Understanding.

Rock, Donald A., and others. 1985. *Psychometric Analysis of the NLS and High School and Beyond Test Batteries.* Government Printing Office.

Shuey, Audrey M. 1966. *The Testing of Negro Intelligence,* 2d ed. New York: Social Science Press.

White, Karl R. 1982. "The Relation between Socioeconomic Status and Academic Achievement." *Psychological Bulletin* 91(May):461–81.

Wonderlic, E. F., and Charles F. Wonderlic. 1972. *Wonderlic Personnel Test: Negro Norms.* Northfield, Ill.: E. F. Wonderlic and Associates, Inc.

Woodworth, Robert S. 1916. "Comparative Psychology of the Races." *Psychological Bulletin* 13(October):388–97.

DAVID GRISSMER
ANN FLANAGAN
STEPHANIE WILLIAMSON

6

Why Did the Black-White Score Gap Narrow in the 1970s and 1980s?

T HE National Assessment of Educational Progress (NAEP) shows a significant narrowing of the gap between blacks and non-Hispanic whites on reading and mathematics tests between 1971 and 1996.[1] Because the NAEP sample is designed to be representative of all American students who were nine, thirteen, or seventeen years old in the year of the test, and because NAEP has used similar questions and testing procedures throughout this period, it is the best available source of evidence about changes in the black-white gap.[2] Larry Hedges and Amy Nowell describe some of these changes in chapter 5. This chapter seeks to explain them.

Although the NAEP did not begin collecting data until 1971, the seventeen-year-olds whom it tested in 1971 were born in 1954 and entered

Support for this chapter came from the Center for Research on Educational Diversity and Excellence (CREDE), supported by the U.S. Department of Education, the Danforth Foundation, and RAND.

1. Hereafter we will shorten the term "non-Hispanic white" to "white."

2. The primary purpose of the NAEP data was to measure trends in achievement, not explain the trends. So NAEP data may not be the best to help explain them. Analysis of the data sets used by Larry Hedges and Amy Nowell in chapter 3 combined with NAEP data will eventually be required to reach an explanation. See Campbell and others (1997), Campbell and others (1996), Johnson and Carlson (1994), and Mullis and others (1993) for descriptions of the NAEP data and for further references on test design, administration, and sampling for the National Assessment.

school around 1960. Their scores reflect the cumulative effects of home and community environments dating from the late 1950s and 1960s, combined with school environments throughout the 1960s. Subsequent changes in NAEP scores by racial or ethnic group reflect the effects of changes in young people's home environments, communities, and schools from the 1960s to the 1990s. The changes we consider include the following.

—National efforts to equalize opportunity and reduce poverty that began in the mid-1960s and continued or expanded in subsequent decades. These efforts included federally funded preschools (Head Start), compensatory funding of elementary schools with large numbers of poor students, desegregation of many schools, affirmative action in college and professional school admissions, and expanded social welfare programs for poor families. The seventeen-year-olds whom the NAEP tested in 1971 were largely unaffected by the changes. Those tested in the 1990s have lived their entire lives in families, communities, and schools influenced by these policies. All these policies are likely to have helped blacks more than whites.

—Educational changes that were not primarily intended to equalize opportunity. These included increased early schooling for nonpoor children, greater per pupil expenditures, smaller classes, increases in the proportion of teachers with masters' degrees, and increases in teachers' experience.

—Changes in families and communities that may have been influenced by efforts to equalize opportunity and reduce poverty but occurred mainly for other reasons. Parents had more formal education, more children had only one or two siblings, fewer children lived with both parents, and the proportion of children living in poverty grew. Poor blacks also became concentrated more in inner cities, while more affluent blacks moved to the suburbs.

Disentangling the effects of these changes is an immensely complex task for which no single data set can provide a complete solution. The NAEP, for example, did not collect much data on children's home environment, their communities, or even their schools.[3] To explain changes in NAEP scores, therefore, we need to combine NAEP data on test scores by

3. Race and parental education are the only family measures available in all years The parent education measures are reported by students and have high levels of missing data for younger students. For students of all ages the missing parent education data are more frequent for lower-scoring students and the reported parental education levels are much higher than reported by similarly aged adults. See for instance, Swinton (1993) and Berends and Koretz (1996).

race, region, age, and year with information about students and schools from other sources. We also need to rely on other data sources to determine which of these changes might actually affect NAEP scores.

Unfortunately, previous research provides less guidance than one might expect about the effects of changes in families, schools, and social policy. Scholars disagree about the impact of the War on Poverty and expanded social welfare programs and about the way communities have changed for black families.[4] Scholars also disagree about the size of the effects of school desegregation on minority children, whether increased school resources have improved achievement, how large the effects from attending kindergarten and preschool are, and how long these effects last.[5] There is even disagreement about whether the net effect on children of recent changes in the family has been beneficial or detrimental.[6]

The NAEP may contribute to resolving some of these controversies because it measures the performance of birth cohorts born before, during, and after most of the changes we have mentioned. In addition the NAEP measures each cohort's performance at three widely separated ages so it can help researchers distinguish the effects of the changes that influence children at specific ages from the effects of changes that are likely to affect children of all ages. Finally the test measures skills that are likely to be sensitive to all the different kinds of changes in families, communities, and schools we have noted.[7] No other national survey has tracked performance at different ages over such a long period.

---

4. For the impact of the War on Poverty see Herrnstein and Murray (1994) and Jencks (1992); for the way communities have changed for black families see Wilson (1987) and Jencks (1992).

5. For the impact of desegregation on minority children see Wells and Crain (1994); Schofield (1994); Armor (1995); and Orfield and Eaton (1996). For the relation between resources and achievement see Burtless (1996) and Ladd (1996). For the effects of kindergarten and preschool see Center for the Future of Children (1995) and Karweit (1989).

6. Cherlin (1988); Zill and Rogers (1988); Fuchs and Rekliss (1992); Popenoe (1993); Stacey (1993); Haverman and Wolfe (1994); and Grissmer and others (1994).

7. Besides the quality of schools and teachers, differences in achievement scores are associated with family characteristics and the "social capital" in our communities. Family characteristics are linked to achievement through innate characteristics passed from parent to child, the different quality and quantity of resources within families, and the different allocation of intrafamily resources—so-called family human capital (Becker, 1981, 1993). Social capital refers to effects that arise mainly from the characteristics of other families within neighborhoods and schools (Coleman, 1988, 1990). It can include peer effects, quality of communication and trust among families in communities, the safety of neighborhoods, and the presence of community institutions that support achievement. An extensive empirical literature provides support for the joint influence of families, communities, and schools on achievement scores.

This chapter is divided into four parts. The first describes changes in black and white students' NAEP scores. Unlike Hedges and Nowell, we focus on how each group's scores changed relative to the group's initial position in the early 1970s. The next part estimates the effects of changes in family characteristics on black and white students' scores. The third part investigates the contribution of changes in schooling that mainly affect a particular age group: the growth of kindergarten and preschools, in tracking and ability grouping, and in what secondary students study. The final part investigates the contribution of desegregation, the pupil-teacher ratio, and teacher characteristics, which are more likely to affect children of all ages.

NAEP Scores

Figure 6-1 shows the changes in black and white seventeen-year-olds' reading and math scores between 1971 and 1996.[8] Figures 6-2 and 6-3 show changes among thirteen-year-olds and nine-year-olds. In all three, both black and white scores are set to a mean of zero and a standard deviation of one for the first year in which the NAEP gave its tests. The fact that black seventeen-year-olds' 1984 reading scores average about 0.6, for example, tells us that the average black seventeen-year-old scored 0.6 stan-

8. The scores have been converted to relative scores by assuming the earliest test score for each race is zero Thus the difference in scores reflects changes in the black-white gap from the earliest test. The scores are converted to standard deviation units by dividing the mean difference from the earliest test by a metric that remains constant over the period: the standard deviations of all students for the earliest year. Another common practice is to measure the gap with respect to the standard deviation in the same year. Because the standard deviation for all students declines for mathematics scores but increases for reading scores, this method would change the metric over time and result in a somewhat different measure of gap reduction.

The 1971 and 1973 scores for non-Hispanic white students were estimated because the only published scores are for combined Hispanic and non-Hispanic white students in those years. Tests after 1973 have separate data for Hispanic and non-Hispanic white students. We make a small correction in the 1971 and 1973 white data by determining the proportion by age group of students who were Hispanic and assuming that the difference between Hispanic and non-Hispanic white scores was the same in 1971 and 1973 as for the 1975 reading and 1978 math tests.

The NAEP scores for seventeen-year-olds are limited to those enrolled in school. To estimate scores for all seventeen-year-olds, we assume that those not enrolled in school would have scored 0.5 standard deviations below the mean score for their race, which is probably a conservative assumption. The October 1970 Current Population Survey (CPS) shows that approximately 88 percent of white and 83 percent of black seventeen-year-olds were in school in 1970, compared with 89 percent of whites and 90 percent of blacks in 1988 (Cook and Evans, 1997).

Figure 6-1. *NAEP Mathematics and Reading Scores for Students Aged 17, by Race, 1971–96*

Standard deviation units

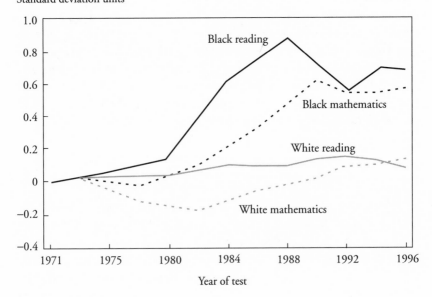

Year of test

Source: See text.

dard deviations higher in 1984 than in 1971. The fact that whites had a mean reading score of 0.1 in 1984 does not mean that the average white scored lower than the average black. It means that whites gained only 0.1 standard deviations between 1971 and 1984. The difference between the black and white means (0.5 standard deviations in this example) represents the change in the black-white gap since 1971.

The following points stand out.

—The black-white gap narrowed for both reading and math at all ages. This happened because black students improved a great deal while white students improved only a little.

—The gap narrowed more for thirteen- and seventeen-year-olds ("adolescents") than for nine-year-olds because black adolescents' scores increased dramatically from the late 1970s to the late 1980s. By the late 1980s black gains were 0.6 to 0.7 standard deviations greater than white gains.

—The gap among adolescents widened again in the 1990s. Black reading scores declined. Black math scores were stable or rose slightly, but white

Figure 6-2. *NAEP Mathematics and Reading Scores for Students Aged 13, by Race, 1971–96*

Standard deviation units

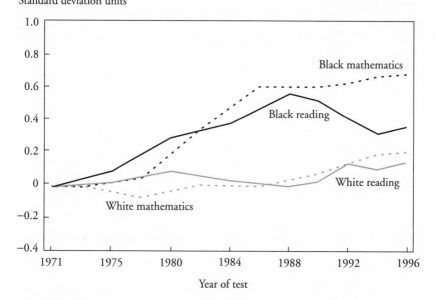

Year of test

Source: See text.

scores rose more. By 1996 black adolescents' gains since the early 1970s exceeded white gains by only 0.2 to 0.6 standard deviations.

—The pattern of gains among black nine-year-olds is very different from the pattern among black adolescents. Black nine-year-olds gained more than older blacks during the 1970s and gained less than older blacks during the 1980s. Black nine-year-olds' math scores continued increasing after 1988. Their reading scores declined between 1988 and 1990 but were back at their 1988 level by 1996. Overall, the black-white gap among nine-year-olds narrowed by 0.25 to 0.35 standard deviations between the early 1970s and 1996.

Even when black gains were largest, they never came close to eliminating the gap. The largest reduction was for seventeen-year-olds' reading scores. In 1971 the median black scored between the 10th and 12th percentiles of the white distribution. By 1988, when the gap was at its narrowest, the median black scored between the 26th and 28th percentiles of the white distribution. For other age groups, the gap remained even wider.

Figure 6-3. *NAEP Mathematics and Reading Scores for Students Aged 9, by Race, 1971–96*

Standard deviation units

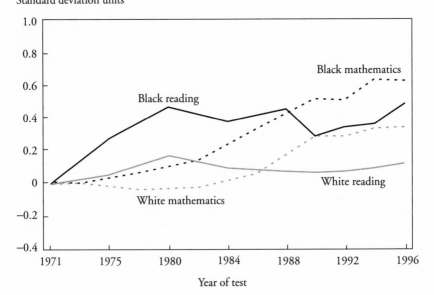

Source: See text.

Cohorts

We ordinarily think of learning as a cumulative process, in which early achievement affects later achievement. We therefore expect achievement gains among nine-year-olds to be followed by gains among thirteen-year-olds four years later. Likewise, we expect gains among thirteen-year-olds to be followed by gains among seventeen-year-olds. This assumption has not always been borne out, however. Preschool, for example, appears to boost achievement in the early grades, but these effects seem to fade as children get older.[9] A rapid expansion of preschooling might therefore lead to an increase in NAEP scores at age nine but not at later ages. Nor do the NAEP data suggest that we always have to improve achievement at age nine to lay the groundwork for higher achievement at ages thirteen or seventeen. Making the high school curriculum tougher without changing the primary school

9. Barnett (1995).

Figure 6-4. *NAEP Reading Scores for Black Students, by Year of School Entry, 1960–94*

Standard deviation units

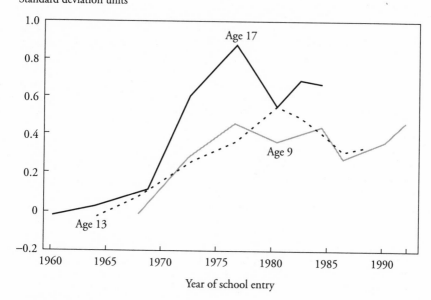

Year of school entry

Source: See text.

curriculum might, for example, boost seventeen-year-olds' test scores even though nine-year-olds' scores remain unchanged.

Tracking the scores of successive school cohorts allows us to see which of these patterns is present. We identify cohorts by the year in which they were six years old. We describe this as the year a cohort entered first grade, although in fact some children enter first grade when they are five and some enter when they are seven.[10] The NAEP did not always administer its tests so as to track the same birth cohort over time, but we can interpolate to estimate what happened to successive birth cohorts. Figure 6-4, for example, shows that the cohort of black children who entered school in 1977 scored 0.44 standard deviations above the earliest cohort at age nine on the NAEP reading test, 0.38 standard deviations above the earliest cohort at age thirteen, and 0.84 standard deviations above the

10. See Koretz (1986) and Koretz (1987) for earlier applications of this technique to NAEP and other data sets. Grissmer and others (forthcoming) also presents and interprets these cohort data.

Figure 6-5. *NAEP Mathematics Scores for Black Students, by Year of School Entry, 1960–93*

Standard deviation units

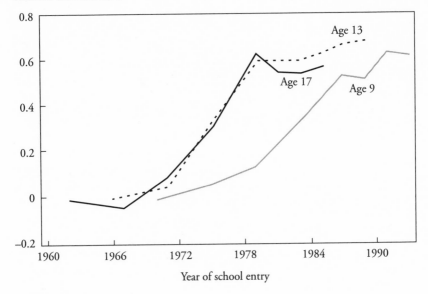

Year of school entry

Source: See text.

earliest cohort at age seventeen. Figure 6-5 shows the corresponding data for the NAEP math test.

The following points stand out.

—For cohorts entering school from 1960 to 1968, older black students' gains were very small. No data are available for nine-year-olds who entered before 1968.[11]

—The most significant black gains occurred in the cohorts entering school from 1968–72 to 1976–80.

11. We have no NAEP data on nine-year-olds who entered school before 1968 or thirteen-year-olds who entered before 1964 The position of the cohort curves for these groups could change if such data were available. The large gain in nine-year-olds' reading between the cohorts entering in 1968 and 1972 may well indicate that there was also some gain at age nine between the 1964 and 1968 cohorts and possibly earlier. If that were the case, benchmarking the data to 1968 or 1964 would raise all subsequent estimates for nine-year-olds and make their pattern closer to the pattern for older groups. For math, however, nine-year-olds in the cohorts that entered in 1970 and 1975 scored at about the same level, making earlier gains appear less likely. For thirteen-year-olds, there appears to be little gain between the 1964–68 cohorts, so earlier gains are probably small.

—Except for nine-year-olds' math scores, black cohorts entering school since 1980 have registered small gains or declines.

—Black reading gains precede mathematics gains. The data show small gains in reading for cohorts entering in the 1960s and dramatic gains for the 1968–1972 cohorts. The math data show no evidence of gains before the 1971 cohort.

The cohort data show little evidence of early gains that fade by later grades. Rather, gains among nine-year-olds are usually sustained and often increased at older ages. For reading, nine-year-olds' gains are followed by similar gains among thirteen-year-olds four years later and then by even larger gains among seventeen-year-olds four years after that. For math, the gains of the cohorts entering after 1970 but before 1980 are not apparent until they reach age thirteen. For cohorts entering after 1980, most gains occur before the age of nine. Thus, some cohorts gain at all ages, while others' gains are age specific. Patterns also differ for reading and math.

Dispersion of Scores

The standard deviation of mathematics scores fell over time for both blacks and whites (Table 6-1). This happened because lower-scoring students of each race gained more than higher-scoring students. The pattern for reading scores is quite different. For nine- and thirteen-year-olds, the standard deviation rose because higher-scoring students gained more. For seventeen-year-olds there is no clear trend.[12]

Regions

Significant black gains occurred in all regions of the country for both reading and math, and these gains are again found at all ages (figure 6-6).[13] Black gains were somewhat larger in the Southeast and smallest in the Northeast. As we shall see, this pattern may reflect the fact that black

12. Hauser and Huang (1996) and Hauser (1996) also identify this pattern. They show the trend even more clearly by analyzing scores at the 5th, 10th, 25th, 50th, 75th, 90th, and 95th percentiles.

13. The means by race and region are unpublished and were provided by Michael Ross of the National Center for Educational Statistics. We only have data regionally from 1971 to 1992 for reading and from 1978 to 1992 for math.

Table 6-1. *Standard Deviation of NAEP Mathematics and Reading Test Scores, by Race, 1971–96*

| | Mathematics | | | | | | | |
Age	1973	1978	1982	1986	1990	1992	1994	1996
White								
Age 9	. . .[a]	34.0	32.8	32.6	31.2	31.0	31.4	32.4
Age 13	. . .	35.7	31.0	29.4	29.0	28.5	29.8	28.7
Age 17	. . .	32.3	30.4	29.1	29.5	28.4	28.6	28.0
Black								
Age 9	. . .[b]	34.5	33.7	31.7	31.5	31.8	30.8	31.1
Age 13	. . .	36.0	31.0	28.3	28.7	30.1	31.5	29.5
Age 17	. . .	31.8	29.2	26.4	27.9	27.5	25.6	27.7

| | Reading | | | | | | | | |
Age	1971	1975	1980	1984	1988	1990	1992	1994	1996
White									
Age 9	. . .[a]	36.1	35.2	38.8	39.3	42.9	37.5	37.4	38.0
Age 13	. . .	32.9	32.7	33.8	33.9	34.5	36.6	37.5	35.9
Age 17	. . .	39.8	37.9	38.2	36.0	39.6	39.8	41.9	40.5
Black									
Age 9	38.3	35.8	37.6	38.9	39.4	41.7	39.8	40.6	40.1
Age 13	33.5	34.9	32.7	34.1	32.1	35.3	39.8	38.0	35.7
Age 17	43.5	43.8	39.5	37.0	35.9	39.2	42.2	42.8	38.6

Source: See text.
a. The 1971 and 1973 white standard deviations not shown because Hispanics and non-Hispanic whites are distinguishable.
b. The 1973 standard deviations for math are not published.

Figure 6-6. *Change in Black NAEP Scores Averaged across Subjects and Ages, by Region, 1970s–92*

Standard deviation units

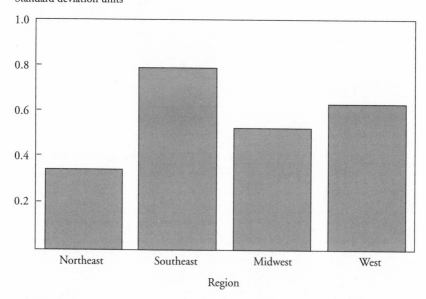

Region

Source: See text.

schools became less segregated in the Southeast and more segregated in the Northeast.[14]

Some Questions

Taken together, the NAEP data raise a number of questions:

—Why did both black and white scores rise for all ages in both reading and math?

—Why did black scores rise substantially more than white scores at all ages and in all subjects?

14. Regional divisions for the NAEP are different from those used by the Census Bureau. In particular, the NAEP places Texas and Oklahoma in the West rather than the South and places Maryland, Delaware, and the part of Virginia around Washington, D.C., in the Northeast. This is important when interpreting black regional scores in the West, since a sizable proportion of "Western" blacks are in Texas.

—Why did black adolescent achievement scores remain stable for cohorts entering from 1960 to 1968–70, suddenly accelerate for cohorts entering school between 1968–72 and 1976–80, and then stabilize or fall in subsequent cohorts?

—Why did black adolescents first gain more and then lose more than black nine-year-olds?

—Why did black reading gains precede black math gains?

—Why were black gains higher in the Southeast and lower in the Northeast?

—Why did low-scoring students gain more in math and less in reading than higher-scoring students, regardless of race?

The most striking feature of the NAEP results for blacks is the size of adolescent gains for cohorts entering from 1968–72 to 1976–80. These gains averaged 0.6 standard deviations for reading and math combined. Such large gains over such a short period are rare; indeed, they may be unprecedented. Scores on IQ tests seem to have increased gradually throughout the twentieth century, both in the United States and elsewhere.[15] Gains on Raven's Progressive Matrices were especially large. But gains on tests similar to the NAEP have averaged less than 0.02 standard deviations a year, a fraction of the black gains in the 1980s. No one has been able to explain the gain in IQ scores.[16]

Gains of this magnitude are unusual even in intensive programs explicitly aimed at raising test scores. Early childhood interventions are widely thought to have the largest potential effect on academic achievement, partly because of their influence on brain development. Yet only a handful of these programs have reported gains as large as half a standard deviation and these were small programs with intensive interventions.[17] Furthermore, when early childhood programs produce large initial gains, the effects usually fade at later ages. Among blacks who entered school between 1968 and 1978, in contrast, gains were largest among older students and occurred nationwide.

Sustained interruptions in schooling can produce large declines in test performance (0.5 standard deviations or more) that persist at older ages.[18] Black students typically gain about 0.4 standard deviations a year on the

15. Flynn (1987).
16. Flynn (1987); and Neisser (1998).
17. Barnett (1995).
18. Ceci and Williams (1997).

NAEP tests between the ages of nine and thirteen. For black thirteen-year-olds, therefore, a gain of 0.6 standard deviations is equivalent to approximately 1.5 years of additional schooling. The large gains among black adolescents during the 1980s are thus what we might expect if the black adolescents who entered school after 1970 had attended elementary schools that qualitatively added 1.5 years of schooling compared with those who entered before 1970.

Family Changes

In most analyses of individuals' test performance, family characteristics account for more of the variance than school characteristics. Many family characteristics that are correlated with test performance changed significantly between 1960 and 1996. The NAEP collects very little data on the characteristics of students' families, but the March Current Population Survey (CPS) provides detailed information on changes in the family characteristics of children born since 1960. Table 6-2 shows how the families of fifteen- to eighteen-year-old students changed between 1970 and 1990.[19] Parents had considerably more education in 1990 than in 1970, and children had fewer siblings living at home, which is also associated with higher academic achievement. These improvements were especially marked for black students. But more teenagers lived with a single parent and more of them had been born to young mothers.[20]

The CPS does not test teenagers, so we cannot use it to estimate the impact of changes in family characteristics on test performance. To do that, we turned to the National Education Longitudinal Survey (NELS) and the National Longitudinal Survey of Youth (NLSY), both of which collected detailed information on family background and gave reading and math tests broadly similar to those in the NAEP. Grissmer and his colleagues estimated the impact of changes in the family characteristics in table 6-2 using NELS and the NLSY.[21] They assumed that the effects in the NAEP would have been the same as in the tests given in NELS and

19. The 1970 CPS does not identify Hispanics, so changes in the characteristics of nonblack families include changes due to the increasing proportion of Hispanic families. Also the CPS variable for siblings includes only those younger than eighteen.

20. The proportion of children born to younger mothers has increased partly because mothers have fewer children, and third and fourth children are usually born to older mothers

21. Grissmer and others (1994).

Table 6-2. *Characteristics of the Families of Black and Nonblack 15- to 18-Year-Olds, Selected Years, 1970–90*
Percent unless otherwise specified

Characteristic	Black				Nonblack			
	1970	1980	1990	Percent change (1970–90)	1970	1980	1990	Percent change (1970–90)
Income (1987 dollars)	23,287	23,121	24,068	3	40,805	43,290	42,545	4
Mother's education								
Less than high school	63.6	45.8	23.8	–63	34.7	24.5	16.0	–54
High school	29.4	39.1	51.4	75	46.7	48.0	46.4	–1
Some college	3.9	10.9	17.0	336	11.3	15.8	20.5	81
College graduate	3.1	4.2	7.8	152	7.2	11.8	17.1	138
Father's education								
Less than high school	72.1	52.2	27.4	–62	38.8	26.9	17.8	–54
High school	21.4	33.8	48.1	125	34.2	35.6	36.1	6
Some college	4.0	10.5	15.3	283	12.3	16.6	21.1	72
College graduate	2.5	3.5	9.2	268	14.6	20.9	25.0	71

Number of siblings								
0–1	30.8	47.1	66.2	115	50.6	60.6	73.5	45
2–3	33.2	34.1	26.9	–19	33.8	32.4	23.0	–32
4 or more	36.0	18.8	7.0	–81	15.6	7.0	3.5	–78
Age of mother at child's birth								
Less than or equal to								
19 years	15.1	16.6	25.3	68	8.5	8.9	11.1	31
20–24 years	26.7	33.1	29.6	11	28.4	32.2	32.2	13
25–29 years	28.0	23.6	24.2	–14	31.3	30.0	35.5	13
Greater than or equal to 30 years	30.3	26.6	20.9	–31	31.8	28.8	21.2	–33
Single mother	36.1	52.1	53.3	48	10.6	14.9	17.9	69
Mother working	54.0	56.5	67.5	25	48.7	59.8	68.7	41

Source: See text.

Table 6-3. *Predicted Gain in NAEP Scores Based on Changes in Family Income, Family Size, Parental Education, Single Parenthood, and Maternal Age, 1970–90*
Gains in standard deviations

	Age 17	Age 13	Age 9[a]
Blacks			
Math	0.30	0.26	0.22
Reading	0.40	0.30	0.20
Non-Hispanic whites			
Math	0.22	0.22	0.22
Reading	0.28	0.22	0.16

Source: Grissmer and others (1994).
a. Estimates for nine-year-olds are linear extrapolations from the estimates for thirteen- and seventeen-year-olds.

the NLSY, that these effects were stable from 1970 to 1990, and that the cross-sectional relationships observed in NELS and the NLSY could be used to estimate the impact of changes in family characteristics between 1970 and 1990.[22]

Table 6-3 shows Grissmer and colleagues' estimates of how family changes altered NAEP scores between the early 1970s and 1990. The net effect of family changes is always positive because the effects of increased parental education and reduced family size always outweigh the adverse effects of declines in the number of two-parent families and older mothers. Changes in family income are too small to make much difference either way. The net improvement in family characteristics between 1970 and 1990 leads to a predicted increase in test performance of 0.16 to 0.40 standard deviations, depending on the age and race of the student.[23] The predicted gains are usually larger for blacks, for older students, and for reading rather than math.[24]

22. Hedges and Nowell in chapter 4 and Evans and Cook (1997) support the premise that family background effects have been stable over time
23. See Grissmer and others (1994, pp 94–97) for the results presented here.
24. When reading and math scores are standardized, family characteristics have more effect on reading scores than math scores. Math scores appear to be more influenced by school characteristics. Changes in family characteristics have more impact on older students because family characteristics improved more in the 1950s, 1960s, and 1970s than in the 1980s.

Even among seventeen-year-olds the predicted changes for blacks exceed those for whites by only 0.08 to 0.12 standard deviations. This implies that changes in family characteristics account for no more than 15 percent of the reduction in the black-white gap between the early 1970s and 1990. To check this estimate, we can compare it to the estimate made by Michael Cook and William Evans using NAEP students' reports of their parents' schooling. They conclude that reducing the black-white gap in parental education accounted for no more than a quarter of the narrowing in the black-white gap in NAEP scores and probably much less.[25]

All these estimates probably overstate the impact of changes in parental education. Parental education is correlated with children's test performance for two reasons. First, education makes parents more effective mentors and helps them provide their children with an environment conducive to learning. Second, parents' educational attainment is a proxy for innate characteristics that parents pass along to their children. These inherited traits then affect the children's test scores. When parents stay in school longer, their child-rearing practices and mentoring ability probably improve, but their innate characteristics do not. Keeping all parents in school longer is therefore unlikely to raise children's test scores as much as we would expect on the basis of the cross-sectional comparisons between parents with more and less schooling. The magnitude of this bias is uncertain.[26]

In this chapter we assume that table 6-3 overestimates the overall effect of changes in family characteristics by a factor of two for both blacks and whites.[27] Table 6-4 uses this assumption to calculate the "residual" (or un-

25. Using NAEP rather than CPS data on parental characteristics allowed Cook and Evans (1997) to make fewer assumptions than Grissmer and others (1994). The disadvantage of using NAEP is that it does not collect data on family size, family structure, maternal age, or family income. But parental schooling is the family characteristic that best predicts children's test scores and that accounts for most of the predicted change in achievement between 1970 and 1990.

26. This bias may be larger for whites than for blacks because unequal educational opportunity may make the genetic component of the correlation between parental education and children's achievement smaller for blacks than for whites. For individuals who face relatively few economic and social obstacles to staying in school, educational attainment may depend mainly on innate characteristics. For those who face greater social and economic obstacles, innate characteristics may be relatively less important. If that were the case, racial convergence in parental education might matter more than we have assumed.

27. Current estimates suggest that heredity explains roughly half the variance in test scores (McGue and others, 1993). If we take account of the possible effect of unequal opportunity by assuming that two-thirds of the effect in black families and one-third of the effect in white families is environmental, this would lower black residuals in table 6-4 by 0.04 to 0.06 and raise the white residuals by 0.03 to 0.05. This assumption would increase to slightly more than one-quarter the portion of the black-white gap reduction for older students that is attributable to family changes.

Table 6-4. *Observed Gain in NAEP Scores after Adjusting for Changes in Family Characteristics, 1970–90*[a]

Standard deviation units

	Age 17	Age 13	Age 9
Blacks			
Math	0.45	0.49	0.41
Reading	0.69	0.44	0.40
Non-Hispanic whites			
Math	−0.07	0	0.13
Reading	−0.03	−0.01	−0.02

Source: See text

a. Observed gain (as shown in figures 6-1 to 6-3) minus half the gain predicted in table 6-3 on the basis of changes in family characteristics.

explained) gain for each group on each test. For whites, we now see small unexplained gains or losses. For blacks, we still see very large unexplained gains. These unexplained gains could be attributable to errors in our assumptions about the effects of measured family characteristics, changes in unmeasured family characteristics such as child-rearing practices, or changes in schools and communities.[28]

Moving is a family change not included in the previous analysis that has a well-documented adverse effect on children.[29] States with high rates of geographic mobility also have lower NAEP scores, even after controlling for other family characteristics.[30] Families with children moved less in the 1990s than in the 1970s, so if all else had been equal, school achievement scores should have risen.[31] But because the decline in geographic mobility was small, the predicted increase in NAEP scores between 1970 and 1990 is no more than 0.02 standard deviations.

28. To account for black-white convergence, unmeasured family characteristics would have to meet three tests: their effects are not captured by the eight family characteristics shown in table 6-2, they changed significantly between 1970 and 1990, and they either changed significantly more for black than for white students or had significantly larger effects on black students' scores than on white students' scores. Changed beliefs, attitudes, and motivations in black families associated with the civil rights movement and War on Poverty might fit this description. We discuss these later.

29. Haveman and Wolfe (1994).

30. Raudenbush (forthcoming).

31. Among children between the ages of five and thirteen, the percentage who had moved within the past year fell from 16.7 percent in 1971 to 15 percent in 1994. See *Statistical Abstract of the United States* (1996, table 33, and 1973, table 45).

In summary, the family changes we examined could account for the small increase in white children's NAEP scores between the early 1970s and the mid-1990s, but these changes can explain about one-third or less of the black gain. However, the changes can account for less than one-quarter of the gap reduction.

Educational Changes Primarily Affecting Scores at Specific Ages

School enrollment among four- and five-year-olds has increased markedly since 1960. This is partly because Head Start, launched in 1965, made preschool more available to low-income families and partly because almost all communities now offer free kindergarten. The labor force participation of mothers with preschool children has also risen, and awareness of the importance of early childhood in cognitive development has spread.[32] Figure 6-6 shows that 16 percent of the cohort that turned six in 1967 (the earliest year for which data are available) was enrolled in kindergarten or nursery school at age four. In the cohort that turned six in 1993 the figure was almost 52 percent.[33] Between 8 and 12 percent of four-year-olds were in kindergarten throughout this period, so almost all the growth in enrollment was due to increases in nursery school enrollment. Figure 6-7 also shows that enrollment rates among five-year-olds (most of whom were in kindergarten but some of whom were in first grade) rose from 66 percent among those who turned six in 1960 to 85–90 percent among those who turned six after 1975.[34]

The consensus among scholars is that participation in large-scale preschool and kindergarten programs leads to significant increases in academic achievement during the first few grades of regular school but that this ad-

32. Head Start has grown. In 1990 it enrolled approximately 10 percent of all four-year-olds. Participation can therefore account for no more than a quarter of the growth in preelementary enrollment. The labor force participation rate of married women with children younger than six has increased from 18.6 to 58.9 percent between 1960 and 1990 (*Statistical Abstract of the United States, 1997*, table 631).

33. *Digest of Educational Statistics: 1996*, table 45.

34. The 1992 *Digest of Educational Statistics*, table 47, also shows a shift toward full-day rather than half-day attendance Among those in nursery school, full-day attendance increased from 23 percent in 1970 to 34 percent in 1990. Among those in kindergarten it increased from 12 percent in 1970 to 41 percent in 1991. By 1990 more than 98 percent of children entering first grade had attended kindergarten. The quoted figure of 89 percent is lower because it includes some children who attended kindergarten at age six and entered first grade at age seven.

Figure 6-7. *Four- and Five-Year-Olds in Kindergarten or Nursery School,*
by Year of School Entry, 1960–92
Percent

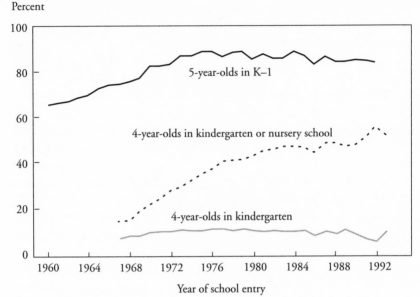

Year of school entry

Source: See text.

vantage fades in later grades, regardless of the race of the children.[35] Steven
Barnett has found that seventeen of twenty-one large programs showed
positive and statistically significant achievement effects in early grades.[36]
By the end of the third grade, only twelve had significant effects. Only six
programs had significant effects at the oldest age measured. Although smaller

35. The best-designed and most intensive small-scale model preschool programs show larger
short-term effects on achievement and IQ for disadvantaged minority children. Ten of twelve model
programs that had control groups showed gains between 0.3 and 0.7 standard deviations at age five
(Barnett, 1995). Eleven of these programs measured achievement and IQ scores at third grade or
older. Approximately one-half showed significant positive effects at these ages. The effects generally
grew smaller at older ages. Only two studies showed significant achievement effects at age fourteen or
older. These model programs focused on small samples of black children. Some interventions started
at birth, while others were directed toward three- to four-year-olds. Almost all included other services
besides preschool. These programs generally had higher-quality staff, higher teacher-pupil ratios, and
more funding than large-scale programs. So the effects generated by these programs would be unlikely
in large-scale preschool programs.
36. Barnett (1995).

and more intensive programs often have much larger short-term effects, large programs like Head Start seldom have effects of more than 0.10 to 0.20 standard deviations at age nine. The limited evidence on kindergarten also shows significant short-term effects for disadvantaged students but little or no long-term effect.[37]

Enrollment rates for five-year-olds increased by 23 percentage points between 1960 and 1990. For four-year-olds the rates increased by 36 percentage points. Black and white rates have grown by about the same amount.[38] Thus if both preschool and kindergarten raised participants' test scores at age nine by 0.10 to 0.20 standard deviations, preschool growth would have raised NAEP scores by about 0.04 to 0.07 standard deviations and kindergarten growth would have raised scores by 0.02 to 0.05 standard deviations. Currently available evidence does not suggest much impact on thirteen- or seventeen-year-olds' scores.

Tracking

If more high school students enroll in the college preparatory (or academic) track, we might expect their test scores to rise, although Ronald Ferguson's review of the evidence finds little support for this expectation (see chapter 8).[39] In any event, the proportion of students in the academic track did not change much in the 1980s, which was the period of the largest test score gains among seventeen-year-olds. Among black high school graduates, the proportion who said they were in the academic or college

---

37. Karweit (1989). The evidence for kindergarten effects is based on the difference between the effects of half-day and full-day attendance. Larger short-term effects might be expected from the change from no attendance to half-day attendance. But since neither preschool nor full-day kindergarten attendance shows long-term effects, it would be surprising if part-day kindergarten showed such an effect. Some small specially designed kindergarten programs appear to have substantial short-term effects (Karweit, 1989). It is also possible that changes in the kindergarten curriculum could have some effects at age nine as well.

38. For three- and four-year-olds, the National Center for Educational Statistics (1972, table 4, and 1996, table 7) shows that black enrollment rose from 22 percent in 1971 to 34 percent in 1975 and 42 percent in 1990, while white enrollment rose from 21 percent in 1971 to 31 percent in 1975 and 47 percent in 1990. The white increase is therefore slightly larger than the black increase. For five-year-olds, 78 percent of whites and 67 percent of blacks were enrolled in 1969 and the percentages were almost the same in 1990.

39. Cook and Evans (1997) estimate the effect of increased enrollment in the academic track between 1980 and 1990 directly from the NAEP data and conclude that such changes might account for 10 to 20 percent of the reduction in the black-white gap. Because track assignment is not random, this estimate is probably an upper boundary.

preparatory track rose from 33 percent in 1982 to 36 percent in 1992. Among whites, the proportion increased from 41 to 46 percent. There were larger shifts from the vocational to the general track, but it is not clear whether this would raise or lower achievement scores.[40]

Elementary Classroom Grouping

Based on his review of the literature, Ferguson concludes that grouping elementary school students by skill level in a mixed classroom can raise their scores by 0.2 to 0.3 standard deviations, at least in the short run. Since these estimates represent the maximum gains possible if such grouping affects all students, there would have to be shifts in groupings affecting one-third or more of students to obtain shifts of 0.1 standard deviations or more. But there is no systematic national evidence about how much elementary school grouping practices have changed. Ferguson also concludes that both high- and low-scoring students appear to benefit from within-classroom grouping, so changes in grouping practices would not be expected to narrow the black-white gap in racially mixed schools. (If predominantly black schools had adopted within-classroom grouping while predominantly white schools had not, this might have narrowed the gap, but there is no evidence that this happened.)

Changes in What Students Study

Figure 6-5 shows that a substantial part of blacks' higher scores in math for cohorts entering school between 1970 to 1980 probably occurred after the age of nine. If blacks took more demanding math courses in middle school and high school during the 1980s, such a change could explain some of the adolescent gains. Although the percentage of high school graduates reporting that they were in the academic track rose slowly between 1982 and 1992, both black and white high school graduates took many more advanced math courses. In 1982 black high school graduates had taken an average of only 1.1 courses in algebra, geometry, or higher-level

---

40. Vocational enrollments declined from 25 percent in 1982 to 11 percent in 1992 for whites and from 32 to 15 percent for blacks. All the tracking data come from National Center for Education Statistics (1996, tables 132, 135, and 136).

math. By 1992 black graduates had taken an average of 2.0 math courses at this level. White graduates averaged 2.5 math courses at this level in 1992, compared to 1.8 in 1982.[41] Thus while the mean rose for both races, it rose more for blacks.

Figure 6-1 shows that seventeen-year-olds' math scores rose about 0.60 standard deviations for blacks and 0.20 standard deviations for whites between 1982 and 1990. Racial convergence in course-taking patterns is probably not sufficient to explain the entire reduction in the math gap during this period, but it could be part of the story. If black students benefit more than white students from more demanding courses, changes in enrollment could explain more of the gap reduction, but we could not find any evidence for this.

In any event, changes in the high school curriculum cannot be the whole story, because figure 6-5 shows that among blacks who completed school between 1982 and 1992 math scores rose as much at age thirteen as at age seventeen. These gains among black thirteen-year-olds were presumably one reason why more of them took algebra and geometry in high school. Unfortunately, we have no data on changes in middle school curriculum for black and white students.[42] Thirteen-year-old white students' scores did not rise much in this period. The middle school curriculum may have changed more for black than for white students, but we cannot be sure.

Reading comprehension is not as tightly linked to specific courses as math skills are. Nonetheless, we might expect reading scores to rise when high school students take more academically demanding courses because such courses give students more practice reading complex material. The percentage of black high school graduates completing four years of English, three years of social science, two years of natural science, and two years of math increased from 32 percent in 1982 to 76 percent in 1994. However, the change was similar for white students (from 33 to 76 percent).[43] Thus if changes in the high school curriculum had the same effect

41. National Center for Education Statistics (1996, table 133).

42. Raudenbush (forthcoming) finds that eighth-graders taking algebra or prealgebra score a full standard deviation above those who are not, even after controlling for diverse family, community, and school characteristics. But selection into these courses is usually based on math skills per se, only part of which is accounted for by general family characteristics, so the observed difference cannot be treated as an effect of taking such courses.

43. An alternative measure of changes in the rigor of the nonscience curriculum is the mean number of foreign language courses taken by black and white high school graduates. These means rose from 0.7 to 1.3 courses for blacks and from 1.0 to 1.7 courses for whites. See National Center for Education Statistics (1996, tables 133 and 136) for data on course taking.

on blacks and whites, we should have seen roughly similar increases in black and white seventeen-year-olds' reading scores. In fact, black seventeen-year-olds' reading scores rose by about 0.45 standard deviations between 1980 and 1992, whereas white seventeen-year-olds' scores rose only 0.15 standard deviations. Increased enrollment in academic courses could explain this if blacks had gained more than whites from taking demanding courses, but we could find no evidence for this.

Changes in Schools That Could Affect All Age Groups

Two types of changes occurred in schools that could affect the scores of nine-, thirteen-, and seventeen-year-old students. We address desegregation first, then changes in teachers and class sizes.

Desegregation

Black adolescents tested in 1971 had entered school in the early 1960s. Averaging across regions, they typically got 60 percent of their education in schools where more than 90 percent of the other students were also minorities (figure 6-8).[44] Between 1968 and 1972 school segregation declined dramatically in the South. As a result, blacks entering school after 1975 got only 35 percent of their education in schools that were more than 90 percent minority. This figure has not changed much for more recent cohorts. NAEP nine-year-olds experienced somewhat less change than older students because southern desegregation began early in their school careers.

Table 6-5 presents bivariate regressions of NAEP scores on desegregation measures. The reading and math scores in these regressions are the unexplained residual after subtracting out the estimated effect of changes in family background, using the same procedures as in table 6-4. Each reading regression is based on nine annual observations. Each math regression is based on eight observations. These regressions therefore serve as only a primitive filter for determining whether the timing of changes in

44. This estimate uses the proportion of blacks in schools that are 90 percent or more minority provided by Michael Ross of the Department of Education to calculate the mean probability of being in such a school for each school cohort. Figure 6-8 shows these probabilities averaged over the years before the time a given cohort reached the age of nine, thirteen, or seventeen.

Figure 6-8. *Estimated Share of Black Schooling in Schools with Greater Than 90 Percent Minority Students, by Age and Year of School Entry, 1960–93*

Percent

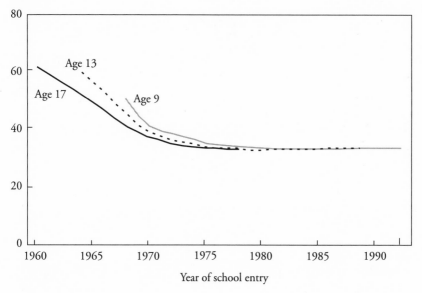

Year of school entry

Source: See text.

segregation matches the timing of changes in NAEP scores. The desegregation measure always has the expected negative sign for blacks and is statistically significant in five out of six cases. Desegregation has no consistent correlation with changes in white scores.

Desegregation has a distinct regional pattern (figure 6-9). Desegregation in the South was concentrated in the four years between 1968 and 1972, and it was more extensive than in any other region. The proportion of southern blacks attending schools that were more than 90 percent minority declined from more than three-quarters to about one-quarter between 1968 and 1972. Some desegregation also took place over a longer time in the West and Midwest. In the Northeast, segregation increased. Figure 6-5 showed that the largest black test score gains also occurred in the South and that the smallest gains occurred in the Northeast. But the direct effect of desegregation cannot account for all black gains, because black scores increased even in the Northeast.

Table 6-5. *Bivariate Regressions of NAEP Gains Adjusted for Family Change on Selected School Characteristics, by Age, Race, and Subject Matter, 1971–92*

	Age 9		Age 13		Age 17	
	Coefficient	*t-statistic*	*Coefficient*	*t-statistic*	*Coefficient*	*t-statistic*
Black math						
Pupil-teacher ratio	-0.068	-6.85	-0.073	-6.32	-0.051	-3.64
Masters degree	0.018	6.14	0.021	8.89	0.015	4.24
Experience	0.006	0.431	0.005	0.360	0.017	1.26
Desegregation	-5.01	-2.21	-2.25	-3.23	-1.32	-2.27
Black reading						
Pupil-teacher ratio	-0.022	-1.35	-0.036	-2.63	-0.061	-3.49
Masters degree	0.006	1.44	0.010	2.52	0.018	3.79
Experience	0.014	2.01	0.023	5.91	0.037	4.52
Desegregation	-1.74	-3.21	-1.24	-3.10	-1.88	-3.47
White math						
Pupil-teacher ratio	-0.039	-2.77	-0.012	-1.25	-0.004	-0.308
Masters degree	0.010	2.50	0.003	1.07	0.001	0.365
Experience	-0.004	-0.415	-0.008	-2.90	-0.009	-1.53
Desegregation	-1.86	-0.904	-0.073	-0.188	0.197	0.532
White reading						
Pupil-teacher ratio	0.004	0.678	0.011	0.197	0.002	0.533
Masters degree	-0.001	-0.636	-0.001	-0.325	-0.000	-0.471
Experience	0.002	0.825	-0.005	-2.04	0.000	0.262
Desegregation	-0.081	-0.271	0.058	0.296	0.039	0.441

Source: See text.

Figure 6-9. *Share of Black Schooling in Schools with Greater than 90 Percent Minority Students, by Region, 1968–91*

Percent

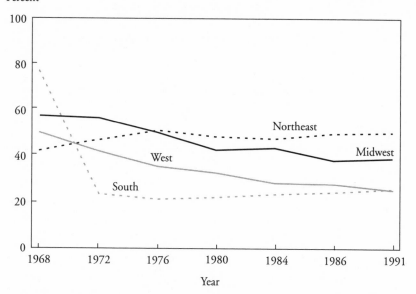

Source: See text.

Although we expect reduced segregation in the Southeast and increased segregation in the Northeast to produce regional differences in black gains, it is not clear when these gains should have occurred. The timing of the gains depends on how the effect of desegregation accumulates as a student spends more time in desegregated schools and on whether early desegregation has effects different from later desegregation. For instance, seventeen-year-old southern blacks who took the NAEP test in 1971 had entered school in 1960 and had spent most of their first eight years in segregated schools. Some then moved to desegregated high schools. Seventeen-year-old blacks who entered school in 1964 were likely to have been in segregated primary schools but often moved to desegregated schools between the fourth and eighth grades. Those who entered in 1973 were the first to experience the full effect of desegregation starting in the earliest grades. If the impact of desegregation depends on attending racially mixed schools from the earliest grades, it would not have appeared for southern black seventeen-year-olds until 1984. If moving to a desegregated middle

Figure 6-10. *Change in NAEP Reading Scores, by Entering School Cohort and Region, for Black Students Aged 9 and 17*

Standard deviation units

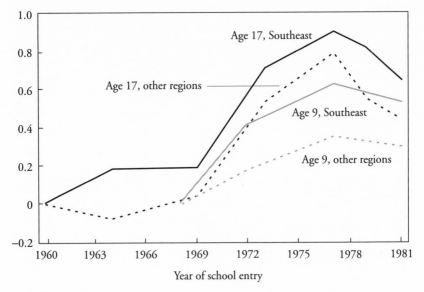

Source: See text.

school or high school after attending segregated elementary schools also helps, black seventeen-year-olds should have gained more in the South than elsewhere before 1984.

Figure 6-10 shows that southern black seventeen-year-olds in the co-hort that entered school in 1964 scored 0.20 standard deviations above those who had entered in 1960. Outside the South black scores dropped slightly during this period. The southern gains could be an effect of deseg-regation. If so, they are mainly an effect of desegregation that began after the sixth grade. For cohorts entering in the late 1960s, however, the pattern is reversed. Black students who entered school in 1969 gained more out-side the South than in the South. Among those entering school between 1969 and 1977, blacks gained dramatically no matter where they lived. Among blacks entering after 1977, reading scores declined everywhere. Fig-ure 6-10 therefore suggests that desegregation boosted southern black seventeen-year-olds' scores by about 0.20 standard deviations and that the effect was relatively immediate rather than cumulative.

Black gains outside the South may, however, have been associated with other social changes, such as the growth of antipoverty and affirmative action programs, that coincided temporally and politically with southern desegregation. All these changes may have signaled to black parents and students nationwide, and also to their teachers, that black children's education was a national priority that would be backed by both money and legal authority. This could have led to a nationwide shift in beliefs, attitudes, and motivation of black parents and students and their teachers that could help explain the subsequent nationwide improvement in black students' performance.

Trends among nine-year-olds provide some additional evidence about the importance of desegregation. Figure 6-10 shows that if we compare nine-year-old blacks who entered school in 1972 to those who entered in 1968, reading scores increased by 0.40 standard deviations in the South compared to only 0.20 standard deviations elsewhere. For later cohorts, the gains were about the same throughout the country.[45]

School Resources

Until relatively recently most social scientists believed that school resources had little impact on student achievement. This counterintuitive view dated back to the so-called Coleman report.[46] Influential reviews by Eric Hanushek argued that evidence from over 300 empirical measurements provided no consistent evidence that increased school resources raised achievement scores.[47] This scholarly consensus began to crack in the early 1990s. When Larry Hedges, Richard Laine, and Rob Greenwald conducted the first formal meta-analysis of the studies that Hanushek had reviewed, they found that many lacked the statistical power to detect resource effects, even when the effects were large. When they pooled data from all the available studies, they found that school spending had a positive and statistically significant effect on achievement.[48]

---

45. We have presented the evidence based on reading scores because we do not have math scores by region and race for 1973. Figure 6-3 shows that nine-year-olds' math scores rose less than reading scores for the early cohorts nationwide. This may be because using a 1973 benchmark lowers subsequent math scores or because math was less affected by desegregation (see chapter 4).

46. Coleman and others (1966).

47. Hanushek (1989, 1994, 1996).

48. Hedges, Laine, and Greenwald (1992); and Hedges and Greenwald (1996).

Nevertheless, Hanushek made one counterargument that Hedges and his colleagues did not try to rebut. Measured in constant dollars, Hanushek said, expenditures per pupil had doubled between the late 1960s and the early 1990s. Yet the NAEP showed little improvement in average reading or math skills. This argument has two major flaws. First, schools' real resources did not come close to doubling. Using the consumer price index to adjust changes in per pupil expenditure for inflation, school outlays do double. But the CPI underestimates price increases for labor-intensive activities like schooling. Using a more appropriate price index yields much lower estimates of growth in schools' real inputs.[49] A second flaw in Hanushek's argument is that a significant part of the increase in schools' real resources went to help students with learning disabilities, many of whom are not tested.[50] Another significant part of the extra spending went for purposes other than raising achievement scores. Using better cost indexes and excluding spending that was not aimed at improving classroom performance, Richard Rothstein and K. H. Miles concluded that the real increase in school resources per regular student was closer to 30 percent than 100 percent.

Additional expenditure aimed at raising regular students' achievement scores went mainly for three purposes: improving the pupil-teacher ratio, creating compensatory programs for low-income students, and paying higher salaries for teachers with more experience and more graduate training.[51] These changes coincided with dramatic increases in black students' test scores. Hispanic students' scores also rose.[52] Among seventeen-year-olds, low-scoring whites also gained, but higher-scoring whites did not gain much.[53] This result makes sense only if low-scoring students, low-income

49. Rothstein and Miles (1995); and Ladd (1996).

50. There is general agreement that an increasing part of school expenditure was directed toward special education during the NAEP period (Lankford and Wyckoff, 1996; Hanuskek and Rivkin, 1997). Hanushek and Rivkin estimate that about a third of the per pupil expenditure increase between 1980 and 1990 was related to special education. NAEP typically excludes about 5 percent of students who have serious learning disabilities. Special education enrollments increased from about 8 percent of all students in 1976–77 to about 12 percent in 1993–94. These figures imply that 7 percent of students taking the NAEP tests were receiving special education resources in 1994 compared with 3 percent in 1976–77. This percentage is too small to have much effect on NAEP trends, but increased special education spending should in principle have had a small positive effect on these students' scores.

51. Rothstein and Miles (1995); and Hanushek and Rivkin (1997).

52. The overall NAEP gains were also lowered by the growth of the Hispanic population in this period.

53. See chapter 4.

students, or minority students received most of the additional resources, or if students with these characteristics benefited disproportionately from a general increase in resources.[54] In addition, the timing of resource changes must match the timing of test score gains. We test the latter hypothesis through simple regressions.

Pupil-Teacher Ratios

Figure 6-11 shows how the pupil-teacher ratio changed for cohorts entering school between 1960 and 1990. It shows the mean pupil-teacher ratio between a cohort's first year of school and the year when the students were tested, with separate trends for nine-, thirteen-, or seventeen-year-olds.[55] Pupil-teacher ratios fell steadily for the cohorts entering school between 1960 and 1980. This trend has continued since 1980 but at a much slower rate. Lower ratios of pupils to teachers imply smaller classes, so declines in the pupil-teacher ratio should be followed by increases in NAEP scores. Table 6-5 shows that this is the case for black students. Changes in the pupil-teacher ratio are significantly correlated with blacks' NAEP scores in five out of six regressions. Because blacks' reading scores decline after 1988 while their math scores do not, pupil-teacher ratios are not as strongly correlated with black reading scores as with black math scores. Among whites, the pupil-teacher ratio has the expected negative sign for math scores and is significant in two out of three cases, but it is insignificant for white reading scores. The effects are also much smaller for whites.

---

54. A number of policies sought to shift resources toward minority or low-income students during these years, including federal compensatory funding based on the percentage of children in poverty, school desegregation, and changes in state funding formulas. However, other changes, such as increased residential segregation by income, could have led to increased funding for schools serving middle- and upper-income children. Cook and Evans (1997) conclude that there was no shift in the relative quality of schools attended by black and white thirteen-year-olds between the early 1970s and 1988. Their school fixed-effect models imply that black students attended schools whose mean score was no higher in the distribution of all school means in 1988 than in the early 1970s, at least after controlling for a few family and community variables. The black-white gap must therefore have narrowed largely *within* schools. Rothstein and Miles (1995) show some redistribution of expenditures, but their data come from only nine school districts. Data on Maryland provided by Evans show little shift in relative spending between high- and low-income school districts between 1970 and 1994.

55. This kind of averaging assumes that school conditions at different ages have the same cumulative impact on scores. If conditions in the early grades have more influence than conditions in later grades, we should observe stronger correlations for nine-year-olds than for older pupils.

Figure 6-11. *Average Pupil-Teacher Ratio during Years of Schooling, by Age of Student and Year of School Entry, 1960–92*

Average pupil-teacher ratio

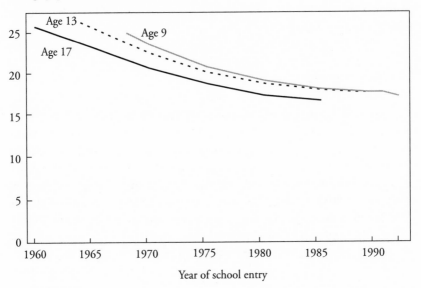

Year of school entry

Source: See text.

Recent research suggests that reductions in class size may, in fact, have more impact on black than on white achievement. A large, multidistrict experiment in Tennessee randomly assigned students to classes of approximately fifteen rather than twenty-three students.[56] It found that reducing class size between kindergarten and third grade raised third grade scores by 0.24 standard deviations for whites and 0.33 standard deviations for blacks.[57] The effects were similar for reading and math. Following the experiment, Tennessee also cut class sizes in the seventeen school districts with the lowest family incomes. Comparisons with other districts and within districts before and after the change showed gains of 0.35 to 0.50 standard deviations.[58] Class size effects therefore appear to be largest for disadvantaged students.

56. Finn and Achilles (1990); Word, Johnston, and Bain (1990); Krueger (1997); and Mosteller (1994).
57. Krueger (1997).
58. Word, Johnston, and Bain (1994); and Mosteller (1994).

For nine-year-olds nationwide, the reduction in the pupil-teacher ratio between 1968 and 1992 was approximately the same amount as the reduction in class size in Tennessee, about eight students per teacher. Table 6-5 implies that reducing the pupil-teacher ratio by eight pupils should raise nine-year-olds' reading and math scores by an average of 0.36 standard deviations for blacks. This is close to the 0.33 standard deviations gain in Tennessee. But Table 6-5 suggests that an eight-pupil reduction in the ratio only raises white scores by 0.14 standard deviations, whereas the Tennessee estimate is 0.24 standard deviations.

There are many possible explanations for the discrepancy between our estimates of class size effects using NAEP and the experimental estimates in Tennessee. One possibility is that the pupil-teacher ratio dropped more for blacks nationwide than for whites. According to Michael Boozer, Alan Krueger, and Shari Wolkon, the pupil-teacher ratio for blacks in the South exceeded that for whites by about three students in the early 1960s.[59] By the late 1980s the gap had vanished. We do not have comparable data for the rest of the country, but if blacks gained more than whites nationwide, table 6-5 will overstate the effect of a one-pupil change on black achievement and understate the effect on whites.

Improving the pupil-teacher ratio may also have had less effect on whites nationally than in Tennessee because Tennessee whites are among the poorest in the nation, and the Tennessee results suggest that cutting class size is more valuable for poor students. Furthermore, Eugene Lewitt and Linda Shumann Baker show that while the schoolwide pupil-teacher ratio fell from about twenty-six in 1961 to seventeen in 1991, actual class size only decreased from about twenty-six to twenty-four. Finally, and perhaps most important, table 6-5 estimates the effect of changing the pupil-teacher ratio without controlling other changes in the educational system.

The Tennessee experiment also leaves a number of other questions unanswered. Tennessee students returned to large classes after the third grade. By the seventh grade the benefits of having been in smaller classes were only half as large as they had been at the end of the third grade, and the benefits to black students were no larger than the benefits to whites.[60] If smaller classes had continued through the seventh grade, the benefits would presumably have persisted and might even have grown.[61] But the Tennessee

59. Boozer, Krueger, and Wolkon (1992).

60. Mosteller (1995).

61. Krueger (1997) finds a small increase in effects for each additional grade spent in smaller classes between kindergarten and third grade.

experiment does not tell us what the cumulative effect of smaller classes from kindergarten through twelfth grade would be. In the NAEP, class size changes affect all grades, and the apparent benefits for blacks are, if anything, larger for older students. But no benefits are detectable for whites after age nine. Although the Tennessee evidence suggests that effects are larger for minority and lower-income children, we need more precise estimates of how smaller classes affect advantaged children.

Finally, the Tennessee experiment did not investigate whether the effects of small classes would change as teachers, children, and parents gained experience with them. Adjustments in teaching style, curriculum, and textbooks take time.[62] In the long run, moreover, smaller classes may change the characteristics of those who become or remain teachers, especially in the poorest schools and districts. The Tennessee experiment cannot capture changes of this kind.

Smaller classes are clearly a viable candidate for explaining some part of the black NAEP gains and some part of the reduction in the black-white gap. But the weak relationship between smaller classes and white NAEP scores is still a puzzle.

Teacher Characteristics

One important side effect of the Tennessee experiment is that it raises new doubts about the validity of estimates derived from nonexperimental studies conducted in a "production function" framework. The Tennessee data show that children gain from smaller classes by the end of their first year in them. Additional years in small classes preserve the (standardized) gain but do not increase it much.[63] As Alan Krueger has pointed out, this finding implies that production functions that include the previous year's scores as a control and simply measure gains measure only a small part of the true benefits accruing after the first year, which take the form of preventing losses rather than ensuring further gains.[64] Until we develop pro-

---

62. Murnane and Levy (1996).

63. Krueger (1997) shows that the big initial-year gain occurred regardless of whether the student entered the experiment in kindergarten, first grade, second grade, or third grade.

64. Two carefully done studies, Ferguson (1991) and Ferguson and Ladd (1996), that used excellent data at the state level and had prior year's test scores as controls were considered to be the most reliable studies. Both showed generally stronger effects of resources than previous studies. However, these specifications may provide downwardly biased results if the first-year effect measured by Krueger is present. The 1996 Ferguson and Ladd study also presents cross-sectional estimates that may more

duction functions that can reproduce these experimental effects and can explain why they work, the results of nonexperimental studies have to be discounted heavily.[65] Unfortunately, we have no experiments that measure the effects of teacher characteristics on student achievement.

Figure 6-12 shows that the mean experience and mean education of teachers increased over the NAEP period.[66] The share of teachers with a master's degree increased from around 25 percent for cohorts entering in the 1960s to more than 50 percent for cohorts entering in the 1980s. The share of teachers with five to twenty years of experience increased from 45 percent for early cohorts to more than 60 percent for cohorts entering in the 1970s, but then decreased to around 50 percent.[67] Production-function studies show no consistent effects of either teachers' advanced study or experience on student achievement.[68] Table 6-5 suggests that teachers' education predicts student achievement about as well as class size does. Teachers' experience has much weaker effects. But without confirming evidence from experiments, we cannot put much weight on these results. Nor do we have much evidence about whether either teachers' preparation or experience changed more for black or white students. In 1986–87, teachers' education and experience were slightly less in schools with high minority enrollment.[69]

---

accurately measure the full effect of school resources. Generally the model without controls for prior scores shows stronger effects for resource variables. Using stringent quality criteria, Hanushek's chapter in Ladd (1996) reviews previous studies including only the ones that had previous years' test scores as controls. He finds no positive effects from these studies, but Krueger's analysis suggests that we should be cautious about these results.

65. Both the constant and the growth components of continuous exposure to smaller classes can depend on how tests are constructed, how curriculum changes, and how teaching styles change when classes shrink. The effect can also depend on whether parents provide more or less time for helping children. Understanding these mechanisms is crucial for specifying models.

66. See Grissmer and Kirby (1997) for an explanation of the shift in teacher characteristics over this period.

67. We use the percentage of teachers with five to twenty years of experience somewhat arbitrarily. There is little evidence about the productivity of groups of teachers who have different levels of experience. Krueger (1997) estimates a peak productivity at twenty years of experience using the Tennessee data, but the size of the effects is small and significance levels are low. We assume a learning curve that increases over the first five years and then assume that productivity falls after twenty years of teaching.

68. Ferguson (1991) and Ferguson and Ladd (1996) find small positive effects from teacher education, while Krueger (1997) finds inconsistent effects. Using state NAEP data for 1992, Raudenbush (forthcoming) finds no master's degree effect but finds that *what* teachers studied in college (math major, math education major) is important, at least for math scores. All these studies find either very small positive effects or no consistent effects from teacher experience.

69. See *Schools and Staffing in the United States: A Statistical Profile, 1987–88*, table 39.

Figure 6-12. *Average Teacher Experience and Education during Years of Schooling, by Age of Student, 1960–90*

Percent

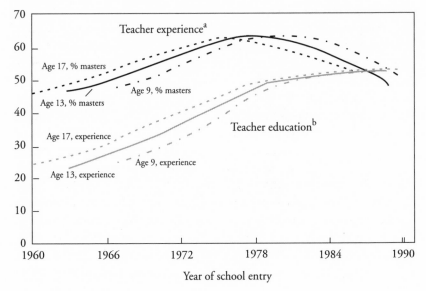

Year of school entry

Source: See text.
a. Percentage of teachers with five to twenty years of experience.
b. Percentage of teachers with advanced degree.

Two other teacher characteristics are important to consider. Teachers' test scores have been more consistently linked to achievement scores than other characteristics (see Ferguson's review in chapter 8). However, there is no reason to think that average teacher scores rose during this period.[70] Demand for new teachers more than doubled between 1960 and 1975, and high demand usually means that school systems cannot be as choosy about the people they hire.[71] The inflow of new, younger teachers could, however, have had a beneficial effect if the teachers had more positive attitudes toward minority students.

70. Controlling for education and experience, Hanushek and Rivkin (1997) found that teachers' salaries fell relative to the distribution of wages for all college-educated workers from 1970 to 1990. This makes it unlikely that teachers' average test scores have risen, either through an increase in the scores of entering teachers or increased retention of high-scoring teachers.
71. Grissmer and Kirby (1992).

In summary, there is little reliable empirical evidence that changes in teachers' characteristics contributed to either the increase in black scores or the narrowing of the black-white gap. The significance of teacher education in regressions with NAEP scores means that it cannot be eliminated from consideration, but we cannot put much weight on these results unless they are confirmed by other evidence.[72]

Violence

Although a number of hypotheses can explain the increase in black and white NAEP scores, the decline in blacks' reading scores after 1988 is much harder to explain. Black reading scores fell markedly at all ages starting in 1988. Only nine-year-olds' scores have recovered. There was no parallel decline in whites' reading scores during this period, so the black-white reading gap among adolescents widened by 0.2 to 0.4 standard deviations (see figures 6-1 to 6-3). Blacks' math scores were relatively flat during this period, while whites' math scores rose. The decline in blacks' reading scores does not appear to be a cohort effect. It started for blacks of all ages in 1988 and continued through 1992 for seventeen- and thirteen-year-olds.[73] The explanation is therefore likely to involve historical shifts that affected blacks of all ages simultaneously.

The effects of changes in schools and communities that gave rise to increasing violence among black teenagers are one possible explanation of this change. Figure 6-13 shows that the murder rate among black teenagers rose dramatically between 1985 and 1990 and remained high through 1992. If murder is a proxy for other adverse changes in black neighborhoods and

72. If we had used a measure of how many teachers had five to forty years of experience, the regression results would have been more similar to those for class size and teacher education. We need better estimates of how experience affects teachers' productivity before eliminating experience from consideration.

73. Dramatic changes starting in one particular year also raise the possibility that changes in sampling procedures or participation rates could be distorting results. One conceivable "explanation" of the trend data is that black adolescents' scores are overestimated in 1988 for some reason. When the 1986 NAEP results for reading looked inexplicably low, the Department of Education suppressed them, even though focused investigations never found methodological problems that might explain the decline. The 1988 scores for black 17-year-old students look abnormally high, and the black reading decline after 1988 would be negligible for seventeen-year-olds if this single data point were eliminated. However, this is not true for thirteen-year-olds, whose reading scores show a steady decline after 1988. Errors that affect only blacks and not whites in 1988, affect blacks of all ages in 1988, and affect black thirteen-year-olds after 1988 appear unlikely.

Figure 6-13. *Homicide Rate per 100,000 Black Males Aged Fifteen
to Nineteen, 1970–92*

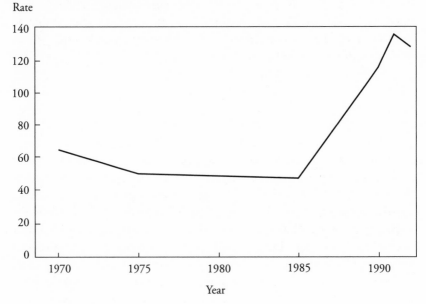

Rate

Year

Source: See text.

schools, it might explain declines in blacks' reading scores. This theory is
appealing because there was no parallel increase in murders among white
teenagers, so it could help explain why blacks' scores declined while whites'
scores remained stable.

Jeff Grogger has used high school principals' reports about violence in
their schools to predict changes in math achievement between the tenth
and twelfth grades.[74] Holding tenth-grade scores constant and treating
schools where the principal said violence was not a problem as his benchmark, Grogger found that twelfth-grade math scores were about 0.20 standard deviations lower when the principal reported a "substantial violent
climate" (about 1 percent of all schools), about 0.10 standard deviations
lower when the principal reported a "moderate violent climate" (10 percent of all schools), and about 0.07 standard deviations lower when the

74. Grogger (1997).

principal reported a "minor violent climate" (62 percent of schools). If these estimates are roughly correct, it would take a very large increase in school violence to lower seventeen-year-olds' scores by 0.2 standard deviations. Furthermore, although the black teenage murder rate rose in the late 1980s, black tenth-graders said they felt safer at school in 1990 than in 1980.[75] Thus it is not clear that school violence increased dramatically. Perhaps most schools took successful steps to maintain security even though violence was increasing on the streets.

A theory that invokes changes in the level of violence among black teenagers must also explain why black adolescents' reading scores fell while their math scores did not. One hypothesis is that if all else had remained equal, increased teenage violence would have depressed both reading and math scores, but that the negative effect of violence on math scores was offset by the fact that black students were taking more demanding math classes. This combination of rising violence among blacks and more demanding math courses for everyone could also explain why adolescents' math scores rose more among whites than blacks during the early 1990s.

Conclusions

What happened? Reading and math scores rose for both black and white students at all ages between 1971 and 1996. But blacks gained much more than whites, narrowing the black-white test score gap by 0.2 to 0.6 standard deviations. Nonetheless, the median black student still scored at the 20th to 25th percentile of the white distribution in 1996.

When did it happen? Blacks who entered school in 1968 did little better than those who entered in 1960. Cohorts of blacks entering school between 1968 and 1980 made large gains. Among blacks entering after 1980, math scores were stable or increased slightly, while reading scores declined.

What explains the gains? Positive changes in family characteristics can explain nearly all the white gains but only a small part of the black gains. Changes in the family may also explain a small part of the gap reduction. The remaining black gains might be explained in two complementary ways, which we can loosely characterize as the civil rights–War on Poverty model and the school-based model.

75. Rasinski and Ingels (1993).

The civil rights–War on Poverty model associates black gains with changes flowing from the civil rights movement and from antipoverty programs initiated in the late 1960s and early 1970s. This explanation requires two assumptions. First, we must assume a nationwide shift in beliefs, attitudes, and motivations among black parents and students, as well as their teachers, triggered by events such as southern school desegregation between 1968 and 1972, which significantly changed the educational experience of black children. Second, we must assume that this change had a large effect on achievement only when students experienced it in early childhood or at the very start of their school careers. If this latter assumption were correct, we would predict big increases in achievement for cohorts of blacks who began school between about 1968 and 1974. Figure 6-4 shows that these were, in fact, the cohorts of blacks whose reading scores rose. For math, however, figure 6-7 suggests some gains for the cohorts entering between 1968 and 1974, but it also shows sizable additional gains for later cohorts.

The school-based model emphasizes the direct (as against the symbolic) effects of school desegregation, along with changes in patterns of course enrollment and reductions in class size. More demanding course work at the middle school and high school level could explain the large gains of older students in the 1980s. Smaller classes might explain black nine-year-olds' gains in the 1970s, as well as some of the gains of older students in the 1980s. The direct effects of school desegregation might also account for some black gains at each age. The main difficulty with this model is that it has trouble explaining why blacks gained more than whites. To explain that fact we have to assume that reducing class size had little effect on most white students and that enrolling in more demanding courses also had far more effect on blacks than whites.

The potential importance of class size, school desegregation, and demanding course work is supported by strong correlations with NAEP scores, corroborating research, or both. Some of the other school-level changes that we analyzed are not similarly supported and probably cannot account for much of the black gain or black-white gap reduction. These failed explanations include reduced geographic mobility, increased preprimary education, and changes in academic tracking. In still other cases, such as more protracted teacher education, increased teacher experience, and ability grouping within heterogeneous elementary school classes, the evidence was too weak to say much either way.

What explains the losses? None of the foregoing changes can explain the decline in black reading scores after 1988–90. Black teenage violence increased dramatically at about this time, and a violent school climate does seem to lower test score gains between the tenth and twelfth grades. But unless teenage violence also has parallel effects on younger students, the cumulative impact does not appear to be large enough to explain the drop in black seventeen-year-olds' reading scores. This important question remains unresolved.

Analysis of the NAEP scores ought to be crucial in the debates about the changes in American families and schools, about policies providing equal opportunity in education, and about how best to invest in education and children. Ignoring the NAEP, as almost everyone has, encourages the proliferation of many beliefs that are inconsistent with NAEP results. The NAEP data do not suggest that families have deteriorated since 1970. Nor do they suggest that schools have squandered money or that social and educational policies aimed at helping minorities have failed.

Instead, the NAEP suggests that overall family environments changed in positive ways from 1970 to 1996, that the implementation of the policies associated with the civil rights movement and the War on Poverty may be a viable explanation for large black reading and math gains, and that changes in our schools may also account for some score gains. Although NAEP scores alone cannot change strongly held beliefs about deteriorating families and schools or the ineffectiveness of social and educational policies, those who believe that families and schools have gotten worse surely have an obligation to explain rising NAEP scores, particularly for minorities. While trends in black achievement since 1988–90 have been more discouraging than trends in the 1980s, white achievement has edged up since 1990 and black achievement rose dramatically during the previous decade. A coherent story about our recent past needs to explain both the long-term gains and the recent reversals for blacks.

References

Armor, D. J. 1995. *Forced Justice: School Desegregation and the Law.* Oxford University Press.

Barnett, Steven. 1995. "Long-Term Effects of Early Childhood Programs on Cognitive and School Outcomes." *Future of Children* 5(Winter).

Becker, Gary. 1981. *A Treatise on the Family.* Harvard University Press.

———. 1993. *Human Capital: A Theoretical and Empirical Analysis with Special Reference to Education,* 3d ed. University of Chicago Press.

Berends, M., and D. Koretz. 1996. "Reporting Minority Students' Test Scores: Can the NAEP Account for Differences in Social Context?" *Educational Assessment.*

Boozer, Michael A., Alan B. Krueger, and Shari Wolkon. 1992. "Race and School Quality since *Brown v. Board of Education.*" *Brookings Papers on Economic Activity, Microeconomics.*

Bureau of the Census. 1983. *Statistical Abstract of the United States, 1982-83.* Department of Commerce.

———. 1997. *Statistical Abstract of the United States, 1997.* Department of Commerce.

Burtless, Gary, ed. 1996. *Does Money Matter? The Effect of School Resources on Student Achievement and Adult Success.* Brookings Institution Press.

Campbell, J. R., and others. 1996. *NAEP 1994 Reading Report Card for the Nations and the States; Findings from the National Assessment of Educational Progress and Trial State Assessment.* Washington: National Center for Education Statistics.

Campbell, Jay, Kristin Voelkl, and Patricia Donahue. 1997. *NAEP 1996 Trends in Academic Progress,* NCES 97-985. Washington: National Center for Education Statistics/Educational Testing Service.

Center for the Future of Children. 1995. "Long-Term Outcomes of Early Childhood Programs." *Future of Children* 5(Winter).

Cherlin, Andrew J. 1988. "The Changing American Family and Public Policy." In A. J. Cherlin, ed. *The Changing American Family and Public Policy.* Washington: Urban Institute Press.

Coleman, James S. 1988. "Social Capital in the Creation of Human Capital." *American Journal of Sociology* 94:s95–s120.

———. 1990. *Foundations of Social Theory.* Harvard University Press.

Coleman, James S., and others. 1966. *Equality of Educational Opportunity.* Washington: Government Printing Office.

Cook, Michael, and William N. Evans. 1977. "Families or Schools? Explaining the Convergence in White and Black Academic Performance," working paper.

Ferguson, Ronald F. 1991. "Paying for Public Education: New Evidence on How and Why Money Matters." *Harvard Journal on Legislation* 28: 465–97.

Ferguson, Ronald F., and Helen F. Ladd. 1996. "How and Why Money Matters: An Analysis of Alabama Schools." In Helen F. Ladd, ed., *Holding Schools Accountable.* Brookings Institution Press.

Finn, Jeremy D., and Helen F. Ladd. 1990. "Answers and Questions about Class Size: A Statewide Experiment." *American Educational Research Journal* 27(3): 557–77.

Flynn, J. R. 1987. "Massive IQ Gains in 14 Nations: What IQ Tests Really Measure." *Psychological Bulletin* 101(2): 171–91.

Fuchs, Victor R., and Diane M. Reklis. 1992. "America's Children: Economic Perspectives and Policy Options." *Science* 255: 41–45.

Grissmer, David, and Sheila Nataraj Kirby. 1997. "Teacher Turnover and Teacher Quality." *Teacher's College Record* 99 (Fall).

———. 1992. *The Pattern of Attrition for Indiana Teachers.* Santa Monica, Calif.: RAND.

Grissmer, David, and others. 1998. "Exploring the Rapid Rise in Black Achievement Scores in the United States (1970–1990)." In Ulrich Neisser, ed., *The Rising Curve: Long-Term Changes in IQ and Related Measures.* Washington: American Psychological Association.

———. 1994. *Student Achievement and the Changing American Family.* Santa Monica, Calif.: RAND.

Grogger, Jeffrey. 1997. "Local Violence and Educational Attainment." *Journal of Human Resources* 32(Fall).

Hanushek, Eric A. 1996. "School Resources and Student Performance." In Burtless, ed., *Does Money Matter?*

———. 1994. *Making Schools Work: Improving Performance and Controlling Costs.* Brookings Institution.

———. 1989. "The Impact of Differential Expenditures on School Performance." *Educational Researcher* 18 (4): 45–51.

Hanushek, Eric A., and Steven G. Rivkin. 1997. "Understanding the Twentieth-Century Growth in U.S. School Spending." *Journal of Human Resources* 32 (Winter).

Hauser, Robert M. 1996. "Trends in Black-White Test Score Differentials: Uses and Misuses of NAEP/SAT Data," CDE working paper 96-29. Center for Demography and Ecology, University of Wisconsin.

Hauser, Robert M., and Min-Hsiung Huang. 1996. "Trends in Black-White Test-Score Differentials," DP # 1110-96. Institute for Research on Poverty, University of Wisconsin.

Haveman, Robert, and Barbara Wolfe, *Succeeding Generations: On the Effects of Investments in Children.* New York: Russell Sage Foundation, 1994.

Hedges, Larry V., and Rob Greenwald. "Have Times Changed? The Relation between School Resources and Student Performance." 1996. In Burtless, ed., *Does Money Matter?*

Hedges, Larry V., Richard D. Laine, and Rob Greenwald. 1992. "Does Monday Matter: Meta-Analysis of Studies of the Effects of Differential School Inputs on Student Outcomes." *Educational Researcher* 23(3): 5–14.

Herrnstein, Richard J., and Charles Murray. 1994. *The Bell Curve: Intelligence and Class Structure in American Life.* Free Press.

Jencks, Christopher. 1992. *Rethinking Social Policy: Race, Poverty, and the Underclass.* Harvard University Press.

Johnson, E. G., and J. E. Carlson. 1994. *The NAEP 1992 Technical Report.* National Center for Education Statistics, Department of Education.

Koretz, Daniel. 1987. *Educational Achievement: Explanations and Implications of Recent Trends.* Congressional Budget Office.

———. 1986. *Trends in Educational Achievement.* Congressional Budget Office.

Krueger, Alan B. 1997. "Experimental Estimates of Education Production Functions," working paper 379. Princeton University, Industrial Relations Section.

Ladd, Helen F. 1996. *Holding Schools Accountable.* Brookings.

Lankford, Hamilton, and James Wyckoff. 1996. "The Allocation of Resources to Special Education and Regular Instruction." In Ladd, ed., *Holding Schools Accountable.*

Lewitt, Eugene, and Linda Shumann Baker. 1997 "Class Size." *Future of Children* 7(Winter):112–21.

McGue, Matt, and others. 1993. "Behavioral Genetics of Cognitive Ability: A Life-Span Perspective." In Robert Plomin and G. E. McClearn, eds., *Nature, Nurture, and Psychology.* Washington: American Psychological Association.

Miller, Paul, Charles Mulvey, and Nick Martin. 1995. "What Do Twins Studies Reveal about the Economic Returns to Education? A Comparison of Australian and U.S. Findings." *American Economic Review* 85 (June 1995).

Mosteller, F. 1994. "The Tennessee Study of Class Size in the Early School Grades." *Future of Children* 5(2): 113–27.

Mullis, I. V. S., and others. 1993. *NAEP 1992 Mathematics Report Card for the Nation and the States: Data from the National and Trial State Assessments.* Washington: National Center for Education Statistics.

Murnane, Richard J., and Frank Levy. 1996. "Evidence from Fifteen Schools in Austin, Texas." In Burtless, ed., *Does Money Matter?*

National Center for Education Statistics. Various years. *Digest of Education Statistics.* Washington: Department of Education.

Neisser, Ulrich, ed. 1998. *The Rising Curve: Long-Term Changes in IQ and Related Measures.* Washington: American Psychological Association

Orfield, Gary, and Susan E. Eaton. 1996. *Dismantling Desegregation: The Quiet Reversal of Brown v. Board of Education.* New Press.

Puma, Michael J., and others. 1997. *Prospects: Final Report on Student Outcomes,* report prepared for the Planing and Evaluation Service, Department of Education. Cambridge, Mass.: Abt Associates.

Popenoe, David. 1993. "American Family Decline, 1960–1990: A Review and Appraisal." *Journal of Marraige and the Family* 55: 27–555.

Rasinski, Kenneth, and Steven Ingels. 1993. *America's High School Sophomores: A Ten-Year Comparison,* NCES 93-087. Washington: National Center for Education Statistics.

Raudenbush, Stephen W., Randall P. Fotiu, and Yuk Fai Cheong. Forthcoming. "Inequality of Access to Educational Resources: A National Report Card for Eighth Grade Math."

Rothstein, Richard, and K. H. Miles. 1995. *Where's the Money Gone? Changes in the Level and Composition of Education Spending.* Washington: Economic Policy Institute.

Schofield, Janet. 1994. In J. A. Banks and C. A. McGee Banks, eds., *Handbook of Research on Multicultural Education.* Macmillan.

Schools and Staffing in the United States: A Statistical Profile, 1986-87, NCES 92-120. 1992. Department of Education.

Stacey, Judith. 1993. "Good Riddance to 'The Family': A Response to David Popenoe." *Journal of Marraige and Family* 55: 545–47.

Swinton, S. 1993. *Differential Response Rates to Open-Ended and Multiple-choice NAEP Items by Ethnic Groups.* Paper presented at the annual meeting of the American Educational Research Association.

Wells, A. S., and R. L. Crain. 1994. "Perpetuation Theory and the Long-Term Effects of School Desegregation." *Review of Educational Research* 64 (Winter): 531.

Wilson, William Julius. 1987. *The Truly Disadvantaged: The Inner City, the Underclass, and Public Policy.* University of Chicago Press.

Word, E. R., J. Johnston, and H. P. Bain. 1994. *The State of Tennessee's Student/Teacher Achievement Ratio (STAR) Project: Technical Report 1985–1990.* Nashville: Tennessee State Department of Education.

———. 1990. *Student/Teacher Achievement Ratio (STAR): Tennessee's K–3 Class Size Study. Final Summary Report, 1985–1990.* Nashville: Tennessee Department of Education.

Zill, Nicholas, and Carolyn C. Rogers. 1988. "Recent Trends in the Well-Being of Children in the United States and Their Implications for Public Policy." In Cherlin, ed., *Changing American Family and Public Policy,* pp. 31–115.

PART III

The Impact of Schools and Culture

MEREDITH PHILLIPS
JAMES CROUSE
JOHN RALPH

7

Does the Black-White Test Score Gap Widen after Children Enter School?

Psychologists have argued about the causes of the black-white test score gap since early in the twentieth century. One of the most controversial empirical questions has been whether the gap widened as children aged. At one time, many psychologists saw age-related changes in the gap as evidence against genetic explanations.[1] Since the 1960s, however, age-related changes have also been invoked as evidence in the debate about whether schools contribute to the gap.[2]

Two competing views shape our thinking about why black teenagers typically leave high school with fewer mathematics and reading skills than

We are indebted to Christopher Jencks for very helpful and extensive comments on numerous drafts of this paper. Arthur Jensen, John Loehlin, and Charles Reichart provided thoughtful comments on an earlier draft. Seminar participants at the University of Chicago and the Kennedy School of Government offered useful suggestions, particularly Norman Bradburn, Thomas Kane, and Christopher Winship. We thank Larry Hedges, Amy Nowell, and William Shadish for technical advice on the meta-analysis. We also thank Karl Alexander for providing us with Beginning School Study analyses and Thomas Hoffer for giving us the Longitudinal Study of American Youth data. Finally, we are grateful for the financial support of the Mellon Foundation and the Spencer Foundation. All errors of fact and interpretation are ours.

1. See, for example, Klineberg (1963).
2. See, for example, Loehlin, Lindzey, and Spuhler (1975).

229

whites. One view, endorsed by many educators and psychologists, is that black children start elementary school with fewer academic skills than white children, and that these initial differences persist for reasons that schools cannot alter. Black-white differences in cognitive skills, in this view, are rooted in children's home environments, over which schools have no control. The other view, endorsed by most African-American parents, many educational reformers, and many sociologists, is that neither home environment nor initial skill differences account for the black-white gap among teenagers. The "strong" variant of this argument, endorsed by some African-American parents, holds that black and white children start out alike and that black children fall behind because their teachers either ask too little of them or teach them incompetently. The "weak" variant of the same argument recognizes that black children enter school with weaker academic skills (smaller vocabularies and less knowledge of numbers, for example), but argues that what starts out as a small gap eventually becomes a much larger gap. Those who endorse this view often cite data showing that black children are less than one year behind whites in second or third grade but have fallen three or four years behind by twelfth grade.

Which view people take on these issues depends partly on how they measure the black-white gap. Roughly speaking, black six-year-olds' vocabulary scores match those of white five-year-olds, so one can say that black children are one year behind whites. Black seventeen-year-olds have vocabularies roughly comparable to those of white thirteen-year-olds, so one can say that at age seventeen blacks are four years behind. But if one compares blacks and whites by asking, for example, what percentage of whites score below the average black at different ages, the percentage will change very little with age. Likewise, if one uses the conventional metric of the social sciences and expresses the black-white gap as a percentage of the overall standard deviation, the gap does not change much with age.

If age-related changes in the black-white gap depend on how one measures the gap, choosing the right measure might seem critically important. In this chapter, however, we do not spend much time on the problem of how we should measure the gap. We argue that measuring it in "years" (or grade levels) makes no sense, because children may not learn the same amount between the ages of sixteen and seventeen as they do between the ages of six and seven. Because we have no good measures of the absolute amount that children know at any age, and because it is not clear that such measures would have any predictive power even if they existed, we will concentrate on "age-standardized" measures of the black-white gap. But readers who think that this decision predetermines our conclusions will be wrong. First, as we shall see, even the standardized gap between blacks and whites grows somewhat between the ages of six and eighteen. Second, and more important, we will argue that even if the standardized gap between blacks and whites did not grow at all, it would not follow that schools had not contributed to racial disparities among their graduates.

Research on how the black-white test score gap changes with age is sparse and contradictory. Arthur Jensen's 1974 review concluded that the standardized gap generally widened with age in cross-sectional surveys but was constant in longitudinal surveys.[3] His own research using sibling comparisons showed that the gap widened on verbal IQ tests.[4] In 1975 John Loehlin, Gardner Lindzey, and J. N. Spuhler concluded from their review that the IQ gap tended "to remain fairly stable during the school years" and inferred that schools could "mostly be exonerated from the charges of creating the black-white difference in average IQ-test performance or of increasing it during the period of school attendance."[5] Robert Gordon's 1984 review also suggested that the black-white IQ gap remained more or less constant with age.[6] The only recent research on age-related trends in the gap is Doris Entwisle and Karl Alexander's longitudinal study of Baltimore elementary school students. They found that blacks and whites started first grade with very similar mathematics and reading skills but that blacks fell behind whites between first and ninth grades.[7] These findings may not generalize to other locations, however, because Baltimore's white students are not at all representative of white students nationally.

Since 1965 eight national surveys have tested black and white students at different ages. This chapter uses these eight surveys to examine how the black-white math, reading, and vocabulary test score gaps change as children grow older. We first present cross-sectional evidence on grade-related trends in the gap and on trends for cohorts born since 1948. From a meta-analysis of these data, we estimate that the math gap widens by about 0.18

3. Jensen (1974).
4. Jensen (1974, 1977).
5. Loehlin, Lindzey, and Spuhler (1975, pp. 156–57).
6. Gordon (1984). Two other studies have briefly discussed age-related changes in the black-white gap. Jones (1984) reported that National Assessment of Educational Progress (NAEP) results from 1975–76 showed that the black-white gap widened by 0.30 standard deviations between ages thirteen and seventeen. In contrast, Hauser and Huang (1996) observed no consistent within-cohort age-related increase in the gap in the NAEP data from the 1970s through 1992.
7. Entwisle and Alexander (1988, 1992, 1994); and Alexander, personal communication, 1997.

standard deviations between the first and twelfth grades, that the reading gap does not widen at all, and that the vocabulary gap widens by 0.23 standard deviations. Like other researchers, we find that the black-white gap has narrowed in recent birth cohorts. Among children born between 1948 and 1978, the gap narrowed by about 0.015 standard deviations a year. Among children born after 1978, however, the gap has remained constant for math and seems to have widened for reading and vocabulary.

We then turn to the question of how one should interpret either stability or changes in the standardized black-white gap. Here, our approach differs somewhat from that of previous analyses because we ask what happens to black and white children who start school with the same "true" test scores. We find that when whites and blacks start elementary school with the same math, reading, and vocabulary scores, they finish elementary school with similar math scores but that the blacks have lower reading and vocabulary test scores. During middle school, blacks may fall farther behind whites in math, but we do not have much confidence in this result. When we compare whites and blacks who start high school with the same math, reading, science, and history scores, blacks finish high school with essentially the same math scores but with slightly lower reading scores. Overall, black children who start elementary school with "true" test scores at the population mean will finish high school with math scores that lie about 0.34 standard deviations below the population mean and reading scores that lie about 0.39 standard deviations below the population mean. This implies that about half of the total black-white math and reading gap at the end of high school can be attributed to the fact that blacks start school with fewer skills than whites. The other half can be attributed to the fact that blacks learn less than whites who enter school with similar initial skills.

This does not necessarily mean that *schools* are a major contributor to the black-white test score gap. Although blacks may attend worse schools than whites, may be treated differently from whites in the same schools, or may be less interested in school than initially similar whites, it is also possible that blacks' parenting practices, peer influences, summer learning opportunities, or beliefs about their academic ability could explain why they learn less between first and twelfth grades than initially similar whites.

Nonetheless, our findings do suggest that public policy must focus *both* on improving black preschoolers' skills *and* on identifying the factors that cause black students to learn less after they start school than their equally prepared white counterparts. Preliminary analyses suggest that differences between black and white children's families and schools play a relatively modest role in exacerbating the initial test score gap. Consequently, we need to consider other possibilities, such as systematic differences in the ways white and black students are treated within the same school, in how white and black children spend their summers, or in white and black children's study habits or perceptions of their academic ability.

Measuring the Black-White Gap

For age-related changes in the size of the test score gap to yield useful information, the tests must meet two criteria: they must measure the same thing at both ages, and the scores must be in the same metric. Prospects: The Congressionally Mandated Study of Educational Growth and Opportunity illustrates both points.[8]

Figure 7-1 presents data on vocabulary growth. On the horizontal axis, 1 represents the fall of first grade, 1.75 represents the spring of first grade, and so on. The scores on the vertical axis come from tests with some overlapping items that have been equated using item response theory (IRT). The lines show the learning trajectories of the average black and white public school student. The black-white gap in vocabulary scores is the difference between the black and white mean at each grade. When blacks and whites learn the same amount, the black-white gap is constant. When blacks learn less than whites, the gap widens with age. Figure 7-1 shows that the black-white vocabulary gap is about the same size at the end of ninth grade as at the beginning of first grade.

To believe that figure 7-1 accurately describes how the black-white vocabulary gap changes with age, one needs to believe that the tests administered at different grades all measure vocabulary skills. Figure 7-1 suggests, for example, that the black-white vocabulary gap widens slightly between the fourth and fifth grades. Suppose, however, that the vocabulary test administered to fifth-graders actually measures reading comprehension as well as vocabulary. If this were the case, the larger black-white gap on the fifth grade test might just indicate that the reading gap is wider than the vocabulary gap, not that blacks learn fewer words than whites between fourth and fifth grades. Test makers try to ensure that similarly named tests measure the same attribute by designing tests that have similar patterns of inter-item correlations and that relate to external criteria in similar ways. But

8. For details, see *Prospects* (1993).

Figure 7-1. *Black-White Differences in Vocabulary Growth between First and Ninth Grades*[a]

Mean vocabulary IRT score

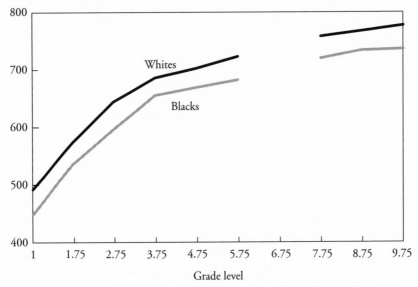

Grade level

Source: Prospects: The Congressionally Mandated Study of Educational Growth and Opportunity, 1991–1993 data set, U.S. Department of Education.

a. Trajectories combine data from three independent cohorts. The first cohort was tested in the fall of first grade, and in the spring of first and second grade. The second cohort was tested in the spring of third, fourth, and fifth grade. The third cohort was tested in the spring of seventh, eighth, and ninth grade.

even when tests look similar, they can still measure different things, and this can affect the size of the black-white gap. Nonetheless, we assume throughout this chapter that similarly named tests measure the same thing.

If we are to compare tests given at different ages, all the tests must also be in the same metric. We can compare the black-white gap at different ages in figure 7-1 because Prospects used tests with enough overlap in their items so they can all be expressed in a single metric. Suppose, however, that we wanted to know whether the black-white vocabulary gap widened between the ninth and twelfth grades. Prospects did not test twelfth-graders. Other surveys did administer vocabulary tests in the twelfth grade, but we have no way of converting those tests to the metric used by Prospects.

Indeed, even the stability of the black-white vocabulary gap on the tests in figure 7-1 may be misleading because some of the scores on these tests become less variable as children age. The figure shows that the black-white vocabulary gap shrinks from 44 points in the first grade to 30 points at the end of the third grade. However, if we divide these raw gaps by the population standard deviation, the standardized gaps are 0.69 standard deviations in both the first and third grades.[9] Standardizing the gap provides a rough measure of overlap between two groups, telling us generally where the mean of one distribution falls in the other distribution. Standardizing gaps also allows us to compare gaps on tests with different metrics.

Because many educators and other users do not understand standardized gaps, test distributors often report scores in "grade equivalents." This leads naturally but misleadingly to expressing the black-white gap at different ages in grade equivalents. If the average black second-grader has the same vocabulary as the average white first-grader, for example, we say the black second-grader is one grade behind. If we retest students two years later and find that the average black fourth-grader's vocabulary is equal to that of the average white second-grader, we say the racial gap has widened from one to two years. Because a difference of one standard deviation always represents a larger grade-level difference as children get older, the black-white gap measured in grade levels will widen even if the overlap between the black and white distributions is unchanged.[10] We do not use grade equivalents in this chapter because we believe that the extent of overlap between the black and white distributions is what matters for future inequalities between black and white adults.

We standardize scores to a population mean of zero and a standard deviation of 1.0. Thus if students score at the population mean for their age or grade level, they get a score of zero. If they score one standard deviation above the mean, they get a score of +1.0 and so on. Readers who find it difficult to think about group differences in terms of standard deviations may find it helpful to think in terms of scores on familiar tests. A 1.0 standard deviation gap on an IQ test is 15 points. A 1.0 standard deviation

9. Because the sample also changes between the first and third grades, the smaller standard deviation may be due to the way the sample was drawn. Once the fourth wave of Prospects data becomes available, we will be able to investigate this possibility.

10. Moreover, whenever a test indicates that children learn less as they get older (that is, when learning curves are convex), the grade-equivalent metric will show that blacks are falling farther behind whites each year unless blacks learn more test items than whites each year. Only when both groups learn the same number of items each year *and* the overall learning trajectory is linear, or when blacks learn more items than whites each year, can the grade-equivalent metric show that the black-white gap remains constant with age.

gap on the math or verbal SAT is 100 points. Thus, a black-white gap of 0.80 standard deviations is equivalent to a 12 point gap on an IQ test or an 80 point gap on the verbal SAT.

Cross-Sectional Evidence

Figure 7-1 suggests that the black-white vocabulary gap is relatively constant between the first and ninth grades. But the data in figure 7-1 come from a single survey (Prospects), a single type of test (the Comprehensive Test of Basic Skills, or CTBS), and a single historical period (the early 1990s). Data from other surveys do not always show the same pattern. We therefore conducted a meta-analysis of the eight national surveys that have tested black and white students since 1965 (table 7-1 and appendix table 7A-1). We included the first wave of each longitudinal study in this analysis, but excluded followups of the longitudinal samples because followups are subject to nonrandom attrition. We measured the black-white gap by subtracting the average score for blacks from the average score for whites and then dividing by the overall standard deviation of the test. The data appendix gives details on our sample and analyses.

Table 7-2 presents results from multivariate models that use both year of birth and grade level to predict the black-white gap. Column 1 shows that with other factors controlled, the math gap widens by about $(0.015)(12) = 0.18$ standard deviations between the first and twelfth grades, the reading gap remains relatively constant, and the vocabulary gap widens by about 0.23 standard deviations. None of these linear trends differs reliably between cross-sectional and longitudinal surveys.[11]

---

11. Table 7-2 does suggest, however, that the first year of a longitudinal survey may yield a smaller black-white gap than do cross-sectional surveys. In addition, tests scaled using Item-Response Theory (IRT) seem to show larger black-white math and reading gaps than tests scored by summing correct answers. These results can be partially attributed to the fact that NAEP observations constitute over half our math and reading samples and the black-white gaps in the NAEP are typically larger than the gaps estimated by other surveys. Hedges and Nowell (chapter 5) attribute the larger NAEP gaps to the fact that NAEP standard deviations have been corrected for measurement error and thus are smaller than the observed standard deviations in other data sets. When we control for whether or not an observation comes from the NAEP, the IRT effect drops by almost half, but remains marginally significant at the .10 level. We did not find any statistically significant evidence that the grade-level trends differed for IRT-scaled tests as opposed to Number Right-scaled tests.

Table 7-1. *Data Sets Used in Meta-Analysis*

Acronym	Name	Test year(s)	Grades
EEO	Equality of Educational Opportunity Study	1965	1, 3, 6, 9, 12
NLSY	National Longitudinal Survey of Youth	1980	10, 11, 12
HS&B	High School & Beyond	1980	10, 12
LSAY	Longitudinal Study of American Youth	1987	7, 10
CNLSY	Children of the National Longitudinal Survey of Youth	1992	Preschool, K, 1, 2, 3, 4, 5
NELS	National Education Longitudinal Study	1988, 1990, 1992	8, 10, 12
Prospects	Prospects: The Congressionally Mandated Study of Educational Growth and Opportunity	1991	1, 3, 7
NAEP	National Assessment of Educational Progress	1971–96	4, 8, 11

Column 2 of table 7-2 shows separate grade-level effects for elementary, middle, and high school.[12] Unlike reading and vocabulary, math has a nonlinear grade-related trend. In fact, the grade-level effects for math are even more complicated than column 2 implies because the form of the nonlinearity differs between cross-sectional and longitudinal surveys. In cross-sectional surveys the math gap widens during elementary school and shrinks during middle school. In longitudinal surveys the math gap shrinks during elementary school and widens during middle school. There is no obvious explanation for this discrepancy. But it strongly suggests that researchers should avoid drawing conclusions about age-related changes in the black-white math gap from any single survey. The grade trends for reading and vocabulary do not differ significantly between elementary, middle, and high school or between cross-sectional and longitudinal surveys. Nonetheless, the point estimates suggest that the vocabulary gap may widen more during elementary school than during high school.

Longitudinal studies that have tested students in both the fall and spring of each school year have sometimes found that schools help equalize students' achievement and that disadvantaged children fall behind during the

12. We estimate the effects of grades one through six with a linear grade-level variable centered at grade one. We also include piecewise splines for grades seven through eight and for grades nine through twelve, so that their overall slopes can be read directly off the table.

Table 7-2. *Effects of Grade at Testing and Year of Birth on Black-White Test Score Gaps*[a]

Independent variables		Mathematics (N = 45) 1	Mathematics (N = 45) 2	Reading (N = 45) 1	Reading (N = 45) 2	Vocabulary (N = 20) 1	Vocabulary (N = 20) 2
Grade level	B	0.015	. . .	0.002	. . .	0.019	. . .
	SE	(0.004)		(0.006)		(0.006)	
Grades 1–6	B	. . .	0.051	. . .	–0.011	. . .	0.034
	SE		(0.014)		(0.023)		(0.012)
Grades 7–8	B	. . .	–0.054*	. . .	0.016	. . .	0.025
	SE		(0.028)		(0.051)		(0.032)
Grades 9–12	B	. . .	0.021*	. . .	0.010	. . .	–0.018
	SE		(0.013)		(0.024)		(0.017)
Month of testing	B	–0.011	–0.007	0.003	0.000	0.015	0.011
	SE	(0.004)	(0.004)	(0.005)	(0.007)	(0.018)	(0.018)
Year of birth before 1978	B	–0.014	–0.014	–0.020	–0.020	–0.010	–0.011
	SE	(0.002)	(0.002)	(0.002)	(0.002)	(0.003)	(0.003)
Year of birth after 1978	B	0.002*	0.004*	0.020*	0.018*	0.031*	0.039*
	SE	(0.006)	(0.005)	(0.009)	(0.010)	(0.011)	(0.012)
Longitudinal survey	B	–0.039	–0.043	–0.069	–0.063	–0.346	–0.273
	SE	(0.033)	(0.033)	(0.047)	(0.051)	(0.157)	(0.161)
IRT metric	B	0.175	0.149	0.159	0.174	0.068	0.000
	SE	(0.033)	(0.035)	(0.046)	(0.051)	(0.082)	(0.088)
Intercept	B	0.765	0.653	0.746	0.792	0.889	0.833
	SE	(0.034)	(0.054)	(0.056)	(0.092)	(0.049)	(0.057)
Adjusted R^2		0.790	0.815	0.693	0.680	0.745	0.806

Source: Authors' calculations using data shown in table 7A-1.

a. The dependent variables are standardized black-white gaps (that is, $(\overline{W} - \overline{B})/SD_t$). Standard errors are in parentheses. The spline coefficient shows the actual slope for that spline. The spline standard error indicates whether the slope differs from zero. An asterisk indicates that the spline's slope differs significantly from the linear slope at the .05 level. Each gap is weighted by the inverse of its estimated sampling variance. See text for more details.

summer.[13] We tried to test this hypothesis by including a variable for month-of-testing in table 7-2. If the cross-sectional black-white gaps in our data sets were systematically smaller at the end of each school year than at the beginning of the next school year, the coefficient of month-of-testing should

13. Heyns (1978); and Entwisle and Alexander (1992, 1994).

be negative. The negative coefficient for month-of-testing in the math equation suggests that the black-white math gap is smaller in the spring than in the fall. The data for reading and vocabulary do not support the summer decrement hypothesis, but the sampling errors of the coefficients are very large.

Table 7-2 also shows the linear effect of the year of birth before 1978 and after 1978.[14] As other researchers have found, the black-white gap narrowed for cohorts born between 1948 and 1978 by about 0.014 standard deviations a year for math, 0.020 standard deviations for reading, and 0.010 standard deviations for vocabulary.[15] Among cohorts born after 1978 the math gap has remained constant, while the reading and vocabulary gaps seem to have widened.

When we compare the results for math and reading in table 7-2, it appears that the black-white reading gap may have narrowed more than the math gap over the past three decades. We cannot test this hypothesis on the entire meta-analytic sample because the math and reading samples are not independent (the same children usually took both math and reading tests), and we do not know all the covariances we would need to estimate the right standard errors. But NAEP participants took either math or reading tests, not both, so we can use them to determine whether the difference between the math and reading trends is significant. Table 7-3 shows that the black-white reading gap in the NAEP did narrow more than the math

14. We estimate the effects of year of birth with a linear year-of-birth variable centered at 1965. We also include a piecewise spline for year of birth after 1978, so that its slope and standard error can be read directly off the table. We chose 1978 as the cut-point for the spline because it provided the best fit across all the outcomes. Nonetheless, 1978 is probably not the magic transition year. More likely, the black-white gap stopped narrowing among cohorts born sometime between the mid-1970s and the early 1980s.

15. Jones (1984) noted a downward trend in reading and math gaps in the NAEP during the 1970s. Many researchers have since confirmed that the black-white math and reading gaps narrowed during the 1970s and 1980s; see, for example, Jaynes and Williams (1989), Grissmer and others (1994), and Hauser and Huang (1996). In chapter 5 of this volume Larry Hedges and Amy Nowell estimate that the black-white gap in non-NAEP surveys narrowed by 0.12 standard deviations per decade for reading, 0.06 standard deviations per decade for math, and did not narrow significantly for vocabulary. They also estimate that the reading gap in NAEP narrowed by 0.26 standard deviations per decade, but that the math gap did not narrow significantly. Like Hauser and Huang, Hedges and Nowell note that the black-white gap among seventeen-year-olds stopped narrowing in the late 1980s and appears to have widened somewhat since then. Hedges and Nowell's estimates of the extent to which the black-white gap narrowed differ from ours both because we combine data from NAEP and the other surveys and because we estimate the trend using data from students of all ages, rather than just seventeen-year-olds.

Table 7-3. *Differential Effects of Grade at Testing and Year of Birth on Black-White Math and Reading Gaps: NAEP Data*[a]

Independent variables		Mathematics (N = 24)		Reading (N = 27)		Difference statistically significant at .05 level	
		1	*2*	*1*	*2*	*1*	*2*
Grade level	B	0.010	. . .	–0.003	. . .	no	. . .
	SE	(0.005)		(0.007)			
Grade 8.0	B	. . .	0.137	. . .	–0.044	. . .	yes
	SE		(0.025)		(0.049)		
Grade 11	B	. . .	0.069	. . .	–0.020	. . .	no
	SE		(0.028)		(0.052)		
Year of birth before 1978	B	–0.014	–0.015	–0.023	–0.023	yes	yes
	SE	(0.003)	(0.002)	(0.003)	(0.003)		
Year of birth after 1978	B	0.002+	0.003*	0.024*	0.023*	no	no
	SE	(0.007)	(0.005)	(0.011)	(0.011)		
Intercept	B	0.929	0.940	0.968	0.971	no	no
	SE	(0.045)	(0.022)	(0.059)	(0.042)		
Adjusted R^2		0.717	0.813	0.708	0.704	. . .	. . .

Source: Authors' calculations using NAEP data from table 7A-1.

a. Dependent variables are standardized black-white gaps (that is, $(\overline{W} - \overline{B})/SD_t$). Standard errors are in parentheses. Grade 8.0 and grade 11.75 are dummy variables; grade 4.37 is the omitted category. The spline coefficient shows the actual slope for that spline. The spline standard error indicates whether the slope differs from zero. Asterisk and plus sign indicate that the spline's slope differs significantly from the linear slope at the .05 or .10 levels, respectively. Each NAEP gap is weighted by the inverse of its estimated sampling variance. See text for more details.

gap (0.23 versus 0.15 standard deviations a decade). However, the relatively flat math trend among cohorts born after 1978 does not differ reliably from the widening gap in reading.[16] This fact underscores an important limitation of all trend analyses using the NAEP: despite its huge overall sample, the samples it uses to estimate trends are relatively small and the resulting trend estimates have large sampling errors.

16. Note also that the grade-related math trend in the NAEP is nonlinear, and that it differs significantly from the relatively flat trend for reading. These results parallel those for the entire sample.

Hedges and Nowell show in chapter 5 that some of the narrowing of the black-white gap during the 1970s and 1980s can be attributed to the historical convergence of blacks' and whites' educational attainment. David Grissmer, Ann Flanagan, and Stephanie Williamson argue in chapter 6 that changes in social and educational policies may also have helped narrow the test score gap. The question of why the black-white reading and vocabulary gaps began to widen among cohorts born in the late 1970s and early 1980s remains unresolved. Indeed, even the magnitude of the change is uncertain. All we can say with confidence is that the gap stopped narrowing. We do not know how much it has widened.

Longitudinal Results

Our cross-sectional results suggest that the standardized black-white reading gap remains relatively constant between the first and twelfth grades. The standardized math and vocabulary gaps widen, but only by about 0.2 standard deviations. These results resemble those from earlier studies of age-related trends in IQ scores. The finding that the black-white test score gap does not widen much between the first and twelfth grades has persuaded some social scientists that schools do not widen the gap.[17] This inference would clearly be correct if students' test scores were perfectly correlated from one year to the next, but that is not the case. When test scores are imperfectly correlated, as they always are, the only way the gap between two social or economic groups can stay the same is if members of the two groups who start out with the same scores typically learn different amounts. Contrary to most people's intuition, for example, a constant black-white gap, like the one we saw for reading, means that black students learn less than whites who start school with the same skills.

If *all* students learned the same amount between the first and twelfth grades, their true first-grade reading scores would be perfectly correlated with their true twelfth-grade reading scores. Consequently, every student, black or white, who scored 0.80 standard deviations below the mean in the first grade would still score $(0.80)(1.00) = 0.80$ standard deviations below the mean in the twelfth grade. In such a world the standardized black-

17. See Loehlin, Lindzey, and Spuhler (1975).

white reading gap would obviously be constant between the first and twelfth grades. So would the gap between high-SES and low-SES students, or between boys and girls. In reality, however, some students improve their reading skills more than others between the first and twelfth grades. Some attend better schools than others, some live closer to libraries, some make more friends who read and recommend books, some go through divorces in which they lose a parent who encouraged reading, others acquire step-parents who encourage reading for the first time. As a result, students' reading scores in the first grade are imperfectly correlated with their reading scores in the twelfth grade.

Suppose students' true reading scores in one year correlate 0.95 with their true reading scores in the following year, 0.95^2 with their true reading scores two years later, and so on. Now, if a white student scores 0.80 standard deviations below the population mean on a reading test in the first grade, he or she will typically score only $(0.80)(0.95) = 0.76$ standard deviations below the mean in the second grade and $(.80)(.95)^{12} = 0.43$ standard deviations below the mean by the twelfth grade. In a color-blind world a black student who scored 0.80 standard deviations below the population mean in the first grade would also score $(0.80)(0.95)^{12} = 0.43$ standard deviations below the mean twelve years later. If black children who scored 0.80 standard deviations below the population mean in the first grade still score 0.80 standard deviations below the mean in the twelfth grade, whereas white students with the same initial score are only 0.43 standard deviations below the mean in the twelfth grade, we need to ask what is causing black children to learn less than white children, given that they entered school with similar skills. Putting this point in slightly more technical terms, if black children regress to the black mean while white children regress to the white mean, the world cannot be color blind. Something besides initial skills must cause this to happen. That "something" could involve genes, families, schools, peers, or other factors.

Cross-sectional surveys provide useful information about age-related trends in the black-white gap because they cover nationally representative samples of many grades and birth cohorts.[18] But because cross-sectional

18. Note, however, that cross-sectional studies may describe grade-related trends in the gap inaccurately because of grade-related changes in sample coverage. The most obvious example is that some high school surveys do not test drop-outs. Because black students are more likely to drop out of school than white students, and because drop-outs tend to have lower test scores than students who stay in school, the black-white gap is likely to be a little smaller among those who remain in school than in the full birth cohort. This would create a spurious picture of convergence at later ages.

surveys do not follow the same individuals over time, they cannot tell us whether individual blacks fall farther behind initially similar whites as they get older. Fortunately, longitudinal surveys can help answer this question. In this section, we analyze longitudinal data from four cohorts of children in Prospects and NELS. Together, these cohorts span most of the years between the beginning of the first grade and the end of the twelfth grade.

Longitudinal samples are subject to nonrandom attrition. If lower-scoring students are more likely to move and less likely to be retested, or if lower-scoring students are more likely to be put in special education classes where they are not retested, sample attrition may distort our picture of both the initial black-white gap and its development over time. Fortunately, nonrandom attrition does not seem to bias the longitudinal data much in Prospects and NELS . When we compare cross-sectional and longitudinal samples drawn from these two surveys, the mean black-white gap differs by less than 0.05 standard deviations across all tests. Although appendix table 7A-2 shows that the longitudinal samples are somewhat more advantaged than the cross-sectional samples, racial differences in attrition are small and mostly involve region of residence and urbanism.[19]

Reduction in the Black-White Gap after Controlling Students' Earlier Scores

Because the longitudinal samples do not differ markedly from their cross-sectional counterparts, longitudinal results from Prospects and NELS should be reasonably generalizable to the national population of black and white school children during the late 1980s and early 1990s. In the analyses that follow, we examine whether black students fall farther behind white students with similar initial scores. We do this by regressing students' scores in one grade on their "true" scores two or four years earlier plus a dummy variable for race.[20]

19. Third-graders in the Prospects longitudinal sample tend to be the most advantaged relative to their cross-sectional counterparts. In two of the three Prospects cohorts and in NELS, attrition in urban schools is higher among blacks than whites. In the Prospects seventh-grade cohort and in NELS, more blacks from the South appear in the longitudinal samples than in the cross-sectional samples. To the extent that not having valid data on race and on each particular demographic variable is correlated with disadvantage, the comparisons in table 7A-2 will understate the extent of nonrandom attrition in the longitudinal samples.

20. An alternative estimation strategy would be to regress the *difference* between students' scores at two time points on a dummy variable for race. Although this "change" strategy has a number of

Tables 7-4 through 7-6 present results for math, reading, and vocabulary for all the cohorts. The first row of each table shows the absolute black-white gap at the end of the second, fifth, ninth, and twelfth grades. The second row shows these gaps after we control students' scores at the beginning of the first, end of the third, end of the seventh, or end of the eighth grade, respectively.[21] The third row shows these gaps when we also correct for measurement error in students' initial scores.[22] Rows 4 and 5 show predicted gaps for students who initially scored at the population mean and one standard deviation below the population mean, calculated from separate equations for blacks and whites.

MATH. Table 7-4 suggests that blacks typically learn about 0.03 standard deviations less math each year than whites with the same initial scores (row 3, last column).[23] Black elementary school students learn only about

---

empirical advantages over our "analysis of covariance" strategy (see Allison, 1990, for an excellent discussion), we cannot use the change approach to investigate whether blacks and whites with similar initial skills regress to the same mean. Even when race is unrelated to how much students learn, the change approach assumes that blacks' and whites' scores will regress toward different means. The change strategy is only mathematically equivalent to our strategy when the correlation between time 1 and time 2 scores is perfect. The absolute (time 2 − time 1) gaps in row 6 of tables 7-4 through 7-6 show the estimates we would have obtained using a change strategy for the Prospects and NELS longitudinal samples.

21. The Prospects equations control math, reading, and vocabulary tests. The NELS equations control math, reading, science, and history tests. We included both linear and quadratic components of the tests whenever the quadratic components were reliably different from zero at the .05 level.

22. We used reliability estimates from the *Prospects Interim Report* (1993) and National Center for Education Statistics, *Psychometric Report for the NELS:88 Base Year through Second Follow-Up* (1995). Because Prospects only reported reliabilities for the components of the total math score, we estimated the reliability of the sum of these components using the following formula: $r_{SUM} = 1 - (\Sigma\sigma_i^2 - \Sigma r_{ji}\sigma_i^2)/\sigma_{SUM}^2$, where σ_i^2 is the variance of each component, r_{ji} is the reliability of each component, and σ_{SUM}^2 is the variance of the sum of the components. Note that the measurement-error models *do not* correct the standard errors for clustered sampling. The other models *do* correct the standard errors for stratified and clustered sampling using a first-order Taylor-series linearization procedure. These corrected standard errors are more accurate and should be used when considering the statistical significance of all the gaps, including those corrected for measurement error. Because the Prospects sampling design is very inefficient, the corrections for design effects in our models are often large and do not allow us to reject the hypothesis that the black-white gap differs statistically from zero. In these instances, the point estimate is our best guess about the sign and magnitude of the gap.

23. Comparing black and white students with the "same" scores raises the possibility that the black and white distributions overlap so little that we actually observe few children with the same scores. If this were the case, our estimates would be based on extrapolations from the data rather than on actual data. Fortunately, in all the longitudinal cohorts we analyze in this chapter, at least 20 percent of the black samples scored at or above the population mean on the time 1 tests.

Table 7-4. *Estimated Effect on Math Scores of Being Black,
Controlling Earlier Scores*

Controlling		Prospects			NELS spring, 12th grade	Annual average[a]
		Spring, 2nd grade	Spring, 5th grade	Spring, 9th grade		
1. Nothing[b]	B	−0.75	−0.51	−0.71	−0.75	...
	SE	(0.10)	(0.10)	(0.12)	(0.05)	
2. All prior scores[c]	B	−0.15	−0.02	−0.22	−0.07	−0.05
	SE	(0.07)	(0.07)	(0.06)	(0.03)	
3. All prior scores corrected for measurement error[d]	B	−0.08	−0.01	−0.20	−0.02	−0.03
	SE	(0.03)	(0.03)	(0.04)	(0.02)	
Predicted gap for students with initial scores[e]						
4. At the population mean		−0.08	0.01	−0.22	−0.05	−0.03
5. −1.0 SDs below population mean		−0.11	−0.10	−0.53	−0.07	−0.08
6. Time_2 Gap − Time_1 Gap		−0.18	−0.11	0.05	−0.02	−0.03
7. $r_{T1,T2}$		0.73	0.72	0.73	0.92	0.90
8. $R_{T1,T2}$[f]		0.75	0.74	0.75	0.93	0.91
White N		3,477	3,221	2,129	8,416	...
Black N		1,395	1,183	474	1,023	...

Source: Authors' calculations based on Prospects data set.

a. Mean annual effects of race and "true" year-to-year correlations, averaged across the ten grades for which we have data (ninth grade counted twice; third, sixth, and seventh grade omitted).

All equations control both linear and quadratic components of prior tests when statistically significant. Standard errors in the measurement-error models have not been corrected for clustered sampling and are thus too small. Standard errors in all other models have been corrected for stratification and clustering using a Taylor-series linearization method. All Prospects data were weighted with the second follow-up weight. NELS data were weighted with the second follow-up panel weight.

b. All equations control gender.

c. Prior scores include math, reading, and vocabulary for Prospects samples; math, reading, science, and history for NELS sample. Prior tests for Prospects second-graders come from the fall of first grade. Prior tests for Prospects fifth-graders come from the spring of third grade. Prior tests for Prospects ninth-graders come from the spring of seventh grade. Prior tests for NELS twelfth-graders come from the spring of eighth grade.

d. We used the following reliability estimates in the measurement error equations: Prospects first-graders (math = 0.80, reading = 0.70, vocabulary = 0.76); Prospects third-graders (math = 0.93, reading = 0.91, vocabulary = 0.82); Prospects seventh-graders (math = 0.94, reading = 0.92, vocabulary = 0.86); NELS eighth-graders (math = 0.89, reading = 0.80, science = 0.73, history = 0.84).

e. We estimated these predicted gaps using separate equations for blacks and whites and race-specific estimates of measurement error when available.

f. "True" multiple correlation from the regression of true time 2 scores on all true time 1 scores.

Table 7-5. *Estimated Effect on Reading Scores of Being Black, Controlling Earlier Scores*

Controlling		Prospects Spring, 2nd grade	Prospects Spring, 5th grade	Prospects Spring, 9th grade	NELS spring, 12th grade	Annual average[a]
1. Nothing[b]	B	−0.80	−0.72	−0.61	−0.67	...
	SE	(0.13)	(0.08)	(0.14)	(0.05)	
2. All prior scores[c]	B	−0.32	−0.22	−0.12	−0.08	−0.07
	SE	(0.09)	(0.07)	(0.10)	(0.03)	
3. All prior scores corrected for measurement error[d]	B	−0.29	−0.19	−0.10	−0.08	−0.07
	SE	(0.03)	(0.03)	(0.05)	(0.02)	
Predicted gap for students with initial scores[e]						
4. At the population mean		−0.36	−0.26	−0.07	−0.16	−0.09
5. −1.0 SDs below population mean		−0.15	−0.36	0.05	−0.13	−0.06
6. Time$_2$ Gap − Time$_1$ Gap		−0.01	0.04	0.05	0.02	0.01
7. $r_{T1,T2}$		0.57	0.68	0.62	0.90	0.86
8. $R_{T1,T2}$[f]		0.67	0.72	0.69	0.91	0.89
White N		3,477	3,221	2,129	8,416	...
Black N		1,395	1,183	474	1,023	...

Source: See table 7-4.

a. Mean annual effects of race and "true" year-to-year correlations, averaged across the ten grades for which we have data (ninth grade counted twice; third, sixth, and seventh grade omitted).

All equations control both linear and quadratic components of prior tests when statistically significant. Standard errors in the measurement-error models have not been corrected for clustered sampling and are thus too small. Standard errors in all other models have been corrected for stratification and clustering using a Taylor-series linearization method. All Prospects data were weighted with the second follow-up weight. NELS data were weighted with the second follow-up panel weight.

b. All equations control gender.

c. Prior scores include math, reading, and vocabulary for Prospects samples; math, reading, science, and history for NELS sample. Prior tests for Prospects second-graders come from the fall of first grade. Prior tests for Prospects fifth-graders come from the spring of third grade. Prior tests for Prospects ninth-graders come from the spring of seventh grade. Prior tests for NELS twelfth-graders come from the spring of eighth grade.

d. We used the following reliability estimates in the measurement error equations: Prospects first-graders (math = 0.80, reading = 0.70, vocabulary = 0.76); Prospects third-graders (math = 0.93, reading = 0.91, vocabulary = 0.82); Prospects seventh-graders (math = 0.94, reading = 0.92, vocabulary = 0.86); NELS eighth-graders (math = 0.89, reading = 0.80, science = 0.73, history = 0.84).

e. We estimated these predicted gaps using separate equations for blacks and whites and race-specific estimates of measurement error when available.

f. "True" multiple correlation from the regression of true time 2 scores on all true time 1 scores.

Table 7-6. *Estimated Effect on Vocabulary Scores of Being Black,*
Controlling Earlier Scores

Controlling		Prospects			Annual average[a]
		Spring, 2nd grade	Spring, 5th grade	Spring, 9th grade	
1. Nothing[b]	B	−0.77	−0.83	−0.78	...
	SE	(0.11)	(0.09)	(0.16)	
2. All prior scores[c]	B	−0.22	−0.27	−0.22	−0.12
	SE	(0.07)	(0.06)	(0.10)	
3. All prior scores corrected for measurement error[d]	B	−0.20	−0.21	−0.14	−0.09
	SE	(0.03)	(0.03)	(0.04)	
Predicted gap for students with initial scores[e]					
4. At the population mean		−0.27	−0.22	−0.05	−0.09
5. −1.0 SDs below population mean		−0.15	−0.21	0.05	−0.05
6. Time$_2$ Gap − Time$_1$ Gap		0.07	0.11	−0.10	0.01
7. $r_{T1,T2}$		0.74	0.84	0.75	0.88
8. $R_{T1,T2}$[f]		0.77	0.85	0.77	0.89
White N		3,477	3,221	2,129	...
Black N		1,395	1,183	474	...

Source: See table 7-4.

a. Mean annual effects of race and "true" year-to-year correlations, averaged across the ten grades for which we have data (ninth grade counted twice; third, sixth, and seventh grade omitted).

All equations control both linear and quadratic components of prior tests when statistically significant. Standard errors in the measurement-error models have not been corrected for clustered sampling and are thus too small. Standard errors in all other models have been corrected for stratification and clustering using a Taylor-series linearization method. All Prospects data were weighted with the second follow-up weight. NELS data were weighted with the second follow-up panel weight.

b. All equations control gender.

c. Prior scores include math, reading, and vocabulary for Prospects samples; math, reading, science, and history for NELS sample. Prior tests for Prospects second-graders come from the fall of first grade. Prior tests for Prospects fifth-graders come from the spring of third grade. Prior tests for Prospects ninth-graders come from the spring of seventh grade. Prior tests for NELS twelfth-graders come from the spring of eighth grade.

d. We used the following reliability estimates in the measurement error equations: Prospects first-graders (math = 0.80, reading = 0.70, vocabulary = 0.76); Prospects third-graders (math = 0.93, reading = 0.91, vocabulary = 0.82); Prospects seventh-graders (math = 0.94, reading = 0.92, vocabulary = 0.86); NELS eighth-graders (math = 0.89, reading = 0.80, science = 0.73, history = 0.84).

e. We estimated these predicted gaps using separate equations for blacks and whites and race-specific estimates of measurement error when available.

f. "True" multiple correlation from the regression of true time 2 scores on all true time 1 scores.

0.02 standard deviations less math each year than whites with comparable initial skills. Because current longitudinal surveys seem to understate the age-related trend in the black-white math gap during elementary school, however, the true figure may be larger than 0.02. Black students appear to fall farther behind initially similar whites between the seventh and ninth grades than in any other grades, but as we have already noted, the cross-sectional results do not support this story, so we do not put much weight on it. When we compare whites and blacks who start high school with the same math, reading, science, and history scores, NELS indicates that they finish high school with essentially the same math scores.[24] These important findings imply that high schools do not make the black-white math gap worse.[25]

READING. Table 7-5 shows that blacks typically learn 0.07 standard deviations less reading each year than whites with the same initial scores. Although well over half of the black-white reading gap at each grade can be explained by black-white differences in initial skills, race appears to have a stronger negative effect on reading growth than on math growth. Even after we control students' scores at the beginning of the first grade and correct these scores for measurement error, blacks' reading scores at the end of the second grade trail whites' by about 0.29 standard deviations. Likewise, even after we control students' scores at the end of the third grade and correct them for measurement error, the black-white reading gap at the end of the fifth grade is about 0.19 standard deviations. Initially similar blacks also learn fewer reading skills than whites during middle school and high school, but the differences are smaller than during elementary school.[26]

24. Ralph, Keller, and Crouse (1997).
25. These longitudinal analyses assume that the tests taken by each cohort measure the same underlying attribute at different grades. Kupermintz and Snow (1997) have shown that this assumption does not hold for the most difficult level of the NELS twelfth-grade math test. They found that the difficult level of the test had a more complex factor structure than either the low or middle levels of the test or the eighth-grade test. This poses a problem for measuring learning between the eighth and twelfth grades among high-scoring students. Fortunately, it poses less of a problem for our analyses because we are mainly interested in comparing blacks and whites with the same initial scores. Since relatively few blacks scored above the population mean in the eighth grade, our comparisons mainly apply to students who scored at or below the population mean. Only 3.1 percent of the students in our longitudinal sample who scored at or below the population mean in the eighth grade took the difficult level of the math test in the twelfth grade (135 whites and 10 blacks).
26. Note that because the association between eighth- and twelfth-grade tests differs by race in NELS, the predicted gaps among students who started high school one standard deviation below the population mean and among students who started high school at the population mean are larger than

VOCABULARY. The vocabulary results resemble those for reading (see table 7-6). Even after we control black-white differences in initial vocabulary, reading, and math scores, and correct these initial scores for measurement error, blacks learn fewer vocabulary skills during elementary and middle school. NELS did not administer vocabulary tests.

Why is it that when blacks start out with the same skills as whites, the subsequent reading gap is larger than the math gap? Recall that blacks can score lower than whites with the same initial skills either because the overall black-white gap is widening or because students' initial scores are imperfectly correlated with their subsequent scores. Row 6 in tables 7-4 through 7-6 shows the change in the math, reading, and vocabulary gaps over each interval (that is, $T_2 - T_1$). Rows 7 and 8 show the estimated true correlations between students' initial and final scores. Race has more effect on reading growth than on math growth both because the mean reading gap widens more over time (or narrows less) and because students' "true" reading scores are not as highly correlated over time as their "true" math scores.

Race also has more impact on vocabulary growth than on math growth during elementary school. But this is solely because the mean vocabulary gap widens more. Students' "true" vocabulary scores in Prospects are at least as highly correlated over time as their "true" math scores.

We also investigated whether any of these findings differed for boys and girls or for students with high and low initial scores. Among those who started first grade with the same skills, the black-white reading and vocabulary gaps had widened more by the end of the second grade among boys than among girls. Despite much theorizing about the special problems of black males, we found no evidence that after we controlled for initial skills the black-white gap widened more among boys than girls after the second grade. Nor did we find much evidence that black students who initially scored below the 20th percentile were especially disadvantaged relative to white students with equally low initial scores.[27] In the Prospects third- and

---

the gaps we estimate for these students when we use the same equation for blacks and whites (–0.13 and –0.16 standard deviations versus –0.08 standard deviations).

27. Blacks who scored in the bottom quintile on the NELS reading test were especially disadvantaged relative to whites with similar initial scores, but this interaction was just significant at the .05 level. The bottom-quintile interaction was also negative for NELS math scores but was statistically significant only at the .10 level. None of the black by bottom-quintile interactions was even marginally significant for the Prospects cohorts. The argument that low-scoring whites will regress to the population mean more than low-scoring blacks will, because low-scoring whites are more atypical, is thus not supported by the Prospects data.

seventh-grade cohorts, however, we actually found that blacks who initially scored above the 80th percentile learned more math than whites with the same initial scores.

All these estimates are very sensitive to our assumptions about the amount of measurement error in students' initial scores. Although we used the best information available, reliability estimates are never perfect. If the reliabilities we use to correct students' initial scores are upwardly biased, we will overestimate the extent to which black students fall behind whites with similar initial skills, and if the reliabilities are downwardly biased, we will underestimate the widening of the gap. To take just one example, recall that we estimated the black-white vocabulary gap in the fifth grade at about 0.20 standard deviations for students who started the third grade with identical skills (see table 7-6). This estimate assumes that 18 percent of the variance in students' third-grade vocabulary scores was random error.[28] If we had assumed, instead, that 30 percent of the variance in the third-grade scores was random error, the estimated effect of race on growth between the third and fifth grades would have disappeared. Although all available evidence indicates that the "true" reliability of the third-grade vocabulary test lies closer to 0.82 than to 0.70, errors in our reliability estimates may still distort the results in tables 7-4 through 7-6.

How Big are the Effects of Race?

After we control for students' initial scores, annual black-white gaps between 0.03 and 0.09 standard deviations look very small compared with the total black-white gap in any given grade. Are these gaps substantively important?

Table 7-7 presents one answer to this question. It expresses the annual decrement associated with being black as a percentage of the amount that white students learn each year. Column 1 shows the annual decrement. Column 2 shows that white students learn more during elementary school than they learn later (see also figure 7-1). Consequently, relatively large standardized decrements during the first and second grades look small relative to the average amount learned in those years (see column 3). During middle school and high school, when students are gaining less in standard-

---

28. For third-grade vocabulary scores, the *Prospects Interim Report* (1993) reported a reliability of .82. The *CTBS/4 Technical Report* (1991) reported a KR20 reliability of .83 and an alternate form reliability of .79.

Table 7-7. *Estimated Annual Effect of Being Black on Math, Reading, and Vocabulary Scores, as Percent of Average Annual White Gain*

Subject and grade	Annual decrement in IRT points[a]	Average annual white gain	Annual decrement as percent of annual white gain
Math			
1st and 2d grades	2.6	59.4	4.4
4th and 5th grades	0.2	20.3	1.0
8th and 9th grades	5.5	9.2	59.8
9th –12th grades	0.1	3.0	3.3
Reading			
1st and 2d grades	13.2	73.8	17.9
4th and 5th grades	5.8	11.9	48.7
8th and 9th grades	2.5	2.1	119.0[b]
9th –12th grades	0.2	1.4	14.3
Vocabulary			
1st and 2d grades	6.5	76.3	8.5
4th and 5th grades	5.7	18.5	30.8
8th and 9th grades	3.7	9.6	38.5

Source: Authors' calculations based on estimates in tables 7-4, 7-5, and 7-6.

a. Because Prospects and NELS used different IRT metrics, IRT scores from these data sets are not comparable. We converted the standardized decrement into an annual IRT decrement by dividing the standardized decrements in row 3 of tables 7-4 to 7-6 by the number of years in each interval and then multiplying this quantity by the population standard deviation of the time 2 test.

b. The Prospects reading test shows very little learning between seventh and ninth grades. Since this pattern does not recur to the same degree for the other Prospects tests or for the NELS reading test, we suspect that the Prospects reading test is badly scaled.

ized terms, relatively small absolute decrements translate into relatively large percentage differences.

Figure 7-2 estimates the effect of being black on cognitive growth in a somewhat different way. It shows predicted scores at each grade for black and white students who start first grade with the same "true" scores. The estimates in the top panel are extrapolated from Prospects and NELS.[29] The top panel probably overstates the cumulative effect of race because we

29. See the data appendix for more details.

Figure 7-2. *Predicted Test Scores for Two Students, One Black, One White, Who Both Started First Grade with True Math, Reading, and Vocabulary Scores at the Mean of the Population Distribution*

A. Using point estimates from tables 7-4 to 7-6
and true multiple correlations from Prospects and NELS

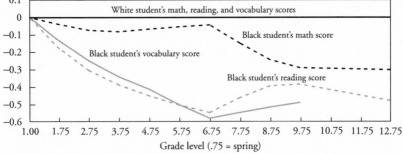

B. Using point estimates from table 7-2 and true year-to-year correlations of .95

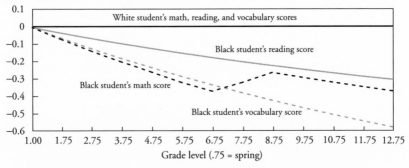

C. Using point estimates and standard errors for reading in table 7-2
and true year-to-year correlations of .93 to .97

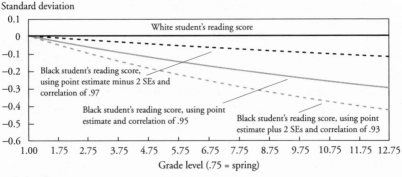

Source: See text.

do not have data on students who were tested in the first grade and retested in the twelfth grade.[30]

The middle panel of figure 7-2 differs from the top panel in that it combines an estimate of the year-to-year correlation between students' test scores with the grade level effects from our meta-analysis. The resulting estimates are less survey specific and test specific than those in the top panel, but they are based on correlations derived from small and unrepresentative samples.[31]

Despite the different approaches used in the two panels, they yield similar conclusions. All else equal, white students who start elementary school with test scores at the population mean can be expected to finish high school with test scores that are still at the mean. Black students who start elementary school with "true" test scores at the population mean can be expected to finish high school with math scores that lie 0.34 standard deviations below the mean and reading scores that lie 0.39 standard deviations below the mean.[32] These gaps are equivalent to a decline of about 35 or 40 SAT points.

30. Unfortunately, no national survey has tested students in the first grade and retested them in the twelfth grade. In splicing together data on several cohorts, we had to assume that after partialing out correlations between adjacent years, the partial correlations between more distant years were all zero. Because this is not quite true, we have almost certainly underestimated the stability of test scores and thus underestimated the contribution of initial test score differences to later differences. We cannot, for example, control for students' first- and second-grade scores when we estimate the gap for the Prospects cohort tested in grades three to five. Likewise, we cannot control for students' first-, second-, third-, fourth-, fifth-, and sixth-grade scores when we estimate the gap for the Prospects cohort tested in grades seven to nine. And so on. This would not be a problem if the relationship between earlier and later test scores followed a first-order Markov model, but at least in the Prospects data for three adjacent years it does not. Thus if we had earlier scores for each of our cohorts, we could probably reduce the magnitude of the estimated black decrements.

31. Reviews of the literature on both achievement and IQ tests generally put the "true" yearly test-retest correlations at .95 to .97 between the first and twelfth grades. We use the .95 estimate in our calculations for the middle panel of figure 7-2 for three reasons. First, "true" test-retest correlations may be slightly smaller for achievement tests than for IQ tests (Bloom, 1964; and Jencks and others, 1972). Second, "true" test-retest correlations may be slightly smaller before the third grade (Bloom 1964; and Humphreys and Davey 1988). And third, correlations based on children who are available for retesting are probably upwardly biased (Jencks and others, 1972). Moreover, we found that the estimated "true" year-to-year correlations between NLSY respondents' IQ scores and their later AFQT scores averaged about .95 after we inflated the observed correlation by 10 percent to correct for measurement error. We used the .95 estimate for the math, reading, and vocabulary calculations because we could not find compelling evidence that "true" test-retest correlations differ systematically across these three types of tests.

32. These estimates are an average of the longitudinal and cross-sectional results. If we obtain estimates for the middle panel of figure 7-2 using "true" year-to-year correlations of .97 instead of .95, our estimates of the gaps are somewhat smaller, but still important. The estimated math gap at the end of the twelfth grade is 0.296 (compared with 0.370), the estimated reading gap is 0.245 (compared with 0.303), and the estimated vocabulary gap is 0.531 (compared with 0.579).

The predictions in the top and middle panels of figure 7-2 should be treated as best guesses about the extent to which black students fall behind whites who start school with the same skills. These estimates are not very precise. The bottom panel shows upper and lower bounds for our cross-sectional predictions for reading.[33] The range of estimates is consistent both with the hypothesis that initial black-white differences explain as much as 82 percent of the observed reading gap at the end of high school and the hypothesis that initial differences explain only 38 percent of gap.[34] The estimates for math and vocabulary are equally uncertain, as are the longitudinal estimates in the top panel.

Nonetheless, if we take our point estimates at face value, they allow us to decompose the total black-white gap at the end of high school into a component attributable to differences in initial skills and a component that is independent of initial skills. Our calculations imply that 56 percent of the math gap and 43 percent of the reading gap can be attributed to the fact that blacks start school with fewer skills than whites. It follows that 44 percent of the math gap and 57 percent of the reading gap is unrelated to racial differences in initial skills.

What Causes the Gap to Widen after Children Enter School?

Why do black children learn less than white children who start out with similar skills? The two most widely cited explanations are lower socioeconomic status and worse schools. To examine the first, we asked how much of the black-white gap among students with initially similar scores was explained by region, urbanism, family composition, household size, and the parents' educational attainment, occupational category, and income (hereafter socioeconomic status). Although these traditional socioeconomic variables do not measure all aspects of a child's home environment that affect test scores (see chapter 4), they do cover the most commonly cited differences between black and white families.

To examine the second explanation, we controlled schools' "fixed effects." This statistical technique in effect controls differences in average

33. We calculated the lower bound using the point estimate in table 7-2 minus two standard errors and a year-to-year correlation of .97. We calculated the upper bound using the point estimate in table 7-2 plus two standard errors and a year-to-year correlation of .93.
34. In the NELS high school class of 1992, the black-white math gap was 0.80 standard deviations and the reading gap was 0.69 standard deviations.

Figure 7-3. *Reduction in the Black-White Math, Reading, and Vocabulary Gaps after Controlling Socioeconomic Status and Between-School Differences*[a]

Standardized black-white gap

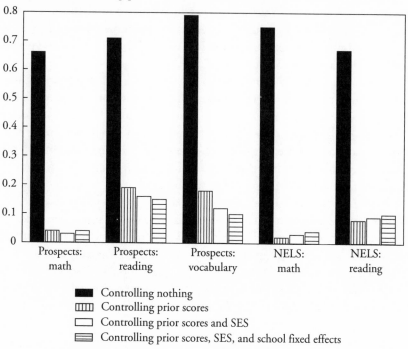

Source: Authors' calculations using data from Prospects and NELS.

a. Prospects estimates are averaged across the three cohorts for which we have data. See appendix table 7A-3 for cohort-specific estimates and for estimates from equations that control SES or school fixed effects but not prior scores.

achievement between the schools that blacks and whites typically attend. That means it controls the effects of such things as differences in racial and socioeconomic mix, per pupil expenditure, and curriculum. But it only controls the average effect of these school characteristics on all students in the school. It does not control for differences in a school's impact on its black and white students.

The black bars in figure 7-3 show the black-white math, reading, and vocabulary gaps in Prospects and NELS. The bars with vertical stripes show the size of these gaps when black and white students have the same "true" test scores at the time of the initial survey. The white bars show the gap after also controlling socioeconomic status. Traditional socioeconomic differences between black and white families seem to explain some of the black-white learning gap in elementary and middle school. But these differences explain none of the learning gap during high school. Readers should keep in mind, of course, that these results do not show the entire effect of socioeconomic status on test scores, because socioeconomic status also affects students' initial scores.[35]

The bars with horizontal stripes show the black-white gap among students who have the same initial scores, the same measured socioeconomic status, and attend the same schools. Between-school differences account for some of the black-white reading and vocabulary gap in elementary and middle school. But between-school differences account for none of the black-white math gap in elementary, middle, or high school. Nor do they account for the reading gap in high school.

Overall, figure 7-3 indicates that neither traditional socioeconomic differences between black and white children's families nor differences between their schools are sufficient to explain why black children learn less than white children with initially similar skills. Even when black and white children have the same prior scores, the same measured socioeconomic status, and attend the same schools, black children still gain on average about 0.02 standard deviations less in math, 0.06 standard deviations less in reading, and 0.05 standard deviations less in vocabulary each year. Future research therefore needs to look for less obvious causes of this learning gap.

Conclusion

Our findings are still tentative. To answer the question in the title of this chapter more confidently, we would need data sets with larger samples of minority students and more efficient sample designs. We would also need to follow the same students all the way through elementary school and ideally through high school.

Despite these limitations, our results have important implications for the way we assess America's efforts to equalize educational opportunity for blacks and whites. If "equal educational opportunity" means that black and white children should start school with the same basic skills, then we have not yet fulfilled that ideal. The average black child starts

35. See appendix table 7A-3 for results after controlling socioeconomic status but not prior scores.

elementary school with substantially weaker math, reading, and vocabulary skills than the average white child. Because these skill differences persist throughout elementary and secondary school, the average black child finishes the twelfth grade with weaker math, reading, and vocabulary skills than the average white child. Our results imply that we could eliminate at least half, and probably more, of the black-white test score gap at the end of the twelfth grade by eliminating the differences that exist before children enter first grade.

If instead "equal educational opportunity" means that black and white children who start first grade with the same skills should learn the same amount during elementary and secondary school, we have not fulfilled that ideal either. Black students who start elementary school with the same test scores as the average white student learn less than the average white student between the first and twelfth grades. Most of this divergence between blacks and whites with initially similar skills seems to occur before high school. Our results imply that we could eliminate about half of the black-white test score gap at the end of the twelfth grade by eliminating the causes of this divergence.

Finally, our results imply that neither differences between the schools that blacks and whites attend nor differences in their socioeconomic status suffice to explain why blacks learn less than whites with similar initial skills. Consequently, we need to investigate whether this learning gap arises because black and white families with similar socioeconomic characteristics differ in other ways, because black and white children have differing perceptions of their own academic ability, because black and white children have different study habits, because blacks and whites who attend the same schools are taught different math and verbal skills, because blacks have fewer opportunities than whites to practice math and verbal skills during the summer, or for other reasons discussed elsewhere in this book.

Data Appendix

Appendix table 7A-1 shows the data used in our meta-analysis. Because we defined our sampling frame as national surveys that had tested children at different ages, we excluded data from the National Longitudinal Survey of 1972 (NLS:72), which only tested twelfth-graders. We reestimated our models with the NLS:72 data included, and the results were very similar. We also excluded data based on tests with poor psychometric

Table 7A-1. *Cross-Sectional Data Used in Meta-Analysis*

Survey[a]	Grade[b]	Year[c]	Black N[d]	White N	Standardized B-W Gap[e]	SE of Gap[f]
Mathematics						
PROS	1.00	1991	2,273	5,388	0.87	0.14
CNLSY	2.00	1992	132	236	0.41	0.13
EEO	3.00	1965	1,000	1,000	0.86	0.05
CNLSY	3.00	1992	133	190	0.74	0.14
PROS	3.75	1991	2,880	6,956	0.67	0.08
CNLSY	4.00	1992	148	169	0.60	0.14
NAEP	4.37	1973	367	1,156	0.97	0.06
NAEP	4.37	1978	984	1,427	0.88	0.04
NAEP	4.37	1982	444	889	0.84	0.06
NAEP	4.37	1986	393	878	0.74	0.06
NAEP	4.37	1990	205	1,521	0.81	0.07
NAEP	4.37	1992	253	1,502	0.82	0.07
NAEP	4.37	1994	371	986	0.74	0.06
NAEP	4.37	1996	493	1,050	0.75	0.05
CNLSY	5.00	1992	145	159	0.58	0.14
EEO	6.00	1965	1,000	1,000	1.10	0.05
LSAY	7.00	1987	341	2,138	0.74	0.18
PROS	7.75	1991	1,375	4,222	0.62	0.11
NAEP	8.00	1973	359	1,573	1.18	0.06
NAEP	8.00	1978	359	1,991	1.08	0.05
NAEP	8.00	1982	375	961	1.02	0.06
NAEP	8.00	1986	151	511	0.79	0.09
NAEP	8.00	1990	156	695	0.87	0.08
NAEP	8.00	1992	251	1003	0.93	0.07
NAEP	8.00	1994	81	1096	0.90	0.11
NAEP	8.00	1996	515	1017	0.92	0.05
NELS	8.75	1988	2,864	15,761	0.78	0.04
EEO	9.00	1965	1,000	1,000	0.98	0.05
NLSY	10.00	1980	249	559	0.98	0.11
LSAY	10.00	1987	282	1,901	0.75	0.23
HS&B	10.75	1980	3,011	16,663	0.87	0.05
NELS	10.75	1990	1,852	12,359	0.77	0.06
NLSY	11.00	1980	403	830	0.95	0.09
NAEP	11.75	1973	598	862	1.15	0.05
NAEP	11.75	1978	598	1,288	1.07	0.05
NAEP	11.75	1982	592	1,141	0.98	0.05
NAEP	11.75	1986	158	847	0.93	0.08

Table 7A-1 *(continued)*

Survey[a]	Grade[b]	Year[c]	Black N[d]	White N	Standardized B-W Gap[e]	SE of Gap[f]
NAEP	11.75	1990	99	870	0.68	0.10
NAEP	11.75	1992	156	1,260	0.87	0.08
NAEP	11.75	1994	202	676	0.89	0.08
NAEP	11.75	1996	266	400	0.89	0.08
EEO	12.00	1965	1,000	1,000	1.12	0.05
NLSY	12.00	1980	405	843	0.91	0.10
HS&B	12.75	1980	2,566	15,331	0.86	0.05
NELS	12.75	1992	1,406	9,928	0.80	0.07
Unweighted mean gap					0.86	
Weighted mean gap					0.91	
Weighted mean gap, 1985–96					0.80	

Reading

Survey[a]	Grade[b]	Year[c]	Black N[d]	White N	Standardized B-W Gap[e]	SE of Gap[f]
PROS	1.00	1991	2,275	5,545	0.74	0.11
EEO	3.00	1965	1,000	1,000	0.87	0.05
CNLSY	3.00	1992	123	182	0.59	0.14
PROS	3.75	1991	2,908	7,143	0.67	0.08
CNLSY	4.00	1992	147	164	0.50	0.14
NAEP	4.37	1971	508	1,916	1.04	0.05
NAEP	4.37	1975	890	2,660	0.92	0.04
NAEP	4.37	1980	436	1,936	0.84	0.05
NAEP	4.37	1984	772	1,859	0.79	0.04
NAEP	4.37	1988	270	788	0.71	0.07
NAEP	4.37	1990	207	1,089	0.79	0.07
NAEP	4.37	1992	327	1,406	0.83	0.06
NAEP	4.37	1994	312	828	0.80	0.06
NAEP	4.37	1996	221	1,003	0.74	0.07
CNLSY	5.00	1992	144	159	0.48	0.13
EEO	6.00	1965	1,000	1,000	0.90	0.04
PROS	7.75	1991	1,397	4,365	0.56	0.09
NAEP	8.00	1971	779	2,209	1.08	0.04
NAEP	8.00	1975	846	2,209	1.02	0.04
NAEP	8.00	1980	475	2,182	0.91	0.05
NAEP	8.00	1984	808	3,173	0.74	0.04
NAEP	8.00	1988	179	950	0.53	0.08
NAEP	8.00	1990	257	1469	0.58	0.07
NAEP	8.00	1992	299	930	0.73	0.06
NAEP	8.00	1994	251	1,162	0.77	0.07

Table 7A-1 *(continued)*

Survey[a]	Grade[b]	Year[c]	Black N[d]	White N	Standardized B-W Gap[e]	SE of Gap[f]
NAEP	8.00	1996	189	1,289	0.82	0.07
NELS	8.75	1988	2,858	15,757	0.70	0.04
EEO	9.00	1965	1,000	1,000	0.96	0.05
NLSY	10.00	1980	249	559	0.90	0.11
HS&B	10.75	1980	3,068	16,812	0.77	0.04
NELS	10.75	1990	1,860	12,371	0.66	0.06
NLSY	11.00	1980	403	830	1.03	0.08
NAEP	11.75	1971	655	1,806	1.15	0.05
NAEP	11.75	1975	480	4,400	1.19	0.05
NAEP	11.75	1980	482	1,773	1.19	0.05
NAEP	11.75	1984	951	1,802	0.79	0.04
NAEP	11.75	1988	224	900	0.55	0.07
NAEP	11.75	1990	290	1,089	0.71	0.06
NAEP	11.75	1992	404	808	0.86	0.06
NAEP	11.75	1994	120	780	0.66	0.09
NAEP	11.75	1996	204	1,139	0.69	0.07
EEO	12.00	1965	1,000	1,000	1.04	0.05
NLSY	12.00	1980	405	843	0.93	0.09
HS&B	12.75	1980	2,687	15,569	0.83	0.04
NELS	12.75	1992	1,406	9,929	0.69	0.06
Unweighted mean gap					0.81	
Weighted mean gap					0.86	
Weighted mean gap, 1985–96					0.70	
Vocabulary						
CNLSY	−2.00	1992	113	172	0.99	0.13
CNLSY	−1.00	1992	125	206	1.22	0.12
CNLSY	0.00	1992	104	193	1.00	0.13
EEO	1.00	1965	1,000	1,000	0.88	0.05
PROS	1.00	1991	2,297	5,525	0.70	0.13
CNLSY	1.00	1992	136	196	0.90	0.12
CNLSY	2.00	1992	131	237	1.01	0.12
CNLSY	3.00	1992	132	188	0.97	0.13
PROS	3.75	1991	2,914	7,149	0.77	0.09
CNLSY	4.00	1992	144	165	0.93	0.13
CNLSY	5.00	1992	144	160	0.85	0.13
EEO	6.00	1965	1,000	1,000	1.15	0.05
PROS	7.75	1991	1,399	4,360	0.77	0.11

Table 7A-1 (continued)

Survey[a]	Grade[b]	Year[c]	Black N[d]	White N	Standardized B-W Gap[e]	SE of Gap[f]
EEO	9.00	1965	1,000	1,000	1.18	0.05
NLSY	10.00	1980	249	555	1.11	0.11
HS&B	10.75	1980	3,062	16,835	0.94	0.04
NLSY	11.00	1980	403	830	1.13	0.08
EEO	12.00	1965	1,000	1,000	1.24	0.05
NLSY	12.00	1980	405	843	1.09	0.09
HS&B	12.75	1980	2,669	15,558	0.82	0.04
Unweighted mean gap					0.98	
Weighted mean gap					1.01	
Weighted mean gap, 1985–96					0.91	

a. EEO (*Equality of Educational Opportunity*): CS, NR; NAEP (*National Assessment of Educational Progress*): CS, IRT. Until 1984 NAEP sampled students on the basis of age rather than grade. After 1984 NAEP used both age and grade-defined samples for reading. In all years, the modal grades of students in the long-term trend samples were 4, 8, and 11. Scores from all long-term trend samples are directly comparable. The percentage of African Americans in the long-term trend samples is smaller than in the main samples because NAEP does not oversample schools with high minority enrollments for the long-term trend samples (Barron and Koretz 1996). Race-specific and overall standard deviations were not available for math for 1973, so we assumed they were the same as those reported for 1978. NLSY (*National Longitudinal Survey of Youth*): CS, NR. NLSY administered the Armed Forces Vocational Aptitude Battery (ASVAB) to 94 percent of the original NLSY cohort. We use an average of scores on the math knowledge and arithmetic reasoning components of the ASVAB to create our math test. Our reading test is the paragraph comprehension subtest; our vocabulary test is the word knowledge subtest. CNLSY (*Children of the National Longitudinal Survey of Youth*): CS, IRT. CNLSY is a longitudinal study, but its data collection procedures are so different from the typical longitudinal study that we treat it as a series of cross-sectional studies. CNLSY is the least representative survey in our meta-analysis. The CNLSY children currently represent about 70 percent of the children born to women who were ages 27 to 34 in 1992. We analyze data for children who were 10 or younger because older children in the CNLSY were born to especially young mothers. We analyze data from the 1992 wave only. CNLSY administered both a reading comprehension test and a reading recognition test. Since none of the other studies we examine included a reading recognition test, we did not analyze it for this chapter. Preliminary analyses suggested, however, that results for the two reading tests are very similar. Preliminary analyses also indicated that scores were kurtotic and skewed on the math test for five- and six-year-olds and on the reading test for five-, six-, and seven-year-olds. Consequently, we excluded these data from our analyses. HS&B (*High School and Beyond*): LG, NR. The tenth grade HS&B cohort took two math tests, which we summed to create our math test. The twelfth grade cohort took two math tests and two vocabulary tests, which we summed to create our math and vocabulary tests. LSAY (*Longitudinal Study of American Youth*): LG, IRT. NELS (*National Education Longitudinal Study*): LG, IRT. PROS (*Prospects: The Congressionally Mandated Study of Educational Growth and Opportunity*): LG, IRT. Prospects respondents took the complete battery of the Comprehensive Test of Basic Skills (CTBS). Prospects first-graders took a math concepts and applications test. Students in all other grades took both a math concepts and applications test and a math computation test, which Prospects combined to form a total math score.

b. For the age-based samples (NAEP, NLSY, CNLSY), we recoded the age at testing to the modal grade at testing. We coded grade level according to whether students were tested in the fall, winter, or spring (for example, since NAEP tested thirteen-year-olds in the fall, we coded their grade level as 8.0.)

c. Indicates the year in which the test was administered.

d. NAEP tested a varying number of black and white students each year. We did not have access to the race-specific numbers for all assessment years. Consequently, we estimated the race-specific sample size from the reported race-specific standard errors and standard deviations in each year. Since NAEP's standard errors are corrected for design effects, the numbers we report do not reflect the actual number of students assessed, but rather the effective number of students assessed after accounting for nonindependence due to within-school clustering.

e. We calculated the gap by subtracting the black mean from the white mean and dividing by the standard deviation for the entire population, including students from other ethnic backgrounds. We estimated all the sample moments using the appropriate cross-sectional weights. We estimated the overall standard deviation based on the sample with test data, regardless of whether sample members had complete data on race. Estimation of the group means required that the sample have complete test data and complete race data.

f. The standard error of the gap is the square root of the estimated sampling variance for each gap. See text for details on the calculation of the variance.

Notes to notes: CS = Cross-sectional Survey; LG = Longitudinal Survey; IRT indicates that students' scores were estimated from their item-response patterns using Item Response Theory. NR stands for "number right" and indicates that the test scores reflect the sum of students' correct responses to the test items. When a data set provided both IRT and NR scores, we used the IRT scores.

properties. Specifically, we excluded the third-grade Equality of Educational Opportunity (EEO) vocabulary test because James Coleman and colleagues reported that it had a low ceiling.[36] We also excluded the Children of the NLSY (CNLSY) reading comprehension data for five-, six-, and seven-year-olds because the tests were skewed and leptokurtic. We excluded CNLSY math data for five- and six-year-olds for the same reason. (The math tests for seven-year-olds were relatively normally distributed, so we included them.) Because NELS used a freshening process to create purportedly nationally representative samples in all three waves of its data collection, we included all three waves of NELS in our analysis. This decision introduces nonindependence into the regression analysis, since most of the same students contributed data to the estimated black-white gaps in the eighth, tenth, and twelfth grades. Nonindependence generally biases the standard errors of regression coefficients downward, making them seem more statistically significant than they should be.

We did not include data from the NAEP "main" samples in the analyses we report. The main sample data are not readily available in most years,

36. Coleman and others (1966, p. 220).

and we had some reason to doubt the accuracy of the data that were available. (We had previously found inaccuracies in the reporting of some of the NAEP "trend" statistics in the same publication from which we had to draw the main sample statistics.) In theory, however, the main samples should provide better estimates of the black-white gap than the trend samples, both because the main samples oversample black students and because the main sample tests are probably more valid measures of achievement. When we included data from the main samples for 1990 and 1992, the reading results reported here did not change much. The math results changed considerably, however. The grade-level effect and the linear time trend both shrank, and the standard errors increased. The predictive power of the entire equation was also reduced by about a third. These results serve as a cautionary tale to researchers who have assumed that the trend results resemble the main sample results. Future research should focus on comparing results from the trend and main samples.

Although the standard meta-analytic convention for calculating effect sizes uses the pooled standard deviation of the two groups, we divided by the overall standard deviation, which included all ethnic groups because that seemed to be the right comparison group. We estimated all sample moments using the appropriate weights, so that the estimates would be nationally representative. For age-based samples, we recoded the age at testing to the modal grade at testing. When we knew the approximate time of year of testing, we coded the grade-level variable accordingly. For example, the NAEP tested nine-year-olds in the winter, so we coded their grade level as 4.37; the NAEP tested thirteen-year-olds in the fall, so we coded their grade level as 8.0; and the NAEP tested seventeen-year-olds in the spring, so we coded their grade level as 11.75. We calculated the variance of the gaps using the following formula from William Shadish and C. Keith Haddock

$$v_i = \frac{n_i^b + n_i^w}{n_i^b n_i^w} + \frac{d_i^2}{2(n_i^b + n_i^w)},$$

where n_i^b is the black sample size, n_i^w is the white sample size, and d_i is the standardized black-white gap.[37] Next, because we had used the overall standard deviation as the denominator of the effect size, we multiplied v_i by the ratio of the pooled variance to the overall variance. We then multiplied this quantity by an estimate of the design effect for each test. When an estimate of the design effect for the test was available in published sources, we used

37. Shadish and Haddock (1994).

it. Otherwise, we calculated the design effects using the strata and primary sampling unit variables in the various data sets. The standard errors reported by the NAEP had already been corrected for design effects. Because we based our EEO calculations on data from the appendix of Coleman and colleagues, we did not have enough information to calculate design effects. We suspect that the design effects are small, however, given that the data in the appendix are based on random draws of 1,000 black and 1,000 white students in each of five grades from an original sample of more than 550,000 students.

We estimated the regressions using weighted least squares regression and standard meta-analytic procedures, where the weight is the inverse of the variance of each standardized gap.[38] We report results from fixed-effects models for math and vocabulary because we could not reject the fixed-effects model for these outcomes. We report results from mixed-effects models for reading. See Hedges (1994) and Raudenbush (1994) for a discussion of the difference between fixed- and mixed- (random) effects models in meta-analysis.

Our NELS longitudinal sample is restricted to students with valid data on race and gender, and on math, reading, science, and history tests at all three time points. Our Prospects longitudinal samples are restricted to students with valid data on race and gender, and on IRT and Number Right (NR) math, reading, and vocabulary tests at all three time points. We report results only for the IRT scores. IRT-equating is the most appropriate way of accounting for guessing on tests and of comparing scores on tests whose items and levels of difficulty vary. The Prospects IRT scores should also provide better estimates of the gaps than the NR scores because a small percentage of students took different forms and levels of the CTBS test at each grade level. However, some of the NR estimates of the gap more closely resemble gaps on other surveys such as the NELS and NAEP. We report results for the IRT tests because the average difference between the IRT-estimated black-white gaps and the NR-estimated black-white gaps is less than 0.05 standard deviations across all the time 1 and time 3 scores we use in this chapter. Also, analyses of the NR scores did not yield substantively different conclusions.

Many students in the Prospects samples had missing data on race in their school records. Some had values on the race variable that conflicted across years. To retain the largest (and most representative) sample of stu-

---

38. See Cooper and Hedges (1994).

dents in each of the cohorts, we constructed a new race variable from all available data. The main source of data on students' race is students' school records. Prospects also surveyed students' parents and asked them to describe the child's race. We first attempted to reconcile conflicting race values by assigning each student the value that corresponded in at least two of the three years. Then, if students had missing data on the race variable in the first year, we assigned them their value from the second year. If they still had missing data on race, we assigned them their value from the third year. We then tried to reconcile parents' reports of their children's race across years and created a parents'-report-of-their-children's-race variable with the least missing data possible by substituting values from year two if values were missing in year one, and values from year three if values were missing in both years one and two. We then substituted the parents' report of the child's race when the child was still missing data on the race variable derived from school records.

Prospects collected family background data from parents each year. Prospects also collected some background information, such as region of residence and urbanism, from schools. NELS collected family background information in the first and third survey waves. We used similar procedures to construct background variables from both surveys. We constructed parents' educational attainment by recoding the variable into years of education, averaging across adult respondent and spouse-partner in each year, and then averaging across all available years. We averaged across people and years to reduce the amount of missing data and to make the measure more reliable. We coded the occupation variable for respondent and spouse into dummy variables, using data from the first wave when available and data from subsequent waves otherwise. We recoded family income to a continuous scale, averaged it across years, and then took its natural log. We recoded household size so that values greater than ten were equal to ten and then averaged it across years. We coded region of residence with dummy variables representing the Northeast, Midwest, and West, with the omitted category as South, and urbanism as urban and suburban, with the omitted category as rural. We coded family composition as a dummy variable indicating whether the child lived in a household with two caregivers. We used data from the first wave when available and otherwise used data from subsequent waves. We dealt with remaining missing data on all the socioeconomic status variables by creating indicator variables for students who had missing data on each of the variables and coding their value to the mean.

We calculated the predicted scores in the top panel of figure 7-2 for students who were initially at the population mean, using the predicted values in row 4 of tables 7-4 through 7-6 and the estimated true multiple correlations between black students' scores at different grades. We first calculated the true multiple correlations between fall-of-first-grade scores and spring-of-second-grade score (math true R = 0.74; reading true R = 0.51; vocabulary true R = 0.76), between spring-of-third-grade scores and spring-of-fifth-grade score (math true R = 0.77; reading true R = 0.69; vocabulary true R = 0.80), between spring-of-seventh-grade scores and spring-of-ninth-grade score (math true R = 0.83; reading true R = 0.60; vocabulary true R = 0.80), and between spring-of-eighth-grade scores and spring-of-twelfth-grade score (math true R = 0.89; reading true R = 0.92) using the observed correlations for blacks and correcting them for estimates of unreliability. (We used reliability estimates for blacks in Prospects. We used reliability estimates for the total sample for NELS because race-specific reliability data were unavailable.) We then took the square root of these true correlations to approximate the true yearly correlations. We used the annual decrements predicted for students whose initial scores were at the population mean that we estimated from separate equations for blacks and whites (row 4 of tables 7-4 through 7-6). For example, suppose we want to calculate how much a black student with scores at the population mean falls behind a white student with comparable skills between the beginning of the first grade and the end of the second grade. Our estimate from row 4 of table 7-4 indicates that black students who score at the mean fall -0.08 standard deviations behind white students who score at the mean, or $-0.08/0.02 = -0.04$ standard deviations annually. Because the true multiple correlation between the fall of first-grade scores and the spring of second-grade scores is 0.74, the estimated annual correlation is $0.74^{1/2} = 0.86$. In the fall of the first grade the black student scores at the mean of the standardized test score distribution, so his or her score is 0. By the end of the first grade the black student's predicted score is $(0)(0.86) - 0.04 = -0.04$ standard deviations below the mean. By the end of the second grade, the black student's predicted score is $(-0.04)(0.86) - 0.04 = -0.074$ standard deviations below the mean. If we continue these calculations through the end of the twelfth grade, we produce the estimates graphed in the top panel of figure 7-2.

We did not have data on correlations or annual decrements for the third, sixth, and seventh grades. We assumed that the annual decrement during the third grade was the average of the annual decrements during the second and fourth grades. Likewise, we assumed that the correlation between end-of-second- and end-of-third-grade scores was the average of the correlation between end-of-first- and end-of-second-grade scores and the correlation between end-of-third-grade and end-of-fourth-grade scores. For the sixth grade we assumed that the annual decrement and the correlation between time 1 and time 2 scores were the same as the decrement and correlation in the fifth grade. For the seventh grade we assumed that the annual decrement and the correlation were the same as the decrement and correlation in the eighth grade. Since Prospects and NELS estimated different annual decrements and true correlations during the ninth grade, we took the average of these estimates.

We calculated the annual black decrements for the middle panel of figure 7-2 by first calculating the predicted black-white gaps from column 2 of table 7-2 for math and column 1 of table 7-2 for reading and vocabulary. (We assumed that the cohort was born in 1974, which is the modal year of birth for the NELS senior cohort, that they took IRT tests, and that they belonged to cross-sectional samples.) We then calculated the predicted black-white gap in the absence of an effect of race, assuming a year-to-year correlation of .95. We subtracted this estimated cumulative gap from the estimated cumulative gap predicted from the meta-analysis, and divided it by 12 to obtain the annual decrement associated with being black. We then used these annual decrements in conjunction with an assumed year-to-year correlation of .95 to produce the estimates in the middle panel of figure 7-2, using calculations similar to those described for the top panel of figure 7-2.

Appendix Tables

Appendix tables 7A-2 and 7A-3 show sample attrition in Prospects and NELS and estimated effects of being white on scores.

Table 7A-2. Sample Attrition, by Race, in Prospects and NELS[a]

	Prospects fall, first grade						Prospects spring, third grade					
	Black mean		White mean		SD	SD	Black mean		White mean		SD	SD
	Cross.	Long.	Cross.	Long.	cross.	long.	Cross.	Long.	Cross.	Long.	cross.	long.
Test scores												
Math (IRT)	434	436	494	498	68	67	653	660	684	689	46	43
Reading (IRT)	440	441	491	493	66	64	651	655	693	695	61	59
Vocabulary (IRT)	448	448	492	493	61	60	651	656	685	687	42	40
Region of residence												
Northeast (%)	20	22	21	19	40	40	24	29	19	23	40	43
Midwest (%)	8	8	24	27	41	43	10	7	27	25	43	42
West (%)	8	6	20	17	38	36	8	6	18	17	37	36
South (%)	63	63	35	36	49	49	59	58	36	34	49	49
Urbanism of school												
Urban (%)	45	42	16	15	41	40	61	55	16	16	42	41
Rural (%)	37	41	45	54	50	50	20	26	38	44	48	49
Suburban (%)	18	17	39	31	48	45	19	19	46	40	49	48
Household size (#)	4.78	4.74	4.46	4.44	1.25	1.21	4.74	4.68	4.45	4.39	1.23	1.13
Two-caregiver family (%)	45	46	83	85	42	41	45	50	83	84	41	40
Parents' educ. attain. (years)	12.38	12.46	13.20	13.21	1.78	1.71	12.56	12.67	13.41	13.58	1.93	1.95
Family income ($)	20,148	20,742	44,908	45,294	33,387	32,859	24,695	29,336	49,426	52,241	34,551	34,483

	Prospects spring, seventh grade						NELS spring, eighth grade					
	Black mean		White mean		SD	SD	Black mean		White mean		SD	SD
	Cross.	Long.	Cross.	Long.	cross.	long.	Cross.	Long.	Cross.	Long.	cross.	long.
Test scores												
Math (IRT)	732	738	762	768	47	42	28	29	37	38	12	12
Reading (IRT)	723	729	749	754	46	41	22	23	28	29	9	8
Vocabulary (IRT)	718	724	755	759	46	42						
Region of residence												
Northeast (%)	16	13	17	19	37	38	14	12	21	21	40	40
Midwest (%)	16	15	30	33	45	46	13	10	32	35	46	47
West (%)	9	9	17	15	36	35	6	4	16	13	35	33
South (%)	59	62	36	34	49	48	66	74	32	31	48	48
Urbanism of school												
Urban (%)	59	50	15	10	41	35	40	29	15	15	39	37
Rural (%)	18	31	44	53	49	50	30	39	38	40	48	49
Suburban (%)	22	19	41	37	49	48	30	32	47	45	50	50
Household size (#)	4.74	4.67	4.46	4.47	1.37	1.25	4.51	4.45	4.30	4.31	1.20	1.17
Two-caregiver family (%)	45	44	83	85	42	40	57	60	85	87	39	37
Parents' educ. attain. (years)	12.56	12.86	13.33	13.43	2.00	1.95	12.71	12.80	13.52	13.62	2.13	2.10
Family income ($)	25,010	27,110	50,738	51,959	33,618	32,704	24,430	25,891	45,018	46,243	32,535	32,692

a. "Cross." stands for cross-sectional sample. "Long." stands for longitudinal sample restricted to students with complete data on three waves of test scores, race, and gender. See text for details on the construction of the socioeconomic variables.

Table 7A-3. *Estimated Effect of Being White on Math, Reading, and Vocabulary Scores, Controlling Earlier Scores, Socioeconomic Status, and School Fixed Effects*

					Controlling			
Subject and grade	Nothing	Prior scores	SES	School fixed effects	SES and school fixed effects	Prior scores and SES	Prior scores and school fixed effects	Prior scores, SES, and school fixed effects
Math								
Second grade	0.75	0.08	0.50	0.57	0.45	0.00	0.13	0.15
Fifth grade	0.51	0.01	0.28	0.28	0.14	−0.03	−0.05	−0.09
Ninth grade	0.71	0.20	0.41	0.39	0.32	0.13	0.09	0.07
Twelfth grade	0.75	0.02	0.42	0.67	0.51	0.03	0.05	0.04
Mean	0.68	0.08	0.40	0.48	0.36	0.03	0.06	0.04
Reading								
Second grade	0.80	0.29	0.60	0.57	0.29	0.25	0.28	0.29
Fifth grade	0.72	0.19	0.45	0.38	0.25	0.12	0.06	0.04
Ninth grade	0.61	0.10	0.38	0.35	0.31	0.12	0.11	0.12
Twelfth grade	0.67	0.08	0.42	0.69	0.56	0.09	0.10	0.10
Mean	0.70	0.17	0.46	0.50	0.35	0.15	0.14	0.14
Vocabulary								
Second grade	0.77	0.20	0.51	0.51	0.35	0.13	0.20	0.21
Fifth grade	0.83	0.21	0.49	0.48	0.33	0.12	0.09	0.06
Ninth grade	0.78	0.14	0.46	0.32	0.28	0.11	0.02	0.03
Mean	0.79	0.18	0.49	0.44	0.32	0.12	0.10	0.10

References

Allison, Paul D. 1990. "Change Scores as Dependent Variables in Regression Analysis." In C. C. Clogg, ed., *Sociological Methodology*, vol. 20, pp. 93–114. Oxford, England: Basil Blackwell.

Barron, Sheila I., and Daniel M. Koretz. 1996. "An Evaluation of the Robustness of the National Assessment of Educational Progress Trend Estimates for Racial-Ethnic Subgroups." *Educational Assessment* 3(3):209–48.

Bloom, Benjamin. 1964. *Stability and Change in Human Characteristics*. John Wiley.

Coleman, James S., and others. 1966. *Equality of Educational Opportunity*. Washington: Government Printing Office.

Cooper, Harris, and Larry V. Hedges, eds. 1994. *The Handbook of Research Synthesis*. Russell Sage Foundation.

The CTBS/4 Technical Report. 1991. Monterey, Calif.: CTB Macmillan/McGraw-Hill School Publishing.

Entwisle, Doris R., and Karl L. Alexander. 1988. "Factors Affecting Achievement Test Scores and Marks of Black and White First Graders." *Elementary School Journal* 88 (5): 449–71.

———. 1992. "Summer Setback: Race, Poverty, School Composition, and Mathematics Achievement in the First Two Years of School." *American Sociological Review* 57: 72–84.

———. 1994. "Winter Setback: The Racial Composition of Schools and Learning to Read." *American Sociological Review* 59: 446–60.

Gordon, Robert A. 1984. "Digits Backward and the Mercer-Kamin Law: Empirical Response to Mercer's Treatment of Internal Validity of IQ Tests." In C. R. Reynolds and R. T. Brown, eds., *Perspectives on Bias in Mental Testing*, pp. 357–506. Plenum.

Grissmer, David W., and others. 1994. *Student Achievement and the Changing American Family*. Santa Monica, Calif.: RAND.

Hauser, Robert M., and Min-Hsiung Huang. 1996. "Trends in Black-White Test Score Differentials." Institute for Research on Poverty discussion paper 1110–96.

Hedges, Larry V. 1994. "Fixed Effects Models." In H. Cooper and L. V. Hedges, eds., *The Handbook of Research Synthesis*, pp. 285–99. Russell Sage Foundation.

Heyns, Barbara. 1978. *Summer Learning and the Effects of Schooling*. Academic Press.

Humphreys, Lloyd G., and Timothy C. Davey. 1988. "Continuity in Intellectual Growth from 12 Months to 9 Years." *Intelligence* 12: 183–97.

Jaynes, Gerald D., and Robin M. Williams Jr., eds. 1989. *A Common Destiny: Blacks and American Society*. Washington: National Academy Press.

Jencks, Christopher, and others. 1972. *Inequality: A Reassessment of the Effect of Family and Schooling in America*. Basic Books.

Jensen, Arthur R. 1974. "Cumulative Deficit: A Testable Hypothesis?" *Developmental Psychology* 10(6): 996–1019.

———. 1977. "Cumulative Deficit in IQ of Blacks in the Rural South." *Developmental Psychology* 13(3): 184–91.

Jones, Lyle V. 1984. "White-Black Achievement Differences: The Narrowing Gap." *American Psychologist* 39 (11): 1207–13.

Klineberg, Otto. 1963. "Negro-White Differences in Intelligence Test Performance: A New Look at an Old Problem." *American Psychologist* 18: 198–203.

Kupermintz, Haggai, and Richard E. Snow. 1997. "Enhancing the Validity and Usefulness of Large-Scale Educational Assessments: III. NELS:88 Mathematics Achievement to 12th Grade." *American Educational Research Journal* 34: 124–50.

Loehlin, John C., Gardner Lindzey, and J. N. Spuhler. 1975. *Race Differences in Intelligence*. San Francisco: W. H. Freeman.

National Center for Education Statistics. August 1995. *Psychometric Report for the NELS:88 Base Year through Second Follow-Up*. Washington: Office of Educational Research and Improvement.

Prospects: The Congressionally Mandated Study of Educational Growth and Opportunity. Interim Report. July 1993. Washington: U.S. Department of Education.

Ralph, John, Dana Keller, and James Crouse. 1997. "The National Education Longitudinal Study: What It Tells Us about High School Academic Achievement."

Raudenbush, Stephen W. 1994. "Random Effects Models." In Cooper and Hedges, *Handbook of Research Synthesis*, pp. 301–39.

Shadish, William R. and C. Keith Haddock. 1994. "Combining Estimates of Effect Size." In Cooper and Hedges, *Handbook of Research Synthesis*, pp. 261–81.

RONALD F. FERGUSON

8

Teachers' Perceptions and Expectations and the Black-White Test Score Gap

A FRICAN-AMERICAN CHILDREN arrive at kindergarten with fewer reading skills than whites, even when their parents have equal years of schooling. In an ideal world, schools would reduce these disparities. Unfortunately, national data show that, at best, the black-white test score gap is roughly constant (in standard deviations) from the primary through the secondary grades.[1] At worst, the gap widens.[2] Among blacks and whites with equal current scores, blacks tend to make less future progress. This is the first of two chapters on how schools might affect this story. It examines evidence for the proposition that teach-

Thanks to Karl Alexander, William Dickens, James Flynn, Christopher Jencks, Meredith Phillips, and Jason Snipes for helpful discussions and comments on earlier drafts. I am also grateful to Lee Jussim and Meredith Phillips for calculations that they conducted at my request for this chapter. Jason Snipes provided able research assistance.

1. See chapter 7. The black-white gap in skills at the beginning of primary school is smaller for more recent cohorts.

2. Existing evidence on group-level disparity at the mean across grade levels within a cohort is not entirely clear, because of measurement issues and data problems. See chapter 7 above for a discussion of methodological decisions that determine whether the gap appears to be constant or to grow wider over time within a cohort.

ers' perceptions, expectations, and behaviors interact with students' beliefs, behaviors, and work habits in ways that help to perpetuate the black-white test score gap.[3]

No matter what material resources are available, no matter what strategies school districts use to allocate children to schools, and no matter how children are grouped for instruction, schoolchildren spend their days in social interaction with teachers and other students. As students and teachers immerse themselves in the routines of schooling, perceptions and expectations both reflect and determine the goals that they set for achievement; the strategies they use to pursue the goals; the skills, energy, and other resources they use to implement the strategies; and the rewards they expect from making the effort. These should affect standardized scores as well as other measures of achievement.

It is a common, if controversial, assumption that teachers' perceptions, expectations, and behaviors are biased by racial stereotypes. The literature is full of seeming contradictions. For example, Sara Lawrence Lightfoot writes: "Teachers, like all of us, use the dimensions of class, race, sex, ethnicity to bring order to their perception of the classroom environment. Rather than teachers gaining more in-depth and holistic understanding of the child, with the passage of time teachers' perceptions become increasingly stereotyped and children become hardened caricatures of an initially discriminatory vision."[4]

Similarly, Reuben Baron, David Tom, and Harris Cooper argue that "the race or class of a particular student may cue the teacher to apply the generalized expectations, therefore making it difficult for the teacher to develop *specific* expectations tailored to individual students. In this manner, the race or class distinction among students is perpetuated. The familiar operation of stereotypes takes place in that it becomes difficult for minority or disadvantaged students to distinguish themselves from the generalized expectation."[5]

---

3. Whenever possible, I present results in terms of "effect sizes" measured in standard deviation units. For example, if one group of students experiences a particular treatment and an otherwise equivalent control or comparison group does not, the effect size of the treatment on test scores is the difference between average scores for the two groups after the treatment, divided by the pooled standard deviation of scores. For an outcome that is normally distributed, an effect size of 0.20 moves a student from the fiftieth to the fifty-eighth percentile; an effect size of 0.50 moves the student to the sixty-ninth percentile; and an effect size of 0.80 moves the student to the seventy-ninth percentile.

4. Lightfoot (1978, pp. 85–86).

5. Baron, Tom, and Cooper (1985, p. 251).

On the other side, Jerome Brophy doubts that bias is important: "Few teachers can sustain grossly inaccurate expectations for many of their students in the face of daily feedback that contradicts those expectations."[6] Emil Haller adds: "Undoubtedly there are some racially biased people who are teachers. . . . However . . . the problem does not seem to be of that nature. Conceiving it so is to confuse the issue, to do a serious injustice to the vast majority of teachers, and ultimately to visit an even more serious one on minority pupils. After all . . . children's reading skills are not much improved by subtly (and not so subtly) labeling their teachers racists."[7]

Some aspects of this debate are substantive, but others are semantic. The chapter begins by distinguishing among alternative definitions of racial bias and reviewing evidence on teachers' perceptions and expectations. Later sections address the ways in which teachers' and students' behaviors might be both causes and consequences of racially disparate perceptions and expectations regarding achievement, and might therefore contribute to perpetuating the black-white test score gap.

Bias in Teachers' Perceptions and Expectations

Expectations, perceptions, and behaviors that look biased under one criterion often look unbiased under another. However, researchers who study racial bias seldom evaluate their findings by more than a single standard. The discourse that results can be quite perplexing. One body of literature alleges bias and another denies it, but much of this disagreement is really over what is meant by "bias." At least three different conceptions of bias appear in this debate.

Bias is deviation from some benchmark that defines neutrality, or lack of bias. One type of benchmark is "unconditional" race neutrality. By this criterion, teachers who are unbiased expect the same, on average, of black and white students. A second type of benchmark is "conditional" race neutrality—that is, conditioned on observable, measurable criteria. For example, unbiased teachers should expect the same of black and white students on the condition that they have the same past grades and test scores. The third type of benchmark is conditioned not on past performance but on

---

6. Brophy (1985, p. 304).
7. Haller (1985, p. 481) is commenting on racial disparity in ability group assignments. See chapter 9 below for more discussion of ability grouping, including Haller's findings.

unobserved potential. It requires neutrality—for example, equal expectations and aspirations—in regard to blacks and whites who have equal potential. Insofar as "potential" differs from past performance, however, it is difficult to prove. Assuming that black and white children are born with the same potential (which seems a fair assumption), there is no distinction at birth between unconditional race neutrality and neutrality conditioned on unobserved potential. However, disparities in potential may develop as children grow older; recent literature on brain development, for example, suggests that experience alters potential. Therefore unconditional race neutrality may or may not remain the best approximation to neutrality conditioned on unobserved potential.

Unconditional Race Neutrality

Unconditional race neutrality requires that teachers' perceptions, expectations, and behaviors be uncorrelated with students' race. By this definition, an unbiased perception, expectation, or treatment has the same average value for all racial groups. This benchmark for racial bias is the standard in experimental studies. Such studies typically find that teachers are racially biased.

In experimental studies researchers systematically manipulate information about students. Although race is included, the sample is selected to avoid any correlation between race and the other characteristics noted.[8] In a typical experiment, teachers receive information about students in written descriptions, photographs, videotapes—or occasionally, real children, who act as the experimenter's confederates. The teachers then predict one or more measures of ability or academic performance for each student. If the experiment is run well, the teachers do not discern that race is a variable in the experiment or that the real purpose is to assess their racial biases.

Baron, Tom, and Cooper conduct a meta-analysis of experimental studies that focus on teachers' expectations, sixteen of which deal with race.[9] Teachers have higher expectations for white students in nine of the studies,

---

8. This immediate discussion concerns experiments. However, this first type of benchmark is also used in naturalistic settings. Specifically, in the absence of reliable information *about individuals* on which to base a benchmark that is not unconditionally race neutral, unconditional racial neutrality may seem the only morally defensible alternative.

9. Baron, Tom, and Cooper (1985).

and for blacks in one study. The differences are statistically significant in five of these studies, all favoring whites. The remaining six studies do not report which group is favored. In these studies, the differences are statistically insignificant. Overall, the hypothesis of identical expectations for black and white students is clearly rejected ($p < 0.002$).[10]

An interesting study by Debra DeMeis and Ralph Turner is not included in Baron, Tom, and Cooper's meta-analysis but supports their conclusion.[11] Sixty-eight white female elementary school teachers, with an average of seven years of teaching experience, were selected from summer school classes at a university in Kentucky during the 1970s. They were played tapes of male fifth-graders responding to the question, "What happened on your favorite TV show the last time you watched it?," and each tape was accompanied by a picture of a black or a white student. DeMeis and Turner asked teachers to rate the taped responses for personality, quality of response, current academic abilities, and future academic abilities. The race of the student in the picture was a statistically significant predictor for each of the four outcomes ($p < 0.0001$).[12]

If the benchmark is unconditional race neutrality, teachers are found to hold racially biased expectations. What should one make of this pervasive racial bias? Consider people who learn from real life that when one flips a coin the odds of getting heads are 60:40. Place these people in an experimental situation where, unknown to them, the odds have been set to 50:50. If each person is then given only one toss of the coin, will their predictions be unbiased? In an environment where real differences in per-

---

10. Baron, Tom, and Cooper (1985) report that effect sizes could be retrieved for only six of the sixteen studies. In these six studies the black-white differences in teacher expectations average half a standard deviation. If nine of the other studies are assumed to have effect sizes of zero and the one with a significant result but no effect size is assumed to have an effect size of 0.36, then the average effect size across all sixteen studies is 0.22.

11. DeMeis and Turner (1978).

12. To compute the effect sizes for each outcome, I use the standard deviation among blacks as the denominator, since the pooled standard deviation is not reported. The standard deviation among whites is virtually the same as that among blacks. Among students speaking standard English, effect sizes for the black-white differences in personality, quality of response, current academic abilities, and future academic abilities are 0.57, 0.52, 0.55, and 0.44 standard deviations, respectively. For black English, the analogous numbers are 0.34, 0.44, 0.23 and 0.14 standard deviations. The fact that effect sizes are smaller for tapes on which students spoke black English is not surprising, since speaking black English would be an especially negative signal for a white student. Across the four outcomes, within-race effect sizes for black English versus standard English range from 0.23 to 0.45 for blacks and from 0.55 to 0.74 for whites, in all cases favoring standard English. All effect sizes reported in this footnote are calculated from numbers in DeMeis and Turner (1978, table 2).

formance between blacks and whites are the norm, if the benchmark for declaring expectations unbiased is unconditional race neutrality, biased expectations are what one should expect.[13] For the same reasons, this type of bias is also pervasive in naturalistic studies—that is, studies in real classrooms, without experimental controls.

Experimental research of this kind establishes that teachers believe certain stereotypes and use the stereotypes in one-time encounters with experimental targets. But it does not establish that the stereotypes would represent biased estimates of the average if they were applied in real classrooms outside the experimental setting. Nor does it prove that teachers in real classrooms treat students inappropriately, or that their stereotypes prevent them from forming accurate perceptions about individual students.

Evidence on Accuracy

For at least two decades, scholars in education have emphasized that teachers' contemporaneous perceptions of students' performance, as well as their expectations of students' future performance, are generally accurate.[14] For example, it has been found that first grade teachers can learn enough about children in the first few weeks of school to predict with some accuracy their rank order on examinations held at the beginning of second grade.[15] Once set, teachers' expectations do not change a great deal. This may be because their early impressions of proficiency are accurate, and the actual rank order does not change much.

There are several possible reasons for stability in rank ordering. First, teachers' perceptions and expectations might be relatively inflexible. Self-fulfilling expectation effects, discussed below, will typically be strongest for the teachers whose expectations are least flexible.[16] For these teachers, cor-

---

13. For whatever reasons, average scores on standardized examinations tend to be lower for blacks than for whites. Hence in general the most accurate prediction is that whites will have higher scores.

14. See, for example, Good (1987); Egan and Archer (1985); Mitman (1985); Hoge and Butcher (1984); Monk (1983); Pedulla, Airasian, and Madaus (1980).

15. See Brophy and Good (1974, table 6.1), which presents correlations from Evertson, Brophy, and Good (1972).

16. Eccles and Wigfield (1985), for example, provide a line of reasoning that might support this outcome. Essentially, in order to deviate from a previously established trajectory, the student may need support from the teacher in begining the process of change. If the teacher continues to treat the student as he or she did before the change, the student may decide that the environment is not sufficiently responsive to attain the new goal, feel a lack of control, and return to the old ways.

relations between beginning-of-year and end-of-year assessments should be among the highest.[17] A second reason for stability might be that few students try hard to change their positions. A third might be that the pace and style of standard teaching offer few effective opportunities for students who are behind to catch up.[18] Most evidence about the accuracy of teachers' perceptions comes from correlations between teachers' predictions and actual test scores, which typically range between 0.50 and 0.90.[19] At least at the low end of this range, one might alternatively focus on the inaccuracy of the predictions, in "glass half empty" fashion.

I know of only three studies that report separate correlations for blacks and whites. Haller finds that the correlation between teachers' subjective assessments of the reading proficiency of fourth, fifth, and sixth graders and students' scores on the Comprehensive Test of Basic Skills is 0.73 for whites and 0.74 for blacks.[20] Jacqueline Irvine asked teachers to rank 213 fifth, sixth, and seventh graders on general academic ability during the second, tenth, and final weeks of the 1983–84 school year. Correlations between these ratings and scores on the California Achievement Test are similar for blacks and whites.[21] Similarly, Margie Gaines finds that teachers' predictions of performance on the Iowa Test of Basic Skills are as accurate for black students as for whites.[22]

17. Experimental studies that expose teachers to different sequences of facts show that their expectations are sufficiently flexible to remain accurate as new information becomes available; see, for example, Shavelson, Cadwell, and Izu (1977). The pattern of flexibility among teachers in real classrooms is not known.

18. Indeed, Guskey (1982) finds that improvements in teacher responsiveness reduce the accuracy of teachers' early predictions for end-of-semester performance; see discussion in text below.

19. See Egan and Archer (1985); Irvine (1985); Brophy and Good (1974); Evertson, Brophy, and Good (1972); Willis (1972).

20. Haller (1985, note 4). This study covers forty-nine teachers and 934 fourth, fifth, and sixth graders in five cities across four census regions.

21. See Irvine (1990, p. 77), discussing findings presented first in Irvine (1985). The correlations between second-week rankings and end-of-year test scores are 0.63 for white males and 0.62 for black males. The correlation for black males dipped in the tenth week, but had returned to the same range as for whites by the end of the school year. Irvine emphasizes this difference in the pattern for black and white boys. It seems to me, however, that similarity is the more salient finding: of three comparisons for boys, in only one (boys at the tenth week) is the racial difference notable; and there is no significant racial difference in the three comparisons for girls. Some teachers in Irvine's study were consistently more accurate than others. For the least accurate teacher, the correlations moved from 0.11 for the second week to 0.56 for the end of the year. At the high end, one teacher had correlations of 0.91, 0.92, and 0.89 for the second week, tenth week, and end of the year, respectively.

22. Gaines (1990).

The similarity in correlations for blacks and whites means that the rank order of achievement among blacks is as stable as that among whites, and that teachers achieve similar accuracy in assessing both racial groups. It does not, however, imply that teachers' perceptions or expectations have the same impact on blacks and whites.[23] Neither does it mean that teachers are racially unbiased. In this context, accuracy is not always the opposite of bias. If self-fulfilling prophecy were always perfect, for example, each student's performance would be exactly what the teacher expected. Therefore if expectations were biased, outcomes would be perfectly predicted but biased.

Race Neutrality Conditioned on Observables

The second type of benchmark for measuring bias is race neutrality conditioned on observables. The assumption is that teacher's perceptions and expectations are unbiased if they are based only on legitimate observable predictors of performance, such as past grades, test scores, attitudes about school, and beliefs about personal abilities (for example, as measured by a survey). In this case, the benchmark is only conditionally race neutral: if past performance or another of these predictors is correlated with race, the benchmark will be too. Bias is the difference between the actual perception or expectation and the benchmark for neutrality.

This type of bias can be estimated by regressing a teacher's perceptions or expectations on both race and one or more other explanatory variables that one regards as legitimate predictors of performance. The coefficient of student race then measures the average racial bias among teachers in the sample. This benchmark is probably more appropriate than unconditional race neutrality when considering, for example, whether teachers rely on biased judgments to nominate students for particular curriculum tracks or ability groups. As I show below, it might also be more appropriate for analyzing whether teachers' biases produce self-fulfilling prophecies of poor performance among black students. However, it is not sufficient to distin-

---

23. Recall that two lines with different slopes can each represent a correlation of one between the variables on the *x* and *y* axes. Similarly, teachers' early perceptions or expectations could have a much larger impact on performance for one race than for the other (as represented by a steeper line), even though the correlation between teachers' perceptions or expectations and end-of-year performance is the same for both groups. The possibility of different slopes is explored by Jussim, Eccles, and Madon (1996), as discussed below.

guish conditional from unconditional race neutrality; the existing literature often makes a further distinction between past performance and future potential.

Race Neutrality Conditioned on Potential

The third type of benchmark—which may or may not equate with either of the two discussed above—is the level of performance that a student could reach at full potential. In this case, bias is found in the perception or estimation of a student's full potential. Full potential equals demonstrated plus latent potential. It is alleged that teachers underestimate the latent potential of blacks more than that of whites.

It is of major concern to African Americans that teachers underestimate the potential of black students, if not necessarily their performance. Consider the following passage from a 1989 report entitled *Visions of a Better Way: A Black Appraisal of American Public Schooling*: "We hold this truth to be self-evident: all black children are capable of learning and achieving. Others who have hesitated, equivocated, or denied this fact have assumed that black children could not master their school-work or have cautioned that blacks were not 'academically oriented.' As a result, they have perpetuated a myth of intellectual inferiority, perhaps genetically based. These falsehoods prop up an inequitable social hierarchy with blacks disproportionately represented at the bottom, and they absolve schools of their fundamental responsibility to educate all children, no matter how deprived."[24]

An earlier description likewise alleges bias, judged against the benchmark of future potential: "In the middle class white school, student inattention was taken as an indication of teacher need to arouse student interest, but the same behavior in a lower class black school was rationalized as boredom due to limited student attention span. In general, the teachers in the lower class black school were characterized by low expectations for the children and low respect for their ability to learn."[25]

24. Committee on Policy for Racial Justice (1989), quoted in Miller (1995, p. 203). The task force that produced the report included a number of noted black scholars at major universities, including Sara Lawrence Lightfoot of Harvard (the principal author), James P. Comer of Yale, John Hope Franklin of Duke, and William Julius Wilson, then at the University of Chicago.
25. Leacock (1969), quoted in Brophy and Good (1974, p. 10).

If, as they surely must, perceptions of children's intellectual potential affect the setting of goals in both homes and classrooms, teachers and parents who underestimate children's potential will tend to set goals that are too low.[26] Such underestimation is undoubtedly a major problem, irrespective of race. A great waste of human potential and much social injustice results from the fact that teachers are not given the incentives and support they need to set, believe in, and skillfully pursue higher goals for all students, and in particular, for African Americans and other stigmatized minorities. The payoff to searching more aggressively for ways to help children learn would surely be higher than most people imagine.

Reliable estimates of bias related to future potential are not possible, because there is no clear basis on which to measure human potential.[27] Surveys find that expressed beliefs in the intellectual inferiority of blacks have moderated over the years.[28] In the General Social Survey, for example, the percentage of whites responding that blacks have less "in-born ability to learn" fell from 27 percent in 1977 to 10 percent in the 1996.[29] There is no way to know the degree to which this reduction is due to changes in beliefs as opposed to changes in social norms. The same survey found in 1990 that when respondents were not constrained to attribute differences to genetic factors, 53 percent agreed that blacks and Hispanics are less intelligent than whites. Indeed, 30 percent of blacks and 35 percent of Hispanics agreed.[30]

Many experts think that genetic differences are at least partially to blame for existing black-white differences in academic achievement. A 1984 survey questioned 1,020 experts on intelligence, most of them professors and university-based researchers who study testing, psychology, and education.

26. Goals are not determined by teachers' expectations alone. The curricular materials that are handed down to teachers from the administration, as well as students' actual behavior, also matter.

27. See Ford (1996) for a useful discussion of the issue in light of theories of multiple intelligences. In the terminology of the present chapter, those who think that potential is very distinct from performance and that ability is equally distributed among the races will favor an unconditionally race-neutral proxy in place of race neutrality conditional on observables. Those who believe that racial differences in performance are good approximations of racial differences in potential might favor a proxy of race neutrality conditional on observables, perhaps augmented by a positive shift factor for all students.

28. Miller (1995, chapter 8) presents a useful review of trends in surveys regarding beliefs about black intellectual inferiority. He points out that numbers in the Harris poll tend to produce smaller percentages because they ask more directly about whether any black-white difference in intelligence is genetic.

29. Kluegel (1990, pp. 514–15, 517); see also the introduction to this volume.

30. Miller (1995, p. 183), based on Tom Smith (1990, p. 6).

Almost half (46 percent) expressed the opinion that black-white differences in intelligence are at least partially genetic. Fifteen percent said that only environment is responsible, 24 percent regarded the available evidence as insufficient, and 14 percent did not answer; in other words, only 15 percent clearly disagreed.[31] With expert opinion slanted so strongly in favor of the genetic hypothesis and widespread media attention paid to books like Richard Herrnstein and Charles Murray's *The Bell Curve*, there is little prospect that "rumors of inferiority" will cease or that racial differences in estimates of students' potential will disappear.[32]

Writers concerned with bias in the estimation of potential often claim that it leads to self-fulfilling prophecies. Their point is that children would achieve more if teachers and other adults expected that they could. In most cases, it might be more appropriate to describe bias of this type as producing expectations that are "sustaining" of past trends.[33] Such an expectation is likely to block the absorption of new information into a decision process, and thereby to sustain the trend that existed before the new information was received.

Self-Fulfilling Prophecy

A self-fulfilling prophecy occurs when bias in a teacher's expectation of a student's performance affects that performance. Self-fulfilling prophecies may be associated with any of the three types of bias discussed above, but only those associated with the second type—where the benchmark is conditioned on observables—can be well measured. The basic concept was introduced into social science by Robert Merton in 1948, and Robert Rosenthal and Lenore Jacobson's work on the topic sparked a small industry of studies during the 1970s and early 1980s.[34] The effect shows up (and sometimes fails to do so) in a wide range of experimental studies with animals and with human subjects.[35] Experimental studies in education typically involve the random assignment of students to groups that have been labeled as high or low performing.

31. Miller (1995, pp. 186-87), based on Snyderman and Rothman (1986, 1987).
32. Herrnstein and Murray (1994); Jeff Howard and Ray Hammond, "Rumors of Inferiority," *New Republic*, September 1989.
33. See, for example, Good (1987).
34. Merton (1948); Rosenthal and Jacobson (1968).
35. See Rosenthal (1994) for a review.

The successful instigation of self-fulfilling prophecies by researchers requires that (1) teachers believe false information about students; (2) teachers act on the information in ways that students can perceive; and (3) students respond in ways that confirm the expectation. The effect can fail to appear—and it often does—if any one of these conditions fails.[36] In experiments that confirm the effect, groups labeled as high performing outperform those labeled as low performing. A meta-analysis by Mary Lee Smith identifies forty-four estimates of effect sizes for reading scores, with an average of 0.48 standard deviations distinguishing students with high and low labels.[37] The average across seventeen effects for mathematics is much smaller, at 0.18. Why the effects should be smaller for mathematics than for reading is unclear. Perhaps mathematics instruction is less flexible, and therefore less affected by teachers' perceptions.

Brophy, a leader since the early 1970s in research on teacher expectations, asserts that on average, teachers' expectations in real classrooms probably make only a small difference to their students' achievement.[38] He adds the caveat, however, that teachers who hold rigid expectations and permit these to guide their interactions with students can produce larger effects. It is plausible, but not established in any literature that I have seen, that expectations of black students might be more rigid than those of whites. Moreover, expectation effects might accumulate from year to year. Surprisingly, there appears to be no good evidence on the degree to which expectation effects accumulate. If small effects accumulate, they could make a larger difference over time. In the short run, even a small difference due to expectations could push a score across the boundary between two grade levels, and thereby become consequential.

In naturalistic studies, the magnitude of self-fulfilling prophecy can be estimated as the coefficient on a teacher's expectation measure in an equa-

36. The most frequent explanation for failure is that the teachers do not believe information about the students. Sometimes teachers figure out the purpose of the experiment. Other times, teachers have their own sources of credible information or have known the students long enough to form opinions before the experiment begins. In a meta-analysis of eighteen experiments in which IQ or a similar measure of ability was the outcome, Raudenbush (1984) shows very clearly that evidence of the effect was primarily found in studies where teachers had no opportunity to form an independent impression of students before the experiment began.

37. Smith (1980). She does not say what percentage of these effect sizes are calculated from the standard deviation of test score levels as opposed to test score gains.

38. Brophy (1985, p. 304). Specifically, he estimates that teachers' expectations make about a 5 percent difference, but he does not say whether he means the difference in gain over a school year or the difference in total achievement (as in the level on a test). Brophy's statement is based on his own review of the literature, where individual studies seldom cover more than a single school year.

tion where the dependent variable is the student's ultimate performance at the end of a school year. Assuming that the estimated effect of the teacher's expectation is not simply a stand-in for omitted variables, the idiosyncratic contribution of the teacher's expectation is the consequence of bias.[39] In some cases, teacher biases exist but do not affect actual scores or grades, either because teachers do not act on their biases or because student performance does not respond to the biased actions that teachers take. Finally, it is also important to note that a teacher's perception of current performance and expectation of future performance can differ, one showing bias while the other does not.[40]

Testing for Racial Differences in Expectancy Effects

Lee Jussim, Jacquelynne Eccles, and Stephanie Madon are the only researchers who have tested for racial differences in the impact of teachers' perceptions on students' test scores.[41] They collected teachers' perceptions of current performance, talent, and effort in mathematics for 1,664 sixth-graders in October 1982.[42] They then tested for what they call racial stereotype bias—that is, whether a student's race predicts teachers' perceptions after controlling for background factors, including previous grades, previous test scores, self-perception of mathematical ability, self-reported level

39. This multivariate equation includes controls for predictors of performance, such as past performance and socioeconomic background. Typically, the estimate of self-fulfilling prophecy may tend to be statistically biased upward, because of omitted variables that are positively associated with both teacher expectations and student performance. Hence any findings of this sort must be taken as suggestive, not definitive.

40. It is not unusual, for example, for a teacher to say, "Betty is doing well now because she is repeating the grade and has seen some of this material before. I don't expect she will do as well for the rest of the year." This teacher might be accurate in the current evaluation of the student, but still biased in the expectation. Or the example might be reversed, with the expectation more positive than the evaluation of current performance. In either case, the expectation might or might not be biased when judged from the perspective of what past performance and attitudes would predict.

41. Jussim, Eccles, and Madon (1996, pp. 350–51). They speculate that the void in the literature stems from the political risk of studying groups that do, in fact, differ. Instead, researchers have tended to focus on experimental studies that assume away differences. See also Jussim (1989) and Jussim and Eccles (1992), which use the same data to study the accuracy of teachers' expectations without emphasizing racial differences.

42. Of the total student sample, seventy-six are African Americans—ideally, a larger number would be preferrable for such a study. The data are taken from the Michigan Study of Adolescent Life Transitions, which was not initially designed to study racial differences; for more on the Michigan study, see Wigfield and others (1991).

of effort, and self-reported time spent on homework. This is an example of the second type of bias defined above, using a benchmark of racial neutrality conditioned on observables, including past performance. They find no evidence of racial stereotype bias in teachers' perceptions of current performance, talent, or effort for this sample of sixth-graders.[43] The coefficient on student race is small and statistically insignificant.[44]

If racial differences in teachers' current perceptions are explained by students' past performance and attitudes, then these perceptions can only be an important source of a *future* black-white test score gap if they affect blacks and whites differently. This is precisely what Jussim, Eccles, and Madon find when they analyze the effects of teachers' perceptions of performance, talent, and effort in October on mathematics grades and scores on the mathematics section of the Michigan Educational Assessment Program (MEAP) the following spring semester, in May 1983.[45] For both grades and scores, the estimated impact of teacher perceptions is almost three times as great for African American students as for whites.[46] Effects are also

---

43. Although they do not report raw means by race, they do report that the correlations of race with grades and standard test scores were -0.12 and -0.14, respectively (in both cases, $p < 0.001$), with black studentss having the lower scores and grades. These correlations are probably smaller than in the typical national sample of (black and white) sixth-graders.

44. Jussim, Eccles, and Madon (1996) perform separate calculations to determine whether the residual variance in teachers' perceptions left unexplained by the background factors is similar for blacks and whites. They find it to be slightly higher for blacks, but by a margin so small as to be inconsequential: "The correlations of ethnicity with the absolute values of the residuals from the models predicting teacher perceptions were 0.06 ($p < 0.05$), 0.07 ($p < 0.05$), and –0.02 (not significant) for performance, talent, and effort, respectively" (p. 355). While two of the three are statistically significant, these suggest only a very small difference in accuracy, and less accuracy for blacks than for whites.

Regarding other effects, they find a small positive relationship between parental education (a proxy for socioeconomic status) and teacher's perception of a student's talent. There are also some small gender effects. Teacher perceptions of performance and effort are higher for girls, after controlling for the factors listed in the text. Hence it appears that teachers relied somewhat on a gender stereotype, although not necessarily a false one.

45. As background variables, the equation to predict scores and grades includes race, mathematics grades from the end of fifth grade, mathematics scores from the end of fifth or beginning of sixth grade, self-perception of ability, self-reported effort at mathematics, self-reported time spent on homework, and indexes of the intrinsic and extrinsic values of mathematics to the student. Interactions of student race with teacher perceptions of effort and talent were tried, but were found to produce strange results, because of collinearity with the interaction for race and performance. The result for performance might best be interpreted as the interaction of race with all aspects of a teacher's perceptions.

46. The effect size for MEAP scores is only 0.14 for whites, but 0.37 for African Americans ($p < 0.001$). This effect size for whites is quite close to that of 0.17 for mathematics achievement scores reported by Smith (1980). For grades, the effect size for African Americans is 0.56, compared with 0.20 for whites ($p < 0.01$).

larger for girls and for children from low-income families. Further, the effect is cumulative across disadvantages or stigmas: black children from low-income backgrounds experience the effects of both race and income. Teachers' perceptions of student effort do not affect MEAP scores but do affect grades, even though they are not strongly correlated with self-reports of effort.[47]

What might explain racial differences in the consequences of teachers' perceptions? One possibility is that the result is simply a statistical artifact due to omitted variable bias. This seems unlikely.[48] More plausibly, teachers are less flexible in their expectations of blacks, females, and students from low-income households. Or, as Rhonda Weinstein speculates, "minority status may play a role in the vulnerability with which students respond to teacher expectations. Differences in cultural values (family compared to school) may serve to immunize some children from the impact of teacher views of their performance or alternately to heighten their susceptibility to the dominant viewpoint."[49] Perhaps the behaviors of both teachers and students are affected by the combination of the student's race and the teacher's perception of performance. These possibilities are addressed below.

Calculations conducted by Jussim after the paper was published use a specification that includes additional interaction terms, including interactions of race with past grades and scores. The effect size for MEAP scores rises from the original 0.37 to 0.58 for African Americans and drops from 0.14 to 0.13 for whites. Moreover, the coefficients on past grades and scores are estimated to be somewhat smaller for African Americans than for whites. Hence it appears that the performance of these black students was more dependent on teachers' current opinions and less anchored in measures of past performance than that of whites. One might speculate that this is because past grades and scores were less accurate measures of the knowledge or potential of the black students than of the whites, but one cannot be sure from the information available.

47. It is not clear what to make of absence of any relationship between self-reports and teachers' perceptions of effort. If teachers' assessments really are grossly inaccurate, this fact could contribute to the disengagement of children who are believed not to be trying when in fact they are. It could also contribute to a lack of challenge for students who are slacking off—even though they might appear to be working hard—and who would work harder if asked.

48. The fact that teacher perceptions are also strong predictors for females and for whites from low-income households makes it more likely that this is a real effect for blacks. Further, since Jussim, Eccles, and Madon (1996) find no unexplained racial differences in the October performance ratings for blacks and whites after controlling for background factors, and only a trivial difference in unexplained variation, it seems unlikely that the ratings have very different interpretations or different implicit scalings for blacks and whites. Still, these results need to be replicated several times in order to be firmly established.

49. Weinstein (1985, p. 344).

Table 8-1. *Spring Standardized Grades and Test Scores in Mathematics and Fall Performance Ratings, Sixth Grade, 1982–83*[a]

Standard deviation units

	Fall performance rating				
Measure and race	1	2	3	4	5
Predicted spring grades					
Blacks	−1.00	−0.57	−0.14	0.28	0.71
Whites	−0.43	−0.25	−0.07	0.11	0.28
Difference	−0.57	−0.32	−0.07	0.18	0.43
Predicted spring scores					
Blacks	−0.79	−0.46	−0.13	0.20	0.53
Whites	−0.30	−0.17	−0.04	0.09	0.21
Difference	−0.50	−0.29	−0.09	0.11	0.31

Source: Author's calculations based on data from Jussim, Eccles, and Madon (1996, pp. 308–11).

a. All other student characteristics are held constant. Grades and test scores relate to the mathematics section of the Michigan Educational Assessment Program. Fall ratings are such that 1 denotes the lowest level of current performance and 5 denotes the highest level. The overall mean is zero and the standard deviation is one.

Table 8-1 shows simulated mathematics scores and grades and teachers' performance ratings, holding all other student characteristics constant. For both blacks and whites, there is a positive relationship between teachers' performance ratings in October and the students' grades and scores in May. However, the effect is stronger for blacks. Blacks who receive the highest performance rating (5) in October are predicted to outperform whites who receive that rating. Conversely, blacks who receive the lowest rating in October lag an estimated half standard deviation behind whites with that rating.

If teachers tend to be accurate both in current perceptions and in expectations of future progress, the findings of Jussim, Eccles, and Madon require that teachers expect the pattern shown in table 8-1.[50] This would

50. Jussim, Eccles, and Madon (1996) assume that current perceptions are good estimates of expectations for the future and they use "perceptions" and "expectations" interchangeably. Jussim has argued in personal communication that this is a reasonable assumption, based on other research regarding the processes by which people form expectations. It might, however, be inappropriate in the present context, for the reasons explained in the text. I do not know of any research that generates data on teachers' perceptions of current performance along with expectations for future performance for both blacks and whites.

represent stereotype bias for expected progress, even if there is no such bias in the evaluation of October performance. The accuracy of the stereotype might reflect self-fulfilling prophecy in the teacher's expectation, or it might not. Evidence that teacher perceptions affect subsequent performance more for blacks than for whites suggests either that black students respond differently than whites to similar treatment from teachers, or that teachers treat black and white students differently, or both.

Do Black and White Children Respond to Teachers Differently?

The finding that black students respond more strongly to teachers' beliefs has not been replicated, but it is consistent with findings from several other studies that ask related questions. In one recent study, Clifton Casteel asks eighth- and ninth-graders whom they most want to please with their classwork.[51] "Teachers" is the answer of 81 percent of black females, 62 percent of black males, 28 percent of white females, and 32 percent of white males. Whites are more concerned with pleasing parents. Doris Entwisle and Karl Alexander find that teachers' ratings of first-graders' maturity have larger effects for blacks than for whites on both verbal and arithmetic scores on the California Achievement Test (CAT).[52] Judith Kleinfeld finds that high-school students' perceptions of their own ability are more correlated with perceived teacher ratings of ability for blacks, but more correlated with perceived parent ratings for whites.[53] Irvine reaches similar conclusions.[54]

Jussim, Eccles, and Madon suggest, and I agree, that Claude Steele's recent work offers one reason why black and white students might respond differently despite identical classroom conditions.[55] Steele identifies a phenomenon that he calls stereotype threat, and the resulting stereotype anxiety, that can affect members of any stigmatized group. When the stereotype concerns ability, "threatened" individuals are anxious not to perform in

51. Casteel (1997). The sample includes 928 whites and 761 African Americans, from twelve classes in nine schools in two public school districts.

52. Entwisle and Alexander (1988).

53. Kleinfeld (1972).

54. See the discussion in Irvine (1990, pp. 46–49). In support of her conclusion that "researchers have found that black and other minority pupils are more negatively affected by teacher expectations than white students are," Irvine cites Baker (1973), Krupczak (1972), and Yee (1968). I have not found any studies that contradict these few.

55. Claude Steele, "Race and the Schooling of Black Americans," *Atlantic Monthly*, April 1992, pp. 68–78; see also chapter 11 below.

ways that might corroborate the stereotype. They fear that the stereotype might become the basis of pejorative judgments by others, as well as of their own self-perceptions.

One effect of this anxiety is "a disruptive apprehension" that can interfere with performance. Under stressful test conditions, Steele finds that women and blacks perform worse when they are primed to be conscious of their race or gender. Steele theorizes that when the anxiety is sufficiently intense, it can provoke a response of "disidentification" with the task at hand or with the general category of tasks. Students decide not to consider performance in that particular domain as important to personal goals or self-perceptions.

Steele has tested this idea only for high-achieving students at highly selective colleges. The degree to which stereotype threat and anxiety might apply to students in primary and secondary schools remains to be investigated. Jussim, Eccles, and Madon's findings were for sixth-graders. Are children this young aware enough of stereotypes to be susceptible to stereotype threat or stereotype anxiety? Perhaps.[56]

Susan Gross studied the mathematics performance of students in a racially integrated suburb of Washington, D.C., during the 1985–86 school year.[57] In fourth grade, 92 percent of blacks and 86 percent of whites who were above grade level on the number of mathematics competencies that they had mastered scored in the eighth and ninth stanines (that is, ninths) of the California Achievement Test for Math (CATM). In the sixth grade, 82 percent of whites who were above grade level in completion of competencies were in the eighth and ninth stanines on the CATM. For blacks, however, the figure was only 68 percent.[58] Gross points out that for the sixth-graders, this pattern of performance on the CATM was inconsistent

---

56. As informal but reliable evidence, I offer my personal experience. As a fifth-grader, I moved from a segregated school to one that was integrated. In my new classroom, the top reading group was white, with one or two exceptions; the middle group was mixed, but mostly black; and the slow group was all black. While I did not believe that this pattern was unfair, I wanted the teacher to know, and I wanted to know for myself, that I was an exception. The teacher placed me in the middle group. I could not understand why she could not see from my records that I belonged in the top group, despite the fact that I was black. I recall being driven to establish myself as an exception to the racial pattern in the classroom and fearing for a while that my performance in the middle group might not be good enough to do so: I might be trapped in the middle group! After a few weeks the teacher moved me up, and my anxiety abated. However, my constant awareness of racial patterns in group memberships remained.

57. Gross (1993).

58. These fourth and sixth grade results are from a single year for two different cohorts, hence while the differences appear consistent with a trend, they do not clearly establish one. Also, Gross does not report sample sizes broken down into those who were above, at, or below a given grade level. Hence it is not clear how many children these percentages represent.

with in-school performance, and hence she cautions against basing ability group placements on test scores alone.

Gross and her team also conducted focus groups with middle school and high school students. She reports "a deep commitment on the part of high-achieving black students to do well in mathematics so that they could move on to good colleges and professional careers." But the same students felt "deep frustration at the incidents of racism they had experienced in the lower expectations they had perceived from teachers and other students. . . . This was particularly true regarding the honors-level black students who reported that each year they had to prove they were capable of doing honors work."[59] Moreover, it was common knowledge that children in upper elementary grades felt the same types of pressure.[60] If the CATM was regarded as a test of ability for sixth-graders, Steele's theory could well explain why black students who were above grade level on competencies got lower CATM scores than their white peers.[61]

Gross appears to find evidence of the type of disengagement that Steele hypothesizes, which could help to explain the larger negative impact on black students that Jussim, Eccles, and Madon find when their performance is perceived to be low. Teachers told Gross that black students were overrepresented among students who were "least studious" and "did not come to their classes prepared to work or in the proper frame of mind to attend fully to instruction."[62]

Both teachers and administrators reported that black parents were less supportive of the school's mission than white parents. However, when Gross convened parents in focus groups, black parents were more supportive of the idea that their children should strive for the higher level classes in mathematics, even if that meant getting lower grades. White parents tended to say that their children should stay in the top sections only if they were likely to do well. Possibly the black parents were sending a mixed message: "Shoot for the top, but if you don't do as well as the white kids, we'll understand."[63] If black children sense more ambivalence from their parents than do white children, their teachers' opinions might take on a special significance for them, as the statistical evidence appears to show.

59. Gross (1993, p. 282).
60. Susan Gross, personal communication.
61. Gross reports, in personal communication, that in a regression analysis using students' classroom performance as a predictor, she found that the CATM test scores of the black high-achievers were below those predicted. These calculations were not published, however, and are no longer available.
62. Gross (1993, p. 281).
63. And this, in turn, might have contributed to the ambivalence that seems to be expressed in the work habits of the black schoolchildren, as shown in figure 8-1 below.

In a study inspired by the work of John Ogbu, Roslyn Mickelson distinguishes "abstract" from "concrete" attitudes in twelfth grade students.[64] She finds that concrete attitudes predict cumulative high school grade point averages, but abstract attitudes do not.[65] Her measure of abstract attitudes reflects mainstream ideology, standard optimistic rhetoric about education and the American dream. Respondents were asked to indicate their level of agreement with the following statements:

—Education is the key to success in the future.

—If everyone in America gets a good education, we can end poverty.

—Achievement and effort in school lead to job success later on.

—The way for poor people to become middle class is for them to get a good education.

—School success is not necessarily a clear path to a better life.

—Getting a good education is a practical road to success for a young black [white] man [woman] like me.

—Young white [black] women [men] like me have a chance of making it if we do well in school.

—Education really pays off in the future for young black [white] men [women] like me.

In contrast, her measure of concrete attitudes includes questions that elicit doubt and ambivalence about education as a route to mainstream success: [66]

—Based on their experiences, my parents say people like us are not always paid or promoted according to our education.

—All I need to learn for my future is to read, write and make change.

---

64. Ogbu (1978, 1983, 1987); Fordham and Ogbu (1986); Mickelson (1990).

65. Mickelson studied 1,193 seniors from eight high schools in the Los Angeles area during the 1982–83 school year. She analyzes only the responses of blacks and whites, who compose 41 and 59 percent, respectively, of her working sample. In predicting grade point averages, the standardized coefficients on concrete attitudes in the full specification are 0.111 ($p < 0.05$) for blacks and 0.190 ($p < 0.01$) for whites. These are not large effects. Still, the facts that such a rough index of beliefs is statistically significant at all, and that the distinction between abstract and concrete attitudes is demonstrated so clearly (see table 8-2), are important. The coefficient for abstract attitudes was about a fifth as large as that for concrete attitudes. The t statistic is about 1 for whites and less than 0.5 for blacks. The regressions control for mother's and father's occupation and education, a locus of control index, student's weekly hours worked, percentage of close friends planning to attend a four-year college, and an indicator variable for each of the eight schools in the sample. Mickelson notes that regressions using standardized test scores as the dependent variable produce the same story as for grades.

66. I think that "concrete" is a gross misnomer for these attitudes, and that it has confused the interpretation of Mickelson's work. They are just as abstract as the others: "fairness" is not concrete. They actually measure ambivalence or doubt about the "abstract" attitudes.

Table 8-2. *Abstract and Concrete Beliefs about the Importance of Education for Success, by Race and Socioeconomic Background, Twelfth Grade, Spring 1983*[a]

Mean score

Socioeconomic status and measure	Males			Females		
	Black	White	Effect size	Black	White	Effect size
White collar						
Abstract beliefs	5.50	5.06	0.58	5.27	5.09	0.24
Concrete beliefs	4.38	4.90	−0.53	4.43	5.00	−0.58
Sample size	56	224	. . .	84	241	. . .
Blue collar						
Abstract beliefs	5.28	4.99	0.38	5.34	5.21	0.17
Concrete beliefs	4.19	4.54	−0.36	4.19	4.81	−0.63
Sample size	138	100	. . .	140	93	. . .

Source: Mickelson (1990).

a. Sample is taken from eight Los Angeles high schools. Classification as white collar or blue collar is based on a combination of standard blue collar–white collar distinctions and parental education. On each index, higher values denote higher levels of agreement with the given abstract or concrete beliefs; see text for details. Racial differences in abstract scores are significant with $p < 0.05$; class differences for concrete scores are significant with $p < 0.0005$; racial differences for concrete scores are significant with $p < 0.0001$. Full sample standard deviations are 0.76 for abstract scores and 0.98 for concrete scores. Each effect size equals the black-white gap in the respective measure divided by the full-sample standard deviation for either abstract or concrete beliefs, whichever applies.

—Although my parents tell me to get a good education to get a good job, they face barriers to job success.

—When our teachers give us homework, my friends never think of doing it.

—People in my family haven't been treated fairly at work, no matter how much education they have.

—Studying in school rarely pays off later with good jobs.

Students might acquire such concrete attitudes from routine, informal, personal interaction with friends, parents, and other adults, as well as from the broader society.

Mickelson finds that blacks express greater agreement than do whites with the optimistic but abstract beliefs about success and the American dream. However, in their concrete attitudes, which are actually expectations for fairness, blacks are less hopeful than whites. Table 8-2 summarizes the pattern (on both indexes, higher values correspond to higher levels of agreement). This finding suggests why surveys usually find that blacks subscribe to mainstream values as much as do whites, but behave in ways that show less commitment to mainstream success.

Do Teachers Treat Black and White Students Differently?

I know of only four experimental studies that deal with teachers' treatment of black and white students, all dating from the 1970s.[67] These studies control differences between students by matching or random assignment. As with most of the experimental literature already discussed, the experiments are contrived one-time encounters. All four experiments find that teachers are less supportive of black than white students.

In Marylee Taylor's experiment, for example, a six-year-old student was said to be watching from behind a screen as college students of education undergoing teacher training taught a prescribed lesson.[68] In each case, the phantom student was described as black or white, male or female, and of high or low ability. The teachers were told that the students could see and hear them and would respond to their instructions by pushing buttons to activate ten lights on a panel. In fact, all of the "student feedback" was provided by a single adult, who was blind to the description of the "student" given to any particular teacher. Taylor finds that black phantom students received briefer feedback after mistakes (the standardized effect size is 0.613), less positive feedback after correct responses (0.423), and fewer "helpful slips of the tongue"—that is, unauthorized coaching (0.536). Each of the experimental studies suggests that some teachers may help white students more than blacks, and that the differences may be large enough to have nontrivial effects on performance.

---

67. Coates (1972); Rubovits and Maehr (1973); Feldman and Orchowsky (1979); Taylor (1979). See also Babad (1980, 1985) for related research from Israel, where teachers in the experiment grade assignments on which the names are randomly either European or Moroccan.

68. Taylor (1979) designed her experiment in response to the possibility that confederate students' behaviors had confounded the findings of racial bias in Rubovits and Maehr (1973). By placing the phantom student behind a one-way glass, where they could allegedly see the teacher and respond to the teacher's questions and instruction, she removed any effects of targets' actual behaviors. Sessions were videotaped and the teachers' behaviors were coded. The participants were 105 white female undergraduates at the University of Massachusetts, Amherst. They were told that the purpose of the experiment was "to examine certain aspects of teaching behavior in a situation where feedback from pupil to teacher was limited." Discussions after the experiment show that they believed this premise.

Studies of real classrooms confirm this hypothesis. While some find no racial differences, more find differences favoring white students.[69] The studies that do find differences are probably more likely to be published. Nonetheless, if the benchmark is unconditional race neutrality, there is strong evidence of racial bias in how teachers treat students. It is nearly impossible in naturalistic studies to determine whether teachers would appear racially biased if one controlled racial differences in students' behaviors, work habits, and social skills. But since students and parents cannot read a teacher's mind, they may *think* that differences in treatment reflect favoritism. And when teachers appear biased, trust may be eroded and relationships spoiled.

Evidence on Possible Reasons for Differential Treatment

In general, there is no way of knowing whether teachers' perceptions of students' attitudes and behaviors are accurate. Jussim, Eccles, and Madon's finding that teacher perceptions of effort predict grades but not standardized test scores suggests that teachers' perceptions of effort may not be accurate, as does their finding that teachers' perceptions of effort were only moderately correlated with students' self-reports.

In 1990 the Prospects survey, conducted for the Department of Education, asked a national sample of teachers to rate specific students in their classes on the following criteria: "cares about doing well," "gets along with teachers," and "works hard at school."[70] The three response categories ranged from "very much" to "not at all." Teachers rated black children lower than whites by a statistically significant margin on all three items. To measure the racial differences in these ratings, I subtract for each racial group the percentage with the lowest ranking from the percentage with the highest ranking in each grade, and then sum the results for the three questions. Higher values of the index are therefore better. The index is standardized to equal 1 for white first-graders.

---

69. There are many sources from which to draw this standard finding. Irvine (1990, table 3.3) tabulates studies conducted in naturalistic classroom settings. Of seventeen findings from sixteen studies, whites are favored in nine, there is no difference in four, the opposite race to the teacher is favored in two, the same race as the teacher is favored in one, and blacks are favored in one. One of these studies is from 1969 and the rest are from the 1970s and early 1980s. For discussion of earlier studies, see Brophy and Good (1974).

70. See Puma and others (1993).

Figure 8-1. *Teachers' Perceptions of Students' Levels of Effort*[a]
Index[b]

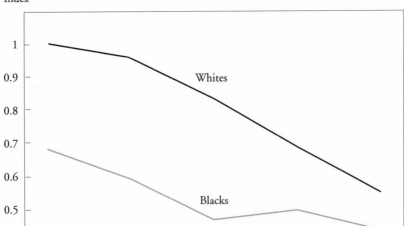

Grade level

Source: Author's calculations based on data collected in the early 1990s for the Prospects study of educational growth and opportunity; see Puma and others (1993).

a. Teachers rated students on the following criteria: cares about doing well, gets along with teachers, and works hard at school. Data for first-graders represent one cohort (1,979 black; 5,333 white); third- and fifth-graders represent a second cohort (1,276 black; 4,045 white); seventh- and ninth-graders represent a third cohort (393 black; 2,424 white). Numbers are weighted to be nationally representative. Chi-square tests on each item for each grade show that through the seventh grade, all black-white differences are statistically significant at the 0.01 level or better. For the ninth grade, the differences are not statistically significant, but the black sample is quite small.

b. Composite index for black and white students in first through ninth grades, constructed such that white first-graders are equal to 1 and higher index values are better; see text for details.

Figure 8-1 shows the means for blacks and whites by grade level. As can be seen, teachers perceive the greatest difference between black and white students in the early years of elementary school. After the fifth grade the gap narrows, but it does not completely close. The apparent similarity in how blacks and whites relate to school by ninth grade is consistent with data on eighth graders from the 1988 National Education Longitudinal Study (NELS). Several authors have remarked on the similarity of black and white attitudes in the NELS.[71] But because that survey did not reach

71. See, for example, Solorzano (1992); Miller (1995); chapter 10 below.

students earlier in their school careers (and also because it did not ask the right questions), it may lead people to underestimate the degree to which racial differences in work habits, behavior, and attitudes below the eighth grade affect teacher-student relations and the black-white test score gap.

Reciprocal Effects between Student Behavior and Teacher Performance

Teachers' judgments about how much they enjoy teaching students inevitably affect their own behaviors. This can apply in regard to entire classrooms and in regard to individual students. Teachers may respond to difficult students by withdrawing support.[72] This could help account for Jussim, Eccles, and Madon's finding that teachers' perceptions at the beginning of the school year, although unbiased, are stronger predictors of end-of-year performance for black students than for whites. Specifically, among equally low-performing black and white students, black students might be perceived as more difficult, and therefore receive less teacher support than whites; while among equally high-performing students, black students might be perceived as less difficult, and therefore receive more teacher support than whites.[73] I have not found any quantitative research in naturalistic settings that controls for initial student performance and systematically measures racial differences in how much positive reinforcement students provide to teachers. However, on average black *students* may give *teachers* less positive reinforcement than do white students with similar levels of beginning-of-year performance.

For example, Willis and Brophy asked twenty-eight first grade teachers to nominate three children to each of four groups, with the following results:[74]

Attachment: If you could keep one student another year for the sheer joy of it, whom would you pick?

Regarding boys in the *attachment groups*, the teachers made more positive comments about their clothing . . . more often assigned them as leaders or

---

72. On the types of student that teachers like to teach, see Brophy and Good (1974) and the literature that they discuss. Also, see below in the present chapter.

73. Teachers' expectations might be less flexible for black students than for whites. Inflexible perceptions, in turn, might lead to teacher behaviors that reinforce problem behaviors in low-performing students and promote good behaviors in high-performing students. This is a ripe topic for future research.

74. Willis and Brophy (1974, p. 132). Extract is from Brophy and Good (1974, pp. 186–93).

classroom helpers . . . high ability [student] who is well-adjusted to the school situation, conforms to the teacher's rules and "rewards" the teacher by being somewhat dependent upon her and by doing well in his schoolwork.

Indifference: If a parent were to drop in unannounced for a conference, whose child would you be least prepared to talk about?

Boys in the *indifference group* were described as more likely to . . . have a "blank" eye expression . . . to have a disinterested or uncooperative parent . . . to have failed to live up to the teachers' initial expectations. . . . Nevertheless, the Metropolitan Readiness Test scores of these boys did not differ significantly from those of their classmates.

Concern: If you could devote all your attention to a child who concerned you a great deal, whom would you pick?

Boys in the *concern group* were especially likely to be described as . . . having a speech impediment . . . being active and vivacious, seeking teacher attention . . . needing readiness work, having generally poor oral and verbal skills . . . and having generally low abilities. . . . [These children are] perceived as making legitimate demands because they generally conform to classroom rules but are in need of help due to low ability.

Rejection: If your class was to be reduced by one child, whom would you be relieved to have removed?

Boys in the *rejection group* were described as being more likely to be non-white than white, coming from intact families in which both parents were living, as being immature and not well-adjusted, as being independent, as being loud or disruptive in the classroom, as being rarely inactive or not vivacious . . . as needing extra help because of generally low ability, as needing readiness work. . . . These children did not differ significantly from their classmates on the Metropolitan Readiness Test scores despite the teachers' comments about low ability.

The rejection group is the only one in which nonwhite boys are over-represented in teachers' remarks. Clearly, much more was involved in shaping the teacher-to-student relationship than simply the child's initial ability or academic performance, at least in first grade. Children's work habits and behaviors (and sometimes even their parents' behaviors) affected teacher preferences. Figure 8-1 has shown that in the 1990s teachers perceive that blacks rate lower than whites on attitudes, effort, and behavior. Based on these patterns, my guess is that *on average* teachers probably prefer to teach whites, and *on average* they probably give whites more plentiful and unambiguous support.

Mismatches of race between teachers and students do not appear to be the central problem. Even black teachers need help in learning to cope with some of the special demands that black children from disadvantaged backgrounds may present.[75] Paula, a young black teacher enrolled in a program to help teachers understand, manage, and teach difficult students, admitted:

> The first thing I knew was that they were just BADD. I know part of the problem was myself because I was saying things that I probably shouldn't have said because they got me so upset and I wasn't able to handle it. . . . I felt that being black I would automatically know more, and so forth, and in ways I think I do, but [the training program] has helped me to understand things from many perspectives. . . . Black teachers who have been in different programs . . . haven't got this cultural awareness and I know that because they're so negative. . . . A lot of them aren't culturally sensitive to their own culture.[76]

It remains an open question how much difference teachers' preferences about whom they teach make to the educational outcomes of students. In difficult schools there may be many "burned out" teachers, who are simply going through the motions and waiting for retirement. It is also unclear to what degree this pattern of bad student behavior and teacher burnout is racially distinct. In many classrooms, teachers and students are embroiled in conflict and confusion that they lack the skills and external support to resolve. Research to analyze the effectiveness and replicability of programs such as that in which Paula was enrolled should be a priority in order to improve the schooling of black children in settings where behavior is a problem.

Indeed, signals about performance can have racial overtones, and these can interfere with teacher-student relations and with learning. A summary of focus group discussions with black males between the ages of nine and nineteen in Fort Wayne, Ind., in 1996 reports: "Students expressed disappointment in their grades when moving from one class to another, but could not explain the differences from year to year with the exception of

---

75. Simply matching the race of the student and the teacher is too simple a prescription: social class and professional competence also appear to be important. In chapter 9 below, I discuss how a teacher's race and social class might affect student performance.

76. Cabello and Burstein (1995, pp. 289–90).

saying that the teacher was prejudiced. Racial prejudice of the teachers was a perception that was common in all the groups. . . . The teacher who encouraged and expected more from the students was always mentioned, but only as the exception."[77] Teachers in integrated schools can be "biased" in ways as simple as reinforcing a propensity of white children to speak more often in class.[78] As a result, black students may assume that the teachers think whites are smarter or like the white students better. How teachers communicate about academic ability—especially in integrated schools where the performance of whites is superior—can affect the degree to which black students disengage from the pursuit of excellence, or alternatively, stay engaged and aim for mastery.[79]

Race and the Role of Peer Culture

What teachers communicate to students about ability is important, because positioning in the hierarchy of *perceived ability* has social significance for both individuals and groups—and this, in turn, has feedback effects on school performance.[80] Readily observable racial patterns in messages from teachers or black-white differences in actual performance can produce stereotype anxiety and can blur the distinction between racial and achievement-related aspects of students' identities.

Shared stereotype anxiety probably encourages black students to form peer groups that disengage from academic competition. Members may secretly want to *be* "smart," like the students (often disproportionately white) whom teachers favor. Nevertheless, they may also resent any effort by black peers to defect from group norms by *acting* smart. In one school district with which I am currently familiar, it is common to hear that some black students accuse their peers of "acting white" when their personal styles seem

---

77. Jones (1997, p. 9).

78. See, for example, Katz (1973), cited in both Brophy and Good (1974) and Irvine (1990).

79. In particular, it is important that teachers make clear that academic ability is not immutable—that sustained effort mobilizes and develops ability. Dweck (1991) and Dweck and Leggett (1988) find statistically significant evidence among white children that those who believe that ability is fixed tend to adopt performance goals, whereas those who believe otherwise tend to adopt mastery goals. Among those who believe ability is fixed and that their own endowment is low, the performance goal serves to hide their ignorance. But both high and low achievers among those who believe that ability can be developed tend toward mastery goals. The same is probably true for blacks, but I do not know of any research that addresses this issue.

80. See the literature review in chapter 10 below.

to resemble those of the smart white kids. However, the same black students who make the accusations resent any insinuation that they themselves are stupid. There is duality. It seems that being smart is valued, but acting smart—or aspiring to move up in the achievement hierarchy, with the associated peer and teacher relationship patterns—is frowned on, at least in others.

How much these factors help to account for the black-white test score gap is uncertain. Philip Cook and Jens Ludwig conclude in chapter 10 below that adolescent peer pressure and the acting white hypothesis bear virtually no responsibility for black-white differences in academic performance. Their study advances the debate, but it leaves the central question unresolved, as I explain in a comment following that chapter. Nevertheless, rather than simply attacking black peer culture, reducing the amount of unresponsive and ineffective teaching is almost surely a more important response to the black-white test score gap.

Responsive Teaching

As noted at the outset of this chapter, the average black child arrives at kindergarten with fewer academic skills than the average white child. Schools may then push students along in ways that sustain or add to racial disparities, validating the expectation that black-white differences in achievement are normal, perhaps even inevitable. But if instruction is appropriately stimulating and responsive to children's progress, teachers' expectations may be neither self-fulfilling nor sustaining. The more inviting and responsive instruction is to children's own efforts to improve, the less teachers' initial perceptions and expectations will predict later success.

Research that measures how instructional methods affect the accuracy of teacher expectations is rare. One relevant set of studies deals with "wait time"—that is, how long a teacher waits for students to raise their hands, for students to begin talking, and for students to continue talking after a pause. Minority students in integrated classrooms participate more when wait time is longer. This improves their performance relative to whites and changes teacher expectations.[81]

81. In a summary of the literature on wait time, Rowe (1986, p. 45) reports that teachers' "expectations change gradually, often signaled by remarks such as 'He never contributed like that before. Maybe he has a special "thing" for this topic.'. . . *This effect was particularly pronounced where minority students were concerned* [emphasis added]. They did more task relevant talking and took a more active

Corrective feedback is probably more significant than wait time, however. In a study that does not mention race, Thomas Guskey looks at forty-four intermediate and high school teachers who taught various subjects in two metropolitan school systems.[82] Each teacher taught two matched classes, after receiving training. One class was instructed using the teacher's standard methods, and the other was taught with a "feedback and corrective" process learned in the training. Both classes received the same final examination and grading standards. Guskey compared teacher ratings of "probable achievement" from early in the semester with final grades and examination scores, and also with end-of-term ratings of "achievement potential."[83] For ten teachers, the training made no difference to their students' performance. However, for thirty-four others—the "positive change" group—the experimental classes did better than the controls on both grades and scores. Among this group, teachers' early expectations were less predictive of students' later achievement as a result of the improved techniques for feedback and correction. Specifically, as shown in table 8-3, correlations between teachers' initial ratings of probable achievement and the students' final grades and examination scores were markedly lower for experimental classes than for classes using customary methods; "no-change" teachers had high correlations in both classes. It seems likely that better feedback and corrective methods could also affect the rank order of performance by race, although Guskey does not investigate this issue.[84]

It is worth noting that responsive teaching can take negative as well as positive forms. For example, some teachers may give incentives and assistance to students who want to improve their positions in the class and penalize students who do not. In an often cited study, Karen Brattesani, Rhonda Weinstein, and Hermine Marshall compare fourth, fifth, and sixth grade classes in which student surveys had indicated various levels of differential treatment.[85] In the classrooms with higher levels of differential

part in discussions than they had before." Rowe also makes other references to the studies that develop these findings. Wait time is shorter for low-performing students (see chapter 8).

82. Guskey (1982).

83. For the ratings on probable achievement in the course and achievement potential, teachers assigned each student to one of five groups of equal size.

84. Studies find mixed results regarding techniques to improve corrective feedback. See, for example, Slavin's (1987) review of the literature on mastery learning.

85. Brattesani, Weinstein, and Marshall (1984). Their point in this paper is that teacher expectations become self-fulfilling prophecies only when communicated through differential treatment. They find that teacher expectations are stronger predictors in classrooms with higher levels of differential

Table 8-3. *Effects of Improved Techniques in Feedback and Correction*[a]

| | Correlation between initial rating and | | | | | |
| | Final rating | | Course grade | | Final examination | |
Teacher sample	Experimental	Control	Experimental	Control	Experimental	Control
Positive change	0.53	0.83	0.51	0.80	0.31	0.50
No change	0.92	0.90	0.77	0.79	0.69	0.75

Source: Guskey (1982).

a. Sample comprises forty-four intermediate and high school teachers of various subjects in two metropolitan school systems; see text for details. The positive change group includes the thirty-four whose classes taught using the improved feedback techniques earned higher final examination scores and course grades than their control classes. For the ten teachers in the no change group, either course grades or scores on the final examination were higher in the control classes.

treatment, more students with below average scores at the beginning of the year made unusually large gains, but fewer students with above average scores made gains.[86]

Both of these studies show that greater responsiveness to individual children can weaken the link between past and future performance, and perhaps also alter trajectories. Both are silent about race and ethnicity. Unfortunately, statistical studies that deal directly with race do not investigate whether particular teaching practices can change the rank order of performance among students.

The Great Expectations Initiative

Great Expectations is a public-private partnership created in 1989 to bring Marva Collins's ideas about teaching into Oklahoma schools.[87]

---

treatment. However, since they collected teachers' expectations in April of the school year, I would regard these as reports from the end of the school year rather than as self-fulfilling predictions. For interesting related work, see Weinstein and others (1987), who show that even first-graders can accurately report teachers' differential treatment of their peers, but that it is not until third grade that students begin to give accurate reports regarding their own differential treatment.

86. See Brattesani, Weinstein, and Marshall (1984, table 4). They find strong evidence that standardized test scores are predicted less well by past performance in classrooms where there is more differential treatment. The sample sizes are small, so that the difference in percentages of low achievers who make large gains does not reach statistical significance. Nevertheless, the magnitudes of the gains are large.

87. This summary draws from Ferguson (1993), which tells the story of the birth and early development of the initiative.

(Collins, an African American, teaches in the inner city in Chicago and is probably the most widely known elementary teacher in the nation.) The initiative includes a range of techniques that Collins has developed over the years. It aims to nurture in all students, not only the most talented, the expectation that they are destined to be important people if they do their best in school to prepare well for the future. Those who misbehave should be reminded regularly that the teacher cares and refuses to give up on them. Teaching methods combine high challenge for students with feedback from teachers *and peers* in forms that make learning fun and emphasize its importance for a happy and effective life. Progress is celebrated, so that every student can earn the opportunity for positive recognition from teachers, peers, and parents. In addition to more standard materials for core subjects, the curriculum includes uplifting, forward-looking poetry, which students memorize and discuss and recite at school and at home. The story of Great Expectations shows real people struggling, with some success, to change teaching practices—and in the process, teachers' expectations—for disadvantaged, mostly minority, children. Whites, blacks, Hispanics, and native Americans are all represented among the poorly performing children that the initiative aims to help. Racial gaps are not an emphasis.

The incentive for the Great Expectations initiative was a threat of takeover of certain Oklahoma schools by the state if test scores for third-graders persisted below the twenty-fifth percentile for three consecutive years on the Iowa Test of Basic Skills. Educators in the schools that joined Great Expectations knew of Marva Collins's reputation for working wonders with children in inner-city Chicago. Her own school had never been independently evaluated, but she appeared to be effective with the types of children that the Oklahoma schools were failing. Although administrators were not certain that these methods could be transferred from Chicago to Oklahoma, they judged it worth a try. For the first training, two teachers from each of twenty-five pilot schools were sent to Collins's Westside Preparatory School in Chicago. There they had a "seeing is believing" experience concerning what children from disadvantaged backgrounds could achieve.

As the initiative spread through the pilot schools in Oklahoma, however, there was substantial resistance from teachers who had not gone to Chicago. The head mentor teacher told me that virtually all of the resistance she encountered represented one or more of the following three perspectives: [88]

88. She maintained that most of the time the resistance could be reduced by a combination of two responses. First, she would assure the teacher that he or she could slip into the Great Expectations

–Time: "I just don't have the time to try this. It's too much. I just can't do it."

–Satisfaction with current practices: "I just don't see the need for doing things differently from what I already do."

–Hopeless students: "You don't know my kids. You couldn't do that with my kids. All that positive stuff is treating kids like babies: discipline has to be tough – you can't mix it with being nice."

Some teachers were insecure: their low expectations for students were partly the consequence of low expectations for themselves as teachers.[89] At the other extreme, some teachers thrived using Collins's ideas and felt professionally rejuvenated. Each summer during the 1990s several hundred teachers have been trained or have received refresher courses through free summer institutes at Northeastern State University. Through the work of the Great Expectations Foundation, funding for the institutes and mentor teachers comes from private donors, philanthropic foundations, the State Board of Regents, and the state Department of Education. School-site training by mentor teachers during the school year reinforces the training received at the summer institutes. Staffs for the institutes comprise professors from several NSU departments and elementary school teachers who have distinguished themselves in the classroom using the Great Expectations teaching methods.

In a baseline survey administered at the Summer Institute in July 1993, I asked teachers with some previous Great Expectations training to describe the improvement in their students' performance since they began using these methods. Table 8-4 presents the results.

The two portraits that follow offer "existence proofs" of the proposition that teaching practices and expectations can change dramatically, even for experienced teachers. At the same time, both of the teachers described express reservations.

---

program gradually, implementing some elements first and others later. Second, she would model the specific practices to which the teacher was resistant. She would do so at that teacher's school, preferably in the teacher's classroom, and always with the greatest respect and tact. When a teacher witnessed a mentor successfully demonstrating a method with the teacher's own students, he or she usually became (or claimed to become) more open to giving it a try.

89. One worst-case example involved a first grade teacher who had failed with a different new method during the previous year. Although several other teachers at her school were using the Great Expectations method and doing well, she was sure that it could not work for her, and she received no pressure to change from the passive principal.

Table 8-4. *Teachers' Assessments of Student Progress due to the*
Great Expectations Program, Oklahoma[a]
Percent

	Aspect of classroom performance			
Assessment	Academic performance	Attitudes	Behaviors	Teachers' job satisfaction
More than I thought was possible	22.37	31.59	25.00	35.53
A lot	55.26	46.05	44.74	48.68
Some	22.37	19.74	28.95	13.16
None	0.00	2.63	1.32	2.16

Source: Author's tabulations from a survey conducted at the Great Expectations Summer Institute, July 1993.

a. Sample comprises seventy-six teachers with some prior training in Great Expectations methods (representing close to a 100 percent response rate of potential interviewees). Participants were asked to complete the following statement: "Because of Great Expectations, the improvement in [aspect of classroom performance] of my students has been. . . ."

Greg Robarts, Fourth Grade Teacher, Beehive Elementary School

Greg Robarts's classroom is a roughly even mix of black, white, Chicano, and Native American children, almost all of whom come from very poor families.[90] Before the Great Expectations initiative, Robarts had taught for seventeen years and believed himself to be a good teacher. But seeing what children at Westside Preparatory School in Chicago could do gave him pause: "I didn't really know how to teach reading. After one workshop in phonics I feel that I know more today than I learned in seventeen years teaching." He describes seeing Westside Preparatory School as "an awakening." "I saw something I'd never seen before; I actually saw education taking place. I saw children interested in learning. After seeing her approach, and seeing that it worked, I thought, 'What I'm doing now isn't working. At best it's just kind of passing.'. . . I had to rededicate myself."

Collins's basic philosophy resonated with Robarts's beliefs about teaching, but he had to unlearn old habits, such as sitting at his desk saying, "Open the book to page 34, here are the instructions. . . ." Even his own

90. In this and the following subsection, names of teachers and schools have been changed, but facts and quotations are real.

principal described Robarts as a "desk sitter" before he changed to the Great Expectations way of running a classroom: "Teach on your feet, not in your seat." Before Great Expectations,

> I was secure with all the books and things. A lot of teachers are where I was. They're embarrassed to say "I don't know." It's that fear of judgment . . . teachers are hesitant to ask. . . . Teaching independently . . . instead of from the book, those are the kinds of things that I wasn't courageous enough to try.
> [How long was it before you felt comfortable with this new style?]
> Oh, I think after about the first day. And I made some horrible mistakes. But my kids just hugged me and said, "Oh, Mr. Robarts, you're so different from when you left!" And they would just say, "Oh, you're doing well." And when I would start kind of maybe, "Well, maybe I need to sit down now; I've kind of done the Marva Collins stuff now, so maybe I need to sit down." The kids would say, "Mr. Robarts, we sense that you're being average again." And so, I said, "Okay." So I always asked them to encourage me when they sensed that I was being average or substandard.

Many people who are not familiar with the Great Expectations approach say that it overemphasizes memorization and underemphasizes higher order thinking. Robarts disagrees. He says these functions are complements, not substitutes: memory is the foundation for higher order thinking. He finds that without practice at memorization many children cannot remember a dictated sentence long enough to write it down. After a few weeks of memorizing poetry and other things, he says, the change is remarkable. He thinks that people who dismiss memory work as outmoded are simply uniformed about how children learn, not only because memory supports higher order thinking, but because children can memorize things that are worth knowing. In addition, by reciting what they have memorized, children build self-confidence and motivation. He says: "If you had told me two years ago that I would have a class of fourth-graders that would know all the states and capitals and would know geographically where things are located, that could spell words, that could read, that could do . . . I would have said, 'Well, maybe if you're in Quail Creek–which is a very affluent area of Oklahoma City—perhaps. But in this area, no, it wouldn't happen. . . . You know, maybe rote memory is not positive in some aspects, but I think that when a child has experienced total failure all through school it can be a major first step."

Much of the memory work in Great Expectations classrooms involves poetry that contains rules for healthy and productive living—messages worth remembering. Robarts reports exciting results from his efforts: "absenteeism is almost nil, refusal to do homework is almost nil, test scores are substantially up." He also describes a "miracle turn-around student" during his first semester using Collins's methods. The student's disciplinary folder was a "blizzard of suspensions." An African-American boy diagnosed as learning disabled, he was "a throw-away child," Robarts says. "He was not supposed to be able to do anything. He came very hostile . . . a tough cracker to break. I didn't understand when Collins said, 'You can look in the eyes of the children when they come, and there's a dullness.' I know what she means now. Children like Jerry have been so programmed to believe that the school is nothing. That *they* are nothing, that the only guarantee they have in school is failure. And it's so exciting to see their eyes brighten, and to see the *child* say that they *can* do." When Jerry transferred to a new school the following year, his classmates teased him for speaking standard English. Jerry persisted, with support from his new teacher. On returning to visit Mr. Robarts, Jerry reported that his new classmates began to change to be more like him, because of the positive responses that he was getting from the teacher.

Robarts realizes that he is not typical. Other teachers need more ongoing support. When I first interviewed him, in December 1991—after the first summer institute but nine months before mentor teachers began working in teachers' classrooms—Robarts was sober about the value of a four-hour demonstration that he and his class were to give the next week for teachers who had not gone to any summer institute: "We'll get them excited. They'll go back to their classrooms, they'll meet with the same failures that they've had. They'll struggle. They'll crash. They'll burn. They'll say, 'To hell with it. It's just another thing that they're doing.' And that will be the end of it. If there is no follow-through, no support person, no person to be supportive and say, 'Well now, this is a possibility,' it will all come to naught." In fact, Robarts was among the teachers who had pushed for the establishment of summer institutes and the use of mentor teachers for ongoing technical assistance. Currently, both programs remain in place, complemented by an academy for principals.

Gloria Chavers, Third Grade Teacher, Lafayette Elementary School

Gloria Chavers recalls not thinking much about Great Expectations at the time that her school applied to participate in the program. However, when the first two teachers came back from Chicago, "They were excited.

There was no doubt about that." The principal asked other teachers to observe in the classrooms of the trained teachers. "So we went to Mrs. Sherrin's [third grade] room. But this excitement that she had, I couldn't pick up on it. Because, and I talked at length with the principal about it at the time, I hadn't experienced what they had experienced. And for them to sit and tell me about what a five-year-old, and they would call these little children's names, you know, they could recite all this. I'd never been around any children who could do this, so it was hard for me to envision."

Chavers also recalls that she saw changes that she did not like in Sherrin's students. She had taught some of these children herself, as a second grade teacher. Now, they were calling themselves "college bound." At that time, Chavers's view was that "in this school system, college is not for everyone. We have a lot of lower socioeconomic people. College is the exception, not the rule."

Finally, the opportunity came to attend the first summer institute. "As it turned out, it was really well worth it," says Chavers. The following semester, she reorganized the way she ran her classroom. "We've gone back to a highly structured way of reading and teaching phonics [using chants]. We'd gotten away from that." She also now teaches the whole class in one group and from one book. She reports that when she first changed, "Some children struggled, but it's surprising when they have their peers reading and reading well, it seems to give them more incentive to read better."

At the summer institute, Chavers learned how to teach addition and subtraction using chants, but the class had not gone on to multiplication and division. So, back at her school, she made up her own chants for multiplication and division. She recalls: "And then I told [the students] one day, I said, 'Well, we'll sing this out.' Well, they didn't know what that was. I told them, 'It's like you're standing on the corner trying to sell something.' And even the children who have more difficulty with math, they have been able to pick up on those multiplication tables. They can not only say them, they can pass their tests! A lot of times after we do them, they'll go out of the room and you'll hear them going down the hall buzzing, singing them. You know, they like to do it. It's really, it's not anything new, it's just the way it's presented."

Chavers talks on about bringing her love of music into the classroom now in ways she never felt authorized to do before. She talks about impressing her friends with her students' written work. She speaks with pride about parents who glow when they see report cards that are better than ever before, who brag that their children are doing work that the parents themselves did not see until junior high school. Parental interest and participation has clearly increased. According to the district superintendent of a rural white community where one of the schools is located, "Some parents here were kind of skeptical about going up and bringing 'this black thing from Chicago,'" into this white, mostly rural section of Oklahoma. The same parents became supporters, however, when they saw the difference that it made for their children.

Chavers says that her children are convinced that they can do anything. When she plays choral music on a tape recorder they beg to learn the songs: "This week they said, 'Oh, won't you play the music?' And, 'Oh, can't we learn the song?'. . . . And they assured me, 'Oh, we can learn it.' So in two afternoons, they pretty well learned it. I was once a music teacher. With this new program I've been able to incorporate it again." When asked who gave her permission to do so, she says, "I just did it. I don't have to feel like this isn't part of my work anymore." Other teachers at other schools expressed similar feelings of a new freedom to bring their personal interests and talents into the classroom.

At the time of our interview, Chavers had been teaching for seventeen years. But, she says, "With the introduction of this program, it's just been different. The whole atmosphere has been different around here. The discipline problems for me have all but just totally disappeared, with this program. And it's not the fact that you're after the kids all the time. It's, 'This is what I expect of you.' You know, 'You are here for a job. This is your job, and my job here is to teach you. Your job is to be the best student you can be. And that is what I expect of you.'"

Robarts and Chavers are examples of what is possible, though perhaps not for all teachers. According to the head mentor teacher, the most important distinction between schools that do very well with Great Expectations and those that do not appears to be having an effective principal who understands the initiative. One characteristic of such principals is that they find ways of removing ineffectual or uncooperative teachers from their schools. The outcomes of the Great Expectations initiative have not yet been rigorously evaluated. However, several teachers bragged during interviews that average test scores in their own classes had risen by 30 or more percentiles in the space of one year.[91] The key for teachers is the apparently

---

91. Chapter 9 discusses the Success for All program, which serves a large number of mostly black and Hispanic children across several states. It shows positive effects for all students, but larger effects for the bottom 25 percent of the class.

effective program of professional development that has helped them to expect more and achieve more for both themselves and their students.

Conclusion

Any conception of bias requires a corresponding conception of neutrality. A major reason that no consensus has emerged from scholarship concerning the importance of racial bias in the classroom is that there is no single benchmark for racial neutrality. Instead, there are at least three: unconditional race neutrality, race neutrality conditioned on observables (including past performance), and race neutrality conditioned on unobserved potential. Moreover, racial biases can exist in teachers' perceptions, expectations, or behaviors, or in any combination of the three.

Consider teacher perceptions of current student performance. If the benchmark for bias is unconditional race neutrality, most teachers are biased, but evidence shows that this is mainly because their perceptions of current performance are correct. When their perceptions early in a school year are inaccurate, the inaccuracies may become true through a process of self-fulfilling prophecy, but there is little evidence that initial inaccuracies or prophecies systematically favor either blacks or whites. In fact, where the benchmark is racial neutrality after taking past performance and other observable predictors into account, evidence favors the conclusion that teacher perceptions of current performance are generally unbiased. Whether the same applies to expectations and behaviors is less clear. I have found no clear evidence on whether teachers' expectations or behaviors are racially biased for students whom they perceive to be equal on past or present measures of performance or proficiency. However, taking unconditional racial neutrality as the benchmark, it is clear that teachers' perceptions and expectations are biased in favor of whites and that teacher behaviors appear less supportive of blacks. Clearly, the benchmark chosen for neutrality affects the conclusions.

Robert Schuller says, "Any fool can count the seeds in an apple, but only God can count the apples in a seed."[92] Similarly, tests can measure what children know, but only God can measure their latent future potential. Neutrality conditioned on latent future potential relates to a third type of bias and a third way in which teachers' beliefs can matter. Since potential

---

92. Robert Schuller is a popular television minister and proponent of positive thinking.

is unobserved, racial bias of this type is virtually impossible to gauge with any reliability. Still, it does seem especially likely that teachers underestimate the potential of students whose current performance is poor, including disproportionate numbers of blacks. Also, blacks are underrepresented among students with the very highest scores, and potential for greater black representation at the top of the distribution is unproven. Thus at both ends of the test score distribution, stereotypes of black intellectual inferiority are reinforced by past and present disparities in performance, and this probably causes teachers to underestimate the potential of black children more than that of whites. If they expect black children to have less potential, teachers are likely to search with less conviction than they should for ways to help these children to improve, and hence miss opportunities to reduce the black-white test score gap.

Simply cajoling teachers to raise their expectations for black children—using phrases such as "All children can learn"—is probably a waste of time. However, good professional development programs can make a difference. Recall that some teachers in Oklahoma responded to the Great Expectations program with the assertion, "My kids couldn't do that." If they had gone on teaching as they had always done, that judgment would have been correct. But when they changed their teaching methods, they learned that they were wrong. Similarly, Guskey shows that teachers can learn responsive teaching methods that weaken the link between past and future performance.[93] Teachers who have been helped to improve their classroom practices can have "seeing is believing" experiences that challenge their prior biases. More research is needed on how professional development programs affect both test score levels and the black-white test score gap.

Even in the absence of the biases discussed above, teachers' beliefs probably affect black students more than whites. The evidence is quite thin, but the few studies that bear on this hypothesis appear to support it. Jussim, Eccles, and Madon find that teachers' perceptions of sixth-graders' mathematics performance in October do not contain a racial bias once they control past performance and attitudes.[94] Nevertheless, the effect of teachers' October perceptions on students' mathematics scores in May is almost three times larger for blacks than for whites. Further, the effect is also larger for females than for males, and larger for both black and white students from low-income households. Findings from other studies are consistent

93. Guskey (1982).
94. Jussim, Eccles, and Madon (1996).

with these results. Casteel finds that black eighth- and ninth-graders are more eager to please their teachers, but their white peers are more concerned about pleasing their parents.[95] These differences may be due to parenting. For example, white parents might exert more consistent pressure for good grades; black parents might be less assertive about grades and more deferential themselves to teachers. Future research should actively pursue these questions, including the implications for policy, teaching, and parenting.

My bottom line conclusion is that teachers' perceptions, expectations, and behaviors probably do help to sustain, and perhaps even to expand, the black-white test score gap. The magnitude of the effect is uncertain, but it may be quite substantial if effects accumulate from kindergarten through high school. The full story is quite complicated and parts of it currently hang by thin threads of evidence. Much remains on this research agenda.

Fortunately, successful interventions do establish that children of all racial and ethnic groups have more potential than most people have assumed. As the evidence accumulates, it should be possible to focus with greater determination on cultivating and harvesting all that youthful minds embody.[96] It would then be no surprise if the black-white test score gap began to shrink again, as it did in the 1980s—and ultimately disappeared.

References

Babad, Elisha Y. 1980. "Expectancy Bias in Scoring as a Function of Ability and Ethnic Labels." *Psychological Reports* 46: 625–26.

———. 1985. "Some Correlates of Teachers' Expectancy Bias." *American Educational Research Journal* 22(Summer): 175–83.

Baker, S. H. 1973. "Teacher Effectiveness and Social Class as Factors in Teacher Expectancy Effects on Pupils' Scholastic Achievement." Ph.D. dissertation. Clark University.

Baron, Reuben, David Y. H. Tom, and Harris M. Cooper. 1985. "Social Class, Race and Teacher Expectations." In Jerome B. Dusek, ed., *Teacher Expectancies*. Hillsdale, N.J.: Erlbaum.

95. Casteel (1997).

96. In addition to strong leadership and professional development for teachers, better-conceived performance incentives, no matter what their expectations of their students, should be a part of this process. The search for ways to design and implement such incentives and standards of accountability is currently quite active; see, for example, Hanushek (1994); Hanushek and Jorgenson (1996); Ladd (1996).

Brattesani, Karen A., Rhonda S. Weinstein, and Hermine Marshall. 1984. "Student Perceptions of Differential Teacher Treatment as Moderators of Teacher Expectation Effects." *Journal of Educational Psychology* 76: 236–47.

Brophy, Jerome. 1985. "Teacher-Student Interaction." In Dusek, ed., *Teacher Expectancies*.

Brophy, Jerome E., and Thomas L. Good. 1974. *Teacher-Student Relationships: Causes and Consequences*. Holt, Rinehart, and Winston.

Cabello, Beverly, and Nancy Davis Burstein. 1995. "Examining Teachers' Beliefs about Teaching in Culturally Diverse Classrooms." *Journal of Teacher Education* 46(September-October): 285–94.

Casteel, Clifton. 1997. "Attitudes of African American and Caucasian Eighth Grade Students about Praises, Rewards, and Punishments." *Elementary School Guidance and Counseling* 31(April): 262–72.

Coates, Brian. 1972. "White Adult Behavior toward Black and White Children." *Child Development* 43: 143–54.

Committee on Policy for Racial Justice. 1989. *Visions of a Better Way*. Washington: Joint Center for Political Studies.

DeMeis, Debra K., and Ralph R. Turner. 1978. "Effects of Students' Race, Physical Attractiveness, and Dialect on Teachers' Evaluations." *Contemporary Educational Psychology* 3: 77–86.

Dweck, Carol. 1991. "Self-Theories and Goals: Their Role in Motivation, Personality and Development." In Richard A. Dienstbier, ed., *Nebraska Symposium on Motivation, 1990*. Lincoln University Press.

Dweck, Carol, and Ellen L. Leggett. 1988. "A Social Cognitive Approach to Motivation and Personality." *Psychological Review* 95: 256–73.

Eccles, Jacquelynne, and Allan Wigfield. 1985. "Teacher Expectations and Student Motivation." In Dusek, ed., *Teacher Expectancies*.

Egan, Owen, and Peter Archer. 1985. "The Accuracy of Teachers' Ratings of Ability: a Regression Model." *American Educational Research Journal* 22: 25–34.

Entwisle, Doris R., and Karl L. Alexander. 1988. "Factors Affecting Achievement Test Scores and Marks of Black and White First Graders." *Elementary School Journal* 88(5): 449–71.

Evertson, Carolyn M., Jerome Brophy, and Thomas L. Good. 1972. "Communication of Teacher Expectations: First Grade," report 91. University of Texas at Austin, Research and Development Center for Teacher Eduction.

Feldman, Robert S., and Stanley Orchowsky. 1979. "Race and Performance of Student as Determinants of Teacher Nonverbal Behavior." *Contemporary Educational Psychology* 4: 324–33.

Ferguson, Ronald F. 1993. "Spreading the Paradigm of a Master Teacher: The Great Expectations Initiative in Oklahoma," working paper. Taubman Center for State and Local Government. John F. Kennedy School of Government, Harvard University.

Ford, Donna Y. 1996. *Reversing the Underachievement among Gifted Black Students*. New York: Teacher's College Press.

Fordham, Signithia, and John Ogbu. 1986. "Black Students' School Success: Coping with the Burden of 'Acting White.'" *Urban Review* 18(3): 176–206.

Gaines, Margie L. 1990. "Accuracy of Teacher Prediction of Elementary Student Achievement." Paper prepared for the annual meeting of the American Educational Research Association.

Good, Thomas L. 1987. "Two Decades of Research on Teacher Expectations: Findings and Future Directions." *Journal of Teacher Education* 38(4): 32–47.

Gross, Susan. 1993. "Early Mathematics Performance and Achievement: Results of a Study within a Large Suburban School System." *Journal of Negro Education.* 62: 269–87.

Guskey, Thomas R. 1982. "The Effects of Change in Instructional Effectiveness on the Relationship of Teacher Expectations and Student Achievement." *Journal of Educational Research* 75: 345–48.

Haller, Emil J. 1985. "Pupil Race and Elementary School Ability Grouping: Are Teachers Biased Against Black Children?" *American Educational Research Journal* 22(4): 465–83.

Hanushek, Eric A. 1994. *Making Schools Work: Improving Performance and Controlling Costs.* Brookings.

Hanushek, Eric A., and Dale W. Jorgenson, eds. 1996. *Improving America's Schools: The Role of Incentives.* Washington: National Academy Press.

Herrnstein, Richard J., and Charles Murray. 1994. *The Bell Curve: Intelligence and Class Structure in American Life.* Free Press.

Hoge, Robert, and Robert Butcher. 1984. "Analysis of Teacher Judgments of Pupil Achievement Level." *Journal of Educational Psychology* 76: 777–81.

Irvine, Jacqueline Jordon. 1985. "The Accuracy and Stability of Teachers' Achievement Expectations as Related to Students' Race and Sex." Paper prepared for the annual meeting of the American Educational Research Association.

———. 1990. *Black Students and School Failure: Policies, Practices, and Prescriptions.* Greenwood Press.

Jones, Joseph, 1997. "The Message Project, Fort Wayne Urban League, Phase I." Urban League of Fort Wayne, Indiana, and Taylor University.

Jussim, Lee. 1989. "Teacher Expectations: Self-Fulfilling Prophecies, Perceptual Biases, and Accuracy." *Journal of Personality and Social Psychology* 57: 469–80.

Jussim, Lee, and Jacquelynne Eccles. 1992. "Teacher Expectations II: Construction and Reflection of Student Achievement." *Journal of Personality and Social Psychology* 63: 947–61.

Jussim, Lee, Jacquelynne Eccles, and Stephanie Madon. 1996. "Social Perception, Social Stereotypes, and Teacher Expectations: Accuracy and the Quest for the Powerful Self-Fulfilling Prophecy." *Advances in Experimental Social Psychology* 28: 281–387.

Katz, M. 1973. "Attitudinal Modernity, Classroom Power and Status Characteristics: An Investigation." Paper prepared for the annual meeting of the American Educational Research Association.

Kleinfeld, Judith. 1972. "The Relative Importance of Teachers and Parents in the Formation of Negro and White Students' Academic Self-Concepts." *Journal of Educational Research* 65: 211–12.

Kluegel, James R. 1990. "Trends in Whites' Explanations of the Black-White Gap in Socioeconomic Status, 1977–1989." *American Sociological Review* 55 (August): 512–25.

Krupczak, W. P. 1972. "Relationships among Student Self-Concept of Academic Ability, Teacher Perception of Student Academic Ability and Student Achievement." Ph.D. dissertation, University of Miami.

Ladd, Helen F., ed. 1996. *Holding Schools Accountable: Performance-Based Reform in Education.* Brookings.

Leacock, E. 1969. *Teaching and Learning in City Schools.* Basic Books.

Lightfoot, Sara Lawrence. 1978. *Worlds Apart: Relationships between Families and Schools.* Basic Books.

Merton, Robert. 1948. "The Self-Fulfilling Prophecy." *Antioch Review* 8: 193–210.

Mickelson, Roslyn A. 1990. "The Attitude-Achievement Paradox among Black Adolescents." *Sociology of Education* 63: 44–61.

Miller, L. Scott. 1995. *An American Imperative: Accelerating Minority Educational Advancement.* Yale University Press.

Mitman, Alexis L. 1985. "Teachers' Differential Behavior toward Higher and Lower Achieving Students and its Relation to Selected Teacher Characteristics." *Journal of Educational Psychology* 77: 149–61.

Monk, Martin J. 1983. "Teacher Expectations? Pupil Responses to Teacher Mediated Classroom Climate." *British Educational Research Journal* 9(2): 153–66.

Ogbu, John. 1978. *Minority Education and Caste: The American System in Cross-Cultural Comparison.* Academic Press.

———. 1983. "Minority Status and Schooling in Plural Societies." *Comparative Education Review* 27(2): 168–203.

———. 1987. "Opportunity Structure, Cultural Boundaries, and Literacy." In Judith Langer, ed., *Language, Literacy, and Culture: Issues of Society and Schooling.* Norwood, N.J.: Ablex Press.

Pedulla, Joseph J., Peter W. Airasian, and George F. Madaus. 1980. "Do Teacher Ratings and Standardized Test Results of Students Yield the Same Information?" *American Educational Research Journal* 17(3): 303–07.

Puma, Michael, and others. 1993. "Prospects: The Congressionally Mandated Study of Educational Growth and Opportunity," interim report. Prepared for the U.S. Department of Education, Planning and Evaluation Service.

Raudenbush, Stephen W. 1984. "Magnitude of Teacher Expectancy Effects on Pupil IQ as a Function of the Credibility of Expectancy Induction: A Synthesis of Findings from 18 Experiments." *Journal of Educational Psychology* 76(1): 85–97.

Rosenthal, Robert. 1994. "Interpersonal Expectancy Effects: A 30-Year Perspective." *Current Directions in Psychological Science* 3(6): 176–79.

Rosenthal, Robert, and L. Jacobson. 1968. *Pygmalion in the Classroom.* Holt, Rinehart, and Winston.

Rowe, Mary Budd. 1986. "Wait Time: Slowing Down May Be a Way of Speeding Up!" *Journal of Teacher Education* 37(1): 43–50.

Rubovits, Pamela C., and Martin L. Maehr. 1973. "Pygmalion Black and White." *Journal of Personality and Social Psychology* 25: 210–18.

Shavelson, Richard J., Joel Cadwell, and Tonia Izu. 1977. "Teachers' Sensitivity to the Reliability of Information in Making Pedagogical Decisions." *American Educational Research Journal* 14(Spring): 83–97.

Slavin, Robert E. 1987. "Mastery Learning Reconsidered." *Review of Educational Research* 57(2): 175–213.

Smith, Mary Lee. 1980. "Teachers' Expectations." *Evaluation in Education* 4: 53–56.

Smith, Tom W. 1990. *Ethnic Images.* GSS topical report 19. University of Chicago, National Opinion Research Center (December).

Snyderman, Mark, and Stanley Rothman. 1986. "Science, Politics, and the IQ Controversy." *Public Interest* 83(Spring): 85.

————. 1987. "Survey of Expert Opinion on Intelligence and Aptitude Testing." *American Psychologist* 42(February): 138–39.

Solorzano, Daniel G. 1992. "An Exploratory Analysis of the Effects of Race, Class, and Gender on Student and Parent Mobility Aspirations." *Journal of Negro Education* 61: 30–44.

Taylor, Marylee C. 1979. "Race, Sex, and the Expression of Self-Fulfilling Prophecies in a Laboratory Teaching Situation." *Personality and Social Psychology* 6: 897–912.

Weinstein, Rhonda S. 1985. "Student Mediation of Classroom Expectancy Effects." In Dusek, ed., *Teacher Expectancies*.

Weinstein, R. S., and others. 1987. "Pygmalion and the Student: Age and Classroom Differences in Children's Awareness of Teacher Expectations." *Child Development* 58: 1079–92.

Wigfield, Allan, and others. 1991. "Transitions at Early Adolescence: Changes in Children's Domain-Specific Self-Perceptions and General Self-Esteem across the Transition to Junior High School." *Developmental Psychology* 27: 552–65.

Willis, Sherry. 1972. "Formation of Teachers' Expectations of Students' Academic Performance." Ph.D. Dissertation, University of Texas at Austin.

Willis, Sherry, and Jerome Brophy. 1974. "The Origins of Teachers' Attitudes towards Young Children." *Journal of Educational Psychology* 66(4): 520–29.

Yee, Albert H. 1968. "Interpersonal Attitudes of Teacher and Disadvantaged Pupils." *Journal of Human Resources* 3(3): 327–45.

RONALD F. FERGUSON

9

Can Schools Narrow the Black-White Test Score Gap?

P ROPOSALS FOR IMPROVING the test performance of black children and closing the black-white test score gap are numerous and varied. This chapter evaluates the evidence for and against six of the most popular proposals that are related to schools: expanding enrollment in preschool programs; reducing ability grouping and curriculum tracking; supporting instructional interventions for youth at risk of failure (mainly in elementary school); matching students and teachers by race; selecting teachers with strong basic skills (as measured by teachers' own test scores); and maintaining smaller classes.[1] To judge the

Thanks to Karl Alexander, John Ballantine, William Dickens, James Flynn, Christopher Jencks, Jens Ludwig, Meredith Phillips, and Jason Snipes for helpful discussions and comments on earlier drafts. I am also grateful to Karl Alexander for calculations provided at my request for this chapter. Jason Snipes provided able research assistance.

1. The fact that I focus on black and white Americans is not an indication that these issues are any less important for other races and ethnicities. The need for research addressing the special patterns and circumstances that apply to Latinos, Native Americans, and Asian Americans remains largely unmet. Similarly, while I focus on test scores, I do not deny that other aspects of children's development may at times be much more important. If there are trade-offs between strategies that would improve scores and those that would benefit children in other ways, great care should be taken to operate in the best interest of the children being served; on this point, see Darling-Hammond (1991, 1994, 1996); Darling-Hammond and McLaughlin (1995); Ford (1996).

effectiveness of these proposals, I focus on studies of the highest methodological quality and pay special attention to whether and to what extent each measure would affect test scores.[2]

Does Preschool Provide a Lasting Head Start?

Most policymakers and advocates for the poor believe that preschools can compensate for factors that place children from disadvantaged backgrounds behind their peers in academic terms before they even enter kindergarten. In reviewing the evidence, two questions are of concern. First, does attending compensatory preschool raise test scores in kindergarten? The best research on this question finds that the answer is yes. Second, do the effects of attending preschool persist into adulthood? The evidence on this question is, at best, mixed.

Experimental and Quasi-Experimental Studies

In the field of education, high-quality studies that use random assignment or good comparison groups, have large samples, and follow subjects over many years are rare. For an evaluation of compensatory preschool programs, Steven Barnett searched out such studies.[3] To qualify for his sample, studies had to cover programs serving children of low-income families and be based in a fixed location. They also had to include data on academic performance through at least the third grade. Eight of the studies that Barnett identified used random-assignment control groups or had comparison groups of similar children who did not attend the program. Almost all of the children in the studies were African American.

These eight studies find IQ gains ranging from 5 points to 13 points during preschool. Such gains are, respectively, equivalent to almost one-third and almost one full standard deviation on the standard scale for measuring IQ. All of the studies, including the Perry Preschool experiment which I discuss below, also show substantial declines in IQ relative to control or comparison groups by the third grade. Only one, the Philadelphia

---

2. Whenever possible, I present results in terms of "effect sizes" measured in standard deviation units; see chapter 8, note 3.

3. Barnett (1992).

Project, reports statistically significant differences as late as fifth grade. These studies yield no firm evidence that preschool programs produce IQ gains that last past the early years of elementary school, but neither do they disprove the possibility.[4]

Five of the eight studies report achievement scores (distinct from IQ scores) for the third grade or higher. Of these five, only Perry Preschool shows a continuing and statistically significant advantage over the comparison group. The other four studies suffer from serious methodological problems. The Early Training Project uses only thirty-three experimentals and fifteen controls. The remaining three rely on achievement tests administered routinely by the schools; there are strong reasons to believe that doing so biases against detecting effects that might be present.[5] On balance, therefore, Perry Preschool is the strongest study.

PERRY PRESCHOOL. From 1962 to 1965, the Perry Preschool experiment randomly assigned five cohorts of children to be participants or members of the control group.[6] Children were eligible if their families had low ratings on a scale of socioeconomic status, their measured IQ was at least one standard deviation below the national mean, and they "showed no signs for organic causation for mental retardation or physical handicap." For the first wave, children enrolled at the age of four, but thereafter at age three. The treatment group attended preschool for 2.5 hours a day, Monday through Friday, from October to May. In addition, a teacher visited these children once a week to provide about 1.5 hours of instruction in a home setting.

An IQ difference of 12 points opened between experimentals and controls by the end of preschool. But this difference was not statistically significant by the time the children were nine years old (see note 4). For

4. Dickens, Kane, and Schultz (forthcoming) point out that the IQ effect of Perry Preschool had not "gone" by the time the children were nine, it just was not statistically significant. The point estimate is positive and the standard error is large enough to allow a fairly large effect. Further, the point estimate is large enough to justify a substantial share of the cost of the treatment. These authors also reanalyze data used for a large meta-analysis of preschool studies by Lazar and Darlington (1982), who conclude that IQ effects disappear by the time children are in their teens. Based on the reanalysis, Dickens, Kane, and Schultz suggest that so strong a conclusion is not warranted.

5. For example, children who attend different schools may be given tests that cannot be fully equated; children retained in grade are seldom tested with their birth cohort; and in many cases, children in special education are not tested at all. Moreover if, as is likely, retention in grade or assignment to special education is greater for the control group, studies based on tests that schools administer are almost certainly biased against finding that preschool has lasting effects.

6. Altogether, across the five cohorts, fifty-eight children were chosen as participants and sixty-five for the control group.

Table 9-1. *Perry Preschool Project: Estimated Standardized Effects on Achievement Scores, Selected Ages*[a]

Item	Age					
	Seven	Eight	Nine	Ten	Fourteen	Nineteen
Effect size	0.23	0.34	0.39	0.42	0.45	0.36
Probability[b]	0.219	0.079	0.042	0.040	0.003	0.059
Sample size						
Treatment group	53	49	54	49	49	52
Control group	60	56	55	46	46	57

Source: Author's calculations based on data from Barnett (1992, table 8).
a. Different examinations were used for different ages; details were unavailable.
b. Values given indicate probability of the estimated effect if the true effect is zero.

achievement, the story is more encouraging. Table 9-1 shows approximate effect sizes for achievement tests.[7] Instead of diminishing over time, the size and statistical significance of the preschool effect on achievement test scores actually increased. The reasons remain unclear: they may be cognitive, motivational, or both.

Perry Preschool is not a typical program. It had more funding, was more intensive, and had better trained staff than most. Given, on the one hand, the small sample size in the Perry Preschool experiment and the fact that the intervention is atypical, and on the other, the weaker results from other experimental and quasi-experimental studies, a large random assignment longitudinal study for a program such as Head Start is overdue. In addition to measuring effects for standard programs, such a large-scale study might enrich a randomly selected sample of programs by strengthening their focus on reading and mathematics readiness, in order to compare the impacts of the basic and enriched interventions.

7. Barnett (1992, table 8) gives the mean scores and sample sizes for the treatment and control groups for each age level; these numbers come from the appendixes of Schweinhart and Weikart (1980) and Berreuta-Clement and others (1984). Barnett's table also gives probability values for the differences in means. As a rough approximation, I take the usual formula for the z value for a test of difference in means, assume that the standard deviation is the same in the treatment and control groups, and using the z value corresponding to the probability value given in the table, solve for the sample standard deviation. I then divide the difference in means by this standard deviation to obtain the effect size. This calculation is only approximate, because the probability values that I use in fact come from an analysis of covariance that controls for several covariates, including gender, mother's employment, and initial IQ. Also, the test taken at age nineteen was not a regular academic achievement test, but the Adult Performance Level test, which measures skills and knowledge associated with educational and occupational success in several domains that are important in adult life.

CHILD-PARENT CENTER, CHICAGO. In a study published after Barnett's review of the literature, Arthur Reynolds and colleagues examine the preschool program of the Child-Parent Center, which has operated since 1967 in low-income neighborhoods of Chicago.[8] The data cover 240 children who finished the preschool program in 1986 and follow them through sixth grade. A comparison group is composed of 120 nonparticipating children from families similar in characteristics to those of the participants and living in the same neighborhoods.

Because the Child-Parent Center study uses a comparison group rather than a randomly selected control group, and because the children were not tested at the time they entered preschool, it is impossible be sure that the treatment and comparison groups were initially equivalent. Nevertheless, as of sixth grade, program participants scored about a third of a standard deviation higher than the comparison group in reading and mathematics on the Iowa Test of Basic Skills, after controlling for gender, age, parental education, eligibility for free lunch, and any additional years of Child-Parent Center participation after preschool. These results are comparable to those from the Perry Preschool program for similar age groups, and hence reinforce the proposition that benefits from preschool can be lasting.

Nonexperimental Evidence

The classic problem with using nonexperimental data to measure program effects of any type is that people are not selected (or do not select themselves) into programs randomly. Therefore statistical analyses that fail to correct for selection bias will tend to over- or underestimate program effects. A recent study of the federal Head Start program by Janet Currie and Duncan Thomas is notable for the way in which it tries to overcome this problem.[9]

Currie and Thomas use the National Longitudinal Survey of Youth's Child-Mother file to estimate effects of Head Start and other preschool programs on several outcomes, including one test score, the Peabody Picture Vocabulary Test (PPVT). Currie and Thomas estimate the difference in PPVT scores between siblings who attend Head Start and those who

8. Reynolds and others (1996).
9. Currie and Thomas (1995).

stay at home.[10] They measure whether the effects of Head Start are lasting by estimating differences between siblings through age ten.

Both African-American and white five-year-olds who attend Head Start score about 7 percentile points higher on the PPVT than their siblings who stay at home. These effects are highly statistically significant. However, while this benefit persists for whites, it decays rapidly for African Americans.[11] By age ten, the estimated effect of Head Start on the PPVT scores of black children has disappeared, but for white children it is roughly 5 percentile points. In addition, Head Start appears to reduce the probability of grade repetition for white children but not for blacks. The finding that effects die out for African Americans is consistent with results from many of the studies reviewed by Barnett that were less methodologically sound than the Perry Preschool study.

These results of Currie and Thomas are not definitive.[12] In order for their results to be unbiased, there must be no systematic difference between the child sent to Head Start and the sibling kept at home. Second, the parents' decision on whether to send the second child to Head Start should not depend on the quality of the first child's experience.[13] Third, the child who stays at home must not benefit from the fact that the sibling attended Head Start. Fourth, the children of families who send some but not all of their children to Head Start must derive the same average benefits as other children. There is some evidence to suggest that the second and third of these assumptions may not hold for African Americans. Specifically, Currie and Thomas report (but do not show) that the effect of Head Start for first-born children is "significantly negative" (that is, smaller) for African Americans.[14]

10. They treat other preschool programs analogously, estimating the difference in PPVT scores between siblings who attend preschool and those who do not. Further, they use a difference-in-difference approach to distinguish the impact of Head Start from other types of preschool program.

11. The benefit of other preschool is zero for whites, but for blacks the point estimate for five-year-olds is 43 percent as large as that for Head Start and almost reaches statistical significance (the coefficient is 1.60 times its standard error). However, this effect for African Americans also dies out, and at roughly the same rate as that of Head Start.

12. Indeed, Currie and Thomas (1995) discuss the necessary assumptions listed here.

13. If parents who have good experiences of Head Start with their first children are more likely to send later children, these families are less likely to be among those with a stay-at-home child. The effective sample will therefore be biased toward households that had a less favorable experience with the program.

14. Currie and Thomas (1995, p. 359). This might result, for example, from positive spillovers from older to younger siblings in black households; or from overrepresentation in the sample of families who had bad experiences—and presumably lower gains than average—with their first-born children in Head Start, and as a consequence, chose not to enroll their later children (see previous note).

Further, the sample of sibling pairs fitting the study's requirements is small.[15] Both Currie and Thomas's study, which finds that achievement effects fade for black children, and the Perry Preschool study, which finds that these effects persist, are small and possibly unrepresentative samples from which to generalize about national impacts of preschool.[16]

DO POOR SCHOOLS SQUANDER GAINS FROM HEAD START? Seeking an explanation for why Head Start's benefits to black children might not persist, Currie and Thomas (1996a) use nationally representative data on eighth graders from the 1988 National Education Longitudinal Study (NELS:88).[17] They examine the proposition that the quality of the schools subsequently attended explains some of the difference in performance between students who attended Head Start and those who did not. Before controlling for school quality, eighth-graders who attended Head Start have lower scores on achievement tests than those who did not. But Currie and Thomas find that "among black children, the gap between Head Start children and other children is virtually eliminated if we include fixed effects for the school the child attends."[18] This suggests that black children who attend Head Start go on to weaker schools than black children who do not attend Head Start.

15. The total sample in the National Longitudinal Survey of Youth's Child-Mother file includes 329 African-American children who attended Head Start; see Currie and Thomas (1995, table 3). Of these, 57.1 percent have a sibling who attended Head Start, 14.2 percent have a sibling who attended another type of preschool, and 28.6 percent have a sibling who did not attended any preschool. This gives 94 African-American sibling pairs (0.286 x 329). The sibling sample for whites is only slightly larger: 134 pairs.

16. In an unpublished critique of Currie and Thomas (1995), Barnett and Camilli (1996) compare the PPVT to intelligence tests for which even the Perry Preschool sample shows fading gains. They write, quoting Schweinhart and others (1993), that the results of the Perry Preschool experiment "were consistent with the findings of Currie and Thomas in that initial effects on the PPVT and other intelligence tests faded away by age eight, and there were no significant effects on grade repetition" (p. 27). In a response, Currie and Thomas (1996b, p. 8) reject the assertion that the PPVT is essentially an intelligence test: "In contrast to Barnett and Camilli, Currie and Thomas are careful to *not* call PPVT a measure of 'cognitive ability' (which it is not) and refer to it as an indicator of 'academic performance'." It is unclear which interpretation is the most appropriate. On the one hand, it seems at least plausible that if the National Longitudinal Survey of Youth's Child-Mother file had used the achievement test instruments used in the Perry Preschool experiment, Currie and Thomas might have discovered more persistent gains for black children. On the other hand, Currie and Thomas report that when they used the Peabody Individual Achievement Test, the results were similar to, but weaker than, those for the PPVT.

17. Currie and Thomas (1996a).

18. Their equations also include controls for gender, family income, whether a foreign language is spoken in the home, number of siblings, and whether the child is the first born.

It would be too big a stretch, however, to conclude from this evidence that the Head Start effect fades as a result of weaker schools. Siblings who are close in age are very likely to attend the same schools. For school quality to explain why Head Start advantages fade for black children but not for whites, one would need to show that inferior schools reduce the difference between higher and lower achieving siblings by depressing high achievement disproportionately. This hypothesis is certainly plausible—even likely—but it awaits evidence other than what the NELS:88 can provide.

There is no disagreement that preschool programs, including Head Start, produce nontrivial gains in children's IQ and achievement scores by the time they enter kindergarten. However, given the nature of the evidence, no strong conclusions are warranted regarding whether these benefits persist. A large-scale random-assignment longitudinal study is needed to answer this question. In the meantime, preschools deserve continuing support.

Do Ability Grouping and Tracking Exacerbate the Black-White Test Score Gap?

In this section, I examine the effects of ability grouping and curricular tracking. Ability grouping usually refers to the practice of clustering elementary school children for instruction, based mostly on demonstrated or expected performance, but also on factors such as motivation, work habits, and behavior. Groups may be taught in the same or different classrooms, for a single subject or for the entire curriculum. Although the practice is not documented by any national survey, it seems that the vast majority of elementary schools in the United States use in-class ability grouping for reading and whole class instruction for other subjects. Most U.S. high schools organize instruction around curricular tracks. Students in a particular track take a sequence of courses that distinguish their multisemester curriculum from that taught in other tracks. Students with greater academic interests and proficiency tend toward academic, as opposed to general or vocational, tracks.[19] This in effect turns tracks into ability groups

---

19. Students and parents often participate in the choice of track. Lee and Eckstrom (1987) report data from the nationally representative High School and Beyond survey, which asked sophomores at public high schools in 1980 how they had ended up in their particular tracks. Only 33 percent of students in academic tracks, 43 percent in general tracks, and 37 percent in vocational tracks reported that they had

much of the time. There are also tracks within tracks: college prep, honors, and advanced placement are some standard labels for progressively more exclusive subdivisions.

Researchers and activists hotly debate the impact of ability grouping on achievement. Fashions in the research literature change with the political climate. James Kulik notes: "In an age of ability testing, reviewers concluded that ability grouping could benefit students. When progressive education was in style and ability testing fell from fashion, reviewers concluded that grouping was more likely to harm than help students. In an era that stressed excellence as an educational goal, reviewers concluded that there were great benefits in the special grouping of higher aptitude students. In an era of educational equity, they concluded that grouping was harmful for disadvantaged and minority students. The times sensitized the reviewers to certain truths about grouping; they also blinded reviewers to other truths."[20]

I consider three questions. First, are blacks distributed among ability groups, curriculum tracks, and courses in equal proportion to their representation in schools? The answer is clearly no. Second, is there evidence that placements in ability groups or curriculum tracks are racially biased? While there are small racial differences in placement associated with socio-economic status, most such differences are associated with measurable differences in proficiency (that is, past performance). But there are no consistent racial differences in placements after controlling for these two factors. Third, is it likely that ability grouping and curriculum tracking help to sustain or exacerbate black-white differences in achievement? The highest quality research suggests that ability grouping and tracking are not harmful—compared to the most likely alternatives.

Critics are not wrong in saying that instructional practices in lower groups and tracks are worse, that instruction in such tracks is not tailored to the needs of low-performing students, or that membership in lower tracks is stigmatizing. But that does not mean necessarily that heterogeneous classrooms are better. Most proposed alternatives to ability grouping and tracking involve changes in teaching, not simply the standard practices of today's heterogeneous classrooms. Without major changes in teacher training—

been "assigned." The proportions of students who chose their tracks without help from anyone else—parents, friends, or counselors—were 25 percent, 23 percent, and 25 percent, for the three options respectively. Only 3 percent of students attended schools where there was no choice to make.

20. Kulik (1992, p. 15).

and probably even with them—there seems little reason to expect that more heterogeneous grouping would be a panacea for any students, black or white. Children can succeed or fail under a variety of grouping arrangements.[21]

Racial Bias in Elementary School Group Placement

Elementary school teachers have virtually complete autonomy in choosing ability group placements for their students. It is therefore very plausible that group placements may be biased by children's race or socioeconomic status. Chapter 8 outlines three types of racial bias, each with a characteristic benchmark: unconditional race neutrality; race neutrality conditioned on past performance and other appropriate criteria; and race neutrality conditioned on future potential. Whether a pattern shows bias or not depends on the benchmark for neutrality that one has in mind.

Discourse on racial imbalance in grouping and tracking often takes any racial imbalance as prima facie evidence of bias. Jomills Braddock and Robert Slavin, for example, cite a study by Emil Haller as evidence of racial imbalance in elementary school and continue: "The U.S. Office of Civil Rights has estimated that more than half of U.S. elementary schools have at least one 'racially identifiable' classroom in its highest or lowest grade. A racially identifiable classroom is one in which the proportion of students of a given race in a class is substantially different from that in the school as a whole. This is considered an indication of discriminatory ability grouping."[22]

Haller asked teachers in the spring of 1982 to assign their current students to reading groups for the next school year.[23] Seventy-eight percent of the children recommended for the highest groups were white, and 63 percent

21. An extended discussion about the interaction of teaching methods and grouping arrangements is beyond the scope of this chapter. However, see Bossert, Barnett, and Filby (1984) for a useful discussion.

22. Braddock and Slavin (1993, p. 55); Haller (1985).

23. Haller collected data from teachers in forty-nine self-contained classrooms serving 934 fourth, fifth, and sixth grade students in five school districts. Two of the districts are in the Northeast, one is in Appalachia, one in the deep South, and one in a relatively affluent, racially integrated suburb of an East-Central state. In interviews averaging 1.5 hours, teachers constructed the reading groups that they would recommend to the following year's teacher. In addition, Haller collected teachers' perceptions of students, using a written survey instrument. She finds that they perceived white students as having more ability, better work habits, and fewer behavioral problems than blacks. The students completed the Comprehensive Test of Basic Skills.

Table 9-2. *Teachers' Comments and Primary Reason for Group Placement,
by Students' Race, Grades Four through Six, 1982*[a]

	White students		Black students	
Comment/reason	Number	Percent	Number	Percent
Comments about students				
Reading ability	1,435	29.1	604	28.9
General ability	848	17.2	317	15.2
Evidence	373	7.6	193	9.2
Work habits	765	15.5	293	14.0
Behavior or personality	869	17.6	382	18.3
Home background	458	9.3	228	10.9
Physical attributes	88	1.8	31	1.5
Miscellaneous	108	2.1	42	2.0
Total	4,938	100.0	2,090	100.0
Primary reason for placement				
Reading ability	238	40.9	89	39.7
General ability	132	22.7	51	22.2
Evidence	40	6.9	28	1.2
Work habits	88	1.5	23	10.0
Behavior or personality	77	13.2	34	14.8
Home background	7	1.2	5	2.1
Physical attributes	0	0	0	0
Miscellaneous	0	0	0	0
Total	582	100.0	230	100.0

Source: Haller (1995, tables 4 and 5).
a. Student sample comprises 667 whites and 267 blacks. For primary reason for placement, chi square is 10.3, $p < 0.07$.

of those recommended for the lowest groups were black. This imbalance is large. Nonetheless, Haller's findings are not an indication of discriminatory ability grouping.

Haller does not find any violation of racial neutrality, once test scores and other reasonable criteria are taken into account. Table 9-2 shows that the criteria teachers applied in judging blacks and whites are nearly identical. If their decisions were racially biased, it seems highly unlikely that teachers would use such similar criteria in discussing students.[24] Table 9-3

24. From table 9-2, the only notable difference relates to "work habits," which is the primary reason for placement for 10 percent of black students but for only 1.5 percent of whites. There is also a (smaller) racial difference for "evidence": 6.9 percent for whites compared with 1.2 percent for blacks.

Table 9-3. *Displacement of Teachers' Group Recommendations Compared with Predictions from Test Scores, by Students' Race, Grades Four through Six, 1982*[a]

	White students		Black students		Total	
Displacement	Number	Percent	Number	Percent	Number	Percent
Upward	121	18.1	47	17.6	168	18.0
None	434	65.1	167	62.5	601	64.3
Downward	112	16.8	53	19.9	165	17.7
Total	667	100	267	100	934	100

Source: Haller (1995, table 8).

a. Comparison is with placement that would have resulted from using a student's class rank in scores on the Comprehensive Test of Basic Skills as the sole criterion. The chi square is 1.23, $p = 0.54$.

compares teachers' reading group recommendations with what placements would be if they were based on students' scores on the Comprehensive Test of Basic Skills, by race. Black-white differences in the percentage of students displaced upward or downward are small and well within the range of simple random variation.[25]

I have found only a few other studies that test for race neutrality conditioned on past performance in ability group placement.[26] None of these find racial bias after controlling for other factors, including test scores. Evidence for bias due to socioeconomic status is more mixed, and may account for a small percentage of the observed racial differences.[27] Still, by far the most important predictor of the black-white disparity in placements is proficiency, which produces large racial imbalances in group membership. The claim of racial discrimination in group placement by teachers is not supported by research.

25. As discussed in chapter 8, the correlations between teachers' perceptions of student reading ability and the test scores are 0.73 for whites and 0.74 for blacks.

26. Sorensen and Hallinan (1984); Pallas and others (1994); Dreeben and Gamoran (1986).

27. Sorensen and Hallinan (1984) do not control for socioeconomic status. While Pallas and others (1994) and Dreeben and Gamoran (1986) do control for socioeconomic status and find that it is a statistically significant predictor even after controlling for test scores, neither study shows the relationship of race to placement when this factor is not controlled. Haller and Davis (1980) report no effects of children's or teachers' socioeconomic status; they do not use race as a variable in their analysis. Thus evidence is mixed on the importance of social class as a predictor of group placement. Moreover, since most studies do not correct for measurement error in prior scores, students' socioeconomic status may simply be proxying aspects of ability or proficiency that are poorly measured by initial test scores, rather than exerting a true "effect" on group placement.

Effects of Ability Grouping

Since black and white students are not equally distributed across groups, ability grouping will contribute to the black-white achievement gap if group placements affect how much students learn. Studies leave no doubt that lower ability groups cover less material than higher groups. This finding says nothing, however, about whether students learn different amounts in ability groups than under heterogeneous arrangements. Indeed, it is conceivable that students in lower ability groups might learn less if placed in heterogeneous groups where material is covered more rapidly.

The best way to estimate the impact of ability grouping is to compare grouped students with similar students who are not grouped. The most extensive meta-analytic reviews of such studies are those of James and Chen-Lin Kulik.[28] Drawing upon their work, tables 9-4 and 9-5 show mean and median effect sizes across studies for five categories of grouping: XYZ, within-class, and across-grade grouping, and enrichment and accelerated classes. Table 9-4 shows effects for grouping versus no grouping in each category. Table 9-5 focuses on the XYZ and within-class grouping categories, showing the same effects separately for high-, low-, and middle-ability groups.[29] The effects are not distinguished for particular racial groups.

In XYZ grouping, which represents the largest number of studies, students are assigned to separate classes based on assessments that often include, but are not restricted to, IQ or achievement test scores.[30] Pedagogically,

28. Kulik and Kulik (1982, 1984a, 1984b, 1987, 1989); Kulik (1992). Although Kulik (1992) is published by an organization that focuses on the gifted and talented, his objectivity should not be questioned: he is thorough and shows no particular propensity for advocacy. See also Slavin (1987, 1990b). The main difference between the reviews by Slavin and the Kuliks is that the former do not include studies of enriched and accelerated classes for the gifted and talented, because Slavin claims that the selection of their comparison groups is biased (see note 37 below). In addition, Slavin's conclusions emphasize the lack of general impact of standard grouping practices, rather than the presence of effects in cases where instruction is adapted to specific students. Slavin's own prescriptive ideas are perfectly consistent with tailoring instruction to students' needs (see the discussion of the Success for All program later in this chapter). His main complaint about standard grouping practices is that they are rigid and can trap children in particular trajectories. Substantively, there is not much difference between Slavin's meta-analytic findings and those based on Kulik's 1992 review of the evidence.

29. XYZ and within-class grouping are the only categories for which separate effects for high-, low-, and middle-ability groups are available from more than one or two studies.

30. XYZ grouping arrangements are typical in upper elementary schools, middle schools, and junior high schools. Of the fifty-one studies of XYZ classes reviewed in Kulik (1992), only four involve grades ten through twelve; only seven involve grade three or below.

Table 9-4. *Estimated Effect Sizes for Selected Types of Ability Grouping* [a]

| Effect size and summary statistic [b] | Type of ability grouping | | | | | | | | | |
| | XYZ | | Within-class | | Cross-grade | | Enriched | | Accelerated [c] | |
	Number	Percent	Number	Percent	Number	Percent	Number	Percent	Number	Percent
Range										
Less than 0	21	41	2	18	2	14	3	12	0	0
0 to 0.25	25	49	5	44	4	29	4	16	0	0
0.26 to 0.50	5	10	2	18	5	36	9	36	3	13
0.51 to 0.75	0	0	1	9	1	7	7	28	2	9
0.76 to 1.00	0	0	1	9	2	14	1	4	10	43
Over 1.00	0	0	0	0	0	0	1	4	8	35
Summary statistic										
Mean	0.03		0.25		0.33		0.41		0.87	
Median	0.04		0.21		0.30		0.40		0.84	
Total studies	51		11		14		25		23	

Source: Author's tabulations from Kulik (1992, tables 1 and 3–6).

a. Sample comprises studies using control or comparison classrooms.

b. Denominator for effect sizes is the pooled standard deviation.

c. In order to average across studies that compare accelerated students to older control groups and those that use same-age comparisons, one standard deviation is added to the effect sizes for studies that use older comparison groups; see text and note 38 for further details.

Table 9-5. Estimated Effect Sizes for XYZ and Within-Class Grouping, by Level of Ability [a]

	Type of ability grouping											
	XYZ						Within-class					
	High ability		Middle ability		Low ability		High ability		Middle ability		Low ability	
Effect size and summary statistic[b]	Number	Percent	Number	Percent	Number	Percent	Number	Percent	Number	Percent	Number	Percent
Range												
Less than 0	12	34	15	52	18	51	0	0	1	17	2	33
0 to 0.25	17	49	11	38	14	40	2	33	3	50	0	0
0.26 to 0.50	3	9	3	10	3	9	4	67	2	33	3	50
0.51 to 0.75	3	9	0	0	0	0	0	0	0	0	1	17
Summary statistic												
Mean	0.10		-0.02		-0.01		0.30		0.18		0.16	
Median	0.13		-0.02		-0.01		0.26		0.22		0.35	
Total studies	35		29		35		6		6		6	

Source: Author's tabulations from Kulik (1992, tables 1 and 4).

a. Sample comprises studies using ungrouped control or comparison classrooms. Note that roughly one-third of the studies in Kulik's meta-analysis that reported overall effect sizes did not report effect sizes separately for different ability groups. Therefore, fewer studies of XYZ and within-class grouping are covered in table 9-5 than in table 9-4.

b. Denominator for effect sizes is the pooled standard deviation.

classes differ in terms of the pace of instruction and the amount of material covered, but not the basic curriculum.[31] In contrast, the four other approaches involve more tailoring of curriculum and instruction to students in the group.

Within-class ability grouping needs no special explanation here; but it should be noted that virtually all of the literature on studies using comparison groups is for mathematics.[32] Cross-grade ability grouping combines students from different classrooms, usually for instruction in a single subject for a small part of each day, after which they return to their regular rooms. Enriched and accelerated programs are for students identified as gifted and talented. Typically, enriched programs not only proceed at a faster pace than heterogeneous classes, but also use more challenging and stimulating materials. Accelerated programs cover material in less time than regular classes, and may or may not use standard curriculums.[33]

For XYZ grouping, the basic finding is that it makes no difference. Table 9-4 shows a mean effect size of 0.03 and a median of 0.04 for fifty-one studies, with a distribution centered quite close to zero.[34] About two-thirds of these studies report separate effect sizes for high, middle, and low groups. Table 9-5 shows that the effect is essentially zero for each ability level.[35]

Studies of the other four types of ability grouping find higher scores for students who are grouped than for those who are not. All the effect sizes for within-class grouping are positive and statistically significant, with small to moderate magnitudes of 0.21 (overall median, table 9-4) to 0.35 (low-ability median, table 9-5). Similarly, the effect sizes for cross-grade grouping are 0.33 (overall mean) and 0.30 (overall median).[36]

31. For example, of the fifty-one studies of XYZ classes in Kulik (1992), only nine involve any curricular adjustment. For these, the average effect size is 0.08, as compared with 0.02 for the others.

32. All but three of the eleven studies of within-class grouping reviewed in Kulik (1992) are for mathematics. Of these three, one is for reading; written in 1927, it is also an outlier historically. The second is for "other," and the third is for reading and mathematics combined. Grade levels range evenly from 2 through 8.

33. Roughly half the accelerated programs reviewed in Kulik (1992) cover a single subject, usually mathematics. Others shortened the time spent at particular grades, enabling students to complete grades seven through nine in two years, for example.

34. Thirty-one studies are from the 1960s, twelve are earlier, and eight are later. Thus most of the evidence here is old.

35. Kulik (1992) examines subsets of these studies, broken down by grade level and a number of other criteria. In no case is the effect size different from zero.

36. Not shown on the table, only two of 14 studies for cross-grade grouping present effect sizes by ability level. One shows no effect for any level of ability, the other finds effect sizes of 0.28 for the high

In regard to enriched and accelerated programs, authors disagree, on methodological grounds, about whether research reviews on ability grouping should include such studies. I believe that they should be included, but with the caution that effects may be overstated and that one has no estimated effect sizes for the students left behind in regular classes.[37] Findings support the claim that for the students smart enough, motivated enough, or lucky enough to be selected, enriched and accelerated programs increase achievement. The median effect sizes are 0.40 for studies of enrichment classes and 0.84 for studies of acceleration.[38] Even if these are overestimates, it seems unlikely that they are so overstated as to warrant ignoring the general finding that tailored instruction appears to promote higher achievement.[39]

---

group and 0.50 for the low group. Most of the studies of cross-grade grouping were for various combinations of grades 3 to 8. Two studies began with first grade and ran for three years, with effect sizes of 0.33 and 0.81.

37. Slavin's (1987) main complaint concerns selection bias: "Much of this research (e.g, Howell, 1962) compares students in gifted programs to students in the same schools who were not accepted for the gifted program, usually matching on IQ or other measures." But even with careful matching, students who are selected probably differ systematically from those who are not. In response, Kulik (1992, p. 19) writes: "Like many other reviewers, we believe that the methodological weaknesses in studies of enriched and accelerated classes are not great enough to warrant their wholesale dismissal." I am inclined to agree with Kulik when students' baseline scores are relatively similar. However, for assessing the effects of moving children among ability groups that differ by one standard deviation or more, I think that Slavin is correct in dismissing such estimates as useless.

The effect sizes for enriched and accelerated groups are not comparable to those of other groups because the standard deviation typically only includes students in gifted and talented classes and their comparison group. Kulik reports, in personal communication, that an earlier effort to replace this with the standard deviation for all students made surprisingly little difference. The reason is that students are selected for gifted and talented programs on criteria (for example, effort and motivation) much broader than the test scores used to measure the impact.

38. Roughly half of the effect sizes for accelerated students reported in Kulik (1992) are measured relative to comparison groups one or more grade levels ahead. For accelerated students compared to control groups of the same age, the Kuliks' typical effect size is about one plus the effect size for accelerated students compared to older control groups. In order to average across studies, table 9-4 adds one standard deviation to the effect sizes for studies that use older comparison groups.

39. Eight of the twenty-five studies of enriched classes reviewed in Kulik (1992) and five of the twenty-three studies of accelerated classes cover grade nine or higher. For these eight enriched classes, the median effect size is 0.40, the same as for enrichment studies overall. The five studies of accelerated classes have a median effect size of 1.1 and a mean of 1.02. In comparison with studies of lower grade levels, these give the most plausible approximations to the possible effects of enriched and accelerated curricular tracking in high school. Five of the enrichment studies reviewed and two of the acceleration studies cover grade three or below. The rest are concentrated in upper elementary, middle, and junior high school.

In summary, XYZ grouping involves very little tailoring to the needs and proficiencies of particular students and produces virtually no effect on test scores. In contrast, when instruction is tailored, for both the top and the bottom of the distribution, all students appear to benefit (and there is not much impact on disparity). However, enriched and accelerated classes probably do increase the test score gap between high and low scorers, since they benefit students who already score high. To estimate the magnitude of this effect, one would need to know how the students who are left in the regular classes are affected by having the top students removed. None of the studies using comparison group methods addresses this question.

READING GROUPS. Ability grouping for within-class reading instruction has not been studied using control or comparison classrooms. Indeed, the practice is so pervasive that comparison classrooms are probably very difficult to find. As an alternative, some studies have used survey data to control for student characteristics that correlate with group placement. This almost invariably leads to the conclusion that all students would benefit from moving to a higher group or be hurt by moving to a lower group. Because such estimates are strongly biased by omitted variables, they are only useful as upper bounds. Small upper bounds can provide assurance that real effects are small, but large upper bounds are not helpful. Unfortunately, the upper bound estimates that I have seen are moderately large.[40]

Slavin is not far off the mark when he writes: "When comparing high- to low-ability groups, pretest or covariate differences of one or two standard deviations are typical. . . . Are the San Francisco Forty-Niners better than the Palo Alto High School football team, controlling for height, weight, speed, and age? Such questions fall into the realm of the unknowable."[41]

Without studies that use control or comparison groups, one simply cannot know how much reading group placement affects student achievement.[42]

---

40. For example, Dreeben and Gamoran (1986) use data from thirteen first grade reading classes in the Chicago area in 1981–82. Shifting a student to a group where the mean aptitude is a standard deviation higher increases the number of words learned by 0.53 standard deviation and reading achievement by 0.45 standard deviations. Similarly, Weinstein (1976) finds that information on reading group placement adds 25 percent to the explained variance in mid-year reading achievement for first-graders, controlling for reading readiness scores. For methodological reasons I describe in the text, I would not draw any conclusions from such estimates. However, see Eder (1981) for a defense, based on classroom observations, of the proposition that such effects are real.

41. Slavin (1990a, p. 505).

42. It is worth noting that the real purpose of Dreeben and Gamoran's (1986) study, cited in note 40, is to isolate the effects of instructional practices by comparing similar students who attend differ-

Racial Bias in High School Track Placement

Studies of tracking that use nationally representative samples of high schools from the early 1980s through the early 1990s find no statistically significant racial differences in placements or courses studied, after socioeconomic status, test scores, and past performance are taken into account.[43] Socioeconomic status, however, does bias placements, such that students from families with more education and income are more likely to be enrolled in challenging tracks, even after controlling for test scores.[44] Consequently, racial differences in socioeconomic status account for small racial differences in track placement among students with similar test scores.[45]

Figure 9-1 shows black-white patterns in reported track placement in 1982 and 1992. Even without controls for socioeconomic status or past academic performance, differences were relatively small in both years. Over the decade, movement out of vocational tracks was more toward the college prep or academic tracks for whites than for blacks, but even these differences are not large.[46] I suspect, however, that track placements are more racially imbalanced in highly integrated schools. I would also expect to find in the same schools that track placements are more racially skewed within the college prep track, with fewer blacks at the highest levels (honors or advanced placement, for example). The data exist to examine these patterns more carefully than past studies have in order to learn more about whether tracking issues differ depending on the level of racial integration.

ent schools; see also Gamoran (1986). Their bottomline conclusion is that instruction, not grouping, explains why black children in the sample learned fewer words and gained less in reading achievement than did whites.

43. See Garet and Delaney (1988); Gamoran and Mare (1989); and Argys, Rees, and Brewer (1996). Even without taking scores into account, racial differences are small. In the nationally representative High School and Beyond sample of tenth-graders in 1980, for example, the simple correlation between track placement and black or Hispanic status is only −0.13, with minorities in lower tracks. The simple correlation between advanced mathematics courses and minority status is −0.20. Moreover, differences in courses taken are predictable by academic background and prior test scores in multivariate equations, with no residual difference due to race. (See Lee and Bryk, 1988, table 6, p. 86.)

44. Studies conducted in the 1960s and 1970s also find higher track placements than measured ability would seem to warrant for students from families of higher socioeconomic status; see Brophy and Good (1974), who cite Douglas (1964); Goldberg, Passow, and Justman (1966); Husen and Svensson (1960).

45. The possibility also exists that the estimated effect of socioeconomic status is in fact due to measurement error in initial test scores; see note 27 above.

46. A related fact is that the number of mathematics and science courses taken by blacks and whites converged between 1982 and 1992, even as both groups increased courses taken in both subjects; see National Center for Education Statistics, *Digest of Education Statistics*, 1996, table 133.

Figure 9-1. *High School Seniors in General, Academic, and Vocational Tracks, by Race, 1982, 1992*[a]

Percent

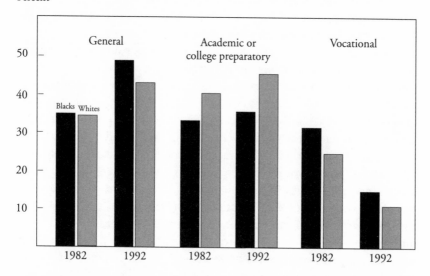

Source: National Center for Education Statistics, *Digest of Education Statistics,* 1996, table 132.

a. Student self-reports. Data for 1982 are from the first follow-up of the High School and Beyond survey; data for 1992 are from the second follow-up survey of the National Educational Longitudinal Study of 1988.

Effects of High School Tracking

Blacks are more heavily represented than whites in less academically challenging tracks. So, if track placement affects test performance, tracking could exacerbate the black-white test score gap even if all track placements were based on race-blind criteria, such as past performance. Since most high schools practice tracking, studies that use control or comparison groups from untracked schools are hard to find.[47] Therefore, just as in the ability grouping literature, an alternative methodology is to use survey data to measure the impact of tracking, by simulating the consequences of moving particular students among tracks. For example, Laura Argys, Daniel Rees, and Dominic Brewer examine the effect of tracking on high school math-

47. As noted above, however, Kulik (1992) reviews thirteen such studies of enriched or accelerated high school classes; see note 39 and related text.

ematics scores using data from the NELS:88.[48] Compared to heterogeneous math classes, they find effect sizes of –0.24 for the below average
classes and 0.37 for the honors classes.[49] Because of inadequate controls for
selection bias, however, their study undoubtedly overestimates the extent
to which tracking helps those at the top and hurts those at the bottom.

Findings from national data probably mask considerable variability
across racial and ethnic groups and across different school and community
settings. Research on the effects of tracking remains very incomplete.

OBSERVATIONAL DIFFERENCES ARE SMALL. Jeannie Oakes is probably the most
influential writer on the negative effects of grouping and tracking. Oakes
concludes that teachers of higher track classes tend to be more enthusiastic,
work harder, prepare more, and respond more supportively than do teachers of lower track classes.[50] I believe that this is so. Indeed, table 9-6, compiled from Oakes's data, shows that time in instruction, time off task, time
spent on learning, and expectations of how much time students will spend
on homework, all favor the high track. However, only the difference in
expected time on homework is impressively large.[51] That most of the differences are surprisingly small may explain why studies of XYZ grouping
show few, if any, effects.

Even though Oakes strongly opposes tracking and ability grouping,
she acknowledges that instruction is remarkably similar among tracks and
groups: "The most significant thing we found is that generally our entire
sample of classes turned out to be pretty noninvolving places. As we expected, passive activities—listening to the teachers, writing answers to questions, and taking tests—were dominant at all track levels."[52] Given this

48. Argys, Rees, and Brewer (1996). For our purposes, the NELS:88 data are special both because
they pertain to the 1990s and, more important, because teachers rather than students identified the
track levels. Earlier studies from survey data rely mostly on students' self-reports, which are known to
be less accurate.

49. These effect sizes are my calculations, using the numbers reported by the authors.

50. Oakes (1985). See also Finley (1984); Schwartz (1981); Metz (1978). All of these sources are
discussed in Gamoran and Berends (1987).

51. Oakes (1985) does not give the standard deviations from which to calculate effect sizes. Neither
does she report comparable numbers from the heterogeneous classes that she observed, which would
be the logical comparison if one were considering the effect of abolishing tracking. Finally, it is not
possible from data such as these to know what consequences the observed differences might have for
disparities in achievement.

52. Oakes (1985, p. 129). Gamoran and Berends (1987) quote this passage in support of the point
that similarity of instruction between tracks may be the reason why the literature is uneven in its
findings.

Table 9-6. *Differences in Instruction between High School Tracks*[a]

Units as indicated

Subject and track	Time in instruction[b]		Observed time off task[b]	Reported rating of class time spent on[d]		Expected homework time[e]
	Reported[c]	Observed		Learning	Behavior	
English						
High track	82	81	2	2.80	1.48	42
Low track	71	75	4	2.44	1.83	13
Mathematics						
High track	77	81	1	2.77	1.43	38
Low track	63	78	4	2.53	1.81	27

Source: Gamoran and Berends (1987, p. 425), constructed from data in Oakes (1985, pp. 98, 100, 101, 103).

a. Sample comprises 160 classes.
b. Percent.
c. By teachers.
d. By students, on a scale from 1 to 3, where 3 denotes the most time spent.
e. By teachers, in minutes.

similarity of teaching styles and classroom procedures, one should not expect large consequences from alternative grouping and tracking arrangements, except where there are substantial differences in curriculum and courses taken.

EFFECTS DEPEND ON TEACHERS. Opponents of tracking also claim that students in lower tracks become resentful and alienated from school, because these tracks confer subordinate status in the school hierarchy. Braddock and Slavin, for example, quote Ollie Taylor, a black eleven-year-old recently assigned to the low track at his school: "The only thing that matters in my life is school, and there they think I'm dumb and always will be. I'm starting to think they're right. Hell, I know they put all the Black kids together in one group if they can, but that doesn't make any difference either. I'm still dumb. . . .Upper tracks? Man, when do you think I see *those* kids? . . . If I ever walked into one of their rooms, they'd throw me out before the teacher even came in. They'd say I'd only be holding them back from their learning."[53]

But is tracking really the problem? Compare Ollie's statement to the following descriptions of life in heterogeneous classrooms, offered in 1996 by black males between the ages of nine and nineteen in the Messages Project in Fort Wayne, Indiana:

> A common message . . . was that teachers . . . favored those kids they believed were smart. Those kids were usually identified as white children. [The black students] reported that they felt unimportant in the classroom and that they were not respected in the classroom. The participants expressed anger and frustration that they were perceived as stupid or of less worth in the classroom. Some suggested that they had been stigmatized by their behavior in a previous grade.
>
> Participants reported an unwillingness to answer questions for fear of appearing stupid. One student reported that his teacher encouraged him in class but then gave him a failing grade. His response to this action: "Makes you want to go home and school not even over and you haven't had lunch yet."[54]

The similarity is evident.

---

53. Braddock and Slavin (1993, p. 51).

54 Jones (1997, p. 9). Jones is the director of the Messages Project, which was established in Fort Wayne, Indiana, in 1996. It began by convening young black males between the ages of nine and

Indications that ability grouping might even make low performers feel better come from Kulik's findings regarding self-esteem. Kulik's meta-analysis of studies with control or comparison groups shows that grouping by ability slightly raises the self-esteem of the lowest groups and slightly lowers the self-esteem of higher groups.[55] Of thirteen studies that estimate the effect of ability grouping on self-esteem, eleven show separate effects for high-ability groups and eleven show separate effects for low-ability groups. Nine of the eleven effect sizes for high-ability groups are negative, with an average of -0.15; nine of the eleven effect sizes for low ability groups are positive, with an average of 0.19. These are small effects, but they clearly run counter to the claim that self-esteem is harmed by ability grouping.

Perhaps more for black children than for whites, teachers play a central role in determining how students feel about their positions in the achievement hierarchy. The focus groups of black students in the Message Project revealed, for example, that "participants in the College Bridge Program and youth in the younger groups all indicated that they received positive expectations and encouragement from *particular* teachers. Even in situations where participants did not suggest any motivation at home, teacher expectations weighed heavily in their motivation to perform well in school."[56]

There is an extensive literature on the ways in which teachers treat students differently, based on their perceived status as high or low achievers. For low achievers, these include waiting less time for them to answer; giving them the answers or calling on someone else, rather than trying to improve their responses by offering clues or repeating or rephrasing questions; accepting inappropriate behavior or incorrect answers; criticizing them more often for failure; praising them less often for success; failing to give feedback to their public responses; paying less attention; calling on them less often with questions; seating them further from the teacher; demanding less from low achievers (teaching them less, providing unsolicited help); interacting with them more in private than in public, and monitor-

---

nineteen in small focus groups in community-based institutions around the city to discuss "things that make you feel good" and "things that make you feel bad" in interactions with parents, teachers, police officers, store clerks, and ministers. This quote is from a summary of the first meetings, in which a total of seventy-three boys participated in ten groups. Each group had ten or fewer participants and was moderated by an adult familiar to the youth. Three groups were aged nine to twelve; two were aged thirteen to fifteen; two were aged thirteen to seventeen, and three were aged sixteen to nineteen.

55. Kulik (1992, table 2).

56. Jones (1997, p. 8).

ing and structuring their activities more closely; in grading tests and assignments, not giving them the benefit of the doubt in borderline cases, in contrast to high achievers; less friendly interaction, including less smiling and fewer other nonverbal indicators of support, attention, and responsiveness (such as eye contact); less use of effective but time-consuming instructional methods when time is limited; and less acceptance and use of their ideas.[57] Moreover, students seem to understand the distinctions of status that these behaviors convey.[58] The distinctions will be more important for black students than for whites if, as discussed in chapter 8, blacks are more affected by teacher perceptions than whites, and more represented among students of whom teachers expect less. Unfortunately, researchers know little about the pervasiveness of these practices in classrooms or their consequences for student achievement.

In the end, the fundamental problem is not ability grouping or tracking per se. Instead, for critics and proponents alike, the problem is the expected quality of instruction for the students about whom they are most concerned. If critics could believe that teachers would be assigned fairly, placements would be flexibly based on students' progress, and teaching would really be tailored to children's needs, they might cease to object. Similarly, if proponents felt assured that the quality of instruction for students at the top of the class would not decline under more heterogeneous arrangements, they might lower their defenses.

Instructional Interventions

Few instructional interventions specifically aim to reduce the black-white test score gap. However, many aim to assist children who are at risk of failure—and these children are frequently black.[59] Improving achievement among black students who are at risk of failure is one way to narrow the black-white test score gap.

Credible claims of remarkable progress for a few students, a few classrooms, or a few schools are common enough. Such successes are regarded

---

57. Multiple references for each of these items are available in Good (1987).

58. See, for example, Weinstein and others (1987).

59. For a review of interventions that focus specifically on African-American students see Levine (1994). For interventions focused on at-risk students in general, see Slavin, Karweit, and Madden, (1989); Slavin and Madden (1989).

as special cases, dependent on a few talented leaders.[60] The more interesting and formidable challenge is to replicate success for many students in many classrooms across many schools, by improving the performance of many average teachers and administrators.[61] Recent news reports of small test score improvements for students in several major city school districts suggest that this might be possible. And there is evidence from a current crop of highly touted interventions for students at risk of failure that makes one hopeful. These include Success for All, the Reading Recovery tutoring program, Henry Levin's Accelerated Schools Program, and James Comer's School Development Program.[62] Evidence of effectiveness is most extensive for Success for All.[63]

Success for All

Success for All is the only well-documented widely replicated program to improve elementary school instruction that uses comparison groups and covers large numbers of black children across several states and cities. While most of the children are African American and many others are nonwhite minorities, the program is based on principles that come from general research findings, where race is not a focus. Similar principles underlie many other programs that have not been so carefully evaluated. Hence the findings discussed below are indicative of broader possibilities.

Based at Johns Hopkins University in the Center for Research on the Education of Students Placed at Risk (CRESPAR), and strongly identified

---

60. A case in point is Marva Collins, whose apparent success with inner-city children in Chicago has been the subject of the CBS television program "Sixty Minutes" and presented in a biographical movie, in which she is portrayed by Cicely Tyson. Collins's work is widely regarded as idiosyncratic. However, in chapter 8 above I discuss an effort to spread her ideas to schools in Oklahoma.

61. For an interesting journalistic account of how difficult this can be, see Sara Mosle, "Public Education's Last, Best Chance," *New York Times Magazine*, August 31, 1997, pp. 30–61.

62. Ross and others (1995) compare the success of Reading Recovery with that of Success for All and find that Success for All is more effective overall, but Reading Recovery appears to have a stronger effect on passage comprehension (one of four measures of reading progress). This is especially true for students who received individualized tutoring. See also Farkas and Vicknair (1995) for a report on another tutoring program that seems to be having some success with disadvantaged students at relatively low cost; and Wasik and Slavin (1993) for a comparison of five tutoring programs. For the Accelerated Schools Program, see Levin (1991a, 1991b); Hoffenberg, Levin, and Associates (1993); cited in Barnett (1996). For the School Development Program, see Haynes and Comer (1993); Becker and Hedges (1992). More extensive reading lists are available from the national offices of these programs.

63. Further, it seems likely that effects on test scores will be smaller for programs that are less directive about the organization of learning and what teachers should do in the classroom.

with Robert Slavin, the Success for All initiative began in a single Baltimore elementary school in 1987. It currently operates in roughly 300 schools in seventy districts in twenty-four states. It aims to head off later school failure by making sure that students placed at risk have a firm foundation in reading.

Success for All preschool and kindergarten programs emphasize language skills and prereading activities, such as story telling, music, and art. An early reading curriculum based on principles that have been established through research begins in the second semester of kindergarten or in first grade. Students spend most of the day in heterogeneous classes. However, for ninety minutes each day students from first through third (and sometimes up to sixth) grade regroup across classes and grade levels into small classes that are more homogeneous in current reading proficiency.

Regrouping in this way for reading instruction allows all children to receive instruction at the same time. This replaces the typical arrangement for elementary schoolrooms where the teacher works with one reading group at a time while other students work at their seats alone. Students who need help receive an additional twenty minutes of one-on-one tutoring by certified teachers each day. Teachers and tutors assess individual progress every eight weeks and adjust group placement accordingly. While "the particular elements of SFA may vary from school to school," Slavin and colleagues report, "there is one factor we try to make consistent in all schools: a relentless focus on the success of every child. . . . Success does not come from piling on additional services, but from coordinating human resources around a well-defined goal, constantly assessing progress toward that goal, and never giving up until success is achieved."[64] This responsiveness pays dividends when the school receives guidance to ensure the quality of implementation. Schools that attempt SFA without help from CRESPAR tend to witness less student progress.[65]

For measuring effects, schools in the program are matched to comparison schools with students that have similar ethnic profiles, poverty levels, and patterns of past performance on standardized examinations.[66] Further, individual students in the Success for All schools are matched on baseline

---

64. Slavin and others (1996, p. 66).

65. Based on a talk that Robert Slavin gave at Harvard's Graduate School of Education, September 26, 1997.

66. For purposes of analysis, each grade-level cohort of students at a school is considered a replication of the program. The summary assessment of twenty-three schools in Slavin and others (1996) includes fifty-five such replications. Some of these cohorts started the program in kindergarten and some in first grade.

Table 9-7. *Effects of Success for All on Standardized Test Scores, First through Fifth Grades*[a]

Effect sizes

Sample, test, and summary statistic	First grade	Second grade	Third grade	Fourth grade	Fifth grade
Top 75 percent					
Durrell Oral Reading	0.46	0.36	0.34	. . .	. . .
Woodcock Passage Comprehension	0.42	0.38	0.44	0.40	0.64
Woodcock Word Attack	0.82	0.68	0.45	0.47	0.70
Woodcock Word Identification	0.51	0.42	0.34	0.42	0.62
Gray Oral Reading Comprehension	. . .	. . .	. . .	0.29	0.48
Gray Oral Passage Reading	. . .	. . .	. . .	0.47	0.73
Summary statistic					
Mean effect size	0.55	0.46	0.39	0.41	0.63
Number of school cohorts	55	36	33	13	6
Bottom 25 percent					
Durrell Oral Reading	0.34	0.43	0.43	. . .	. . .
Woodcock Passage Comprehension	0.41	0.50	0.72	1.29	0.84
Woodcock Word Attack	0.71	0.79	0.46	0.47	0.87
Woodcock Word Identification	0.43	0.66	0.53	1.17	0.99
Gray Oral Reading Comprehension	. . .	. . .	. . .	0.88	0.91
Gray Oral Passage Reading	. . .	. . .	. . .	0.62	0.50
Summary statistic					
Mean effect size	0.47	0.60	0.53	0.88	0.82
Number of school cohorts	55	36	33	13	6

Source: Author's calculations based on Slavin and others (1996, tables 2-6).

a. All effects are different from zero at $p < 0.01$. Note that effect sizes reported for the bottom 25 percent are computed using the overall pooled standard deviation, and therefore differ from those presented by Slavin and colleagues, who use the standard deviation for the bottom 25 percent.

test scores to individuals in the comparison schools. Table 9-7 shows effect sizes for various examinations for the top 75 percent and the bottom 25 percent of students on pretests.[67] These effect sizes compare scores for Success for All and control students, divided by the pooled standard deviation across all students in the sample, so that the effect sizes for the top 75

67. Hanushek and others (1994) point out that early testing using the California Achievement Test gave less encouraging results, and the test was not used in later evaluations. It is possible that the tests currently used (see table 9-7) are better measures of the specific skills emphasized in Success for All.

percent and those for the bottom 25 percent are directly comparable.[68] All effect sizes are statistically significant at the 0.01 level or better, in favor of Success for All. Moreover, after first grade, effect sizes are larger for the bottom 25 percent of students.[69] In other words, the program not only increases overall performance—it also helps low-scoring students the most.

Aside from the cost of setting up preschool and full-day kindergarten programs, most of the expenses for Success for All can be covered by redirecting funds from existing state and federal programs.[70] Success for All shows that it is possible to produce sustained improvement in students' achievement test scores when schools and communities make the commitment to do so. Commitment alone is not sufficient, however. Success for All draws on years of research on reading instruction, and it also has a well-oiled machine—albeit with less than infinite capacity—to manage dissemination and replication.

Should Instruction Differ for Black and White Students?

For now, I see little reason to believe that different instructional methods or curriculums are required for black and white students—the same work for both.[71] This is not inconsistent with the view that schools should pay special attention to race, ethnicity, and social class, so that students,

---

68. Thus for the bottom 25 percent, the effect sizes shown in table 9-7 differ from those reported by Slavin and others (1996), who use the standard deviation only among the bottom 25 percent. Their procedure facilitates direct comparison with other programs that serve students similar to those in the bottom 25 percent, but the results may be misleading when compared with effect sizes computed using the overall standard deviation.

69. This tendency for effect sizes to be larger at higher grade levels may be due to the fact that the older cohorts tend to be at schools that start Success for All in kindergarten or prekindergarten, while the younger cohorts more often started the program in first grade. In addition, schools that have been implementing the program longer produce larger effect sizes, which suggests that schools improve with practice.

70. See Barnett (1996) for an assessment of the cost-effectiveness of Success for All, the Accelerated Schools Program, and the School Development Program. Hanushek (1994) points out that an effective tutoring program, such as Reading Recovery, may be more efficient for some schools and some students than the more elaborate schoolwide programs like Success for All.

71. Admittedly, scholars continue to disagree about which "traditional" approaches do in fact work. For example, whole language instruction in reading (whereby children learn to read whole words in context, instead of using phonics) is currently under attack because recent research finds that it is not effective; see the exchange of views in *Education Week*, March 20, 1996. Indeed, the value of this approach has been questioned for some time, because it does not normally give students the word attack skills that they need to become good readers. For a review of many meta-analyses of techniques of instruction in education, see Wang, Haertel, and Walberg (1993). See also Tomlinson and Walberg (1986); Waxman and Walberg (1991); Slavin, Karweit, and Madden (1989).

teachers, and parents from disparate backgrounds might understand one another and collaborate more effectively. Further, it makes sense that some teaching styles and school environments are better suited to children from particular backgrounds. One common hypothesis is that all children learn more when their home and school environments are well matched—that is, when there is cultural congruence. Some black children, especially those from low-income households, come from home environments that differ systematically from the typical white mainstream to which schools and teachers are usually oriented.

Wade Boykin of Howard University, and several of his former students, lead current research on this topic. They find that black children in early elementary school tend to do better on both memory and reasoning tasks, relative to matched whites, when teachers allow "verve." Allowing verve means mixing or switching back and forth between tasks, rather than focusing on one task at a time for longer periods. Both black and white children tend to improve when tasks are mixed, but black children improve more.[72]

In several other projects, Boykin and Brenda Allen find that black children from low-income backgrounds do better when classes include physical movement, when music plays in the background or is directly part of the instruction, and when they work in teams for group rather than individual rewards.[73] The authors report that these features of the classroom are consistent with the children's descriptions of their home environments. They are careful to say that their findings are context-specific to the children in their samples and may not be applicable to other times and places. This work is in the early stages of development, but it is clearly worth pursuing and broadening.

Do Black Teachers Raise the Test Scores of Black Children?

One version of the cultural congruence hypothesis is that black children should learn more in classes taught by black teachers. The evidence is mixed, however. Richard Murnane studied the learning gains of black students in first through third grade classrooms in New Haven, Connecticut,

---

72. Boykin and others (1997). They report one exception: they find that black children of high socioeconomic status do not improve under the verve condition.

73. See Allen and Boykin (1991); and Allen and Boykin (1992). Although the research varies in quality, other writers also suggest that the learning styles of black children are more holistic (Cooper, 1989; O'Neil, 1990; Venson, 1990), and that black children are helped by verbal communication and cooperative social arrangements (Hale-Benson, 1982, 1990; Madhere, 1989; Boykin, 1986; Clark, 1990; Nelson-LeGall and Jones, 1990; Patchen, 1982; Shade, 1989).

in 1970–72.[74] He found that black teachers with less than six years of experience were more effective at raising children's reading and mathematics scores than white teachers with the same level of experience. In his multivariate analysis for gains in both reading and mathematics scores, black teachers were more effective by between a quarter and a half standard deviation, with the greatest difference for reading. Black and white teachers with more than six years of experience were more similar to one another in effectiveness, but black teachers still held a small advantage.

George Farkas and colleagues studied a large school district in the late 1980s.[75] They found that black seventh- and eighth-graders were absent from school less frequently when they had black teachers, other things equal. However, being taught by an African American did not affect students' scores on a social studies test matched to the district-level curriculum. Ronald Ehrenberg, Daniel Goldhaber, and Dominic Brewer use data for eighth- and tenth-graders from the NELS:88 to study gains in tests on history, reading, mathematics, and science.[76] They do not find statistically significant effects of teachers' race on scores for whites, blacks, or Hispanics. Finally, Ehrenberg and Brewer analyze data for 1966 from the Equality of Educational Opportunity study.[77] After controlling for teachers' verbal scores and other characteristics, they find that compared with white teachers, black teachers were associated with lower gains for elementary students and white high school students, and with higher gains for black high school students.

Karl Alexander, Doris Entwisle, and Maxine Thompson analyze data from twenty Baltimore schools in the Beginning School Study in the 1982-83 school year, looking at gains in scores on the California Achievement Test from the beginning to the end of the first grade. They report that "black performance falls short of white only in the classrooms of high-SES [socioeconomic status] teachers."[78] However, tables 9-8 and 9-9 here show new calculations by Alexander, which suggest that teacher's race and socioeconomic status interact. Compared with all other teachers, high status

74. Murnane (1975).
75. Farkas and others (1990).
76. Ehrenberg, Goldhaber, and Brewer (1995).
77. Ehrenberg and Brewer (1995).
78. Alexander, Entwisle, and Thompson (1987, p. 674). Two points are important here. First, the Beginning School Study is unusual in that the black and white students are much more similar academically than in most other studies. Second, in the analysis, teacher's socioeconomic status is based on the occupation of the head of household when the teacher was a child.

Table 9-8. *Teachers' Socioeconomic Status and Fall-to-Spring Test Score Gains, by Race of Teachers and Students, First Grade, Baltimore, 1982–83*[a]

Teachers' race and measure	Low socioeconomic status teachers		High socioeconomic status teachers	
	Black students	White students	Black students	White students
Black teachers				
Fall verbal scores	284.5	283.7	280.7	286.6
Gain through spring	54.9	56.2	56.3	85.4
Fall mathematics scores	292.7	298.1	292.5	301.0
Gain through spring	50.4	41.7	39.3	69.1
White teachers				
Fall verbal scores	290.9	274.4	265.6	273.3
Gain through spring	40.7	53.4	61.8	70.0
Fall mathematics scores	274.3	279.3	278.3	289.2
Gain through spring	47.7	61.6	55.5	55.3

Source: Data are from the Beginning School Study for the 1982–83 school year. Data were provided by Karl Alexander, Johns Hopkins University. Sample sizes appear in table 9-9.

a. Scores are on the California Achievement Test for a random sample of first-graders from twenty Baltimore schools.

black teachers are the best at producing gains in both verbal and mathematics scores for white students, but for black students they are average in producing gains in verbal scores and below average for mathematics scores. Only black teachers of low socioeconomic status produce higher gains for black students than for white students, and then only in mathematics, where they produce very low gains for white students.

On the one hand, black teachers of high socioeconomic status may have expected more of white students or worked harder with them than other teachers. On the other, the best results for black students, especially in mathematics, were associated with black teachers of low socioeconomic status and white teachers of high socioeconomic status. It seems quite plausible that low status black teachers and high status white teachers are the most comfortable with black children of low socioeconomic status.[79]

79. To explain this point in more detail would require venturing on quite delicate and speculative ground in psychoanalyzing teachers. Here, let me simply suggest that these particular groups of teachers might feel the least "threatened" by black children of low socioeconomic status, and be the most inclined to believe that such children can achieve at high levels.

Table 9-9. *Effect Sizes of Teachers' Socioeconomic Status on Fall-to-Spring Test Score Gains, by Race of Teachers and Students, First Grade, Baltimore, 1982–83*[a]

	Black teachers		White teachers	
Item	Black students	White students	Black students	White students
Effect size for verbal scores	0.03	0.64	0.46	0.37
p value[b]	0.17	0.001	0.05	0.17
Number of students with				
High socioeconomic status teachers	83	42	38	50
Low socioeconomic status teachers	124	102	17	16
Effect size for mathematics scores	–0.37	0.92	0.26	–0.21
p value[b]	0.005	0.0001	0.32	0.44
Number of students with				
High socioeconomic status teachers	83	40	38	49
Low socioeconomic status teachers	120	100	20	28

Source: Author's calculations based on data used for table 9-8.

a. Scores are on the California Achievement Test for a random sample of first-graders from twenty Baltimore schools. Effect sizes are calculated as the mean gain with teachers of high socioeconomic status minus the mean gain with teachers of low socioeconomic status, divided by the overall standard deviation of student-level gains in verbal or mathematics scores. For both reading and mathematics, the standard deviation in gains (45.4 and 29.9, respectively) is roughly the same as the standard deviation in fall levels (38.2 and 30.4, respectively), so either can be used to compute the effect size.

b. *P* values are for the within-race effect of teachers' socioeconomic status.

These findings for black teachers of high socioeconomic status are reminiscent of the findings for high status black children by Boykin and colleagues. One might say that in both cases, blacks of high socioeconomic status responded more like whites than whites did: the teachers were the most effective with white students, and the students were the least responsive to teaching practices allowing for verve. Both findings indicate that distinctions of social class may be as important as racial distinctions for understanding the black-white achievement gap and how to reduce it.

The Test Scores of Teachers

Teachers differ greatly in effectiveness. The difference between a good teacher and a bad teacher can be a full grade level of achievement in a school year.[80] But social scientists are unable to identify and measure most of the characteristics that make one teacher more effective than another. No one characteristic is a reliable predictor of a teacher's performance. Nor are most teachers uniformly good or bad in every subject or with all types of students. Nevertheless, research tends to find that teachers who have attended better colleges or scored higher on standardized examinations are more successful at helping their students to score higher.[81] One hypothesis is that teachers who score high on tests are good at teaching students to do well on tests or that they place greater emphasis on test-taking skills. By this reasoning, test score differences overstate differences in how much children have learned. I have found no research that tries to test the validity of this hypothesis or to gauge the magnitude of any associated overstatement of differences in learning.

In this section, I review evidence from Texas in the 1980s showing that teachers' scores were lower in districts where larger percentages of students were black or Hispanic.[82] I also present evidence that this contributed to Texas's black-white test score gap among students. Finally, I use data from Alabama to show that certification testing reduces the number of people who enter the teaching profession with weak basic skills. In the process, it narrows the skill gap between new black and white teachers. I suggest that because rejected candidates would probably have taught disproportionately in black districts, initial certification testing for teachers is probably helping to narrow the test score gap between black and white students.

Teachers' Scores and the Percentage of Black Students

In 1986 the State of Texas tested all of its teachers with the Texas Examination of Current Administrators and Teachers (TECAT), a basic test of literacy skills. Table 9-10 examines teachers' TECAT scores and their

---

80. See Hanushek (1992).

81. See the meta-analysis in Greenwald, Hedges, and Laine (1996, table 1). In a response in the same journal, Hanushek (1996a) disputes their interpretation of the evidence, but he does not question the findings regarding teachers' test scores. For other evidence on college training and test scores for teachers, see Ehrenberg and Brewer (1994, 1995); Ferguson (1991a, 1991b); Ferguson and Ladd (1996); Hanushek (1972); Straus and Sawyer (1986); Winkler (1975).

82. For additional statistical estimates using these data, see Ferguson (1991a, 1991b). Also, John Kain is currently assembling a large data set for Texas with which to study student performance at the individual level; see Kain (1995); Kain and Singleton (1996).

Table 9-10. *Effects of Percent Minority on Teacher Test Scores and of Teacher Test Scores on Student Mathematics Achievement, Texas*[a]

	Dependent variable						
	TECAT scores		Mathematics scores, 1988				Difference in gains[b]
			Fifth grade		Eleventh grade		
Explanatory variable	*Black teachers*	*White teachers*					
	(1)	*(2)*	*(3)*	*(4)*	*(5)*	*(6)*	*(7)*
TECAT scores							
High school teachers	...	...	...	...	...	0.128	0.164
						(3.83)	(2.09)
Elementary teachers	...	...	...	0.146	...	...	−0.179
				(2.96)			(2.13)
Percent minority students[c]							
Black	−0.031	−0.014	−0.006	−0.0004	−0.019	−0.015	−0.012
	(3.52)	(9.58)	(1.81)	(0.12)	(7.83)	(5.70)	(2.07)
Hispanic	−0.013	−0.010	−0.008	−0.007	−0.014	−0.013	−0.007
	(2.93)	(14.03)	(3.35)	(2.78)	(8.33)	(7.73)	(1.91)

Mathematics scores, 1986

Third grade	...	...	0.394	0.367	...	...	...
			(12.08)	(11.41)			
Ninth grade	...	...	...	...	0.455	0.438	...
					(16.92)	(16.15)	
Additional variables[d]	*	*	yes	yes	yes	yes	yes
Summary statistic							
Number of districts	386	919	884	884	853	853	849
$\bar{R}^2$	0.03	0.19	0.46	0.47	0.72	0.73	0.04

Source: Author's calculations using data from the Texas Education Agency. For a detailed description of the data, see Ferguson (1991a).

a. Observations are for districts and data are district-level averages; Houston and Dallas are not included in the analysis. Teachers' scores on the Texas Examination of Current Administrators and Teachers and students' mathematics scores are measured in standard deviations of the mean scores among districts. In both cases, this standard deviation is roughly one-third the standard deviation of the state-wide distribution of scores among individuals. To correct for heteroskedasticity, each observation in each regression is weighted by the square root of student enrollment. t statistics are in parentheses.

b. Ninth through eleventh grades minus third through fifth grades.

c. Scaled from 0 to 100.

d. Asterisk denotes that constant term is the only control variable. Otherwise, control variables include teachers per student; percent of teachers with master's degrees; percent of teachers with five or more years of experience; percent adult population with more than high school education; percent of adult population with high school education; log per capita income; percent children in poverty; percent female-headed families; percent in public schools; percent migrant farm worker students; percent English is second language; and indicator variables for city, suburb, town, non-metro city, rural, Mexican border high-poverty district.

students' scores on mathematics achievement tests. Black teachers had lower scores than white teachers by more than one standard deviation, and black teachers were more likely than white teachers to teach in districts with many black students (table 9-10, column 1).[83] Moreover, white teachers who taught in districts with higher concentrations of black students tended to have lower scores than other white teachers (table 9-10, column 2). In Texas, as certainly in other states, attracting and retaining talented people with strong skills to teach in the districts where black students are heavily represented is part of the unfinished business of equalizing educational opportunity.[84]

Teachers' Scores and the Black-White Test Score Gap for Students

Estimates using the Texas data and standard econometric specifications for education production functions show that teachers' scores on TECAT are important predictors of their students' mathematics scores (table 9-10, columns 4 and 6).[85] In addition, teachers' scores help to explain why average mathematics scores are lower in districts with higher proportions of black students.[86] However, one cannot be sure that teachers' test scores affect students' scores, because teachers' scores might be standing in for some omitted variables that are correlated with both teachers' and students' scores. Fortunately, the availability of separate scores for elementary and high school teachers allows me to circumvent this problem.[87] I compare gains in test scores for high school students to those of elementary school students in the same district, and ask whether the difference in gains is larger in districts where the TECAT gap between high school and elementary school teachers is larger.[88] Using this approach, a change of one stan-

---

83. The standard deviation in the text is for the statewide distribution of scores among individual teachers.

84. Arkansas is the only other state that has tested all of its teachers. In Texas, not many teachers lost their jobs as a result of this initiative, because most passed the test with second and third chances; see Shepard and Kreitzer (1987).

85. For a detailed description of the data, see Ferguson (1991a). Houston and Dallas are not included in my analysis.

86. Compare the coefficient on "percent black among students" in column 3 with that in column 4; and the same coefficient in column 5 with that in column 6.

87. Assuming that unmeasured factors affecting differences between the test score gains of elementary and high school students are not positively correlated with differences between the TECAT scores of elementary and high school teachers.

88. The dependent variable in table 9-10, column 7 is the difference between two differences: that

dard deviation in teachers' TECAT scores predicts a change of 0.17 standard deviations in students' scores over the course of two years.[89]

If the impact of skilled teachers is important and it accumulates, unusually high (or low) TECAT scores in a district should help to pull up (or push down) students' scores, and this impact should become more apparent the longer children are in school. For example, among Texas districts where students do poorly in the early years of elementary school, those in which TECAT scores are unusually high should present much higher scores for students at the end of high school than those in which TECAT scores are unusually low. To test this proposition, I group districts into four sets: unusually high TECAT scores but low first and third grade mathematics scores (sample size is three districts); unusually high TECAT scores and high first and third grade mathematics scores (thirty-seven); unusually low TECAT scores and low first and third grade mathematics scores (twenty-five); and unusually low TECAT scores and high first and third grade mathematics scores (four).[90]

Figure 9-2 graphs the district-average math score for odd-numbered grades from one through eleven for the 1985–86 school year in each of the four sets of districts.[91] Compare the patterns for districts with similar teachers' scores. The dashed lines are districts where teachers' scores are more than a standard deviation above the state-wide mean. Even though they start at opposite extremes for first and third grade scores, the two converge completely by the eleventh grade. The solid lines are districts where teachers' scores are more than a standard deviation below the state-wide mean. Here too, students' scores have converged by the eleventh grade, but at a far

---

is, the district's mean gain in mathematics scores between the ninth and eleventh grades minus the district's mean gain between third and fifth grades. TECAT scores for elementary teachers and high school teachers are included as separate variables.

89. This number is the average of 0.164 (the coefficient on high school teachers' scores) and 0.179 (the absolute value of the coefficient on elementary school teachers' scores), both from column 7.

90. For teachers' scores, I define "unusually high" (or low) as a district-average TECAT score of more than one standard deviation above (or below) the statewide mean, where the relevant standard deviation is that among district-level means. For students' scores, "low" first and third grade mathematics scores are more than one-half standard deviation below the statewide mean for both years. Again, the relevant standard deviation is that among district-level means. For both students' and teachers' scores, the ratio of this standard deviation to that of individuals statewide is about 3 to 1. Districts with high scoring teachers and low scoring students or low scoring teachers and high scoring students are rare; from roughly 900 districts, I could identify only a few.

91. Reading scores exhibit the same general pattern, as do equivalent data for Alabama, albeit less dramatically (results not shown).

Figure 9-2. *Effect of Teachers' Test Scores on District-Average Mathematics Test Scores across Grades, Texas, Selected Districts, 1985–86*[a]

Students' score (standard deviation units)

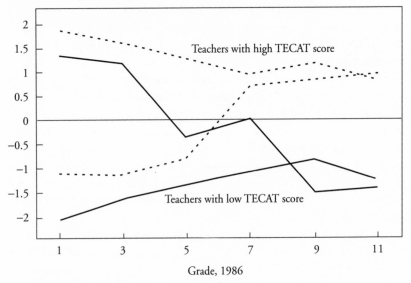

Grade, 1986

Source: Author's calculations based on data obtained from the Texas Education Agency.

a. Sample comprises three districts with unusually high teacher scores on the Texas Examination for Current Administrators and Teachers and unusually low student scores on mathematics achievement tests; four districts with low teacher scores and high student scores; thirty-seven districts with high scores for both teachers and students; and twenty-five districts with low scores for both teachers and students. For TECAT scores, "high" and "low" mean one standard deviation or more above and below, respectively, the Texas mean; for mathematics scores, the respective criteria are 0.50 standard deviations above and below the Texas mean. Standard deviations for both teachers' and students' scores are from the distribution of district-level means. In each case, the ratio of this standard deviation to that for individuals statewide is 3 to 1.

lower level. Teachers' TECAT scores seem to dominate outcomes by the eleventh grade.

Figure 9-2 is not absolute proof of causation, but it is exactly what one would expect under the assumption that teachers' measured skills are important determinants of students' scores. Also, the magnitude of the change from elementary through high school is almost exactly what one would predict with the regression estimates from table 9-10, column 7. Specifically, for two districts that start with equal student scores but with teacher's scores separated by two standard deviations, the difference in student scores would over ten years accumulate to 1.70 standard deviations.[92] This is a large effect.

Certification Testing and the Black-White Test Score Gap for Students

About twenty-five years ago, working with data from the 1966 Coleman report, David Armor wrote: "Even though black teachers' formal training seems as extensive as that of white teachers, if not more so, their verbal scores indicate that they have far less academic achievement. It is especially ironic that, when schools are concerned with raising black student achievement, the black teachers who have the major responsibility for it suffer from the same disadvantage as their students."[93] Certification testing began in earnest in the early 1980s and, as of 1996, policymakers in forty-three states had enacted some form of initial competency testing for teachers, albeit relying less on research evidence than on their own judgment.[94] Thirty-nine of these states include a test of basic reading, and some also test mathematics skills. This initial testing is usually supplemented by an additional test of professional knowledge, such as the National Teachers Exam, which is used in twenty-one states.

Initial certification testing limits entry into the teaching profession. For example, figure 9-3 shows that after certification testing was introduced in Alabama in 1981, the test score gap between new black and white teachers fell sharply.[95] Since districts with more black students also have more black teachers in Alabama, a change that increases the average level of skill among incoming black teachers should disproportionately benefit black children.[96] If, as seems likely, this pattern recurs in other states, one should

92. That is, 0.17 times two standard deviations times five two-year intervals. This is not simply regression to the mean for student scores. Note that there are two sets of districts whose student scores are far below the mean as of the first and third grades. Only those with high teacher scores have student scores above the mean by the end of high school. Scores do regress toward the mean for the districts with low teacher scores, but these student scores nevertheless remain substantially below the mean. These statements apply correspondingly to the districts with first and third grade scores above the mean.

93. Armor (1972).

94. National Center for Education Statistics, *Digest of Education Statistics,* 1996, table 154. The number of states that implemented certification testing increased from three in 1980 to twenty in 1984 and to forty-two in 1990.

95. The data are calculated from teachers' ACT scores when they applied to college. For more detail on the ACT data for Alabama, see Ferguson and Ladd (1996).

96. The simple correlation between "percent black among students" and "percent black among teachers" is 0.91 among 129 districts in Alabama.

Figure 9-3. *Difference between Mean College Entrance Examination Scores of White and Black Teachers by Year of Entry into the Profession, Alabama, 1976–88*[a]

Test score points

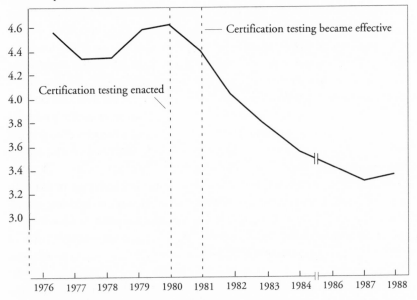

Source: Author's calculations based on unpublished data.

a. Teachers' scores are on the ACT and are not associated with any professional certification tests. The mean score is 20.3, the median score is 20.0, the standard deviation among individual teachers is 3.7, and the standard deviation among district means is 1.4.

find that black children's scores improve more than do white children's scores after states implement certification testing for teachers.

In the 1980s, certification test passing rates for black teaching applicants in some states were half those for whites.[97] Certainly, some of the black candidates who failed would have become good teachers. However, the relevant question is whether students are, on average, better off with the policy in place. I think that the answer is yes.

97. "In California, the passing rate for white test takers was 76 percent, but 26 percent for blacks; in Georgia, 87 percent of whites passed the test on the first try, while only 34 percent of blacks did; in Oklahoma, there was a 79 percent pass rate for whites and 48 percent for blacks; in Florida, an 83 percent pass rate for whites, 35 percent for blacks; in Louisiana, 78 percent for whites, 15 percent for blacks; on the NTE [National Teachers Exam] Core Battery, 94 percent of whites passed, compared with 48 percent of blacks"; Irvine (1990, p. 39) based on Anrig (1986).

Class Size

Reducing class size is a standard prescription for improving the quality of public education. Currently, the national ratio of pupils to teachers is low by historical standards. Also, as table 9-11 shows, it is quite similar at schools with a high percentage of black students and those with a high percentage of whites.[98] Despite the strong convictions of many teachers, parents, and advocates of policy that small classes are better, there is no research consensus on whether reducing class size matters, or how much. I summarize this debate briefly and then review recent evidence that reductions in class size may matter more for black children than for whites. If black children have less effective work habits and pose more behavioral challenges, the greater opportunities for individual attention afforded by small classes may be especially important for them.[99]

Recent summaries of the research literature on education production functions have reached diametrically opposed conclusions regarding the effect of resources, including class size, on student achievement. This research tries to estimate the effect of class size by comparing student achievement in schools or districts with large and small classes. To obtain valid conclusions, all the correlates of class size that might affect student achievement must be held constant. In a series of influential summaries, Eric Hanushek finds that there is no consistent relationship between class size and student achievement.[100] He reaches this conclusion by counting the number of statistically significant and insignificant, and positive and negative estimates in the literature. However, this "vote counting" method of synthesizing different studies can easily fail to detect effects that actually do exist.

Larry Hedges, Richard Laine, and Robert Greenwald use formal methods of meta-analysis, which have greater statistical power.[101] They analyze most of the same studies as Hanushek and find that several kinds of re-

---

98. It is in fact rather complicated to obtain accurate black-white comparisons for class size. Hence, the numbers in table 9-11 are only approximate. Classes of different types (for example, regular, special education, gifted and talented, remedial) have different standard sizes. If blacks are more often in those classes that are typicallly smaller, such as special education classes, it may still be the case that within any given type of class, blacks are in larger classes. Boozer and Rouse (1995) find this to be so in New Jersey.

99. See chapter 8 for the greater sensitivity of black children to teachers' perceptions, and the discussion of behavioral issues and teachers' assessments of work habits above. Also in chapter 8, see figure 8-1.

100. Hanushek (1986, 1989, 1991, 1996a, 1996b).

101. Hedges, Laine, and Greenwald (1994a, 1994b); Greenwald, Hedges, and Laine (1996); Hedges and Greenwald (1996).

Table 9-11. *Mean Class Sizes, by Percent Black Students and Percent Free Lunch Students, 1987–92*[a]

Ratio

	Percentage range				
Basis	0 to 20	20 to 40	40 to 60	60 to 80	80 to 100
Black students	17.86	17.40	16.87	16.66	17.55
Free lunch students	17.92	17.37	17.22	17.30	17.32

Source: Author's calculations based on data from the Department of Education's Common Core of Data Surveys, School-Level File.

a. Table reports mean ratio of pupils to full-time equivalent instructional staff. See text for complications in calculating this ratio.

sources, including class size, have beneficial effects on student outcomes. In the debate that has ensued, each party has applied assumptions that, if correct, favor its own position. However, the pivotal assumptions are not testable, so there is an intellectual standoff.[102]

My own view is that the literature on educational production functions is sufficiently flawed, especially in the way that it treats class size, that neither vote counting nor meta-analysis is reliable. The data are often inadequate and the quality of available studies is variable. Typically, such studies cannot compensate adequately for the possibility of reversed causation. Districts may aim for smaller classes at schools where children are performing poorly, just as individual schools provide smaller classes for children whose past and expected levels of performance are low. Hence classes are sometimes smaller precisely because the children in them have special needs for more individualized attention. This type of reverse causation might obscure any tendency for smaller class size, per se, to produce higher achievement.

Experimental studies offer a more methodologically sound alternative. Tennessee's Project Star (for student-teacher achievement ratio), funded by the state legislature in 1985, is the largest experimental study of class size ever to be conducted.[103] It operated in roughly eighty schools, with

102. Greenwald, Hedges, and Laine interpret their findings to mean that resources are used productively in most schools, but they feel that individual studies do not have enough statistical power to establish this. Hanushek rejects their interpretation and asserts that they merely answer the uninteresting question of whether resources "might matter somewhere." He points out that they would obtain the same results if resources were used effectively only in a small minority of schools—but a larger number than would occur merely by chance—which Hanushek believes is closer to the truth.

103. See Word and others (1990); Nye and others (1993, 1994); Mosteller and others (1995); Boyd-Zaharias (1994).

330 classrooms serving 6,500 students. Students were randomly assigned to small classes (thirteen to seventeen students) and large classes (twenty-two to twenty-five students), beginning in kindergarten and continuing through third grade.[104]

Children in small classes gained more in both reading and mathematics achievement than those in large classes from kindergarten through the end of first grade, but the advantage shrank between first and third grades.[105] No one knows what would have happened to the test score advantage if the children in the small classes had shifted to large classes for the second and third grades.[106] However, while the experiment ended at third grade, children who had been in the smaller classes remained at an advantage at least through seventh grade.[107] This was true for both black and white children.

The effect of small classes was larger for black children than for whites, and racial differences in scores were smaller in small classes. Table 9-12 reports effect sizes on the Stanford Achievement Test for kindergarten through third grade. It shows that after kindergarten, the effects for both reading and mathematics were typically twice as large for blacks as for whites. Other analysis shows that the effects for blacks in inner cities were even larger than the average effects for blacks.[108] Recent reanalysis conducted by Alan Krueger has found these results to be robust.[109]

---

104. Note that even these "large" classes may be below the level at which large class size is most harmful to performance. Ferguson (1991a) and Glass and Smith (1979), for example, suggest that class size may have threshold effects. The existence of these effects has not been widely explored, however, and once again, problems of obtaining appropriate data make it difficult to be certain of the levels of such thresholds. Perhaps a more dependable method is to ask teachers. Surveys by the Educational Research Service have repeatedly found, over the years, that teachers report that class size shifts from being a minor problem to a more important one in the range of twenty-four students per class; see Robinson and Wittebods (1986). If this is the case, the Tennessee experiment may have missed some of the effect.

105. Analysis of these data is ongoing. It appears that class sizes were not consistently maintained: some of the small classes became larger, and some of the large classes became smaller. This drift may partially account for the slight downward drift in the measured advantage of small classes in the second and third grades. For a discussion of this issue, see Boyd-Zaharias and others (1994). Indeed, Krueger (1997) reanalyzes the data adjusting for the drift in class sizes and finds a slight additional annual gain of 1 percentile for each successive year after the first year in a small class.

106. Hanushek and others (1994b, p. 144) assert that in the second and third grades, smaller classes "made no difference in achievement." The experiment did not test this.

107. Nye and others (1994a).

108. Krueger (1997, table 11).

109. Krueger has reanalyzed the Tennessee Star data to test the sensitivity of the results to each of several limitations. He concludes: "Adjustments for school effects, attrition, re-randomization after kindergarten, nonrandom transitions, and variability in actual class size do not overturn the main findings: Students in small classes scored higher on standardized tests than students in regular-size classes" (Krueger 1997, p. 26).

Table 9-12. *Project Star, Tennessee: Effects of Small Classes Relative to Large Classes on Reading and Mathematics Test Scores, by Race, Kindergarten through Third Grade*[a]

Effect sizes[b]

	Grade			
Test and sample	Kindergarten	One	Two	Three
Reading				
Whites	...	0.17	0.13	0.17
Blacks	...	0.37	0.33	0.40
Total	0.18	0.24	0.23	0.26
Mathematics				
Whites	0.17	0.22	0.12	0.16
Blacks	0.08	0.31	0.35	0.30
Total	0.15	0.27	0.20	0.23

Source: Nye and others (1993, table 3).

a. Small classes have between thirteen and seventeen children; large classes have between twenty-two and twenty-five children. Scores are on the Stanford Achievement Test.

b. Effect sizes equal differences in scores for small versus large classes, divided by the pooled standard deviation of scores within the respective grade-level cohort.

If smaller classes help blacks more than whites in Tennessee, the same is probably true in other states. Nationally, the pupil-to-teacher ratio in elementary schools fell by roughly 25 percent between 1970 and 1990. Therefore, this drop should be reflected in national data on black-white test score differences for elementary students. To examine this hypothesis, I chart the national trend in the black-white gap in test scores, using data from the National Assessment of Educational Progress (NAEP), the only continuing, nationally representative assessment of educational progress for the United States. Its periodic report, *The Nation's Report Card*, shows trends in the performance of nine-, thirteen-, and seventeen-year-olds (or fourth-, eighth-, and eleventh-graders). NAEP scores are standardized, on a scale from 0 to 500, to be comparable not only across time but also across age groups. I discuss only the reading and mathematics trends for nine-year-olds, since this sample is the closest in age to the children in the Tennessee experiment.[110]

Figure 9-4 presents pupil-to-teacher ratios and black-white test score gaps for reading and mathematics for nine-year-olds. It can be seen that nearly all of the inflections in the lines for pupils per teacher are matched in

110. See chapter 6 above for more on NAEP scores and effects of class size.

Figure 9-4. *Average Class Size and the Black-White Test Score Gap in Reading and Mathematics, Nine-Year-Olds*[a]

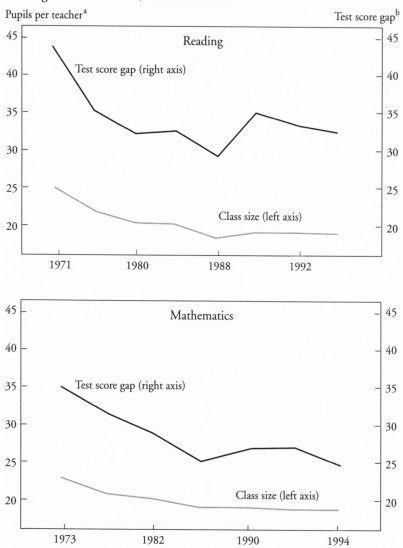

Source: Data on test scores are from National Center for Educational Statistics (1996). Pupils per teacher are from the center's Digest of Educational Statistics: data through 1989 are from the 1991 edition; data for 1990–94 are from the 1996 edition.

a. Data up to 1990 were later revised and subjected to smoothing, but this graph represents the original numbers.

b. Average score for whites minus that for blacks from the National Assessment of Educational Progress.

the lines for racial disparity in reading and mathematics scores. Since the NAEP data cover only eight observations for reading and seven for mathematics over a period of twenty-three years, this finding should not be taken as proof of a relationship. However, it seems highly improbable that so many of the inflections match by chance.[111] A simple regression analysis supports this view.[112] Therefore, I strongly suspect that the patterns in figure 9-4 reflect a systematic causal relationship between class size and the black-white test score gap. One possible explanation is that class size has fallen more in schools that serve blacks. Another interpretation, consistent with the findings from Tennessee, is that even when the reductions have been equally distributed, their impact has been greater for black students. The effect sizes implied by figure 9-4 are similar in magnitude to those in the Tennessee experiment.[113]

111. Some might argue that the appropriate class size variable is some combination of class sizes from each of the years that the nine-year-olds have been in schools. I have tried, for example, using the average class size from the years that the students were in grades one through four. In that case, the line for pupils per teacher mirrored the disparities in test scores almost, but not quite, as well as the concurrent pupil-to-teacher ratio (that is, for grade four alone) shown in the figure. Specifically, with the average ratio for grades one through four there is no inflection at 1975, and there is a slight downward slope between 1988 and 1990—otherwise, the picture is essentially the same.

112. Regressions using the eight observations for reading and the seven mathematics observations separately each produce an adjusted R^2 of 0.99. This is true both with and without the inclusion of a simple time trend. The coefficient on pupils per teacher in the reading regressions has t statistics of 5.29 with the trend variable and 4.91 without it; for mathematics, the corersponding t statistics are 2.16 and 7.91, respectively.

113. For example, the ratio of pupils to teachers in the national data dropped from 24.9 in 1971 to 18.0 in 1988. Assuming that teachers only spend about 80 percent of their time in the classroom, this change represents a drop of about 8.6 in average class size: from roughly 31.1 pupils in 1971 to 22.5 in 1988. (In translating pupils per teacher into average class size, it is commonly assumed that teachers spend 80 percent of their time in the classroom, because they have periods off during the day for class planning and administrative responsibilities. I find this assumption confirmed in data for Alabama, where measures of both class size and pupils per teacher are available.) The difference in class sizes in Tennessee's Project Star, between the midpoints of the "large" and "small" ranges, is 8.5. For Tennessee, this change reduced the black-white difference by 0.23 standard deviation (0.40 minus 0.17 standard deviations) in third grade reading scores (see table 9-12). In figure 9-4, the change in the national black-white gap from 1971 to 1988 is 14.7; the standard deviations in NAEP reading scores among all nine-year-olds are 41.2 in 1971 and 42.1 in 1988. Using the standard deviation from 1971, a change of 14.7 produces a national black-white difference in effect sizes of 0.36 (14.7 divided by 41.2). This is comparable to the differential effect size of 0.23 from the Tennessee experiment. The difference between 0.36 and 0.23 could easily be accounted for if class sizes nationwide decreased more for blacks than for whites.

Chapter 6 above provides additional analysis of the NAEP data and reaches conclusions similar to mine. The authors also show that the apparently contradictory findings of a recent analysis by Cook and Evans (1997) are not in fact contradictory.

Given that researchers cannot agree about whether resources such as class size make any difference at all, it is premature to assert that class size affects the black-white test score gap. Nor is it known whether reducing class size does more good for younger or older children. Nevertheless, the matching inflections in trends in the pupil-to-teacher ratio and differences in scores between blacks and whites in figure 9-4, and the similarity of effect sizes for third-graders in the Tennessee data and those implied by the NAEP data for nine-year-olds, make it quite plausible that much of the reduction in the test-score gap among nine-year-olds in NAEP data may be the consequence of changes in class size after 1971. Smaller classes in the early grades probably help black students more than whites: racial and socioeconomic differences in the effects of class size warrant more research attention than they have received to date.

Summary and Conclusion

The opening section of this chapter strongly confirms that compensatory preschools raise achievement test scores for both blacks and whites by the time they enter kindergarten, but studies disagree on whether the effect is lasting for blacks. I speculate that it might last longer and be more consistent if the primary and secondary schools that blacks attend were more effective. Ironically, if the gains from preschool persist for whites and those for blacks do not, the ideal of universal access to preschool might actually add to the black-white test score gap.

In reviewing the evidence on ability grouping and curriculum tracking, I find no evidence for racial bias in placements, once past performance is taken into account. There is, however, a tendency for children from families of higher socioeconomic status to be in higher ability groups and tracks than measured past performance would predict. In some cases, this contributes to racial differences in placement patterns. The mechanisms that produce these differences should be addressed in future research. In addition, heavily integrated schools should be examined separately from more segregated schools. I suspect that grouping and tracking patterns in heavily integrated schools may have a more distinctly racial component than one sees in the aggregated data.

Because a larger share of black elementary school children are in lower within-class ability groups and lower ability classrooms, any negative effect of ability grouping on children in slower groups adds to the black-white achievement gap. Research shows that grouping children into different classes by ability and varying the pace, but not the curriculum or instructional methods, has little effect on achievement. By contrast, when curriculum or instruction is tailored well to the needs of the different groups, as in cross-grade grouping or enriched and accelerated classes, some children are helped. But it is not known whether it is necessary to separate children in different classes to achieve these positive effects. For within-class ability grouping for mathematics, the little sound evidence that exists suggests that the impacts of ability grouping may be positive for both high and low groups. There is no methodologically sound evidence on the effects of within-class ability grouping for reading. Despite strong opinions on both sides of the debate, the available research yields no general prescription about separating children by ability.

For high schools, black-white differences in curriculum track placement are smaller than in the past, but blacks still remain underrepresented in the most challenging tracks. This is not necessarily evidence of bias. Blacks are represented in rough proportion to what one would predict, given the proficiencies with which they enter high school. The potential consequences of making classes more heterogeneous in terms of student preparation or motivation are unclear.

The most common complaint about ability grouping and curriculum tracking is that students in lower ability groups and in less academically challenging curriculum tracks receive lower quality teaching. Ethnographic research supports this contention. But evidence also indicates that "lows" are taught less well than "highs" when groups and classrooms are heterogeneous. Poor teaching in low ability groups is probably no more harmful than poor teaching to the same students in groups that are less homogeneous. One arrangement appears no better than the other.

When all is said and done, the main concern is quality of teaching. Any instructional regime that is responsive to the needs of individual children and flexible enough not to place ceilings on their progress is likely to benefit all children and, by the very nature of what it means to be responsive, to enhance the opportunities for those who start behind to catch up. Most children in the Success for All program gain relative to comparison groups; those in the bottom 25 percent on baseline measures gain the most. The program mainly serves minorities, most of whom are black. Success for All shows that children can make impressive progress if instruction is good and if problems such as the need for reading glasses or clothing or health care that might interfere with learning are monitored and managed.

Black children do not require exotic instructional strategies that allegedly suit black children better than whites. At the same time, there is some evidence that the fit between home and school learning environments can be improved. A few researchers have identified changes in classroom management for early elementary grades which, compared to standard practices, can help both black and white children, but appear to benefit black children from households of lower socioeconomic status the most. In at least one study, black children from households of high socioeconomic status are the only ones who do not benefit. The school performance of such children receives far less attention than it warrants, since black children are grossly underrepresented among top achievers (see chapter 5 above), whom one would expect mainly to be of high socioeconomic status.

I also consider the evidence on the effects of matching black children with black teachers. On balance, I do not find clear support for the proposition that black teachers are significantly better than white teachers in helping black children to improve their scores on standardized examinations. Indeed, questions about racial differences in teacher effectiveness have not been well researched. The little evidence that we have is mixed. In addition, there is tentative evidence that teachers' social class backgrounds might be as important as race, and in complicated ways. In any case, what surely matters most is that teachers of any race have the skills they need to be effective in the classroom. Some of these skills can be measured by standardized exams. Studies tend to show that teachers' exam scores help to predict students' scores, irrespective of teachers' racial backgrounds.

Teacher certification tests can measure skills that predict student performance and can be effective for screening potential teachers. Most states adopted certification testing for new teachers during the 1980s; Texas and Arkansas are the only states that have tested incumbent teachers for recertification. Scores from Texas suggest that the impact of teachers' basic skills on students' test scores accumulates over time. Texas districts that have more black students have lower scoring teachers, and the latter contribute to lower scores for black students.

In Alabama, testing for new teachers has narrowed the gap in basic skills between incoming black and white teachers. Since black teachers are more often matched with black students, this may gradually increase the quality of teaching in the schools where black teachers tend to be employed—in schools with predominately black student populations. Continued use of certification testing seems warranted, especially if the tests are refined and validated for their ability to identify effective classroom teachers.

Finally, I review evidence from Tennessee's Project Star that class size matters more for black students than for whites, and matters more in the inner city. Like many of the other findings discussed in this chapter, those of Project Star need to be confirmed (or refuted) through replication. Still, the interaction of class size and race is not an especially surprising finding, given the issues discussed in chapter 8 above. If, as the evidence indicates, black children are more sensitive than whites to teachers' perceptions, and black children's work habits and behavioral problems present greater challenges to teachers, smaller classes that are easier for teachers to manage may have more impact on improving black students' scores than whites'. It is probably correct that having fewer pupils per class can improve learning outcomes and reduce racial disparities. There is no consensus on how small classes should be, but few experts who think that class size matters would condone a pupil-to-teacher ratio much above twenty.

This and the previous chapter show that schools can and do affect test scores and the black-white test score gap. Further, both teachers and students have latent aptitudes that can be realized if parents and other stakeholders create the incentives and provide the resources to help elicit these potentials. Whether the black-white test score gap would narrow if schools and teachers became more effective is uncertain. I believe it would. However, if the gap were to remain because *all* children improved, that too would be quite acceptable.

References

Alexander, Karl L., Doris R. Entwisle, and Maxine S. Thompson. 1987. "School Performance, Status Relations, and the Structure of Sentiment: Bringing the Teacher Back In." *American Sociology Review* 52(October): 665–82.

Allen, Brenda A., and A. Wade Boykin. 1991. "The Influence of Contextual Factors on Afro-American and Euro-American Children's Performance: Effects of Movement Opportunity and Music." *International Journal of Psychology* 26: 373–87.

———. 1992. "African American Children and the Educational Process: Alleviating Cultural Discontinuity through Prescriptive Pedagogy." *School Psychology Review* 21: 586–96.

Anrig, G. R. 1986. "Teacher Education and Teacher Training: The Rush to Mandate." *Phi Delta Kappan* 67: 447–51.

Argys, Laura M., Daniel I. Rees, and Dominic Brewer. 1996. "Detracking America's Schools: Equity at Zero Cost?" working paper 9501. University of Colorado, Denver, Center for Research on Economic and Social Policy.

Armor, David. 1972. "School and Family Effects on Black and White Achievement: A Reexamination of the USOE Data." In Frederick Mosteller and Daniel P. Moynihan, eds., *On Equality of Educational Opportunity*. Random House.

Barnett, W. Steven. 1992. "Benefits of Compensatory Preschool Education." *Journal of Human Resources* 27(2): 279–312.

————. 1996. "Economics of School Reform: Three Promising Models." In Helen F. Ladd, ed., *Holding Schools Accountable: Performance-Based Reform in Education*. Brookings.

Barnett, W. Steven, and Gregory Camilli. 1996. "Definite Results from Loose Data: A Response to 'Does Head Start Make a Difference?'" Rutgers University (January).

Becker, Betsy J., and Larry V. Hedges. 1992. "A Review of the Literature on the Effectiveness of Comer's School Development Program," report to the Rockefeller Foundation. Yale University, Child Study Center School Development Program.

Berreuta-Clement, J. R., and others. 1984. *Changed Lives: The Effects of the Perry Preschool Program on Youths through Age 19*. Ypsilanti, Mich.: High/Scope Press.

Boozer, Michael, and Cecilia Rouse. 1995. "Intraschool Variation in Class Size: Patterns and Implications," working paper 5144. Cambridge, Mass.: National Bureau of Economic Research.

Bossert, Steven T., Bruce G. Barnett, and Nikola N. Filby. 1984. "Grouping and Instructional Organization." In Penelope L. Peterson, Louise Cherry Wilkinson, and Maureen Hallinan, eds., *The Social Context of Instruction: Group Organization and Group Processes*. Academic Press.

Boyd-Zaharias, Jayne, and others. 1994. "Quality Schools Build on a Quality Start." Tennessee State University, Center of Excellence in Basic Skills.

Boykin, A. Wade. 1986. "The Triple Quandary and the Schooling of Afro-American Children." In Ulrich Neisser, ed., *The School Achievement of Minority Children*. Hillsdale, N.J.: Erlbaum.

Boykin, A. Wade, and others. 1997. "Social Context Factors, Context Variability and School Children's Task Performance: Further Explorations in Verve." *Journal of Psychology* 131(4): 427–37.

Braddock, Jomills II, and Robert E. Slavin. 1993. "Why Ability Grouping Must End: Achieving Excellence and Equity in American Education." *Journal of Intergroup Relations* 20(2): 51–64.

Brophy, Jerome E., and Thomas L. Good. 1974. *Teacher-Student Relationships: Causes and Consequences*. Holt, Rinehart and Winston.

Clark, Maxine L. 1990. "Social Identity, Peer Relations, and Academic Competence of African-American Adolescents." *Education and Urban Society* 24: 41–52.

Cook, Michael, and William N. Evans. 1997. "Families or Schools? Explaining the Convergence in White and Black Academic Performance," working paper.

Cooper, Grace C. 1989. "Black Language and Holistic Cognitive Style." In Barbara R. J. Shade, ed., *Culture, Style and the Educative Process*. Springfield, Ill.: Charles C. Thomas.

Currie, Janet, and Duncan Thomas. 1995. "Does Head Start Make a Difference?" *American Economic Review* 85(3): 341–64.

————. 1996a. "Report on Definite Results from Loose Data: A Response to 'Does Head Start Make a Difference?'" University of California at Los Angeles.

————. 1996b. "Does Subsequent School Quality Affect the Long-Term Gains from Head Start?" University of California at Los Angeles.

Darling-Hammond, Linda. 1991. "The Implications of Testing Policy for Quality and Equality." *Phi Delta Kappan* 73(3): 220–25.

————. 1994. "Who Will Speak for the Children?" *Phi Delta Kappan* 76(1): 21–34.

————. 1996. "The Quiet Revolution: Rethinking Teacher Development." *Educational Leadership* 53(6): 4–10.

Darling-Hammond, Linda, and Milbrey W. McLaughlin. 1995. "Policies That Support Professional Development in an Era of Reform." *Phi Delta Kappan* 76(8): 597–604.

Dickens, William, Thomas Kane, and Charles Schultz. Forthcoming. *Does the Bell Curve Ring True?* Brookings.

Douglas, J. 1964. *The Home and the School.* London: MacGibbon and Kee.

Dreeben, Robert, and Adam Gamoran. 1986. "Race, Instructions, and Learning." *American Sociological Review* 51(October): 660–69.

Eder, Donna. 1981. "Ability Grouping as a Self-Fulfilling Prophecy: A Micro-Analysis of Teacher-Student Interaction." *Sociology of Education* 54(3): 151–62.

Ehrenberg, Ronald G., and Dominic J. Brewer. 1994. "Do School and Teacher Characteristics Matter? Evidence from *High School and Beyond.*" *Economics of Education Review* 13(1): 1–17.

————. 1995. "Did Teachers' Verbal Ability and Race Matter in the 1960s? Coleman Revisited." *Economics of Education Review* 14: 1–21.

Ehrenberg, Ronald G., Daniel D. Goldhaber, and Dominic J. Brewer. 1995. "Do Teachers' Race, Gender, and Ethnicity Matter? Evidence from the National Education Longitudinal Study of 1988." *Industrial and Labor Relations Review* 48: 547–61.

Farkas, George, and Kevin Vicknair. 1995. "Reading 1-1 Program Effect, 1994–95." Center for Education and Social Policy, University of Texas at Dallas.

Farkas, George, and others. 1990. "Cultural Resources and School Success: Gender, Ethnicity, and Poverty Groups within An Urban District." *American Sociological Review* 55(1): 127–42.

Ferguson, Ronald F. 1991a. "Paying for Public Education: New Evidence on How and Why Money Matters." *Harvard Journal on Legislation* 28(2): 465–98.

————. 1991b. "Racial Patterns in How School and Teacher Quality Affect Achievement and Earnings." *Challenge* 2(1): 1–26.

Ferguson, Ronald F., and Helen F. Ladd. 1996. "How and Why Money Matters: An Analysis of Alabama Schools." In Ladd, ed., *Holding Schools Accountable.*

Finley, Merrilee K. 1984. "Teachers and Tracking in a Comprehensive High School." *Sociology of Education* 57(4): 233–43.

Ford, Donna Y. 1996. *Reversing the Underachievement among Gifted Black Students.* New York: Teacher's College Press.

Gamoran, Adam. 1986. "Instructional and Institutional Effects of Ability Grouping." *Sociology of Wisconsin* 59(October): 185–98.

Gamoran, Adam, and Mark Berends. 1987. "The Effects of Stratification in Secondary Schools: Synthesis of Survey and Ethnographic Research." *Review of Educational Research* 57(4): 415–35.

Gamoran, Adam, and Robert G. Mare. 1989. "Secondary School Tracking and Educational Inequality: Compensation, Reinforcement, or Neutrality?" *American Journal of Sociology* 94: 1146–83.

Garet, Michael S., and Brian Delaney. 1988. "Students, Courses and Stratification." *Sociology of Education* 61: 61–77.

Glass, Gene V., and Mary Lee Smith. 1979. "Meta-Analysis of Research on Class Size and Achievement." *Educational Evaluation and Policy Analysis* 1(1): 2–16.

Goldberg, M., A. Passow, and J. Justman. 1966. *The Effect of Ability Grouping.* New York: Teachers College Press.

Good, Thomas L. 1987. "Two Decades of Research on Teacher Expectations: Findings and Future Directions." *Journal of Teacher Education* 38(4): 32–47.

Greenwald, Robert, Larry V. Hedges, and Richard D. Laine. 1996. "The Effect of School Resources on Student Achievement." *Review of Educational Research* 66: 361–96.

Hale-Benson, Janice E. 1982. *Black Children: Their Roots, Culture and Learning Styles.* Brigham Young University Press.

———. 1990. "Visions for Children: Educating Black Children in the Context of Their Culture." In K. Lomotey, ed., *Going to School: The African-American Experience.* New York University.

Haller, Emil J. 1985. "Pupil Race and Elementary School Ability Grouping: Are Teachers Biased against Black Children?" *American Educational Research Journal* 22(4): 465–83.

Haller, Emil J., and Sharon A. Davis. 1980. "Does Socioeconomic Status Bias the Assignment of Elementary School Students to Reading Groups?" *American Educational Research Journal* 17(4): 409–18.

Hanushek, Eric. 1972. *Education and Race.* Lexington, Mass.: Heath-Lexington.

———. 1986. "The Economics of Schooling: Production Efficiency in Public Schools." *Journal of Economic Literature* 24(September): 1141–77.

———. 1989. "The Impact of Differential Expenditures on School Performance." *Educational Researcher* 18(4): 45–62.

———. 1991. "When School Finance 'Reform' May Not Be Good Policy." *Harvard Journal on Legislation* 28(2): 423–56.

———. 1992. "The Trade-Off between Child Quantity and Quality." *Journal of Political Economy* 100: 84–117.

———. 1994a. *Making Schools Work: Improving Performance and Controlling Costs.* Brookings.

———. 1994b. "Money Might Matter Somewhere: A Response to Hedges, Laine, and Greenwald." *Educational Researcher* 23(4): 5–8.

———. 1996a. "A More Complete Picture of School Resource Policies." *Review of Educational Research* 66: 397–409.

———. 1996b. "School Resources and Student Performance." In Gary Burtless, ed., *Does Money Matter? The Effect of School Resources on Student Achievement and Adult Success.* Brookings.

Haynes, Norris M., and James P. Comer. 1993. "The Yale School Development Program: Process, Outcomes, and Policy Implications." *Urban Education* 28(2): 166–99.

Hedges, Larry V., and Robert Greenwald. 1996. "Have Times Changed? The Relation between School Resources and Student Performance." In Burtless, ed., *Does Money Matter?*

Hedges, Larry V., Richard D. Laine, and Robert Greenwald. 1994a. "Does Money Matter? A Meta-Analysis of Studies of the Effects of Differential Inputs on Student Outcomes." *Educational Researcher* 23(3): 5–14.

———. 1994b. "Money Does Matter Somewhere: A Reply to Hanushek." *Educational Researcher* 23(4): 9–10.

Hoffenberg, Wendy A., Henry M. Levin, and associates. 1993. *The Accelerated Schools Resource Guide.* San Francisco: Jossey Bass.

Howell, W. 1962. "Grouping of Talented Students Leads to Better Academic Achievement in Secondary School." *Bulletin of the NASSP* [National Association of Secondary School Principals] 46: 76–73.

Husen, T., and N. Svennson. 1960. "Pedagogic Milieu and Development of Intellectual Skills." *Schools Review* 68: 36–51.

Irvine, Jacqueline J. 1990. *Black Students and School Failure.* Westport, Conn.: Greenwood.

Jones, Joseph. 1997. "The Messages Project, Fort Wayne Urban League, Phase I." Urban League of Fort Wayne, Ind., and Taylor University (January).

Kain, John F. 1995. "Impact of Minority Suburbanization on the School Attendance and Achievement of Minority Children." Harvard University, Department of Economics.

Kain, John F., and Kraig Singleton. 1996. "Equality of Educational Opportunity Revisited." *New England Economic Review* (May–June): 87–111.

Krueger, Alan B. 1997. "Experimental Estimates of Education Production Functions." Princeton University.

Kulik, Chen-Lin C., and James A. Kulik. 1982. "Effects of Ability Grouping on Secondary School Students: A Meta-Analysis of Evaluation Findings." *American Educational Research Journal* 19: 415–28.

———. 1984a. "Effects of Ability Grouping on Elementary School Pupils: A Meta-Analysis." Paper prepared for the annual meeting of the American Psychological Association.

———. 1984b. "Effects of Accelerated Instruction on Students." *Review of Educational Research* 54: 409–26.

———. 1987. "Effects of Ability Grouping on Student Achievement." *Equity and Excellence* 23: 22–30.

———. 1989. "Meta-Analysis in Educational Research." *International Journal of Educational Research* 13: 221–340.

Kulik, James A. 1992. "An Analysis of the Research on Ability Grouping: Historical and Contemporary Perspectives." University of Connecticut, National Center on the Gifted and Talented.

Lazar, Irving, and Richard Darlington. 1982. "Lasting Effects of Early Education: A Report from the Consortium for Longitudinal Studies." Monograph of the Society for Research in Child Development 196-47(2-3).

Lee, Valerie E., and Anthony S. Bryk. 1988. "Curriculum Tracking as Mediating the Social Distribution of High School Achievement." *Sociology of Education* 61(April): 78–94.

Lee, Valerie E., and Ruth B. Ekstrom. 1987. "Student Access to Guidance Counseling in High School." *American Educational Research Journal* 24(Summer): 287–310.

Levin, Henry M. 1991a. "Accelerating the Progress of ALL Students." Paper prepared for Nelson A. Rockefeller Institute of Government Educational Policy Seminar.

———. 1991b. "Learning from Accelerated Schools." *Policy Perspectives.* Philadelphia: Pew Charitable Trusts, Higher Education Research Program.

Levine, Daniel L. 1994. "Instructional Approaches and Interventions That Can Improve the Academic Performance of African American Students." *Journal of Negro Education* 63: 46–63.

Metz, Mary H. 1978. *Classrooms and Corridors: The Crisis of Authority in Desegregated Secondary Schools.* University of California Press.

Madhere, Serge S. 1989. "Models of Intelligence and the Black Intellect." *Journal of Negro Education* 58(2): 189–201.

Mosteller, Frederick. 1995. "The Tennessee Study of Class Size in the Early School Grades." *Future of Children* 5(2): 113–27.

Murnane, Richard. 1975. *The Impact of School Resources on the Learning of Inner City Children.* Ballinger.

National Center for Education Statistics. 1996. *NAEP 1994 Trends in Academic Progress.* Department of Education.

———. Various years. *Digest of Education Statistics.* Department of Education.

Nelson-LeGall, Sharon, and Elaine Jones. 1990. "Classroom Helpseeking Behavior of African-American Children." *Education and Urban Society* 24(1): 27–40.

Nye, Barbara A., and others. 1993. "Tennessee's Bold Experiment: Using Research to Inform Policy and Practice." *Tennessee Education* 22(3): 10–17.

———. 1994a. "The Lasting Benefit Study: A Continuing Analysis of the Effect of Small Class Size in Kindergarten through Third Grade on Student Achievement Test Scores in Subsequent Grade Levels: Seventh Grade, 1992–1993, Technical Report." Tennessee State University, Center of Excellence for Research in Basic Skills.

———. 1994b. "Project Challenge, Fourth-Year Summary Report: An Initial Evaluation of the Tennessee Department of Education 'At-Risk' Student/Teacher Ratio Reduction Project in Sixteen Counties, 1990 through 1993." Tennessee State University, Center of Excellence for Research in Basic Skills.

———. 1994c. "The Lasting Benefits Study Seventh Grade: Executive Summary." Tennessee State University, Center of Excellence for Research in Basic Skills.

Oakes, Jeannie. 1985. *Keeping Track: How Schools Structure Inequality.* Yale University Press.

O'Neil, J. 1990. "Making Sense of Style." *Educational Leadership* 48: 4–9.

Pallas, Aaron M., and others. 1994. "Ability-Group Effects: Instructional, Social, or Institutional?" *Sociology of Education* 67: 27–46.

Patchen, Martin. 1982. *Black-White Contact in Schools: Its Social and Academic Effects.* Purdue University Press.

Reynolds, Arthur J., and others. 1996. "Cognitive and Family-Support Mediators of Preschool Effectiveness: A Confirmatory Analysis." *Child Development* 67(3): 1119–40.

Robinson, Glen E., and James H. Wittebods. 1986. *Class Size Research: A Related Cluster Analysis for Decision Making.* Research Brief. Arlington, Va.: Educational Research Service.

Ross, Steven M., and others. 1995. "Increasing the Academic Success of Disadvantaged Children: An Examination of Alternative Early Intervention Programs." *American Educational Research Journal* 32(4): 773–800.

Schwartz, Frances. 1981. "Supporting or Subverting Learning: Peer Group Patterns in Four Tracked Schools." *Anthropology and Education Quarterly* 12(2): 99–121.

Schweinhart, L. J., and D. P. Weikart. 1980. *Young Children Grow Up: The Effects of the Perry Preschool Program on Youths through Age 15.* Ypsilanti, Mich.: High/Scope Press.

Schweinhart, L. J., and others. 1993. *Significant Benefits: The High/Scope Perry Preschool Study through Age 27.* Ypsilanti, Mich.: High/Scope Press.

Shade, Barbara R. J. 1989. "Afro-American Cognitive Patterns: A Review of the Research." In Shade, ed., *Culture, Style and the Educative Process.*

Shepard, Lorrie A., and Amelia E. Kreitzer. 1987. "The Texas Teacher Test." *Educational Researcher* 16(6): 22–31.

Slavin, Robert E. 1987. "Grouping for Instruction in the Elementary School." *Educational Psychologist* 22(2): 109–27.

————. 1990a. "Ability Grouping in Secondary Schools: A Response to Hallinan." *Review of Educational Research* 60: 505–07.

————. 1990b. "Achievement Effects of Ability Grouping in Secondary Schools: A Best-Evidence Synthesis." *Review of Educational Research* 60(3): 471–99.

Slavin, Robert E., Nancy L. Karweit, and Nancy A. Madden. 1989. *Effective Programs for Students at Risk.*. Boston: Allyn and Bacon.

Slavin, Robert E., and Nancy A. Madden. 1989. "What Works for Students at Risk: A Research Synthesis." *Educational Leadership* (February): 4–13.

Slavin, Robert E., and others. 1996. "Success for All: A Summary of Research." *Journal of Education for Students Placed at Risk* 1: 41–76.

Sorensen, Aage B., and Maureen Hallinan. 1984. "Effects of Race on Assignment to Ability Groups." In Peterson, Wilkinson, and Hallinan, eds., *Social Context of Instruction.*

Straus, Robert P., and Elizabeth A. Sawyer. 1986. "Some New Evidence on Teacher and Student Competencies." *Economics of Education Review* 5(1):41–48.

Tomlinson, Tommy M., and Herbert J. Walberg, eds. 1986. *Academic Work and Education Excellence: Raising Student Productivity.* Berkeley, Calif.: McCutchan.

Venson, S. 1990. *Let's Education Together.* Chicago: Alternative Schools Network.

Wang, Margaret, Geneva D. Haertel, and Herbert J. Walberg. 1993. "Toward a Knowledge Base for School Learning." *Review of Education Research* 63(3): 249–94.

Wasik, Barbara A., and Robert E. Slavin. 1993. "Preventing Early Reading Failure with One-to-One Tutoring: A Review of Five Programs." *Reading Research Quarterly* 28(2): 179–99.

Waxman, Hersholt C., and Herbert J. Walberg, eds. 1991. *Effective Teaching: Current Research.* Berkeley, Calif.: McCutchan.

Weinstein, Rhonda S. 1976. "Reading Group Membership in First Grade: Teacher Behaviors and Pupil Experience over Time." *Journal of Educational Psychology* 68: 103–16.

Weinstein, Rhonda S., and others. 1987. "Pygmalion and the Student: Age and Classroom Differences in Children's Awareness of Teacher Expectations." *Child Development* 58: 1079–92.

Winkler, D. R. 1975. "Educational Achievement and School Peer Group Composition." *Journal of Human Resources* 10:189–204.

Word, Elizabeth, and others. 1990. "Student/Teacher Achievement Ratio (STAR) Tennessee's K–3 Class Size Study, Final Summary Report, 1985–1990." Tennessee State Department of Education.

PHILIP J. COOK
JENS LUDWIG

10

The Burden of "Acting White": Do Black Adolescents Disparage Academic Achievement?

The academic learning and performance problems of black children arise not only from a limited opportunity structure and black people's response to it, but also from the way black people attempt to cope with the burden of "acting white."[1]

R ECENT ETHNOGRAPHIC WORK suggests that some minority students condemn academic success as a rejection of their cultural identity. The research on African-American students has been particularly influential: a study by Signithia Fordham and John Ogbu has played a major role in making this one of the "chestnut"

We wish to thank William Ascher, Laurie Bassi, Gary Burtless, Charles Clotfelter, Michael Cook, Ron Ferguson, Francine Frazier-Floyd, William Gormley, Willis Hawley, Christopher Jencks, Thomas Kane, Alan Kerckhoff, Helen Ladd, Richard Murnane, John Ogbu, Steve Pischke, Alison Reeve, Mark Rom, Robin Turner, and an anonymous referee for helpful comments. Thanks also to Brian Komar for excellent research assistance, and to Peggy Quinn at the U.S. Department of Education's National Center for Education Statistics for help with all our questions about the National Education Longitudinal Study. All errors of fact or interpretation are, of course, our own.

This chapter is a revised version of a paper previously published in the *Journal of Policy Analysis and Management* (Cook and Ludwig, 1997).

1. Fordham and Ogbu (1986, p. 201).

explanations for black-white differences in educational outcomes.[2] According to these authors, "one major reason that black students do poorly in school is that they experience inordinate ambivalence and affective dissonance in regard to academic effort and success." Due to the history of racial discrimination in the United States, African Americans "began to doubt their own intellectual ability, began to define academic success as white people's prerogative, and began to discourage their peers, perhaps unconsciously, from emulating white people in academic striving, i.e., from 'acting white.'"[3]

The "acting white" hypothesis seems to suggest that if African Americans were as committed as whites to achievement, the educational gap between blacks and whites would narrow. This may be true, but before one accepts the argument, one needs to ask whether African-American youth really is alienated from school and hostile to academic effort. While ethnographic and anecdotal evidence indicates that some black students see academic success as selling out, it cannot say how pervasive this perspective is nor whether it is more common among blacks than whites. To answer this question, one needs data on nationally representative samples of both blacks and whites.

In this chapter we use the National Education Longitudinal Study (NELS), which provides recent data on American tenth graders, to answer three questions:

—Do African-American adolescents report greater alienation from school than non-Hispanic whites?

—Does academic success lead to social ostracism among black adolescents?

—Do the social costs or benefits of academic success differ by race?

Our analysis suggests that the answer to each of these questions is "apparently not."

We begin by discussing the acting white hypothesis in greater detail, tracing its evolution from an ethnographic finding to a popular media story to conventional wisdom, and reviewing earlier surveys that have explored the issue. We then describe the NELS data. We compare the alienation from school of black and white tenth graders in 1990, and also look at the social costs of academic success for blacks and for whites.

---

2. Fordham and Ogbu (1986); Claude M. Steele, "Race and the Schooling of Black Americans," *Atlantic Monthly*, April 1992, pp. 68–78. Similar attitudes have been documented among Chicano students and various other ethnic groups; see Portes and Zhou (1994).

3. Fordham and Ogbu (1986, p. 177).

The Acting White Hypothesis

The notion that blacks view upward mobility as selling out has been around since at least the 1950s.[4] But concern about the effects of this attitude on the educational efforts and aspirations of blacks appears to have increased in the past decade.[5] In their 1986 study, Fordham and Ogbu argue that the history of discrimination in the United States has led African-American adolescents to value educational achievement less than other groups, and that blacks have come to associate academic success with acting white. Subsequently, Ogbu suggested that African Americans had developed a "folk theory of getting ahead that does not necessarily emphasize the strategy of academic pursuit." He contrasts this with the "folk theories" of most white Americans, who allegedly saw education as a key strategy for upward socioeconomic mobility, and concluded that "castelike minorities [such as African Americans] tend to equate . . . learning standard English and academic aspects of the school curriculum . . . with linear acculturation, which is threatening to their culture/language, identity, and sense of security."[6]

More recently, Ogbu has introduced the term "cultural inversion," which he describes as "a process whereby subordinate group members come to define certain forms of behaviors, events, symbols, and meanings as inappropriate for them because these are characteristic of their oppressors. . . . The target areas in which an oppositional cultural frame of reference is applied appear to be those traditionally defined as prerogatives of white Americans, first defined by whites themselves and then acceded to by blacks. . . . Intellectual performance (IQ scores), scholastic performance, and performance in high-status jobs in [the] mainstream economy represent such areas."[7]

Shelby Steele argues similarly in his 1990 book *The Content of Our Character*: "The middle-class values by which we [middle-class blacks] were raised—the work ethic, the importance of education, the value of property

---

4. See, for example, Frazier (1957).

5. Petroni (1970), in an early description of this phenomenon, notes that black school children were afraid of being called an "Uncle Tom" or accused of "acting white" if they exerted themselves too much at school work; cited by Ogbu (1987, p. 168).

6. Ogbu (1987, pp. 154, 156). Ogbu appears to have changed his view somewhat in recent years: "It is true that in spite of the historical experience of blacks in the opportunity structure, black folk theories for getting ahead stress the importance of education. But this verbal endorsement is not to be accepted at face value. It is often not accompanied by appropriate or necessary effort" (1994, p. 289).

7. Ogbu (1994, pp. 274, 275).

ownership, of respectability, of 'getting ahead,' of stable family life, of initiative, of self-reliance, et cetera—are, in themselves, raceless and even
assimilationist. . . . But the particular pattern of racial identification that
emerged in the sixties and still prevails today urges middle-class blacks
(and all blacks) in the opposite direction." He writes that one of "the most
damning things one black can say about another black [is that] so-and-so is
not really black, so-and-so is an Oreo."[8]

Claude Steele argues that African-American students "disidentify" with
academic achievement. He describes "the basic assimilationist offer that
schools make to blacks" as follows: "You can be valued and rewarded in
school (and society) . . . but you must first master the culture and ways of
the American mainstream, and since that mainstream (as it is represented)
is essentially white, this means you must give up many particulars of being
black—styles of speech and appearance, value priorities, preferences—at
least in mainstream settings. This is asking a lot."[9] He cautions that "once
disidentification occurs in a school, it can spread like the common cold. . . .
Pressure to make it a group norm can evolve quickly and become fierce.
Defectors are called 'oreos' or 'incognegroes.' One's identity as an authentic
black is held hostage, made incompatible with school identification."[10]

Fordham and Ogbu's study focuses on one almost entirely black high
school in Washington, D.C., but they suggest that the phenomenon also
occurs in other parts of the United States. However, Diana Slaughter-Defoe
and colleagues argue that this study probably is not representative of high
schools nationally. Indeed, Fordham has acknowledged that the findings
are "not necessarily generalizable to all black adolescents."[11]

From Media Story to Conventional Wisdom

Since Fordham and Ogbu first suggested that fear of acting white is "a
very important but as yet widely unrecognized dilemma of black students,"
this dilemma has received considerable attention in the mainstream press.[12]

8. Steele (1990, pp. 71, 95, 96).
9. Claude M. Steele, "Race and the Schooling of Black Americans," *Atlantic Monthly*, April 1992,
p. 77.
10. Claude M. Steele, "Race and the Schooling of Black Americans," *Atlantic Monthly*, April 1992,
p. 75. Shelby Steele and Claude Steele offer different explanations for this phenomenon, but nonetheless their predictions for the effort of African-American students relative to whites are strikingly similar to those of Fordham and Ogbu (1986).
11. Fordham and Ogbu (1986, p. 200); Slaughter-Defoe and others (1990); Fordham (1988, p. 55).
12. Fordham and Ogbu (1986, p. 202).

A 1992 *Time* magazine feature, with the tag line "Talented black students find that one of the most insidious obstacles to achievement comes from a surprising source: their own peers," described the problem as follows:

> Of all the obstacles to success that inner-city black students face, the most surprising—and discouraging—may be those erected by their own peers. . . . Many teenagers have come to equate black identity with alienation and indifference. "I used to go home and cry," says Tachelle Ross, 18, a senior at Oberlin High in Ohio. "They called me white. I don't know why. I'd say, 'I'm just as black as you are.'". . . Promising black students are ridiculed for speaking standard English, showing an interest in ballet or theater, having white friends or joining activities other than sports. . . .
>
> Honor students may be rebuked for even showing up for class on time. The pattern of abuse is a distinctive variation on the nerd bashing that almost all bright, ambitious students—no matter what their color—face at some point in their lives. The anti-achievement ethic championed by some black youngsters declares formal education useless; those who disagree and study hard face isolation, scorn and violence. While educators have recognized the existence of an anti-achievement culture for at least a decade, it has only recently emerged as a dominant theme among the troubles facing urban schools. . . .
>
> Social success depends partly on academic failure; safety and acceptance lie in rejecting the traditional paths to self-improvement.[13]

These themes are echoed in a 1994 story in the *Wall Street Journal* about a summer program for minority teenagers at the Massachusetts Institute of Technology: "At a lunch table, over cold cuts on whole wheat, talk turns to the ultimate insult: 'wanting to be white.'" The story describes an African-American participant from a low-income area of Washington, D.C., as knowing few whites; in his world, whites have always been the unseen oppressors: "'The charge of 'wanting to be white,' where I'm from . . . is like treason.'"[14]

In an op-ed piece published in the same newspaper a few weeks later, Hugh Pearson connects acting white rhetoric to the rise of the Black Power movement. Of his childhood in Fort Wayne, Indiana, in the late 1960s he

---

13. Sophronia Scott Gregory, "The Hidden Hurdle," *Time*, March 16, 1992, pp. 44–46.
14. Ron Suskind, "Poor, Black, and Smart, an Inner City Teen Tries to Survive MIT," *Wall Street Journal*, September 22, 1994, p. A1.

recalls: "Schoolwork, my two Black Power-chanting classmates decided, was for white people. Our take on Black Power meant . . . that we were supposed to stop excelling in 'the white man's school.'" His own attitude toward school changed, and by the sixth grade he had achieved "the greatest improvement in test scores of any student in my predominantly white school." But he quotes a black classmate commenting, "I guess you think you're like the white students now." Even today, Pearson writes, "numerous black students tell of being made to feel uncomfortable if they apply themselves and get good grades. Such a tactic is the legacy of the type of behavior that I experienced in the sixth grade." He suggests that simply changing black attitudes toward schooling "could mean that within fifteen years the 15-point gap in black and white IQ averages would be closed."[15]

Although conventional wisdom has now incorporated the notion that black youths who strive to excel in school are subject to extremely powerful peer sanctions, the evidence that peer pressure accounts for current black-white differences in test performance is hardly compelling. Ethnographers have documented the existence of antiachievement norms among black adolescents. But they have not compared the strength of antiachievement norms to that of proachievement norms. Furthermore, while black teenagers disparage high achievers for acting white, white teenagers disparage high achievers for being nerds. Without some evidence that antiachievement norms are stronger among blacks than whites, one cannot conclude that they contribute to racial differences in achievement.

Previous Surveys

Laurence Steinberg, Sanford Dornbusch, and Bradford Brown explore these issues in a survey of nine high schools in California and Wisconsin conducted in 1987–88, which includes interviews with 15,000 students of different races. Their conclusions seem to support Ogbu and Fordham: "Although [African-American] parents were supportive of academic success, these [African-American] youngsters, we learned from our interviews, find it much more difficult to join a peer group that encourages the same goal. Our interviews with high-achieving African-American students indicated that peer support for academic success is so limited that many successful African-American students eschew contact with other

15. Hugh Pearson, "The Black Academic Environment," *Wall Street Journal*, November 23, 1994, p. A14.

African-American students and affiliate primarily with students from other ethnic groups."[16]

Jan Collins-Eaglin and Stuart Karabenick draw quite different conclusions from their interviews of approximately two hundred African-American students at Michigan schools, almost three-fourths of whom were attending an academic summer institute.[17] Their sample was probably more academically inclined than the average black student in Michigan. On the one hand, therefore, the interviewees may have been more aware than other blacks of whether peer pressure affected their academic behavior. On the other hand, they may have been drawn disproportionately from schools with unusually peer-supportive environments. Only a fifth of the sample reported any agreement with the statement that academic success would be viewed by black schoolmates as "selling out." Only a quarter reported any agreement with the statement that their black friends viewed success in school as "acting white."

The National Education Longitudinal Study

The National Education Longitudinal Study sponsored by the U.S. Department of Education surveyed a national sample of eighth grade students in 1988 and interviewed them again in 1990 and 1992. The original sample covered 815 public schools and 237 private schools. From each school, twenty-six students were chosen to participate in the study, deliberately excluding those with mental handicaps, serious physical or emotional problems, or inadequate command of the English language. We use data from the 1990 followup, when most students were in tenth grade. Our sample includes 17,544 students: with appropriate weights, it is intended to be representative of all tenth graders who met the criteria for inclusion. Descriptive statistics for the sample are reported in appendix table 10A-1.

Most of our data come from a self-administered questionnaire. This raises the possibility that differences between black and white students in the accuracy of reports could bias our results. Kurt Bauman finds that black tenth-graders in the 1980 High School and Beyond survey overestimate their grades by about a quarter of a letter grade, whereas whites only over-

---

16. Steinberg, Dornbusch, and Brown (1992, p. 728).
17. Collins-Eaglin and Karabenick (1993).

state them by a fifth of a letter grade. But blacks do not seem more likely than whites to overstate time spent on homework.[18] Fortunately, the NELS provides two measures of student behavior that do not rely on self-reports: absences and dropping out. Data on absences are gathered from high school transcripts, and dropout data come from other school records.

In contrast with the ethnographic data, the NELS does not describe students' speech or behavioral patterns, attitudes toward racial identity, or social interactions. But it is a nationally representative sample, and it does allow one to compare blacks with whites in ways that existing ethnographic studies do not.

Alienation from School

To measure alienation from school among tenth graders, we look at their educational expectations, their dropout rates, the effort they devote to classes, and parental involvement in their schooling. We first compare the observed means for blacks to those for non-Hispanic whites. Then we estimate the black-white difference for students whose parental income, mother's education, and family structure are the same.

Educational Expectations

If African-American teenagers see a conflict between preserving their cultural identity and succeeding in school, one would expect them to de-value staying in school. Table 10-1 shows, however, that about 60 percent of both black and white tenth graders expect to earn a four-year college degree. This does not mean that blacks and whites do in fact graduate from college in equal numbers. In the early 1990s, only about 24 percent of whites and 13 percent of blacks completed college.[19] Nonetheless, comparing the NELS measures for blacks and whites from similar socioeconomic backgrounds, blacks on average expect to stay in school longer than whites.

Dropout Rates

In 1990, almost all the tenth graders surveyed said that they expected to graduate from high school. The 1992 followup survey found that 6.9

18. Bauman (1996).
19. National Center for Education Statistics (1994a).

Table 10-1. *Educational Expectations, NELS Tenth Graders, 1990* [a]

Measure and summary statistic	Non-Hispanic whites	Blacks
Percent expecting to complete		
High school or less	9.4	11.2
Some college	29.6	30.5
College or more	61.0	58.3
Expected years of school	15.9	16.0
Adjusted mean[a]	15.8*	16.4*
Summary statistic		
Sample size	12,311	1,742

Source: Authors' calculations based on data from National Center for Education Statistics (1994b). Asterisk denotes black-white difference statistically significant at the 0.05 level.

a. Adjusted for socioeconomic status, using a probit regression analysis evaluated at the non-Hispanic white mean for gender, race, father in the home, mother's education, and family income.

percent of the whites and 9.8 percent of the blacks were no longer enrolled in school. But this difference disappears when one adjusts for family background. Earlier studies also find that among students from similar socioeconomic backgrounds, blacks actually stay in school longer than do whites.[20]

Effort

If the African-American adolescent community does discourage academic achievement, one would expect blacks to skip class and miss school more often than whites. The NELS suggests otherwise. Table 10-2 shows that about 35 percent of both racial groups admit to skipping class at least once during the fall term. And about 10 percent of both groups report missing more than ten days of school during the fall. After adjusting for family characteristics, whites miss slightly more days than blacks. School transcripts for the full academic year tell essentially the same story.

Another indicator of effort is the amount of time students spend on schoolwork when they are not in school. Sixty-eight percent of white and 65 percent of black respondents said they spent at least two to three hours a week outside school doing homework. Even this small difference disappears

20. Jaynes and Williams (1989); Cook and Moore (1993); Ludwig (1994); Haveman and Wolfe (1994).

Table 10-2. *Low Levels of Effort, NELS Tenth-Graders, 1990*[a]

Percent

Measure and summary statistic	Non-Hispanic whites	Blacks
Skipped a class, fall 1989		
Observed	34.9	35.5
Adjusted	34.8	33.4
Missed more than ten days of school, fall 1989		
Observed	10.1	9.2
Adjusted	9.7*	6.5*
Transcript shows missed more than ten days of school, 1989–90		
Observed	28.5	28.0
Adjusted	28.4	20.8*
Does less than two hours of homework out of school		
Observed	31.9*	34.8*
Adjusted	31.6	31.1
Summary statistic		
Sample size	12,311	1,742

Source: Authors' calculations based on data from sources for table 10-1.

a. Data are self-reported, unless otherwise indicated. Adjusted percentages are controlled for socioeconomic status; see table 10-1, note a. Asterisk denotes black-white difference statistically significant at the 0.05 level.

once one controls for family background. Note that regardless of race, a third of tenth-graders spend less than two hours on homework each week.[21]

Similarities in the levels of effort of the typical black and the typical white student may mask differences between the hardest working students.

21. By way of comparison, in a survey of 8,000 students enrolled in Wisconsin and San Francisco public high schools, Brown and Steinberg (1991) find that respondents spend about four to five hours on homework per week, figures apparently similar to those from other national surveys. Brown and Steinberg's survey may include time spent on homework during school hours, while the NELS focuses on homework time after school. Using data on sophomores in the High School and Beyond survey for 1980, Bauman (1996) finds that black students spend an average of approximately 30 minutes less on homework than whites. This difference is fully accounted for by sociodemographic factors. Ainsworth-Darnell and Downey (forthcoming) perform an exercise similar to ours using data from the NELS tenth-graders, but focus on the mean (rather than the median) time spent on homework by black and white students. They find a statistically significant difference between blacks and whites, even after controlling for socioeconomic status, but it is quite small: about 15 minutes per week.

Table 10-3. *High Levels of Effort, NELS Tenth-Graders, 1990*[a]

Percent

Measure and summary statistic	Total	Non-Hispanic whites	Blacks
Spends four or more hours on homework per week			
Unadjusted	39.6	40.5	34.7*
Adjusted	40.1	40.6	37.4*
Spends ten or more hours on homework per week			
Unadjusted	13.3	14	9.6*
Adjusted	12.9	13.4	10.1*
Participated in science or mathematics fair			
Unadjusted	10.3	9.6	14.9*
Adjusted	10.6	9.6	17.5*
Participates in academic honor society			
Unadjusted	7.6	7.4	8.4
Adjusted	7.2	6.9	8.9*
Receives mostly A's in mathematics			
Unadjusted	18.5	19.6	13.0*
Adjusted	18.8	19.4	15.4*
Receives mostly A's in English			
Unadjusted	19.4	20.1	16.0*
Adjusted	19.3	19.5	18.4
Won an academic honor			
Unadjusted	16	15.6	18.6*
Adjusted	15.9	15.3	19.6*
Summary statistic			
Sample size	17,753	12,311	1,742

Source: Authors' calculations based on data from sources for table 10-1.

a. Unadjusted percentages are calculated from a probit regression that includes a constant term and a dichotomous variable for gender, evaluated at the white mean for percent male. Adjusted percentages are controlled for socioeconomic status; see table 10-1, note a. Asterisk denotes black-white difference statistically significant at the 0.05 level.

Table 10-3 suggests that among these students, blacks and whites differ somewhat in the time that they spend on homework. Focusing on students who spend four or more hours per week on homework (roughly, 40 percent of all students) and those who spend ten or more hours (roughly 13 percent), whites are somewhat more likely than blacks to spend large amounts of time on homework, even after controlling for socioeconomic status.[22] To put these results in perspective, if one compares the homework effort of black students at the 75th and 90th percentiles of the black distribution with whites at similar points in the white distribution (after controlling for socioeconomic status), whites spend about one to one-and-a-half more hours on homework per week, or about ten to fifteen more minutes per day.[23]

Participation in science or math fairs may be another good measure of effort among the hardest workers. In the 1990 NELS survey, blacks are somewhat more likely than whites to participate in these events, as shown in table 10-3. Moreover, the table shows that blacks and whites are equally likely to be recognized by their schools for hard work and high performance. Black students are as likely as whites to receive an academic award, participate in an honor society, or receive mostly A's in English, although they are somewhat less likely to receive high marks in mathematics.

Parental Involvement

Table 10-4 suggests that African-American parents are at least as involved in their children's education as white parents with similar socioeconomic characteristics. Black children are more likely than white children to report that their parents have telephoned a teacher or attended school meetings. Once family socioeconomic status is controlled, African-American children are also more likely to say their parents have attended other school events. Finally, table 10-4 shows that African-American parents are at least as likely as white parents to check their children's homework.

Social Costs of Academic Success

Although black and white adolescents have remarkably similar expectations and exert similar amounts of effort, they might still differ in how much they value doing well in school. Academic success could bring more peer derision or ostracism to blacks than to whites.

Many sociological studies have noted that high school students self-select

22. In the 1990 NELS survey, homework time is reported in discrete categories (for example, two to three hours per week), so we have chosen the categories that contain the 75th and 90th percentiles.

23. These estimates are based on a linear regression of total homework time on our socioeconomic measures and a race variable. We then compare the regression residuals for white students with those for blacks (after adding together the residual and the coefficient for the race variable for black students). The differences at the 80th and 95th percentiles are around 1.5 hours and 1 hour, respectively.

Table 10-4. *Parental Involvement in Students' Education,*
NELS Tenth-Graders, 1990[a]
Percent

Measure and summary statistic	Non-Hispanic whites	Blacks
Telephoned teacher at least once, fall 1989		
Observed	57.8	64.5*
Adjusted	57.8	65.9*
Attended school meeting at least once, fall 1989		
Observed	56.4	64.7*
Adjusted	56.8	70.8*
Attended at least one school event, fall 1989		
Observed	62.3	63.1
Adjusted	62.6	68.1*
Checks homework at least sometimes		
Observed	53.1	54.4
Adjusted	53.1	57.3*
Summary statistic		
Sample size	12,311	1,742

Source: Authors' calculations based on data from sources for table 10-1.
a. Adjusted percentages are controlled for socioeconomic status; see table 10-1, note a. Asterisk denotes black-white difference statistically significant at the 0.05 level.

into different social cliques, such as "jocks," "populars," "brains," "loners," "nerds," "average students." The affiliation of each student seems to be widely known throughout the school, even across racial lines.[24] Student support for academic achievement is highest among the "brains," lowest among the oppositional crowd, and moderate for other groups.[25]

In this balkanized social system, a student's status is likely to depend on two factors: how the student ranks within a given group and how that group ranks in the school. If each group enjoyed equal social standing, the status of an individual would depend entirely on his or her standing within a group. But this is probably not the case. James Coleman writes about the 1950s that "in every school, most students saw a leading crowd, and were willing to say what it took to get in." He notes that while a few students

24. Steinberg, Dornbusch, and Brown (1992).
25. In the northern California high schools that they survey, Brown and Steinberg (1991) refer to the oppositional crowd as "druggies."

Table 10-5. *Low Social Standing, NELS Tenth-Graders, 1990*

Percent

Measure	Non-Hispanic whites	Blacks
Often feels put down by students in class	19.8	22.3
Says someone threatened to hurt him or her at school last fall	24.3	20.9
Answers "not at all" to whether other students think of him or her as popular	15.9	15.6
Says is not very popular with opposite sex[a]	21.0	26.5
Answers "not at all" to whether other students think of him or her as part of leading crowd	33.0	33.4

Source: Authors' calculations based on data from sources for table 10-1.
a. Includes those reporting "true," "mostly true," or "more true than false."

objected to the idea of such a social hierarchy, a friend of one such student offered a poignant retort: "You don't see it because you're in it."[26] As the junior author of the present chapter can attest, there is no reason to think that today's schools are any less hierarchical than those that Coleman studied.

The NELS asks students a number of questions about their social standing and how they are treated by their peers. Table 10-5 presents results on five of these measures: experience of put-downs and physical threat; whether a student thinks he or she is popular in general, and with students of the opposite sex, in particular; and whether other students think the respondent is part of the "leading crowd."

With these data, table 10-6 relates social standing to academic success for high achieving tenth graders. We measure academic success with two indicators: receiving mostly A's in mathematics (reported by 20 percent of whites versus 13 percent of blacks) and membership in an academic honor society (7 percent of whites versus 8 percent of blacks).[27] We measure the social cost of high achievement as the percentage of high achievers who are "unpopular" minus the percentage of other students who are "unpopular." When this value is positive, it indicates that high achievers are paying a social price for their academic success.

26. Coleman (1961, p. 36).
27. In regard to the first indicator, we find qualitatively similar patterns to "mostly A's in mathematics" when we use "mostly A's in English" as the criterion (not reported here). For the second indicator, the question is worded, "Which of the following activities have you participated in during this school year?" Possible answers include "National Honor Society or other academic honor society."

Table 10-6. *Effects of High Achievement on Low Social Standing,*
by Race and Gender, NELS Tenth-Graders, 1990[a]
Percent[b]

	Measure of low social standing				
Measure of high achievement and sample	Feels put down by students	Threatened at least once last fall	Not popular	Not part of leading crowd	Not popular with opposite sex
Mostly A's in mathematics					
Whites (10,284)	−1	−2	3[†]	2	0
Blacks (1,289)	−1	−3[†]	−4	−5	4
Predominantly white schools[c]					
Whites (8,715)	−2	−3[†]	0	0	−2
Blacks (472)	−1	4	6	10	4[††]
Predominantly black schools[d]					
Blacks (399)	7	6	−3	0	−15[†, ††]
Honor society					
Whites (11,586)	−2	−8[†]	−5[†]	−11[†]	−4[†]
Blacks (1,653)	−1	−6	−12[†]	−21[†]	−18[†*]
Predominantly white schools[c]					
Whites (9,732)	−2	−9[†]	−4[†]	−9[†]	−4[†]
Blacks (588)	−10	−1	−7	5[††]	−1[††]
Predominantly black schools[d]					
Blacks (514)	6	−5	−18[†]	−32[†, ††]	−21[†, ††]

Source: Authors' calculations based on data from sources for table 10-1.

a. † denotes "penalty" statistically significant at the 0.05 level; †† denotes "penalty" differs between predominantly black and predominantly white schools (statistically significant at the 0.05 level). * denotes black-white difference statistically significant at the 0.05 level. Sample size is shown in parentheses.

b. Percent of high achievers who report a given measure of low social standing minus percent of other students who report the same measure.

c. At least 60 percent of total student population is non-Hispanic white. In these schools, fifty-five black students earn mostly A's in mathematics and thirty-four are members of an honor society.

d. At least 60 percent of total student population is black. In these schools, fifty-eight black students earn mostly A's in mathematics and sixty-three are members of an honor society.

Ethnographic evidence suggests that the social cost should be positive for high achieving blacks. Table 10-6 does not support this hypothesis. Black tenth-graders who mostly earn A's in mathematics appear to be marginally more popular than those who mostly earn B's or C's, although the difference is never statistically significant. Black honor society members are substantially more popular than their classmates, and these differences are statistically significant.

The acting white hypothesis could still help to explain why blacks score lower than whites on standardized tests, however, if the positive correlation between academic success and social standing were weaker among blacks than whites. But table 10-6 does not offer any support for this view either. The social benefits of academic success are generally greater for blacks than for whites. This racial difference is neither statistically significant nor substantively significant for math grades, but it is large and sometimes statistically significant for honor society members.

If whites support high achievement more than do blacks, academic success might be less costly in predominantly white schools than in predominantly black schools. Recall that Fordham and Ogbu base their conclusions on data from a predominantly black high school. But table 10-6 does not support this hypothesis either. Although our samples of high-achieving blacks are fairly small, several of the differences between predominantly black and predominantly white schools are statistically significant. These suggest that academic success is more socially beneficial in black than in white schools.

Conclusion

Black high school students are not particularly alienated from school. They are as likely as whites to expect to enter and complete college, and their actual rate of high school completion is as high as that among whites from the same socioeconomic background. Also, black and white students report that they spend about the same amount of time on homework and have similar rates of absenteeism.

The story is somewhat more complicated for the hardest working students. Although the typical black student spends as much time on homework as the typical white student, after controlling for socioeconomic status, the hardest working white students do about ten to fifteen more minutes of homework a day than the hardest working black students. This difference may exist because schools have lower expectations of their top black students than their top white students. Despite the fact that the hardest working black students do less homework than their white counterparts, blacks are actually more likely than whites to be members of academic honor societies or to win academic awards, and they are equally likely to receive high marks in English.

Moreover, black and white tenth-graders who excel in school are no more likely to be unpopular than other students. This finding suggests that both black and white students are able to find peer groups that accept high achievement. Indeed, our evidence indicates that membership in an academic honor society is a social advantage. While ethnographers observe that black adolescents sometimes taunt high-achieving black students for acting white, it appears that either these taunts do not inflict especially grievous social damage or high achievement has offsetting social benefits.

Are there other reasonable interpretations for our results? It is possible that surveys like the National Education Longitudinal Study are misleading, because blacks are more likely than whites to exaggerate their level of effort. Bauman's results based on tenth-graders in the 1980 High School and Beyond survey suggest that blacks overstate their grades somewhat more than do whites.[28] Blacks may also overstate their commitment to school. It might be that black students are heavily influenced by an oppositional culture that penalizes doing well in school, but deny this alienation in response to survey questions, representing themselves as more engaged in schoolwork than they really are. Alienation and misrepresentation would then cancel out, to produce our NELS results.

But if this theory were correct, indicators of effort taken from school records should tell a different story than self-reports. As we have shown, that is not the case. School records show little difference between blacks and whites on attendance or graduation rates. Differing bias in survey responses between blacks and whites is even less likely to account for our findings concerning popularity: because these are based on comparisons of blacks with blacks and whites with whites, any generalized "race effect" should cancel out.

There is another, more complex, challenge to our interpretation. Suppose students choose between two types of clique: the A's, who tolerate effort, and the D's, who impose prohibitive penalties on effort among themselves but ignore nonmembers. If black students tend to find the D's more attractive, high-achieving black students would suffer no social penalty, but antieffort norms would have a more negative effect on blacks than whites, just as ethnographers have suggested. But this theory implies that blacks should devote less time to schoolwork than whites, which does not appear to be the case— at least, for the average black and white students. Furthermore, ethnographic accounts do not, in fact, suggest that high-achieving blacks are completely insulated from oppositional norms in this way. Quite the contrary.

28. Bauman (1996).

How, then, is one to account for the discrepancy between the NELS survey and the reports in the ethnographic literature and the press? One possible answer is that such accounts are correct but incomplete. Ethnographers, journalists, and some high-achieving blacks have stressed the social costs of achievement. They have not had much to say one way or the other about the possible social *benefits* of high achievement. To put this point slightly differently, ethnographic accounts of social norms in black schools say very little about the social costs of *not* doing well. The NELS suggests that the social costs and benefits of academic achievement roughly offset each other.

The notion that blacks pay a higher social price than whites for doing well in school may also reflect the absence of careful ethnographic comparisons between blacks and whites. White students do not criticize one another for "acting white," but they have many other derogatory terms for classmates who work "too hard." Blacks stigmatize effort in racial terms whereas whites do so in other ways, and one cannot predict a priori which form of stigma will be most effective. To answer that question, one would need to measure effort directly. When we try to do this using NELS, we find little difference between typical black and white students and only moderate differences between the top black and white students.

In sum, our results do not support the belief that group differences in peer attitudes account for the black-white gap in educational achievement. In contrast, disparities in the family backgrounds of blacks and whites do account for the modest differences in effort that we find between the average black and white students. Policymakers, therefore, should not allow concern about the so-called oppositional culture to distract them from more fundamental issues, such as improving schools and providing adequate motivation, support, and guidance for students weighed down by the burdens of poverty.

That the problem may be more fundamental than racial differences in peer group norms is illustrated by the troubling story of Scott Baylark and Telkia Steward, two of the top students in the class of 1986 at DuSable High School in Chicago.[29] Both took numerous honors classes. Both were given every encouragement by the faculty. Far from being ostracized by their peers, both were elected class officers and served as class leaders. Both went on to matriculate at the University of Illinois. There, they both discovered that they were poorly prepared for the academic demands of freshman year. For that reason among others, both soon dropped out.

29. Alex Kotlowitz, "Upward Fragility," *New York Times Magazine*, April 2, 1995, pp. 36–40, 49, 62–63, 85, 87

Appendix: The NELS Sample

Table 10A-1 presents descriptive statistics for our sample of tenth-graders from the 1990 followup of the National Education Longitudinal Study.

Table 10A-1. *The NELS Tenth-Grade Sample*[a]

Percent

Characteristic and summary statistic	Total sample	Non-Hispanic whites	Blacks
Male	50.0	50.3	49.1
Race			
Non-Hispanic white	71.4	n.a.	n.a.
African American	12.5	n.a.	n.a.
Hispanic	10.5	n.a.	n.a.
Asian	4.0	n.a.	n.a.
Other	1.6	n.a.	n.a.
Family income, 1988			
Less than $10,000	9.7	5.6	28.3
$10,000–$20,000	14.8	12.5	21.5
$20,000–$35,000	29.7	30.2	27.1
$35,000–$50,000	21.5	24.2	12.1
$50,000–$75,000	16.0	18.1	8.8
More than $75,000	8.1	9.5	2.3
Mother's education			
Less than high school	14.6	10.5	17.5
High school	38.3	40.1	36.4
Some postsecondary	23.0	23.6	27.3
College degree	14.5	15.8	10.7
Postgraduate	9.5	10.1	8.2
No father or male guardian in home	15.0	11.8	38.4
Black tenth graders in high school			
0–25 percent	82.2	90.7	27.8
26–50 percent	9.0	6.7	27.7
51–75 percent	4.6	2.1	20.5
76–100 percent	3.3	0.2	24.2
Summary statistic			
Sample size	17,753	12,311	1,742

Source: Authors' calculations based on data from NCES (1994b)

a. Missing values for variables are as follows: school demographics, 6.6 percent; family income, 18.5 percent; mother's education, 15.8 percent.

Comment by Ronald F. Ferguson

The first published version of this chapter won Philip Cook and Jens Ludwig the award for the most important paper published by the *Journal of Policy Analysis and Management* in 1997. Its inclusion in this volume is further testament to its impact. Many people seem to believe that the authors have put to rest the popular hypothesis that fear of acting white is an impediment to closing the black-white achievement gap. I disagree with this interpretation of their findings.

Before explaining my reasons, however, let me state some points of agreement. First, I agree that the 1988 National Education Longitudinal Study data offer no clear support for the proposition that high-achieving black students are less popular than low-achieving black students. Second, the ethnographic literature probably does overstate the amount of negative peer pressure in fact experienced by high-performing black students. Third, I strongly agree that the black-white test score gap is, as Cook and Ludwig write, much more fundamental than racial differences in peer group norms. Indeed, my own chapters in this volume describe many other factors that contribute to the gap. Finally, I agree with Cook and Ludwig that policymakers "should not allow concern about the so-called oppositional culture to distract them from more fundamental issues, such as improving schools and providing adequate motivation, support, and guidance for students weighed down by the burdens of poverty."

Two conditions must be met for the acting white hypothesis to be true. First, black and white adolescents must be faced with different peer norms for academic achievement. Second, these norms must affect their academic achievement. Like most other researchers who have tested "cultural" theories about racial differences in behavior, Cook and Ludwig have no measures of peer norms or pressures. Instead, they use measures of academic behavior—such as time spent doing homework, school attendance, and school completion—that they say should be influenced by differential norms if such norms vary by race. When they find that these behaviors hardly differ by race, they conclude that peer norms regarding academic achievement do not differ by race either.

In my judgment, however, the NELS survey does not measure the behaviors that are most indicative of adolescent norms. For example, black students may hesitate to raise their hands in class, to participate in class discussions, or to seem eager to learn because they fear social ostracism by their peers. Some blacks may moderate their speech because they worry about sounding too much like an "Oreo." Others may try to "act ghetto" in an effort to assert their racial authenticity, but as a consequence may convince teachers that they are disruptive and uncommitted to academic matters. Indeed, a forthcoming study by James Ainsworth-Darnell and Douglas Downey, using the same NELS data that Cook and Ludwig used, finds that teachers rate black students as more frequently disruptive and as putting forth less effort. Both effects remained statistically significant after accounting for family income, parental occupation, and parental education. White students may exhibit similar behaviors, but I suspect that the social pressures against acting white are stronger and more effective than those against acting nerdy. This is an empirical question, but it requires assessment of a range of behaviors more subtle than those that the NELS measures. These subtler behaviors might not be correlated at all with attendance rates or homework hours, especially when even whites do very little homework.

Cook and Ludwig also try to assess racial differences in peer norms regarding academic achievement by examining whether high-achieving students report being less popular than low-achieving students. I do not dispute their basic finding that black and white tenth-graders who excel in school are no more likely to be unpopular than other students. I do wonder, however, about the generality and relevance of this conclusion.

First, the prevalence of accusations about acting white probably varies by context. Although Fordham and Ogbu developed the acting white hypothesis based on data from an all-black high school, one would expect peer pressure against acting white to be stronger for black students in racially mixed schools. Cook and Ludwig's data suggest that this could be the case. In table 10-5, for example, blacks in predominantly white schools who get mostly A's in mathematics have been threatened more and are more likely to be "not popular," "not part of the leading crowd," and "not popular with the opposite sex." None of these differences, taken singly, is statistically significant. But the sample is very small: only fifty-five blacks in white schools earn mostly A's in mathematics. Nonetheless, this pattern differs from the pattern for whites in the same schools, and it contradicts Cook and Ludwig's overall conclusion. Conversely, answers for students in honor societies in predominantly white schools (only thirty-four such students are black) indicate no penalty for blacks, and perhaps even an advantage. Why does the pattern for students who get A's differ so much from the pattern for students in an honor society? Is it just statistical noise? One needs to examine much larger samples of high-achieving blacks in racially mixed settings and more appropriate variables before one can draw any conclusions about whether antiacademic peer pressure discourages achievement in such settings.

I also believe that Cook and Ludwig's analysis is too static. Imagine two runners nearing the end of a one-mile race, separated by forty yards. Like the bottom three-quarters of black and white students, who spend very little time outside of school on homework, the runners in this race are jogging along at a leisurely pace. One could ask one of two questions. The first is: why are the runners forty yards apart? In effect, this is the question that Cook and Ludwig ask, and they come to the conclusion that the acting white hypothesis is not an important part of the answer. I agree. To my mind, however, as one looks to the future the more relevant question is: why is the distance between the runners not closing more rapidly? Or, why is the second runner not running faster in order to catch up? After all, the front runner is only jogging. The acting white hypothesis probably *does* help to explain why black students are not closing the gap with whites who make relatively little effort.

At bottom, then, my criticism is that the NELS data are not adequate for testing the acting white hypothesis. Cook and Ludwig recognize this possibility when they suggest that their analysis of peer pressure would be invalid if students self-segregated into peer groups with different norms, and if these peer groups did not interact much. They offer the hypothetical example of students who sort themselves "between two types of clique: the A's, who tolerate effort, and the D's, who impose prohibitive penalties on effort among themselves but ignore nonmembers. If black students tend to find the D's more attractive, high-achieving black students would suffer no social penalty, but antieffort norms would have a more negative effect on blacks than whites, just as ethnographers have suggested." I believe that this approximates reality in many schools. If so, closing the black-white achievement gap would probably require group-level "cross-overs" by black students. To learn whether fear of acting white is an impediment to crossing over from the D's to the A's, one would need data on peer group membership, on students' perceptions of how their peers might respond to changes in their academic behavior or group affiliations, and on what happens to black and white students when they try to change peer groups. This goes far beyond what the NELS can provide.

Cook and Ludwig have helped to stimulate a more carefully crafted debate on the acting white hypothesis. For this they should be applauded. Still, I think the NELS data miss the subtle ways in which peer norms influence black students' effort. I also think that the acting white hypothesis is most relevant to the question of why the black-white gap does not close more during high school. In any case, there is still a lot to learn about the importance of the acting white hypothesis for explaining the persistence of the black-white achievement gap.

Comment by Philip J. Cook and Jens Ludwig

We thank Ronald Ferguson for his thoughtful comments on our chapter. We agree with him that our views overlap considerably. In what follows, we focus on three remaining points of disagreement.

The first concerns African-Americans in mixed-race schools. Ferguson suggests that our findings for predominantly white schools contradict our overall conclusion that high-achieving black students are not more likely to be unpopular than other black students, and may be inconsistent with our findings for blacks who earn A's in mostly white schools. Yet none of the "achievement penalties" that we estimate for black students in predominantly white schools using either of our achievement measures is statistically significant, which means that the confidence intervals around these estimates are consistent with achievement being a social help *or* a hindrance. Of the ten achievement penalties for African-American students in mostly white schools, five are positive (high-achieving blacks are less popular than other blacks) and five are negative (high-achievers are more popular)— exactly the pattern that we would expect if the true effect were zero.

Since all the statistically significant estimates for the achievement penalties tell the same story—that high-achieving blacks are no more likely to be unpopular than other black students—we think the results in our study are quite consistent. Nevertheless, we agree with Ferguson that additional research on African-American students in mixed-race schools would be valuable, given the small sample of such students in NELS.

The second point concerns potential limitations of our effort measures. If peer norms for student achievement differed by race, we should find differences in the levels of black and white students' engagement with school. Instead, we find that the typical black and white student have similar attendance rates and spend similar amounts of time on homework. Ferguson argues that more subtle measures of school engagement might turn up more racial differences. We agree that it would be valuable to uncover other types of student effort that differ by race and to investigate how these different kinds of effort influence academic achievement. However, the absence of racial differences in school attendance and homework effort makes us doubt that differences in other types of effort would be large. The study by James W. Ainsworth-Darnell and Douglas B. Downey, "Assessing the Oppositional Culture Explanation for Racial/Ethnic Differences in School Performance," forthcoming in *American Sociological Review* provides support for our view. On the one hand, teachers report that African-American students put forth less effort and are more disruptive than whites, and student self-reports suggest that blacks are in trouble more frequently than whites. On the other hand, these differences are quite small, equal to .12, .17, and .01 standard deviations, respectively.

Furthermore, if peer norms differed by race, high-achieving students would need to be socially isolated from other students in order to explain why high-achieving blacks are as popular as other blacks. Newspaper accounts of African-American valedictorians and honors students who are elected officers in student government provide some support for our view that high-achieving blacks are not particularly socially isolated.[30] It seems unlikely that these high achievers would have been elected class president or vice president had their popularity been limited to one small clique within the school.

The third point concerns implications for public policy. One way to narrow the achievement gap between blacks and whites is to ask black students to work harder than whites from similar backgrounds. But, assuming that effective strategies for improving student motivation can be identified, some students who are currently in low-effort peer groups may receive grief from their friends if they try to increase their effort. In this way, the acting white phenomenon could act as an impediment to reducing the black-white test score gap. Ferguson is correct that our chapter provides few clues about this possibility.

The concern that motivates our study, however, is that the widespread belief that black students do not work as hard in school as whites might distract attention from the need to equalize the educational opportunities of black and white students. We hope we have dispelled the notion that the acting white hypothesis is likely to explain much of the black-white test score gap.

30. Examples include Scott Baylark and Telkia Steward of DuSable High School in Chicago and Lauren Powell of Washington-Lee High School in Arlington, Virginia; see, respectively, Alex Kotlowitz, "Upward Fragility," *New York Times Magazine*, April 2, 1995, pp. 36–40, 49, 62–63, 85, 87; Eric L.Wee,"Students Go the Extracurricular Mile for Admission to Elite Colleges," *Washington Post*, May 7, 1996, p. A1.

References

Ainsworth-Darnell, James W., and Douglas B. Downey. Forthcoming. "Assessing the Oppositional Culture Explanation for Racial/Ethnic Differences in School Performance." *American Sociological Review.*

Bauman, Kurt. 1996. "Trying to Get Ahead: School Work and Grades in the Educational Advance of African-Americans," working paper. Madison, Wis.: Institute for Research on Poverty.

Brown, B. Bradford, and Laurence Steinberg. 1991. "Final Report: Project 2. Noninstructional Influences on Adolescent Engagement and Achievement." Paper prepared for the U.S. Department of Education.

Coleman, James S. 1961. *The Adolescent Society: The Social Life of the Teenager and Its Impact on Education.* Free Press.

Collins-Eaglin, Jan, and Stuart Karabenick. 1993. "Devaluing of Academic Success by African-American Students: On 'Acting White' and 'Selling out.'" Paper prepared for the annual meeting of the American Educational Research Association.

Cook, Philip J., and Michael Moore. 1993. "Drinking and Schooling." *Journal of Health Economics* 12: 411–29.

Cook, Philip J., and Jens Ludwig. 1997. "Weighing the Burden of 'Acting White'": Are There Race Differences in Attitudes toward Education?" *Journal of Policy Analysis and Management* 16(2): 656–78.

Dornbusch, Sanford, Philip Ritter, and Laurence Steinberg. 1991. "Community Influences on the Relation of Family Statuses to Adolescent School Performance: Differences between African Americans and Non-Hispanic Whites." *American Journal of Education* 99(4): 543–67.

Fordham, Signithia, and John Ogbu. 1986. "Black Students' School Success: Coping with the Burden of 'Acting White.'" *Urban Review* 18(3): 176–206.

Fordham, Signithia. 1988. "Racelessness as a Factor in Black Students' Success." *Harvard Educational Review* 58(1): 54–84.

Frazier, Franklin. 1957. *Black Bourgeoisie: The Rise of a New Middle Class in the United States.* Free Press.

Haveman, Robert, and Barbara Wolfe. 1994. *Succeeding Generations: On the Effects of Investments in Children.* Russell Sage.

Jaynes, Gerald, and Robin Williams Jr. 1989. *A Common Destiny: Blacks and American Society.* Washington: National Academy Press.

Ludwig, Jens. 1994. "Information and Inner City Educational Attainment." Ph.D. dissertation, Duke University.

National Center for Education Statistics. 1994a. *Digest of Education Statistics, 1994.* NCES 94-115. Department of Education.

———. 1994b. *National Education Longitudinal Study of 1988 Second Follow-Up: Student Component Data File User's Manual,* NCES 94-374, 94-376. Department of Education.

Ogbu, John. 1987. "Opportunity Structure, Cultural Boundaries, and Literacy." In Judith Langer, ed. *Language, Literacy, and Culture: Issues of Society and Schooling.* Ablex.

———. 1994. "Racial Stratification in the United States: Why Inequality Persists." *Teachers College Record* 96(2):264–98.

Petroni, Frank A. 1970. "'Uncle Tom': White Stereotypes in the Black Movement." *Human Organization* 29(4): 260–66.

Portes, Alejandro, and Min Zhou. 1994. "Should Immigrants Assimilate?" *Public Interest* 116(Summer): 18–33.

Slaughter-Defoe, Diana, and others. 1990. "Toward Cultural/Ecological Perspectives on Schooling and Achievement in African- and Asian-American Children." *Child Development* 61(2): 363–83.

Steele, Shelby. 1990. *The Content of Our Character: A New Vision of Race in America.* HarperPerennial.

Steinberg, Laurence, Sanford Dornbusch, and Bradford Brown. 1992. "Ethnic Differences in Adolescent Achievement: An Ecological Perspective." *American Psychologist* 47(6): 723–29.

CLAUDE M. STEELE
JOSHUA ARONSON

11

Stereotype Threat and the Test Performance of Academically Successful African Americans

NOT LONG AGO the novelist Philip Roth, explaining his lifelong preoccupation with the American Jewish experience, said in a National Public Radio interview that it was not Jewish culture or religion, per se, that fascinated him, but what he called the Jewish predicament. This is an apt term for the problem that we examine here, namely, the way in which African Americans deal with negative stereotypes about their mental ability. We argue that widely known negative stereotypes can place any group in a predicament. Terms like "yuppie," "feminist," "liberal," and "white male," can all conjure up unflattering images. Members of these groups are familiar with such images. They must deal with the possibility of being judged or treated stereotypically, or of doing something that would confirm the stereotype. We call this predicament stereotype threat. When a negative stereotype is particularly hurtful, we argue, stereotype threat can seriously disrupt the lives of those to whom it might apply.

This research was supported by the National Institutes of Health, through grant MH51977, and the Russell Sage Foundation, through grant 879.304, to Steele; and by the Spencer Foundation and the James S. McDonnell Foundation, through postdoctoral fellowships to Aronson. We thank John Butner, Emmeline Chen, Matthew McGlone, the editor of the *Journal of Personality and Social Psychology*, and several reviewers for helpful comments on earlier drafts.

This chapter describes our research on how stereotype threat affects the performance of talented, strongly school-identified African Americans on standardized tests. We argue that African-American students know that any faltering could cause them to be seen through the lens of a negative racial stereotype. Those whose self-regard is predicated on high achievement—usually the stronger, more confident students—may feel this pressure so greatly that it disrupts and undermines their test performance.

It is important to stress that academically successful black students are the most likely to be affected by this pressure. Confirming a negative stereotype about academic ability threatens something that they care about: their attachment to a domain in which they have invested. Those who identify less with school—often weaker, less confident students—feel such threats less intensely because they do not care so much about academic success. Thus stereotype threat may impair the test performance of school-identified African-American students in two ways. First, it adds a pressure that may directly undermine that performance. Second, if it persists as a chronic feature of the school performance domain, it may force the affected students to disidentify with that domain.[1]

Background

The educational achievement and school retention rates of African-American children have lagged behind those of whites for as long as records have existed. At the college level, for example, only 38 percent of black entrants graduate within six years, compared with 58 percent of white entrants. Those African Americans who do graduate typically earn grade point averages (GPAs) two-thirds of a letter grade below those of white graduates.[2]

These differences in academic performance reflect the effect of historic and ongoing socioeconomic disadvantages, segregation, and discrimination. Such deprivation can directly impede school preparation. It can also lead black students to make unfavorable assessments of their educational prospects, which, in turn, encourage disidentification with school. But there is evidence that the crisis has other roots as well. Even among blacks and

---

1. C. Steele (1992, 1997).
2. For college entrants, see American Council on Education (1994–95). On GPAs, see, for example, Nettles (1988).

whites who enter college with comparable skills—as measured by the Scholastic Assessment Test (SAT), for example—the black students earn lower GPAs, take longer to graduate, and indeed are less likely to graduate.[3] This kind of underachievement is often described as overprediction, because standardized tests predict that black students will do better than they actually do. The problem suggests that black-white differences in college performance cannot be caused entirely by differences in preparation. Blacks earn lower grades than whites even when their grades and test scores suggest that they are extraordinarily well prepared for college work.

We argue that black underachievement derives in part from the stereotype threat that is a chronic feature of African-American students' academic environment. The psychic distress that negative stereotypes can cause their targets has been a concern of many social scientists.[4] Some have hypothesized that such distress may be a factor in the underperformance of African-American students.[5] Most of these authors assume that the stereotype, or rather the prospect of being stereotyped, triggers an internalized anxiety or low expectancy about one's ability that has already been established as a result of prior exposure to the stereotype. The present model, in contrast, assumes that the prospect of being negatively stereotyped can be threatening, and thus disruptive, in its own right, whether or not it triggers self-doubt or internalized low expectancies.

When a negative stereotype about one's group becomes relevant to the situation that one is in, it signals the risk of being judged or treated stereotypically, or of doing something that would inadvertently confirm the stereotype. Whether this predicament affects behavior depends not on whether one has internalized the stereotype as self-doubt, but on whether one cares about the domain in which the stereotype applies. In the case of African-American students, we argue that stereotype threat primarily affects those who care most about academic success, namely, those who have enough confidence in their own ability to have formed an academic identity.[6] For students who are less school-identified, this situational predica-

---

3. Jensen (1980); see also chapter 13 below. Up to 1995 the SAT was known as the Scholastic Aptitude Test; see chapter 2 above.

4. See, for example, Allport (1954); Goffman (1963); Howard and Hammond, "Rumors of Inferiority," *New Republic*, 1985, pp. 18–23; C. Steele (1975); S. Steele (1990).

5. See, for example, Clark (1968); and S. Steele (1990).

6. C. Steele (1997).

ment is likely to be less threatening, because it affects something that is less important to them.

The experimental work of Irwin Katz and his colleagues in the 1960s suggests that black test performance is influenced by factors that could well involve stereotype threat. For example, Katz, Roberts, and Robinson find that blacks perform better on an IQ subtest when it is presented as a test of eye-hand coordination—a nonevaluative and thus threat-negating description—than when it is presented as a test of intelligence. Katz, Epps, and Axelson find that black students perform better on an IQ test when they believe that their performance will be compared to that of other blacks than when they believe that it will be compared to the performance of whites. Our work builds on these earlier experiments.[7]

Any test that purports to measure intellectual ability might induce stereotype threat in African-American students. These feelings may interfere with performance in several ways. The emotional arousal that accompanies them can reduce the range of cues that students use to solve test problems. It can divert attention from the task at hand to irrelevant worries. It can also cause self-consciousness or overcautiousness.[8]

In order to test our hypothesis that stereotype threat leads school-identified blacks to underachieve in test situations, we conduct five experiments. Under the assumption that in general students at Stanford University are rather strongly identified with academic performance, in each experiment we randomly assign black and white Stanford undergraduates to different "treatments," or conditions. These experiments help one to understand both what kinds of testing conditions provoke stereotype threat and the ways in which the threat can interfere with black students' performance.[9]

Study One

For the first study, we recruited 114 Stanford undergraduates and randomly assigned them to one of three experimental conditions. Approximately half of the participants were white and half were black. When they

---

7. Katz, Epps, and Axelson (1964); Katz, Roberts, and Robinson (1965).

8. For example, on cue utilization, see Easterbrook (1959); on irrelvant worries, see Sarason (1972) and Wine (1971); on self-consciousness, see Baumeister (1984); and on overcautiousness, see Geen (1985).

9. We summarize the experiments below; for further detail, see Steele and Aronson (1995).

arrived at the laboratory, a white male experimenter explained that for the next thirty minutes they would work on a set of verbal problems in a format identical to the SAT, and then they would answer some questions about the experience. The experimenter then asked the participants to read a page that states the purpose of the study, describes the procedure for answering questions, stresses the importance of indicating guessed answers, describes the test as very difficult, says that participants should not expect to answer many of the questions correctly, and says that they will be given feedback on their performance at the end of the session. Except for changes in a few key phrases of this description, the procedure was the same for all three groups.

In the first experimental condition ("diagnostic"), the test is described as diagnostic of intellectual ability, making the racial stereotype about intellectual ability relevant to the performance of black participants and establishing the threat that they might be seen stereotypically, or might fulfill the stereotype. Participants are told that the study is concerned with "various personal factors involved in performance on problems requiring reading and verbal reasoning abilities." They are told that after the test they will receive feedback that "may be helpful to you by familiarizing you with some of your strengths and weaknesses" in verbal problem solving. The difficulty of the test is justified as a means of providing a "genuine test of your verbal abilities and limitations so that we might better understand the factors involved in both." Participants are asked to try hard in order to "help us in our analysis of your verbal ability."

In the second experimental condition ("nondiagnostic only"), the same test is described simply as a laboratory problem solving task, not intended as diagnostic of ability. Instead, participants are told that the purpose of the research is to better understand the "psychological factors involved in solving verbal problems." They are also told that they will receive performance feedback, but as a means of familiarizing them "with the kinds of problems that appear on tests [they] may encounter in the future." The difficulty of the test is justified in terms of a research focus on difficult verbal problems, and participants are asked to try hard in order to "help us in our analysis of the problem solving process." The experimenter himself told participants in the nondiagnostic condition to try hard "even though we're not going to evaluate your ability."

In the third experimental condition ("nondiagnostic challenge"), participants are encouraged to view the difficult test as a challenge. For practical reasons, we are interested in finding out whether emphasizing the challenge inherent in a difficult test might increase participants' motivation and performance in comparison with the nondiagnostic only condition. The study description is the same as in the second experimental condition, except that the nondiagnostic challenge condition is explained as an attempt to provide "even highly verbal people with a mental challenge." In this case, the experimenter told participants to "please take this challenge seriously, even though we will not be evaluating your ability."

Participants took a thirty minute test composed of twenty-seven difficult verbal items (only 30 percent of earlier samples had answered these items correctly) and three difficult anagram problems, all taken from Graduate Record Examination (GRE) study guides. The most complex items are presented first. Participants then completed an eighteen item self-report measure of their current thoughts about academic competence and personal worth; such as, "I feel confident about my abilities," "I feel self-conscious," or "I feel as smart as others." Participants also completed a twelve item measure of cognitive interference frequently used in test anxiety research, on which they indicated the frequency of several distracting thoughts during the exam; such as, "I wondered what the experimenter would think of me," "I thought about how poorly I was doing," or "I thought about the difficulty of the problems."[10] They also rated the test on difficulty and bias. Participants then evaluated their own performance by estimating the number of problems that they had solved correctly and comparing their own performance to that of the average Stanford student.[11] Finally, as a check on whether the experimental manipulation had worked as intended, participants selected an answer to the following: "The purpose of this experiment was to: (a) provide a genuine test of my abilities in order to examine personal factors involved in verbal ability; (b) provide a challenging test in order to examine factors involved in solving verbal problems; (c) present you with unfamiliar verbal problems to measure verbal learning."[12]

---

10. See Sarason (1980).

11. The academic competence and personal worth items are measured on five-point scales ranging from 1 (not at all) to 5 (extremely). Scoring on the cognitive interference items ranges from 1 (never) to 5 (very often). The difficulty and bias measure ranges from 1 (not at all) to 15 (extremely). The relative performance measure ranges from 1 (much worse) to 15 (much better).

12. Chi-square analyses of the manipulation check reveal that participants are more likely to believe that theexperiment is intended as an evaluation of ability in the diagnostic condition (65 percent) than in the nondiagnostic (3 percent) or the challenge (11 percent) conditions.

Results

Figure 11-1 presents the mean test performances of blacks and whites in each experimental condition in Study One. The figure shows the mean number of items that blacks and whites answer correctly in each condition, after adjusting for individual differences in self-reported SAT scores.[13] If describing the test as diagnostic of ability subjects black students to stereotype threat, the performance of blacks should be lower in this condition than under the other two. Blacks' scores should also be lower than whites' scores in this condition. By contrast, there should be no difference between the scores of blacks and whites in the other two conditions.

Black participants in the diagnostic condition perform significantly worse than those in either the nondiagnostic condition ($p < 0.01$) or the challenge condition ($p < 0.01$). In addition, blacks perform worse than white participants in the diagnostic condition ($p < 0.01$).[14] But the overall interaction between race and experimental condition does not reach conventional levels of statistical significance ($p < 0.19$). It may be that the overall interaction effect is weakened by the fact that whites slightly outperform blacks in the nondiagnostic challenge condition. When one excludes the challenge condition and compare the race effects in the diagnostic and nondiagnostic conditions, the difference is somewhat more significant ($p < 0.08$).

We measure accuracy by the percentage of items attempted that a respondent answered correctly. Black participants in the diagnostic condition have the lowest adjusted mean accuracy of any group in this study. Black participants in the diagnostic condition are reliably less accurate than either black participants in the nondiagnostic only condition ($p < 0.01$) or white participants in the diagnostic condition ($p < 0.05$).[15]

For the self-reported measures, experimental condition does not appear to have significant effects on academic competence, personal worth, or disruptive thoughts and feelings during the test. Black participants in each condition believe the test more biased than do white participants ($p < 0.001$). However, black participants' estimates of how many problems they have solved correctly and how their scores compare to those of other par-

---

13. The mean SAT score for black participants is 592; for white participants it is 632.

14. We use the Bonferonni procedure for all comparisons of adjusted means reported in this paper.

15. We do not find any statistically reliable interactions of race and condition for either number of items completed or number of guesses recorded.

Figure 11-1. *Test Performance, Study One*

Mean score[a]

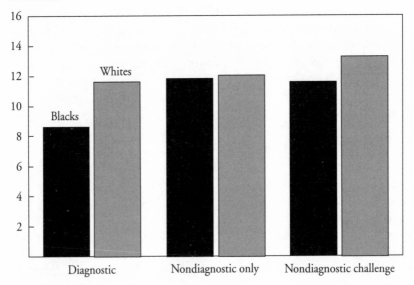

Source: See text.
a. Mean number of items solved, adjusted by SAT score.

ticipants are significantly lower in the diagnostic condition than in the other two. Test description has no effect on the self-evaluations of white participants.

Discussion

After controlling for SAT scores, blacks perform worse than whites when the test is presented as a measure of their ability. The performance of blacks improves dramatically and matches that of whites when the test is presented in a different way. Nonetheless, the relation between race and experimental condition interaction is only marginally significant, even when participants from the nondiagnostic challenge condition are excluded from the analysis. Likewise, despite our hypothesis that stereotype threat might increase the occurrence of interfering thoughts during the test, the diagnostic condition affected neither self-evaluation nor thoughts about the self in the immediate situation.

Study Two

To further test the reliability of the hypothesized interaction and explore the role played by stereotype threat, in the second study we randomly assigned twenty black and twenty white female Stanford undergraduates to the diagnostic and nondiagnostic conditions used in Study One (that is, we omitted the challenge condition).[16] The test is the same as that used in Study One, except that we cut the test period to twenty-five minutes, deleted the three anagram problems, and presented the test on a Macintosh computer. Participants could control how long each item or component of an item was on the screen and could access whatever material they wanted to see at their own pace. In addition to recording participants' answers, the computer recorded both the amount of time each item or item component was on the screen and the number of referrals between item components (for example, in the reading comprehension items).

After the test, participants completed a version of the Spielberger State Anxiety Inventory. This scale has been used successfully in other research to detect anxiety induced by evaluation apprehension. Participants also answered the cognitive interference questions used in Study One. In addition, they indicated the extent to which they guessed at items they found difficult, expended effort, persisted on problems, limited time on problems, read items more than once, became frustrated and gave up, and felt that the test was biased.

Results

Figure 11-2 presents the mean test performances of blacks and whites in each condition in Study Two, adjusted for self-reported SAT scores.[17] In this experiment, the overall interaction effect for race and experimental condition is statistically reliable, and planned condition contrasts support our hypothesis. Blacks in the diagnostic condition perform significantly worse than blacks in the nondiagnostic condition, whites in the diagnostic

---

16. We use female participants in this experiment because, due to other on-going research, we had considerably easier access to black female undergraduates than to black males at that time. This decision is justified by the finding of no gender differences in the first study; nor, as it turns out, in any of the subsequent studies reported in this chapter, all of which use both male and female participants.

17. The mean SAT score for black participants is 603; for white participants it is 655.

Figure 11-2. *Test Performance, Study Two*

Mean score[a]

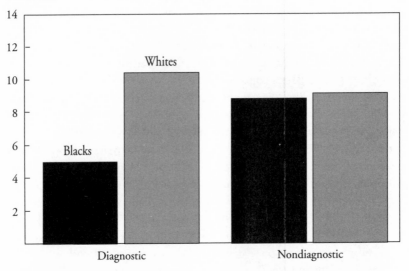

Source: See text.

a. Mean number of items solved, adjusted by SAT score.

condition, and whites in the nondiagnostic condition.[18] Blacks in the diagnostic condition are also less accurate than either blacks in the nondiagnostic condition or whites in either condition.[19]

In terms of rate of work, blacks complete significantly fewer items than whites ($p < 0.01$). Both black and white participants in the diagnostic condition complete fewer items than their counterparts in the nondiagnostic condition ($p < 0.007$). Black participants in the diagnostic condition finish fewer items (the mean is 12.38) than blacks in the nondiagnostic condition (18.53), whites in the diagnostic condition (20.93), and whites in the nondiagnostic condition (21.45).[20]

18. The analysis of covariance (ANCOVA) for number of items solved correctly yields a significant main effect of race—$F(1, 35) = 10.04$, $p < 0.01$—qualified by a significant interaction effect for race and test description—$F(1, 35) = 8.07$, $p < 0.01$. All p values for the planned condition are statistically significant at below the 0.05 level.

19. This interaction of diagnosticity and race is statistically significant ($p < 0.05$), but the planned contrasts of the black diagnostic condition against the other conditions were only marginally significant.

20. For all contrasts, $p < 0.05$.

We find no condition or group differences on any of the remaining self-reported measures: effort, cognitive interference, and anxiety.

Discussion

The results of this study establish the reliability of the interaction effect of race and diagnosticity that was only marginally significant in Study One. They also show that the diagnostic nature of a test impairs the rate as well as the accuracy of blacks' performance. It is precisely the type of impairment that other researchers find in test takers subject to evaluation apprehension, test anxiety, or competitive pressure.[21]

Study Three

The third study examines *why* framing tests as measures of ability impairs the performance of black participants. We randomly assigned thirty-five (nine male, twenty-six female) black and thirty-three (twenty male, thirteen female) white Stanford undergraduates to diagnostic, nondiagnostic, or control conditions; that is, ten to twelve participants in each experimental group. The diagnostic and nondiagnostic conditions are essentially the same as those used in Study One. However, in Study Three participants did not actually take a test; they were asked to complete a battery of measures immediately after reading the instructions, just before the test ostensibly was to be administered.

As they arrived for the study, a white male experimenter gave participants in the diagnostic and nondiagnostic conditions a booklet explaining that the study sought to examine the relationship between two types of

---

21. See, for example, Baumeister (1984). Why is speed impaired in this study but not in the first study? In the second study the test is five minutes shorter than in the first, but in both studies the more complicated items are presented at the beginning of the test. If stereotype threat slowed the pace of black participants in the diagnostic conditions of both experiments, this five minute difference may have made it harder for the blacks in the second study to move on to the more quickly answered items at the end of the test. This fact may also explain the generally lower scores in this study. Black participants in the diagnostic condition were, in fact, slower on the first five test items than participants in the other conditions. On average, these participants spent ninety-four seconds answering each of these items, compared with seventy-one seconds for black participants in the nondiagnostic condition, 73 seconds for whites in the diagnostic condition, and 71 seconds for whites in the nondiagnostic condition (in all cases, $p < 0.05$).

412 THE IMPACT OF SCHOOLS AND CULTURE

cognitive processes: lexical access processing (LAP) and higher verbal reasoning (HVR).[22] Participants were told that they would be asked to complete two tasks, one measuring LAP—"the visual and recognition processing of words"—and the other measuring HVR—"abstract reasoning about the meaning of words." They were then shown one sample item of lexical access processing and three sample items of higher verbal reasoning, all difficult verbal GRE problems. The purpose of the HVR sample items was to alert participants to the difficulty of the test and the possibility that they might perform poorly, thus invoking the relevance of the racial stereotype in the diagnostic condition.

Participants in the control condition did not expect to take any test. When they arrived at the laboratory, they found a note of apology from the experimenter for not being present. The note instructed them to complete a set of measures left on the desk in envelopes marked with the participants' names. Each envelope contained the LAP word fragment and stereotype avoidance measures described below, with detailed instructions on how to complete them.

The measures used in this study test the proposition that if the diagnostic nature of a test threatens black participants with a specifically racial stereotype, black participants in the diagnostic condition should demonstrate greater cognitive activation of racial stereotypes and doubts about their own abilities, greater motivation to disassociate themselves from the stereotypes, and greater performance apprehension than participants in the other conditions.

STEREOTYPE AND SELF-DOUBT ACTIVATION. If anticipation of a difficult, intellectually diagnostic test makes black participants feel threatened by a racial stereotype, one might expect it to activate the stereotype in their thought and information processing. That is, the racial stereotype, and perhaps also the self-doubt associated with it, should be more cognitively

---

22. The diagnostic and nondiagnostic conditions are more strongly differentiated in the written instructions for Study Three than those for Study One. In Study Three, participants in the diagnostic condition read the following: "Because we want an accurate measure of your ability in these domains, we want to ask you to try as hard as you can to perform well on these tasks. At the end of the study, we can give you feedback which may be helpful by pointing out your strengths and weaknesses." Participants in the nondiagnostic condition read the following: "Even though we are not evaluating your ability on these tasks, we want to ask you to try as hard as you can to perform well on these tasks. If you want to know more about your LAP and HVR performance, we can give you feedback at the end of the study."

activated for black participants in the diagnostic condition than for black participants in the nondiagnostic condition or for white participants in either condition.[23] To assess this possibility, participants were asked to perform a word fragment completion task (the "LAP task"), which has been shown to measure the cognitive activation of constructs that either have been recently primed or are self-generated.[24] The task consists of eighty word fragments with missing letters specified as blank spaces.

For twelve of these fragments, the possible solutions include a word that reflects either a race-related construct or an image associated with African Americans: __ __ C E (RACE); L A__ __ (LAZY); __ __A C K (BLACK); __ __ O R (POOR); C L __ S__ (CLASS); B R __ __ __ __ __ (BROTHER); __ __ __ __ T E (WHITE); M I __ __ __ __ __ __ (MINORITY); W E L __ __ __ __ __ (WELFARE); C O __ __ __ (COLOR); T O __ __ __ __ (TOKEN).[25] We include a fairly high number of these target fragments so that ceiling or floor effects on some fragments do not damage the overall sensitivity of the measure. To reduce the likelihood that participants will become aware of the racial nature of the target fragments, these items are spaced out, with at least three other items between them, and there are only two target fragments on any page in the booklet. Participants were instructed to work quickly, spending no more than fifteen seconds on each item.

Seven word fragments reflecting self-doubt related to competence and ability are also included among the eighty items of the LAP task: L O __ __ __ (LOSER); D U __ __(DUMB); S H A __ __ (SHAME); __ __ __ __ E R I O R (INFERIOR); F L __ __ __ __ (FLUNK); __ A R D (HARD); W __ __ K (WEAK). These are separated from one another, and from the racial fragments, by at least three other items.

STEREOTYPE AVOIDANCE. If the diagnostic nature of a test makes black participants apprehensive about fulfilling or being judged by a racial stereo-

---

23. Dovidio, Evans, and Tyler (1986); Devine (1989); Higgins (1989).

24. Gilbert and Hixon (1991); Tulving, Schacter, and Stark (1982).

25. The list was generated by asking forty undergraduates (white students from the introductory psychology pool) to provide a set of words that reflected their images of African Americans. From these lists, the research team identified the twelve most common constructs (for example, lower class, minority) and selected single words to represent them. For each word to be included in the task, at least two letter spaces were omitted and the resulting word stem was reviewed to determine whether other associations, unrelated to the stereotype, were possible. Leaving at least two letter spaces blank, rather than only one, greatly increases the number of ways in which a fragment might be completed, and thus reduces the chance of ceiling effects, when virtually all participants think of the race-related solution.

type, one might expect black participants in the diagnostic condition to disassociate themselves from that stereotype more than do participants in the other conditions. Brent Staples, an African-American editorialist for the *New York Times*, offers an example of this phenomenon in his recent autobiography, *Parallel Time*.[26] When he began graduate school at the University of Chicago, he found that as he walked the streets of Hyde Park, he made people uncomfortable; they grouped more closely when he passed, and some even crossed the street to avoid him. He eventually realized that dressed as a student in an urban context, he was being perceived through the lens of a race-class stereotype, as a potentially menacing black male. To deflect this perception, he learned a trick: he whistled music by Vivaldi. On hearing this, people around him visibly relaxed and he no longer felt suspect. If apprehension about being judged in light of the racial stereotype affects black participants in the diagnostic condition, these students, like Staples, might want to show that the broader racial stereotype is not applicable to them.

To test this possibility, Study Three asks participants to rate their preferences for a variety of activities and interests, and how descriptive of themselves are various personality traits. Some of these activities and traits are stereotypic of African Americans.[27] Participants in the diagnostic and nondiagnostic conditions were told that these ratings would provide a better understanding of the underpinnings of LAP and HVR processes. Control participants were told that the ratings assessed the typical interests and personality traits of Stanford undergraduates. The measure contains fifty-seven items. Activities and interests include reading for pleasure, socializing, shopping, traveling, types of music (such as jazz, rap music, classical music), and sports (such as baseball, basketball, boxing). Personality traits include extroverted, organized, and humorous. The stereotype-relevant questions about activities are "How much do you enjoy sports?" and "How much do you enjoy being a lazy 'couch potato'?" For music and sports, the stereotypic preferences are rap music and basketball. For personality, the stereotypic ratings are lazy and aggressive-belligerent.

PERFORMANCE APPREHENSION. By adding the risk of validating a racial stereotype to the normal risks of being evaluated, the diagnostic condition

---

26. Staples (1994).

27. Items selected as stereotypic were generated by 65 percent of a pretest sample of forty white participants asked to list activities and traits that they believed to be stereotypic of African Americans.

should make black participants more apprehensive about their test performance. We measure this apprehension by the degree to which participants endorse excuses for poor performance before the test. The directions state: "As you know, student life is sometimes stressful, and we may not always get enough sleep, etc. Such things can affect cognitive functioning, so it will be necessary to ask how prepared you feel." Participants were then asked to indicate the number of hours they had slept the night before and to answer the following questions: "How able to focus do you feel?" "How much stress have you been under lately?" "How tricky/unfair do you typically find standardized tests?"

Participants also completed a brief demographic questionnaire, asking their age, gender, major, and so forth, just before they expected to begin the test. The second item of this questionnaire gives the option of recording race. We reasoned that participants who wanted to avoid having their performance viewed through the lens of a racial stereotype would be less willing to indicate their race.

Results

Figure 11-3 presents results on the stereotype activation, self-doubt activation, and stereotype avoidance measures in Study Three. The figure shows that blacks in the diagnostic condition produce more race-related word completions than blacks in the other two conditions and whites in any of the conditions (in all cases, $p < 0.05$).[28] Blacks in the diagnostic condition also complete significantly more words in ways that suggest anxiety related to self-doubt than any other group (in all cases, $p < 0.05$).

To assess stereotype avoidance, we sum scores on the six items with stereotypic preferences and attributes.[29] Figure 11-3 shows that blacks in the diagnostic condition avoid conforming to stereotypic images of African Americans more than do blacks in the other conditions and whites in any of the conditions (in all cases, $p < 0.05$). The findings on the willing-

---

28. Analysis of the number of target word fragments completed stereotypically yields significant main effects for both race—$F_{(1,61)} = 13.77$, $p < 0.001$—and experimental condition—$F_{(2,61)} = 5.90$, $p < 0.005$—as well as a statistically significant interaction of race and condition—$F_{(2,61)} = 3.30$, $p < 0.05$—in the expected direction.

29. The scale ranges from 6 to 42, with a higher score indicating lower avoidance and 42 indicating low avoidance (Cronbach's alpha = 0. 65). An ANCOVA on the sum yields a significant effect of condition—$F_{(2, 61)} = 4.73$, $p < 0.02$—and a significant interaction of race and experimental condition—$F_{(2, 61)} = 4.14$, $p < 0.03$.

Figure 11-3. *Indicators of Stereotype Threat, Study Three*

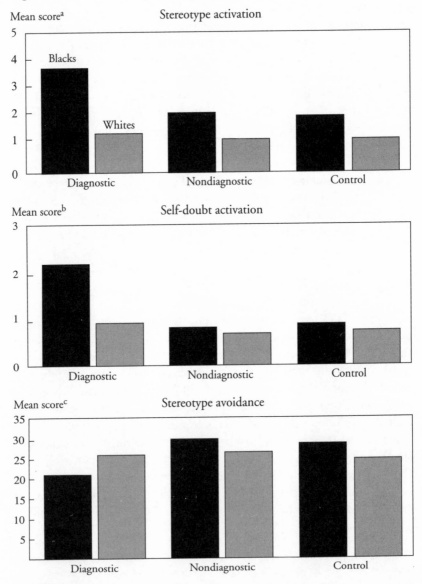

Source: See text.

a. Mean number of race-related word completions.

b. Mean number of word completions suggesting self-doubt.

c. Stereotype avoidance measure is the sum of scores on six items asking particpants to categorize themselves in terms of preferences and attributes. Scale ranges from 6 to 42, where a lower score indicates greater avoidance; see text for details.

Table 11-1. *Performance Apprehension Responses, Study Three* [a]
Units as indicated

| | Experimental condition | | | |
| | Diagnostic | | Nondiagnostic | |
Measure and summary statistic	Blacks	Whites	Blacks	Whites
Hours of sleep	5.10$_a$	7.48$_b$	7.05$_b$	7.70$_b$
Ability to focus	4.03$_a$	5.88$_b$	5.85$_b$	6.16$_b$
Current stress	5.51$_a$	5.24$_a$	5.00$_a$	5.02$_a$
Tests are unfair	5.46$_a$	2.78$_b$	3.14$_b$	2.04$_b$
Summary statistic				
Sample size	12	11	11	10

Source: See text.

a. Table shows mean scores on each measure. Means that do not share a subscript differ at the 0.01 level, according to Bonferroni procedure. Means with a common subscript do not differ.

ness of participants to report their race on the questionnaire are even more striking. Among black participants in the diagnostic condition, only 25 percent indicate their race, in contrast to 100 percent of participants in the other conditions.[30]

Table 11-1 reports the results for the four measures used to assess participants' willingness to make excuses for their performance. Blacks in the diagnostic condition are more likely than blacks in the nondiagnostic condition and whites in either condition to report not having slept much before the test, being relatively less able to focus, and thinking that standardized tests are typically tricky and unfair.[31] We do not find significant differences in participants' ratings of current levels of stress.

30. Using a 0/1 conversion of the response frequencies (where 0 denotes refusal to indicate race and 1 denotes indication of race), a standard ANCOVA reveals a marginally significant effect of race— $F(1, 61) = 3.86$, $p < 0.06$—a significant effect of condition, $F(2.61) = 3.40$, $p < 0.04$—and a significant interaction of race and experimental condition—$F(1,61) = 6.60$, $p < 0.01$—all due to the unique unwillingness of black participants in the diagnostic condition to indicate their race.

31. The ANCOVA for hours of sleep yields a significant effect of race—$F(1,39) = 8.22$, $p < 0.01$—a significant effect of condition—$F(1,39) = 6.53$, $p < 0.02$—and a significant interaction of race and condition—$F(1,39) = 4.1$, $p < 0.01$. The ANCOVA for ability to focus yields main effects of race—$F(1,39) = 7.26$, $p < 0.02$— and of condition—$F(1,39) = 0.67$, $p < 0.01$—and a significant interaction of race and condition—$F(1,39) = 5.73$, $p < 0.03$. The same pattern of effects emerges for participants' ratings of how tricky or unfair they generally find standardized tests: a race main effect, $F(1,39) = 13.24$, $p < 0.001$; a condition main effect, $F(1,39) = 13.42$, $p < 0.001$; and a marginally significant interaction of race and condition, $F(1,39) = 3.58$, $p < 0.07$.

Discussion

The results in Study Three provide dramatic support to our hypothesis that presenting an intellectual test as diagnostic of ability will arouse a sense of stereotype threat in black participants. Compared with blacks in the nondiagnostic condition and whites in both conditions, black participants in the diagnostic condition show significantly greater activation of African-American stereotypes, greater activation of concerns about their own ability, a greater tendency to avoid racially stereotypic preferences, a greater tendency to make excuses for their performance, and a greater reluctance to make their racial identity known. The instructions in the diagnostic condition clearly cause these participants to experience a strong, racialized apprehension.

Taken together, Studies One, Two, and Three show that presenting a difficult test as diagnostic of ability can undermine blacks' performance and make them feel threatened by racial stereotypes. But our findings raise two important questions. First, is stereotype threat itself, even in the absence of an explicit statement that a test measures ability, sufficient to disrupt blacks' performance on a difficult test? Second, is the disruptive effect of the experimental manipulation really mediated by stereotype threat? Our fourth study addresses these questions.

Study Four

In this study we did not tell any of the participants that the test measures ability. To learn whether stereotype threat depresses the performance of blacks even when a test is not labeled as diagnostic of ability, we asked some participants to record their race on a demographic questionnaire before taking the test ("race priming"). We reasoned that doing so might suffice to make these participants think about racial stereotypes, feel stereotype threatened when they took the test, and as a result perform worse on the test.

We randomly assigned twenty-four black and twenty-three white Stanford undergraduates to the race-primed or unprimed conditions by drawing questionnaires (labeled "personal information") from a shuffled stack.[32] The questionnaires were virtually identical, except that in the race-

32. We discarded all data from two black participants who arrived with suspicions about the racial nature of the study, as well as data from one white student who failed to provide an SAT score. We added new participants to bring the number of participants in each condition to eleven.

primed condition the final item asked participants to indicate race. A white male experimenter explained the purpose and format of the test in the same way as for the nondiagnostic conditions in Studies One and Two. The twenty-five minute test used in Study Three is the same as that for Study Two, but administered on paper rather than on computer. During the test, participants marked their guesses, and after the test they indicated the extent to which they guessed when they were having difficulty, expended effort, persisted on problems, limited their time on problems, read problems more than once, became frustrated and gave up, and felt that the test was biased. Participants also completed a questionnaire expressing their agreement or disagreement with each of eight statements, such as, "Some people feel I have less verbal ability because of my race," "The test may have been easier for people of my race," "The experimenter expected me to do poorly because of my race," "In English classes people of my race often face biased evaluations," and "My race does not affect people's perception of my verbal ability." Nine additional items explore the effect of the race-primed condition on the perceived importance of verbal and mathematics skills for participants' education and career plans; for example, "Verbal skills will be important to my career," "I am a verbally oriented person," and "I feel that math is important to me."

Results

Figure 11-4 presents the mean test performances of blacks and whites in each condition in Study Four, adjusted for self-reported SAT scores. As the figure shows, blacks in the race-primed condition perform significantly worse than either blacks in the unprimed condition or whites in the race-primed condition.[33] In the absence of race-priming, blacks perform as well as whites with comparable SAT scores.

Blacks in the race-primed condition are also less accurate than blacks in the unprimed condition and whites in either of the conditions, although the difference between blacks in the primed and unprimed conditions is only marginally significant ($p < 0.08$). Race-primed blacks also complete fewer items than whites (the means are 11.58 and 20.15, respectively), whereas unprimed blacks and whites answer roughly the same number of items (15.32 and 13.03, respectively).[34]

33. Black participants in the race-primed condition also perform worse than whites in the unprimed condition, but this difference is not statistically significant.

34. The interaction of race and race priming for the number of test items completed is statistically significant ($p < 0.01$).

Figure 11-4. *Test Performance, Study Four*

Mean score[a]

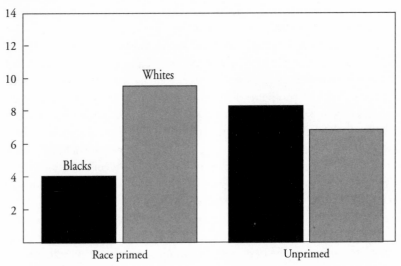

Source: See text.

a. Mean number of items solved, adjusted by SAT score.

Although participants' ratings reveal no difference in the degree to which they report that they guessed on the test, black participants note fewer guesses on their answer sheets when race is primed (the mean is 1.99) than when it is not (2.74). White participants, in contrast, tend to guess more when race is primed (4.23) than when it is not (1.58).[35]

Participants' estimates of how well they performed and how much having to indicate their ethnicity bothered them during the test (or would have bothered them, in the case of the unprimed condition) did not differ in the two conditions. In postexperiment interviews, several participants stated that they did not find recording their race noteworthy, because they have to do it so often in everyday life. Analysis of the stereotype threat scale reveals that black participants feel more stereotype threat than white participants ($p < 0.01$); but contrary to our expectations, race-primed blacks seem no more threatened than unprimed blacks. Black participants also

35. The interaction of race priming and race is significant at the 0.03 level.

report valuing sports less than whites ($p < 0.05$), and this effect does not differ between conditions either.[36]

Discussion

Asking black participants to report their racial identity depresses their performance on a difficult verbal test even when it is not presented as diagnostic of intellectual ability. We argue that this happens because race priming makes stereotypes about mental capability more salient to black participants. But black participants in the race-primed condition do not show more stereotype threat (as determined by the stereotype threat and stereotype avoidance measures) than black participants in the unprimed condition. One possible explanation for this finding is that the stereotype threat measures were presented after the test, not before it, as in Study Three. After experiencing the difficult, frustrating examination, all black participants may have felt somewhat stereotype threatened and stereotype avoidant, regardless of the condition.

The findings in Study Four do not suggest that black participants underperform because they withhold effort from the experiment. Black participants in the race-primed condition report expending as much effort as others on the test; they were no more disturbed at having to list their race; and they do not report guessing more than others. Moreover, black participants in both conditions reread the test items more than do white participants.

Study Five

The fifth study is designed to establish whether the race-prime effect can be replicated and explore the possible mediating role of anxiety, as in Study Two. We randomly assigned ten black students to the race-prime condition and nine black students to the unprimed condition used in Study

---

36. Correlations between participants' numerical estimates of performance and their ratings of the importance of sports show that the worse blacks believe they have performed, the more they devalue sports, in the unprimed condition ($r = 0.56$), and particularly in the race-primed condition ($r = 0.70$). These results support the findings of Study Three in suggesting that black participants try to distance themselves from the stereotype of the academically untalented black athlete.

Four, but this time the test was administered by computer, so that we could record the time participants spent on each item. In addition, participants took the same anxiety measure as used in Study Two.

Results

As in Study Four, race-primed participants answer significantly fewer items correctly than do unprimed participants (means are 4.4 and 7.7, respectively; $p < 0.04$). Race-primed participants are also marginally less accurate than unprimed participants ($p < 0.10$). Participants in the race-primed condition answer fewer items than unprimed participants (13.2 and 20.1, respectively; $p < 0.01$). And while all participants completed the first five test items, race-primed participants spent more time on these (79 seconds and 61 seconds, respectively; $p < 0.04$). Race-primed participants are significantly more anxious than unprimed participants (48.5 and 40.5, respectively; $p < 0.04$). These results confirm that race priming depresses the performance of black participants on a difficult examination, and that it causes reactions that could be responses to stereotype threat.

Conclusions

The existence of a negative stereotype about a group to which one belongs means that in situations where it is potentially applicable, one risks confirming that stereotype, both to oneself and to others. Such situations create what we have called stereotype threat. When the stereotype in ques-tion demeans something as important to one as intellectual ability is to good students, it can impair performance.

Our experiments show that making African Americans more conscious of negative stereotypes about their intellectual ability as a group can de-press their test performance relative to that of whites. Conditions designed to alleviate stereotype threat, in turn, can improve the performance of blacks. These findings come from Studies One and Two, which variously present the test as diagnostic or nondiagnostic of intellectual ability. That is, these studies vary the extent to which the stereotype about blacks' ability seems relevant to the test they are taking. Study Three provides direct evidence that describing a test in a particular way can arouse stereotype threat in black participants. Describing the test as a measure of ability activates the racial stereotype, provokes self-doubt relating to the stereotype, and leads blacks to distance themselves from other stereotypes about African Americans. Study Four shows that merely asking black students to record their race is enough to impair their test performance, even when the test is not described as a measure of ability. This is presumably because race priming makes the stereotype salient in the minds of these participants. Study Five replicates these results. Taken together, the five studies show that stereotype threat can impair the test performance of African Americans even if it is created by quite subtle changes of environment. Eliminating stereotype threat can dramatically improve blacks' performance.

Effect of Stereotype Threat on Performance

Study Three provides clear evidence that the mere prospect of a difficult test that is diagnostic of ability is enough to make African-American participants experience stereotype threat. But the mechanisms by which stereotype threat affects test performance are less clear. Participants who experience stereotype threat do not seem to give up on such tests. They report expending as much effort as other participants. In Studies Two and Five, those subjected to stereotype threat actually spend more time per item than the others. They guess no more than particpants who are not threatened and they report rereading the items more than white participants. Weaker black students with relatively low investment in seeing themselves as academically competent might have responded differently. But for the presumably school-identified black students in these studies, giving up is not a way out of their predicament.

Stereotype threat seems to exert its influence by reducing efficiency. Participants who experience stereotype threat spend more time doing fewer items less accurately. This reduction in the efficiency of mental processing is probably the result of dividing their attention, alternating between trying to answer the items and trying to assess the significance of their frustration. Stereotype threat may also increase test anxiety for blacks—we find increased anxiety in the replication study, but not in Study Two. Overall, the impact of stereotype threat seems to be similar to that of other evaluative pressures.[37]

37. See, for example, Geen (1985); Wine (1971); Sarason (1972); Bond (1982); Baumeister (1984).

Generalizing from the Results

Our experiments suggest that stereotype threat lowers the performance of high-scoring black college students on a difficult verbal test. It is not yet clear to what extent one can generalize from these findings to other kinds of students and tests. Several questions remain unanswered.

First, would the findings hold if one gave the same students an easier test, so that they answered more items correctly and experienced less frustration? Our theory suggests that an easy test would not threaten black students with the possibility of fulfilling the negative stereotype about academic competence. But perhaps *any* test that purports to measure mental ability arouses such fears, at least in advance of taking it. In this case, the performance of black students might be adversely affected even when they take easy tests.

Uncertainty about whether stereotype threat affects performance on tests that individuals find relatively easy also introduces some ambiguity in interpreting the comparisons between blacks and whites reported above. All the analyses control students' self-reported SAT scores. Since all participants report high SAT scores, we assume that they experience relatively little frustration while taking the SAT, and hence that their SAT scores are not depressed by stereotype threat. And our findings provide some indirect support for this assumption. If black students' SAT scores were depressed by stereotype threat, they would underestimate these students' performance in situations where that threat is reduced or removed, as it is supposed to be for most of our control groups. If stereotype threat lowers the performance of able black students on the SAT but not in our nondiagnostic groups, blacks in the nondiagnostic groups should perform *better* than whites with the same SAT scores. This rarely occurs. Nonetheless, future research should try to verify this argument.[38]

A second question is whether the findings would hold if one gave an easier test, such as the SAT, to students who were less well prepared? Our model assumes that stereotype threat arises when black students think they are in a situation that might, in principle, confirm a negative stereotype

38. If stereotype threat significantly undermines the performance of black students on the SAT, is it appropriate to use the SAT to equate the skill levels of black and white participants in our experiments? Even if black participants' SAT scores were depressed by stereotype threat, using depressed scores as a covariate would adjust black performance more in the direction of reducing the black-white difference in the stereotype threat condition. Thus even if stereotype threat commonly depresses the standardized test performance of black test takers, our results probably are not compromised.

about African Americans, and when they also have enough difficulty with most of the test items that they fear confirming the stereotype. Less well prepared black students, taking a test in which they get most of the items wrong, should experience a high level of frustration and should be subject to stereotype threat. But if less adept students are less identified with academic performance, the threat may be less salient and the effect on performance greatly reduced. This topic also requires more research.

A closely related issue is whether stereotype threat would make less difference to high-scoring students at a less selective university than Stanford. Such students may be less concerned about academic ability, and thus less threatened by stereotypes about the academic competence of African Americans.

Third, would the results hold for other kinds of tests? The studies examine whether stereotype vulnerability lowers the performance of black students on multiple choice tests of verbal skills. Our theory predicts that one would find the same pattern with a mathematics test, for example. It is less clear whether one should expect to find the same pattern for tests that are seen as measuring achievement or effort, rather than ability. A chemistry or history test, for instance, might produce different findings.

Policy Implications

The studies described in this chapter seek to explain why blacks underperform in college relative to equally well-prepared whites. But an important implication of our research is that stereotype threat may be an underappreciated source of blacks' poor performance on IQ tests. The same logic may also apply to other groups subject to stereotype threat, such as people of lower socioeconomic status or women studying mathematics.[39] In addition to the particular environmental or genetic endowments that an individual brings to the testing situation, our research suggests that testing situations are unlikely to be neutral in relation to group identity.

By asking how social context and group identity come together to mediate an important behavior, we have reached some hopeful—though still tentative—conclusions. To explain African American students' underachievement as a byproduct of either socioeconomic conditions or "black culture" offers little realistic basis for improving the situation. Our analysis

39. Herrnstein (1973); Jensen (1969, 1980); Spencer and Steele (1994).

uncovers a social and psychological predicament that is rife in the standardized testing environment, but, as our manipulations illustrate, is amenable to change.

References

Allport, G. 1954. *The Nature of Prejudice.* Addison-Wesley.

American Council on Education. 1994–95. *Minorities in Higher Education.* Office of Minority Concerns.

Baumeister, R. F. 1984. "Choking under Pressure: Self-Consciousness and Paradoxical Effects of Incentives on Skillful Performance." *Journal of Personality and Social Psychology* 46(3): 610–20.

Bond, C. F. 1982. "Social Facilitation: A Self-Presentational View." *Journal of Personality and Social Psychology* 42: 1042–50.

Clark, K. B. 1965. *Dark Ghetto: Dilemmas of Social Power.* Harper and Row.

Devine, P. G. 1989. "Stereotypes and Prejudice: Their Automatic and Controlled Components." *Journal of Personality and Social Psychology* 56: 5–18.

Dovidio, J. F., N. Evans, and R. B. Tyler. 1986. "Racial Stereotypes: The Contents of Their Cognitive Representations." *Journal of Experimental Social Psychology* 22: 22–37.

Easterbrook, J. A. 1959. "The Effect of Emotion on Cue Utilization and the Organization of Behavior." *Psychological Review* 66: 183–201.

Geen, R. G. 1985. "Evaluation Apprehension and Response Withholding in Solution of Anagrams." *Personality and Individual Differences* 6: 293–98.

Gilbert, D. T., and J. G. Hixon. 1991. "The Trouble of Thinking: Activation and Application of Stereotypic Beliefs." *Journal of Personality and Social Psychology* 60(4): 509–17.

Goffman, I. 1963. *Stigma.* Simon and Shuster.

Herrnstein, R. 1973. *IQ in the Meritocracy.* Boston: Little Brown.

Higgins, E. T. 1989. "Knowledge Accessibility and Activation: Subjectivity and Suffering from Unconscious Sources." In J. S. Uleman and J. A. Bargh, eds., *Unintended Thoughts.* New York: Guilford.

Jensen, Arthur R. 1969. "How Much Can We Boost IQ and Scholastic Achievement?" *Harvard Educational Review* 39: 1–123.

———. 1980. *Bias in Mental Testing.* Free Press.

Katz, Irwin. 1964. "Review of Evidence Relating to Effects of Desegregation on the Intellectual Performance of Negroes." *American Psychologist* 19: 381–99.

Katz, Irwin, E. G. Epps, and L. J. Axelson. 1964. "Effect upon Negro Digit Symbol Performance of Comparison with Whites and with Other Negroes." *Journal of Abnormal and Social Psychology* 69: 963–70.

Katz, Irwin, S. O. Roberts, and J. M. Robinson. 1965. "Effects of Task Difficulty, Race of Administrator, and Instructions on Digit-Symbol Performance of Negroes." *Journal of Personality and Social Psychology* 2: 53–59.

Nettles, Michael T. 1988. *Toward Undergraduate Student Equality in American Higher Education.* New York: Greenwood.

Sarason, I. G. 1972. "Experimental Approaches to Test Anxiety: Attention and the Uses of Information." In C. D. Spielberger, ed., *Anxiety: Current Trends in Theory and Research,* vol 2. Academic Press.

————. 1980. "Introduction to the Study of Test Anxiety." In I. Sarason, ed., *Test Anxiety: Theory, Research, and Applications.* Hillsdale, N. J.: Erlbaum.

Spencer, S. J., and C. M. Steele. 1994. "Under Suspicion of Inability: Stereotype Vulnerability and Women's Math Performance." State University of New York, Buffalo, and Stanford University.

Spielberger, C., R. Gorsuch, and R. Lushene. 1970. *Manual for the State-Trait Anxiety Inventory.* Palo Alto, Calif.: Consulting Psychologists Press.

Staples, Brent. 1994. *Parallel Time.*

Steele, Claude M. 1975. "Name-Calling and Compliance." *Journal of Personality and Social Psychology* 31: 361–69.

————. 1992. "Race and the Schooling of Black America." *Atlantic Monthly* (April): 68–78.

————. 1997. "A Threat in the Air: How Stereotypes Shape the Intellectual Identities and Performance of Women and African Americans." *American Psychologist* (June).

Steele, Claude M., and Joshua Aronson. 1995. "Stereotype Threat and the Intellectual Test Performance of African Americans." *Journal of Personality and Social Psychology* 69(5): 797–811.

Steele, Shelby. 1990. *The Content of Our Character.* St. Martin's Press.

Tulving, E., D. L. Schacter, and H. A. Stark. 1982. "Priming Effects in Word-Fragment Completion Are Independent of Recognition Memory." *Journal of Experimental Psychology: Learning, Memory, and Cognition* 8: 336–42.

Wine, J. 1971. "Test Anxiety and Direction of Attention." *Psychological Bulletin* 76: 92–104.

PART IV

Do Test Scores Matter?

THOMAS J. KANE

12

Racial and Ethnic Preferences in College Admissions

C OLLEGE ADMISSIONS COMMITTEES, not markets, ration access to many of the most selective U.S. colleges. As the labor market payoff to a college education has risen and competition for admission to elite universities has become more keen, racial preference in college admissions has become increasingly controversial, particularly at public institutions. In the spring of 1996 the Fifth Circuit Court of Appeals dramatically narrowed the latitude to use race in determining admissions to colleges within its jurisdiction, and the Supreme Court subsequently refused to review this decision. The following fall, voters in California approved a proposal to end the use of racial and ethnic preferences in admissions to state institutions. A number of other states are also reconsidering the role of race and ethnicity in admissions and financial aid.

I began work on this paper while a visiting fellow at the Brown Center for Education Policy at the Brookings Institution. I thank William Dickens, George Akerlof, Christopher Jencks, Chris Avery, William Bowen, Helen Ladd, Meredith Phillips, Charles Schultze, Doug Staiger, and David Wise for many helpful comments and discussions. Seminar participants at the University of Chicago, Harvard University, and the National Bureau of Economic Research offered a number of helpful suggestions; in particular, Charles Clotfelter, Ron Ehrenberg, Robert Hauser, Robert Meyer, Derek Neal, and Michael Rothschild. Tony Shen and Susan Dynarski provided excellent research assistance in the early stages of this research. Any errors are my sole responsibility.

Some will wait for the Supreme Court to clarify the legal issues at stake, but some may not.[1] Because colleges shroud their admissions procedures in mystery, the public knows little about the extent to which racial preference is practiced. Even less is known about the impact of such preferences on the later careers of black and white youth. This chapter explores these questions using data collected from the high school class of 1982.

The first section uses the High School and Beyond (HSB) survey to analyze the importance of race to college admission decisions in the early 1980s. It shows that racial preference is confined to "elite" colleges and universities, namely, the most academically selective fifth of all four-year institutions, where scores on the Scholastic Aptitude Test (SAT) averaged 1,100 or more.[2] The proportion of minority students at these colleges would be extremely low if admissions committees ignored the race or ethnicity of applicants. In fact, African-American applicants enjoy an advantage equivalent to an increase of two-thirds of a point in high school grade point average (GPA)—on a four-point scale—or 400 points on the SAT. However, at the less exclusive four-year colleges that 80 percent of students attend, we could not respect the hypothesis that race plays almost no role in admission decisions.

The second section examines the costs and benefits for minority students and students with low SAT scores of attending an elite college. The most damning charge against racial preference policies is that they harm their intended beneficiaries by enticing unqualified students to colleges where they cannot do the work. The HSB data do not support this claim. For the class of 1982, attending a more selective college is associated with higher graduation rates and higher earnings for both minority and nonminority students. Since one cannot control all the initial differences between students admitted to different kinds of colleges, one cannot be sure that the higher graduation rates and higher pay of those attending more selective institutions are pure "value added." What looks like an effect of attending an elite college may really be an effect of unmeasured preexisting differences in academic or earning potential. However, there is no evidence that the benefits associated with attending an elite school are

---

1. The attorney general for the State of Georgia, for example, has recommended that public educational institutions stop using race in deciding admissions; *Chronicle of Higher Education*, April 19, 1996, p. A40.

2. Note that since 1995, the SAT has been known as the Scholastic Assessment Test; see chapter 2 above.

any lower for black and Hispanic students than for white non-Hispanic students.

The final section of the chapter explores what would happen if colleges used class-based preferences instead of race-based preferences. Unless elite colleges dramatically reduce their reliance on high school grades and standardized test scores, class-based preferences cannot do much to cushion the impact of the elimination of race-based preferences. Although blacks and Hispanics would benefit disproportionately from policies favoring low-income applicants, minorities constitute only a small fraction of all high-scoring disadvantaged youth. As a result, substituting class-based for race-based preferences would not suffice to maintain racial diversity at academically selective colleges. Most academically selective colleges probably cannot have both race-blind admissions and racial diversity on campus.

The Nature and Extent of Affirmative Action in Higher Education

Black and white parents have on average different amounts of education and income, and their children often attend different high schools. On the average, black and white college applicants also have different high school grades and scores on standardized tests. Without direct knowledge of the weight that admissions committees attach to each of these characteristics, it is a difficult to know how important race, per se, is to committee decisions.

Richard Herrnstein and Charles Murray use differences in the average SAT scores of black and white students as evidence that elite colleges favor black applicants. Table 12-1 shows that these differences were quite large, ranging from 288 points at the University of California, Berkeley, in 1988 to 95 points at Harvard in the early 1990s. On the basis of these data, Herrnstein and Murray conclude that "the edge given to minority applicants to college and graduate school is not a nod in their favor in the case of a close call, but an extremely large advantage that puts black and Latino candidates in a separate admissions competition."[3]

But table 12-1 might well be misleading for two reasons.[4] First, it is known there are large differences between the mean SAT scores in the population of black and white high school graduates. It is also known that fac-

3. Herrnstein and Murray (1994, p. 447).
4. For a more detailed discussion, see Dickens, Kane, and Schultze (1998).

Table 12-1. *Racial and Ethnic Differences in SAT Scores,*
Selected Four-Year Colleges, 1998 and Early 1990s

Test score points

	Difference relative to whites	
Institution	Blacks	Asians
Rice	−271	70
University of California, Berkeley	−288	2
University of Virginia	−246	−22
Dartmouth	−218	49
Oberlin	−206	−57
University of Rochester	−219	−37
Wesleyan	−219	27
University of Chicago	−207	−28
Stanford	−171	58
Columbia	−182	42
Duke	−184	38
Williams	−181	36
Northwestern	−180	35
Wellesley	−175	34
Swarthmore	−200	−6
Amherst	−178	18
Princeton	−150	40
Brown	−150	40
Cornell	−162	21
University of Pennsylvania	−150	23
Harvard	−95	65
Georgetown	−147	3
Massachusetts Institute of Technology	−122	−5

Source: Herrnstein and Murray (1994, p. 452). Data for the University of Virginia and the University of California, Berkeley, are for 1988; others are from early 1990s.

tors other than SAT scores, such as high school grades, personal references, and sometimes even luck, can affect admission decisions. This means that even if admissions committees were color blind, any racial differences in the mean SAT scores of applicants would persist in attenuated form among those admitted. To see why, suppose that a college admitted students either if they had an SAT score above 1,100 or if their last name began with a vowel. Such a process is race blind. But the differences in SAT scores in the population at large will tend to be reflected among the students admitted because those admitted on the basis of their last names will have test scores similar to the scores of the population as a whole (assuming that SAT scores are only weakly related to whether the last name begins with a vowel).

Second, even if students were admitted solely on the basis of SAT score, one would expect some racial difference in their mean scores, because the distribution of SAT scores above the admission threshold would be different for blacks and whites. The College Entrance Examination Board reports that blacks in the high school class of 1982 represented 2 percent of those scoring over 500 on the mathematics SAT, 1 percent of those scoring over 600, and 0.6 percent of those scoring over 700.[5] Blacks are thus increasingly underrepresented at higher levels of performance. It follows that if a college admitted all students who scored above 500, blacks would be disproportionately likely to have scores in the 500 to 600 range, while whites would be overrepresented at higher levels. As a result, even a color-blind college that admitted only students with mathematics scores above 500 would find that on average its black students scored lower than its white students.

Using data from the high school class of 1982, I estimate that if a college relied entirely on high school GPA to rank students and admitted only those in the top third of their class, its white freshmen would score 180 points higher on combined verbal and mathematics SAT scores than its black freshmen.[6] Even if the college based admissions solely on SAT scores and admitted the top third of high school students, whites would have mean SAT scores 34 points higher than blacks. Therefore, an elite college could satisfy Herrnstein and Murray's standard only by discriminating *against* blacks and Hispanics because race-blind rules would continue to produce differences in SAT scores by race.[7]

---

5. Ramist and Arbeiter (1984).

6. To simulate college admission decisions based on high school GPA alone, I sort students by grade point average in academic subjects at high school, and for the top third, calculate mean SAT scores by race and ethnicity. To simulate admissions based solely on SAT scores, I follow the same procedure, after initially sorting students by SAT score.

7. Although this chapter is concerned with inferring racial preference in college admissions, the same problems arise when trying to infer discrimination in hiring, for example. In that context the relevant question is: "Among those with a given level of academic preparation, did blacks and whites end up at different levels?" Observers without access to a representative sample of the population may tend to base their inferences on the sample at hand—on the job, in their school, in their neighborhood—asking whether blacks and whites have different mean qualifications. Surveys suggest that whites think there is strong affirmative action in the labor market. Yet in chapter 14 below, William Johnson and Derek Neal show that black males have lower annual earnings than similarly qualified whites. The popular impression may rest on the same mistaken reasoning as Herrnstein and Murray's argument. For a discussion of the problems of inferring discrimination by studying differences in qualifications among those with similar earnings, see Goldberger (1984).

To learn about the actual effect of affirmative action in college admissions, one must look at which applicants specific colleges admit and reject. To answer this question, I use data from the High School and Beyond survey, a longitudinal survey of the high school class of 1982. The base year sample was drawn from 1,015 public and private high schools in the United States. Students were first surveyed in 1980, when they were in tenth grade, and followed up in 1982, 1984, 1986, and 1992. For students who attended a four-year college, I add data on that college's undergraduate enrollment, the mean SAT score of its entering freshmen, whether the college was historically black, and the percent of the student body that was black and Hispanic.[8]

The 1984 followup asked respondents to list their top two choices among the colleges to which they had applied, and to say whether they had been accepted by them.[9] The HSB survey includes students' scores on tests administered during their sophomore and senior years in high school, high school grades and activities, family income, and parental education.[10] Holding these characteristics constant, I estimate the effect of race and ethnicity on the likelihood of being admitted to various types of colleges.

8. Mean SAT scores for colleges and universities were obtained from the Higher Education Research Institute (HERI) of the University of California, Los Angeles. HERI gathers these data from college guides, such as Peterson's and Barron's. The SAT scores published in such guides are reported by the schools and are not verified. The data manager for the Peterson's guide reports sending out yearly mailings to 1,950 four-year schools. Schools are asked to indicate what percentage of their admitted students fall within one-hundred-point ranges on the mathematics and verbal sections of the SAT. The means in this chapter are calculated using weighted averages of the mid-points of these ranges. Each school's form also carries that school's responses from the previous year. The school has the option to indicate that the data are unchanged; approximately 50 percent do so each year.

9. HSB respondents report higher acceptance rates than do colleges. Nine-tenths (89 percent) of the HSB sample who applied to a four-year college reported that they were accepted; the College Entrance Examination Board (1994), by contrast, reports acceptance rates of 70 percent at public institutions and 60 percent at private institutions. There are at least three possible explanations for the divergence. First, only 39 percent of public colleges and 49 percent of private institutions responded to the College Board survey. If more selective institutions were more likely to respond, the estimated acceptance rate would be biased upward. Second, colleges are probably more likely than students to report an incomplete application as a denial. Colleges have an incentive to overstate selectivity, while students may be reluctant to admit being denied admission. Indeed, there is some evidence in the HSB data that colleges overstate average SAT scores of their students. Third, students were only asked to name their first two choices. A disproportionate share of students may have chosen not to list the most selective schools among the top two, to shield themselves from having to admit that they were not accepted.

10. For the sample of students without SAT scores on their high school transcripts, I imputed SAT scores by first regressing SAT scores on sophomore and senior HSB test scores for those with SAT scores and then using the regression coefficients on sophomore and senior test scores to impute SATs for those without them.

Table 12-2 shows the difference in the probability of acceptance associated with different characteristics. The first column shows the effect on the predicted acceptance rate of a one unit change in each characteristic when the applicant's other characteristics were at the mean of the applicant

Table 12-2. *Determinants of Admission to Four-Year College*[a]

Variable	All colleges	Quintile of college selectivity[b]				
		Lowest	Second	Third	Fourth	Top
Race[c]						
Black, non-Hispanic	0.021	–0.001	–0.014	–0.020	0.031	0.103
	(0.010)	(0.014)	(0.016)	(0.027)	(0.011)	(0.028)
Hispanic	0.022	0.010	0.000	–0.021	0.032	0.086
	(0.010)	(0.010)	(0.016)	(0.028)	(0.013)	(0.031)
Other, non-Hispanic	–0.045	. . .	–0.053	–0.046	–0.087	–0.067
	(0.018)		(0.037)	(0.043)	(0.059)	(0.040)
Academic credentials						
High school acade-	0.072	0.025	0.020	0.048	0.082	0.151
mic GPA[d]	(0.007)	(0.008)	(0.009)	(0.015)	(0.012)	(0.023)
SAT score[e]	0.016	0.008	0.015	0.007	0.020	0.025
	(0.003)	(0.003)	(0.004)	(0.006)	(0.004)	(0.009)
High school activities						
Student government	0.019	0.002	0.026	0.009	0.002	0.053
	(0.007)	(0.010)	(0.010)	(0.017)	(0.012)	(0.020)
Athletics	0.011	0.016	0.002	0.016	0.004	0.006
	(0.007)	(0.010)	(0.011)	(0.014)	(0.011)	(0.020)
College selectivity						
Mean college SAT[f]	–0.077	–0.026	–0.035	–0.078	–0.025	–0.165
	(0.005)	(0.013)	(0.026)	(0.079)	(0.039)	(0.018)
Summary statistic						
Sample size	5,888	928	991	1,070	1,097	1,696
Probability of admission for average applicant	0.927	0.978	0.967	0.938	0.957	0.812

Source: Author's calculations based on data from the High School and Beyond survey.

a. Calculated from a probit regression analysis. The effect of being "other, non-Hispanic" is not identified for the lowest quintile, since no such students were denied admission at those schools. Equations include indicators for eight categories of family income, five categories of parental education, and eight categories of high school sample stratum. Standard errors, shown in parentheses, are calculated using a method proposed by Huber (1967) and White (1980), which allows the errors to be correlated among those applying to the same college.

b. Quintile breaks are set in such a way that equal numbers of students enrolled in each quintile.

c. Relative to non-Hispanic whites.

d. Scale is 0(F) to 4 (A).

e. Scale is 4 (400) to 16 (1600).

f. Scale is 4 (400) to 16 (1600).

pool. Overall, it shows that blacks and Hispanics were 2.1 percent and 2.2 percent, respectively, more likely to be admitted at the schools to which they applied than non-Hispanic whites (hereafter, "whites") with similar credentials.[11] This advantage is roughly as large as the advantage associated with being a member of student government, having a B+ rather than a B average in high school, or scoring 1,130 rather than 1,000 on the SAT.

However, the other five columns show that the admissions process differs substantially at different types of school. To measure selectivity, I rank colleges by their students' mean SAT scores and then divide them into five groups of equal size.[12] At the least selective 60 percent of colleges, being black or Hispanic had little effect on an applicant's chances of admission. This is mainly because these colleges admitted almost all of those who applied. Insofar as these colleges were selective, they seem to have relied largely on high school grades and SAT scores. A high school grade point average of B rather than C raised an applicant's chances of admission to a college in the middle quintile by 5 percent, for example, whereas being black or Hispanic had no statistically identifiable effect.

Racial and ethnic differences in the probability of admission are most pronounced at the most selective colleges. At these colleges, otherwise average applicants were 8 to 10 percent more likely to be admitted if they were black or Hispanic. Such a differential is comparable to the effect of having an A- rather than a B average in high school or a total SAT score of 1,400 rather than 1,000.[13]

Table 12-3 investigates whether race affects the weight that elite colleges put on an applicant's other characteristics. Colleges seem to put less weight on high school GPA when evaluating minority applicants. Other characteristics, including SAT scores, evidently have about the same impact on black and white students' chances of admission.

---

11. Students of primarily Asian ethnicity seem to be 4.5 percentage points *less* likely than whites to be admitted.

12. The quintile breaks are set so as to ensure that an equal number of students enrolled in each quintile. Note that the more selective colleges receive a disproportionate share of applicants. The results in table 12-2 assume that within each quintile, the cutoffs used by more selective schools are a linear function of the college's mean SAT score. Appendix table 12A-1 reports similar results when college fixed effects are included.

13. The High School and Beyond survey retrieved SAT scores from high school records, when such scores were available. For the remaining cases, I estimate SAT scores from the HSB test battery, using an ordinary least squares equation estimated for students who had both SAT and HSB scores.

Table 12-3. *Racial Preference in Admissions and Characteristics of Students and Colleges, Four-Year Colleges in Top Quintile of Selectivity*[a]

| Variable | Difference in predicted probability, evaluated at sample mean | | | |
	(1)	*(2)*	*(3)*[b]	*(4)*[c]
Black, non-Hispanic	0.145	0.115	0.073	0.101
	(0.085)	(0.028)	(0.038)	(0.028)
Hispanic	0.139	0.096	0.055	0.121
	(0.090)	(0.030)	(0.043)	(0.032)
Minority*own SAT score	0.012	...	...	...
	(0.018)			
Minority*high school GPA	−0.081	...	...	...
	(0.039)			
Minority*high school student government	0.040	...	...	...
	(0.047)			
Minority*high school athletics	0.052	...	...	...
	(0.042)			
Minority*low income	...	−0.098	...	...
		(0.074)		
Minority*private college	...	...	0.064	...
			(0.041)	
Black, non-Hispanic southern state[d]	...	...	...	0.105
				(0.061)
Black, non-Hispanic Hispanic state[e]	...	...	...	−0.009
				(0.155)
Hispanic, southern state[d]	...	...	...	−0.040
				(0.098)
Hispanic, Hispanic state[e]	...	...	...	−0.078
				(0.080)

Source: Author's calculations based on data from sources for table 12-2.

a. Calculated from a probit regression analysis. Equations include indicators for participation in high school athletics, high school student government, and other high school activities; the student's own SAT score; the college's mean SAT score; the student's high school GPA in academic subjects; eight categories of family income; five categories of parental education; and eight categories of high school sample stratum. The specification in column 4 also includes an indicator for Hispanic states and southern states. Standard errors, shown in parentheses, are calculated using the method proposed by Huber (1967) and White (1980); see table 12-2, note a.

b. Includes an indicator for private colleges.

c. Includes indicators for colleges in "southern" and "Hispanic" states; see notes d and e below.

d. Southern states include Delaware, Maryland, District of Columbia, Virginia, West Virginia, North Carolina, South Carolina, Georgia, Kentucky, Tennessee, Mississippi, and Alabama.

e. Hispanic states include California, New Mexico, Arizona, Texas, and Florida.

Tables 12-2 and 12-3 describe racial and ethnic differences in the likelihood of admission, after controlling for the student characteristics reported in the HSB survey. Elite colleges also ask applicants to provide other types of information, such as letters of recommendation, that are not measured by the HSB survey. If blacks look better than whites on these "unobservables," table 12-2 overstates the extent of racial preference in college admissions. If minority applicants look worse than white applicants on these unobservables, the table understates the degree of racial preference.

One way to examine whether the limited range of data available from the HSB questionnaire biases my estimates of racial preference is to focus on students who applied to more than one college and compare their chances of admission at more and less selective institutions. This comparison effectively controls both observed and unobserved characteristics of students. One can then ask whether the chance of admission falls more for whites than for blacks as the selectivity of the colleges to which they apply increases. Table 12-4 shows that applying to a college with a mean SAT score 100 points higher reduces the average applicant's probability of admission by 28 percent.[14] For black and Hispanic applicants, this trade-off seems to be somewhat less pronounced: a 100 point increase in a college's mean SAT score reduces the probability of admission by only 21.6 percent (0.281 – 0.065). Although this black-white difference is on the margin of statistical significance, it is consistent with the earlier and more statistically robust finding that elite colleges put more weight on race in their admissions decisions.[15]

The Benefits of Attending a Selective College

One of the more provocative charges leveled against racial preference in college admissions is that the policy actually hurts the intended beneficiaries, by enticing minority youth to enter colleges for which they are underprepared and in which they are more likely to fail because of the competition from other students. Indeed, some have claimed that reverse

14. The probit specification used to generate table 12-4 can be estimated only for the sample of students who applied to two four-year colleges and were accepted at one, but not both.

15. Because the sample is limited to those who applied to two colleges and were accepted at only one of these, the racial differential in likelihood of admission at higher quality schools has a large standard error, with a two-sided p value of 0.19.

Table 12-4. *Racial Difference in the Probability of Being Admitted to a More Selective Four-Year College* [a]

Effect on probability of admission (admitted to first choice – admitted to second choice)	Change in probability of admission
100 point difference in colleges' mean SAT	−0.281
(mean SAT of 1st choice − mean SAT of 2nd choice)/100	(0.065)
100 point difference in colleges' SAT*Black, Hispanic	0.065
	(0.049)

Source: Author's calculations based on data from sources for table 12-2.

a. Calculated from a probit regression analysis. Standard errors are in parentheses. The sample is limited to students who applied to two four-year colleges and were accepted at only one. Sample size is 467.

discrimination explains the high dropout rates and low grade point averages of minority undergraduates. This section examines the payoff to attending a selective college for both minority and nonminority students.

A student's college performance is likely to depend on at least three distinct factors: prior educational preparation (as measured by a standardized test score), the quality of the college (proxied by the mean standardized test score of the other students attending that college), and the match between the student's preparation and the preparation of other students at the same college (as measured by the difference between the student's standardized test score and the mean score of other students at the college). Observers are not always careful to distinguish these effects. For instance, in an article in the *Public Interest*, John Bunzel catalogued the poor grades and high dropout rates of black students admitted under an affirmative action program at the University of California, Berkeley.[16] His discussion implies that these high dropout rates were the result of the difference between the SAT scores of black students and those of most other students at Berkeley.[17] But given their lower test scores and high school grades, it is perfectly possible that these black students would have dropped out in large numbers no matter which college they attended. In order to learn about the net effect of attending a more selective school, one must compare graduation rates for academically similar students at different schools.

16. Bunzel (1988).
17. Herrnstein and Murray (1994) draw a similar conclusion.

Table 12-5. *Students' College Grade Point Average and College Selectivity*[a]

Variable	(1)	(2)	(3)	(4)	(5)	(6)	(7)
Black or Hispanic	-0.315 (0.034)	-0.129 (0.030)	-0.132 (0.030)	0.025 (0.188)	0.015 (0.240)	-0.095 (0.307)	0.123 (0.332)
College selectivity[b]	...	...	-0.027 (0.012)	-0.020 (0.014)	-0.020 (0.014)	...	...
Selectivity*minority	...	...	...	-0.016 (0.019)	-0.014 (0.024)	-0.005 (0.030)	-0.027 (0.033)
Historically black institution*minority	...	...	...	...	0.016 (0.100)	...	...
Selectivity*individual SAT score[c]	...	...	...	...	...	...	-0.015 (0.007)
College fixed effects	No	No	No	No	No	Yes	Yes
Controls for family background, high school grades, SAT	No	Yes	Yes	Yes	Yes	Yes	Yes

Source: Author's calculations based on data from sources for table 12-2.

a. All specifications include indicators for high school sample stratum. Family background and academic controls include five dummies for parental education, eight dummies for family income, gender, student's SAT score, and high school grade point average. Sample size is 2,912. Standard errors, shown in parentheses, are calculated using the method proposed by Huber (1967) and White (1980); see table 12-2, note a.

b. College's mean total SAT score scale is 4 (400) to 16 (1600).

c. Scale is 4 (400) to 16 (1600).

Table 12-5 shows the determinants of the college grade point averages of students in the HSB survey. In all of the estimates reported, students' high school records and family backgrounds are held constant.[18] Column 1 shows that without adjustment for SAT scores or high school grades, the college GPAs of black and Hispanic students are roughly 0.3 points lower than those of white and Asian students—equivalent to a B rather than B+ average, for example. This is consistent with the evidence presented by Bunzel. Column 2 estimates the college GPA gap between blacks and whites with the same SAT score, high school GPA, family income, and parental education. I find, as do many other authors, that blacks and Hispanics have lower college GPAs than whites with apparently similar academic credentials and family background.[19] This suggests that Bunzel would have found that black and Hispanic students "underperformed" relative to whites even if Berkeley had exercised a race blind admissions policy in the 1980s.

The third column of table 12-5 shows that when one holds applicants' characteristics constant, those who attended more selective colleges earned lower grades—but the effect of selectivity is rather small. All else equal, a 100 point increase in a college's mean SAT score is associated with a 0.027 point drop in a student's GPA. Since the mean SAT is only 200 points higher in the top quintile of colleges than in the bottom quintile, attending a more selective college has a small effect on a student's GPA.

Table 12-6 performs an equivalent exercise to show the effect of college selectivity on college graduation rates, rather than grades. Attending a more selective college is associated with a 3 percent increase in the likelihood of graduating. In other words, the net effect of attending a more selective institution on completion rates for students with similar test scores is positive, not negative. Since studying at a selective college surely puts

18. The sample is limited to those who reported attending a four-year college. The GPA results are based on grades from the first four-year college attended. For the B.A. completion and earnings results, I analyze the characteristics of the first four-year college attended. To limit the influence of outliers, I exclude those with annual earnings of less than $1,000 or more than $100,000 from the earnings equation.

19. See Cleary (1968); Crouse and Trusheim (1988); Nettles, Theony, and Gosman (1968); Ramist, Lewis, and McCamley-Jenkins (1994); chapter 13 below. Vars and Bowen report in chapter 13 that the black-white gap in college GPAs is widest among students with the highest SAT scores. When I test for evidence of a racial difference in the relationship between SAT scores and college GPA, I cannot reject the hypothesis that the relationship is the same for blacks and whites. I suspect that my results differ from Vars and Bowen's because our data come from different samples. In contrast to their sample of students from highly selective colleges, the HSB data probably do not have enough power to distinguish among students at the very top of the SAT distribution.

Table 12-6. Completion of B.A. by 1992 and College Selectivity[a]

Variable	(1)	(2)	(3)	(4)	(5)	(6)	(7)
Black or Hispanic	-0.160	-0.033	-0.030	0.269	0.006	0.030	0.173
	(0.020)	(0.020)	(0.020)	(0.114)	(0.240)	(0.186)	(0.200)
College selectivity[b]	…	…	0.031	0.044	0.045	…	…
			(0.007)	(0.008)	(0.008)		
Selectivity*minority	…	…	…	-0.030	-0.006	-0.009	-0.023
				(0.011)	(0.013)	(0.018)	(0.020)
Historically black institution*minority	…	…	…	…	0.172	…	…
					(0.053)		
Selectivity*individual SAT score[c]	…	…	…	…	…	…	-0.010
							(0.004)
College fixed effects	No	No	No	No	No	Yes	Yes
Controls for family background, high school grades, SAT	No	Yes	Yes	Yes	Yes	Yes	Yes

Source: Author's calculations based on data from sources for table 12-2.

a. All specifications include indicators for high school sample stratum. Family background and academic controls include five dummies for parental education, eight dummies for family income, gender, student's SAT score, and high school grade point average. Sample size is 3,671. Standard errors, shown in parentheses, are calculated using the method proposed by Huber (1967) and White (1980); see table 12-2, note a.

b. College's mean total SAT score scale is 4 (400) to 16 (1600).

c. Scale is 4 (400) to 16 (1600).

students at some competitive disadvantage relative to their classmates, this finding suggests that such colleges have offsetting advantages. Perhaps better prepared classmates or better teachers make attending these colleges more interesting. Selective colleges may also establish social norms that favor staying in school.

Table 12-7 shows that holding an entering student's measured characteristics constant, a 100 point increase in a college's mean SAT score is associated with a 0.056 increase in the log of earnings in 1991, nine years after high school graduation. That is equivalent to a 5.8 percent increase in actual earnings.[20] There is also some evidence that this payoff may have risen over time.[21]

From their analysis of data on the high school class of 1972, Linda Loury and David Garman conclude that greater college selectivity is associated with higher graduation rates for whites, but lower rates for blacks.[22] In table 12-6, column 4 shows, consistent with Loury and Garman, that the relationship between college selectivity and completion of the B.A. is significantly weaker for minority youth than for whites and Asians, although it is not negative. Column 5 shows why this is the case. College selectivity has less impact on blacks in this context because many black undergraduates attend historically black institutions, which have low mean SAT scores but high graduation rates. These institutions have traditionally generated a disproportionate share of black college graduates in the United States. For the 1980s, the HSB shows that blacks who attended historically black institutions still had completion rates 17.2 percent higher than apparently similar minority students in historically white schools. After taking this fact into account, one finds that among students in historically white institutions, selectivity has about the same effect on the graduation rates of minority and nonminority students. Table 12-7 shows that college selectivity is positively associated with earnings and that the payoff is similar for blacks and whites. However, although attending an HBI was positively related to B.A. completion, there is no statistically significant relationship with earnings.[23]

---

20. Since completion of the B.A. is not included in the earnings equation, the estimated relationship between college selectivity and earnings includes the net effect of college quality on degree completion.

21. Brewer, Eide, and Ehrenberg (1996). The finding that college selectivity is related to earnings is also consistent with Daniel, Black, and Smith (1995), James and others (1989), and Wales (1973).

22. Loury and Garman (1995).

23. For insightful discussions of the economic importance of historically black institutions in the

Table 12-7. Students' Log Earnings in 1991 and College Selectivity[a]

Variable	(1)	(2)	(3)	(4)	(5)	(6)	(7)
Black or Hispanic	-0.086	-0.013	-0.006	-0.094	-0.179	-0.055	0.208
	(0.026)	(0.026)	(0.025)	(0.188)	(0.223)	(0.308)	(0.332)
College selectivity[b]	...	...	0.056	0.052	0.052	...	...
			(0.010)	(0.013)	(0.013)		
Selectivity*minority	...	...	...	0.009	0.017	0.005	-0.021
				(0.019)	(0.022)	(0.030)	(0.033)
Historically black institution*minority	...	...	...	...	0.056	...	...
					(0.087)		
Selectivity*individual SAT score[c]	...	...	...	...	...	...	-0.019
							(0.007)
College fixed effects	No	No	No	No	No	Yes	Yes
Controls for family background, high school grades, SAT	No	Yes	Yes	Yes	Yes	Yes	Yes

Source: Author's calculations based on data from sources for table 12-2.

a. All specifications include indicators for high school sample stratum. Family background and academic controls include five dummies for parental education, eight dummies for family income, gender, student's SAT score, and high school grade point average. Sample size is 3,686. Standard errors, shown in parentheses, are calculated using the method proposed by Huber (1967) and White (1980); see table 12-2, note a.

b. College's mean total SAT score scale is 4 (400) to 16 (1600).

c. Scale is 4 (400) to 16 (1600).

In tables 12-5, 12-6, and 12-7, column 6 controls for all differences between colleges, using a fixed effects model. Column 6 therefore estimates the impact of different influences on students who attend the same institution. Using this approach, the relationship between college selectivity, college GPA, completion of the B.A., and earnings never varies significantly by race. Column 7 tests for an interaction between the student's own test score and the mean score at the college that the student attended. The interaction is significantly negative for both graduation rates and earnings. This would suggest that the gains associated with attending a more selective school are higher for those with lower test scores.[24]

As noted above, selective colleges ask applicants for more information than does the HSB survey. This additional information substantially improves the ability of elite colleges to predict college grades.[25] Since most selective colleges also use this information to select students, one must assume that the students that they admit differ from those at other colleges in ways that the HSB does not measure. That makes it difficult to infer the true value added by more selective institutions. All one can say is that the estimates in tables 12-6 and 12-7 probably overstate the benefits of attending a more selective college. But there is no reason to think that this bias is larger for minority students than for other students—in fact, one might expect the bias

---

careers of their graduates, see Constantine (1995); Ehrenberg and Rothstein (1994). The statistically insignificant earnings differential associated with attending a historically black institution is consistent with the finding reported by Ehrenberg and Rothstein (1994), who use the same survey as Loury and Garman (1995). Constantine (1995) also finds a small earnings differential for attending a historically black institution using ordinary least squares, but she reports a positive and significant earnings payoff to attending such an institution when she attempts to control for differences in students' unobserved characteristics. This points to another important difference between these results and those of Loury and Garman: Loury and Garman's estimation strategy implicitly assumes that B.A. completion has the same impact on earnings regardless of the college attended. Since they find a weaker relationship between college selectivity and completion rates for black and Hispanic youth, they necessarily find a weaker relationship between college selectivity and earnings for minority youth. However, because the earnings results reported in table 12-7 are not conditional on degree completion, the coefficient of the mean SAT score implicitly includes any effects of college quality that operate through completion rates. If Loury and Garman had estimated only the gross relationship between college selectivity and earnings for blacks and whites, they might well have found it the same for blacks and Hispanics as for others—even without considering the effects of attending a historically black institution.

24. None of the results in tables 12-5 to 12-7 are sensitive to the linear specifications used. I obtain similar results by using a wide range of polynomials for a student's own SAT, the college's mean SAT, and the difference between the two.

25. See chapter 13 below.

to be smaller for minority students, since it is primarily the most selective schools that use racial preferences in admissions decisions. In terms of both B.A. completion and earnings, the racial difference in the payoff to attending a more selective college is small and insignificant. To the extent that more selective institutions offer benefits to their students, these payoffs seem to be as large for black and Hispanic youth as for white youth.

Class-Based Affirmative Action

As political support for the use of racial and ethnic preferences in college admissions has eroded, some have argued that colleges should replace racial preferences with a system of class-based preferences.[26] Indeed Michael Williams, who opposed race-based scholarships as an official in George Bush's administration, recently suggested that "the end of racial preferences is here, but . . . with some ingenuity and creativity, America's campuses can continue to represent the wide variety that is America."[27]

As table 12-8 shows, class is a very poor substitute for race for selective colleges seeking racial diversity. The problem is simply one of demographics. To illustrate the point, I tabulate a representative sample of youth from the high school class of 1992. The top panel of table 12-8 presents the cross-tabulation of race by family income for the full sample of those graduating in 1992; the bottom panel presents a similar cross-tabulation for the subsample of youth with combined math and reading test scores in the top 10 percent of the class. (Row proportions are reported in parentheses and column proportions are reported in square brackets.)

As reported in the top panel of table 12-8, blacks and Hispanics were roughly three times as likely as white and other non-Hispanic students to come from families with incomes at or below $20,000 (51.2 percent of blacks and Hispanics as opposed to 17.5 percent of whites and others). Such facts are the source of the intuition that income-based preference in college admissions would disproportionately benefit black and Hispanic youth since they are more likely to be from low-income backgrounds than whites and other non-Hispanics. However, as reported in the row percentages in the top panel of table 12-8, less than half (47 percent) of those who were low-income were black or Hispanic. The simple reason for the paradox is that blacks and His-

---

26. For a summary of the case for class-based preferences, see Kahlenberg (1996).

27. Michael L. Williams, "Racial Diversity without Racial Preferences," *Chronicle of Higher Education*, November 15, 1996, p. A64.

Table 12-8. *The Demographics of Race and Income, High School Class of 1992*

Among Those Graduating from High School in 1992
(Row proportion)
[Column proportion]

	Blacks and Hispanics	Whites and other non-Hispanics	Row total
Income > $20,000	266,700 (0.152) [0.487]	1,493,100 (0.848) [0.825]	1,759,800 (1.000) [0.747]
Income < $20,000	280,100 (0.470) [0.512]	316,200 (0.530) [0.175]	596,300 (1.000) [0.253]
Column total	546,800 (0.232) [1.000]	1,809,300 (0.768) [1.000]	2,356,100

Among Those Graduating from High School in 1992
Who Had Combined Reading and Math Test Scores in the Top Tenth of the Class
(Row proportion)
[Column proportion]

	Blacks and Hispanics	Whites and other non-Hispanics	Row total
Income > $20,000	11,800 (0.061) [0.828]	182,000 (0.939) [0.939]	193,800 (1.000) [0.932]
Income < $20,000	2,400 (0.173) [0.172]	11,700 (0.827) [0.061]	14,200 (1.000) [0.068]
Column total	14,200 (0.068) [1.000]	193,800 (0.932) [1.000]	208,000

Source: Author's calculations based on National Education Longitudinal Study (NELS) data.

panics are a minority of the population and, as a result, are a minority of most subgroups of the population, including low-income youth.

However, as reported in the bottom panel of table 12-8, this paradox is even more telling among the youth with test scores in the top 10 percent of the class of 1992. Again, black and Hispanic youth are three times as likely to be low-income: 17.2 percent of blacks and Hispanics and 6.1 percent of white and other non-Hispanic students with high scores came from families with incomes at or below $20,000. However, among the high-scoring youth who were also low-income, only 17.3 percent (roughly one out of six) were black or Hispanic.

In other words, if a selective college with an application pool of students with test scores in the top ten percent granted a preference to students with family incomes below $20,000, only one out of six would be black or Hispanic. The reason is not that high-scoring black or Hispanic youth have higher incomes than white and other non-Hispanic youth. Clearly, they do not. As in the full sample of high school graduates in 1992, black or Hispanic youth with test scores in the top 10 percent were three times as likely to be low income than white and other non-Hispanic youth. Rather, the source of the apparent paradox is that blacks and Hispanics are a minority of the population, and a very small minority of students with test scores in the top ten percent (6.8 percent) and as a result, represent a minority of most subgroups of the population, including low-income youth.

There may be other characteristics that are more highly correlated with race than income alone, such as family wealth or neighborhood poverty rates, that a college might use to construct a "race-blind" measure for promoting racial diversity. However, since blacks and Hispanics are only 6.8 percent of the highest-scoring youth, it would be difficult to find a preference that would yield even a majority of black or Hispanic youth. For instance, even if high-scoring black or Hispanic youth were thirteen times more likely to meet some combination of wealth, neighborhood, and family income criteria than other youth, they would still represent less than half of the high-scoring youth meeting the criteria.[28]

---

28. This is a simple application of Bayes' Rule. For example, suppose that $P(D|BH)$ and $P(D|O)$ are the proportions of black and Hispanic and other youth that meet some definition of "disadvantaged" respectively. Suppose further that $P(BH)$ is the proportion of the population in question that is black or Hispanic. Bayes' Rule implies that the proportion of disadvantaged youth that are black or Hispanic $[P(BH|D)]$ can be expressed as

$$P(BH|D) = \frac{P(D|BH)P(BH)}{P(D|BH)P(BH) + P(D|O)(1 - P(BH))} = \frac{kP(BH)}{kP(BH) + (1 - P(BH))},$$

where k is the relative likelihood that blacks and Hispanic youth meet the definition of disadvantage, $P(D|BH)/P(D|O)$. Within a pool of youth that is only 6.8 percent black or Hispanic $[P(BH) = .068]$, it can be shown that $P(BH|D)$ is greater than 0.5 only if k is greater than 13.7.

Table 12-8 also illustrates another implication of the demographics of race, income, and test scores. Although high-scoring black or Hispanic youth are three times as likely to have incomes less than $20,000 than whites and other non-Hispanic youth, only 17.2 percent of high-scoring black or Hispanic youth come from such low-income families (as compared with 51.2 percent of all black or Hispanic youth). Because test scores are so strongly related to family income, a small share of the high-scoring minority youth—those most likely to benefit from a race-based criterion at selective schools—are actually low-income.

Highly selective colleges have four options. First, they can continue current policies. That is, they can continue to admit students primarily on the basis of test scores and high school grades, but boost black and Hispanic enrollments with some form of racial preference near the academic margin.

Second, they can replace current racial preferences with much larger scale class-based programs, at the same time becoming less academically selective. This would mean deemphasizing high school grades and especially SAT scores, which put minority students at a substantial disadvantage, and emphasizing nonacademic selection standards that have less adverse impact on minority applicants.

Third, they can remain as academically selective as at present, replace race-based preferences with class-based preferences, and allow the number of black and Hispanic youth on campus to drop sharply. And fourth, they can abandon racial preferences and allow minority enrollment to drop even more than it would if they adopted class-based preferences instead.

In short, there is an inescapable trade-off between race blindness and racial diversity. Class-based preferences do not offer a way out of the quandary.

Conclusion

Although twenty years have passed since the Supreme Court decision in the *Bakke* case affirmed the use of race as one factor in college admissions, many of the most basic questions regarding the magnitude of racial preference in college admissions have remained unanswered. In this chapter, I have attempted to provide some answers using data from the high school graduating class of 1982. The evidence suggests that use of race in college admissions appears to be limited to the most selective 20 percent of four-year institutions. Yet at these institutions, race weighs heavily in admission decisions: being black or Hispanic has approximately the same effect on one's chances of admission as two-thirds of a grade point performance in high school or roughly 400 points on the SAT test.

Two claims are often made in the debate over racial preferences that, if true, would greatly simplify the impending decisions regarding the fate of racial preference policies. The first is that racial preferences actually harm the intended beneficiaries, leading to lower college completion rates by black and Hispanic youth, putting them at a competitive disadvantage relative to their classmates. If such a claim were true, all racial groups could be made better off by ending affirmative action in college. However, the evidence suggests that the matter is not so simple: even if a student's characteristics are held constant, attendance at a more selective institution is associated with higher earnings and higher college completion rates for minority students as well as white and other non-Hispanic students. College retention rates are lower for black and Hispanic students, apparently because of differences in academic preparation emerging from high school and racial differences in performance among otherwise similar students within most colleges. But to the extent that affirmative action leads minority students to attend more selective colleges than they would otherwise, affirmative action may actually lead to narrower rather than wider gaps in college retention rates by race, since the net relationship between college selectivity, earnings, and college graduation rates appears to be positive for minority and other students.

The second claim is that colleges could achieve the same extent of racial diversity on campus without using race explicitly by granting preferences in admissions on the basis of other factors such as family income or family wealth. To the extent that society values both race blindness and racial diversity on elite campuses, the prospect of a race-blind rule producing an equivalent degree of racial diversity on campus is an attractive one, since it would seem to achieve the goal of diversity at less cost in terms of an explicit racial preference. However, the evidence suggests that a race-blind route to racial diversity is likely to be hard to find. Because blacks and Hispanics represent such a small share of students with standardized test scores in the top of their class, colleges are likely to have a difficult time finding any subgroup of high-scoring students in which blacks or Hispanics are anything but a small minority. For instance, although high-scoring black or Hispanic youth are more likely to be from low-income backgrounds, they represent only one out of six low-income students with test scores in the top tenth of the class of 1992.

The debate over affirmative action in college admissions will depend on a careful weighing of the value of racial diversity on college campuses against the real costs imposed on the students who are not admitted. In social policy debates, the easy answers—promising social benefits without social costs—usually prove ephemeral. The debate over affirmative action in college admissions is likely to be no different. Although one might make a case for class-based preferences in their own right, they are unlikely to serve as an easy substitute for race-based preferences in generating racial diversity. Likewise, however large the gains in terms of equity or increased access to college for white and other non-Hispanic youth, an end to racial preferences would seem to impose real costs on minority youth. Thus there is no avoiding the difficult trade-offs to be made.

However, the political debate over affirmative action in college admissions is likely to be complicated by the fact that it is difficult for white and other non-Hispanic youth to assess how racial preferences affect their own chances of admission to elite colleges. Handicapped parking policy provides a useful analogy.[29] Suppose that one parking space in front of a popular restaurant is reserved for disabled drivers. Many of the nondisabled drivers who pass by the space while circling the parking lot in search of a place to park may be tempted to think that they would have an easier time finding a space if the space had not been reserved. Although eliminating the space would have only a minuscule effect on the average parking search for nondisabled drivers, the cumulative cost perceived by each passing driver is likely to exceed the true cost simply because people have a difficult time thinking about small probability events.

In the same way, many families are likely to misperceive the impact of racial preference in college admissions. Harvard College, for example, accepts roughly 10 out of 100 applicants. Only 1.5 out of the 10 that are admitted (15 percent of students) are black or Hispanic. Even if ending racial preferences excluded all black and Hispanic students (an upper-bound estimate, since many minority applicants would be admitted using color-blind procedures), only 1.5 out of the 90 students who were denied admission would now find a space. Yet, if more than 1.5 out of the 90 students who are now denied think they would be the next person in line when racial preferences are ended, the perceived costs of affirmative action are likely to exceed the actual costs.

---

29. I am grateful to George Akerlof for suggesting this analogy.

Therefore, whatever the true costs of affirmative action in college admissions, the perceived costs are likely to be overstated. The implications of this insight could be used both by supporters and opponents of racial preferences. On the one hand, whatever pedagogical benefits racial diversity produces on campus are being compared with a perceived cost that is likely to be exaggerated. To the extent this is true, the political process is likely to underprovide diversity on campus. On the other hand, whatever benefit is being generated by affirmative action in admissions, the resentment that is produced is likely to be disproportionate. Even if the perceived costs are exaggerated, they represent a real social cost. Therefore, the "handicapped parking" analogy provides an apt description of the quandary college presidents, judges, and voters now face as the future of affirmative action in college admissions is debated.

Appendix : Determinants of Admission to a Four-Year College

Table 12A-1 shows the probability of acceptance by a four-year college for applicants with different characteristics, similar to table 12-2, but including college fixed effects.

Table 12A-1. *Determinants of Admission to Four-Year College, College Fixed Effects Included* [a]

Variable	Quintile of college selectivity [b]				
	Lowest	Second	Third	Fourth	Top
Race [c]					
Black, non-Hispanic	0.004	–0.009	–0.012	0.039	0.168
	(0.013)	(0.028)	(0.045)	(0.015)	(0.022)
Hispanic	–0.021	0.018	0.028	0.023	0.122
	(0.028)	(0.017)	(0.035)	(0.019)	(0.031)
Other, non-Hispanic	. . .	–0.100	0.008	–0.139	–0.022
		(0.099)	(0.055)	(0.093)	(0.044)
Academic credentials					
High school academic GPA [d]	0.054	0.038	0.108	0.104	0.219
	(0.027)	(0.015)	(0.025)	(0.019)	(0.026)
SAT score [e]	0.010	0.029	0.016	0.027	0.049
	(0.006)	(0.008)	(0.009)	(0.006)	(0.009)
High school activities					
Student government	0.011	0.032	0.019	0.004	0.090
	(0.006)	(0.017)	(0.027)	(0.017)	(0.024)
Athletics	0.029	0.006	0.007	–0.008	0.028
	(0.019)	(0.016)	(0.026)	(0.015)	(0.027)
Summary statistic					
Number of college effects estimated	25	37	49	42	105
Sample size	215	380	579	725	1,393

Source: Author's calculations based on data from sources for table 12-2.

a. The effect of being "other, non-Hispanic" is not identified for the lowest quintile, since no such students were denied admission at those schools. Equations include eight categories of family income, five categories of parental education, and eight categories of high school sample stratum. Standard errors, shown in parentheses, are calculated using the method proposed by Huber (1967) and White (1980); see table 12-2, note a.

b. Quintile breaks are set in such a way that equal numbers of students enrolled in each quintile.

c. Relative to non-Hispanic whites.

d. Scale is 0(F) to 4 (A).

e. Scale is 4 (400) to 16 (1600).

References

Brewer, Dominic J., Eric Eide, and Ronald Ehrenberg. 1996. "Does It Pay to Attend an Elite Private College?" NBER Working Paper 5613. Cambridge, Mass.: National Bureau of Economic Research.

Bunzel, John. 1988. "Affirmative Action Admissions: How It 'Works' at UC Berkeley." *Public Interest* 93 (Fall):111–29.

Cleary, Anne T. 1968. "Test Bias: Prediction of Grades of Negro and White Students in Integrated Colleges." *Journal of Educational Measurement* 5(Summer):115–24.

Coate, Stephen, and Glenn C. Loury. 1993. "Will Affirmative-Action Policies Eliminate Negative Stereotypes?" *American Economic Review* 83(5):1220–40.

College Entrance Examination Board. 1994. *Summary Statistics: Annual Survey of Colleges, 1992–93 and 1993–94.* New York.

Constantine, Jill. 1995. "The Effect of Attending Historically Black Colleges and Universities on Future Wages of Black Students." *Industrial and Labor Relations Review* 48(3):531–46.

Crouse, James, and Dale Trusheim. 1988. *The Case against the SAT.* University of Chicago Press.

Daniel, Kermit, Dan Black, and Jeffrey Smith. 1995. "College Quality and the Wages of Young Men." University of Pennsylvania, June.

Dickens, William T., Thomas J. Kane, and Charles Schultze. Forthcoming. *Does the Bell Curve Ring True?* Brookings.

Ehrenberg, Ronald, and Donna Rothstein. 1994. "Do Historically Black Institutions of Higher Education Confer Unique Advantages on Black Students?" In Ronald Ehrenberg, ed., *Choices and Consequences: Contemporary Policy Issues in Education.* Ithaca, N.Y.: ILR Press.

Goldberger, Arthur S. 1984. "Reverse Regression and Salary Discrimination." *Journal of Human Resources* 19(3): 293–318.

Herrnstein, Richard, and Charles Murray. 1994. *The Bell Curve: Intelligence and Class Structure in American Life.* Free Press.

Huber, P. J. 1967. "The Behavior of Maximum Likelihood Estimates under Non-Standard Conditions." *Proceedings of the Fifth Berkeley Symposium on Mathematical Statistics and Probability,* vol. 1. University of California Press, pp. 221–33.

James, Estelle, and others. 1989. "College Quality and Future Earnings: Where Should You Send Your Child to College?" *American Economic Review* 79(2): 247–52.

Kahlenberg, Richard D. 1996. *The Remedy: Class, Race, and Affirmative Action.* Basic Books.

Loury, Linda Datcher, and David Garman. 1995. "College Selectivity and Earnings." *Journal of Labor Economics* 13(2):289–308.

Nettles, Michael T., A. Robert Theony, and Erica Gosman. 1986. "Comparative and Predictive Analyses of Black and White Students' College Achievement and Experiences." *Journal of Higher Education* 57(May-June):289–318.

Ramist, Leonard, and Solomon Arbeiter. 1984. *Profiles, College-Bound Seniors, 1982.* New York: College Entrance Examination Board.

Ramist, Leonard, Charles Lewis, and Laura McCamley-Jenkins. 1994. *Student Group Differences in Predicting College Grades: Sex, Language and Ethnic Groups.* New York: College Entrance Examination Board.

Wales, Terence. 1973. "The Effect of College Quality on Earnings: Results from the NBER-Thorndike Data." *Journal of Human Resources* 8:306–17.

White, H. 1980. "A Heteroskedasticity-Consistent Covariance Matrix Estimator and a Direct Test for Heteroskedasticity." *Econometrica* 48(4):817–38.

FREDRICK E. VARS
WILLIAM G. BOWEN

13

Scholastic Aptitude Test Scores, Race, and Academic Performance in Selective Colleges and Universities

M OST PEOPLE, even if they are not inveterate surveyors of the political landscape, know that the role of race in determining admission to selective colleges and universities is intensely controversial at present. Competition for places in the most prestigious colleges and universities is keener than ever, and in the admissions process there is an inescapable tension between the claim of "individual merit," which focuses on a candidate's qualifications, and the claim of "institutional diversity," which also emphasizes broad educational goals, moral imperatives, and societal needs.[1]

This chapter investigates how well one measure of individual merit, scores on the Scholastic Aptitude Test (SAT), predicts academic achieve-

This chapter is part of a larger study being carried out by staff at The Andrew W. Mellon Foundation. We are indebted to many colleagues for help with preparation and analysis of the data and for comments on earlier drafts, including Elizabeth Duffy, Thomas Nygren, Douglas Mills, James Shulman, Sarah Turner, and Harriet Zuckerman. We have also been helped greatly by David Card, Ronald Ehrenberg, Christopher Jencks, Daniel Kahneman, Randall Kennedy, Alan Krueger, Michael McPherson, Meredith Phillips, Cecilia Rouse, Robert Solow, Stephen Stigler, and Charles Vars. Finally, we wish to thank the individuals at participating colleges and universities who assembled data from their institutional records. Responsibility for interpretations, errors, and confusions is, of course, ours alone.

1. For an excellent exposition of the history of the case for diversity within a single institution of high quality, see Rudenstine (1996). See also Bowen (1987, 1995).

ment for black and white students at highly selective colleges and universities.[2] We ask whether SATs predict college success equally well for blacks and whites, or for women and men within these racial groups. We also ask how well high school grades predict college grades, and how much of the observed difference in academic achievement between blacks and whites can be attributed to differences in family background.

This subject is so fraught with emotional baggage and "principled convictions" that facts can seem almost out of place. The race-specific data on test scores and academic performance assembled in this chapter can easily be misinterpreted or quoted out of context, even by well-meaning readers. Nonetheless, we believe that the underlying issues of educational and social policy are so important that these risks have to be accepted. Only by confronting evidence, and learning from experience, can policies be evaluated and improved. Moreover, nightmares are almost always worse than daytime realities.

Our principal findings are as follows. First, while SAT scores are related to the college grades of both black and white students, the relationship is weaker for blacks than for whites. More important, and more disturbing, at every level of SAT score, blacks earn lower grades than their white counterparts, and this remains true after controlling (at least crudely) for other variables, including high school grades and socioeconomic status. Most sobering of all, the performance gap is greatest for the black students with the highest SATs. The reasons for this gap are not well understood; nevertheless, we believe that many gifted African-American students at academically selective institutions are not realizing their full academic potential.

Conceptual Framework and Data

We focus primarily on two educational outcomes: graduation—that is, earning a degree—and grade point average (GPA).[3] For the present purpose, we treat these academic outcomes as a function of three sets of influences:

2. Note that since 1995, the SAT has been known as the Scholastic Assessment Test; see chapter 2 above.

3. For a study that defines success in college much more broadly, see Willingham (1985). Through the survey component of the present study, we also plan to examine a wide range of long-term outcomes, from income to civic involvement to life satisfaction. For a discussion of the economic benefits of high GPAs—and more generally, of attending different types of institution—see James and others (1989).

—Applicants' academic qualifications, which include test scores, rank in high school class, and the type of secondary school attended.

—Individual and family characteristics, which include gender, race, and parental socioeconomic status (measured, imperfectly, by educational attainment, occupational status, and receipt of need-based aid, which serves as a proxy for family income).

—College environment, which at this stage of our research consists only of the distinction between a liberal arts college and a research university.[4]

Our data cover all of the 10,558 students who entered six private universities and five selective liberal arts colleges in fall 1989.[5] These data are described in appendix table 13A-1. Roughly three-quarters of these students were enrolled in the six universities, and one-quarter in the five colleges. The total number of women and men is almost exactly the same; more men enrolled in the universities, but the inclusion of two women's colleges offsets this imbalance. There are 758 African-American students and 7,673 white students, and the remaining 2,127 students are mostly Asian or Hispanic. We also have data for students who entered the six universities in the fall of 1976, with which we can examine changes over time.

The eleven universities and colleges we study are all highly selective and in no way typical of American higher education. Among first-year students in 1989, verbal SAT scores averaged 617, mathematics scores averaged 672. This put the typical student near the ninety-fifth percentile of all test takers. The typical African-American student at these eleven institutions was just above the ninety-seventh percentile of the national distribution for African-American students, and at about the eighty-fourth percentile of the distribution for all test takers.[6]

Graduation rates at these eleven institutions were also unusually high. Ninety percent of those who entered in 1989 graduated within six years compared with 54 percent of all students who entered the 298 National

---

4. As we include more schools in our database, it will also be possible to study the effects of size, degree of selectivity, coeducational status, and location (urban versus rural). Ideally, one would also consider campus climate, faculty attitudes, residential patterns, and availability of counseling among other factors.

5. The eleven institutions included in this analysis are drawn from a larger group of thirteen private universities (Columbia, Duke, Emory, Northwestern, Princeton, Rice, Stanford, Tufts, Tulane, University of Pennsylvania, Vanderbilt, Washington University in St. Louis, Mo., and Yale) and eleven colleges (Barnard, Bryn Mawr, Denison, Hamilton, Kenyon, Oberlin, Smith, Swarthmore, Wellesley, Wesleyan, and Williams). Our subset was chosen entirely on the basis of early availability of data; even for these schools, the findings are provisional, in that we continue to pursue missing pieces of data.

6. These estimates are based on data from the College Entrance Examination Board (1989).

Collegiate Athletic Association Division I schools in 1986. Among the African-American students who entered these eleven institutions, 78 percent graduated within 6 years, compared with 34 percent for all Division I schools.[7] Unfortunately, we do not know how many of those who did not graduate earned degrees elsewhere.

We focus on highly selective institutions for three reasons. First, the controversy over admissions criteria rightly focuses on the most selective institutions; in colleges that accept a high percentage of applicants, admission policies make far less difference. Second, the student populations at these eleven schools are similar enough to permit rather precise comparisons among various categories of students (black versus white, male versus female). Third, such schools attract a large share of all African-American students with high SAT scores; and a disproportionate number of future leaders is likely to emerge from this group.[8] The strength of our database is also its weakness: because we focus on a high-achieving population, our findings cannot be extrapolated to other institutional settings.

Graduation Rates

Although many studies of the economic returns to education treat each additional year of school as equally valuable, it is widely believed that completing a particular stage of education confers added value.[9] Nonetheless, surprisingly little is known about the predictors of college graduation.

---

7. "Within six year" graduation rates are for full-time students only (National Collegiate Athletic Association, 1993, p. 608). It is mildly ironic that data collected for the purpose of monitoring the academic performance of athletes constitute the best regularly reported source of national graduation rates. The National Center for Educational Statistics of the Department of Education is now publishing such data, based on the 1990 Beginning Postsecondary Students (BPS) Longitudinal Study, but at the time of this writing, only five-year graduation rates are available. The high graduation rates at the eleven institutions in our study are consistent with Kane's finding in chapter 12 above that black students at selective schools graduate at higher rates than comparable black students at less selective schools. Unfortunately, we lack the data to conduct a similar comparison for GPAs.

8. Less than 1 percent of the African Americans who took the SAT in 1990 ended up at one of the eleven schools in our sample, but of blacks who scored at or above 700 on the verbal section, almost one-fifth matriculated at one of these schools; College Entrance Examination Board (1990).

9. This is sometimes referred to as a sheepskin effect; see Jaeger and Page (1996). As noted above, we are unable to distinguish between nongraduates who drop out, never to complete college anywhere, and those who leave college A to complete a degree at college B. We have experimented with identifying students who leave college A "in good standing," but so far we have not found a real answer to the overall problem. We are currently collecting data that will provide information on degrees obtained at other institutions.

Figure 13-1. *Graduation Rates by Mathematics and Verbal SAT Scores, 1989 Entering Cohort*[a]

Percent

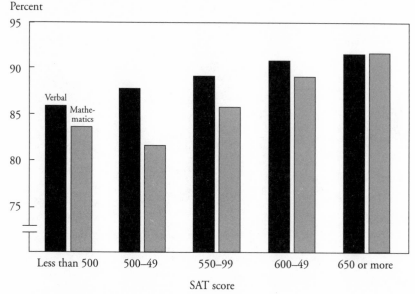

Source: Authors' calculations based on data from sources for table 13-1.
a. Sample includes eleven selective institutions: six universities and five liberal arts colleges. Rates are based on six years of matriculation.

Figure 13-1 shows the relationship between graduation rates and SAT scores. Students with high SAT scores are somewhat more likely to graduate than students with lower scores. Mathematics scores influence degree completion more than do verbal scores.[10] This may be because disappointing performance more often earns F's in mathematics-based courses, in contrast to C's in "verbal" courses.

Figure 13-2 shows that graduation rates also vary by race and gender. African-American students have lower graduation rates than white students at every level of SAT score ($p < 0.01$).[11] Both white and black women have

10. The mathematics SAT score is statistically significant in a logistic regression predicting degree completion (which also includes dummy variables for race, gender, and institution); the verbal score is not. This finding also holds for colleges and universities separately.

11. The probability values are derived from a logistic regression model that includes race, gender, and interaction variables between race and gender. The interaction term is not statistically significant. The following table reports the cell sizes for the subgroups in figure 13-2:

Figure 13-2. *Graduation Rates by Mathematics SAT Score, Race, and Gender, 1989 Entering Cohort*[a]

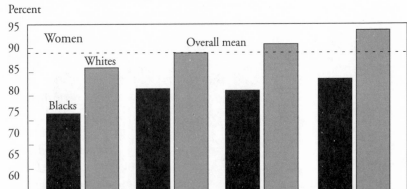

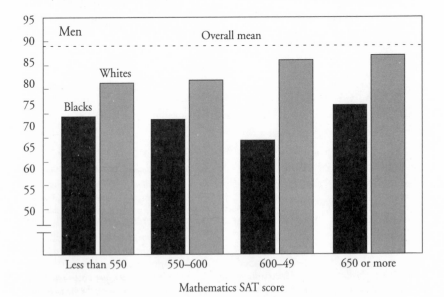

Source: Authors' calculations based on data from sources for table 13-1.
a. Sample includes eleven selective institutions: six universities and five liberal arts colleges.

higher graduation rates than their male counterparts ($p < 0.05$). Moreover, SAT scores are better predictors for women than for men, regardless of race.

Cumulative Grade Point Averages

As important as is college graduation, a student's cumulative grade point average is a more discriminating measure of academic performance. Grade point averages—expressed on a five-point scale, from 0 (F) to 4 (A)—are continuous rather than dichotomous, and they are not contaminated by as many nonacademic factors as graduation. Not surprisingly, the students in our sample who fail to graduate have lower cumulative GPAs (mean is 2.78) than graduates (3.29). But some of those who do not graduate have high GPAs, and many undoubtedly graduate elsewhere. Cumulative GPAs tell one about students' academic achievement during the years they spent at an educational institution, even if they chose to leave.[12]

Table 13-1 shows that, controlling for gender, race, participation in varsity athletics, college or university attended, and major field of study, SAT scores are statistically significant predictors of cumulative grade point averages.[13] The coefficient on the combined SAT score implies that a 100

Math SAT	Black women	White women	Black men	White men
< 550	165	243	66	94
550–599	127	449	72	192
600–649	77	704	52	388
≥ 650	71	2,226	98	3,196

12. Alan Krueger has pointed out that the GPA measure has the disadvantage that it is somewhat arbitrarily scaled across schools. The use of dummy variables for school attended and major field addresses this problem in part, but the dispersion of the variable also needs to be considered. Following Krueger's suggestion, we ran our regressions again, substituting percentile rank within school for GPA. Within the 1989 cohort, our basic findings were unchanged; however, using percentile rank has a major effect in comparisons between the 1976 and 1989 cohorts, as we explain below.

13. Of these eleven institutions, five (four liberal arts colleges and one university) have usable data on high school rank in class. In these cases, high school rank is a slightly weaker predictor of GPA than is SAT score; a combination of SAT score and high school rank predicts better than either one alone. High school size also correlates with GPA, albeit in complicated ways; we hope eventually to be able to say more about the effects of a range of secondary school characteristics on academic performance in college. Robert Solow, in particular, has urged us to examine secondary school environment in greater detail.

Table 13-1. *Effects of Gender, Race, Varsity Athletics, and SAT Scores on Cumulative GPA, 1989 Entering Cohort* [a]

Variable	Eleven institutions			Six universities	Five colleges
	(A)	(B)	(C)	(D)	(E)
Intercept	3.336	1.790	1.828	1.672	2.255
	(0.015)	(0.053)	(0.054)	(0.064)	(0.098)
Female	0.069	0.100	0.094	0.094	0.098
	(0.009)	(0.008)	(0.008)	(0.009)	(0.019)
Black	−0.527	−0.332	−0.341	−0.333	−0.357
	(0.016)	(0.017)	(0.017)	(0.019)	(0.034)
Athlete	−0.205	−0.114	−0.111	−0.116	−0.091
	(0.012)	(0.012)	(0.012)	(0.016)	(0.019)
Combined SAT score[b]	...	0.111	...	...	...
		(0.004)			
Verbal SAT score[b]	...	...	0.130	0.134	0.112
			(0.006)	(0.007)	(0.011)
Mathematics SAT score[b]	...	...	0.088	0.108	0.042
			(0.007)	(0.008)	(0.012)
Summary statistic					
R^2	0.198	0.265	0.266	0.286	0.225
Sample size	10,095	10,095	10,095	7,538	2,557

Source: Authors' regressions, as described in text. Underlying data are from the College & Beyond database.

a. Sample includes eleven selective institutions: six universities and five liberal arts colleges. All coefficients are statistically significant at $p < 0.01$. Base group for all five regressions is white males in the humanities. We exclude 464 individuals for whom either SAT scores or GPA are missing. Dummy variables for institution, major field of study, and other racial-ethnic groups were included in each regression, but are omitted here. Standard errors are in parentheses. For a complete summary of regression C, see table 13A-2.

b. In 100 point ranges.

point increase in SAT score (for example, from 1100 to 1200) raises a student's predicted GPA by roughly 0.11 (from 3.00 to 3.11, for example). Taking verbal and mathematics scores separately, the coefficients on both are statistically significant, but—consistent with conventional wisdom—verbal scores predict grades better than do mathematics scores. Mathematics scores are appreciably more powerful in the universities than in the colleges; indeed, they are nearly as important as verbal scores in predicting GPAs in the six universities. This is because mathematics scores are especially important in predicting success in science and engineering fields, which are more popular in the six universities than in the five colleges in our sample.[14] The higher percentage of women in the colleges may also help to explain why mathematics scores are less strongly related to grades in these institutions than in the universities.

Gender

Column A of table 13-1 shows that women typically earn grades 0.07 points higher than do men of the same race, in the same major field of study, and at the same institution. Adding SAT scores to the basic regression raises women's advantage to about 0.10 points (column B), because in these eleven schools women have slightly lower SATs than men. To put the matter more directly, women do better academically than men *despite* having slightly lower SAT scores. This relationship holds for both the universities and the colleges. When we add high school grades to the model (not shown in the table), the women's advantage is reduced somewhat—again, reflecting women's tendency to do better when success is measured by grades than when it is measured by test scores. This pattern is consistent with previous research.[15] Mathematics SAT scores are better predictors of grades for men than for women; verbal scores predict grades equally well for both.

Race

Against this backdrop, we turn to the role of race. At the eleven institutions in our sample, African Americans on average have an appreciably lower GPA than whites (2.80 versus 3.30, a difference of 0.50 grade points). Controlling for black-white differences in gender, athletic participation, institution attended, and major field of study increases the differential to 0.53 (table 13-1, column A). The primary reason for this small increase is that African Americans are less likely to major in science

---

14. When we introduce a new set of interactive variables, which combine mathematics and verbal SAT scores and the main fields of study, we find that mathematics scores predict grade point averages more strongly in the natural sciences and engineering than in the humanities and social sciences. Conversely, the coefficients on verbal SAT scores are significantly smaller in science and engineering than in the humanities and social sciences.

15. See, for example, Linn (1973).

or engineering, where average grade levels are lower than in the humanities or social sciences.

Since African-American students have a lower average SAT score than white students (1131 versus 1306 in these institutions), one would expect the GPA differential to be narrowed when one holds SAT scores constant. Controlling for differences in SAT scores does reduce the GPA gap: from 0.53 to 0.33 grade points. We estimate that only about 19 percent of blacks earn GPAs above the mean predicted for white students with otherwise equivalent characteristics.[16] The black-white gap is therefore substantively significant, as well as statistically so. The average gap is very similar in the five colleges and in the six universities (table 13-1, columns D and E), though it varies appreciably by institution within each group.[17]

While high school grades and size of high school both influence grade point average, adding these variables to the analysis has a negligible effect on the GPA gap in the five institutions for which we have such data (regressions not shown). Moreover, we find that dropping SAT scores and relying solely on high school records overpredicts black performance by an even greater margin than when we use SAT scores alone.[18]

In short, African-American students have lower GPAs than one would predict on the basis of SAT scores and high school grades.[19] In our analysis, this overprediction, or underperformance, is present among both males and females, and in both colleges and universities. While it is most pronounced in the sciences, it exists in all major fields of study.

16. Stephen Stigler suggested that we provide this estimate of "predicted overlap" as an indicator of substantive significance.

17. While our results pertain only to highly selective institutions, they are remarkably consistent with the results from the nationally representative High School and Beyond data set reported in chapter 12 above. Kane finds that the GPA gap ranges from 0.3 to 0.4 grade point, depending on the control variables included.

18. Both of these findings are roughly consistent with those of Ramist, Lewis, and McCamley-Jenkins (1994), who find that adding high school GPA to their basic model reduces the overprediction of black students' performance from 0.23 to 0.16. We suspect that the greater narrowing of the gap in their study results from their use of a much more diverse student population. Ramist and colleagues also report that high school grades alone tend to overpredict black GPAs by 0.35. The fact that, on average, African Americans attend poorer quality secondary schools is a plausible explanation for this pattern. As of this writing, our only proxy for high school quality is whether the school is public, private, or parochial. In a regression using data from the six schools where this information is available, high school type does not predict college GPA, and the black-white gap is not affected.

19. Overprediction of black students' performance is not a new discovery; see Cleary (1968); Breland (1979); Jensen (1980). Nor is it limited to the undergraduate level in higher education; for a discussion of underperformance at law school and medical school, see Klitgaard (1985, pp. 162–64).

Socioeconomic Status

It is known that socioeconomic status affects academic success and that, on average, black students come from less advantaged backgrounds than their white counterparts. Thus the apparently negative effects of race on grade point average could be attributable to the fact that black students' parents have less education, less desirable occupations, and less income than white parents with children at the same colleges. Table 13-2 shows the relationship between socioeconomic status and cumulative GPAs at the two universities and three colleges for which we have reasonably complete data on parental socioeconomic status. The socioeconomic status measures have the expected effects, but these effects are small: taken together, they only reduce the black-white GPA gap from 0.37 points to 0.33 points (compare columns B and E).

Looking at the individual indicators of socioeconomic status, we find that controlling for receipt of financial aid, which within these schools is a rough proxy for family income, reduces the GPA gap only from 0.37 points to 0.36 points (compare columns B and C). Adding controls for parental educational attainment explains another 2.5 percent of the variance in GPA but only reduces the black-white GPA gap from 0.36 to 0.34 points (see column D). The third proxy, parental occupations, depends on descriptions provided by students on their applications. Cryptic responses like "businessman" make it difficult to gauge the prestige or income associated with an occupation. In any case, we find that it is marginally advantageous to have a father who is a professor or a social or natural scientist; it is marginally disadvantageous to have a mother who is a homemaker (see column E). But differences in parental occupations, insofar as we are able to measure them, do not explain why black students earn lower grades than whites. Indeed, blacks still underperform by a third of a grade point after controlling all our measures of socioeconomic status.

Exceptionally High SAT Scores

Do SAT scores overpredict the performance of African-American students along the full range of scores, or is underperformance especially pronounced at one end of the SAT distribution? When we limit the analysis to black and white students and allow for differences in the predictive power of SAT, we find that a 100 point increase in total SAT score raises cumulative GPA by 0.12 points for whites, but only 0.08 points for blacks

Table 13-2. *Effects of Socioeconomic Status on Cumulative GPA, 1989 Entering Cohort*[a]

Variable	(A)	(B)	(C)	(D)	(E)
Intercept	3.310	1.814	1.829	1.817	1.844
	(0.017)	(0.084)	(0.085)	(0.085)	(0.086)
Female	0.079	0.100	0.100	0.094	0.094
	(0.013)	(0.013)	(0.013)	(0.013)	(0.013)
Black	−0.553	−0.370	−0.361	−0.336	−0.331
	(0.025)	(0.026)	(0.027)	(0.026)	(0.027)
Athlete	−0.190	−0.101	−0.102	−0.109	−0.108
	(0.017)	(0.017)	(0.017)	(0.017)	(0.017)
Verbal SAT score[b]	. . .	0.138	0.138	0.131	0.131
		(0.010)	(0.010)	(0.009)	(0.009)
Mathematics SAT score[b]	. . .	0.080	0.079	0.071	0.071
		(0.011)	(0.011)	(0.010)	(0.010)
Need-based aid	. . .	. . .	−0.020[†]	−0.004[†]	−0.005[†]
			(0.013)	(0.013)	(0.013)
Dad may have completed college	. . .	. . .	. . .	−0.275[†]	−0.231[†]
				(0.381)	(0.381)
Dad completed college	. . .	. . .	. . .	0.061	0.049*
				(0.021)	(0.022)
Dad has graduate degree	. . .	. . .	. . .	0.081	0.057*
				(0.026)	(0.029)
Missing data on Dad's education	. . .	. . .	. . .	−0.017[†]	0.006[†]
				(0.044)	(0.046)
Mom may have completed college	. . .	. . .	. . .	0.144[†]	0.129[†]
				(0.270)	(0.270)
Mom completed college	. . .	. . .	. . .	0.066	0.058
				(0.016)	(0.016)
Mom has graduate degree	. . .	. . .	. . .	0.082	0.066
				(0.023)	(0.024)

($p < 0.01$).[20] It follows that the GPA gap between white and black students increases as SAT scores rise.

Table 13-3 shows overprediction for black students by SAT level; column B shows the average gap between the GPAs of black and white students, controlling for gender, participation in varsity athletics, institution attended, and major. Among those with combined SAT scores below 1000, the grades

---

20. This finding is consistent with results obtained by Nettles, Thoeny, and Gosman (1986, table 2), who report a significant negative coefficient for the interaction of race and SAT.

Table 13-2 (*continued*)

Variable	(A)	(B)	(C)	(D)	(E)
Missing data on Mom's education	...	...	...	−0.144 (0.043)	−0.095* (0.044)
Dad is professor	...	...	...	...	0.046** (0.027)
Dad is high-level executive	...	...	...	...	0.021† (0.018)
Dad is doctor, lawyer	...	...	...	...	0.024† (0.017)
Dad is natural, social scientist	...	...	...	...	0.052** (0.030)
Dad in service occupation	...	...	...	...	−0.013† (0.025)
Dad is dead, unemployed, missing data	...	...	...	...	−0.045† (0.028)
Mom is homemaker	...	...	...	...	−0.027** (0.017)
Mom is dead, unemployed, missing data	...	...	...	...	−0.032† (0.019)
Summary statistic					
R^2	0.170	0.235	0.236	0.261	0.263
Sample size	4,312	4,312	4,312	4,312	4,312

Source: Authors' regressions, as described in text, using data from College and Beyond database.
a. Sample includes five selective institutions: two universities and three liberal arts colleges. All coefficients are statistically significant at $p < 0.01$, unless otherwise noted as follows: * denotes $p <$ 0.05, ** denotes $p < 0.10$, † denotes statistically insignificant. All coefficients are statistically significant at $p < 0.01$. See table 13-1, note a, for other control variables. Standard errors are in parentheses.
b. In 100 point ranges.

of black students are 0.21 point lower than those of whites with similar characteristics. Moving up the SAT scale, the gap then increases modestly but steadily, before jumping to 0.43 of a grade point for those with SAT scores above 1300 (which is roughly the mean for students other than African Americans in these institutions). In short, at this exceptionally high level of SAT score, blacks earn GPAs almost half a grade point lower than do whites.[21]

21. Because a higher percentage of whites than blacks have SAT scores well above 1300, and therefore the highest range is very broad, it is possible that the black-white difference in mean SAT within

Table 13-3. *Black Overprediction (Underperformance) in Cumulative GPA and Percentile Rank, by SAT Level, 1976 and 1989 Entering Cohorts*[a]

| | Cumulative GPA | | Percentile rank | |
| | 1976 | 1989 | 1976 | 1989 |
Combined SAT score	(A)	(B)	(C)	(D)
400–999	–0.335	–0.209	–10.546	–0.334
	(0.042)	(0.052)	(2.401)	(3.408)
1000–99	–0.372	–0.309	–15.511	–12.660
	(0.045)	(0.041)	(2.518)	(2.666)
1100–99	–0.379	–0.299	–19.074	–17.603
	(0.046)	(0.031)	(2.595)	(2.049)
1200–99	–0.563	–0.345	–24.557	–20.424
	(0.064)	(0.034)	(3.618)	(2.250)
1300–1600	–0.635	–0.431	–27.623	–26.025
	(0.111)	(0.044)	(6.242)	(2.900)
Summary statistic				
R^2	0.292	0.287	0.212	0.251
Sample size	6,919	7,538	6,919	7,538

Source: Authors' regressions, as described in text, using data from College and Beyond database.
a. Sample includes six selective universities. All coefficients are statistically significant at $p < 0.01$. This model differs from table 13-1, column B by allowing a different black coefficient in each range of SAT scores. See table 13-1, note a, for other control variables. Standard errors are in parentheses.

The black-white GPA gap is also larger for students majoring in the natural sciences or engineering than for students with other majors. The grade point averages of blacks majoring in engineering or the natural sciences are 0.51 grade point lower than those of their white counterparts, whereas the black-white gap is only 0.34 points for the social sciences and 0.38 points for the humanities. However, even after taking account of interactions with field of study, the GPA gap still grows wider as SAT scores rise.

The principal finding seems inescapable: in selective colleges and universities, black students at the highest levels of SAT score are especially

this range magnifies the size of the gap between grade point averages. However, our substantive conclusions do not change when the analysis is applied to the range 1300–99, where the black-white difference in mean SAT is narrow—here too, the black-white GPA gap is much larger than at lower levels of SAT. In fact, the gap is actually slightly larger in the 1300–99 range (–0.50) than in the 1300+ range (–0.44).

likely to underperform relative to white classmates with similar scores and characteristics.[22]

Alternative Interpretations: Precollege versus College Effects

Broadly speaking, there are two possible explanations for the black-white gap in academic performance in our set of schools. One is that at the time of matriculation, apparently similar black and white students differed in ways that we fail to measure.[23] Alternatively, the college experience may have had an adverse impact on the academic performance of black students relative to white classmates who arrived with the same SAT scores and other attributes. Both explanations seem plausible.

What unobserved differences between apparently comparable black and white freshmen might affect their final grade point averages? First, their families and home environments differ in ways we do not measure. For example, the parents of today's black students did not have the same opportunities as their white counterparts to attend the most academically selective educational institutions, so black and white parents with the same amount of schooling may not have had schooling of similar quality—their college degrees are not necessarily equivalent. As another example, more black than white students may come from single-parent families. Nonetheless, we are struck by how little impact the conventional indicators of socioeconomic status (including parental occupation as well as education) have on the black-white GPA gap: they reduce it by no more than about 10 percent. Thus we are skeptical that more refined measures of family background would come close to eliminating the gap.

---

22. We do not believe that this pattern can be mainly attributed to measurement error. David Card and Cecilia Rouse have suggested that there could be more measurement error in SAT scores for blacks than for whites, and that this greater degree of "noise" might explain the lower predictive power of SAT scores for blacks. To test this hypothesis, we used 1989 data for the 6,178 whites and 480 blacks who supplied more than one set of SAT scores to the most selective of our eleven institutions. The correlation between the two most recent scores is 0.77 for whites and 0.90 for blacks. If anything, the SAT scores are more reliable for black students than for whites (who may be more likely to "prep" for a second test). Following a suggestion by Alan Krueger, we also examined the correlation between mathematics and verbal SAT scores for blacks and whites at the eleven schools in our sample. The correlations are 0.48 for blacks and 0.37 for whites.

23. Thus the black-white GPA gap could largely be a statistical artifact, created by the inability of SAT scores to capture fully the academic promise of a student in combination with a lower mean SAT score for black students. This line of thinking presumes that there is something else "out there" driving both SAT scores and GPAs. We are indebted to Stephen Stigler for demonstrating the importance of this possibility, in correspondence.

Second, there might be differences that we do not measure in the secondary school preparation of black and white students. But any stable trait that affects college grades, such as motivation to learn or disciplined study habits, should also have affected high school grades. Our regressions show that while high school rank does affect college GPA (raising the R^2 substantially when included with SAT scores), it has very little effect on the magnitude of the black-white GPA gap.

A third possibility is that college admission officers are more selective in choosing among white applicants than among black applicants. Several commentators on our research have suggested that because there are proportionately more white than black applicants with high SAT scores and superior secondary school grades, colleges interested in diversity may choose a smaller, more "select," fraction of white applicants at a given level of SAT scores. As a result, white matriculants may be more likely to be exceptionally strong in academic credentials not captured by the SAT. Were this the case, SAT scores would underpredict white GPAs, but a more sophisticated academic rating would not.[24]

Admission officers base their estimates of applicants' academic potential on a wide array of information in addition to SAT scores. For one institution, we are fortunate to have a detailed admission file that includes both "academic ratings" and "personal ratings" for the 1989 entering cohort. The academic ratings integrate all the objective information that is used to predict academic performance: test scores of all kinds, including SATs and achievement scores, high school grades in core subjects, advanced placement data, and the quality of the secondary school. These academic ratings do predict college grades much better than do SAT scores alone (the R^2 is 0.368 versus 0.276). As we would expect, using academic ratings to predict GPA also narrows the average black-white gap, but only by about 15 percent—and the gap remains highly significant statistically. Moreover, consistent with our findings for SATs, the resulting GPA gap is widest

---

24. Ronald Ehrenberg and Michael McPherson have both advanced this selection bias hypothesis, in correspondence. There are also many other forms of selection bias: self-selection in application and matriculation, preferences by schools for children of alumni(ae), recruitment of athletes, "development" cases (applicants who are given extra attention in the admission process because they are from wealthy families likely to support the "development" (fund-raising) objectives of the institution), and so on. As noted, we do include a varsity athletics variable in these regressions and find that, other things equal, athletes perform less well academically than other students. We also find that including an athletics variable increases—rather than reduces, as some commentators have hypothesized—the black-white GPA gap.

among students with high academic ratings. The personal ratings do not predict college grades at all.

Thus, while we do find some evidence that blacks and whites with similar SAT scores differ in other ways that affect their college grades, these differences appear to be modest. Strong conclusions would be premature, given the large amount of variance to be explained, but it seems unlikely that unobserved variables would explain the entire black-white GPA gap at these colleges.

Therefore we turn to our main alternative explanation, that college experiences play a significant role in determining academic outcomes. The fact that the black-white GPA gap varies markedly from campus to campus supports this hypothesis. Among the eleven institutions that we study, the GPA gap varies by as much as 0.29 grade points.[25] The pattern of differences also varies across institutions. At seven of the eleven schools, the gap grows wider as one moves up the SAT scale. At two of the six universities, however, the gap in GPAs is around a third of a grade point across the entire range of SAT scores. At two of the liberal arts colleges, the GPA gap narrows at higher levels of SAT score. These findings highlight the need to examine how educational practices and assumptions at a given institution affect the academic performance of its students.

A Then and Now Comparison

Although the existence of a pervasive gap between the academic performance of black and white students is cause for serious concern, it is important to note that some progress has been made in addressing the problem. For the six universities in our sample, we have data on students who entered in 1976 as well as those who entered in 1989. The combined SAT scores of African Americans entering these schools rose substantially over this interval, from a mean of 1050 in 1976 to 1153 in 1989. Although the mean SATs of white students at these institutions also rose (from 1269 to 1323) over this period, the mean black-white difference narrowed (from

---

25. We have run the regressions reported above adding race-by-major and race-by-institution dummy variables, as well as the race-by-SAT dummies. The differences among many of the institutions are statistically significant, and they also appear to be substantively significant. Moreover, we find that controlling for socioeconomic status (in the subset of schools for which this is possible) leaves these results intact.

Figure 13-3. *Distribution of African-American College Students by Combined SAT Score, 1976 and 1989 Entering Cohorts*[a]

Percent

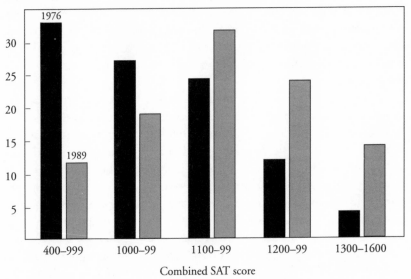

Combined SAT score

Source: Authors' calculations based on data from the College and Beyond database.
a. Sample includes six selective universities.

219 to 170 points). As can be seen from figure 13-3, the shift in the entire distribution of SAT scores for African-American students is striking.

Because black students' SAT scores rose, and underperformance is most pronounced for blacks with high scores, one might expect that the overall black-white GPA gap grew wider between 1976 and 1989. In fact, the reverse is true. Controlling for gender, athletic participation, SAT score, major field of study, and institution attended, the overall black-white GPA gap at these six universities fell from 0.40 points in 1976 to 0.33 points in 1989.

This change does not, however, mean that black students are doing better relative to whites. As these institutions became more selective, grades rose, and the entire GPA distribution became somewhat more compressed. When we measure academic performance using students' percentile rank in their college class, we no longer find that the black-white gap has been closing. Controlling for SAT scores and other attributes, a black student in the 1976 cohort was 16.9 percentage points lower in the schoolwide distribution of GPAs than a white student who entered with similar qualifications; in the 1989 cohort, the percentile gap was 17.4 points (regressions not shown). In relative terms, black students in the 1989 entering cohort underperformed to almost precisely the same degree as did black students in the 1976 entering cohort.[26] Converting grade point averages into class rankings strengthens our finding that the black-white gap widens as SAT scores rise. Furthermore, table 13-3 shows that this result holds for both the 1976 and the 1989 cohorts.

Conclusion

We see no simple explanation for our findings. We do not believe that the black-white GPA gap reflects blatant discrimination by faculty members. In our experience, most white faculty members want very much to assist and encourage minority students. We also reject any interpretation that would "blame the victim." It seems utterly implausible that African-American students with high test scores and excellent secondary school grades suddenly become uninterested in academic success or unwilling to do academic work once they enroll in selective colleges and universities.[27]

Rather, subtle forces appear to be at work. In chapter 11 above, Claude Steele and Joshua Aronson propose an imaginative—and to our minds, persuasive—interpretation. They argue that vulnerability to stereotypes can harm the academic performance of the most talented minority students in highly competitive environments. Our findings are particularly consonant with this research, since they direct attention to underperformance among the best and the brightest African-American students at the most selective institutions.

Modest SAT scores (by the high standards of these institutions) condemn no one to failure; nor do any of the other variables included in this analysis. Taken together, these variables account for only about a quarter of

26. The changes over time in graduation rates at these six universities are complex and hard to interpret. In brief, between 1976 and 1989 the graduation rate for all students increased from 83 to 89 percent; the overall gap in raw graduation rates between black and white students increased from 12 to 15 percentage points; and the black-white gap in graduation rates at the highest levels of SAT scores (over 1200) decreased from 22 to 13 percentage points.

27. Some commentators have argued that affirmative action in the workplace weakens incentives for black students to perform academically, because they know that a good job will be waiting for them. However, even if affirmative action were to shift upward career prospects for black graduates, the *marginal* payoffs to academic achievement should remain constant.

the variance in academic performance—a result common to almost all models of individual behavior. Clearly, much remains to be explained.[28] The relatively weak relationship between SAT scores and academic performance, especially for black students, underscores why admission officers must be free to consider factors other than grades and SATs when choosing among candidates. The large amount of unexplained variance also cautions against drawing more than tentative conclusions about the relative importance of precollege versus college effects on performance.

The issues discussed in this paper represent far more than intellectual puzzles. For those who believe in the need for wider educational opportunity, in the benefits of diversity, and in the need to address the problems posed by the persistence of the "color line," the gap in college grades between African Americans and whites (after controlling many other variables) is a fact that is crucial to face. African Americans are grossly underrepresented among those who earn the highest SAT scores and grades in secondary school.[29] It is therefore critically important to ensure, as best one can, that those black students who do have strong academic qualifications thrive in college. Otherwise, society will be deprived of the full potential of exceptional students, who clearly have the capacity to fill important leadership roles.

Our findings suggest that academically selective colleges and universities need to redouble their efforts to find the most effective ways of educating the most able African-American students—that is, to encourage high expectations and provide settings in which such expectations are routinely realized. This task cannot be accomplished in a single day; the underlying problems have been generations in the making. A long-term approach is needed, and more persistence than many seem wont to display.

28. As Heckman (1995) points out, a shortcoming of Herrnstein and Murray's (1994) book is that, while emphasizing the predictive power of "general intelligence," these authors fail to report the R^2 for either their analyses or those that they cite in support of their conclusion. We agree with Heckman that the low R^2 values characteristic of all these models tell an important story in their own right: test scores explain only a small part of the variance in important life outcomes. (But see chapter 14 for evidence that the black-white test score gap accounts for much of the difference in earnings between blacks and whites.)

29. See Miller's (1995) authoritative discussion.

Data Appendix

Table 13A-1 describes the student cohort that entered our sample of six universities and five liberal arts colleges in 1989. Table 13A-2 provides a complete summary of regression C, as reported in table 13-1.

Table 13A-1. *Descriptive Statistics, 1989 Entering Cohort at Eleven Selective Institutions*[a]
Units as indicated

Item	Total	Whites	Blacks
Population			
Women	5,323	3,726	453
Men	5,235	3,947	305
Total	10,558	7,673	758
SAT scores			
Verbal mean			
Women	613	624	553
Men	621	630	548
Total	617	627	551
Mathematics mean			
Women	649	657	565
Men	695	699	602
Total	672	679	580
Combined mean			
Women	1263	1282	1118
Men	1316	1330	1150
Total	1289	1306	1131
Combined standard deviation			
Women	130	114	133
Men	126	114	149
Total	131	117	140
Cumulative GPA			
Mean			
Women	3.28	3.34	2.87
Men	3.21	3.26	2.69
Total	3.25	3.30	2.80
Standard deviation			
Women	0.40	0.37	0.44
Men	0.48	0.45	0.58
Total	0.44	0.42	0.51
Graduation rate			
Mean			
Women	89	90	79
Men	88	89	77
Total	89	90	78

Source: Authors' calculations based on data from the College and Beyond database.
a. Sample includes six universities and five liberal arts colleges. Noncitizen students are excluded.

Table 13A-2. *Summary of Table 13-1, Regression C*[a]

	Analysis of variance				
Source	Degrees of freedom	Sum of squares	Mean square	F Value	Probability > F
Model	26	526.3102	20.2427	140.161	0.0001
Error	10,068	1,454.0679	0.14442	...	...
C Total	10,094	1,980.3781	...	...	...

Root mean standard error	0.3800	R^2	0.2658	
Dependent mean	3.2498	$\bar{R}^2$	0.2639	
C.V.	11.6940			

	Parameter estimates				
				T for hypothesis 0	
Variable	Degrees of freedom	Parameter estimate	Standard error	Parameter = 0	Probability > |T|
INTERCEPT	1	1.8275	0.0539	33.901	0.0001
FEMALE	1	0.0940	0.0085	11.119	0.0001
BLACK	1	−0.3407	0.0167	−20.406	0.0001
ATHLETE	1	−0.1110	0.0123	−8.991	0.0001
SATVRBL	1	0.1301	0.0058	22.367	0.0001
SATMATH	1	0.0879	0.0067	13.201	0.0001
ASIAN	1	−0.0710	0.0121	−5.884	0.0001
HISP	1	−0.1524	0.0176	−8.667	0.0001
EOTHER	1	−0.2188	0.0726	−3.013	0.0026
EMISSING	1	−0.0382	0.0271	−1.411	0.1583
NATSCI	1	−0.0082	0.0125	−0.652	0.5145
SOCSCI	1	0.0089	0.0097	0.919	0.3580
ENGINEER	1	−0.1075	0.0142	−7.572	0.0001
BUSINESS	1	−0.0048	0.0220	−0.218	0.8278
EDUC	1	0.0904	0.0626	1.443	0.1491
OTHER	1	−0.1196	0.0226	−5.285	0.0001
MISSING	1	−0.4749	0.0229	−20.766	0.0001
INST1	1	0.1448	0.0173	8.389	0.0001
INST2	1	0.0143	0.0154	0.929	0.3527
INST3	1	0.0211	0.0160	1.313	0.1891
INST4	1	0.0192	0.0200	0.958	0.3382
INST5	1	0.1517	0.0155	9.784	0.0001
INST6	1	0.0040	0.0242	0.165	0.8690
INST7	1	0.1011	0.0195	5.187	0.0001
INST8	1	0.0225	0.0210	1.069	0.2853
INST9	1	0.0555	0.0213	2.603	0.0092
INST10	1	0.2014	0.0217	9.295	0.0001

Source: See table 13-1.

a. Dependent variable is cumulative GPA. Base group is white males in the humanities.

References

Bowen, William G. 1987. "Admissions and the Relevance of Race." In *Ever the Teacher.* Princeton University Press.

———. 1995. "No Limits." Paper prepared for symposium, "The New American University: National Treasure or Endangered Species?" Cornell University.

Breland, Hunter M. 1979. *Population Validity and College Entrance Measures,* research monograph 8. New York: College Entrance Examination Board.

Cleary, Anne T. 1968. "Test Bias: Prediction of Grades of Negro and White Students in Integrated Colleges." *Journal of Educational Measurement* 5(2):115–24.

College Entrance Examination Board. 1989. *College Bound Seniors: 1989 Profile of SAT and Achievement Test Takers.* New York.

———. 1990. *1990 College-Bound Seniors: Ethnic and Gender Profile of SAT and Achievement Test Takers.* New York.

Heckman, James J. 1995. "Lessons from the Bell Curve." *Journal of Political Economy* 103(5):1091–120.

Herrnstein, Richard J., and Charles Murray. 1994. *The Bell Curve.* Free Press.

Jaeger, Dave, and Marianne Page. 1996. "Degrees Matter: New Evidence on Sheepskin Effects in the Returns to Education." *Review of Economics and Statistics* 78(4):733–40.

James, Estelle, and others. 1989. "College Quality and Future Earnings: Where Should You Send Your Child to College?" *American Economic Review* 79(2):247–52.

Jensen, Arthur R. 1980. *Bias in Mental Testing.* Free Press.

Klitgaard, Robert. 1985. *Choosing Elites.* Basic Books.

Linn, Robert L. 1973. "Fair Test Use in Selection." *Review of Educational Research* 43(2):139–61.

Miller, L. Scott. 1995. *An American Imperative: Accelerating Minority Educational Advancement.* Yale University Press.

National Collegiate Athletic Association. 1993. *1993 NCAA Division I Graduation-Rates Report.* Overland Park, Kans.

Nettles, Michael T., A. Robert Thoeny, and Erica J. Gosman. 1986. "Comparative and Predictive Analyses of Black and White Students' College Achievement and Experiences." *Journal of Higher Education* 57(3):289–318.

Ramist, Leonard, Charles Lewis, and Laura McCamley-Jenkins. 1994. *Student Group Differences in Predicting College Grades: Sex, Language, and Ethnic Groups,* College Board report 93-1, ETS RR 94-27. New York: College Entrance Examination Board.

Rudenstine, Neil L. 1996. "Diversity and Learning." In *The President's Report: 1993–1995.* Harvard University Press.

Willingham, Warren W. 1985. *Success in College: The Role of Personal Qualities and Academic Ability.* New York: College Entrance Examination Board.

WILLIAM R. JOHNSON
DEREK NEAL

14

Basic Skills and the Black-White Earnings Gap

T HE DISPARITY between black and white incomes has been a central problem of American public life for decades. Although the gap is smaller than it was a generation ago, progress has been slow and fitful, leading many to doubt whether true parity can be achieved without substantial government intervention in the labor market.[1] No rigorous appraisal of such policies can be undertaken without first knowing the root causes of this economic disparity. In previous work, we have shown that the disparity in hourly pay between young blacks and whites can largely be traced to a gap in basic skills that predates their entry into the labor market.[2] Black teenagers lag well behind their white counterparts in reading and mathematics, and this skill deficit explains most of the racial difference in wage outcomes among young adults.

We appreciate very useful comments from Christopher Jencks and Meredith Phillips. Johnson acknowledges support from the Bankard Fund of the University of Virginia. Neal's work was supported by a grant from the Sarah Scaife Foundation to the George Stigler Center for the Study of the Economy and the State at the University of Chicago.

1. For an excellent survey of the literature on black economic progress, see Smith and Welch (1986). For a survey of the economic impacts of Civil Rights legislation, see Donahue and Heckman (1991).

2. Neal and Johnson (1996).

In this chapter, we extend our previous work by examining the relationship between basic skills and annual earnings (hereafter, "earnings"). We show that black-white differences in skills before entering the labor market do account for a significant portion of the black-white earnings gap in the early 1990s. But even when we compare blacks and whites with the same premarket skills, large earnings differences remain. Only black workers at the top of the skill distribution report earnings close to those of their white counterparts.

Since earnings are the product of hourly wages (hereafter "wages") and hours of paid work, earnings differences can arise from wage differences, differences in employment, or both. We document important racial differences in employment that contribute significantly to the black-white earnings gap. Young white employees work significantly more hours than young blacks with similar skills. The main exceptions are young black college graduates, who work almost as many hours as equally skilled white college graduates. As a result, they earn almost as much per year. Finally, we show that the disparity in hours worked has a cumulative effect. At all skill levels, the black-white wage gap stems partly from black-white differences in weeks of past work experience.

We begin by describing the effect of black-white skill differences on wages. We then examine racial differences in earnings and their relation to skill differences, among women and among men. The results for men lead to an examination of the relationship between past and current employment. We close by discussing possible interpretations of our results.

Wage Rates and Basic Skills

The National Longitudinal Survey of Youth (NLSY) is an annual survey sponsored by the Bureau of Labor Statistics that documents the educational and work experiences of more than 10,000 young people born between 1957 and 1964. Data have been collected from these individuals since 1979. The data set is uniquely suited for our purposes, because in 1980 most respondents were given a common test of basic skills, the Armed Forces Qualification Test (AFQT). This test is used by the Department of Defense to screen applicants for military service, and it is considered to be a racially unbiased predictor of military job performance.[3]

---

3. This assessment is supported by Wigdor and Green (1991).

We restrict our analysis to respondents born between 1962 and 1964, because these individuals took the AFQT before they turned nineteen. At the time of the test, they had just begun to make choices about post secondary schooling or employment. Because these AFQT scores measure skills at the beginning of careers, they should not be contaminated by discrimination in either the labor market or postsecondary education. The data appendix describes the construction of our data set.

Although the standardized AFQT score distributions for blacks and for whites overlap, blacks typically score substantially lower than whites. The racial difference in average scores is roughly one standard deviation, for both men and women.

To measure wages, we average a respondent's inflation-adjusted wages from 1990 to 1993. By using a four-year average, we come slightly closer to estimating "permanent" differences in wages between blacks and whites. We are also able to include respondents who worked at any point in a four-year span, but not necessarily in all four years. This is important when studying people with weak attachment to the labor force.[4]

Table 14-1 examines some of the determinants of our measure of wages. Columns 1 and 3 estimate the racial gap in wages for men and women, controlling only for age. Among men, for example, the mean of the log of wages is 0.277 lower for blacks than whites. This difference implies that black men earn 24 percent less per hour than white men. For women, the log wage gap of 0.183 implies that black women earn 17 percent less per hour than white women of the same age. Controlling for AFQT score completely changes these residual wage gaps (see columns 2 and 4). For men, the wage gap narrows by roughly two-thirds, to about 9 percent. For women, the outcome is actually reversed. Black women earn 5 percent *more* per hour than white women with the same AFQT score.[5]

AFQT score is not simply a proxy for race in these regressions. Table 14-2 shows the relationship between AFQT score and wages for blacks, whites, and Hispanics. Columns 2 and 5 show that AFQT score has as

4. In Neal and Johnson (1996), we use a two-year averaging period. The sample in the present study includes more people who do not work very often.

5. For men, the black-white wage gap after controlling for AFQT score is slightly larger in absolute value than the corresponding gap of −0.072 reported in our previous study. A significant portion of the difference reflects the fact that the present sample contains an additional ninety-seven workers with very weak attachment to the labor market. If we use the 1990–93 average wage but restrict the sample to our original sample of workers, the adjusted log wage gap is −0.084. See Neal and Johnson (1996) for an extended treatment of selection bias in these regressions.

Table 14-1. *Effect of AFQT Score on Wage Rates* [a]

Independent variable and summary statistic	Men		Women	
	(1)	*(2)*	*(3)*	*(4)*
Black	–0.277	–0.098	–0.183	0.052
	(0.024)	(0.025)	(0.028)	(0.029)
Hispanic	–0.132	–0.009	–0.024	0.160
	(0.028)	(0.028)	(0.032)	(0.031)
Age	0.041	0.034	–0.002	0.010
	(0.013)	(0.012)	(0.015)	(0.014)
AFQT	. . .	0.175	. . .	0.249
		(0.011)		(0.014)
Constant	5.79	5.92	6.72	6.27
	(0.356)	(0.332)	(0.407)	(0.373)
Summary statistic				
Sample size[b]	1,689	1,689	1,546	1,546
Adjusted R^2	0.075	0.194	0.028	0.189

Source: Authors' calculations based on data from the NLSY.

a. Dependent variable is log wage rate, where the wage rate is the average real wage rate over 1990–93. Sample includes respondents with valid AFQT scores and born after 1961 who report valid wage observations between 1990 and 1993. Standard errors are in parentheses.

b. Starting with 1,881 men and 1,805 women, we eliminate 59 men and 163 women who report, in each interview, that they have not worked since the previous interview; and 133 men and 96 women because their records contain no valid wage or employment information for the period 1990–93.

large an effect on wages within the black population as it has in the national population. Basic cognitive skills, as measured by the AFQT, raise the wages of blacks at least as much as they raise the wages of whites. In short, basic skills do influence wages and a large fraction of the black-white wage gap reflects a skill gap that predates labor market entry.

Earnings depend not only on hourly wages, but also on how many hours employees work. Even if firms pay workers strictly according to productivity, without regard to race, they might still be less inclined to hire black workers in the first place.[6] Differences in earnings may provide a different and more complete picture than do wage differences of the economic consequences of both labor market discrimination and black-white differences in premarket skills.

---

6. As we show below, difficulty in finding employment may also translate into less work experience and slower wage growth, which implies an additional drag on earnings growth for black workers.

Table 14-2. *Effect of AFQT Score on Wage Rates, by Race* [a]

Independent variable and summary statistic	Men			Women		
	White (1)	Black (2)	Hispanic (3)	White (4)	Black (5)	Hispanic (6)
Age	0.041	0.043	−0.004	0.018	0.003	0.002
	(0.016)	(0.023)	(0.032)	(0.021)	(0.022)	(0.030)
AFQT	0.176	0.193	0.148	0.262	0.252	0.215
	(0.014)	(0.022)	(0.028)	(0.021)	(0.025)	(0.029)
Constant	5.73	5.59	6.92	6.06	6.50	6.63
	(0.436)	(0.619)	(0.877)	(0.572)	(0.592)	(0.809)
Summary statistic						
Sample size	870	500	319	767	459	320
Adjusted R^2	0.156	0.136	0.074	0.166	0.185	0.146

Source: Authors' calculations based on data from sources for table 14-1.

a. Dependent variable is log wage rate, where the wage rate is the average real wage rate over 1990–93. See note to table 14-1 for description of data. Standard errors are in parentheses.

Basic Skills and Women's Earnings

Table 14-3 shows how women's AFQT scores affect their earnings.[7] The earnings measure is the log of average annual inflation-adjusted earnings from 1990 to 1992 for everyone who reported any earnings during this period.[8] Black women, on average, enjoy a substantial earnings advantage over white women with similar AFQT scores. Although columns 3 and 4 show that the earnings gap is smaller among highly skilled women, predicted earnings for black women remain above predicted earnings for their white counterparts over almost the entire range of black AFQT scores.

At first glance, tables 14-1 and 14-3 suggest that, holding premarket skills constant, black women earn more per year and are paid slightly higher wages than white women. However, these results should be interpreted cautiously for two reasons. First, we do not observe potential wages and potential earnings for every woman in our sample, because some women

7. We present results from a specification which uses a quadratic function of AFQT. We have also tried linear, cubic, and quartic specifications. For black women, the linear specification performs poorly. For men, however, the same basic pattern of black-white earnings gaps emerges in all four specifications.

8. The NLSY asks questions about current wages and about earnings during the past calendar year. Therefore although wage data are available through 1993, earnings data are available only through 1992.

Table 14-3. *Effect of AFQT Score on Earnings Differences, Women*[a]

Independent variable and summary statistic	All races		White	Black
	(1)	(2)	(3)	(4)
Black	−0.271	0.191	. . .	. . .
	(0.078)	(0.084)		
Hispanic	−0.095	0.270	. . .	. . .
	(0.088)	(0.089)		
Age	−0.049	−0.028	−0.042	−0.017
	(0.042)	(0.040)	(0.056)	(0.078)
AFQT	. . .	0.506	0.541	0.419
		(0.043)	(0.075)	(0.097)
AFQT^2	. . .	−0.035	−0.025	−0.206
		(0.038	(0.061)	(0.100)
Constant	10.56	9.78	10.12	9.75
	(1.13)	(1.08)	(1.51)	(2.11)
Summary statistic				
Sample size[b]	1,442	1,442	728	421
Adjusted R^2	0.007	0.097	0.105	0.076

Source: Authors' calculations based on data from sources for table 14-1.

a. Dependent variable is log annual inflation-adjusted earnings over 1990–92. Sample includes female respondents with valid AFQT scores and born after 1961 who report positive earnings in at least one survey year. Standard errors are in parentheses.

b. Starting with 1,805 respondents, we eliminate 96 because their records contain no valid earnings data for any of the years in question; and 267 who report zero earnings in all valid interview years.

do not work or work part time. Second, the missing wage and earnings data do not represent a random sample from the overall distribution. This raises the possibility that these results may misrepresent the relative economic status of black women.

Missing observations create a complex problem in our analyses of women's wages and earnings. Although researchers commonly assume that prime-age men who are not working have lower potential wages than apparently similar men who are working, this may not be a tenable assumption for women. Many women with relatively high potential wages choose not to work for pay, particularly if they have young children or husbands with high incomes.[9]

9. Many less skilled women with children, especially those who are not married, also choose not to work. Some of these women are on public assistance and have decided that, given child care expenses and other fixed costs of work, they are better off at home.

Table 14-4. *Women's Wages by Marital Status in 1993*[a]

Independent variable and summary statistic	Never married (1)	(2)	Ever married (3)	(4)
Black	−0.312	−0.024	−0.128	0.085
	(0.050)	(0.054)	(0.035)	(0.035)
Hispanic	−0.016	0.184	−0.035	0.146
	(0.064)	(0.061)	(0.037)	(0.036)
Age	−0.042	−0.012	0.016	0.019
	(0.027)	(0.025)	(0.018)	(0.016)
AFQT	. . .	0.242	. . .	0.247
		(0.025)		(0.016)
Constant	7.87	6.88	6.23	6.03
	(0.736)	(0.668)	(0.485)	(0.447)
Summary statistic				
Sample size	392	392	1,154	1,154
Adjusted R^2	0.109	0.283	0.010	0.161

Source: Authors' calculations based on data from sources for table 14-1.

a. Dependent variable is log wage rate, where the wage rate is the average real wage rate over 1990–93. Standard errors are in parentheses.

Further, even if we knew the potential wage of each woman in our sample, we would still have a related problem. Working women often choose whether to work part-time or full-time. For those who choose to work part-time, actual earnings will understate potential earnings.

A complete analysis of female labor supply is beyond the scope of this chapter, but we can show why we are reluctant to take the results in tables 14-1 and 14-3 at face value. Table 14-4 provides wage analyses for samples of women defined by marital status: a "never-married" woman is one who said in 1993 that she had never been married, and all other women fall in the "ever-married" group. Although ever-married black women receive wages over 8 percent higher than their white counterparts, never-married black women receive wages quite similar to those of never-married whites.[10] If highly skilled, married, black women have less wealth than their white counterparts, it is possible that the correlation between potential wages and the

10. In similar analyses for men, we cannot reject the hypothesis that the black-white wage gap is the same in both samples. Further, the difference in the estimated gaps is roughly half as large as that for women (compare columns 2 and 4 of table 14-4).

probability of participation is stronger among black wives than among white wives. If this is the case, overall black-white wage comparisons based only on participants may overstate the relative economic status of black women. Black and white women also differ substantially in the observed patterns of their labor supply. Among whites, never-married women work on average six weeks more per year than ever-married women. Among blacks, the situation is reversed: never-married women work six weeks less than ever-married women.[11] The relationship between marital status and labor supply clearly differs by race. If we assume that marital status is correlated with unmeasured aspects of skill, we confront the possibility that the relationship between unmeasured skills and labor supply also differs by race.

Basic Skills and Men's Earnings

Hereafter we focus on explaining the black-white earnings gap among men. While the selection biases that plague the analysis of women might also influence men, such effects should be smaller, both because few married men are secondary earners and because our sample includes every respondent who worked at all during 1990, 1991, or 1992.

Table 14-5 shows how AFQT scores affect the earnings of men. Column 1 parallels the analysis of wages in table 14-1: it presents the differences in log earnings between black, white, and Hispanic men, controlling only for age. Comparison of tables 14-1 and 14-5 shows that the earnings gap between black and white men is over twice as large as the wage gap. Black men earn 48 percent less per year than whites of the same age, even though their wages are only 24 percent lower.[12] When we control for AFQT

11. While 92 percent of the ever-married black women report that they have worked for some number of weeks during 1990–92, only 77 percent of single black women do likewise. White women exhibit the reverse pattern: 95 percent of single women report working, while only 91 percent of married women do so.

12. The log earnings gap that we report is roughly twice as large as the black-white gap in log earnings based on annual earnings data from the Current Population Surveys of the Census Bureau, a common resource for research on black-white earnings differences. There are three reasons for this disparity. First, our three-year average includes all persons who report valid earnings over as short a period as one year. The inclusion of workers with weak labor force attachment increases the black-white earnings gap. Second, the Current Population Survey's definition of "white" includes some Hispanics, whereas the NLSY definition does not. Finally, the NLSY includes more black workers who report relatively meager earnings in any given year than does the Current Population Survey. This has little effect on the black-white ratio of average annual earnings, but has noticeable effects on the

Table 14-5. *Effect of AFQT Score on Earnings Differences, Men*[a]

Independent variable and summary statistic	All races		White	Black
	(1)	(2)	(3)	(4)
Black	–0.653	–0.318	...	...
	(0.057)	(0.060)		
Hispanic	–0.302	–0.087	...	...
	(0.066)	(0.066)		
Age	0.074	0.059	0.098	0.000
	(0.031)	(0.029)	(0.031)	(0.070)
AFQT	...	0.337	0.318	0.447
		(0.027)	(0.031)	(0.080)
AFQT^2	...	–0.054	–0.032	–0.016
		(0.024)	(0.028)	(0.071)
Constant	7.85	8.17	7.09	9.46
	(0.828)	(0.791)	(0.852)	(1.89)
Summary statistic				
Sample size[b]	1,638	1,638	850	483
Adjusted R^2	0.077	0.159	0.133	0.080

Source: Authors' calculations based on data from sources for table 14-1.

a. Dependent variable is log annual inflation-adjusted earnings over 1990–92. Sample includes male respondents with valid AFQT scores and born after 1961 who report positive earnings in at least one survey year. Standard errors are in parentheses.

b. Starting with 1,881 respondents, we eliminate 124 because their records contain no valid earnings data for any of the years in question; and 119 who report zero earnings in all valid interview years.

in column 2 of table 14-5, the earnings gap between black and white men is cut almost in half. Consequently, while premarket skills explain a significant part of the earnings gap, they account for a smaller fraction of the earnings gap than of the wage gap.

Nevertheless, columns 3 and 4 of table 14-5 show that AFQT score has a substantially greater impact on log earnings among blacks than among whites.[13] Among twenty-seven-year-old men with AFQT scores one stan-

---

ratio of average log annual earnings. Restricting the log earnings regressions to men who earned over $1,000 in 1990, the estimated black-white gaps in log earnings in the NLSY and Current Population Survey are almost identical, given appropriate adjustments in the NLSY classification of whites.

13. In pooled specifications that involve different slopes by race, we reject the null hypothesis that the relationships between AFQT score and earnings are the same for both black and white men.

Table 14-6. *Men's Wages, Earnings, and Labor Supply,*
by Education and Race[a]

Education and race	Log of wage rate (1)	Log of earnings (2)	Average annual hours (3)	Average annual weeks (4)
High school dropout				
White	6.73	9.42	1,932	42.4
	(0.39)	(0.95)	(754)	(12.9
Black	6.49	8.60	1,441	33.8
	(0.38)	(1.55)	(780)	(16.6)
Black-white ratio	0.787	0.440	0.745	0.797
High school graduate				
White	6.87	9.84	2,175	47.4
	(0.36)	(0.73)	(630)	(10.2)
Black	6.65	9.41	1,894	42.7
	(0.40)	(0.92)	(745)	(13.7)
Black-white ratio	0.795	0.651	0.871	0.901
College graduate				
White	7.19	10.28	2,274	48.8
	(0.40)	(0.549)	(633)	(7.3)
Black	7.09	10.10	2,248	48.7
	(0.39)	(0.826)	(564)	(8.4)
Black-white ratio	0.905	0.835	0.989	0.998

Source: Authors' calculations based on data from sources for table 14-1.

a. Samples for columns 2–4 include 1,326 individuals: the black and white respondents in the sample for table 14-5 less 12 who have invalid labor supply records. For the wage sample (column 1), we eliminate an additional 21 respondents who report invalid wages. Sample standard deviations are in parentheses.

dard deviation above the sample mean, blacks earn only about 12 percent less than white men. But only 5 percent of the black sample have AFQT scores in this range. The earnings gap for most black men is much larger.

Why is the black-white earnings gap for men larger than the corresponding wage gap? And why is the earnings gap for men smaller among highly skilled workers? Schooling provides at least part of the answer. Table 14-6 shows earnings, wages, and labor supply for workers of different races with various levels of education. Among men without a high school diploma, blacks work and earn significantly less than whites. For both hours

Table 14-7. *Effect of AFQT Score and Education on Earnings, Men*[a]

Independent variable and summary statistic	White (1)	Black (2)
High school graduate	0.308	0.726
	(0.065)	(0.119)
College graduate	0.341	0.521
	(0.072)	(0.194)
Age	0.103	0.051
	(0.031)	(0.067)
AFQT	0.184	0.220
	(0.036)	(0.086)
AFQT^2	−0.057	−0.038
	(0.029)	(0.069)
Constant	6.73	7.46
	(0.832)	(1.83)
Summary statistic		
Sample size	850	483
Adjusted R^2	0.180	0.161

Source: Authors' calculations based on data from sources for table 14-1.

a. Dependent variable is log annual inflation-adjusted earnings over 1990–92. Sample excludes respondents with zero earnings. See notes to table 14-5 for details of the earnings variable. Standard errors are in parentheses.

and weeks worked, the ratio of black labor supply to white labor supply is 0.8 or less. Among high school graduates, the racial gap in labor supply is smaller but still substantial. Among college graduates, however, the gap is trivial.

Since AFQT scores are correlated with future educational attainment, the results in table 14-6 raise the possibility that the strong relationship between test scores and log earnings for blacks reported in table 14-5 operates, at least in part, through post secondary education. Table 14-7 confirms this hypothesis. The relationship between log earnings and AFQT scores is much more similar for blacks and whites when we control for educational attainments.

Two forces drive this result. Youth with strong basic skills are more likely to attend college, and in addition, the return to college education is greater for black students than white students. Among students who begin college with roughly the same basic skills, black students who graduate

Figure 14-1. *Predicted Earnings by Race and Education, Men*[a]
Thousands of dollars

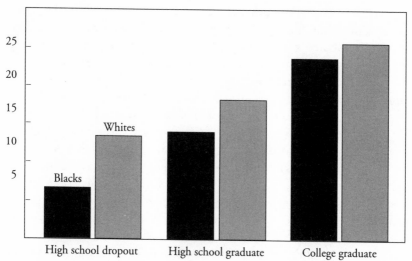

Source: Authors' calculations based on data from sources for table 14-1.
a. Estimated for twenty-seven-year-old males with AFQT scores at the sample mean.

earn much higher returns than white students who graduate. Assuming that workers supply labor inelastically, these higher returns take two forms. The college wage premium is greater for black workers, and as table 14-6 indicates, college degrees appear to have a greater effect on the employment opportunities of black workers.[14]

To see the total impact of these effects, consider two 27-year-old men, one black and one white, both with college degrees and both with AFQT scores equal to the sample mean. As figure 14-1 shows, the black man's predicted earnings are only 7 percent lower than those of his white counterpart. In contrast, the same comparison for two men who are high school dropouts reveals an enormous gap in predicted earnings.

14. The appendix to Neal and Johnson (1996) provides separate estimates of the college wage premium by race conditional on AFQT. This premium is notably larger for blacks. Similar results hold in our present sample. Further, although table 14-6 provides the raw differentials in employment by education category, a similar pattern holds conditional on AFQT.

Lower Employment Rates among Less Educated Black Men

Table 14-6 shows that black men with less than a college education work significantly fewer hours than similarly educated white men. This clearly contributes to the black-white earnings gap. Although black men earn lower wages than white men in all educational categories, observed differences in weeks and hours worked between blacks and whites are too large to be explained as a voluntary labor supply response to lower wages. Because most estimates of the response of men's labor supply to a permanent increase in wages are small and often negative, the observed black-white gap in hours worked among men who do not finish college must have other sources.[15] These sources may include, among other things, employer discrimination or racial differences in access to job networks. Whatever the source of the racial gap in work experience among men without a college degree, one does know that working less today reduces wages in the future. To the extent blacks work less than whites in their early working-age years, theories of learning by doing and on-the-job training predict that older blacks will have lower wages as a result. Thus, the effects of racial differences in access to jobs could compound, over the course of a decade, into wage differences such as those shown in table 14-1, column 2.

Table 14-8 shows the effect of experience on men's wages. Columns 1, 3, and 5 report the results of regressing log wages on race, age, and AFQT score. Each regression is restricted to workers with the same amount of education. The coefficients on the black dummy variable in these regressions describe the skill-adjusted wage gap between blacks and whites in a given educational category. As one would expect from table 14-6, these gaps decline with educational attainment. In fact, black male college graduates in this sample earn higher wages than white male graduates with similar AFQT scores, although the difference is not statistically significant. However, even holding AFQT scores constant, black high school dropouts and graduates earn substantially lower wages than do their white counterparts.

Can differences in past work experience account for these gaps? In the regressions reported in columns 2, 4, and 6 of table 14-8, we add a measure of total weeks employed between the year in which the respondent turned eighteen and 1990, which is the first year in our measure of average wages.

---

15. On labor supply response, see Pencavel (1986).

Table 14-8. *Effect of Work Experience on Wages, Men*[a]

Independent variable and summary statistic	Education					
	High school dropout		High school graduate		College graduate	
	(1)	(2)	(3)	(4)	(5)	(6)
Age	0.030	−0.021	0.038	−0.005	0.060	0.035
	(0.023)	(0.024)	(0.016)	(0.017)	(0.029)	(0.031)
Black	−0.144	−0.100	−0.133	−0.066	0.074	0.087
	(0.045)	(0.044)	(0.034)	(0.034)	(0.071)	(0.071)
Hispanic	0.052	0.054	−0.028	−0.008	−0.110	−0.121
	(0.046)	(0.045)	(0.038)	(0.017)	(0.076)	(0.077)
AFQT	0.150	0.131	0.087	0.088	0.189	0.188
	(0.024)	(0.024)	(0.017)	(0.017)	(0.038)	(0.038)
Total weeks employed	...	0.0010	...	0.0010	...	0.0005
		(0.0001)		(0.0001)		(0.0002)
Constant	5.955	6.991	5.800	6.607	5.341	5.836
	(0.633)	(0.630)	(0.445)	(0.436)	(0.787)	(0.818)
Summary statistic						
Sample size	480	480	847	847	292	292
Adjusted R^2	0.131	0.197	0.085	0.160	0.105	0.115
Addendum						
Mean weeks worked						
Whites		320		358		319
Blacks		267		290		290

Source: Authors' calculations based on data from sources for table 14-1.

a. Dependent variable is log wage rate, where the wage rate is the average real wage rate over 1990–93. Sample includes the 1,689 males with valid wage observations (see table 14-1) less 70 respondents who have at least one invalid record of annual weeks worked. Standard errors are in parentheses.

The bottom panel of table 14-8 shows the average weeks worked by each group. Columns 2, 4, and 6 show that prior work experience is strongly associated with wages for workers in each educational group, but especially for those without a college education. For high school dropouts and high school graduates, each additional year of work experience adds roughly 5 percent to the wage rate. Among high school graduates, roughly half of the unexplained black-white wage gap can be attributed to differences in past work experience (compare the race coefficients in columns 3 and 4). Among dropouts, experience explains about 30 percent of the remaining black-white gap (compare columns 1 and 2).[16]

If these racial differences in past work experience result from employment discrimination, then discrimination contributes significantly to the observed wage and earnings gaps between black and white men. However, it is possible that they are not primarily caused by employer discrimination. Workers in general, and young people in particular, often learn about job opportunities from informal networks of friends, family, and associates. This may be particularly true for less educated workers.[17] If the informal job search networks available to young black men are less extensive than those of their white counterparts, racial differences in work experience may reflect a black disadvantage in access to information about employment opportunities. This disadvantage might be the result of employer discrimination against past generations of blacks, but it could persist even when employers no longer discriminate.

Conclusions

In this chapter, we use scores on the Armed Forces Qualification Test for the younger members of the National Longitudinal Survey of Youth panel as a measure of the skills that young adults bring to the labor market. We measure labor market outcomes when workers are in their late twenties and early thirties. Our findings are as follows.

First, skills are important determinants of wages and earnings. Skill differences explain a substantial part of the wage and earnings variation among blacks, among whites, and between blacks and whites.

Second, for men, the black-white gap in annual earnings is more than twice as large as the gap in hourly wages. Further, the racial difference not explained by skills is three times as large for annual earnings as for hourly wages.

Third, the low earnings of black men are partly attributable to the fact that less educated black men work significantly fewer hours and weeks

16. The specifications in table 14-8 force the AFQT effects to be the same for blacks and whites in a given educational group. We have used more flexible functional forms to estimate the impact of past work experience on the residual black-white wage gap, with similar results.

17. See, for example, Rees and Gray (1982). Employed family and friends may also bring responsible potential employees to the attention of employers.

than their white counterparts. This phenomenon probably cannot be attributed to the fact that black men are offered lower wages.

Fourth, less work experience during their early years in the job market has a notable effect on the wage gap faced by less educated black men in their late twenties and early thirties.

Finally, the relationship between basic skills and eventual earnings is stronger among black men than white men. This reflects, in large part, a racial difference in the economic benefits of post secondary schooling.

We have identified two important reasons why black men earn less than white men. First, black men enter the labor market with fewer basic skills. Second, black men get less work experience early in life. Discrimination in the labor market may play a direct role in reducing wages for black men, by impeding the accumulation of valuable experience. However, the black-white gap in basic premarket skills remains a prominent cause of black-white earnings inequality.

Data Appendix

This chapter draws on data taken from the National Longitudinal Survey of Youth. The data include respondents from the national cross-section subsample (Sample ID < 9), and from the Hispanic and black supplemental samples. We do not use data from the poor white or military supplemental samples. Therefore, although our resulting sample contains a disproportionate share of blacks and Hispanics, the data are nationally representative within each racial category. In our analyses we also use eight variables that are not taken directly from the NLSY, but are created from the information available in that survey: age-adjusted AFQT score, high school graduate, college graduate, average wage, average earnings, average hours worked, average weeks worked, and total weeks worked before 1990.

The age-adjusted AFQT variable is based on the 1989 scoring formula for the AFQT (see Center for Human Resource Research, 1995). We regress AFQT on dummies for year of birth. We then capture the residuals from this regression and standardize them to a mean of zero and a standard deviation of one. These standardized residuals are the age-adjusted AFQT scores.

The high school and college graduation variables identify those who actually graduated from high school or college. Individuals who received general equivalency diplomas (GED) are not counted as high school graduates. In most cases, a college graduate is a respondent who reports both receiving a college degree and also completing a total of at least fifteen years of schooling. Among those for whom degree information is not available, college graduates are defined as persons who have completed at least sixteen years of schooling.

Average wages are defined as the average reported hourly wage over the 1990–93 survey years. The wage observations come from the current or most recent job at the time of the interview. Reported wages of less than $1 per hour or more than $75 per hour are treated as coding errors. If a person lacks a valid wage observation for a given year or years, the average is computed from the balance of the wage observations.

Average earnings are defined as the average reported annual earnings over the 1991–93 survey years. The earnings observations are total labor earnings in the previous calendar year. When a respondent reports zero earnings for one or two years, these observations enter the calculation of average earnings. However, if earnings data are missing or invalid for a given year, the average earnings are computed by using data from the other years. Since earnings data do not include military pay, we treat earnings data as invalid if respondents served in the military for any part of the calendar year in question. Persons who report zero earnings in all survey years, but otherwise have valid data, are given an average of zero and excluded from the regressions involving log earnings.

Average weeks and hours worked are calculated using data from the 1991–93 surveys on weeks and hours worked in all jobs during the past calendar year. For person-years with fewer than fifty-two weeks covered in the data, we impute annual weeks worked using the "weeks unaccounted for" variables. If imputed total weeks exceed fifty-two, the record is declared invalid. For cases involving imputations, we top code annual hours at 3,500.

The total weeks worked before 1990 variable is also calculated using the weeks worked during the past calendar year variable. Invalid cases are identified using the rule described above. If data are missing for a given year, and data are available in both adjacent years, we impute annual weeks as the average of reported annual weeks worked in the two adjacent years. All other imputations are based on the average of all annual weeks worked reported in valid interviews between the eighteenth year following the worker's birth and 1990.

References

Center for Human Resource Research. 1995. *N.L.S. Users' Guide*. Ohio State University.

Donohue, John J., III, and James J. Heckman. 1991. "Continuous versus Episodic Change: The Impact of Civil Rights Policy on the Economic Status of Blacks." *Journal of Economic Literature* 29(December 4): 1603–43.

Neal, Derek, and William R. Johnson. 1996. "The Role of Premarket Factors in Black-White Wage Differences." *Journal of Political Economy* 104(October 5): 869–95.

Pencavel, John. 1986. "Labor Supply of Men: A Survey." In Orley Ashenfelter and Richard Layard, eds., *Handbook of Labor Economics*, vol. 1. Amsterdam: Elsevier.

Rees, Albert, and Wayne Gray. 1982. "Family Effects in Youth Employment." In Richard Freeman and David Wise, eds., *The Youth Labor Market Problem: Its Nature, Causes and Consequences*. University of Chicago Press.

Smith, James P., and Finis Welch. 1986. *Closing the Gap: Forty Years of Economic Progress for Blacks*, R-3330-DOL. Santa Monica, Calif.: Rand.

Wigdor, Alexandra K., and Bert F. Green, eds. 1991. *Performance Assessment in the Workplace*. 2 vols. Washington: National Academy Press.

PART V

Commentary

WILLIAM JULIUS WILSON

15) The Role of the Environment in the Black-White Test Score Gap

IN THEIR controversial book, *The Bell Curve*, published in 1994, Richard Herrnstein and Charles Murray argued that success or failure in the United States, including class and racial differences in performance, is largely determined by genetic endowment. They therefore question the extent to which the social environment influences group social outcomes, including performance on cognitive tests, and whether intervention programs such as Head Start or affirmative action can overcome the handicaps of innate intelligence. The attention their best-selling book has received has made it important, especially in terms of public policy, for social scientists to advance definitive empirical evidence on the powerful and complex role of the social environment in group social outcomes. The carefully written and persuasive chapters in this volume provide an important set of initial findings on the strong relationship between the social environment and one widely discussed social outcome, the black-white test score gap.

If this volume and other recent studies are any indication, *The Bell Curve* has had one notable positive effect.[1] It has prompted social scientists to respond to the book's arguments emphasizing genetic endowment by

---

1. For another recent discussion see Fischer and others (1996).

examining more closely and carefully the role of the social environment in the success rate of African Americans. For a number of years many social scientists, often influenced by ideological considerations, have been polarized into two camps when discussing environmental influences on minority groups. Liberals highlight social factors, such as racial discrimination, low wages, inadequate schooling, lack of jobs, and so on. Conservatives emphasize cultural factors, such as values, attitudes, habits, and styles.[2] Because the environment includes both social and cultural opportunities and constraints, and social and cultural variables often interact, this ideological split results in incomplete analyses of the influence of the environment on social behavior.

This volume takes us in a more constructive direction because several of the authors not only try to account for the influence of both social and cultural variables but also try to integrate psychological variables into their explanatory frameworks. The evidence they produce reveals the powerful influence of the environment in maintaining the black-white test score gap. However, even with their persuasive analysis of environmental influences, a good deal of the gap remains unexplained by the measures they use. Accordingly, the authors point out that additional studies are necessary to uncover other unmeasured aspects of the social environment.

I would like to suggest that the unexplained variance does not just stem from the rudimentary environmental measures used in these studies. There is indeed a more fundamental problem that derives from the use of a framework that features only individual-level analysis. By "individual-level analysis" I mean a study of social inequality that focuses on the different attributes of individuals (gender, race, human capital, psychological traits) or their social situations (the schools they attend, the industries in which they are employed, the social networks of which they are a part). Thus whether the analysis focuses on the attributes of individuals or their social situations, it involves the properties of individuals.[3] On the basis of these attributes these individuals are then sorted into social positions that accord them differential awards. "With this type of analysis," Charles Tilly comments, "collective outcomes (e.g., racial differences in poverty) are derived entirely from individual effects."[4]

2. For a discussion of the liberal-conservative split on the role of the social environment, see Wilson (1987, chap. 1).

3. Tilly (1998); and Fischer and others (1996).

4. (Tilly, 1998, p. 23). My discussion of the limitations of individual analysis here and later is indebted to Tilly.

Frameworks featuring individual-level analyses make it difficult if not impossible to consider empirically the impact of the *social structure of inequality* on racial group social outcomes, including the impact of relational, organizational, and collective processes.[5] Before I attempt to address this issue in greater detail, let me spell out what I take to be the major arguments presented in this volume, arguments derived from careful and sophisticated individual-level analyses that clearly challenge the biogenetic explanations of Herrnstein and Murray.

The Contributions of Individual-Level Analyses of the Environment

Although IQ scores for all groups have risen over the years, the gap in black-white IQs has narrowed because of significant improvements in black children's physical and social environments. The available evidence reviewed by several authors in this volume provide, as Richard E. Nisbett puts it, "no evidence for genetic superiority for either race while providing strong evidence for a substantial environmental contribution to the black-white IQ gap." Indeed, he argues, IQ scores and cognitive skills have been improved by rigorous interventions at "every stage of the life course." Larry V. Hedges and Amy Nowell's careful review of every major national survey since 1965 that encompasses tests of cognitive skills (including mathematics, science, and reading) shows that the racial gap in test scores has narrowed. What all of these tests measure is achievement. And the evidence suggests that rates of achievement vary in terms of environmental conditions.

Accordingly, although the environment of blacks has improved, it is still far from comparable to that of whites and some other groups. Indeed, even though the black-white gap in cognitive test scores has narrowed in recent years, Meredith Phillips, James Crouse, and John Ralph point out that black children enter school not only with fewer math and reading skills than white children but that the disparity increases as they move through primary and middle school. Even when they compare blacks and whites who begin school with the same test scores, blacks fall behind as they progress through school. And large racial differences remain even after the standard measures of family background are controlled.

However, several of the authors in this volume make it clear that the standard measures of family background hardly capture the complex di-

5. Tilly (1998).

mensions of the environment. Although family background still accounts for a significant portion of the black-white test score gap, its importance has diminished over the years. And social scientists have become increasingly aware that other environmental influences have to be taken into account. As Phillips, Crouse, and Ralph write, we need to consider possibilities "such as systematic differences in the ways white and black pupils are treated within the same school, in how white and black children spend their summers, or in white and black children's study habits or perceptions of their academic ability."

Some social scientists have cited the research of the anthropologist John Ogbu, who argues that in the black community adolescents pressure one another not to "act white," which includes not doing too well in school. This, he says, is partly responsible for the black-white difference in academic performance, including lower test scores. However, Philip J. Cook and Jens Ludwig find no support for this thesis in their analysis of a national survey of tenth-grade students in 1990. They therefore suggest that instead of addressing the problem of an "oppositional culture," policymakers should direct their attention to other adverse aspects of black students' environment—poor schools and inadequate student guidance and support.

Ronald Ferguson's discussion of teacher perceptions is especially relevant in this connection. Based on the limited evidence available, he raises the possibility that teachers' perceptions and expectations of black youngsters affect how much these children learn. Teachers' lack of faith in black children's potential, even when it is not based on racial bias per se but on the children's past behavior, can adversely affect these children's future test scores.

The extent to which teachers' perceptions of black children are derived from knowledge or beliefs about the neighborhoods and families from which they come is a topic of future research. What we do know from a number of empirical studies is that there are significant differences in the family environment and neighborhood environment of blacks and whites, differences that are understated when standard measures of socioeconomic status (SES) are employed.

Consider, for example, family environment. As this volume shows, even when white and black parents report the same average income, white parents have substantially more assets than do black parents. White parents have also usually attended better schools and colleges than black parents with the same amount of schooling. Furthermore, children's test scores are affected not only by the socioeconomic status of their parents, but also by that of their grandparents. In other words, the SES of the grandparents has a delayed effect on their grandchildren's test scores in addition to its effect on the SES of the children's parents. This means that it could take several generations before reductions in socioeconomic inequality produce their full benefits.

But the problems associated with the use of the conventional measures of SES (parental education and income) are not limited to their failure to take account of differences in assets between blacks and whites or family background effects that span more than one generation. Conventional measures of SES also capture only a small component of a child's total family environment. Accordingly, instead of relying solely on the conventional measure of socioeconomic status, which explains roughly a third of the black-white IQ gap, in chapter 4 Phillips and her colleagues use data from the Children of the National Longitudinal Study of Youth (CNLSY) to develop a broader index of a child's family environment. They are consequently able to explain more than half the gap. The more measures of family environment they control, the narrower the black-white IQ gap becomes. This suggests, as they point out, that their measures of black-white family background differences are not only incomplete but probably underestimate the importance of such differences. The authors stress that additional measures of family environment might account for the remainder of the black-white gap.

Phillips and her colleagues also emphasize the potential importance of child rearing practices in explaining the gap. Their analysis suggests that racial differences in child rearing practices are related to differences in IQ scores independent of socioeconomic status. As Richard Nisbett points out in this connection, mixed race children with a black mother and a white father have lower IQs than mixed-race children with a white mother and a black father. One possible explanation is that white mothers tend to be more supportive in patterns of interaction that involve their children's work on cognitive tasks. Different child rearing practices represent cultural differences that exert a major influence on the learning of black and white students at school, including their performance on cognitive tests.

As far as differences in the black-white neighborhood environment are concerned, Phillips and her colleagues report that whereas only 7 percent of white children in the Panel Study of Income Dynamics (PSID) national sample who were born between 1978 and 1980 lived in poor neighborhoods (areas with poverty rates of at least 20 percent), 57 percent of comparable black children did. Even children from *nonpoor* black families are far more likely than poor white children to live in relatively impoverished neighborhoods. Between 1980 and 1985 almost half the children from nonpoor black families lived in areas in which at least a fifth of their neighbors were poor. Only 7 percent of nonpoor white families lived in such areas. The impact of neighborhood differences on test scores has yet to be fully explored in the empirical research.

The importance of black-white differences in environmental experiences can be acknowledged in other ways. For example, in their study of the black-white earnings differential, William R. Johnson and Derek Neal point out that young black men have significantly less work experience during their early years in the job market. In addition to the traditional problem of discrimination in the labor market, they raise the possibility that this discrepancy could be accounted for by the fact that young black men "have less extensive informal job search networks than their white counterparts."

The effect of different environments on black and white social outcomes is seen even among black adolescents who have been reared in white homes. Black adolescents raised by white parents will still have more exposure to or involvement in a "black" environment than white adolescents. Given the categorical racial distinctions in the United States and the pressures on young blacks to join or participate in their own informal subgroups, black adolescents raised by white parents are more likely to be involved in black adolescent networks than comparable white networks.[6]

Finally, I would argue that even the different black-white psychological reactions to competitive academic situations that Claude Steele and Joshua Aronson document stem from different environmental experiences. Fredrick E. Vars and William G. Bowen speculate that the research of Steele and his colleagues may help to explain their puzzling findings on the relationship between black academic grades and SAT scores at academically selective colleges and universities. Vars and Bowen find that regardless of their SAT score, blacks earn lower grades than their white counterparts even after controlling socioeconomic status and high school grades. Furthermore, the disparity between black and white students' grades was greatest among those with the highest SAT scores. Thus, at academically selective institutions many talented African-American students are not reaching their full potential. There are currently no clearly definitive explanations for this

6. On black adolescents' involvement, see Smith and Moore (1997).

gap, but Vars and Bowen, referring to the research of Steele and his colleagues, state that there may be subtle forces at work, such as the effects of negative stereotypes on minority students.

As pointed out by Steele and Aronson, even the academic performance of the most talented minority students in highly competitive environments suffers because of their vulnerability to stereotypes. The experiments reported in Steele and Aronson's chapter reveal that conditions designed to increase African-American students' awareness of negative stereotypes about blacks' intellectual ability depress their test performance relative to that of white students. Conditions intended to lessen consciousness of stereotypes can, in turn, improve the academic performance of blacks. Given the absence of good empirical evidence, it is reasonable to assume that black students' reaction to negative stereotypes in competitive academic settings is associated with their unique collective experience in America's racially restricted social environment. In this sense the influence of the environment on academic performance is mediated by settings or conditions that involve the relative presence or absence of negative stereotypes.

Collectively, the studies in this volume make a substantial contribution in presenting clear and detailed findings from systematic empirical research on the powerful role of the environment in the black-white test score gap. In the process they devastate many of the assumptions and arguments that Herrnstein and Murray make about the role of genetic endowment in that gap.

However, as I pointed out earlier, even the sophisticated studies in this volume can only account for a fraction, albeit a significant fraction, of the black-white test score gap. One reason is that the measures of the environment are still incomplete. The other, and perhaps more fundamental, reason is that these measures are derived from frameworks based on individual-level analysis and therefore fail to capture the impact of the social structure of inequality. I raise this point not as a criticism of the authors of these impressive studies, but to strengthen their arguments as to why much of the remaining influence of the environment is left unexplained.

The real challenge for social scientists is to supplement studies of social inequality that demonstrate the powerful impact of the environment through individual-level analyses with studies that are able to capture the complex and important influence of the social structure of inequality. Of the studies in this volume, only Ferguson's chapter 8 on the effect of teacher perceptions and expectations of black youngsters represents the latter. Teachers share ideologies of group differences, including those that highlight social and cultural differences. These ideologies justify or prescribe "appropriate" ways of handling the education of black and white students. For black students this often results in teacher expectations and institutional practices that ultimately undermine academic achievement.

The Missing Link: The Impact of the Structure of Inequality

As I pointed out, an individual-level analysis of social inequality focuses on the different attributes of individuals or their social situations. It involves an examination of the properties of individuals. On the basis of these attributes the individuals are then sorted into social positions that afford them differential rewards and privileges. Collective outcomes are then derived from individual effects.[7]

This individualistic framework is not designed to capture the impact of relational, organizational, and collective processes that embody the social structure of inequality. Included among these processes are the institutional influences on mobility and opportunity; the operation and organization of schools; the mechanisms of residential racial segregation and social isolation in poor neighborhoods; categorical forms of discrimination in hiring, promotions, and other avenues of mobility; ideologies of group differences shared by members of society and institutionalized in organizational practices and norms that affect social outcomes; unequal access to information concerning the labor market, financial markets, apprenticeship programs, and schools; the activities of employers' associations and unions; government policies involving taxation, service, investment, and redistribution; and corporate decisions concerning the location and mobility of industries.[8]

Since organizational, relational and collective processes are omitted, the individualistic framework is unable to specify fully the mechanisms by which certain individual attributes produce certain social outcomes, or spell out how and why these attributes result in individuals being sorted into different social positions. "The crucial causal mechanisms behind categorical inequality," argues Tilly, "operate in the domain of collective experience and social interaction."[9] I mentioned earlier that an important aspect of

---

7. Tilly (1998).
8. Fischer and others (1996); and Tilly (1998).
9. Tilly (1998, p. 24).

the environment is the interaction between social and cultural factors. In considering the domain of collective experience and social interaction, culture, the sharing of modes of behavior and outlook within a community is most fully understood as being "intertwined closely with social relations, serving as their tools and constraints instead of constituting an autonomous sphere."[10]

The extent to which communities differ on some aspects of outlook and behavior depends in part on the extent of each community's social isolation from the broader society, the material assets or other resources that members of the community control, the privileges and benefits they derive from these resources, the cultural experiences community members have accumulated from political and economic arrangements, both current and historical, and the influence community members wield because of these arrangements. In the final analysis, the exposure to different cultural influences—as reflected in culturally shaped habits, styles, skills, values, and preferences—has to be taken into account and related to various types of social relations if one is to really appreciate and explain the divergent social outcomes of human groups.[11] In several of the chapters in this volume, cultural influences are discussed in terms of individual attributes, but the discussion of cultural influences is vague, not only because of an inadequate conceptual and empirical analysis of culture, but also because the treatment of culture is not integrated into a broader discussion of social relations.

Finally, if an understanding of the role of culture requires a more comprehensive analysis of the structure of inequality, so too does an understanding of the psychological dynamics associated with black academic underachievement require that they be related to the social processes that constitute the structure of inequality. If blacks react differently to negative stereotypes in academic settings, the reasons will be found in the discovery of the social processes that generate this collective reaction.

For public policy purposes it is important to understand this complex relationship between individual outcomes and the structure of inequality. Some short-term policy options do not require knowledge of this more comprehensive relationship. Examples include changes in the certification of teachers, as Ferguson suggests; changes in test labels to make clear that they measure developed abilities, as Jencks suggests; creating academic set-

10. Tilly (1998, p. 21).
11. Wilson (1996).

tings that reduce the salience of racial stereotypes, as Steele and Aronson propose; encouraging college admission officers to consider criteria other than SATs or grades, as Vars and Bowen advocate; and continuing racial preferences at elite colleges, as Kane's findings seem to me to warrant.

But in the long term the programs that will have the greatest effect are those that attack *all* aspects of the structure of inequality. Only then can we drastically reduce and eventually eliminate the environmental differences that create the present gap in black and white achievement.

References

Fischer, Claude S., and others. 1996. *Inequality and Design: Cracking the Bell Curve Myth.* Princeton University Press.

Herrnstein, Richard J., and Charles Murray. 1994. *The Bell Curve: Intelligence and Class in American Life.* Free Press.

Smith, Sandra, and Mignon Renee Moore. 1997. "What It Means to Be Black: Interracial Alienation among Black Students at a Predominantly White College." Paper presented at the annual meeting of the American Sociological Association.

Tilly, Charles. 1998. *Durable Inequality.* University of California Press.

Wilson, William Julius. 1987. *The Truly Disadvantaged: The Inner City, The Underclass, and Public Policy.* University of Chicago Press.

———. 1996. *When Work Disappears: The World of the New Urban Poor.* Alfred A. Knopf.

Contributors

Joshua Aronson
University of Texas, Austin

William G. Bowen
Andrew W. Mellon Foundation

Jeanne Brooks-Gunn
Columbia University

Philip J. Cook
Duke University

Jonathan Crane
National Center for Research on Social Programs

James Crouse
University of Delaware

Greg J. Duncan
Northwestern University

Ronald F. Ferguson
Harvard University

Ann Flanagan
RAND

David Grissmer
RAND

Larry V. Hedges
University of Chicago

Christopher Jencks
Harvard University

William R. Johnson
University of Virginia

Thomas J. Kane
Harvard University

Pamela Klebanov
Columbia University

Jens Ludwig
Georgetown University

Derek Neal
University of Wisconsin, Madison

Richard E. Nisbett
University of Michigan

Amy Nowell
University of Chicago

Meredith Phillips
University of California, Los Angeles

John Ralph
*National Center for Education
Statistics*

Claude M. Steele
Stanford University

Fredrick E. Vars
Yale University

Stephanie Williamson
RAND

William Julius Wilson
Harvard University

Index

513